Personal Wealth from a Global Perspective

The UNU World Institute for Development Economics Research (UNU-WIDER) was established by the United Nations University as its first research and training centre and started work in Helsinki, Finland, in 1985. The purpose of the institute is to undertake applied research and policy analysis on structural changes affecting developing and transitional economies, to provide a forum for the advocacy of policies leading to robust, equitable, and environmentally sustainable growth, and to promote capacity strengthening and training in the field of economic and social policymaking. Its work is carried out by staff researchers and visiting scholars in Helsinki and via networks of collaborating scholars and institutions around the world.

United Nations University World Institute for Development Economics Research
(UNU-WIDER)
Katajanokanlaituri 6 B, FIN-00160 Helsinki, Finland
www.wider.unu.edu

Personal Wealth from a Global Perspective

Edited by
James B. Davies

A study prepared for the World Institute for
Development Economics Research of the United
Nations University (UNU-WIDER)

OXFORD
UNIVERSITY PRESS

OXFORD
UNIVERSITY PRESS

Great Clarendon Street, Oxford OX2 6DP

Oxford University Press is a department of the University of Oxford.
It furthers the University's objective of excellence in research, scholarship,
and education by publishing worldwide in

Oxford New York

Auckland Cape Town Dar es Salaam Hong Kong Karachi
Kuala Lumpur Madrid Melbourne Mexico City Nairobi
New Delhi Shanghai Taipei Toronto

With offices in

Argentina Austria Brazil Chile Czech Republic France Greece
Guatemala Hungary Italy Japan Poland Portugal Singapore
South Korea Switzerland Thailand Turkey Ukraine Vietnam

Oxford is a registered trade mark of Oxford University Press
in the UK and in certain other countries

Published in the United States
by Oxford University Press Inc., New York

British Library Cataloguing in Publication Data

Data available

Library of Congress Cataloging in Publication Data

Personal wealth from a global perspective / edited by James B. Davies.
     p. cm—(Wider studies in development economics)
  Includes bibliographical references and index.
  ISBN 978–0–19–954889–7
  1. Wealth. 2. Economic development. 3. Income distribution. I. Davies, James B.,
1951–
  HC79.W4P47 2008
  339.2′2–dc22

2008031569

Typeset by SPI Publisher Services, Pondicherry, India
Printed in Great Britain
on acid-free paper by
CPI Antony Rowe, Chippenham, Wiltshire

ISBN 978–0–19–954888–0 (Hbk.)
     978–0–19–954889–7 (Pbk.)

1 3 5 7 9 10 8 6 4 2

Foreword

When Adam Smith wrote about the wealth of nations he was concerned with the flows of production and resources that distinguish the living standards of rich and poor countries. Nowadays economists tend to use terms like 'income' and 'consumption' to refer to such flows, reserving 'wealth' for the stock of assets owned, for example, individually by persons or collectively by countries. This volume deals with wealth in this modern sense, focusing specifically on the net worth of households as measured by the market value of physical property plus financial assets less debts.

Judging by the popular media, there is an insatiable appetite for news about the activities of the super rich. But personal wealth is also important for those lower down the economic hierarchy. It provides a stock of consumption power for retirement years and a cushion against unanticipated adverse events such as crop failure, unemployment, and medical emergencies. In addition, it provides a source of finance for entrepreneurial pursuits, and collateral for loans for business purposes or house purchase. These benefits of wealth are particularly compelling in poor countries that tend to lack well-functioning capital markets or any form of social insurance protection. Yet on the global scale in comparison with income, wealth is more skewed towards rich countries, and more skewed towards rich households within countries.

Data on the level and distribution of household wealth is much less common than information on income or consumption. A few countries have wealth series dating back for a century or more. A number of other countries—in the main OECD members—have recent wealth data. This volume reviews the available evidence on time trends and compares the figures across countries, as others have done before. However, unlike earlier works, this book goes much further; looking at personal wealth from a global perspective. Individual chapters document what is known about asset holdings in developing and transition countries. Others focus on specific aspects such as financial assets, housing, and the gender dimension. The volume also contains the first attempt to estimate how world household wealth is distributed across countries and across the global population.

The material in this book will appeal to members of the general public interested in global economic issues as well as social scientists in universities and business schools. It contains powerful ammunition for those who see increasing inequality as an inevitable consequence of globalization. But at the same time, the growing prosperity of China, India, and other emerging market economies suggests that the pattern of wealth ownership observed in the past is unlikely to be replicated in the future.

Anthony Shorrocks
Director, UNU-WIDER

Contents

Contents

Part IV   The Global Picture

List of Figures

List of Figures

List of Tables

Notes on Contributors

Janine Aron is a Research Fellow at the Centre for the Study of African Economies in the Department of Economics, University of Oxford. She has consulted for the World Bank, IMF, and other international organizations. She publishes mainly in the areas of macroeconomics, monetary and exchange-rate policy in Africa, especially South Africa.

Juliano Assunção is Assistant Professor of Economics at the Pontifical Catholic University in Rio de Janeiro. His research interests are primarily focused on microeconomic aspects of economic development such as land markets and rural households, immigration, informality, and economic implications of tax systems.

Sir A. B. Atkinson is Professor of Economics at the University of Oxford. He was previously Warden of Nuffield College, Oxford. His research interests include the economics of inequality and global public economics.

Frikkie Booysen is a Professor of Economics and is attached to the Department of Economics and Centre for Health Systems Research and Development at the University of the Free State. His main areas of expertise include development indicators, health and poverty, and health economics.

Ronelle Burger is a researcher at the Economics Department of Stellenbosch University. Her research is focused upon poverty alleviation and development in African countries.

James B. Davies is Director of the Economic Policy Research Institute at the University of Western Ontario, where he was Chair of the Department of Economics 1992–2001. His research has looked at human capital and tax policy, tax incidence, inequality measurement, and the distribution of wealth.

Carmen Diana Deere is Professor of Food and Resource Economics and Director of the Center for Latin American Studies at the University of Florida. She is the co-author of *Empowering Women: Land and Property Rights in Latin America* (2001) and co-editor of a special issue on 'Women and Wealth' in *Feminist Economics* (2006).

Cheryl Doss is a development economist, whose work focuses on gender and development issues in Africa. She has been the Director of Graduate

Studies for the MA Program in International Relations and a Lecturer in Economics at Yale since 1999. Her publications focus on issues of gender and agricultural technology, intra-household resource allocation, and the gender–asset gap.

Sergei Guriev is Rector of the New Economic School in Moscow. He has published on topics related to development and transition economics, as well as income and wealth inequality.

Patrick Honohan is Professor of International Financial Economics and Development at Trinity College Dublin and a research fellow of CEPR. Previously he was a senior adviser at the World Bank, and his career has also included periods at the IMF, the Central Bank of Ireland, the Economic and Social Research Institute, Dublin, and as economic adviser to the Taoiseach.

Markus Jäntti is Professor of Economics at Åbo Akademi University, Research Director at the Luxembourg Income Study, and a research associate at UNU-WIDER. His research interests centre on international comparisons of and methods for the study of income inequality, income mobility, and poverty.

D. Jayaraj is a professor at the Madras Institute of Development Studies. He publishes on themes related to women's well-being and sex ratio, child labour, structural transformation of rural workforce, and poverty.

Shi Li is Professor of Economics at the School of Economics and Business, and Director of the Centre for Income Distribution and Poverty Studies, Beijing Normal University. His research interest has focused on issues related to income inequality, poverty, and rural migration in China.

Jim MacGee received his Ph.D. in economics from the University of Minnesota. He has published in publications including *Journal of Monetary Economics*, *American Economic Review*, and *Review of Economic Dynamics*. His research focuses on consumer credit, bankruptcy, and international business cycles, and has been supported by the Social Science and Humanities Research Council of Canada.

John Muellbauer is Professor of Economics at Oxford and has been an Official Fellow of Nuffield College since 1981. He is a Fellow of the British Academy, the Econometric Society, and the European Economic Association. His research in macroeconomics has particularly concerned monetary policy, housing, credit markets, and consumer behaviour, and the consequences of institutional differences.

Henry Ohlsson is Professor of Economics at Uppsala University, and was previously at Umeå University. His research is mainly within the fields of public and labour economics. He is currently on the board of the Swedish National Employment Services and a member of the Economic Council of Swedish Industry.

Sangeeta Pratap is Associate Professor of Economics at Hunter College and the Graduate Center of the City University of New York. She has worked on the effect of financial constraints on firm investment at the theoretical and empirical level, and is currently working on financial crises and their effects on the real economy.

Johan Prinsloo studied at the University of the Free State in South Africa. In 1980 he joined the South African Reserve Bank, where he was Head of the National Accounts Division in the Research Department. He has published articles related to South Africa's national accounts, saving and household debt, and since November 2007 he has worked as regional adviser for the IMF.

Erwan Quintin is a senior economist and policy adviser at the Federal Reserve Bank of Dallas. His research interests include growth and development economics, financial economics, and macroeconomics, with an emphasis on Latin American issues.

Andrei Rachinsky is an economist at the Centre for Economic and Financial Research, New Economic School, in Moscow. He has published on topics related to corporate governance in Russia and on Russian oligarchs.

Christian Rogg is a senior economic adviser at the UK Department for International Development (DFID) and is currently based in Accra, Ghana. He is also a research associate at the Centre for the Study of African Economies (CSAE) of the University of Oxford.

Jesper Roine is Assistant Professor at SITE at the Stockholm School of Economics. His recent research has focused on long-run income and wealth inequality in Sweden, and he has also worked on topics in the fields of political economy and economic growth.

Susanna Sandström is a research associate at UNU-WIDER. She has previously held positions at the Luxembourg Income Study and Statistics Finland.

Anthony Shorrocks is Director of UNU-WIDER, having previously held positions at the London School of Economics and the University of Essex. He has published widely on topics related to income and wealth distribution, inequality, and poverty.

Eva Sierminska is a research economist at CEPS/INSTEAD and a research affiliate at DIW Berlin. In the past she was director of the Wealth Project (LWS) at the Luxembourg Income Study and worked at Georgetown University. Her current research focuses on cross-country and demographic differences in wealth portfolios and distribution, the link between consumption, income, and wealth, inequality measurement, and methodological issues in cross-country wealth analysis.

Seymour Spilerman is the Julian C. Levi Professor of Social Sciences at Columbia University, where he co-directs the Center for the Study of Wealth and Inequality. His publications cover issues in inequality and intergenerational financial linkages, as well as social violence.

S. Subramanian is a professor at the Madras Institute of Development Studies. He has research interests in the fields of social and economic measurement, development economics, and the theory of collective choice.

Florencia Torche is Assistant Professor of Sociology at New York University, and Associate Director of the Center for the Study of Wealth and Inequality, Columbia University. Her research focuses on inequality reproduction in the educational, occupational, and wealth spheres in an international comparative perspective. She has conducted national mobility surveys in Chile and Mexico.

Servaas van der Berg is Professor of Economics at the University of Stellenbosch, South Africa. His research interests are mainly in the fields of poverty and inequality, and in the economics of education.

Michael von Maltitz is a lecturer in the Department of Mathematical Statistics at the University of the Free State, South Africa. His research specialities include multivariate statistical methods, time-series analysis, and social capital theory.

Daniel Waldenström earned his Ph.D. at the Stockholm School of Economics, has taught at UCLA, and is currently a research fellow at the Research Institute of Industrial Economics in Stockholm. His research deals mainly with income and wealth inequality and the development of financial markets.

Edward Wolff is Professor of Economics at New York University and a senior scholar at the Levy Economics Institute of Bard College. He is also a research associate at the National Bureau of Economic Research. He served as Managing Editor of the *Review of Income and Wealth* during 1987–2004 and was a visiting scholar at the Russell Sage Foundation in New York in 2003–4. His principal research areas are productivity growth and income and wealth distribution.

Ruslan Yemtsov is a lead economist in the Social and Economic Development Group, Middle East and North Africa Region, at the World Bank. He was a professor at the Moscow State University before joining the Word Bank in 1993. Until 2007 he focused on transition economies, coordinating World Bank work on poverty in the ECA region, but he has since moved to work on poverty, labour issues, and social policy in Egypt, Morocco, and Tunisia.

Renwei Zhao is a professor and former Director of the Institute of Economics at the Chinese Academy of Social Sciences, and was a visiting fellow at St Antony's College and All Souls College, University of Oxford. He specializes in transition economics, income distribution, and wealth distribution in China.

Acknowledgements

The chapters of this volume are the outcome of a UNU-WIDER research project on personal assets from a global perspective carried out in 2005–6. The original idea for this project came from Tony Shorrocks, Director of UNU-WIDER, who has been a great help throughout the project. Branko Milanovic of the World Bank took part enthusiastically in our project meeting in May 2006 in Helsinki and gave invaluable comments on the papers. UNU-WIDER researchers Tony Addison, Indranil Dutta, Basudeb Guha-Khasnobis, George Mavrotas, and Mark McGillivray provided ideas and helpful comments as well.

UNU-WIDER staff provided excellent assistance. Many thanks are due to our project assistant, Lorraine Telfer-Taivainen, who handled administrative aspects, organized the project meeting, and provided editorial assistance. Adam Swallow provided valuable advice throughout. Sincere thanks are also due to Barbara Fagerman, Ara Kazandjian, Sherry Ruuskanen, and Bruck Tadesse for their assistance.

I am most grateful to all the contributors to this volume for their inputs and insights and to the two anonymous referees, whose comments were very useful in revising the volume. Finally, I would like to thank my wife, Laurel, for her strong support and encouragement for my work on this volume.

UNU-WIDER acknowledges with thanks the financial contributions to its research programme by the governments of Denmark (Royal Ministry of Foreign Affairs), Finland (Ministry for Foreign Affairs), Norway (Royal Ministry of Foreign Affairs), Sweden (Swedish International Development Cooperation Agency (Sida)), and the United Kingdom (Department for International Development).

Jim Davies
London, Ontario
February 2008

List of Acronyms and Abbreviations

AIRDIS	All-India Rural Debt and Investment Survey
APH	agricultural population per holding
BIS	Bank for International Settlements
BREAD	Bureau for Research in Economic Analysis of Development
CASS	Chinese Academy of Social Sciences
CCI	credit conditions index
CEDAW	Convention on the Elimination of All Forms of Discrimination against Women
CEE	Central and Eastern Europe
CIA	Central Intelligence Agency (USA)
CIS	Commonwealth of Independent States
CSAE	Centre for the Study of African Economies (Oxford University)
CSDS	Centre for Security and Defence Studies (Carleton University)
CSO	Central Statistical Office (Poland)
CSS	CentER Savings Survey (Netherlands)
CV	coefficient of variation
DC	defined contribution
DCLG	Department for Communities and Local Government (UK)
DHS	Demographic and Health Surveys (Ghana)
EAS	Economic Activity Surveys (South Africa)
ECA	Eastern Europe and Central Asian
ECB	European Central Bank
ECM	error correction models
ERHS	Ethiopia Rural Household Survey
EVS	Einkommens- und Verbrauchsstichprobe (Germany)
FAO	Food and Agriculture Organization (United Nations)
FSU	former Soviet Union
GLSS	Ghana Living Standards Survey
GQ	general quadratic

HBS	household budget survey
HDW	household disposable wealth
HILDA	Household, Income and Labour Dynamics in Australia survey
HMT	Her Majesty's Treasury (UK)
IBGE	Brazilian Census Bureau
IBRA	Brazilian Institute for Agrarian Reform
ICRW	International Center for Research on Women
IDRC	International Development Research Centre (Canada)
IDS	Income Distribution Surveys
IFLS	Indonesian Family Life Survey
ILO	International Labour Organization
IMF	International Monetary Fund
INCRA	National Institute for Rural Settlement and Agrarian Reform (Brazil)
ISWGNA	Inter-Secretariat Working Group on National Accounts
LDC	less developed country
LINDA	Longitudinal INdividual DAta (Sweden)
LSMS	Living Standards Measurement Survey (World Bank)
LWS	Luxembourg Wealth Study
MCA	multiple correspondence analysis
MF	multi-family
MFRC	Micro-Finance Regulatory Council (South Africa)
MLD	mean logarithmic deviation
MPC	Monetary Policy Committee (Bank of England)
MST	Landless Rural Worker's Movement (Brazil)
MWA	mean wealth above
NATSEM	National Centre for Social and Economic Modelling (Australia)
NBER	National Bureau of Economic Research (USA)
NBS	National Bureau of Statistics
NCAER	National Council of Applied Economic Research (India)
NDA	National Institute for Agricultural Development (Brazil)
NGO	non-governmental organization
NIESR	National Institute of Economic and Social Research (UK)
NPO	non-profit organization
NSSO	National Sample Survey Organization (India)
ODPM	Office of the Deputy Prime Minister (UK)
OECD	Organization for Economic Cooperation and Development
OLS	ordinary least squares

List of Acronyms and Abbreviations

ONS	Office of National Statistics (UK)
PCA	principal component approach
PDI	personal disposable income
PEP	Poverty and Economic Policy research network (Canada)
PIM	perpetual inventory method
PNAD	National Household Survey (Brazil)
PPP	purchasing power parity
PPSA	Personal Property Security Act (Canada)
PSID	Panel Study of Income Dynamics (USA)
RBI	Reserve Bank of India
RLMS	Russia Longitudinal Monitoring Survey
RRIFs	registered retirement income funds (Canada)
SARB	South African Reserve Bank
SAYE	save-as-you-earn
SEBI	Securities and Exchange Board of India
SCF	Survey of Consumer Finances (USA)
SCST	scheduled caste and scheduled tribe (India)
SHIW	Survey of Household Income and Wealth (Italy)
SNA	System of National Accounts
SOE	state-owned enterprise
SOU	Statens Offentliga Utredningar (Sweden)
SPI	Survey of Personal Incomes
UNECE	United Nations Economic Commission for Europe
UNSD	United Nations Statistics Division
USAID	United States Agency for International Development
WIID	World Income Inequality Database (UNU-WIDER)

1

An Overview of Personal Wealth

James B. Davies

This volume examines personal assets or wealth from a global perspective. Wealth is the value of physical and financial assets minus debts. It is a crucial determinant of well-being, and is being studied carefully in an increasing number of countries. While valuable international comparisons have been made, there has, so far, not been an attempt to integrate national perspectives fully and to look at personal wealth from a global viewpoint.

1 Why Study Wealth?

Wealth is one of the two major sources of household income. The other is human capital. For income there is a huge literature on the distribution within countries, and there is also now a sizeable literature on the global distribution. As part of that work, researchers study the flow of income from human capital—that is, labour earnings—without estimating the distribution of human capital itself. Why then can we not confine ourselves to the study of capital income? Why is it important also to study the stock of personal wealth that generates this flow?

A short answer is that, whereas labour earnings are easy to measure while the value of human capital is not, the situation is the opposite for physical and financial capital. In the latter case, income is often unobserved or badly measured and the value of the stock is more easily estimated. Most assets are bought and sold and have values that can in principle be observed. To take an example of practical importance, the imputed rent on an owner-occupied house is generally more difficult to establish than the value of the house.

While it might be agreed that, in principle, it is desirable to study the distribution of wealth, it may be pointed out that there are measurement difficulties in this area too. Furthermore, it could be argued, the bulk of personal resources and income are on the human rather the non-human side.

Since on average about 60–70 per cent of personal income comes from human capital, is it not good enough for most purposes just to look at labour earnings? The answer is no, for a number of reasons. One of these is that the share of labour income is not so high in many developing countries. Also, household wealth is less equally distributed than labour earnings or family income. As estimated in Davies et al. (Chapter 19, this volume), the world Gini coefficient for household wealth is about 0.89. The world Gini for household income is only about 0.80 (Milanovic 2005).

Since personal assets, unlike human capital, can be bought and sold, they provide a store of value. This gives assets functions that cannot be played by human capital. First, people can self-insure by 'saving against a rainy day'. This function is especially important in poor countries, where social safety nets are lacking, there is more dependence on agriculture with all its risks, and vulnerability to disasters is greater. Saving for retirement and other predictable future needs is also important.

Personal assets can be used as collateral for loans. This is often important in starting a business. And, if loans cannot be obtained, personal assets can be transformed into cash and thereby into business equity. Again this may be especially important in poor countries where financial markets are less developed. Having personal wealth can also give people more independence in other ways. It is easier to insist on your rights when you have the resources to hire a good lawyer, for example. Political power may also be related to wealth.

Is it always equally important to include wealth in one's analysis? The significance of wealth depends on the environment. In a corrupt society wealth may buy more power. Where there are public pensions, a good supply of rental housing, free health care, and low-cost education, many people may be able to have a good life with little private wealth. However, lack of assets may be a big problem in a country where people face high income risk and there is little social security. The distribution of wealth may therefore be of most concern in poor, developing, and transition countries.[1]

2 Definitions and Conceptual Issues

The definition of wealth is deceptively simple: the value of assets minus debts. However, there is some debate about which assets should be included, and there are valuation problems. Difficulties centre on the asset rather than

---

[1] It is probably also more important in a country like the USA, where many people lack health insurance, public schooling is poor in many areas, and transfer payments are less generous or more difficult to get than in other high-income OECD countries. It is not *only* in poor, developing, or transition countries that personal wealth can be important for well-being.

debt side. For example, should pension rights be included? Occupational or employer-based pensions might be regarded as deferred labour compensation, and therefore part of the return on human capital. Even if such pension rights are included in non-human wealth, should this be at a discount in view of their illiquidity? And what is the status of public pension rights, given that the benefits could legally be altered without permission or compensation of the 'owners'? Is there really a property right to such pensions?

The question of whether to include pension rights is often moot, due to lack of data. Where data are available, they are sometimes only partial. For example, the US Survey of Consumer Finance includes defined contribution pension plans (readily measured) but excludes defined benefit plans (difficult to measure). Attempts to include all private pensions have been made in some cases. In the UK, for example, the Inland Revenue's series 'D' and 'E' estimates include private pensions, and private plus public pensions. Private pensions pushed the wealth share of the top 1 per cent down from about 18 per cent in the mid-1980s to 14 per cent, and adding both private and public pensions decreased the share further to 11 per cent (Davies and Shorrocks 2000: 605–76). In the USA, on the other hand, Wolff and Marley (1989: 765–844) found that adding private pensions had little impact on overall inequality, but that after public pensions were added the share of the top 1 per cent fell from 30 to 20 per cent in 1981. Adding private pensions may have an equalizing or disequalizing effect depending on how important they are at different wealth levels in a particular country. Public pension rights are generally rather equally distributed.

It may be unclear whether some assets should be classified as belonging to the state or to households. Some countries have extremely wealthy rulers or heads of state. In some cases—for example, the UK—a careful distinction is made between the ruler's personal wealth and state assets like official residences. However, in some transition, developing, and resource-rich countries, it is not clear that such a line can be readily drawn.[2]

Even after the list of personal assets has been determined, there remain conceptual difficulties associated with valuation. For many assets there is a difference between a 'going concern' versus 'realization' valuation (see, e.g., Atkinson and Harrison 1978). For a going concern, it would be normal to use replacement value for real assets. However, the realization approach is more commonly used in household surveys. This is appropriate if we are interested

---

[2] An interesting case is that of oil-rich monarchical states, of which Saudi Arabia is the leading example. Saudi Arabia has a large royal family, and its members share much of the ownership of the country's oil. Their affairs are, however, intimately connected with those of the state (see Cahill 2006). In this and similar cases the question of whether the assets should be considered personal or state assets could have practical implications for measurement. Estimates of the value of oil and other natural resources by country are available; see, e.g., World Bank (2006a).

in such questions as how much wealth people can draw on in emergencies.[3] Since each approach has its own uses, though, it can pay to have estimates prepared on the two alternative bases, as in Atkinson and Harrison (1978).

An example where realization and going-concern valuations lead to very different results is life insurance. In household surveys it is common to value insurance on a 'cash surrender'—that is, realization—basis. In this approach term insurance has no value. If one takes a dynastic view of the family, this is odd. An actuarial valuation would be more appropriate. While 28 per cent of American families had life insurance according to the 2001 Survey of Consumer Finances (SCF), it accounted for only 5.3 per cent of total financial assets. That small share reflects only the savings component, and leaves out the actuarial value of death benefits entirely.

A difficulty in international comparisons lies in the classification of different kinds of assets and debts. A central example concerns business assets and debts. In some household surveys respondents are simply asked to report their 'business equity'. In other cases, however, they are asked to detail business assets and debts, and these may be aggregated by type with the household's other assets and debts. This will result in a different apparent composition of household wealth than classifying business equity as a separate asset. Within countries this is not a problem. However, international comparisons of portfolio composition become more difficult when not all countries use the same approach.

There are other international differences in classification. Not all countries distinguish between mortgage and consumer debt. Among real assets, 'housing' generally refers to the gross value of owner-occupied housing, including the land occupied. However, this is not always clear. In Italy, for example, in the Survey of Household Income and Wealth (SHIW), housing includes all houses owned by the household, owner-occupied or not. And in China the value is net of mortgage debt, and land is not included. For financial assets, varying levels of detail are seen. In some cases, for example, all forms of deposit are lumped together; in others, they are separated. Sheltered retirement savings may be separated, or the underlying assets held in this form may be aggregated with stocks, bonds, and so on.

As in income distribution studies there is an important question of the choice of unit—households, families, individuals, or perhaps adults. Some of the considerations are similar to those for income, but others differ.

---

[3] It has been argued by some that, if a major purpose of personal wealth is to offset risk, in addition to the usual measures of wealth we should look at more narrow measures that omit illiquid assets—for example, houses, vehicles, and other durables (see, e.g., Shorrocks 1987b; Jenkins 1990). E. N. Wolff (1990b) provides a wealth variant in his study of wealth and poverty in the USA, fungible wealth that omits durables and household inventories. Omitting housing or durables results in a more unequal distribution of wealth, emphasizing the vulnerability of many households to income or other risk.

A household or family basis is often used in income studies, since it is believed either that members share their income for consumption purposes or that they should. However, the presumption of sharing does not necessarily apply to wealth. For example, the bulk of a family's wealth might legally be in the husband's name. Or the husband and wife may have independent ownership of assets they brought to the marriage or inherited. The adult children may have no legal claim on the family's assets. These considerations may make the choice of an individual or adult unit more attractive in the case of wealth than for income.

Many countries have wealthy citizens living offshore for tax or other reasons. This raises the question of whether the distribution of wealth should be estimated on a residence or citizenship basis. The residence basis is normally used, but—for example, in making lists of the rich—journalists sometimes use citizenship. A related problem is that wealthy individuals may hold much of their assets offshore. These assets should be included, but it may be very difficult to estimate their value.

A further conceptual issue is the relationship between personal and national wealth. Ultimately, all wealth must belong to *people*. It might therefore seem that a country's personal wealth and its national wealth should be the same. However, national balance sheets recognize the separate wealth of non-personal sectors—for example, non-profit organizations (NPOs), private corporations, and the state. It is sometimes argued that the net worth of these sectors should be imputed to persons. While this may appear to be an attractive argument, note that a similar argument can be made for income. Also, there are considerable conceptual and practical difficulties in performing the imputations. Finally, the net worth of non-personal sectors is generally much less than their assets, so that the quantitative impact of the proposed imputation is not necessarily large. For such reasons, it is not common to make imputations for the wealth of non-personal sectors when studying the distribution of wealth, and such calculations are not made in this volume.

National wealth includes the value of foreign assets and is net of liabilities to the rest-of-the-world. For some countries foreign investments are much larger than liabilities, so that national wealth is significantly larger than domestic wealth. Estimates of the latter have been provided for 120 countries in World Bank (2006a), which pays particular attention to natural resources. In order to put the World Bank numbers on a personal basis, it would be necessary to add net foreign wealth and to deduct the wealth of the state, NPOs and other non-personal sectors. There can be large differences between domestic and personal wealth in countries with a large (positive or negative) net foreign balance, or in countries with state ownership of large natural resources. It appears that no one has yet attempted to generate national or personal sector wealth numbers from the Bank's estimates.

3 Data Sources

For some purposes—for example, estimating macroeconomic relationships—interest centres on aggregates. A balance sheet for the personal sector as a whole is needed, preferably on an annual basis. As discussed in Chapter 19, such balance sheets are currently available for fifteen high-income Organization for Economic Cooperation and Development (OECD) countries, as well as the Czech Republic and South Africa. In fifteen additional cases, including most of Central Europe, a balance sheet of financial assets and liabilities is available.

While the balance sheet of the personal sector is interesting, it tells us nothing about the distribution of wealth, or about differences in portfolios. Evidence on the distribution and composition of wealth can be generated from three major sources: data on investment income, wealth and estate tax records, and household surveys. The investment income multiplier approach has been used where direct information on wealth is not available. If the distribution of investment income, by type of asset, is known, one can estimate the corresponding wealth by multiplying by the inverse of an asset-specific rate of return. In recent years the best example of the use of this approach has been in Australia (Dilnot 1990; Baekgaard 1997). While this can be a useful method, it is generally better to seek direct estimates. As household wealth surveys become more widespread and reliable, we may expect even less use of the investment income multiplier method.[4] However, it can still be useful where information on the upper tail of the wealth distribution from other sources is poor, or in countries that lack surveys.

Wealth tax records have been used to estimate the distribution of wealth, notably in the Nordic countries, and the estate tax source has been used for a long time in the UK and USA. The methods involved and results obtained are discussed in several places in this volume, for example by Jäntti and Sierminska (Chapter 2), Ohlsson et al. (Chapter 3), Atkinson (Chapter 4), and Davies et al. (Chapter 19). Unlike the investment income method, estimation based on wealth and estate tax records is not becoming less important over time. Recently, new studies using such data have been done for France, Spain, Switzerland, and the USA by Thomas Piketty, Emmanuel Saez, and co-authors (see Kopczuk and Saez 2004b; Alvaredo and Saez 2006; Piketty et al. 2006; Dell et al. 2007; Ohlsson et al., Chapter 3, this volume). The UK still does not have a regular wealth survey, although that may change.[5] And, while

---

[4] Australia now has good direct evidence from the Household, Income and Labour Dynamics in Australia (HILDA) survey—for example, reducing the need to apply the investment income multiplier method in that country (see Headey et al. 2005).

[5] The UK is an official participant in the Luxembourg Wealth Study (LWS), which aims to develop internationally comparable household wealth survey data.

the USA has excellent survey evidence, attention is still paid to estate tax-based results as a check and an alternative way of viewing the distribution.[6]

Finally, there are household surveys. While these have many advantages, they are subject to both sampling and non-sampling error. The former is a significant problem, since the distribution of wealth is highly skewed, and it has been known for a long time that this reduces reliability. Non-sampling error may arise from systematic variation in response rates with wealth (for example, lower rates among the rich), and misreporting (generally under-reporting) of assets by respondents. Survey organizations have developed sophisticated methods to combat these errors. One of the most useful is to oversample households expected to have high wealth—for example, on the basis of income tax records. Such oversampling is required for a household survey to provide reliable estimates of the upper tail. The technique is used in the USA, Canada, Finland, Spain, and a few other countries. It should be applied more widely.

4 Contribution of this Volume

This volume is divided into four parts. The middle two, which are the longest, cover wealth distribution in developing and transition countries and the role of major asset types in economic development and performance. The final section has a single chapter that presents the first available estimates of the global distribution of household wealth. The first section sets the stage by looking at wealth in the developed world, where we have the best data.

4.1 *The Rich and the Super-Rich*

The volume begins with three chapters that study the 'rich and the super-rich'—the world's wealthiest countries and the richest people who live in those countries. We begin in Chapter 2 with a snapshot of personal wealth in OECD countries today, mainly as revealed in household surveys. As Markus Jäntti and Eva Sierminska outline, sample surveys of wealth have become increasingly sophisticated and have spread. They summarize results from twelve countries. Asset coverage varies, and, while most countries use interviews, the Nordic countries use wealth tax records. Several, but not all, countries use a high-income sampling frame. Because of these differences in

---

[6] The estate tax-based estimates are on an individual basis, whereas the SCF results are on a household basis, and there are other differences—for example, in asset coverage. The two sources show somewhat contrasting pictures with regard to changes in inequality over time; see the discussion by Ohlsson et al., Chapter 3, this volume.

methods, the data allow only rough comparisons.[7] In terms of means, it is found that the USA is the wealthiest, followed by Italy, Japan, Australia, the Netherlands, and Canada.

Jäntti and Sierminska also look at asset composition and incidence. They find that home ownership rates have risen over time. This rate is at its highest (68 per cent) in the USA, followed by Italy (66 per cent), Canada (60 per cent), and the UK (57 per cent). While always important, the value of housing varies considerably: from 38 per cent of non-financial assets in Italy to 80 per cent in Germany. On average, housing makes up about 40 per cent of net worth (see Chapters 5 and 19 as well as Chapter 2). Considerable variation is also seen in the composition of financial assets, with greatest variation in mutual funds and retirement accounts—both very important in the USA, for example, but unimportant in some other countries.

To date, consistent measures of wealth inequality have not been available for many countries. In Chapter 19 this problem is tackled by fitting smooth distributions for each country and comparing the inequality measures generated. Jäntti and Sierminska instead use a simple indicator of inequality that can be computed for eight OECD countries from published data. This is the difference in the logs of mean and median wealth. Among the seven high-income countries in this group, the USA has the highest value (1.45) and Sweden the lowest (0.37). In three countries where comparisons can be made over time (Finland, Italy, and the USA), wealth inequality rose over the 1990s.

In Chapter 3 Ohlsson et al. examine historical evidence on the evolution of wealth inequality in seven OECD countries, using wealth and estate tax data as well as survey evidence. Data are available for the UK and USA going back to 1740 and 1774 respectively—before the Industrial revolution—and for France from 1807. Series begin for Denmark, Norway, Sweden, and Switzerland in the early twentieth century. Since the Nordic countries were late to industrialize, some of these data also go back to a pre-industrial time.

As originally suggested by Kuznets, one might expect an inverse U-shaped path of inequality during development. Ohlsson et al. find roughly such a pattern for wealth in France, the UK, and the USA. On the other hand, wealth inequality has been stable in Switzerland, and in the Nordic countries we do not find rising inequality in the early years. Finally, after the downswing observed in most countries, wealth inequality reached considerably lower levels than before industrialization. Thus a better description is an inverse J- rather than U-shaped path.

The declining wealth inequality seen in six of the seven countries in the mid-twentieth century is associated with a fall in income inequality. There was

[7] A major international project, the Luxembourg Wealth Study (LWS), is developing comparable wealth data for ten countries: Austria, Canada, Cyprus, Finland, Germany, Italy, Norway, Sweden, the UK, and the USA; see www.lisproject.org/lws.htm.

a spread of wealth holding to wider circles, and a growth of 'popular assets'—automobiles, other durables, and owner-occupied housing. Two world wars, the depression, and redistributive taxation may also have played a role.

Trends over the last three decades are of interest. A continuing increase in income inequality began in the mid-1970s in the USA, and roughly similar patterns have been seen in the UK and elsewhere. With deregulation of financial markets, a spread of share holding, and buoyant stock markets, an increase in wealth inequality might be expected. Surprisingly, although an upward trend over the twenty years beginning in the early 1980s can be detected in each country in the Ohlsson et al. sample, except for France, which does not have enough data points to allow a conclusion, the expected upward trend is not as strong as one might have expected. This has attracted particular attention in the USA, where estate multiplier data show no upward trend in the share of the top 1 per cent, and where the Survey of Consumer Finance shows only a mild increase in concentration. Shares of the top 1 and 5 per cent rose in the SCF from the 1983 survey to surveys conducted from 1989 to 1995. However, the share of the top 5 per cent fell after 1995 and that of the top 1 per cent dropped from 38.1 per cent in 1998 to 33.4 per cent in 2001, taking it back very close to the 1983 value of 33.8 per cent.

The lack of a stronger upward trend in top wealth shares in the last few decades of the twentieth century may be partly due to the strength of house prices in this period. A rise in house prices tends to increase the wealth share of middle groups, for whom housing is a very important component of the household portfolio, and to decrease shares for top groups, since housing is relatively less important for them. Wolff (2005) has identified another important part of the puzzle for the USA. The standard measure of wealth in the USA includes only a part of pension wealth—that is, defined contribution (DC) pension plans. The Gini coefficient for this measure of wealth rose from 0.799 in 1983 to 0.826 in 2001, an increase of just 3.4 per cent. However, when all forms of pension and social-security wealth are included, the Gini rose from 0.590 to 0.663, a rise of 12.4 per cent. Thus the impression that wealth inequality in 2001 was not very different from that in 1983 is dispelled if a more complete measure of wealth is used.

In Chapter 4 Tony Atkinson examines how the 'head count' of the rich and inequality within this group have changed over time in France, Germany, the UK, and the USA. This parallels studies of poverty, which estimate the number below the 'poverty line' and inequality among the poor. Atkinson defines the rich as those with more than 30 times mean income. He finds that concentration in this group is very high. Typically the Gini coefficient of wealth is about 0.5 in this group, and its top quarter holds about one half of the group's wealth. There were also major changes in the number of the rich and concentration among them in the twentieth century, although these changes differed across countries. Atkinson's longest time series are for France and Germany, where he finds that there was a large drop in the percentage rich from the First World War to the period immediately after the Second World War. During this time, though, trends in concentration differed, with inequality among the wealthy declining in France but changing little in Germany. After 1950 the percentage rich rebounded in both France and Germany, as the wealthy rebuilt their war-damaged fortunes. The trend was in the other direction in the UK and USA, where both the percentage rich and the degree of concentration among them declined. After about 1980 we find, however, that both the percentage rich and the degree of concentration rose in the USA. Concentration also increased in Germany, although not in France. (Atkinson's UK data do not extend into this period.) The *Forbes* billionaire list indicates, however, that *globally* concentration rose over this period. It has been suggested by some that one reason for this trend could be the increasingly 'winner takes all' character of markets resulting from globalization. Lists of the wealthy, such as those published by *Forbes* magazine, allow one to identify sources of wealth to an extent. The highest echelons tend to be dominated by self-made fortunes. The force of inheritance is reduced by estate division, which is typically more equal now than it was in former times. As Atkinson points out, this provides reason to expect that the relative importance of inheritance may be less at the very top than lower among the wealthy.

4.2 Wealth in the Developing World and Transition Countries

The second part of the volume begins with chapters on wealth distribution in China and India, and moves on to European transition countries, Latin America, and Africa. China is both the largest developing country and the largest transition country. It had 20.6 per cent of the world's population in 2000. Along with India it is also one of just two developing countries that have had repeated wealth surveys. The fact that China and India both have evidence on wealth holding over a significant period of time gives us an important window on trends in a large segment of the developing world— one comprising 37.4 per cent of the world's population in 2000. This is complemented by a wealth survey conducted by the Rand Corporation in 1997 for the third most populous developing country, Indonesia, as part of the Indonesian Family Life Survey (IFLS) panel study (see Davies and Shorrocks 2005, and Davies et al., Chapter 19, this volume).

Chinese wealth surveys are available for 1988 (rural areas only), 1995, and 2002. The latter two surveys look at rural and urban sectors separately and together. As set out by Li and Zhao in Chapter 5, wealth inequality, while apparently still low by international standards, has been rapidly increasing. This parallels the trend in income inequality. In 1995 the Gini coefficient for wealth in China as a whole was 0.40 while in 2002 it had risen to 0.55.

The increase was due mostly to a rise in the rural–urban gap. In 1995 rural wealth averaged 83 per cent of urban, but by 2002 urban wealth had risen so much that this ratio was down to 28 per cent. The fastest growing urban asset was housing, reflecting partly housing privatization but mostly rising prices and new construction.[8]

The Chinese wealth surveys (like those in India) do not over-sample the rich and probably understate the importance of the upper tail. However, this problem may not be more severe than in the several developed countries that do not over-sample at the top. It could even be less severe. The survey response rate is about 95 per cent in both China and India, suggesting that the differential response problem may be less than in developed countries, where typical response rates are 60–70 per cent. Also, in high-income countries one usually finds many people on the *Forbes* list of billionaires, making it clear that there is indeed a very long upper tail. China, however, still had relatively few billionaires on the *Forbes* list when the 2002 survey was conducted (just one, versus five in India).

There have now been five modern wealth surveys in India, conducted at roughly decennial intervals. The evidence they provide is examined closely by Subramanian and Jayaraj in Chapter 6. The first survey, in 1961–2, was confined to rural areas, but both urban and rural areas have been covered since. The most recent survey is for 2002–3. Fairly consistent definitions and concepts have been used throughout. Sample sizes are very large: 143,285 in 2002–3, for example. This allows reliable disaggregation by occupation, caste, and state.

While there are similarities between China and India, there are also great differences. One of these is that India is not a transition country. Substantial wealth inequality was found in India from the time of the first surveys, and there has been no evident upward trend since that time. While, as mentioned above, the estimated upper tail is probably too short, the Gini coefficient of 0.689 for wealth in the country as a whole in the most recent survey is about average in international terms, and much higher than the Gini in China. There is a large rural–urban gap: in 2002–3 rural wealth averaged 73.9 per cent of urban. Inequality is fairly high in both sectors, with Ginis of 0.629 and 0.664 for rural and urban areas respectively. The share of the top 1 per cent is 15.7 per cent in the 2002–3 survey, and rises to 17.8 per cent if the 178 most wealthy Indians reported by the *Business Standard* magazine are added on. There is considerable horizontal wealth inequality in India. Mean wealth in

---

[8] The tendency for housing privatization in urban areas to raise measured wealth inequality can be criticized as partly spurious. The value of use-rights in public housing is not normally included in the data, which exaggerates the inequality-increasing effect of privatization, as explained by Li and Zhao, Chapter 5, and as also discussed by Yemtsov, Chapter 15, both this volume.

the rural area of the most prosperous state exceeds that in the least wealthy state by a factor of 9.2, and the corresponding urban ratio is 3.1. Wealth is also very low for members of the scheduled tribes and castes, and for rural labourers. On the bright side, mean wealth has been rising quite quickly in India, approximately doubling in both rural and urban areas between 1981–2 and 2002–3. This rate of growth is less than observed in China, but it is more evenly shared between rural and urban areas. Overall wealth inequality did not change appreciably between 1991–2 and 2002–3, a period during which wealth inequality was rising rapidly in China. The fact that India grew fairly rapidly during that period without an apparent rise in wealth inequality is encouraging.

The survey evidence for Indonesia indicates even higher concentration than is apparent in India (see Davies et al., Chapter 19). The share of the top 10 per cent in 1997 was 65.4 per cent versus 52.9 per cent in India and 41.4 per cent in China in their most recent surveys. At 0.764, the Gini coefficient estimated for Indonesia by Davies et al. is high compared to those for China and India reported above. Gini figures imputed for Bangladesh and Vietnam by Davies et al. are similar to that for India. The Ginis for Pakistan and Thailand are somewhat higher, but still below Indonesia's.

In contrast to the largest countries in Asia, the European transition countries, Africa, and Latin America have not had wealth surveys at the national level. There are some balance-sheet data, evidence on the distribution of land and the incidence of some other assets, and information that can be used to estimate the distribution of housing wealth. For these areas we have *some* pieces of the puzzle. A series of chapters take the existing pieces and assemble as much of the puzzle as possible, starting with the European transition countries.

In Chapter 7 Sergei Guriev and Andrei Rachinsky discuss the evolution of personal wealth in the former Soviet Union (FSU) and Central and Eastern Europe (CEE), telling how industrial assets and natural resources were privatized and how their ownership has changed over time—Yemtsov's Chapter 15 complements this discussion by estimating the distribution of housing wealth in Russia, Poland, and Serbia. The most fascinating story is that of the Russian oligarchs, men who quickly became fabulously wealthy by obtaining state assets at low prices in the early transition. Although the oligarchs appear to have run their enterprises efficiently, how they obtained their wealth is heavily resented by many Russians. President Putin enforced his famous pact with the oligarchs, under which they stayed out of politics and paid taxes, while he left them alone to run their businesses. However, renationalization is now underway. What happens to the distribution of wealth in Russia in coming years depends in part on the extent and nature of this renationalization.

While there are no household surveys or tax-based information on wealth in the FSU or CEE countries, we do have the *Forbes* lists of billionaires, and estimated numbers of millionaires from Merrill-Lynch. The most striking feature, once again, is the Russian situation. As Guriev and Rachinsky point out, the combined wealth of the 26 Russian billionaires in 2004 was 19 per cent of Russian GDP, whereas, for comparison, the total wealth of the 262 USA billionaires was only 7 per cent of USA GDP. Even without any overall estimates, it seems likely that the Russian wealth distribution is one of the most unequal in the world.

The evolution of wealth inequality in the other European transition countries is also interesting. In the CEE countries, the prospect of EU accession has encouraged the development of property rights, financial institutions, and the rule of law. Together with relatively transparent privatization, these conditions have stimulated private enterprise and have produced a more equal distribution of wealth than in Russia. In the FSU countries aside from Russia, oligarchs are also apparently missing. However, Guriev and Rachinsky point out that autocratic rulers have effectively captured state assets in a number of cases. They suggest that these rulers may be regarded as the 'ultimate oligarchs'.

In Chapter 8, Florencia Torche and Seymour Spilerman outline what is known about the distribution of personal assets in Latin America. They show that a great deal can be said, even though full wealth surveys are not available. There has been considerable attention to the distribution of *land* in Latin America, since it is less equally distributed there than in most other parts of the world. The inequality is less extreme in Bolivia, Mexico, and Nicaragua, where substantial land reforms took place at various times. In most of Latin America there is relatively high access to land, but there is enormous concentration among landowners—a pattern that began with large estates being given to an elite group in colonial times. While land is still an important asset in Latin America, its dominance has been reduced, since most of the population now lives in urban areas. Here housing is very important. Fortunately, it is possible to impute house values by applying a multiplier to reported rental values (Yemtsov uses similar techniques in Chapter 15). Using this method, Torche and Spilerman find that housing wealth in Latin America is more unequal than income, which is itself very unequal. Gini coefficients of housing wealth range from 0.5 to 0.6. This helps to confirm the high wealth inequality in this region, although it should be noted that housing wealth is less unequal in several countries, for example, Chile, where governments have had programmes to assist home-buyers. The picture is rounded out by a study of the distribution of investment income, based on national household surveys from across the region, which confirms the view of informed observers that capital income is very unequally distributed in Latin America.

Juliano Assunção studies the distribution of land and the impact of land reform in Brazil. Although Brazil has become a largely urban society, Assunção finds that 39 per cent of households still own land. Land ownership is popular partly for a range of non-agricultural purposes: as a hedge against inflation, as collateral, as a tax shelter, and even to launder illegal funds. There is a tension between these motives and the principle in Brazilian law, now enshrined in the 1988 Constitution, that ownership is contingent on the land being used. Recent major land reforms, from 1985–9 under the Sarney government, and after 1992 under Cardoso, have been confined to the 'disappropriation' of idle land. Assunção estimates the impact of land disappropriations in a state on the likelihood that households will own land. When household characteristics are held constant, there is only a positive effect for poor and less-educated households. The impact on inequality of land holding among landowners is positive, since the land is redistributed in relatively small parcels mainly to poor households. If inequality in land holding among the population as a whole were considered, however, it would probably decline, because of the reduction in the number of non-holders.

An interesting theme that emerges from Latin America is that, in countries with very high inequality, redistribution may occur via assets as well as, or instead of, via income. This happens in part spontaneously, through squatting, but also in part through official programmes of land reform and housing access. There is an attempt, in Sen's language, to redistribute *capabilities* (see Subramanian and Jayaraj, Chapter 6). Such a tendency adds to the importance of studying personal wealth.

The last three chapters in Part II are on Africa. Chapter 10, by Aron, Muellbauer, and Prinsloo, estimates household balance sheets for South Africa over the period 1975–2003. Along with distributional data, balance sheets are one of the two essential tools for studying household wealth. Unfortunately, with the exception of Mexico, no other developing countries currently have balance-sheet data. Such data are being developed, however, in a number of emerging market and transition countries, such as the Czech Republic, Poland, and Hungary. Chapter 10 explores the problems faced in generating such data.

In some developed countries, such as Australia, Canada, the UK, and the USA, complete national balance sheets have been developed. These include balance sheets not only for the household sector, but for the corporate, government, external, and other sectors. Especially since estimates for many household sector totals are obtained by subtracting the holdings of other sectors from economy-wide aggregates, it might appear that a household sector balance sheet cannot be produced on its own. Fortunately, it *is* possible to assemble good household balance sheets without generating complete balance sheets for other sectors.

Estimates of many financial assets and liabilities can be made from 'counterpart data'. Bank deposits, for example, have their counterpart in a liability of the banks. While in such cases the holdings of the household sector can be identified, in others, such as that of notes and coins, educated guesswork is needed. Estimating household share holdings is particularly difficult. Aron et al. estimate these by cumulating past acquisitions of shares shown in flow-of-funds data. In countries without flow-of-funds data, total share holding would have to be divided between the household and other sectors by some other means, perhaps on the basis of dividends reported for tax purposes. Tangible assets can be estimated using perpetual inventory and other methods.

Aron et al. use their balance sheets to identify some interesting trends. Prior to 1989, the personal wealth to disposable income ratio fluctuated between about 3.5 and 4.0 in South Africa, but after that it fell to the range 2.5–3.0. This was related to a rise in debt, and also a decline in housing wealth. In recent years housing wealth, which is strongly affected by price changes, has rebounded, and there are signs that the overall wealth to income ratio rose after 2003. Other trends have been a decline in liquid assets and a rise in pension wealth. These trends show that household wealth can be very dynamic, and that balance sheets can add to our knowledge of changes in household circumstances. It is to be hoped that researchers in more countries will be able to assemble household balance sheets.

In Chapter 11 Christian Rogg focuses on rural Africa, which accounts for about 63 per cent of the continent's population. He briefly discusses the evidence for various countries and then focuses on the Ethiopia Rural House-hold Survey (ERHS), a panel study of fifteen representative villages that provides some of the most detailed and reliable evidence on wealth in rural Africa. Villagers in Ethiopia are mainly engaged in agriculture and, although relatively poor, hold assets in the form of food and crops, livestock, and farming equipment in addition to some housing and consumer durables. Cash or liquid assets are of little importance. Under the Ethiopian constitution land cannot be bought or sold. It is more equally distributed than other assets, but its inequality is about average for African countries. Wealthier households invest particularly in additional livestock, which is riskier than, for example, food and crops. Villagers in locations with more variable rainfall, however, invest less in livestock. These observations are consistent with economists' ideas about how portfolio choice should vary with wealth and the riskiness of assets. Rogg finds that the main motives for saving in rural Ethiopia are for precautionary reasons, investment, and to some extent bequest. Life-cycle motives are less important than in developed countries. He also finds, interestingly, that, while assets are more unequally distributed than consumption, they are less unequal than income. This reflects variable returns and uncertainty in farm incomes, and is suggestive of the role of assets in providing self-insurance.

The last chapter in Part II, by Ronelle Burger and co-authors, uses information on whether people own particular assets from the Demographic and Health Surveys (DHS) for Ghana to construct an *asset index*. Similar approaches have been applied in various countries for two purposes. Where both asset indices and measures of income or consumption are available, they correlate fairly highly. Researchers therefore have used asset indices as a measure of welfare or resources in cases where other indicators were not available. A second use of asset indices has been as a *supplement* to information on income or consumption. Burger et al. ask to what extent asset indices can substitute for direct evidence on wealth. If such a substitution can be made, it may be helpful in many other developing countries.

The data used by Burger et al. record whether households own nine assets. In addition, the type of flooring in the home enters the index. Multiple correspondence analysis (MCA) is used. The results are appealing. Owning a car increases the index value by about 24 times as much as a bicycle, for example; a radio is 'worth' about half as much as a TV; and a tractor bumps up the index more than twice as much as a horse and cart. The 'values' of the assets in the index reflect not only the market value of the asset but the significance of related assets. Owning a video recorder turns out to have the largest impact on the index, reflecting the fact that video recorders are owned mainly by the wealthiest households, who hold many related assets. Burger et al. are able to evaluate their index using the 1998 Ghana Living Standards Survey (GLSS). The GLSS lacks data on livestock and debt, but otherwise has fairly complete asset coverage. It is found using the GLSS data that an index based on the same ten characteristics as the asset index constructed using the DHS data is moderately correlated with broad measures of household wealth, and behaves similarly to them in important ways. This suggests that DHS-type data can be used to construct asset indices that can stand in for wealth, at least for some purposes, in countries that lack full wealth data.

An interesting sidelight is that all three studies for Africa show household wealth increasing, either for a significant period in the 1990s (Ethiopia) or both in the 1990s and the early 2000s (South Africa and Ghana). The studies for Ethiopia and Ghana also find a strong positive effect of education on wealth. These findings make clear that progress in building household wealth is quite possible in Africa, and in some cases has indeed been occurring.

4.3 *Role of Personal Assets in Economic Development and Performance*

Part III begins with two studies that look at major asset types—financial holdings, and housing. These are followed by chapters on housing privatization in transition economies, the impact of land titles and credit markets, gender-related aspects of wealth holding, and the informal sector.

In Chapter 13 Patrick Honohan discusses the role of household financial assets in development. Financial assets make up 30–40 per cent of net worth in typical developed countries according to survey evidence. The ratio appears to be smaller in developing countries; as low as 6 per cent in India. Reported debt is also less important in developing countries. In addition, some patterns observed in developed countries, such as the decline in riskiness of portfolios at higher ages, and the increase in risk-taking with wealth, are not so evident in developing countries. There is a widespread belief that increasing access to financial institutions and products is important for welfare and development. Honohan assembles data on financial access in 150 countries and shows that the relationship between financial access and poverty is not robust. On the other hand, there *is* a robust (negative) relationship between financial depth, measured, for example, by the ratio of deposits or credit to GDP, and poverty. There are competing explanations for this, but so far no consensus. It seems likely though that it is the *use* of financial products, including loans, not access to those products, that is crucial in reducing poverty.

The single most important asset in the personal sector is housing. As discussed by John Muellbauer in Chapter 14, the evidence from developed countries indicates that housing market activity may have strong effects on macroeconomic behaviour. One important pathway in the 'monetary transmission mechanism' lies from interest rates through home borrowing to housing demand and new construction. And the housing market itself may be the source of macroeconomic disturbances resulting from changes in consumer expenditure in response to house prices. In recent years there has been anxiety that house prices in several important OECD countries have risen unsustainably. Muellbauer argues that, while such concerns should not be dismissed, they have been overblown. He also demonstrates that the macroeconomic significance of the housing market is related to key institutional features that vary greatly between countries.

While the role of housing in monetary transmission might seem a remote concern in many poor countries, some developing countries are growing rapidly, and such concerns may soon become relevant. Increased development of mortgage finance in developing countries, for example, may have important effects. As noted earlier, in developed countries a high fraction of new businesses is financed through mortgages on homes. Also, housing is the most important of those popular assets whose spread helped to equalize the distribution of wealth in developed countries through much of the twentieth century. The development of good mortgage finance and high rates of home ownership may be an important element both in achieving growth and in reducing inequality.

Housing wealth has also been a centre of interest in transition countries, as discussed by Ruslan Yemtsov in Chapter 15. There the rate of home ownership increased greatly in a few years because of privatization. A number of studies have concluded that privatization reduced income or consumption inequality, when in-kind benefits of housing are taken into account. Yemtsov, however, points out measurement difficulties, particularly the lack of attention to differences in quality and market value of housing. He argues that, if such a large wealth transfer was really equalizing, one should see a downward impact on inequality in consumption *omitting* housing benefits, but across eighteen transition countries, from the former USSR and Central Europe, there is no such relationship. Yemtsov goes further, using survey data on housing, income, and consumption to construct estimates of the market value of housing and rental values for Russia, Poland, and Serbia. In all three countries there was little variation with income in the value of a privatized dwelling. Thus, if the percentage of households experiencing privatization had been the same across income groups, it would have been equalizing. However, the incidence of privatization rose sharply with income—for example, from 19 per cent in the bottom consumption quintile in Russia to 41 per cent in the top quintile. This contributes to the result that the effect of housing services (both from privatized and non-privatized dwellings) on consumption inequality is small and negative in Russia and Poland, and also small but positive in Serbia.

The impact of privatization on inequality *in housing wealth* is somewhat negative in each country Yemtsov studies, in the sense that inequality of overall housing wealth is less than that of non-privatized housing alone. This equalizing effect is obtained because, although privatized houses are, on average, worth more than non-privatized, the inequality in value of privatized housing is estimated to be much smaller. Since housing is such a sizable asset and both financial assets and debts are low for households in transition countries, the effect of privatization on inequality in total wealth may also have been negative, although the data required to test this hypothesis are not available.

In Chapter 16 Jim MacGee looks at the role of land titling, first explaining the elements that are required for it to be effective. These include efficient registration of land transactions, a comprehensive database on land titles, known as a cadastre, and a register of mortgages and other liens on property. Developed countries have these elements, and also enforce property rights and the rights of mortgagors. However, the same is not true in many developing and transition countries. MacGee asks what impacts this may have on growth and development, and also on wealth distribution. There is a range of empirical evidence indicating that lack of formal land titling reduces investment and productivity, as well as borrowing. These are anti-growth impacts. The effect on wealth inequality is less easy to predict. In a world with poor land titles and underdeveloped credit, households need to accumulate wealth in order to be able to purchase housing or start a business, or for precautionary reasons. Secure land titles and better credit markets may reduce wealth holding of low-income or young people by reducing these motives for saving. Such effects may raise wealth inequality. This conclusion is supported by a number of dynamic simulation exercises in recent years. Thus not all increases in wealth inequality are necessarily 'bad'.

Chapter 17 looks at gender-related aspects. As Carmen Deere and Cheryl Doss detail, gender is potentially more important in wealth studies than for income or consumption. There can be more gender inequality in asset ownership within the family, for example, than there is in consumption. Also, 'ownership' is multi-faceted. The right to receive income from an asset may belong to one person, while the right to sell or the right to inherit may belong to others, including people outside the immediate family. These rights are often fractured along gender lines. Deere and Doss document that there is a considerable gender gap in asset ownership in the developing world. They outline four constraints on women's ownership: state, family, community, and market, paying particular attention to legal regimes, since these come to the fore in comparative analyses. Both marital and inheritance regimes are important. An important step forward for marital property regimes was the 1981 Convention on the Elimination of All Forms of Discrimination against Women (CEDAW), now ratified by most UN member countries. Under CEDAW women must have equal rights to own, transact, and benefit from property whether married or not. The convention has had significant impact in Latin America, but apparently less effect in Africa and India. In many parts of Africa, matters are difficult, since marital rights are affected by overlapping legal systems based on civil, religious, and customary law.

An important aspect of inheritance regimes is the degree of testamentary freedom. In India, legislation in the 1950s conferred complete testamentary freedom, which provides the least protection for widows. In Latin America, there has been a move towards reserving a share of the estate for widows, adding to their protection in most of this region through a half share in marital community property. In Africa, inheritance rules tend to be complex and are heterogeneous across countries and communities. The inheritance rights of women are generally weak, and are even so where matrilineal lineage is practised. This reinforces the tendency of the marital regime to make women's access to land dependent on marriage. There have been improvements in women's access to land in Latin America, but progress has been relatively slow in Africa. There is evidence that wives' land ownership not only increases their welfare, but is positively related to the fraction of the household budget spent on food and the amount of child schooling.

A large fraction of wealth in developing and transition countries lies in the informal sector. In Chapter 18 Pratap and Quintin report a shift in thinking about the informal sector that de-emphasizes barriers to workers in obtaining jobs in the formal sector, and highlights instead institutional deficiencies, such as unnecessary bureaucracy and poor tax administration. Given the latter, many entrepreneurs will find it more profitable to stay in the informal sector, despite the resulting poor access to credit. Lack of credit leads to under-capitalized firms, lower output, and lower wages throughout the economy than could be achieved with better institutions and a smaller informal sector.

De Soto (2000) has argued that the amount of untitled real estate in the informal sectors of developing and transition countries is huge. His point estimate for the year 1997, based on extrapolating from four or five countries studied in detail, is $US9.34 trillion. He refers to this wealth as 'dead capital', arguing that it cannot be used as collateral and has limited marketability. Other investigators have criticized de Soto's estimates, and have found that people in the informal sector typically do have significant access to loans. However, there is a consensus that the problem de Soto identified is nonetheless significant. This has given impetus to titling programmes in many countries. Woodruff (2001) reviews the evidence and gives a best guess of $US3.4 trillion for the amount of informal sector capital. For comparison, this is 21 per cent of the total household wealth that Davies et al. estimate (in Chapter 19) was held in the world's 162 low- and middle-income countries in the year 2000.[9]

5 The Global Picture

The final section of the volume has just one chapter, by James Davies, Susanna Sandström, Tony Shorrocks, and Ed Wolff (DSSW hereafter). This chapter provides the first available estimate of the world distribution of household wealth. The authors require two key inputs: country wealth levels and the distribution of wealth within countries. Data on wealth levels are available for thirty-nine countries, from either balance-sheet or survey sources. Estimates of the distribution of wealth are available for twenty countries from household surveys, wealth tax, or estate tax-based studies. The countries with wealth data include 56 per cent of the world's population and it is estimated that they have 80 per cent of the world's wealth. Evidence from these countries is used to develop techniques that allow the imputation of wealth levels and distributions to the remaining countries.

The results of the DSSW study are striking. The top 2 per cent of the world's adults are estimated to hold 50 per cent of the world's household wealth. The Gini coefficient for world wealth is 0.89, which is the same value one would obtain in a population of ten people if one person had $US1,000 and the other nine had just $US1. Clearly, the world distribution of wealth is highly unequal. North America, Europe, and the high-income Asian countries (for example, Japan, Korea, Hong Kong, and Singapore) each have between about 25 and 35 per cent of the world's wealth. Latin America, Africa, the transition countries, and much of Asia share the rest. Interestingly, while

---

[9] Chapter 19 estimates that $US104.4 trillion was held in the 24 high-income OECD countries, $US4.6 trillion in 43 high-income non-OECD countries, and $US16.3 trillion in low- and middle-income countries.

world wealth inequality is certainly greater than average inequality within countries, the difference is not as great as in the case of income. One reflection of this is that wealth inequality in the USA is at almost the same level as world wealth inequality. In contrast, there is a significant step-up from USA income inequality to world income inequality.

A further finding of DSSW is that portfolio patterns differ considerably across countries. Predictably, land and agricultural assets are relatively more important in developing countries. However, even within the OECD there are very large variations. In some countries, such as Japan, Italy, and a number of European transition countries, there is a strong preference for safe liquid assets, such as bank deposits. Participation in share holding, and ownership rates for other risky assets, are low. In contrast, in the USA, the UK, and some other countries, there is much wider ownership of corporate shares and far less emphasis on safe assets. In the long run these differences ought to have consequences for the distributions of both wealth and income.

6 Conclusions

A number of important conclusions can be drawn from the above discussion and from the studies in this volume. Most of these are of a positive nature, but some are normative. It is clear that low wealth and poor access to credit exacerbate poverty problems in developing and transition countries. Providing institutions, programmes, and policies that will help the poor to build their wealth and borrow on appropriate terms is, therefore, an objective that should have wide support. Broad consensus can also be expected that people should not be able to build fortunes through corruption or unfair competition, and that action to prevent this is important. Whether there should also be attempts to *redistribute* wealth, and what form they should take, is a more controversial matter, and one that is beyond the scope of this volume. We have seen, however, that in developing countries with very unequal distribution of land, and in transition countries with questionable privatization practices, there tends to be great inequality of income and wealth. If equitable land reforms or redistribution of privatized assets can be performed in an orderly fashion, and have broad popular support, then they would seem to have much to recommend them.

Some of the key conclusions from the research reported in this volume are:

- Household wealth is highly unequal, both within countries and in the world as a whole.
- During industrialization wealth inequality first rose in most developed countries, but then experienced a long decline, with the spread of popular

assets and a decline in income inequality. This trend continued until the 1970s. The pattern can be described as an inverse J-shape.

- Within most countries the trend in the last three decades has been towards higher wealth inequality. In transition countries, this is partly a result of the replacement of socialist patterns of ownership by those of a market economy. Elsewhere it is associated with the rise in income inequality, deregulation of financial markets, and increases in share prices. The rise in wealth inequality has not been as strong as might have been expected in all countries, however. Using standard measures it has been especially weak in the USA. One force holding back the shares of the top 1 and 5 per cent has been rising house prices, which have a greater impact for middle groups. But recent evidence also suggests that the impression of little increase in wealth inequality in the USA may be misleading, since, when all forms of retirement wealth are included and attention is paid to overall inequality—that is, not just top shares—there is a significant upward trend in wealth inequality.

- Wealth differences between countries have on average probably been declining in recent years, because of the rapid increase in wealth in China and India.

- There has been a tendency in recent decades towards increased wealth concentration *among* the truly rich. This may be related to the increasingly 'winner-takes-all' nature of global markets.

- Trends in house prices and mortgage lending can have important implications for consumer expenditure and therefore for macroeconomic performance. The strength of these impacts varies across countries, depending on the nature of institutions and the level of financial development.

- In developing countries, whether people have access to financial institutions does not appear to affect poverty. The extent to which they *use* financial products is, however, negatively associated with poverty. This suggests that programmes that reduce practical barriers to the use of credit and savings vehicles by the poor are important.

- Lack of formal title to land and housing may slow income growth and hold back development. Such property cannot be used as collateral for loans from financial institutions. Continuing to promote titling programmes should help more households to access credit and build wealth in developing countries.

- Household portfolio choices differ considerably between countries. Research is needed to investigate why this is the case, and to establish whether there is a link between these differences and those in wealth inequality.

- Wealth is probably more important for welfare, particularly for the poor and low-income groups, in developing and transition countries than in high-income countries. Where social safety nets and credit availability are poor or lacking, household assets serve as an important form of self-insurance.

They also allow self-financing for business start-ups and operation. It is, therefore, especially important to study household wealth in developing and transition countries—precisely the countries where data are currently the poorest.

We hope that the research reported in this volume will be effective in demonstrating the great importance of personal assets in economic development, poverty reduction, and patterns of inequality. Future national and international assessments of poverty and inequality should make the best possible use of data on household assets and wealth, in addition to studying consumption and income. And much more needs to be done to increase the quality and availability of household wealth data. Central banks and national statistical agencies should work to produce household balance-sheet estimates. Wealth questions should be included on household surveys, and wealth surveys should over-sample the upper tail in order to obtain the most accurate possible results. Finally, international cooperation must be established in order to compare methods and experiences and to spread best practices in the development of household wealth data.

Part I

The Rich and the Super-Rich

2

Survey Estimates of Wealth Holdings in OECD Countries: Evidence on the Level and Distribution across Selected Countries

Markus Jäntti and Eva Sierminska

1 Introduction

Comparisons of income levels across countries and within countries across time are common ways to assess the extent to which living standards vary. As large disparities in incomes are thought to reduce the level of well-being that is associated with a given income level, comparisons of income levels across countries have long been augmented by comparisons of income distribution across countries (see Atkinson et al. 1995).

Wealth may also be important for understanding differences in economic well-being. While we tend to think that well-being depends on the flow of goods and services consumed by persons, the stock of wealth is important for understanding that level. At the household level, the stock of wealth is important both for generating income and, potentially, as a source of reserve funds that allow consumption to be smoothed in case of temporary fluctuations in income. Thus, analyses of cross-country levels and distribution of wealth are an important complement to analyses of income levels and distribution.

There are many other reasons to study household wealth, including, importantly, the analysis of household portfolio choice. This chapter, however, is motivated by distributional issues. There are many ways of defining wealth. If our interest lies in the overall distribution of well-being, wealth defined as human and non-human capital would be of central interest. In this chapter, the term wealth refers to the more commonly used concept of net worth, which measures the value of all non-human assets less liabilities. The problem is not so much in defining the general concept of wealth or net worth, but more in actually measuring it or defining it based on data that are already available.[1] For this reason, researchers have analysed wealth using instruments ranging from proxy variables that indicate the socio-economic status of individuals to very broad net worth concepts. Many current net worth definitions seem to be data driven, but are not consistently used across studies (Sierminska 2005).

Three commonly used notions of wealth distinguished by E. N. Wolff (1990a) include *household disposable wealth* (HDW), *augmented wealth* and *capital wealth*. The first is an accounting notion of wealth and refers to the market value of assets less liabilities that are directly tradable. Augmented wealth refers to the neoclassical notion of the present value of the discounted future stream of net income (including human capital or other comparable measure of future earnings possibilities). In practice, it includes among other wealth components some type of valuation of pension rights from public and private sources, even if these do not meet the more stringent criteria for being wealth. In this respect, it is to be a better indicator of potential future consumption, but quite problematic to estimate.[2] The third concept is a narrower concept than HDW and refers to the ownership of income-producing assets as a store of value and measure of power. In more recent studies, E. N. Wolff (1996, 1998, 2004) uses the concept of marketable wealth (*a*) and augmented wealth (*b*) using data created from estate tax registers along with survey data. These concepts appear to be the most widely used in the literature (Davies and Shorrocks 2000).

As expected, we have come across certain difficulties in cross-country comparisons. One of these is the different definitions that have been used for wealth. In some countries, broader concepts are used, while in others, very detailed wealth questions have been asked. This should be considered when making more general statements about the levels of wealth across countries. Through our literature search, we have found very few comparative studies. In what follows, we compile evidence on wealth composition and distribution to give an overview of the existing data, based on secondary sources. We should also note that a major project to provide comparable wealth survey data for researchers, the Luxembourg Wealth Study (LWS) was finalized too late to be used extensively in this study.[3]

2 Wealth Definitions and Sources across Countries

In order to be able to compare wealth levels across countries, we need to know, among other things, about differences in the definitions of wealth used in the

---

[1] See Jenkins (1990) for a discussion of other conceptual issues in defining wealth.

[2] Social-security and private pension wealth are quite often excluded from the concept of net worth owing to measurement difficulties.

[3] See http://www.lisproject.org/lwstechdoc.htm for information on LWS.

different countries and surveys. Differences in sampling and data collection, while highly technical in nature, can also be very important for cross-country comparisons of wealth—for instance, oversampling of the wealthy can have a very large impact on the estimated level of wealth, as well as its distribution. We must also choose a common metric in which to compare wealth. We have chosen to convert the national currencies first to year 2002 prices using the OECD's price indices for actual private consumption, then to use purchasing power parities (PPPs) for actual private consumption, and then to further convert the data to international US dollars.[4]

The exact definition of net worth varies depending both on what is available in the data and on the purpose of each study. For Australia, Headey et al. (2005) are able to provide a rather complete concept of wealth in relation to aggregate wealth sources. They use the Household, Income and Labour Dynamics in Australia Survey (HILDA), which excludes only information on pre-paid insurance premiums and consumer durables aside from vehicles. For Canada, Morissette et al. (2003) exclude from their concept of net worth the value of the contents of the home, collectibles and valuables, annuities and registered retirement income funds (RRIFs) in order to have comparable wealth definition for their 1984 and 1999 waves. Brandolini et al. (2004) define household wealth in Italy as the total market value of dwellings, consumer durables, and financial assets, net of debts. The value of small unincorporated businesses is excluded, as well as the value of life insurance and private pension funds. Jappelli and Pistaferri (2000), who use the same survey, include the latter in their concept of net worth.

In Finland, net worth includes financial and non-financial assets, including housing and consumer durables net of debts. The main omission is that the value of forests is not included. In Norway, net worth includes the tax-assessed value of real capital and financial capital, less all debts. Using tax assessment is cost effective for data-gathering purposes, but is associated with many well-known problems, such as large undervaluations of different assets and the fact that whatever is not included in the tax assessments is missed altogether. While we include information for Norway for completeness, we are quite sceptical as to its comparability with the numbers for other countries—which is already much in doubt.

In Japan, net worth, as defined by Kitamura et al. (2003), includes financial assets (excluding social-security wealth), the value of principal residence, durables less gulf club membership certificates, and debt. Banks et al. (2002)

---

[4] The source for price indices is OECD (2005a: table A.14) and for PPPs OECD (2005b: table 1.12). Undervaluations of different assets and the fact that whatever is not included in the tax assessments is missed altogether. While we include information for Norway for completeness, we are quite sceptical as to its comparability with the numbers for other countries—which is already much in doubt.

look at the distribution of financial wealth in Great Britain and provide some analysis of pensions and housing wealth. Their concept of net worth includes savings, investments (excludes pensions and housing), and debt. A comprehensive analysis of British wealth at this time is not possible owing to the lack of a survey that would measure all dimensions of wealth.

For the USA, we provide results from two surveys, the Panel Survey of Income Dynamics (PSID) and the Survey of Consumer Finances (SCF). The SCF is one of the most complete wealth surveys in the world. In addition to asking multiple wealth questions, it over-samples the wealthy, which allows for more accurate measurement of wealth at the top of the distribution and therefore also of both total and mean wealth. The SCF also multiply imputes missing values, which also improves its accuracy. The PSID uses some imputation methods, has substantially fewer wealth questions, and does not over-sample the wealthy. Juster et al. (1999) find that the SCF net worth concept over-samples the Federal Reserve Flow of Funds by about 8 per cent. Meanwhile, the PSID total net worth is about 75 per cent of the SCF value, and the correspondences vary across tangible assets.

Sampling is particularly important in wealth surveys, since wealth is much more highly concentrated than income. Questions about wealth are often deemed sensitive, potentially leading to large non-response rates. If non-response increases with the level of wealth, the total level of wealth can be seriously underestimated if special care is not taken to ensure sample responses at the higher end of the wealth distribution. The Australian HILDA has information on a wide range of wealth components. All the same, it under-represents the amount of wealth held by Australians, since the very wealthy, who hold a disproportionate share of total wealth, are under-represented. This is also likely to be true of the US PSID, which understates Flow of Funds data from the Federal Reserve between 22 and 28 per cent.

The German data we report stems from the Income and Expenditure Surveys conducted by the German Statistical Offices. The data are top coded for income. The data have been obtained from self-assessments of wealth, which are considered to understate true wealth (Eymann and Börcsh-Supan 2002; Hauser and Stein 2003; Ammermüller et al. 2005). The Dutch data in turn stem from the Center Savings Survey (CSS), an annual panel that has a substantial over-sampling of high-income earners. The data have quite comprehensive information on different components of household wealth.

Both the Finnish and Norwegian samples are based on Income Distribution Surveys (IDS). In Finland, the IDS over-samples high-income earners, but does not specifically target the wealthy. The main difference between the Finnish and the Norwegian data is that the wealth variables in Finland are based on extensive interviews, while in Norway wealth data are taken from administrative registers, primarily those of the tax authorities. Such information is also available for Finland. A comparison of interview with register data in the

Finnish case suggests that average gross wealth from tax data is estimated to be about one half of that based on detailed interviews (Jäntti 2006). For debts, administrative data are estimated to be a little higher than the interview information. Tax data thus tend to undervalue assets and value debts at close to their true value. The Swedish sample is based on a household panel survey, the HUS.

Davies et al. (2007; see also Chapter 19, this volume) offer a rich source of information about wealth levels and portfolio composition for the countries we study (and many others). In the part of their data that are based on national balance sheets, financial assets are relatively more important than in survey data.

3 Comparisons of the Level of Wealth across Countries

A comparison of wealth levels in the late 1990s and early 2000 can be found in Table 2.1. The broadest measure of wealth, net worth, indicates that the USA has the highest wealth holdings and is followed by Italy, Japan, Australia, the Netherlands, and Canada, if we consider the US Survey of Consumer Finances as our benchmark. If, instead, we consider the US PSID, then Italy, Japan, and Australia surpass the USA in the level of net worth. However, these numbers are skewed upwards by a relatively small number of wealthy households. German net worth is close to that of the Netherlands, whereas the Nordic countries—of which we include information for Finland, Sweden, and Norway—are much lower. Norway, in particular, has a high level of GDP but very low net worth. Even though taxable wealth is expected to be less than survey wealth (Jäntti 2006), and the Norwegian tax rules are different, the comparison to Finland is open to some doubt, as the Norwegian levels do appear implausibly low. Even a doubling of Norwegian net worth would leave it with lower wealth on average than Mexico. As mentioned, differences in sample design and in particular whether the wealthy are over-sampled may have a large impact on the estimated average wealth levels. The analysis of median, rather than mean, wealth levels therefore is warranted.

The typical or 'median' household across countries in 2002 $US is richest in Japan, followed by Australia and the USA. Once we switch to this measure, the specific survey in the USA has no effect on our conclusions. We can gain some idea of wealth inequality in the USA by noting that USA net worth, taking the much lower PSID average of $US296,000, is about 2.5 times that in Sweden, $US121,000. The median net worth in Sweden in 1997, by contrast, is $US83,000, which is quite close to the US (PSID) figure of $US96,000.

It is also tempting to speculate that the Nordic countries' low levels of net worth might in part be explained by the presence of legislated earnings-related pensions. While the details vary across countries, and also change over time

Table 2.1. Wealth levels, selected countries (means and medians in 2002 $US000)

Mean or Median	Country and Year													
	Australia 2002	Canada* 1999	Finland 1998	Germany 1998	Italy 2000	Japan 1994	Mexico 2002	Netherlands 1998	Norway 2002	Sweden 1997	UK 2000	USA PSID 2001	USA* SCF 2001	USA* SCF 2004
Mean														
Net worth	308.6	174.9	78.0	141.5	354.1	345.0	96.0	137.4	18.5	121.1	—	296.4	428.1	430.4
Assets	360.9	207.8	91.7	166.4	359.1	—	96.9	181.4	72.2	155.1	—	—	486.8	506.1
Financial assets	113.9	61.0	17.3	40.6	102.3	102.9 (2)	—	50.1	39.5	43.6	26.6	122.1	204.5	180.8
Non-financial assets	247.0	121.4	96.7	—	256.8	187.1 (2)	—	—	32.8	—	153.0	180.6 (4)	282.5	325.3
Housing (main)	157.1	78.7	40.2	—	133.5	—	30.5	—	—	79.1	—	76.5 (4)	132.4	163.8
Other property	—	16.4	—	—	68.8	—	22.6	—	—	32.5	—	34.9	22.8	32.1
All property	195.6	95.1	56.5	125.8	202.3	—	53.1	—	—	111.6	153.0	111.4	155.2	195.8
Debt	52.3	32.8	13.7	24.9	4.9	—	0.9	44.0	53.8	34.0	3.9 (3)	7.2 (4)	58.9	75.9
Mortgages	39.2	25.4	10.0	23.2	—	—	—	38.9	—	—	—	—	44.3 (5)	57.1 (5)
Median														
Net worth	166.8	—	51.9	47.9	—	219.8	12.9	—	—	83.3	—	96.5	93.1	89.4
Assets	219.9	119.6	68.9	56.8	—	—	14.5	—	—	—	—	—	159.3	166.0
Financial assets	39.3	14.5	60.7	19.0	—	61.5 (2)	0.0	—	—	—	—	—	30.3	22.1
Non-financial assets	166.3	90.2	56.1	—	—	100.1 (2)	—	—	—	—	124.8	38.6 (4)	122.8	141.9
Housing (main)	122.1	109.5	—	—	—	—	9.6	—	—	—	—	0.0	133.1	153.6
Other property	—	56.9	—	—	—	—	0.0	—	—	—	—	—	86.5	96.0
All property	137.4	—	—	—	—	—	12.9	—	—	—	—	—	—	—
Debt	7.6	25.4	0.2	0.0	—	—	0.0	—	—	—	0.0 (3)	0.2 (4)	41.9	53.1
Mortgages	0.0	60.4	—	—	—	—	0.0	—	—	—	—	—	75.8 (5)	91.2 (5)

Note: *median for those with item (1) for median household of net worth and not the median over the entire distribution. (2) Net financial assets = financial assets − debt; net housing assets = housing assets − housing debt. (3) Non-housing debt. (4) Includes main home equity not value of main home. For debt refers to 'other debt'. (5) Primary residence mortgage.

Sources: Australia: Headey et al. (2005); Canada: Statistics Canada (2006); Finland: Jäntti (2006); Germany: Ammermüller et al. (2005); Italy: Brandolini et al. (2004); Japan: Kitamura et al. (2003) (only net worth and net assets are available); Mexico: Bernal (2006); Netherlands: Alessie et al. (2002); Norway: Statistics Norway (various years); Sweden: Klevmarken (2006); UK: Banks et al. (2002); USA: Gouskova and Stafford (2002), Bucks et al. (2006).

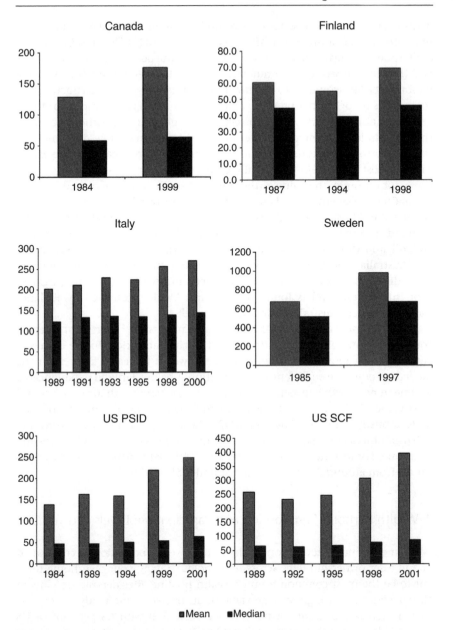

Figure 2.1. Mean and median net worth, selected countries, selected years

within countries, the presence of pension legislation that makes future bene-fits a function of earnings—or, after recent reforms in Sweden and in Finland, of lifetime earnings—will almost certainly affect the perceived need for savings and therefore of wealth accumulation. A partial correction for this in cross-national studies would be to impute, based on labour-market characteristics, some measure of the net present value of future expected pensions for those who have not yet retired. Such corrections are not possible without access to the household level microdata. Because of the non-negligible differences in the net worth concepts used by authors, it may be more meaningful to exam-ine the most comparable or specific components of net worth across coun-tries—for example, the value of the principal residence.[5] The owned home is the main component of assets in most countries (over 70 per cent) except for Germany and Japan (OECD 2000). Across countries, the highest average value is found in Australia, followed by the UK, Italy, the USA, Sweden, Canada, Finland, and Mexico. Once we turn to medians, the USA leads, followed by the UK, Australia, and Canada. However, assessing cross-country differences is quite difficult, as information is incomplete and scattered. Turning next to debt, the lowest level is found in Italy and Mexico, followed by Finland, Canada, Sweden, Australia, Norway, and the USA.

Finally, we show in Figure 2.1 mean and median net worth for selected countries across selected years (measured in constant prices in the domestic currencies). In most cases, the mean of net worth increases faster than the median, a point we shall return to in Section 4 below. Finland experienced a decline in net worth between 1987 and 1994, associated with lower house and asset values. In Sweden, both the mean and the median appeared to increase quite robustly between 1984 and 1997. The USA (measured here using the PSID) exhibits a large gap between the mean and the median, which is growing over time. For instance, between 1994 and 2001, net worth increased by two-thirds, from around $US150,000 to just under $US250,000.

4 Wealth Portfolio Composition and Participation: Levels and Trends

We next examine what components household wealth portfolios are constituted of and asset ownership rates across households. Having your own home turns out to be the most common form of wealth holding after deposit accounts in all our countries. A high average value of an owned home tends to coincide with a high rate of home ownership (see Table 2.2) with 68 per cent of US households owning their home, followed by Italy (66 per cent), Canada (60 per cent), and the United Kingdom (57 per cent). Home ownership is most prevalent

---

[5] Even in this respect surveys vary; e.g., the US PSID provides information on the net value of owned homes.

in Mexico, with 74.4 per cent. Owning other types of housing is most common in Italy.

In terms of the portfolio composition of financial assets, deposit accounts are held by a majority of households in all countries except Mexico. Here, only 18 per cent of the population has financial assets, while over 80 per cent has non-financial assets. There are some differences in the types of financial investments held. In Canada and Italy, households invest in bonds and mutual funds, while in the USA more risky instruments in the form of stocks are more prevalent. Participation in financial assets is, however, highest in the USA, then Canada, followed by Italy. Over half of the population holds debt in Canada, Finland, the Netherlands, and the USA (with the UK just below one half). The numbers are much lower for Germany (42 per cent), Italy (21 per cent), and Mexico (31 per cent). The major component of household wealth is housing, followed by pensions. However, many countries do not include information on pensions at all. As discussed, some may in fact have low levels for institutional reasons.

Trends in ownership indicate that in Italy from 1989 to 1998 non-financial ownership was quite stable, with about 65 per cent owning their main residence, 26–34 per cent owning investment real estate, and 13–17 per cent owning their own business (Guiso and Jappelli 2002). There were some changes in financial asset participation. Bonds were popular among over 30 per cent of the population until 1995, at which point stocks and mutual funds became more popular (7 and 10 per cent respectively), as they have emerged as an alternative investment tool in the Italian market. By international standards, direct and indirect stock holding in Italy is quite low. This is due, in part, to high entry and management fees. Another feature of the Italian stock market is high volatility in relation to other markets. For example, the standard deviation of returns in the past four decades was twice as high as in other European countries (France, Germany, and the UK) and in the USA. During the sample period, there was also an increase in private pension plan participation (17 in 1989, to 29 in 1998) because of reforms of the social-security system and life insurance (14 to 23) stimulated by tax incentives. An expansion of consumer credit and personal loans has caused an increase in participation of non-housing debt.

Brandolini et al. (2004) construct for Italy an aggregate time series from the mid-1960s that indicates that the value of housing in total wealth fluctuated between 51 and 66 per cent. At least from 1989, this change was largely due to a change in real-estate prices rather than changes in home-ownership rates (Guiso and Jappelli 2002). The stock of durables was steadily declining, to below 10 per cent by 2002, and debt, although very low (below 5 per cent) compared to other OECD countries, has for the past twenty-five years been increasing as a share of total wealth. In terms of the financial portfolio composition, they observe a steady decline in the share of deposit accounts (19 per cent in the 1970s to below 10 per cent in 2002) in favour of equities and

Table 2.2a. Asset participation, selected countries (%)

Asset	Country and Year									
	Canada 1999	Finland 1998	Germany 1998	Italy 1998	Mexico 2002	Netherlands 1998	UK 2000	USA PSID 2001	USA SCF 2001	USA SCF 2004
Financial assets	93	—	—	—	15.8	95.4	—	—	93	94
Deposit accounts	88	92.3	82.2	83	—	93.2	76	82	91	91
Bonds	14	—	8.5	15	—	3.5	—	—	17	18
Stocks	10	—	17.1	7	—	15.4	46 (1)	30	21	21
Mutual funds	14	—	17.7	11	—	21.6	—	—	18	15
Retirement accounts	61	—	56.6	8	—	25.4	—	35	52	50
Non-financial assets	100	—	—	—	82.2	79.2	—	—	91	93
Housing (main residence)	60	73.2	46.2 (4)	66	74.4	50.8	57	68 (3)	68	69
Other housing	16	—	—	26	23.6	4.5	—	16	11	13
Business	19	—	—	12	17.7	5.1	—	13	12	12
Debt	68	60.7	—	21	26.1	65.7	48 (2)	51 (3)	75	76
Mortgages	35	—	24.7	—	—	42.6	—	—	45	48

Note: (1) investment wealth; (2) non-housing debt; (3) includes main home equity not value of main home, debt refers to 'other debt'; (4) total real estate.

Sources: Canada: Statistics Canada (2006); Finland: Jäntti (2006); Germany: Ammermüller et al. (2005); Italy: Guiso and Jappelli (2002); Mexico: Bernal (2006); Netherlands: Alessie et al. (2002); UK: Banks et al. (2002); USA: Gouskova and Stafford (2002), Bucks et al. (2006).

Table 2.2b. Asset composition, selected countries (in percentage share of total)

Asset	Australia 2002	Canada 1999	Germany 1998	Italy 2000	Mexico	Netherlands	Sweden 1997	UK	USA
Financial assets	31.6	36.7	28.6	28.9	45.2	27.6	28.1	—	35.7
Deposit accounts	4.6	7.5	11.0	11.4	—	9.7	—	—	13.2
Bonds	—	—	1.6	5	—	0.6	—	—	5.3
Stocks	—	—	2.4	—	—	6.6	—	—	17.6
Mutual funds	6.6 (1)	10.9	2.8	12.5	—	3.7	—	46 (5)	14.7
Retirement accounts	16.3	15.9	8.7	—	—	5.9	—	—	32
Other assets	7.8 (2)	2.4	—	—	—	—	—	—	17.2
Non-financial assets	68.4	84.5	88.9	72.5	54.8	67.5	71.9	—	64.3
Housing	54.2	62.2	—	37.7	—	63.7	51	—	50.3 (4)
Business	9.5	16.5	—	7.4	—	3.7	—	—	25.9
Total assets	100	121.3	100.0	101.4	100.0	100.0	—	—	100
Debt	100	21.3	17.6	1.4	0.89	24.3	21.9	—	—
Mortgages	75	14.1	16.4	—	—	21.5	—	—	70.2 (4)
Net worth	100	100	100.0	100	100	75.7	78.1	100	100

Note: (1) shares, managed funds, etc.; (2) includes vehicles, cash investments, trust funds, cash-in value of life insurance and collectibles; (3) stocks and bonds; (4) total real estate; (5) the question related to financial assets lists deposit accounts, retirement accounts, stocks and bonds, and the respondent is just asked to give the total value of all of these assets. The information on retirement accounts and deposit accounts (or savings) comes from other questions unrelated to the total value of financial assets. Therefore it is impossible to determine what is their share of the total financial assets. (6) The percentages are of total (gross) wealth, not net worth.

Sources: Australia: Headey et al. (2005); Canada: Morissette et al. (2003) (mututal funds also includes stocks and bonds); Germany: Ammermüller et al. (2005); Italy: Brandolini et al. (2004); Mexico: Bernal (2006); Netherlands: Alessie et al. (2002); Sweden: Klevmarken (2006); UK: Banks et al. (2002); USA: Gouskova and Stafford (2002), Bucks et al. (2006).

mutual funds. The share of financial assets in overall wealth has been fluctuating (between 30 and 40 per cent) and is related to economic expansions in the past decades.

For the USA, data from 1983 to 2004 indicate relative stability in non-financial ownership. There was a steady increase in home ownership, from 63 to 69 per cent, over the past twenty years. After 1983, business ownership was steady at 11 per cent. Roughly, only 10 per cent of households did not own any type of non-financial asset, but the number fell to less than 8 per cent in 2004 (Bertaut and Starr-McCluer 2002; Bucks et al. 2006). During this period, more traditional investments, such as certificates of deposits, bonds, and life insurance, became less popular. Households turned to financial tools with higher rates of return, such as mutual funds (5 per cent in 1983 to 18 per cent in 2004), although there was a drop to 15 per cent in 2004. After 1992 stock ownership increased, from 15 per cent in 1995 to 21 per cent in 2001, and declined slightly by 2004. The share of households with tax-deferred retirement accounts increased steadily from 1983 (31 per cent to 52 per cent in 2001). This also declined slightly by 2004, despite which the actual amounts held have been on the rise. The per cent of households with debt—both mortgages and personal loans—rose steadily. The importance of financial assets was also on the rise during this period, because of a growing value of equities and retirement accounts in the wealth portfolio and a declining relative role of home equity.

In Canada, evidence compiled by Chawla (1990) and Morissette et al. (2003) for 1984 and 1989 suggests that, similarly to the trends observed in the other countries we discuss, there have been more changes to participation among financial, rather than non-financial assets. Over the 15-year period, there was a slight increase in home ownership (58 to 60 per cent) and investment real estate (13 to 16 per cent). The share of the main home in total net worth increased by less than two percentage points, and there was a slight decline in the share of other real estate. The biggest decline occurred for business equity—from 25 per cent to 17 per cent of total net worth—although this was accompanied by increased participation, from 14 per cent in 1984 to 19 per cent in 1989, which indicates that average business equity for units with a business declined. For financial assets, we observe a decline of 3 percentage points in stock and 14 points in bond participation, but the overall share of equities in total wealth increased. The biggest increase in the share of total net worth is observed for retirement accounts.

The British Household Panel Study is a popular source for wealth analysis in the UK. The range of questions and comparability across years allow Banks et al. (2002) to compare savings and investment for 1995 and 2000. Their analysis includes household units that did not change in composition during the five years except for the addition or leaving of children. Most of the analysis is therefore performed by age groups, as the probability that household composition changes varies with age. If the household head is younger than 60, less wealthy benefit units are more likely to change composition. In benefit units where the head is over 60, the wealthier are more likely to change composition. The results indicate that over half of units with zero wealth in 1995 improved their position in 2000, whereas 21 per cent with medium levels of wealth in 1995 had zero wealth in 2000. The youngest and the oldest group were most likely to remain in the zero-wealth group. Looking at those over 30 years old, of those with zero wealth in 1995, 40 per cent owned a home. There is not much spread in the mean and median value of the house, regardless of the wealth position in 1995. The highest mean and median is for those in the highest wealth group in 2000 who had zero wealth in 1995. House values on average increased by £GB33,000; the median increased by £GB23,000. Those with zero wealth in both years saw the smallest increase in the mean and median (£GB27,000 and £GB16,000, respectively). Only 25 per cent of those in the group own their home compared to 40–60 per cent in the other wealth groups.

5 The Inequality of Wealth

The limits of comparing wealth across countries based on secondary sources are very obvious when trying to assess the degree on inequality in wealth. Some studies provide quantiles, such as deciles, quintiles, or quartiles, which can be used to calculate quantile ratios. Others provide quantile group shares or means, while still others show summary income inequality indices such as the Gini coefficient. Thus, a comparison of the level and change in wealth inequality across countries based on secondary sources is very difficult. Of course, details of the data choices limit the extent to which any two estimates of the same statistic can be compared across countries.

We opt for a very simple solution. Namely, many of the studies we looked at in Table 2.1 include two pieces of information that can be used to assess, in a rather crude way, the degree of inequality in the distribution of wealth. Theil's mean log deviation for a variable, say income, is defined as the difference between the mean of log income and the log of the mean of income. While Table 2.1 does not provide us with the mean of log wealth, we can do a crude version of this by taking the difference between the log of median wealth (which equals the median of log wealth) and the log of mean wealth. The difference between the mean and the median is, of course, closely related to the skewness of a distribution.

The results, shown in Table 2.3, suggest that this fairly crude method may be able to capture some interesting aspects of the distribution of wealth. First, this measure allows us to order by inequality of net worth the countries for which we have both the mean and the median net worth in Table 2.1. The ordering suggests that, in the latter half of the 1990s and the early 2000s, Mexico had the most unequal distribution of wealth, followed by the USA. Canada, Italy,

Table 2.3. Inequality of net worth, selected countries

Country	Average inequality			Gini index	
	Before 1990	1991–5	1995–2001	LWS	DSSW
Australia	—	—	0.62	—	0.62
Canada	0.79	—	1.00	0.75	0.69
Finland	0.30	0.33	0.41	0.68	0.62
Germany	0.00	0.32	0.47	0.78	0.67
Italy	0.50	0.50	0.62	0.61	0.61
Japan	—	—	0.45	—	0.55
Mexico	—	—	2.01	—	0.75
Sweden	0.27	—	0.37	0.89	0.78
UK	—	—	—	0.66	0.70
USA PSID	1.15	1.13	1.40	0.81	—
USA SCF	0.00	1.31	1.45	0.84	0.80

Note: Inequality is measured in the first three columns by the difference in mean and median net worth averaged across survey years.

Sources: Columns 1–3: Authors' calculations from sources in Table 2.1, Column 4 (LWS): Sierminska et al. (2006a); Column 5 (DSSW): Davies et al. (2007).

and Australia are next, and Japan, Finland, and Sweden are at the low end of the inequality of wealth. Second, for a few countries we observe this indicator of wealth inequality across several years. In all cases, at least by this measure, inequality in the last available year is more unequally distributed than early on, suggesting that disparities in wealth are increasing in several countries.

We also show in Table 2.3 Gini coefficients taken from two sources. The fourth column shows Gini coefficients for net worth, based on the beta phase of the Luxembourg Wealth Study (LWS) (Sierminska et al. 2006a, 2006b). The fifth shows Gini coefficients for net worth from Davies et al. (2007). The two sets of Gini coefficients suggest similar orderings of the countries, but different magnitudes, and are different again from that suggested by our measure based on the comparison of the mean and the median. For instance, Sweden has the highest Gini coefficient based on the results in Sierminska et al. (2006a, 2006b) and the next highest Gini coefficient in the estimates in Davies et al. (2007) but one of the lowest values based on the mean and median results. On the other hand, there are similarities as well. In particular, the USA and Mexico have high levels of net worth inequality using all three measures. However, the differences in levels of net worth inequality from different sources underline the importance of researchers being able to make their own data definitions and choices using microdata from several countries in drawing conclusions about both wealth levels and distribution.

6 Concluding Comments

Attempts to summarize descriptive statistics for the level, composition, and distribution of wealth across countries is known to be difficult because of differences in definitions and measurement. These kinds of concerns are what prompted, for instance, Kessler and Wolff (1991) to use microdata from France and the USA, together with household balance sheets for the two countries, carefully to construct a comparison between the two countries. These concerns are also behind the effort to construct a micro database of comparable wealth data, the LWS described in Sierminska et al. (2006b).

To some extent, the patterns we do observe correspond to what we might expect. The USA, for instance, does have high levels of net worth, as do many other 'rich' countries as measured by the level of GDP per capita. Housing is, as expected, an important component in net worth across all our countries. The story is not as simple as that, however. First, the differences across US surveys suggest that means can be a bad gauge of central tendency for wealth, in that the median, a much more robust measure, is fairly similar across the surveys. The Nordic countries are relatively close in national income to many of the countries that appear to be much richer in terms of net worth.

The authors are grateful to James Davies and Edward Wolff, as well as to participants of the UNU-WIDER project meeting 'Personal Assets from a Global Perspective', Helsinki, 4–6 May 2006, for helpful comments on earlier drafts of the study.

3

Long-Run Changes in the Concentration of Wealth: An Overview of Recent Findings

Henry Ohlsson, Jesper Roine, and Daniel Waldenström

1 Introduction

In this chapter we review the latest findings on historical wealth concentration in a number of Western countries. We also present new series for Scandinavia, and, finally, we compare these developments over time. The aim is to distinguish between common trends and changes that are more likely to be country specific. In particular, we revisit the question of whether wealth inequality increased in the initial phase of industrialization and to what extent later stages of development saw a reversal of such a trend. Ultimately the goal is to present new insights about the dynamics of wealth distribution over the development path. This, in turn, may have implications for countries currently in early stages of development.[1]

We are grateful to Tony Atkinson, James Davis, Markus Jäntti, Jean-Laurent Rosenthal, and conference participants at the UNU-WIDER project meeting 'Personal Assets from a Global Perspective', Helsinki, 4–6 May 2006, for comments. Lennart Berg and Mats Johansson have generously provided some of the Swedish data.

[1] There is a large theoretical literature on the interplay between wealth distribution and development that emphasizes wealth distribution as a determinant of individual possibilities to pursue different occupations, especially in the presence of credit constraints, when assets are essential as collateral or as a means of directly financing entrepreneurial undertakings. This literature does not, however, give a uniform message about the dynamics of wealth distribution over development. Indeed, recent models can be classified according to their predictions about how markets affect the distribution of wealth in the long-run (see, e.g., Mookherjee and Ray 2006). Some promote an equalization view, in which the intergenerational transmission of wealth causes convergence (e.g., Becker and Tomes 1979; Loury 1981). Stiglitz (1969) also showed long-run equalization to be the predicted outcome under quite general assumptions in a standard neoclassical framework. Others take the completely opposite view that markets in the long run increase wealth inequality (e.g., Ljungqvist 1993; Mookherjee and Ray 2003). In between these extremes we find models that permit both initial inequalities and initial equalities

We believe that there are several reasons why it is interesting to study the evolution of wealth concentration in Scandinavia compared to other countries. First, compared to most countries for which data on wealth concentration exist, the Scandinavian countries were late to industrialize. This, combined with the fact that we have data stretching as far back as around 1800, means that we can follow wealth concentration over the whole transition from before industrialization up to now.[2] A second reason for comparing Scandinavia to other Western countries is that the Scandinavian countries are well known to be extremes in the spectrum of welfare states, and their achievements in terms of equalizing income and wealth are renowned.[3] However, it is not equally established how much of the equalization took part before the welfare-state expansion, and, in particular, it is not clear why it happened.[4] Finally, a common theme stressed in several recent studies is that a number of exogenous shocks to wealth holdings during the first half of the twentieth century are the main explanation to the dramatic declines in top wealth shares. As Sweden did not take part in the world wars and was less affected by the Great Depression compared to many other countries, the development of wealth concentration over these periods is interesting. If Swedish wealth concentration falls at the same time as in other countries, then different mechanisms must be at work, which would not be the case if Sweden (and other countries not involved in the wars) showed no decline in wealth inequality.

We will focus on the most recent studies for France (Piketty et al. 2006), Switzerland (Dell et al. 2007), and the USA (Kopczuk and Saez 2004b), but we also include UK data from Lindert (1986, 2000) for the nineteenth century, UK data from Atkinson and Harrison (1978) and Atkinson et al. (1989) for the twentieth century, and US wealth distribution data from Lindert (2000). Our hope is that by focusing on these recent studies we can update the parts of the picture given by Davies and Shorrocks (2000).[5] For Scandinavia we rely on new

---

to persist. Typically, history determines where a society ends up in the long-run view (Banerjee and Newman 1993; Galor and Zeira 1993; Aghion and Bolton 1997; Piketty 1997; Matsuyama 2000; Ghatak and Jiang 2002). Data on wealth distribution over the transition from agrarian to industrial society are therefore also important to evaluate the various theoretical predictions.

[2] The first observation for Sweden is 1800, and for Denmark and Norway 1789. These early estimates are due the pioneering work by Soltow (1980, 1981, 1985). In terms of new data, our earliest observations are 1868 for Norway, 1873 for Sweden, and 1908 for Denmark.

[3] See, e.g., Esping-Andersen's famous categorization (1990) of different types of welfare states.

[4] Spånt (1978) studies Sweden during the period 1920–75 and establishes that wealth shares did fall substantially before the welfare state expansion. We provide new data for earlier periods and more details for the period 1920–75, allowing us to draw new conclusions about when the major changes took place.

[5] In a way, these recent studies can be seen as a renewed interest in the long-run development wealth concentration, despite the obvious shortcomings of early data. As noted by Davies and Shorrocks (2000), the emphasis in the past decades had been shifting away from general distributional characteristics to causes of individual differences in wealth holdings. Such questions require micro-data, typically not found before the 1960s, and, therefore, much

data based on wealth tax statistics as well as some new estate tax data. For the case of Sweden, using new data allows us to construct comparable series from 1908 until today, while for Denmark and Norway we compile data from a number of previous publications trying to link comparable estimates. These series are the result of our first analysis of the new Scandinavian data and our future work may contain adjusted estimates.[6]

2 Recent Country Studies

2.1 *Some Measurement Issues*

The main conceptual and measurement issues relevant when studying the historical development of wealth inequality relate to how wealth and wealth holders are defined in the different sources and to how this affects the calculation of wealth concentration. More elaborate discussions can be found in, for example, Davies and Shorrocks (2000) and Atkinson (Chapter 4, this volume).

The wealth definition in historical sources is usually *net wealth* (also called net worth or net marketable wealth), defined as the sum of real and financial assets less debts. This is the most common concept appearing in the historical tax-based sources (that is, wealth and estate taxes) and the main concept used throughout this chapter. For the post-war years, however, *augmented wealth*, defined as net wealth and pension wealth (contributions into pension schemes and future social-security payments), has been proposed as an alternative.

Wealth and estate taxation provide the most common sources of historical wealth data. These fiscal instruments have been levied for centuries, and the authorities have often been interested not only in collecting the revenues but also in calculating the sizes of the tax bases. In the present study, the series from France, the UK, and the USA are based on the estate tax, specifically on samples of individual estate tax returns.[7] The wealth data from Denmark, Norway, and Switzerland are based on wealth taxes, in most cases as tabulated distributions published by each country's tax authorities. For Sweden we have data based both on wealth and on estate taxes.

---

of the long-term perspective had, until recently, been considered, if not less important, then impossible to study owing to the lack of data. New research, following Piketty (2001), Piketty and Saez (2003), and Atkinson (2004), focusing first on income but then also on wealth distribution (some of which we review here), has lately changed this. See Atkinson and Piketty (2007) for more on this research agenda.

[6] More complete details on the sources as well as some additional tables can be found in the working paper version of this chapter and the data appendix therein (Ohlsson et al. 2006).

[7] These are generally adjusted to reflect the distribution of the living population by use of inverse mortality rates for age, sex, and social-status classes; see Atkinson and Harrison (1978: ch. 3) for a thorough description of the estate multiplier method.

Tax-based statistics have some well-known problems, the most obvious relating to tax evasion and avoidance. Whether such activities lead to errors in estimated wealth shares is, however, not clear. If non-compliance and tax planning are equally prevalent in all parts of the distribution—they may, of course, take very different forms—this affects the reported wealth levels but not the shares. The same goes for comparisons over time and across countries. Unfortunately there is little systematic evidence on this. Overviews, such as Andreoni et al. (1998), and Slemrod and Yitzhaki (2002) (which are mainly concerned with personal income taxes) suggest that, while avoidance and evasion activities are important in size, there are no clear results on the incidence of overall opportunities nor on these activities becoming more or less important over time.[8] Furthermore it is not clear whether to expect more or less avoidance and evasion in countries with higher tax rates. While incentives to engage in avoidance and evasion clearly increase with taxes, so do the incentives for tax authorities to improve their information.[9] Concerning wealth and estate taxes, it seems plausible to think that estate tax data are more reliable since it is typically in the interest of the heirs formally to establish correct valuations of the estate.[10] At the same time, tax planning aimed at avoiding the estate tax is an important industry in the USA and elsewhere. This may affect the reliability of the data. For wealth tax data, problems of under-reporting are likely to be similar to those for income data, with items that are double reported being well captured while other items are more difficult. Finally, the use of tax shelters may be a problem. Given the large fixed costs related to advanced tax planning, it is likely that such activities are limited to the very top of the distribution. If this has become more important over the past decades—something that seems likely—then estimates of wealth concentration for recent periods may understate wealth holdings in the very top and not be directly comparable with estimates produced earlier; in particular top wealth shares may be underestimated for recent decades.[11]

[8] For example, Gordon and Slemrod (1988: 89–130) and Agell and Persson (1990) argue that tax arbitrage opportunities generally benefit those at the bottom and the top of the tax rate distribution (typically correspondingly low- and high-income earners) to the disadvantage of those in the middle. Tax evasion (in developed countries) seems to be a relatively minor problem when it comes to income from wages and salaries, and capital income from dividend and interest, but more of a problem for self-employment income and informal small business income (e.g., Slemrod and Yitzhaki 2002), but, again, it is not clear that these activities on aggregate are unevenly spread across the distribution.

[9] Friedman et al. (2000) provide evidence supporting the idea that higher taxes also leads to better administration across a broad sample of countries as they find that higher taxes are associated with less unofficial activity.

[10] For 2001, the most recent year for which the IRS has final figures, the tax gap in the USA (i.e. the difference between taxes owed and taxes paid) was around 16%. Out of the $US345 billion that make up the tax gap, only about $US4 billion were associated with estate and excise taxes.

[11] Dell et al. (2007) find that the number of wealthy foreigners living in Switzerland has increased sharply since the 1950s. However, they also find that the amounts earned in Switzerland from all non-residents is very small relative to the amounts reported by high incomes in the

Even if there are problems with tax statistics, emphasizing the need for caution especially when comparing long series across countries, there are some positive aspects as well. First, tax statistics are often available for long time periods. They are also typically quite comprehensive in their coverage, which would imply smaller sampling errors. The fact that tax-based data stem from an administrative process that is part of enforcing the tax legislation means that declining to respond is typically not an option. This means that the 'response rate' in tax-based data is likely to be higher than in survey data.[12]

The definition of wealth holders in the tax statistics—that is, the tax units—differs across the wealth and estate taxes and, therefore, also across the countries studied here. The wealth tax (in Sweden, Denmark, and Switzerland) uses variants of the *household* as tax unit. This, in principle refers to families (that is, married couples and their under-aged children living under the same roof) and single adults who then make up the relevant tax population.[13] The estate tax data (in France, the UK, and the USA) are based on (deceased) *individuals* and hence the tax population consists of all adults.[14] The tax unit definition actually matters for the distributional estimates, as shown by Atkinson and Leigh (2007). Unless husbands and wives have equal wealth, individual-based data tend to (but must not) give rise to a more unequal wealth distribution than do the household-based data. The wealth-holder concept also matters when wealth inequality trends are studied over very long time periods—for example, from periods when a significant share of the population was represented by slaves, unfree women, or improperly registered immigrants. Shammas (1993) shows that the US historical wealth concentration is different depending on how one chooses to include these different subgroups in the reference tax population. Our aim has been to use whichever historical estimate generates the highest degree of consistency over time for all countries.

USA (less than 10% of all incomes earned by the top 0.01% income earners in the USA). But, as they also note, there are other tax havens, and, especially for relatively small open economies such as the Scandinavian countries, wealth held abroad may have an important impact on top wealth shares. Roine and Waldenström (2007) show that the share of the top wealth percentile in Sweden increases substantially if one adds the amounts of estimated household wealth placed abroad using capital flow data in the balance of payments statistics.

[12] Johansson and Klevmarken (2007) compare survey and register wealth data and find that there is no general tendency of survey data to underestimate mean wealth with the exception of the last percentile. This underestimate is, however, due not to under-reporting but rather to selective nonresponse.

[13] It should be noted that households and families are not fully equivalent, e.g., in the, often historical, cases when households also include servants and other non-related persons. We disregard these distinctions for practical reasons and treat family- and household-based tax systems as essentially identical.

[14] An additional problem is that the age cut-off may vary across countries and even within countries over time, which could introduce measurement errors and problems of comparability.

2.2 France

The long-run evolution of French wealth inequality is particularly interesting to study given France's important role for Europe's economic and political development. Recently Piketty et al. (2006) presented new data on wealth concentration for Paris and France over almost 200 years, from the Napoleonic era up to today. No previous study on any country has produced such a long homogenous time series offering a complete coverage of the effects of industrialization on wealth inequality. The French wealth data come from estate sizes collected in relation to an estate tax that was established in 1791 and maintained for more than two centuries. For every tenth year during 1807–1902, the authors manually collected all estate tax returns recorded in the city of Paris—Paris was chosen both for practical reasons but also because it hosted a disproportionally large share of the wealthy in France. Based on summary statistics on the national level for the estate tax returns, the top Paris wealth shares were 'extrapolated' to the national level. For the post-1902 period, tabulated estate size distributions published by French tax authorities were used.

Figure 3.1 shows the evolution of the wealth shares for some fractiles within the top wealth decile in Paris (1807–1902) and France (1947–94). The estimates are from the population of deceased—that is, directly from the estate tax returns—but comparisons with the equivalent wealth shares for the distribution of the living population (computed using estate multipliers) reveal practically identical trends and levels.[15] The figure shows that wealth concentration increased significantly for the top 1 and 0.1 percentiles over the nineteenth century, first slowly up to the 1870s then more quickly, until a peak at the eve of the First World War. By contrast, the two lower groups in the top decile are much less volatile during the period. The bottom 5 per cent (P90–95) held about 9 per cent of total wealth until the First World War, when its share started to increase slowly until it had doubled by the 1980s. The next 4 per cent (P95–99) stayed put on a level around 27 per cent of total wealth throughout the period. These patterns suggest that the French industrialization, which took off around mid-century, greatly affected personal wealth. It was already doing so after a couple of decades, but only in the absolute top group. This conclusion is further supported by two other observations. First, the composition of top wealth went from being dominated by real-estate assets (mainly land and palaces) in the first half of the century to being dominated by financial assets (cash, stocks, and bonds), which were supposedly held by successful industrialists and their financiers. Second, over the same period the share of aristocrats among top wealth holders decreased from about 40

---

[15] From data in Piketty et al. (2004: tables A2 and A4) over top wealth shares for both the dead and living populations in Paris and France, it is evident that the trends in wealth shares over time are practically the same for all fractiles and even the levels do not differ much, on average 0.4% for the top decile and 5.1% for the top percentile.

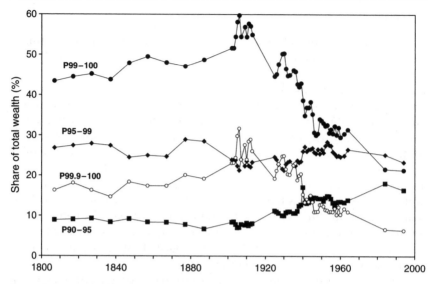

Figure 3.1. Top wealth shares among the deceased, France, 1800–2000
Source: Piketty et al. (2004: tables A3 and A7).

per cent to about 10 per cent.[16] From the First World War to the end of the Second World War, top wealth shares declined sharply, which, according to Piketty (2003), is directly linked to the shocks to top capital holdings that inflation, bankruptcies, and destructions meant. The post-war era was quieter with regard to changes in the wealth concentration, although its decline continued, probably in relation to the increase of progressive taxation (Piketty et al. 2006).

2.3 Switzerland

Switzerland is an interesting point of reference to any cross-country analysis of industrialized countries because of its specific institutional setting, with little central government interference and low overall taxation levels. Moreover, Switzerland did not take part in the world wars. Data on the Swiss wealth concentration are based on wealth tax returns compiled by tax authorities for disparate years between 1913 and 1997 (Dell et al. 2007). The Swiss wealth tax was levied on a highly irregular basis and the authors have spliced several different point estimates from local as well as federal estimates to get a fairly continuous series for the whole country.

---

[16] These facts are shown in Piketty et al. (2004: figures 4–6).

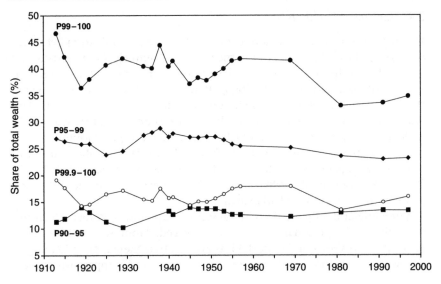

Figure 3.2. Top wealth shares, Switzerland, 1913–1997
Source: Dell et al. (2007: table 3).

Figure 3.2 depicts top wealth shares within the Swiss top wealth decile over the twentieth century. In stark contrast to the other countries surveyed in this study, wealth concentration in Switzerland appears to have been basically constant throughout the period. The wealth shares at the top of the distribution have decreased but the movements are small compared to all other countries studied.[17] This refers not only to the top decile vis-à-vis the rest of the population, but perhaps most strikingly also to the concentration of wealth within the top decile. The highest percentile and the top 0.1 percentile have not gained or lost considerably compared the bottom 9 per cent of the top decile, except for some short-run fluctuations. It is not obvious how to account for this long-term stability in terms of the country's relatively low level of wealth taxation, nor can the fact that Switzerland stayed out of both the world wars alone account for this, as Sweden, which also escaped both world wars, does not share the Swiss pattern of development of the wealth distribution. In any case, the Swiss top wealth share series seriously questions the hypothesis that significant economic development always leads to a lower level of wealth inequality over time either for reasons of redistribution or simply because of the relatively quicker accumulation of household wealth among the middle class.

---

[17] A simple trend regression yields small but significant negative coefficients.

2.4 The United Kingdom

The historical data on UK wealth concentration are available from before the country's industrialization. Prior to the twentieth century, however, data have to be collected from scattered samples of probate records and occasional tax assessments (see Lindert 1986, 2000). It was not until the Inland Revenue Statistics started publishing compilations of estate tax returns after the First World War that the series are fully reliable (see Atkinson and Harrison 1978; Atkinson et al. 1989).[18] It should be noted that the geographical unit of analysis changes over time, with pre-Second World War numbers almost always being England and Wales while the post-war ones reflect all of the UK. Data in Atkinson et al. (1989: table 1) show, however, that the differences between these entities are fairly small.

When England industrialized in the second half of the eighteenth century, the build-up of personal wealth also changed. From the overall wealth concentration shown in Figure 3.3 it is evident that there is great heterogeneity within the top 5 per cent of the distribution.[19] Apparently, wealth

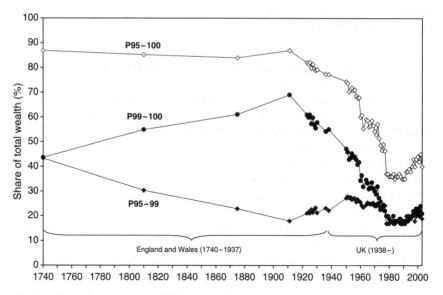

Figure 3.3. Top wealth shares, UK (and England and Wales), 1740–2003
Source: See Ohlsson et al. (2006: data appendix).

[18] Some sources of variation remain, however, such as the fact that for 1911–13 estate multipliers were based only on age, whereas from 1923 onwards they were based on both age and gender.
[19] The reader should keep in mind that this figure, and several others in this study, contains spliced series coming from different sources, which naturally may impede the degree of homogeneity over time.

concentration at the very top increased, while, by contrast, the wealth share of the next 4 per cent saw its wealth share decline during the same period. Using supplementary evidence on personal wealth, Lindert (1986, 2000) shows that wealth gaps were indeed increasing in the absolute top during the nineteenth century, with large landlords and merchants on the winning side. At the same time, Lindert points out that the middle class (that is, those between the 60th and 95th wealth percentiles) were also building up a stock of personal wealth, and this is probably what is causing the drop in the share of the next 4 per cent shown in Figure 3.3.

After the First World War, the pattern was reversed. While the top percentile wealth share dropped dramatically from almost 70 per cent of total wealth in 1913 to less than 20 per cent in 1980, the share of the next four percentiles remained stable and even gained relative to the rest of the population. Atkinson et al. (1989) argue that this development was driven by several factors, but that the evolution of share prices and the ratio of consumer durables and owner-occupied housing (that is, popular wealth) to the value of other wealth were the most important ones. According to the most recent statistics from the Inland Revenue, the top 1 per cent wealth share increased by about one-third between 1990 and 2003, but this increase has not yet been explained by researchers. Possibly, it reflects the surge in share prices following the financial market deregulation of the 1980s (the 'big bang'), as financial wealth is most concentrated at the absolute top of the wealth distribution.[20]

2.5 *The United States*

The historical development of US wealth concentration has been extensively studied by economists and historians. Inequality estimates are available back to the time of the American Revolution. In this study, we combine pieces of evidence to create long (fairly) homogenous series of wealth inequality for the USA. There are several problems with the final series concerning consistency and comparability over time (for reasons discussed in Section 3.1). For the twentieth century we compare complementary series based on different sources and definitions of wealth to get an idea of how large these problems may be.

In Figure 3.4, the evolution of the US top wealth decile is shown over the period 1774–2001, with the top percentile drawn from two different distributions: adults and households. Specifically, the top wealth shares for adults in 1774 come from Shammas (1993), who in turn adjusted earlier estimates of Alice Hanson Jones by adding unfree men and women to the reference total population, and for the years 1916–2000 from Kopczuk and Saez (2004b), who

---

[20] This is a stylized fact that is true for many developed countries (see, e.g., the overview of 'stylized facts' in Davies and Shorrocks 2000).

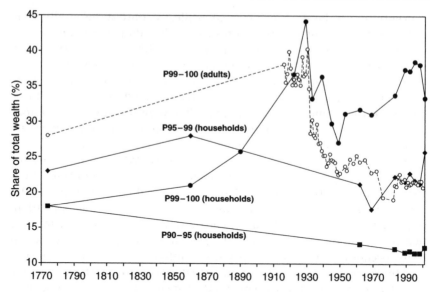

Figure 3.4. Top wealth shares, adult and household populations, USA, 1774–2001
Source: See Ohlsson et al. (2006: data appendix).

use federal estate tax returns. For the household distribution, data come from Shammas (1993), Lindert (2000) and various twentieth-century estimates by E. N. Wolff (1987, 2006).[21] The two top percentile series seem inversely U-shaped over the period, with wealth shares increasing slowly between the late eighteenth and the mid-nineteenth centuries but then much faster between 1860 and 1929, when they more than doubled. The long-run pattern of the lower 9 per cent of the top wealth decile, however, exhibits stable or even decreasing shares of total wealth (although based on rather few observations). This inequality increase in the absolute top coincides with the industrialization era in the USA around the mid-nineteenth century. Although the few pre-First World War estimates are uncertain, their basic message is supported by researchers using other sources. For example, Rosenbloom and Stutes (2005) also find in their cross-sectional individual analysis of the 1870 census that regions with a relatively high share of its workforce in manufacturing had relatively more unequal wealth distributions (see also Moehling and Steckel 2001). Another anecdotal piece of evidence in support of a linkage between industrialization and increased inequality is that the fifteen richest Americans in 1915 were industrialists from the oil, steel, and railroad industries and their financiers from the financial sector.[22]

---

[21] While the pre-Second World War data are drawn mainly from censuses, the post-1962 observations from E. N. Wolff (1987, 2006) are based on survey material.

[22] See the listing of the top 20 fortunes in 1915 by De Long (1996).

The twentieth-century development in Figure 3.4 suggests that wealth concentration peaked just before the Great Depression in 1929–30, when the financial holdings of the rich were highly valued on the markets. In the depression years, however, top wealth shares plummeted as stocks lost almost two-thirds of their real values. Kopczuk and Saez (2004b) show that corporate equity represented more than half of the net wealth of the top 0.1 percentile wealth holders in 1929. Another contributing factor to wealth compression was surely the redistributive policies in the New Deal. After the Second World War, the top percentile wealth shares remained low until the 1980s, when the top household percentile's share increased significantly, peaking around mid–late 1990s and then declined somewhat in 2001 (E. N. Wolff 2006). By contrast, the top adult percentile wealth share from the estate series in Kopczuk and Saez (2004b) exhibits no such increase, which is surprising given that this period also saw a well-documented surge in US top incomes (Piketty and Saez 2003). Whether the difference in trends between the household and adult distributions reflects inconsistencies in the data or some deeper dissimilarity in the relation between income and wealth accumulation remains to be examined by future research.

2.6 Denmark

For Denmark, there exist historical estimates of wealth concentration from as early as 1789 and then more frequently from the beginning of the twentieth century onwards. The comparability of these observations is not perfect and the composite series must thus be interpreted cautiously. Nevertheless, this study is the first to present a full range of wealth-inequality estimates from the periods before, during, and after the industrialization of Denmark that took place in the late nineteenth century. The earliest data for Danish wealth concentration come from a comprehensive national wealth-tax assessment in 1789, from which Soltow (1981) has collected a large individual sample of the gross wealth of households. After this year, however, there is a gap in the data until the early twentieth century, when the modern wealth tax had been introduced. For 1908–25, Zeuthen (1928) lists tabulated wealth distributions (number of households and their wealth sums in different wealth size classes) for Danish households, adjusted so as to include also those households with no taxable wealth. Similar tabulated wealth-tax-based data are published in Bjerke (1956) for 1939, 1944, and 1949 and in various official statistical publications of Statistics Denmark for a few years thereafter until the wealth tax was abolished in 1997.[23]

---

[23] The estimates in 1995 and 1996 were constructed from only the tabulated number of wealth holders (families) and the total net wealth in the whole country. Supplementary Danish top wealth shares exist for the 1980s in Bentzen and Schmidt-Sørensen (1994), but unfortunately wealth size has been top-coded in their data and the resulting estimates are not fully comparable with the other tax-based data.

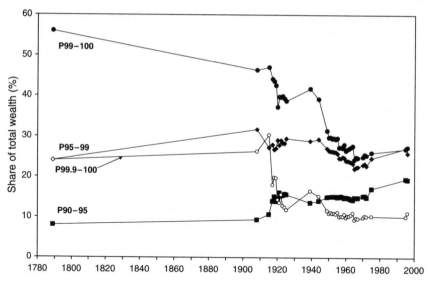

Figure 3.5. Top wealth shares, Denmark, 1789–1996
Source: See Ohlsson et al. (2006: data appendix).

Figure 3.5 shows the wealth shares of groups within the top decile between 1789 and 1996. The lowest 5 per cent (P90–95) exhibits a flat trend up to 1908 and thereafter doubles its share from 10 to 20 per cent over the twentieth century. The next 4 per cent (P95–99) lies constant between 25 and 30 per cent of total wealth over the entire period, whereas the top percentile (P99–100) decreases significantly over the period, with particularly marked decreases after the two world wars. At the very top of the distribution, the top 0.1 percentile (P99.9–100), there is no decrease at all up to 1915, but instead there is a dramatic drop by almost two-thirds of the wealth share between 1915 and 1925. Overall, the Danish wealth concentration decreased over the course of industrialization, and this continued throughout the twentieth century, although the development was not uniform at all times and across all groups.

Explaining the wealth compression of the Danish industrialization can be done by comparing the identities of the Danish top wealth holders before and after the late nineteenth century. In 1789, the dominant groups in the top of the wealth distribution were owners of large agricultural estates. Soltow (1981: 126) cites a historical source, saying that 'some 300 Danish landlords owned about 90 per cent of the Danish soil'. By contrast, in 1925 the group with the largest private fortunes was the stock brokers (*Veksellerere*), although landlords (*Godsejere, Proprietærer og Storforpagterere*) were still wealthy, both groups having more than 50 times larger average wealth than the country average.[24]

The drops in top wealth shares after the two world wars were partly associated with the sharply progressive wartime wealth taxes.[25] According to Bjerke (1956: 140), however, the fall after the Second World War was also largely due to new routines in the collection and valuation of wealth information of the tax authorities, which in particular made middle-class wealth more visible. Towards the end of the century, the wealth concentration continued declining up to the 1980s, largely because of the increased share of the relatively equally distributed house ownership in the total portfolio (Lavindkomstkommissionen 1979: ch. 5), but thereafter started to increase up to the mid-1990s.

2.7 Norway

As for the case of Denmark, the Norwegian wealth concentration data also come mostly from various kinds of wealth taxation. The first observation is from 1789, when the wealth tax assessment that was also launched in Denmark came into place (the two countries were in a political union at this time). As in Denmark, both real and personal assets were taxed, including land, houses, or farms, factories, livestock, mills, shops inventories, and financial instruments. Debts were not deducted, and hence the wealth concept is gross wealth.[26] Our second observation is from 1868, when the Norwegian government launched a national wealth tax assessment. Mohn (1873) presents totals for wealth and households and a tabulation of the wealth held by the top 0.27 per cent (P99.73–100) of all households, including a detailed listing of the fifteen overall largest fortunes.[27] For 1912, we use wealth tax returns from the taxation of 1913–14 (exempting financial wealth), which are presented in tabulated form in Statistics Norway (1915b).[28] Similarly, for 1930 we use tabulated wealth distributions (number of wealth holders in wealth classes along with totals for wealth and tax units) presented in Statistics Norway (1934). From 1948 onwards, we use the tabulation of wealth holders and wealth sums in wealth classes published in the Statistical Yearbook of various years. In the early 1980s the wealth statistics started being reported for

---

[24] The average net personal wealth in 1925 was Danish kronor (DKR) 6,826 for all of Denmark, DKR366,000 for brokers and DKR359,000 for large landlords (Zeuthen 1928: 447).

[25] On the historical development of Danish wealth taxation, see Christensen (2003: 8, 14).

[26] We use Soltow's distributional estimates (1980) based on 'males or families aged 26 and older', which is not identical to what is used for latter years and probably implies that the 1789 inequality should be adjusted upwards to be fully comparable.

[27] There is no information about whether it was the gross or net wealth that was taxed.

[28] We use tables of wealth holders in wealth classes in Statistics Norway (1915b: 20–1), corroborated by information about reference wealth and tax unit totals in Statistics Norway (1915a: 13–14) and Kiær (1917: 22). The fact that financial assets were exempt in the Norwegian wealth taxation before 1922 is discussed in Statistics Norway (1934: 1).

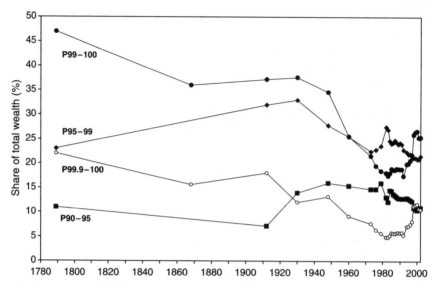

Figure 3.6. Top wealth shares, Norway, 1789–2002
Source: See Ohlsson et al. (2006: data appendix).

individual taxpayers instead of, as before, for households. In order to keep our series as consistent as possible, we attempted to convert the post-1982 observations from reflecting the individual distribution to reflect the household distribution, using a listing of both types by Statistics Norway for the year of 1979.[29]

Figure 3.6 presents the trends in Norwegian wealth concentration between 1789 and 2002. The figure shows the top wealth decile broken up into the bottom 5 per cent (P90–95) of wealth holders, the next 4 per cent (P95–99), the top percentile, as well as the top 0.1 percentile. Norway's top wealth holders experienced quite different trends in their relative positions over the period. As for the bottom 5 per cent of the top decile, its share decreases between 1789 and 1912 and then jumps up sharply between 1912 and 1930 to land on a fairly stable (though slowly declining) level thereafter. The wealth share of the next 4 per cent exhibits an inverse-U-shaped pattern, increasing sometime in the nineteenth century (we do not know exactly when because of a lack of

[29] The Statistical Yearbook of Norway of 1981 tabulates the net wealth of both households (table 380: 316) and personal taxpayers (table 368: 306). In the latter case, however, we have no data on the sum of personal wealth of all wealth holders in each wealth class. We therefore insert the sums of wealth observed in the household case into the individual case for the exact corresponding wealth classes. The comparison of wealth shares across these two distributions shows that the individual distribution produces shares that are 25%, 21%, 30%, 44%, and 60% higher than the household distribution for the top 10%, 5%, 1%, 0.1%, 0.01% fractiles, respectively.

data), peaking in 1930 and then declining almost monotonically over the rest of the twentieth century. Finally, the share of the top wealth percentile decreases significantly between 1789 and 1868, both dates being before Norway's industrialization period. The share then goes up slightly to 1912, only to start decreasing again. The most dramatic falls occur in the post-war period, with the top percentile dropping from 34.6 per cent to 18.5 per cent during 1948–79 and the top 0.1 percentile going from 13.2 per cent to 5.7 per cent over the same period. In the 1990s, there is a rapid recovery, which may be related to the oil fortunes being built up in recent times, and to the rise in world stock markets prices that produces a rise in the top shares in other countries over this period. The sizeable increase between 1997 and 1998 can also be explained by a change in the Norwegian tax laws, specifying an increase in the assessed values of corporate stock on personal tax returns.[30]

Despite the seeming disparate trends among Norway's top wealth holders, the evidence presented in Figure 3.6 corresponds well with the official economic and political history of Norway over this period. The Norwegian economy was badly hit by the economic crisis after the Napoleonic wars, when there was a shift in the political power from the great landlords and landed nobility to a class of civil servants.[31] When merchant shipping expanded in the world after 1850, Norwegian ship owners and manufacturers experienced a tremendous economic boost. The list of the average wealth of various occupations in 1868 in Mohn (1873: 24) shows that the four richest groups were manufacturers (having 160 times the country average household wealth), merchants (124 times), ship owners (96 times), and civil servants (87 times). Half a century later, in 1930, a similar comparison between the wealth of top occupations groups and the country average was made (Statistics Norway 1934: 6), and only ship owners had kept the distance from the rest of the population (having 119 times the country average wealth), while merchants (22 times) and manufacturers (19 times) had lost wealth relative to the average.

2.8 Sweden

Recent studies of wealth distribution in Sweden have mainly used data from household surveys collected in the last three decades (see, e.g., Bager-Sjögren and Klevmarken 1998; Klevmarken 2004).[32] The only previous comprehensive

---

[30] The tax-assessed values of stocks were raised in 1998, for stocks listed at the Oslo Stock Exchange from 75% to 100% of the market value and for non-listed stocks from 30% to 65% of an assumed market value.

[31] Historical account taken from the section on Norway's history during 'The Napoleonic Wars and the 19th Century' in *Encylopedia Britannica Online*.

[32] The main data source in these studies was the panel survey database HUS (for more information see web page http://www.nek.uu.se/faculty/klevmark/hus.htm).

studies on the Swedish historical wealth concentration are those by Spånt (1978, 1979), which are based on wealth tax statistics and published in the Censuses, and some special public investigations of the wealth distribution, covering the period 1920–75.[33] Wealth is defined as share of net worth (taxation values). We extend these available data both in scope and detail, first by complementing the years covered by Spånt with a number of years for which we have found satisfactory reference totals for 'total wealth' and data on distribution (sometimes only for the very top of the distribution, as in 1937) in the tax statistics. Moreover, we present new series using the same type of tax data for as long as they remain available, which is the period 1978–93. Hence, we are able to construct fully homogenous series of wealth concentration over the period 1920–93, which is the longest available series for Sweden so far. We also add to these series observations based on similar data for the years 2000–2.[34]

We complement the wealth tax returns-based series with new data coming from estate tax material for 1873–7, 1906–8, 1954–5, 1967, and 2002–3,[35] as well as with a number of alternative series for wealth concentration over the past decades.[36] We also add the observation for the year 1800 made by Soltow (1985).[37] Overall, we believe our series give a good sense of the evolution of wealth concentration in Sweden at least from the beginning of the twentieth

---

[33] The material used was the censuses for 1920, 1930, 1935, 1945, 1951, and surveys done in 1966, 1970, and 1975. The surveys oversampled rich households, so coverage for studying wealth concentration is likely to be good in these studies. For previous periods, Soltow (1985) also reports data for 1800.

[34] The data for 2000–2 are taken from the Longitudinal INdividual DAta (LINDA) for Sweden database, which in turn relies on wealth tax returns (LINDA is a register-based longitudinal data set intended to complement survey databases used in much of the previous work on wealth distribution in Sweden; see web-page http://linda.nek.uu.se/ for more on LINDA).

[35] The sources of the estate data are Finansdepartementet (1879, 1910) and SOU (1957, 1969, 2004). The 1908 wealth data are based on applying the estate multiplier method to the estate data; see Finansdepartementet (1910: 14–34).

[36] The main complements for the past decades are series from Statistics Sweden based on their HINK-database. This is a population sample where data on wealth are taken from the taxation material and other administrative records using the same household definition as we do in our main series (counting individuals over the age of 18 as individual units, even if they still live with their parents). This household definition is the main difference between HINK and HUS, a much used detailed household survey but with a relatively small sample, where instead 'kosthushåll' is used, meaning roughly that everyone living together counts as one household. This difference is the major source of discrepancies between estimates from the two sources. The fact that individuals over the age of 18 who live with their parents form separate households in HINK (and in our historical data) means that we get a substantial number of observations of individuals with very low wealth but who still may enjoy access to the wealth of their parents. This is potentially problematic if we are concerned with issues of living standards but not if we want to estimate the distribution of wealth (in terms of ownership and control).

[37] This observation is based on a wealth census carried out in 1800 and describes the wealth distribution for the population of males aged 20 and older.

century until the present day. We also note that wealth tax data and estate tax data indicate similar patterns of development over the twentieth century.

Looking first at the pattern over the nineteenth century, our observations indicate a relatively stable wealth distribution that by today's standards was very unequal. As there are no observations between 1800 and 1873, there is little that can be said about the development over this period, but, given the fact that industrialization is typically considered to have started around 1850 and to have accelerated around 1870, we do not, a priori, think that we miss any major changes in the wealth distribution relating to the industrialization.

Over the twentieth century the picture is much clearer. We can draw on multiple sources that overlap in time, and, even though there is still uncertainty about the levels over time, the trends seem relatively certain. The long-run trend in wealth concentration in Sweden over the twentieth century is that the top decile saw its wealth share drop substantially, from around 90 per cent in the early decades of the century, to around 53 per cent around 1980, and then recovering slightly to a level around 60 per cent in recent years. Looking just at this general trend is, however, incomplete if one is really to comprehend the evolution of wealth concentration. Decomposing the top decile and looking separately at the top per cent (P99–100) and the 9 per cent below that (P90–99), we see that the majority of the top decile actually experiences substantial gains in wealth shares over the first half of the century. The overall drop in the top decile share is explained by such dramatic decreases in the top percentile share that this outweighs the increase for the P90–99 group. In the period 1950–80 both groups experience declines in wealth shares, but the decrease is larger for the top percentile, and after 1980 the trend is again the same for both groups, but now the gains in wealth shares are somewhat larger for the top percentile.

From the decompositions of wealth shares in Figure 3.7, the Swedish wealth distribution exhibits a 'Kuznets-type pattern' over the first eighty years of the twentieth century, with a gradual spread of increasing shares to lower fractiles beginning with the biggest increases in the wealth share of the P95–99 group before 1930 (even P99–99.5 increases until 1930), followed by increases for P90–95 up until the end of the Second World War, and then continued and large increases for the rest of the population (P0–90) after that.

How can we account for these developments? Focusing first on the decreases at the very top of the distribution over the first half of the century, we note that most of the decrease takes place between 1930 and 1950, with the sharpest falls in the early 1930s—a time of financial turbulence and in particular the Kreuger crash—and just after the Second World War.[38] The period after 1945 was a time

[38] While Sweden was not as affected by the Great Depression as many other countries, the so-called Kreuger crash in 1932, the bankruptcy of Ivar Kreuger's industrial empire, led to major loses of wealth in Sweden. As an indication of how important this event was, 18% of all bank lending in Sweden at the time was to companies controlled by Kreuger.

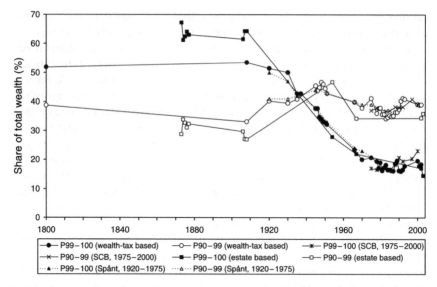

Figure 3.7. Top 10% wealth shares, showing a bottom 9% (P90–99) and a top 1% (P99–100) share, Sweden, 1800–2003

Source: Authors' calculations.

when many of the reforms discussed in the 1930s, but put on hold by the war, were expected to happen and politically the Communist Party gained ground forcing the Social Democratic Party to move to the left.[39] In particular, the progressive taxes that had been pushed up during the war remained high and also affected wealth holdings, as Sweden had a joint income and wealth tax until 1948. However, the main reason for the decreasing share at the very top is likely to be the increasing share for the lower 9 per cent of the top decile, and the reason for this in turn is likely to be increased wealth accumulation among relatively well-paid individuals. After 1945 the trend of increased accumulation of wealth continues down the distribution. Over the next thirty years the most important change is the increased share of owner-occupied housing in total wealth, which increases from being 17 per cent of all wealth to 45 per cent in 1975 and remains around that in 1997, when owner-occupied apartments and houses, and holiday homes are included (consumer durables also increase a lot but stay a relatively small share of the total).[40] Even if this type of wealth was far from evenly accumulated across the distribution, it accrued to relatively large groups in the distribution, causing wealth concentration to keep falling. Today about half of all households in Sweden own their homes. Over the past decades fluctuations in wealth shares have depended largely on

[39] See, e.g., Steinmo (1993).
[40] See Spånt (1979: 78–80) and Statistics Sweden (2000: 19–21).

movements in real-estate prices and share prices. Increases in the former have a tendency to push up the share of the upper half of the distribution at the expense of the very top, causing inequality to go down, while increases in share prices make the very top share larger, because of share ownership still being very concentrated, which causes inequality to increase. In the year 1997 the top percentile in the wealth distribution owned 62 per cent of all privately held shares and the top 5 per cent held 90 per cent.[41]

2.9 Comparing the Long-Run Wealth Concentration across Countries

Above we have presented a compilation of recent information as well as some new evidence on the long-run evolution of wealth inequality in seven Western countries: France, Switzerland, the UK, the USA, Denmark, Norway, and Sweden. Figure 3.8 shows the top wealth percentile in each of these countries for various periods during 1740–2003. Even though great caution should be taken when comparing these series, we still believe that some conclusions can be drawn about the developments of wealth inequality in these countries over the past 200 years.

Two broad results can be drawn from the series. First, the evidence does not unambiguously support the idea that wealth inequality increases in the early

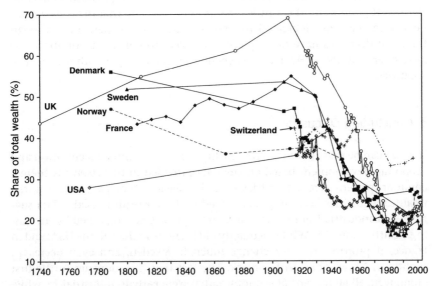

Figure 3.8. Top 1% wealth shares (P99–100), seven Western countries, 1740–2003

Source: See Ohlsson et al. (2006: table 1 and data appendix).

[41] Statistics Sweden (2000: 38–40).

stages of industrialization. Looking at the development of the wealth share of the top percentile among the countries analysed here, the Scandinavian observations exhibit slightly falling (Denmark and Norway) or fairly stable (Sweden) inequality levels over the initial stages of industrialization (in the late nineteenth century). The UK series (England and Wales) show increasing wealth shares for the top percentile in the period of the two industrial revolutions (1740–1911), as do the US and French series over the nineteenth century. Overall this suggests that going from a rural to an industrial society, with entirely new stocks and types of wealth being created, may, but does not necessarily, give rise to a large increase in wealth concentration. It also suggests that carefully studying smaller fractiles of the distribution is necessary to get a more complete picture of the development.

Second, while the series do not indicate a clear common pattern over the nineteenth century when industrialization took place (first in the UK, later in the USA and France, and towards the end of the century in Scandinavia) the development over the twentieth century seems unambiguous. Top wealth shares have decreased sharply in all countries studied in this chapter with the exception of Switzerland, where the fall has been small. The magnitude seems to be that the top percentile has decreased its share of total wealth by about a factor of 2 on average (from around 40–50 per cent in the beginning of the century to around 20–25 per cent at the time of writing). It also seems that the lowest point in most countries was around 1980 and that the top percentile wealth share has increased in most countries since then. Even though the main decreases have taken place at the very top of the distribution, the next 4 per cent (P95–99) have also experienced decreasing wealth shares in all countries.

3 Concluding Discussion

So what can be said about the relationship between wealth concentration and economic development based on the data provided in this study? Is there a common pattern across countries over the development path? Have initial wealth inequalities been amplified or reduced? Our reading of the data suggests that industrialization was not unambiguously accompanied by increasing wealth inequality. While inequality did increase in the UK, the USA, and in France, it probably did not change much in Sweden, and even decreased slightly in Norway and in Denmark. The fact that the countries in the first group were all large, central economies that were early to industrialize, while the Scandinavian countries were small peripheral economies that industrialized much later, may hold clues to the different experiences, but it does not change the fact that industrialization did not increase wealth concentration everywhere.

The twentieth-century experience seems to have been much more homogenous. As the countries continued to develop, top wealth concentration also dropped substantially. Looking at the details of the pattern by which different fractiles gain wealth shares indicates that this drop was due to a gradual process of wealth spreading in the population—confirming the increase of 'popular wealth' identified in, for example, Atkinson and Harrison (1978). In a sense, this pattern is consistent with a Kuznets-type process, where inequality eventually decreases as the whole economy becomes developed. However, it has recently been suggested that this development was probably not driven by such a process, but mainly by exogenous events. Piketty et al. (2006) argue that it was primarily adverse shocks to top wealth during the period 1914–15, mainly in the form of the world wars, that decreased French wealth inequality, and the subsequent introduction of redistributive policies that prevented them from recovering. A similar explanation is given by Kopczuk and Saez (2004b) for the USA. This reasoning has been supported by the fact that Switzerland, which did not take part in either of the wars, exhibits rather stable top wealth shares. Our data on Sweden, which also did not participate in any of the world wars, shows an example of equalization taking place without decreases in top wealth shares driven by exogenous shocks. Even though events such as the Kreuger crash in 1932 hit top wealth holders in Sweden as well, this does not explain the entire drop. Policy may, at least in Sweden, have played a more active role in equalizing wealth than merely holding back the creation of new fortunes after the Second World War. Suggesting that rising taxation and increased redistribution have been important for the decline of wealth inequality is also consistent with the largest drops taking place in the Scandinavian countries, as well as with the smaller decline in Switzerland, with its smaller government.

Overall the data seem to suggest (1) that there was a mixed impact of industrialization and (2) that, in later stages, after countries had become industrial, significant wealth holding spread to wider groups, bringing down wealth inequality. In terms of the often-discussed inverse U-shape over the path of development, the first upward part does not seem to be present everywhere, while the later stage decrease in inequality does fit all countries we have studied. An important addition to this characterization is that this analogy misses an important point which is present in the series. While the inverse U-shape suggests that the distribution of wealth starts at some level in a non-industrialized society, then rises, and later returns to the same level of inequality, all our series indicate that development has unambiguously lowered wealth concentration. The proper characterization of wealth inequality over the path of development hence seems to be that it follows an inverse J-shape, with wealth being more equally distributed today than before industrialization started.

4

Concentration among the Rich

Anthony B. Atkinson

Introduction

The aim of this chapter is to examine the degree of wealth concentration among the very rich and how it changed over the twentieth century. I ask, not what happened to the share of the top 1 per cent, say, in total wealth, but about the size of the group defined as rich and about what happened *within* this group of rich wealth holders. The definition of 'the rich' adopted in this chapter, which is the subject of Section 1, typically identifies a small group of the population above a wealth cut-off. In this respect, it differs from many wealth studies, such as the annual study of wealth by Statistics Sweden (for example, 2004), which gives results by decile groups. My concern is with the very top of the distribution, and in how the *shape of the distribution* at the top has changed over time.

The chapter focuses on the concentration of wealth for a positive reason and for a negative reason. The positive reason is that it helps us understand what is happening to top shares. In most advanced countries, changes over the past century in the wealth distribution have reflected two major factors. The *first factor* is the growth of 'popular wealth': consumer durables, houses, and small savings. Tawney remarked of the soldiers of the First World War that most of them went off to war with their possessions on their back. Today, most households in OECD countries have significant assets, even if debts and mortgages are also large. The growth of popular wealth has been a major

The first version of this study was prepared while I was visiting the Economic Research Department of the Bank of Italy. I am most grateful for their hospitality, but the views expressed are solely mine and do not reflect those of the Bank of Italy. The study was revised while I was holding a Chaire Blaise Pascal at the Paris School of Economics. I am most grateful to Jim Davies and Tony Shorrocks for their penetrating and constructive advice, and to other participants at the UNU-WIDER project meeting 'Personal Assets from a Global Perspective', Helsinki, 4–6 May 2006, for their very helpful comments.

element reducing the relative share of the top wealth groups (Atkinson and Harrison 1978). The *second factor* is the change in the shape of the distribution at the top. A number of studies have found that the downward trend in wealth shares over much of the twentieth century was limited to the top: for example, in Britain the results of Atkinson and Harrison (1978: ch. 6) for the period 1923–72 show a clear downward trend for the share of the top 1 per cent, but no significant trend for the next 4 per cent. The estimates of wealth concentration in France by Piketty et al. (2006) show that between 1947 and 1994 the share of the top 1 per cent fell by 8 percentage points but that of the next 4 per cent was virtually unaltered. Progressive inheritance taxation and other forces have been reducing the top fortunes relative to those just below them. By focusing on the concentration among the rich, the study singles out this changing shape.

The negative reason is that we can study concentration among the rich without needing to make estimates of total wealth. We do not require figures for the wealth of people below the cut-off that defines 'rich'. This is important, since the sources used, discussed in Section 2, are all partial in their coverage of wealth: wealth tax data are limited to those above the tax threshold, estate data do not cover those dying with wealth insufficient to be recorded, investment income data are typically limited to those in the upper ranges, and *Forbes* magazine and other journalistic sources are interested only in the really rich. The advantage of focusing on the upper part of the distribution may also apply to survey data where there are differences in the treatment or coverage of smaller wealth holdings.

To illustrate what can be learned by focusing on the top of the distribution, I present in Section 3 results for four countries: France, Germany, the UK, and the USA (evidence for a wider range of countries is presented by Ohlsson et al., Chapter 3, this volume) The results are derived from sources that differ, and they cover different periods, so that cross-country comparisons are not possible.[1] My emphasis is rather on the changes within countries over time. This is a further reason why I concentrate on non-survey evidence. While wealth surveys have a distinguished record, they are best in the most recent period, and cannot typically take us far back in the past. Nor can they always provide the frequent observations necessary if one is to avoid being unduly influenced by years in which valuations are particularly high or low. The main findings are summarized in the concluding Section 4, where I speculate about their explanation, taking account of both 'new' wealth, created by today's self-made rich, and wealth inherited from previous generations.

---

[1] For an international comparison covering eight countries, including the four studied here, see Wolff (1996).

1 Definition of the 'Rich'

The group of 'rich' with whom I am concerned could be defined in a number of different ways. The definition closest to the existing literature would specify a percentage of the total (adult) population, like the top 1 per cent or 0.5 per cent. Or the definition could take the top N persons, as in the *Sunday Times Rich List* in the UK. Such approaches do, however, miss the possibility, indeed probability, that the rich are a changing proportion of the population, which is one of the questions I wish to explore. Moreover, the arbitrary nature of the choice of percentage (why 1 per cent?) serves to underscore the point made by Shorrocks (1987a: 46) that studies of wealth often fail to make clear their rationale.

A different approach, suggested by Stark (1972) in the context of high incomes, is to define an upper cut-off analogously to the definition of a poverty line. This could be a 'focal' value, as with the $US1 billion cut-off for the *Forbes* list used below. Or, as with the definition of poverty, the cut-off could be a relative line. As was noted long ago by Watkins (1907: 3–4), 'the "large fortune" is a more or less relative quantity... The rich of former days would not even be "respectably poor" in New York City today.' This may lead us to define as 'rich' those who have more than x times the median wealth. This does not, however, resolve the question of arbitrariness. Moreover, it has the practical problem that we need to know enough about the distribution to be able to estimate the median, which is often not the case with the sources used here. For example, the wealth tax returns may cover only a small percentage of the population.

Instead, I employ here a definition based on a multiple of mean *income* per person (or per tax unit). Mean income also has to be estimated, and figures are not always easy to obtain for earlier periods, but we are better placed than seeking to estimate total wealth, in view of the guidance provided by national income accounts.[2] What multiple do we choose? The definition adopted here treats as rich those *individuals whose wealth exceeds 30 times mean income*. The wealth cut-off per person is referred to below as W^*. So that in the UK in 2000, when mean income per person was around £14,000, the cut-off is £420,000 per person. In the USA in the same year the mean income per tax unit was $US42,500. In what follows, I apply a simple adjustment of 1.5 to convert tax units to adult population, which implies a cut-off for the USA in 2000 of some $US850,000 per person. What is the rationale for a multiple of 30? The choice of 30 is based on the fact that at a real yield of $3\frac{1}{3}$ per annum this level of wealth generates an amount equal to mean income per person. A person with W^* could live off the interest at an average standard of living. An assumed

---

[2] The estimation of total individual income is discussed in Atkinson (2007), drawing on a number of studies for different countries.

return of 3⅓ per cent does not seem unreasonable as a measure of the long-run real return. While a higher rate of 4 per cent is used by some institutions as a measure of the long-run sustainable expenditure while maintaining the real value of their endowment (US charitable foundations are required to take the still higher rate of 5 per cent), I have applied a lower figure to take account of the importance of owner-occupied housing and its incomplete representation in personal income. The cut-off is not dissimilar to the Cap Gemini definition of High Net Worth Individuals, which in 2006 was $US1 million excluding home real estate.[3] On the other hand, it is considerably higher than the level taken for the USA by Danziger et al. (1989) to define 'rich' in their article 'How the Rich Have Fared, 1973–87', where the cut-off was 9 times the poverty line, or $US95,000 for a family of four in 1987 dollars (my definition would have yielded a figure around $US475,000).

In addition to the above definition of 'the rich', I also define 'super-rich' to be those individuals with 30×30 times mean income per person, and the 'mega-rich' as those with $30 \times 30 \times 30$ times mean income per person. For the USA in 2000 these cut-offs are approximately (per individual) $US25 million, and $US0.75 billion, respectively (billions in this study are American billions). This means that most of the mega-rich should feature on the *Forbes* list of billionaires. If the rich are those who could live off their interest, the super-rich are those who could live off the interest on their interest, and the mega-rich are those who could live off the interest on the interest on their interest.

1.1 Methods of Analysis

As has been set out clearly by Sen (1988), the measurement of wealth, or 'affluence' in the case of income, can proceed along the same lines as the measurement of poverty, with indicators such as the proportion rich (head-count) and the concentration of wealth among the rich (parallel to the Sen poverty index).[4] The first indicator used here is indeed the headcount: the proportion of the adult population classified as rich or super-rich. (It should be noted that, while this does not require a control total for total wealth, it does require a control total for the adult population.) The proportion is not, of course, sensitive to the extent to which people surpass the cut-off. Just as with the measurement of poverty, we may want to take account of the distribution beyond the cut-off. Following the parallel with the literature on industrial concentration, I examine, as a second indicator, the 'market share' of the top 25 per cent of wealthy individuals. How much does the top quarter own of the total wealth of this group?

---

[3] Website of Capgemini, 21 Feb. 2006.
[4] I am most grateful to S. Subramanian for drawing my attention to this reference.

The third indicator involves the shape of the distribution above the wealth cut-off. It is widely believed that the upper tail of the wealth distribution has a Pareto form, which can be fitted without reference to total wealth or total population. In this case, the number of people with wealth in excess of W is given by $N = AW^{-\alpha}$, where α is the Pareto exponent and A is a constant. If we then plot the logarithm of the rank of billionaires (their number in the *Forbes* list) as a function of the logarithm of their wealth, we should observe a downward sloping line with slope α. Alternatively, we may note that the mean wealth of people above W is given by, where the Pareto distribution holds for all wealth levels above W, a multiple $\alpha/(\alpha - 1)$ of W. The 'mean wealth above' (MWA) ratio is constant. So $\alpha = 3$ implies that people above you have on average a wealth 50 per cent higher than yours; $\alpha = 2$ implies that people above you have on average a wealth twice yours. In this sense, a higher value of α corresponds to less concentration. In the same way, the 'incomplete' Gini coefficient measured considering only the rich is equal to $1/(2\alpha - 1)$, so that a value of 2 implies a Gini coefficient of a third. The coefficient can also be related to the share of the top quarter. Where the Pareto formula applies, the within-group share of the top quarter is given by $(0.25)^{(1-1/\alpha)}$. A share of 50 per cent for the top quarter implies a value for α of 2, a share of 60 per cent implies a value for α of around 1.6.[5] The third indicator of concentration used here is, therefore, the Pareto exponent, α, measured in one of these ways. However, one of the questions considered in Section 3 is the extent to which the Pareto distribution does indeed provide a reasonable fit to the observed data. If we plot the *Forbes* billionaires by rank in a double logarithmic diagram, do we find a straight line?

With the exception of the journalist lists, I do not use microdata (although microdata exist for certain recent years in some countries and are being collected in other countries from archives; see Piketty et al. 2006). The typical data therefore consist of the number of people (or tax units) with wealth in excess of W and the amount of their wealth, for a range of values of W above my cut-off to define 'the rich'. This has, therefore, involved interpolation, where I have applied a logarithmic (Pareto) interpolation to either cumulative numbers or cumulative amounts.[6]

---

[5] This method of estimating the Pareto coefficient was proposed by Macgregor (1936), who noted that it made a bridge between Pareto and Lorenz. For this reason, to draw a distinction from other methods of estimating the Pareto coefficient, I refer to it as the Pareto–Lorenz coefficient.

[6] The validity of this method of interpolation does not depend on the Pareto distribution providing a good fit to the upper part of the distribution. The logarithmic interpolation in effect fits a Pareto curve to each interval, so that the implied Pareto exponent varies from interval to interval.

2 Sources of Data on the Rich

Sources of data on the distribution of wealth are extensively described by Davies and Shorrocks (2000: sect. 3), who identify five main types. The most widely used today are sample surveys, but the group of the population with which I am concerned here is that typically least well covered. Considerable efforts are made to ensure good coverage of wealthy individuals in surveys— for example, by over-sampling of those with high incomes. But coverage of the very wealthy remains problematic. Nor does survey evidence typically provide a long run of data. The first survey for the USA cited by Davies and Shorrocks (2000) is for 1962; the first Canadian survey provides information for 1964. In the UK, the Oxford Savings Surveys provided information on net worth for the early 1950s (Straw 1956), but the surveys were not continued. I shall, therefore, concentrate here on four other sources of evidence: lists of named wealth holders constructed by journalists, wealth tax data, estate tax data, and investment income tax data—Ohlsson et al. (Chapter 3, this volume) make extensive use of wealth tax and estate tax data.

2.1 Lists of Named Wealth Holders

As described by Davies and Shorrocks (2000: 642) in the USA for many years, *Forbes* magazine and *Fortune* have provided lists of the very wealthy,[7] and this practice has spread to other countries, examples being the *Sunday Times Rich List* in the UK (Beresford 1990, 1991) and *Business Review Weekly* in Australia (Shann 1998). As Davies and Shorrocks make clear, this source has considerable interest, and it has been used to augment information from other sources, as in the estimates for Canada produced by Davies (1993). These lists do however suffer from several disadvantages:

The validity of the list depends on the extent to which wealth holdings are public knowledge, which is likely to vary across countries and over time, and on the efforts made by the investigators to obtain adequate coverage. As survey researchers in the USA have noted (see Kennickell 2003), their interviews have thrown up people missing from the journalist lists. Many of the assets may be difficult to value, such as holdings in unquoted companies, or collections of art (well illustrated by the difficulty in predicting the price that works will fetch at auction).

The lists often combine individual wealth holdings, those of couples, and those of 'families', where the last of these extends beyond the immediate

---

[7] Such lists go back at least to 1892, when the New York *Tribune* published a list of 4,047 American millionaires (Watkins 1907: note to ch. III).

nuclear family; it may, therefore, be difficult to reduce them to a common basis. For example, in the 2006 *Forbes* list of world billionaires, number 8 is 'Kenneth Thomson and family', whereas numbers 17 to 21 are five people with the surname 'Walton'. If the wealth of the latter were added, it would put them at the top of the list.

Assets may be more visible than debts, causing net worth to be overstated. Davies and Shorrocks (2000) cite the example of the UK publisher Robert Maxwell, who appeared in the *Sunday Times* list of top wealth holders shortly before his death revealed massive debts. The coverage of national lists is affected by the geographic criteria for the inclusion of individuals. For example, in the 2006 *Forbes* list of world billionaires, number 11 is Roman Abramovich, shown as having Russian citizenship but UK residence.

2.2 Wealth Tax Data

As discussed by Ohlsson et al. (Chapter 3, this volume), in a number of European countries there are annual taxes on wealth that may be used to derive statistics about the distribution of wealth (for a recent review, see Hansson 2002). There has been some tendency to dismiss these data. Harrison (1979: 51), in his valuable survey of the distribution of wealth in ten countries, says simply of the German wealth tax data used below that they 'are widely recognised as being of little value'. He equally deems the Norwegian estimates based on wealth tax returns to be so unreliable as not to warrant inclusion. He noted that total recorded personal wealth in the Norwegian case was less than total personal income. This does not, however, mean that the data cannot be employed to throw light on the upper tail of the distribution. Indeed, as Spånt (1987) has shown for Sweden, they can be used to construct long-run series (covering the period 1920–83). Tuomala and Vilmunen (1988) have used the wealth tax data for Finland. Ohlsson et al. (Chapter 3, this volume) have extended the series for Sweden and used similar data for Denmark and Norway to produce long-run series for those countries.

The wealth tax data have the advantage, compared with the two methods that follow (the estate method and the investment income method), of measuring directly the variable and the population with which we are concerned. At the same time, there are several problems that limit use of wealth tax data:

1. The definition of wealth follows the wealth tax law, so that the data omit classes of assets that are not taxable, and classes of liabilities that are not allowed against taxable wealth. Variations in the tax law across countries limit the extent of comparability across countries and changes over time limit the extent of consistency over time.

2. The valuation of assets follows the wealth tax law, and this may be below the market valuation, as a result of tax concessions (such as those for certain business assets under the German wealth tax).[8]

3. Tax evasion means that wealth holdings are understated. In the case of Sweden, Spånt (1987: 53) notes that 'a major problem with tax return data is the extent of under-reporting and avoidance through evasion and legal tax exemptions'.

2.3 Estate Data

One of the oldest methods of obtaining information about the distribution of individual wealth is to use the dead as a sample of living. If we assume that those persons dying in a particular year are representative of the living population, the overall distribution may be obtained by 'blowing up' the estate data by an appropriate mortality multiplier, equal to the reciprocal of the mortality rate. So, if the mortality rate is 2 per cent, we multiply by 50. In the earliest calculations, a single multiplier was applied to all estates, but this led, as described by Mallet (1908: 66), to 'the most disquieting discrepancies', since both wealth and mortality tend to increase with age. Following the suggestion of the Australian statistician, Coghlan (1906), Mallet used multipliers that varied with age at death, and this has now become standard practice (see, e.g., Lampman 1962 for the USA and Lydall and Tipping 1961 for the UK). Restriction to data giving the distribution by age of estates limits the time period that can be covered. In the UK, data are available for the distribution of estates classified by age and gender only from 1923.

The fact that small estates are not liable for estate tax, and that small wealth holdings are therefore missing, is not a problem for the present application. At the same time, the estate multiplier method has the following disadvantages:

1. Those dying in a given year are not necessarily representative of the living population. For example, those dying are likely to have had below-average health, which would have affected their wealth accumulation (for example, they may have stopped work sooner). Those with shorter life expectancy may have taken steps to avoid estate tax, for instance, by making transfers of property.

2. The 'predictability' of death may have changed over time, affecting the scope for estate tax planning.

3. The war years are unrepresentative.

[8] Although it may be noted that a study for Finland of wealth tax data concludes that 'the share of the top wealth holders (in 1981) is practically speaking invariant with respect to the transformation of tax values to market values' (Tuomala and Vilmunen 1988: 185).

4. The valuation for estate tax purposes (a 'sell-up' value) may be different from, typically lower than, the valuation on a 'going-concern' basis (an exception is, of course, the value of life assurance policies).

5. Typically estate tax law exempts certain types of property, such as that settled in certain types of trust, or applies a discount to the value of certain types of property.

In recent years, a number of studies have used estate data without mortality multipliers, and this is true of the estimates for France used below (and in Ohlsson et al., Chapter 3, this volume), based on the work of Piketty (2001). From the examination of the theory of mortality multipliers by Atkinson and Harrison (1975), it is clear that the implications of making no adjustment for differential mortality depend on the end-statistics in which one is interested. The finding of Mallet (1908) was that total wealth would be significantly overstated.[9] The impact on the *distribution* of wealth is, however, less straightforward. Piketty et al. (2006) compare the results for wealth in Paris obtained with and without multipliers from 1807 to 1902, and show that the estimates obtained without multipliers gave higher shares for the top 1 per cent but that the overall upward trend is similar.[10]

2.4 Investment Income Data

Estimation of wealth holdings via the capitalization of investment income as declared for income tax was much used in early studies of total national wealth, and the method is particularly associated with Sir Robert Giffen (in the UK, it is known as the *Giffen Method*). In the USA, it was used before the Second World War by Lehmann (1937) and Stewart (1939) to estimate the size distribution of wealth. Since then, it has been little used, perhaps in part because the tabulated income tax data in the USA do not provide a size distribution of investment income (as opposed to amounts of investment income classified according to ranges of total income). (The necessary investment income data could be obtained from the US microdata, which are available from 1960.) The method has been used in Australia, employing investment income data from household surveys, by Dilnot (1990), Baekgaard and King (1996), and Kelly (2001).

The essence of the investment income method is to apply a yield multiplier to work back from the distribution of taxable investment income to the

[9] Mallet estimated total wealth among the living as around £6 billion in England in 1905–6, whereas the lowest previous figure cited was close to £8 billion. As was noted by Bowley, 'most people, when they first saw this paper [of Mallet], must have felt that somebody had robbed them of at least £2 billion' (discussion of Mallet 1908: 88–9).

[10] The earlier study by Fouquet and Strauss-Kahn (1984) for one year (1977) showed that moving from general mortality multipliers to social-class multipliers had the effect of reducing the share of the top 1% in France from 22.9% to 19.1%.

distribution of wealth. If the yield on all wealth were x per cent, then we would simply multiply up the recorded investment income by $100/x$. In reality, the yield varies with the form in which wealth is held, and the multiplier varies by range. Where, as is the case below, the investment income data come from income tax records, the multiplier has to be based on taxable yield. This means that the yield is typically the money yield, with no adjustment for inflation, but that it excludes capital gains (in most countries) and that we have to take account of assets whose yield is not taxed, such as (commonly) owner-occupied housing or tax exempt bonds.

The investment income data cover the living population, but they provide only indirect evidence about wealth, causing several problems in their use:

The method allows for variation in asset composition by wealth level, but not for the possibility that yields vary with the level of the holding. For example, banks commonly pay higher rates of interest on larger accounts. In the opposite direction, those with a higher marginal tax rate are likely to choose asset vehicles with a lower taxable component. Corresponding to any portfolio, there will be a distribution of ex post returns: income y is the product of the return, R, and the wealth, w. Where R and w are independently distributed, the coefficient of variation of y exceeds that of w, so that the investment income method overstates the dispersion of wealth holdings (Atkinson and Harrison 1978: app. VII). Applied to tabulated data, the method does not allow for variation in portfolio choices by individuals with the same level of wealth, such as those due to differences in the degree of risk aversion.

2.5 Conclusion

The non-survey data on the distribution of wealth described in this section are subject to a number of qualifications. None of the sources is ideal. Nonetheless, they all seem well worth investigation. If, as in this chapter, we are interested in the concentration of wealth among the rich, then they may be more informative than household surveys. Davies and Shorrocks (2000: 664), in their review of alternative data sources, conclude that 'estate and wealth tax data probably yield more reliable information on the upper tail of the distribution'.

3 The Rich in the Twentieth Century

I now consider what can be learned about the rich from these four sources, referring first to the global distribution, and then to the distributions in individual countries, evidence being presented for the USA, Germany, France, and the UK. It should be noted that we do not have statistics for all four countries from all four sources, and that no cross-country comparison is possible of the levels of concentration. At the country level, the chapter focuses on the changes over time.

3.1 *Evidence from Lists of Named Wealth Holders: The World and the USA*

It is natural to start with the *Forbes* magazine list of 'The World's Richest People' (Kroll and Fass 2006). By taking the global population, we avoid the problems associated with identifying the geographical location of the rich. At the same time, as noted earlier, one of the problems in using this list is that, in some cases, family holdings are reported, rather than individual holdings. In what follows, no correction is made. In February 2006, this list consisted of 793 billionaires, with net worth of $US1 billion or more. The total wealth of $US2,645 billion is itself quite concentrated. A quarter of the 793 own 59.9 per cent of the wealth of the group; and just 42 own a quarter of the total. The Gini coefficient for the population of billionaires is 46 per cent.

Figure 4.1 shows the cumulative distribution, with the logarithm of rank on the vertical and the logarithm of wealth (in billions) on the horizontal. The right hand part reflects the sparseness of the data. Bill Gates and Warren Buffett (number 2) stand out. If the distribution were exactly Pareto Type I, there would be a linear relation, with downward slope given by the Pareto coefficient. Judged by eye, the fit does not appear good. The partisans of the Pareto distribution may reasonably say that it cannot be expected to fit well where people are sparse. On the other hand, if we exclude the top 50 (broadly above $US10 billion), there remains a distinct downward curvature of the line.

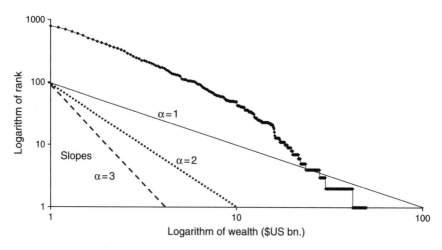

Figure 4.1. The world's billionaires, 2006

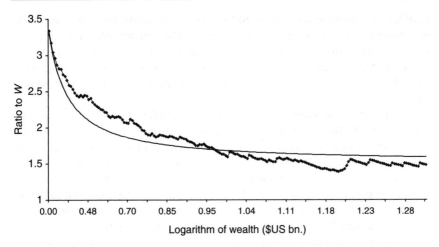

Figure 4.2. Ratio to W of mean wealth above W among world billionaires, 2006

Such a downward curvature has been found in other wealth studies: see, for example, the UK estate data in Shorrocks (1975: fig. 1). If, however, we consider only US billionaires in the *Forbes* list, then the downward curvature is not observed.[11]

An alternative representation is provided by Figure 4.2, which shows the MWA ratio curve, where attention is restricted to those with $US20 billion or less (this means that the top seven people are not shown, although their wealth is included in the calculation). The ratio is not constant but falls with wealth. Starting from a value of around 3.3, corresponding to a Pareto coefficient of 1.43, the ratio converges downwards to a value around 1.5, which corresponds to a Pareto coefficient around 3. In other words, the implied Pareto coefficient rises. One obvious first approach to modelling this convergence is to take the Pareto Type II distribution, where the ratio is given by the limiting value times $(1 + B/W)$, where B is a constant.[12] As, however, is shown by the illustrative curve in Figure 4.2, a value of B that is consistent with the initial values implies a faster initial convergence than observed in the data.

One of the attractions of the journalists' lists is that we can see who is who in the upper tail. Inspection of the *Forbes* list of world billionaires suggests that those at the very top are largely self-made. Bill Gates has topped the list for twelve years, and others in the top twenty-five in 2006 include Paul Allen, Steven Ballmer, Michael Dell, and Lawrence Ellison, with Sergey Brin and Larry Page of Google at numbers 26 and 27. But also near the top is Lakshmi Mittal, whose father was also a successful businessman, and the Thomson and Walton

---

[11] I owe this point to Tony Shorrocks.
[12] For references to Pareto distributions Types I and II, see Atkinson and Harrison (1978: 314–15).

families, the Rausing daughters, and the Duke of Westminster, where wealth was inherited. In the latter case, the origins of the family's wealth date back to the sixteenth century. While self-made fortunes may appear to dominate the list, and while some of those at the top have given away substantial parts of their fortunes to charitable foundations, inheritance remains an important mechanism.

Nearly half of the world's billionaires are US residents, and they correspond quite closely to the 400 richest Americans who feature on another *Forbes* list (*400 Richest Americans*) that has been published annually since 1982. These data have been considered in a number of US studies to examine their coherence with other sources of evidence. Here I simply consider the list on its own terms. To this end, I make use of the table prepared by Kopczuk and Saez (2004a: table C2), where they calculate the shares in total US wealth of the top 100 and top 400. Here I am interested not in their shares of total wealth, but in their *relative* shares—that is, the degree of concentration within the very rich. This shows that over the past twenty years the share of the top quarter of the 400 richest Americans rose from around a half at the start of the 1980s to around two-thirds at the time of writing. As Kopczuk and Saez (2004a: 31) bring out, the top 100 have pulled ahead quite markedly. The implied Pareto coefficient has fallen from around 2 to around 1.4.

3.2 Evidence from Wealth Tax Data in Germany

Those in the *Forbes* list for the USA are mostly 'mega-rich' on my definition and all are 'super-rich'. I now descend to the level of the merely rich, defined as having more than 30 times mean income per person, and consider the evidence from the wealth tax data for Germany, covering the former German Reich 1924–35 and West Germany for the period 1953–95.

Wealth tax data, as noted in Section 2, are subject to a number of shortcomings. In the case of Germany, the merits of the wealth tax data have been extensively reviewed by Ring (1998), who draws a careful comparison with other sources, notably the income and expenditure survey: the Einkommens- und Verbrauchsstichprobe (EVS).[13] The wealth tax data cover only a small fraction of the population: the official estimate is that in 1989 the statistics covered 3.4 per cent of households (Schöffel 1993: 752).[14] As noted by Föhl (1964: 44), this limits any analysis of the wealth tax data to larger wealth holdings, but this is precisely the group with whom I am concerned in this chapter. The wealth tax data have the advantage of being readily available: the

---

[13] The EVS data on wealth are used by Hauser and Stein (2003) in their study of the distribution of wealth in Germany for the period 1973–98.

[14] The comparison is with the Mikrozensus of April 1989. Ring (1998: 166) gives the percentage covered from 1953 to 1993. The lowest value is 1.85% in 1974; the highest 3.84% in 1993.

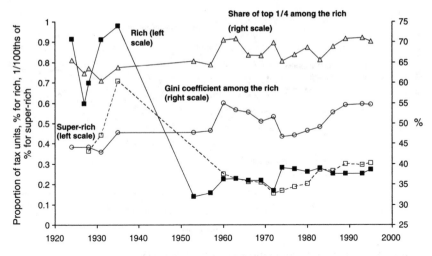

Figure 4.3. Wealth concentration, Germany, 1924–1995

German data used below are published in the *Statistisches Jahrbuch*, or in *Wirtschaft und Statistik*, or in the special series of *Finanzen und Steuern* dealing with the wealth tax (Fachserie 14). Furthermore, the data require no further manipulation to arrive at estimates of the distribution of wealth.[15]

The wealth cut-off applied to the German data in this chapter is 30 times the mean income per tax unit. For 1995, the last year for which the data exist, the cut-off is around €700,000 per tax unit.[16] In 1924, the first year for which data are used below, it meant wealth in excess of some 50,000 Reichsmark. For the super-rich, the cut-off is 30 times these figures. Figure 4.3 shows on the left-hand axis the proportions of rich and super-rich in Germany, the latter being measured in 1/100ths of per cent (basis points), and two measures of concentration, measured on the right-hand axis. The proportions of rich and super-rich were higher in the pre-war period, although it should be noted that this covered a different geographical entity. At that time, the rich constituted about 1 per cent of tax units. In 1953 the proportion classified as 'rich' was under 0.15 per cent, but the figure increased over the next forty years to approximately 0.3 per cent. The main increase took place in the 1950s and up to 1974; after 1974 the proportion rich remained broadly stable.

[15] Apart from interpolation. In the case of the super-rich calculations, this has in some cases involved extrapolating the top open interval; this has been done only where the cut-off is less than 50% higher than the starting point of this interval. The Gini coefficient is not calculated where there are fewer than 4 points.

[16] The mean income per tax unit is taken from Dell (2007). The figures for West Germany for 1993 and 1995 are extrapolated from the growth over time in those for unified Germany.

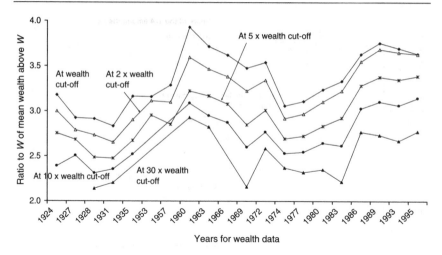

Figure 4.4. Mean wealth above ratio, Germany, 1924–1995

The scale for the proportion of super-rich is 100 times that for the rich, and the closeness of the graphs indicates that the super-rich were about 1 in 100 of the rich. With a wealth difference by a factor of 30, this would be consistent with a Pareto distribution with exponent about 1.35, indicating a high degree of concentration. The share of the top 25 per cent, and the Gini coefficient among the rich (calculated where there are 5 or more points on the Lorenz curve), shown in Figure 4.3 bear out that there was a high level of concentration. A Gini coefficient of 55 per cent, as found for 1960 and 1989–95, corresponds, with a Pareto upper tail, to a Pareto coefficient of 1.4. The share of the top quarter is around 70 per cent. Over time, there have been clear changes. Concentration in the early 1950s was similar to that in the German Reich. It then rose up to 1960; it fell in the 1960s and early 1970s, before rising again over the last twenty years.

The distribution is not necessarily closely approximated by the Pareto distribution. An indication of the closeness of fit is provided in Figure 4.4 by the ratio to W of MWA at different values of W: the cut off W^*, $2W^*$, $5W^*$, etc. Reading the curves vertically, we can see that the MWA ratio falls steadily as we move to higher levels of wealth. The implied Pareto coefficient rises. For example, in 1980 the ratio is 3.23 at W^*, corresponding to a Pareto coefficient of 1.45, whereas, at 30 times W^* (the threshold to be super-rich), the ratio is 2.35, corresponding to a Pareto coefficient of 1.75. Reading Figure 4.4 horizontally, we can see even more clearly the wave-like motion. Up to 1960 there was a rise in concentration; there was then a reversal up to 1974, after which concentration again increased. It may also be noted that concentration, measured this way, is higher in the 1990s than in 1953 and higher than for the German Reich.

It is interesting to compare these findings with those of earlier studies for Germany using the wealth tax and other data. Ring (1998: 209), who provides a summary of studies up to 1992, shows a graph (p. 233) for the shares of the top 0.5 per cent, 1 per cent, 1.5 per cent, and 1.7 per cent that moves over time in the same wave-like fashion as Figure 4.4.[17] As he notes, in the decades after the Second World War, Germany did not exhibit the decline in wealth concentration observed in other countries. There was a decline from 1960, followed by a rise after 1972. On the other hand, the total shares, influenced by the spread of popular wealth arising from increased prosperity, end up at around their 1953 level, whereas our measures of wealth concentration among the rich are distinctly higher.

3.3 Evidence from Estate Data

Use of estate data to estimate the distribution of wealth involves additional assumptions, but the method has long been applied successfully. In the USA and the UK, it provides one of the major sources of evidence about the distribution of wealth, in that the estimates cover a long run of years. The recent study by Kopczuk and Saez (2004a, b) for the USA covers the period 1916–2000; the estimates of Atkinson and Harrison (1978) for the UK start in 1923. Here I make use of the Kopczuk and Saez estimates for the USA, concentrating on the period since 1945 (the coverage of the estate data before then is less extensive, and does not extend to all the group defined as 'rich' according to the criterion adopted in this chapter).

The estimates of Kopczuk and Saez show that the share of the top 1 per cent in total wealth declined up to 1949, when it was around 22.5 per cent. It then recovered slightly, reaching 25 per cent in the 1960s, before falling to less than 20 per cent in 1976. It then rises again back to around 22 per cent in the early 1980s, but after that remains 'remarkably stable' in the 1990s (Kopczuk and Saez 2004a: 8). It is indeed remarkable, since the top *income* shares rose substantially over this period. Part of the explanation is, however, to be found in the fact that wealth holdings as a whole have increased, relative to total personal income. This is picked up by the measure adopted in this chapter, since it is based on a wealth cut-off defined relative to mean income. If all wealth holdings are increasing faster than income, then the shares may remain constant, while the proportion of rich, and super-rich, is increasing.

As may be seen from Figure 4.5, this is what appears to be happening. Figure 4.5 shows the proportions of rich and super-rich in the USA,[18] the former being shown by the solid squares and lines, and the latter by hollow squares

[17] Hauser and Stein show results for 1973–98, but these do not cover groups smaller than the top 10%.
[18] The mean income per tax unit is taken from Piketty and Saez (2007: table 4.A.0), divided by 1.5 to give an individual income figure used here. The definition of income excludes capital

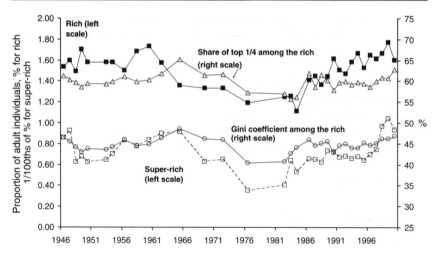

Figure 4.5. Wealth concentrations, USA, 1946–2000

and dashed lines. As for Figure 4.4, the scale for the proportion of super-rich is 100 times that for the rich, and the position of the graphs indicates that the super-rich were about 1 in 200 of the rich. With a wealth difference by a factor of 30, this would be consistent with a Pareto distribution with exponent about 1.55. The percentages of rich and super-rich behave rather differently from the top shares. The decline in the 1960s and 1970s is more evident. In 1960 some 1.75 per cent of US adults are classified as rich according to the criterion adopted here; by 1982 this had fallen to 1.25 per cent. The super-rich had fallen from 1 in 12,000 in 1960 to 1 in 25,000 in 1982. In the recent period, there is the same rise in the 1980s, but it continues in the 1990s. At the beginning of the 1990s, the super-rich were 1 in 14,000; at the end of the decade, they were 1 in 11,000.

Judged in relation to the aggregate economy, top wealth holdings have been becoming more dominant in the USA. Moreover, as noted by Kopczuk and Saez (2004a, b) and shown by the *Forbes* evidence, among the rich, wealth is becoming more concentrated. Figure 4.5 shows on the right-hand axis the percentage of the wealth of the rich owned by the top quarter. This began around 60 per cent, and rose from 1950 up to the mid-1960s; there was then a fall in concentration, reversed from 1982. The Gini coefficient among the rich shows a similar pattern. In 1965 the Gini was 48.6 per cent; it fell to 40.4 per cent in

gains and is expressed in 2000 prices. The wealth data are interpolated from table B2 in Kopczuk and Saez (2004a); i.e., using the thresholds 2%, 1%, 0.5%, etc., and the mean values implied by the wealth shares. The numbers of rich and super-rich are expressed relative to the population of adults (defined as aged 20 plus). The data for 1985 are not used, as they appear to lead to implausible results.

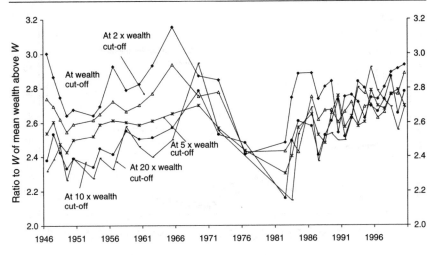

Figure 4.6. Mean wealth above ratio, USA, 1946–2000

1976, and then rose, reaching 46.9 per cent in 2000. This may not seem a large rise, but it means that the implied Pareto coefficient fell from 1.74 to 1.57.

In the German wealth tax data, we saw the distinct tendency for the Pareto exponent to rise with W, or for the MWA W to fall with W. The MWA ratio for the USA is shown in Figure 4.6. This demonstrates the same movement over time in concentration, with the ratio tending to rise in the 1950s and the first part of the 1960s, and then to fall. From 1982 there is an upward trend, indicating increased concentration. On the other hand, the evidence obtained by reading the graph vertically is different. It is true that, in the early period, there is a definite downward movement as we move to higher wealth levels (for example, comparing those above the wealth cut-off, with the MWA 20 times the cut-off), but this ceases to be the case as we move to later years. In the recent period the lines are much closer together and cross. In this period, the Pareto distribution appears to provide a better fit than in the German case. The MWA ratio is close to 2.7, corresponding to a Pareto coefficient of 1.6.

I turn now to the evidence for France. As noted earlier, these estimates relate to *estates* rather than wealth holdings. They are limited in their coverage of the period since 1964 and are also limited in the number of ranges for certain years, which means that neither the proportion super-rich nor the Gini coefficient can be calculated for those years. The data are used are those published by Piketty (2001), although I have used the total decedents aged 20 plus from Piketty et al. (2006). The wealth cut-off is based on mean 'revenue fiscal' per tax unit, divided by 1.5, and adjusted by a factor 1/0.8 to convert from a net to gross basis. In 1994, the most recent year covered, the cut-off was FF3.2 million per person, or around €500,000 per person.

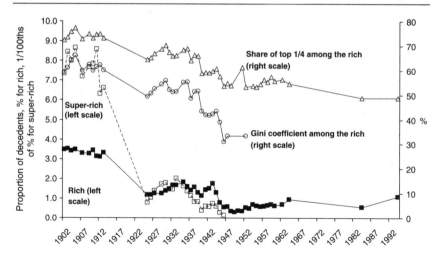

Figure 4.7. Concentration of estates, France, 1902–1994

One of the advantages of the estate data for France is that they allow us to go back to the beginning of the twentieth century. Figure 4.7 shows how different was the period before the First World War with regard to the proportions of rich and super-rich, which were much higher (above 3 per cent in the rich category) before 1913. Moreover, the super-rich line was about twice as high as that for the rich, which, allowing for the scale being different by a factor of 100, means that the super-rich were 2 per cent of the rich. After the First World War, they were reduced to 1 in a 100. In order to accommodate these larger differences, the scale in Figure 4.7 is smaller, and it should be noted that the changes over time in more recent years in the proportion rich are quite large. The proportion recovered a part of the lost ground after the First World War, but then fell sharply again after the Second World War. During the 1950s and early 1960s there was a further recovery. The degree of concentration, shown on the right-hand axis of Figure 4.7, was much higher before the First World War. A situation where the top quarter of the rich own three-quarters of their wealth corresponds to a Pareto coefficient of around 1.25.

One merit of the estate data is that, coupled with the French inheritance laws restricting disposal of estates outside the family, we can see that substantial inheritances must have been taking place. In 1902, for example, there were twenty-seven estates with mean wealth more than 9 times the threshold for the super-rich category. Even allowing for equal division among several heirs, such sums allow a considerable role for inheritance.[19] Moreover, the estate

[19] See Piketty (2001: app. J) for references to the (limited) statistical information on the division of estates by parts.

documents have been preserved as microdata, a fact that has been exploited by Piketty et al. (2006) to explore the causes of wealth concentration from 1807 to 1994. They find that concentration increased until the First World War, largely driven after 1860 by the growth of large industrial and financial estates, accompanying a decline of aristocratic fortunes. The subsequent decline was caused by the First World War and the ensuing shocks. In the UK, there has been a long tradition of using the estate records to examine the sources of individual fortunes, dating back to Wedgwood (1928, 1929). Given the freedom of bequest in the UK, particular attention focused on the division of estates. Wedgwood (1928: 48) found that 'among the very wealthy, equal division . . . is not the general rule'. On the other hand, Menchik (1980) found in the USA that in most cases there was equal division. The same source allows the pattern of marriage to be investigated. In the UK, Harbury and Hitchens (1979: 96) found that 'approximately 60 per cent of rich sons (daughters) of rich fathers marry daughters (sons) from wealthy families'.

3.4 Evidence from Investment Income Data

Investment income data have been relatively little used for the purposes of estimating the distribution of wealth. In part, this reflects the paucity of such data. The UK is one of the few countries to have published distributions of investment income over a long run of years. These data, which start in 1948, come from the surtax data and from the Survey of Personal Incomes (SPI). The surtax data have the advantage of being annual, but they end in 1972 with the merging of surtax into the general income tax; the SPI is a survey of all income tax records, but was carried out only every five years before 1962 (when it became annual), and tabulations of investment income have not been published since the 1970s.

In part, the relatively little use of the investment income method reflects the problems described in Section 2. Davies and Shorrocks (2000: 642) emphasize the sensitivity of the resulting distributional estimates to the coverage of assets and the underlying assumptions. We need, however, to distinguish between, on the one hand, the sensitivity of the overall wealth shares or the proportions of rich, and, on the other hand, the concentration among the wealthy, which is the principal concern of this chapter. Taking the UK results of Atkinson and Harrison (1978: table 7.3a) for those with investment income in excess of £3,000 (approximately 5 times mean tax unit income), we can examine the sensitivity of the ratio of concentration by comparing the findings with their estimated yield multipliers and those applying a common multiplier. For 1968, the top quarter of this group are estimated to own 51.2 per cent of total wealth using the varying yield multipliers and 49.2 per cent with a common multiplier. These appear close.

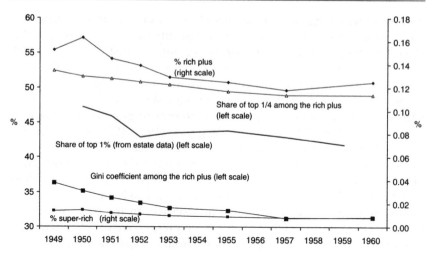

Figure 4.8. Concentration of wealth, investment income method, UK, 1949–1960

For the present application, we have also to bear in mind that the selected cut-off for the rich population was motivated by reference to mean income. This means that a different choice of level for the yield multiplier could also be construed as implying a correspondingly different cut-off. In the light of these considerations, I have opted here to work directly in terms of investment income, sidestepping the problems associated with the choice of yield multiplier. The 'rich' are taken to be those who have investment income in excess of mean income. Although, given that the surtax data cover only a fraction of the population defined as 'rich' according to the criterion adopted in this chapter, I work with a 'rich-plus' group, defined as tax units who have investment income in excess of 7½ times the mean overall income.

The surtax data provide evidence for the period 1949–72.[20] Here I consider 1949 to 1960. This period is of interest, since top wealth shares in the UK fell considerably—the estimates of Atkinson et al. (1989: table 1) show a fall from 1950 to 1959 of more than 5 percentage points (see the line without markers in Figure 4.8). It is therefore interesting to ask whether there was a comparable fall in the degree of concentration among the rich. Was the falling share of the top 1 per cent simply a reflection of the increased post-war affluence of the remaining 99 per cent? Figure 4.8 shows the estimated proportions of 'rich plus' (those with investment income more than 7½ times overall mean income) and super-rich (defined as before). Both of these fell quite markedly: the

---

[20] Data exist for the tax year 1948–9, but there appears to be a problem with the classification by ranges, as the implied means lie outside the ranges below £4,000. I have therefore used the data from the tax year 1949–50. In each case, the tax year 19xx − 19xx + 1, starting in April 19xx, is referred to as 19xx.

proportion of super-rich nearly halved. Figure 4.8 also shows that the degree of concentration among the 'rich plus' fell over the period. The Gini coefficient, calculated just for this group, was around 36 per cent at the beginning of the 1950s but had fallen by 5 percentage points by 1960. The limiting value of the Pareto coefficient had been around 2 but rose to 2.2 by 1960. There was definitely a reduction in concentration among the rich-plus group during this period of progressive income and estate taxation.

4 Summary of Evidence and towards Explanations

In this chapter, I have looked at the distribution of wealth through a particular lens, focused on those with wealth sufficient to place them in a very advantageous position relative to the average income recipient. I have presented evidence, not in the form of the more usual analysis of the share of the top x per cent in total wealth, but in terms of the proportion 'rich' and 'super-rich', defined as having wealth at least 30 times, or 30×30 times, average income. Moreover, I have considered not just the number of rich, but also the distribution *within* this group: for example, the Gini coefficient among the rich. For this purpose, household surveys are of limited use, and I have concentrated on what can be learned from wealth tax data, estate data, investment income data, and journalists' lists. These sources are subject to a number of qualifications, which have been summarized in Section 2, and they are not easy to compare across countries, but the data seem well worth investigation, and allow a long-run perspective.

The first finding is that wealth among the rich is indeed highly concentrated. Of the 793 world billionaires on the 2006 *Forbes* list, just 42 own a quarter of the total wealth of this group. The Gini coefficient for the population of billionaires is 46 per cent. Within individual countries, the Gini coefficient among the rich is close to 50 per cent in Germany (wealth tax data) and the USA (estate data based estimates of wealth). Among estates in France, the share of the top quarter was around half, and the same was true in the UK in 1960 for the share of investment income received by the top quarter.

The second finding is that there have been major changes over time. The estate data for France show that the rich constituted a much larger fraction of the population before the First World War, and that the concentration within this group fell. The same French data show that there was equally a major decline between the 1930s and the period after the Second World War. For Germany, there was a fall in the proportion rich, but no apparent decline in concentration, between the German Reich of the 1930s and the post-war Bundesrepublik. The changes over time are not indeed the same across the four countries. The 1950s saw, in the UK investment income data, a fall in the proportions of rich and super-rich, and a decline in concentration. The other three countries saw a rise in these proportions and in wealth concentration. In the past two decades, the (limited) evidence for France does not suggest a rise in the proportion of rich or in concentration. In contrast, in the USA there has been a clear rise in the proportions of rich and super-rich, and a rise in the Gini coefficient among the rich. This casts a rather different light on the evidence of stability in top wealth shares described by Kopczuk and Saez (2004a) as 're-markable'. It reflects the fact that we are here defining the cut-off in relation to average incomes, and, judged in relation to the aggregate economy, wealth holdings are becoming more important. Moreover, as these authors note, using the *Forbes* list, the degree of concentration among the rich has increased.

The third main finding concerns the shape of the distribution. While it is certainly reasonable to treat the distribution as having a Pareto upper tail, it is not necessarily a good approximation for the group of rich wealth holders considered here. The MWA curves drawn for France and Germany indicate an increasing Pareto exponent (declining concentration) as we move to higher wealth levels. Even with the mega-rich group of world billionaires in the *Forbes* list, the distribution only approaches the Pareto distribution in the limit. However, the USA has become an exception in recent decades, in that the Pareto distribution provides a better approximation. It may be the case, as noted for the *Forbes* list of billionaires, that the US distribution has acquired a different shape.

The fourth, suggestive, finding is that the upper part of the wealth distribution appears to be a subtle blend of self-made fortunes and fortunes acquired through inheritance or marriage. This can be seen from the *Forbes* lists and from microdata studies based on estate records. These sources would repay further investigation.

4.1 *Towards Explanations*

In 1907 the American Economic Association published a study 'The Growth of Large Fortunes' (Watkins 1907: 1). The author noted: 'The nature and causes of the wealth of nations have long been subjects of scientific interest . . . But it is time that the causes of the welfare and "fortune" of individuals should receive a share of attention . . . No thorough study of the general subject of large fortunes has yet been made. It is necessary, therefore, to study not merely concrete conditions, but also general causes and underlying general principles.'[21]

Watkins (1907) goes on to argue that 'ours is an age of new and striking characteristics' in that the origin of large fortunes, in contrast to the past, are economic rather than political: 'modern great fortunes . . . have come as a

[21] For more recent reviews of the literature on the explanation of the distribution of wealth, see Jenkins (1990) and Davies and Shorrocks (2000).

phase of a beneficent process of industrial and commercial development . . . It is an obvious inference that their appearance is probably correlated with our modern developments in technology and industrial organization' (p. 3). In an analysis that has many resonances today, he cites the impact of world trade 'formerly isolated and outlying communities and countries, from Ceylon to the edge of the one-time "great American desert", have been drawn into the swirl of exchange . . . The opportunity of the business man in any line to profit by value-increase is multiplied by the increase in the breadth and in the number of exchanges' (pp. 62–3). Watkins similarly identifies the role of technological progress:

prices of products do not fall so promptly as cost of production, and their tardier fall gives the gain, in the first instance, to the entrepreneur. The consumer and labourer come in for their share later, meanwhile often leaving a very great margin of profit to the entrepreneur, which he gives up only gradually, as forced to by competition. Or monopolistic devices may sometimes enable him to retain it indefinitely. Thus great advances in production are favourable to the acquisition of riches. (p. 107)

These forces of technological change and globalization may be expected to have left their mark on the distribution of self-made fortunes. The list of the rich is in part a mirror of economic history: railway and steel magnates and brewers were replaced by people like Henry Ford, Lord Nuffield, and John Paul Getty, who have in turn been replaced by those who made their money as a result of the ICT revolution. Rubinstein (1971) classified the industrial origins of British fortunes as 'old' (agriculture, textiles, etc.), 'intermediate' (brewing, engineering, etc.) and 'new' (retail, newspapers, property, etc.), and showed how there had been a steady shift towards industries that were growing more rapidly.

How can these mechanisms be formalized? Consideration of the origins of such fortunes suggests that many are made in 'winner-take-all' markets (as is evidenced by the fact that I am writing this chapter using Microsoft Word, not WordPerfect, which I used ten years ago). A natural starting point is therefore to model them as an extreme value distribution. If we consider only values that exceed some threshold, then, for sufficiently high values of the threshold, the extreme value distribution has the generalized Pareto form (see, e.g., Coles 2001: 75). But this in turn needs to be related to the underlying microeconomics of entrepreneurship. The distribution of prizes is not necessarily exogenous, and may be influenced by the number of incipient entrepreneurs and the degree to which they pool their activities. A promising model of this kind has been proposed by Shorrocks (1988), who distinguishes two stages of entrepreneurship (low and high risk), where success at the first stage is necessary to enter the high stakes stage. The relationship between self-employment and wealth inequality is examined empirically for Sweden by Lindh and Ohlsson (1998).

When, to the distribution of current self-made fortunes, we add those created in previous generations, we have to allow for accumulation and decumulation. Self-made fortunes do not simply continue unchanged. From the total stock of those created in the past, we have to subtract those that have disappeared completely, as with the collapse of a business empire or where a fortune is left at death to charity. People may build on the fortune through further accumulation or entrepreneurial activity. Their capacity to do so depends on the extent and effectiveness of progressive income and wealth taxation. Fortunes may be eroded through division among a number of heirs, or augmented through marriage. Again, progressive estate or inheritance taxation may cut wealth transmission, or provide incentives to distribute wealth more widely. These factors are investigated by, among others, Meade (1964) and Blinder (1973). The resulting distribution depends on the balance of these influences. They are not, however, necessarily exogenous. There may be feedback from the distribution of wealth to the aggregate economy, affecting the rate of return and the growth rate. The model of Stiglitz (1969) provides an example. He assumes that 'new' wealth is created each generation and that all estates are equally divided. The evolution of inherited wealth then depends on whether the rate of accumulation (which depends on the rate of return) less the rate of division is greater or less than the rate of growth of the economy. He shows that, with a standard aggregate production function, aggregate wealth converges to a level where savings out of inherited wealth cannot keep up. We would then observe a distribution where inherited wealth became progressively less important as we move up the rich list.

Appendix

Table 4.A1. Sources of wealth tax data, Germany

Year	Source
1924	SJ 1927: 477
1927	W&S 1929: 765
1928	SJ 1932: 508–9
1931	SJ 1936: 490
1935	W&S 1937: 692
1953	SJ 1959: 388
1957	W&S 1960: 642
1960	SJ 1963: 440–1
1963	SJ 1966: 458
1966	SJ 1969: 408
1969	F&S 1972: 60–1
1972	F&S 1972: 22–3
1974	F&S 1974: 26–7
1977	F&S 1977: 24–5
1980	F&S 1980: 21
1983	F&S 1983: 21
1986	F&S 1986: 23
1989	F&S 1989: 23
1993	SJ 1997: 550–1
1995	F&S 1995: 21

Sources: SJ denotes *Statistisches Jahrbuch*, W&S denotes *Wirtschaft und Statistik*, and F&S denotes *Finanzen und Steuern Fachserie* 14.

Table 4.A2. Sources of investment income data, UK, 1949–1960

Year	Source
1949–50	*AR* 1950–1: 139
1950–51	*AR* 1951–2: 157
1951–52	*AR* 1952–3: 87
1952–53	*AR* 1953–4: 85
1953–54	*AR* 1954–5: 82
1955–56	*AR* 1956–7: 148
1957–58	*AR* 1958–9: 85
1960–61	*AR* 1961–2: 209

Source: AR denotes *Annual Report of the Commissioners of the Inland Revenue*.

Data sources

World Billionaires (Figures 4.1 and 4.2): website of *Forbes* magazine, downloaded 22 Mar. 2006.

Richest Americans (Figure 4.3): Kopczuk and Saez (2004a: table C2).

Germany Wealth Estimates (Figures 4.4 and 4.5): wealth tax data from sources listed in Table 4.A1.

United States Wealth Estimates (Figures 4.6 and 4.7): Kopczuk and Saez (2004a: table B2).

France Estate Estimates (Figures 4.8 and 4.9): number of decedents aged 20+ from Piketty et al. (2006: table A5). Estate data from Piketty (2001: table J1). Average income per tax unit from Piketty (2001: table G2, col. 6).

United Kingdom Investment Income Data (Figure 4.8): investment income data from sources listed in Table 4.A2.

Part II

Wealth Holdings in the Developing World and Transition Countries

5

Changes in the Distribution of Wealth in China, 1995–2002

Shi Li and Renwei Zhao

1 Introduction

In the last twenty-five years, China has moved from a centrally planned to a market-oriented economy, leading to rapid economic growth and substantial improvement in the living standard of Chinese households.[1] Given the fact that, like other Asian countries, China has quite a high propensity to save, wealth accumulation and growth have become significantly faster with rapid income growth. Moreover, the land reform in rural areas and the privatization of public housing in urban areas have also speeded up the process of wealth accumulation of Chinese households. Along with the rising income inequality, however, household wealth displays an even more unequal distribution at the beginning of the new millennium. As indicated in this chapter, the Gini coefficient of the wealth distribution for the country as a whole was 0.55 in 2002, compared with 0.45 in 1995. That means inequality in the distribution of wealth has experienced a rapid increase in a rather short period.

This chapter attempts to investigate some major changes in the wealth distribution in rural and urban areas and in China as a whole using the data from two national household surveys conducted in 1995 and 2002. The surveys

This study was presented at the UNU-WIDER project meeting 'Personal Assets from a Global Perspective', Helsinki, 4–6 May 2006. The authors thank Jim Davies for his constructive and detailed comments. The authors would also like to thank Jesper Roine and other participants for their comments.

[1] It should be noted that 'China' in this chapter means mainland China. Hong Kong, Macau, and Taiwan are not included in our analysis. Given the fact that the three regions are much wealthier than mainland China, their inclusion in the analysis would inevitably lead to a significantly higher wealth level and wider wealth distribution in China as a whole.

collected rich information on household wealth and its components, enabling a detailed analysis of changes in wealth distribution among Chinese households. Our analysis indicates that the wealth distribution in China as a whole became much more unequal in 2002 than it was in 1995. The rising inequality is largely due to a striking increase in the wealth gap between urban and rural households. The housing reform, in which public apartments were sold to urban households at extremely low prices, has speeded up the accumulation of wealth among urban households, widening the wealth gap between urban and rural areas. Another contributor to the widening wealth gap between urban and rural households is declining land values in rural areas, which have led to a slowdown of wealth growth for rural households.

The chapter is organized as follows. The next section discusses some key issues related to the growth and distribution of household wealth in the last two decades, and provides a background for understanding the institutional settings and policies. In the third section, the survey and data used in the chapter are described. As China is a rural–urban divide society, the wealth distribution and its changes in urban and rural areas are investigated separately, in Sections 4 and 5 respectively. Then the wealth distribution in China as a whole is examined in Section 6. The chapter is concluded with some policy implications in Section 7.

2 Settings

In the pre-reform period private property rights were not fully recognized, and with an extremely low income level the accumulation of household wealth was very limited in China. The great majority of urban families lived in public housing. Private and individual business, and even self-employment, were strictly prohibited. As a result, the wealth accumulation of urban households principally took the form of financial assets from savings and durable consumer goods. In 1978 the total amount of time deposit savings in China as a whole was 12.9 billion yuan (NBS 1999: 25), which is equivalent to 13 yuan per capita and less than $US2 billion at the current exchange rate. From a distributive point of view, financial assets were more concentrated in urban areas than in rural areas, since rural people had a large part of their assets in the form of housing. Although rural people occupied more living space than their urban counterparts,[2] the market value of their housing was extremely low, reflecting the fact of a huge number of rural people living in poverty.[3] Since the average

[2] Housing space averaged 3.6 m^2 per capita for urban residents and 8.1 m^2 for rural residents in 1978 (NBS 1999: 25).

[3] There are different estimates of the number of the poor in rural China in the pre-reform period, depending on the poverty thresholds adopted. If the official line is used, there were 250 million poor people in 1978. The number would increase to 450 million if the $US1 line were adopted (see World Bank 2000).

level of wealth was so low, the distribution of household wealth was not a concern either of academia or of the government. Even in the early stages of economic reform in the 1980s, wealth distribution did not attract much attention. Consequently, there were few studies specifically focusing on the issues of inequality of wealth distribution in China.

Economic reforms started in rural areas in the late 1970s, with land reform widely and rapidly spreading over the entire rural sector in a short period. Collective land was distributed to rural households within villages mainly according to household size. Households obtained only usage rights rather than land property rights. Generally speaking, even today the land distribution is highly equal within villages and even within townships, although the inequality increases with an administrative region getting larger. The land reform allowed rural households more autonomy in farming their land and gave them a claim to the economic returns from using land, although the land remained collectively owned by law. From an economic point of view, the land can be regarded as a part of the wealth of rural households (McKinley 1993; Brenner 2001).

While the land reform increased the wealth of rural people, the housing reform has undoubtedly augmented the wealth of urban people. The housing reform started in the early 1990s and speeded up later in the decade. The principle of the reform was to sell the public housing to urban households at extremely low prices. The official selling prices were set by local governments with considerations of income level, living costs, and construction costs locally. There were almost no differences in the selling prices within a city. Variation of the official prices was insignificant across cities and provinces, but the regional *market* prices of housing were remarkably different. Even within a city, the market housing prices were different from one location to another. While the housing reform benefited urban households on average in terms of wealth accumulation, it also had a big impact on the wealth distribution in urban areas. Those households living in apartments with a good location, high quality, and a lot of space before the reform benefited more from purchasing their apartments than others. Housing reform had a significant effect in widening the wealth gap between urban and rural areas as the reform took place for urban households, precisely for those living in public housing. The percentage of the urban households living in public housing fell dramatically, from 84 per cent in 1988 to 16 per cent in 2002, as indicated in the data from 1988 and 2002 household income surveys.[4]

When looking at the changes in wealth distribution, we cannot ignore the changes in income distribution in China. One of most striking features in the

---

[4] The data from the 2002 household income survey are described in the next section in this chapter and the data from the 1988 survey are introduced in Eichen and Zhang (199). The authors of this chapter were deeply involved in the data collection of the two surveys.

income distribution during the period under study is the widening income gap between urban and rural areas. The official statistics, although more or less biased, indicate a rising urban–rural income gap from 1997 to 2003—the ratio of urban to rural household income per capita jumped from 2.5:1 to 3.2:1 (NBS 2004). This is also demonstrated in Khan and Riskin (2006) and Sicular et al. (2007).

3 Data

The data used in this chapter come from two household surveys conducted by the research team of the household income project formed by researchers in the Institute of Economics, Chinese Academy of Social Sciences (CASS), and international scholars. The first survey refers to 1995 and was conducted in the spring of 1996; the second survey refers to 2002 and was conducted in early 2003. The samples in the 1995 and 2002 surveys were drawn from the large sample used by the National Bureau of Statistics (NBS) in its annual household survey. The NBS adopts a slightly different sampling procedure for its rural survey from that for urban surveys. The sampling method for the urban survey can be described as follows. The respondent households are selected using a two-stage stratified systematic random sampling scheme. In the first stage cities and county towns are selected; in the second stage households within the selected cities and towns are chosen.

The procedure to select cities and county towns is designed as follows. First, all cities and county towns are classified into five categories on the basis of their population size. The categories are: extremely large cities, large cities, medium-sized cities, small cities, and county towns. Second, the cities and towns in each category are grouped into the six geographical regions (north-east, north, east, centre, north-west, and south-west). In each region, the cities and county towns of each category are arranged according to the average wages of their staff and workers with urban *hukou* (registration). Third, the numbers of individuals who are staff and workers in the cities are added up, and the sample cities or counties are selected using an interval of one million staff and workers (NBS 2004).

At the second stage, the households are selected in each of the sample cities by a multi-phase sampling scheme. In the extra large and large cities, the procedure is a so-called three-phase sampling method. In the first phase, the sample sub-districts in each city or county town are selected. In the second phase, the sample resident committees are selected from the sample sub-districts. And in the last phase, the sample households are selected from the sample resident committees (*jumin weiyuan hui*). In the medium-sized and small cities and counties, the procedure is a two-stage sampling method. First, the sample resident committees are selected; second, the sample households are selected from the sample resident committees. Unfortunately, the NBS does not document how the sub-districts, resident committees and households are selected. It is believed that a more or less random selection method is adopted. The NBS rural household surveys follow a slightly different procedure from its urban surveys. The difference exists in the sampling procedure, which consists of two steps. First, the sample villages are selected directly in each province, and second the sample households are drawn from each of the sample villages. Generally, ten households are selected from each village.

The 1995 survey conducted by CASS covers 19 provinces and 102 counties in rural China, and 12 provinces and 69 cities in urban China. The number of provinces in the 2002 rural survey increases to 22 and counties to 120, while the 2002 urban survey contains the same number of provinces and cities as the 1995 survey. The increase in the number of provinces in the 2002 survey has only a small effect on the estimated wealth distribution, as the newly included provinces have income and wealth close to the average level of the surveyed provinces.[5] Table 5.1 presents the sample distribution of cities/counties and households among the provinces surveyed. The sample size increases with the size of the provincial population, but not exactly in proportion.

The surveys collected detailed information on household wealth and its components, including financial assets, market value of private housing, production assets, and value of durable consumer goods. For the rural households, the value of land is estimated following the procedure that was adopted in McKinley (1993) and Brenner (2001).[6] The housing value is estimated by asking households to assess the market value of their owned housing. For a few homeowners housing space is reported, but, with no reported housing value, we make imputations following the method used in Gustafsson et al. (2006). The value is calculated as the average value per square metre in the county/city, times the reported space. Here housing property is defined as the net value, meaning the total value of housing minus outstanding housing

[5] Chongqing was a part of Sichuan in 1995 and separated from Sichuan as a provincial level administration region in 2002, so actually two provinces, Guangxi and Xinjiang, are added into the 2002 survey as new provinces. An exercise shows that wealth per capita would increase by 2.8% if the two provinces were removed from the survey.

[6] The procedure consists of the following steps. First, land area is adjusted for quality; 1 mu (equivalent to 0.06 hectare) of paddy field is set equal to 2 mu of dry fields. Second, net agricultural income per household is gross income minus production costs. Finally, according to measurements in 1988 and 1995, 25% of net agricultural income came from land, and the rate of return on land was 8%. Based on these definitions and assumptions, we calculate land value. In the 2002 survey, gross agricultural income and production costs are not reported. Using reported land area and average net agricultural income in the country, which is computed from the survey data, we calculate land value per household. It should be pointed out that the difference in calculation of land value in 2002 may result in an underestimate of inequality of land value in rural areas, since disparity of land productivity within counties is not taken into account.

Table 5.1. Distribution of households in the 1995 rural and urban surveys, by province, China

Province	Rural				Urban			
	Number of counties		Number of households		Number of cities		Number of households	
	1995	2002	1995	2002	1995	2002	1995	2002
Beijing	1	2	100	160	1	1	500	484
Hebei	5	5	498	370				
Shanxi	6	6	300	400	7	7	650	640
Liaoning	5	6	300	450	5	5	700	697
Jilin	5	5	300	480				
Jiangsu	5	5	500	440	9	9	800	729
Zhejiang	5	6	400	520				
Anhui	5	5	450	440	6	6	500	493
Jiangxi	5	6	350	430				
Shandong	7	7	700	630				
Henan	6	6	700	530	8	8	600	680
Hubei	6	6	402	520	7	7	742	673
Hunan	4	5	500	450				
Guangdong	7	7	500	530	8	8	546	544
Guangxi		5		400				
Chongqing		2		200		2		279
Sichuan	8	6	798	500	7	6	848	585
Guizhou	5	6	300	400				
Yunnan	5	5	300	260	9	8	648	636
Shaanxi	6	6	300	370				
Gansu	6	5	300	320	3	3	400	395
Xinjiang		8		400				
Total	102	120	7,998	9,200	69	70	6,934	6,835

Source: See text.

debt. Households were also asked to value their durable consumer goods, and most households reported the present market value. For some farmers who failed to report the value of durable goods, but reported the holdings of televisions, bicycles, washing machines, etc., we specify and estimate a linear consumer durable function over the households reporting the values and then apply the coefficients to the households that hold these goods but did not report values. The value of net wealth is used for our analysis, which is then the sum of all wealth items minus non-housing debt. Finally, we derived the household wealth per capita in rural and urban areas and China as a whole for 1995 and 2002 respectively.

4 The Distribution of Wealth in Rural China

As China has a striking urban–rural divide, it is best to begin by looking at descriptive statistics of wealth size and composition in rural and urban areas separately. According to the information collected in the surveys, the wealth

Table 5.2. Net values of household wealth per capita and its composition, rural, urban, and all China, 1995 and 2002

	1995		2002		Growth, 1995–2002
	Mean value (yuan)	Share (%)	Mean value (yuan)	Share (%)	
Rural areas					
Total wealth (net value) of which:	11,427	100.00	12,938	100.00	13.2
land value	5,350	46.82	3,974	30.72	−25.7
net value of housing	3,599	31.50	5,565	43.01	54.6
financial assets	1,131	9.90	1,593	12.31	40.8
fixed production assets	664	5.81	1,182	9.14	78.0
durable consumer goods	750	6.56	793	6.13	5.7
non-housing liabilities	−67	−0.59	−169	−1.31	152.2
Urban areas					
Total wealth (net value) of which:	13,698	100.00	46,134	100.00	236.79
financial assets	3,841	28.04	11,958	25.92	211.33
net value of housing	5,985	43.69	29,703	64.38	396.29
fixed production assets	165	1.20	815	1.77	393.94
durable consumer goods	3,156	23.04	3,338	7.24	5.77
other assets	612	4.47	620	1.34	1.31
non-housing liabilities	−61	−0.45	−301	0.65	593.44
China as a whole					
Total wealth (net value) of which:	12,102	100.00	25,897	100.00	113.99
land value	3,828	31.63	2,421	9.35	−36.76
financial assets	1,908	15.77	5,643	21.79	195.75
net value of housing	4,289	35.44	14,989	57.88	249.48
fixed production assets	525	4.34	1,037	4.00	97.52
durable consumer goods	1,441	11.91	1,784	6.89	23.80
other assets	175	1.45	242	0.93	38.29
non-housing liabilities	−65	−0.54	−219	−0.85	236.92

Note: Mean value of wealth and its components are measured in 2002 prices.

Sources: Household income survey, 1995 and 2002.

of rural households can be divided into six items: land, housing property, financial assets, fixed production assets, durable consumption goods, and non-housing liability (see Table 5.2).

There are many remarkable changes taking place in the level and structure of household wealth in rural areas between 1995 and 2002. The household wealth per capita is 11,427 yuan in 1995 (in 2002 yuan) and then rises to 12,938 yuan in 2002, increasing by 13 per cent during seven years. Of the net wealth, land and housing are the two largest assets, accounting for 78 per cent in 1995 and 74 per cent in 2002 respectively. All the wealth components except for land value have some increase. However, the land value decreases dramatically by 26 per cent during the period under study. As a result, the share of land in net wealth falls from 47 per cent in 1995 to 31 per cent in 2002. Why does the land value of rural households decline? We believe there are several explanations. First, industrialization, urbanization, and construction of the transportation system use more farmland and cause a reduction in the

Table 5.3. Cumulative share of wealth in decile groups, rural, urban, and all China, 1995 and 2002 (%)

Decile	Rural		Urban		All China	
	1995	2002	1995	2002	1995	2002
1 bottom	3.1	2.0	0.7	0.2	2.0	0.7
2	7.8	5.7	2.9	2.8	5.8	2.8
3	13.6	10.6	6.1	6.8	10.8	5.8
4	20.3	16.6	10.4	12.1	16.9	9.6
5	28.0	23.7	16.0	18.6	24.1	14.4
6	36.8	32.1	23.3	26.6	32.5	20.6
7	47.0	42.0	32.6	36.5	42.3	28.9
8	59.0	54.0	44.7	49.1	54.1	40.7
9	73.9	69.6	61.6	66.3	69.3	58.6
10 top	100	100	100	100	100	100
Gini	0.33	0.40	0.52	0.48	0.40	0.55

Note: The observations with negative value of wealth are not included in computation of Gini coefficients. Observations are for individuals rather than for households.

Sources: Household income survey, 1995 and 2002.

land size per capita in rural China. The surveys indicate that the land size per capita declines from 1.73 mu or 0.104 hectares per capita in 1995 to 1.47 mu (0.088 hectares) in 2002. Second, the returns to farming land have been falling since the mid-1990s, with the decline in the prices of agricultural products and stagnation of farming productivity.

Unlike land value, the shares of housing and production assets increase rapidly, as shown in Table 5.2. The former increased by 55 per cent and the latter by 78 per cent between 1995 and 2002. As a result, the share of housing value rose from 32 per cent to 43 per cent and that of production assets from 5.8 per cent to 9.1 per cent. Meanwhile, the share of financial assets went up modestly, from 10 per cent to 12 per cent, although the absolute growth of financial assets was fairly high.

The distribution of wealth among Chinese rural households can be examined by making a comparison of the shares of net wealth in the decile groups and then computing the Gini coefficient—the results appear in Table 5.3. It is clear that the distribution of wealth was becoming more unequal from 1995 to 2002; the Gini coefficient increased from 0.33 to 0.40. Looking at the shares of net wealth obtained by the decile groups, we see that the share for the top decile is 26.2 per cent in 1995 and then rises to 30.5 per cent in 2002. At the same time the wealth shared by the bottom decile falls from 3.1 per cent in 1995 to 2 per cent in 2002. Furthermore, the ratio between the highest two deciles and lowest two deciles rises from 5.3:1 in 1995, to 8.1:1 in 2002. Widening inequality of the wealth distribution can also be observed in Figure 5.1, which shows the Lorenz curve of the wealth distribution of rural households in the two years. Clearly, the 2002 curve lies completely outside the 1995 curve.

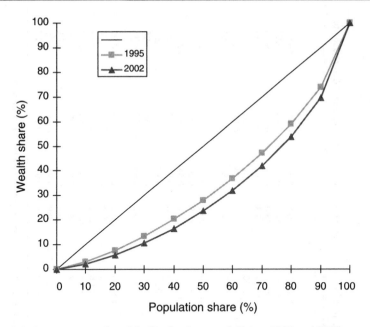

Figure 5.1. Lorenz curve of wealth distribution, rural China, 1995 and 2002

Note: Observations are for individuals rather than households. Those with a negative value of wealth are not included.

To find out how the wealth components and their distribution contribute to the distribution of net wealth, we decomposed the Gini coefficient of net wealth by using the formula:[7]

$$G_t = \sum_{j=1}^{J} \theta_j C_j \qquad (5.1)$$

where G_t is the Gini coefficient of net wealth, and θ_j and C_j are the share and concentration ratio of the jth wealth component.

The change in wealth distribution in rural China can also be examined decomposing the Gini coefficient (G_t) of net wealth into two items as indicated by (5.1), the concentration ratio (C_j) and the share (θ_j) of the j components. That means the contribution of each of the components to the inequality of net wealth depends on its share and concentration ratio. Comparing the Gini of net wealth with the concentration ratio of the jth component, one can consider that the component has an equalizing effect if its concentration ratio is smaller than the Gini of net wealth; otherwise it has a disequalizing effect.

---

[7] This formula is examined in more detail by Pyatt et al. (1980).

Table 5.4. Wealth inequality and its decomposition by factor, rural, urban, and all China, 1995 and 2002

	1995				2002			
	Share (%)	Gini	Concentration ratio	Contribution to total inequality (%)	Share (%)	Gini	Concentration ratio	Contribution to total inequality (%)
Rural areas								
Total wealth (net value) of which:	100.0	0.33	0.33	100.00	100.0	0.40	0.40	100.00
land value	46.8	0.37	0.29	40.44	30.7	0.45	0.26	20.02
net value of housing	31.5	0.47	0.38	36.46	43.0	0.54	0.46	49.15
financial assets	9.9	0.62	0.44	13.19	12.3	0.68	0.49	15.18
fixed production assets	5.8	0.63	0.32	5.60	9.1	0.67	0.39	9.02
durable consumer goods	6.6	0.40	0.22	4.45	6.1	0.66	0.38	5.79
non-housing liabilities	-0.6	0.95	0.06	-0.11	-1.3	0.95	-0.25	0.81
Urban areas								
Total wealth (net value) of which:	100.0	0.52	0.52	100.00	100.0	0.48	0.48	100.00
financial assets	28.0	0.60	0.42	22.8	25.9	0.60	0.44	24.22
net value of housing	43.7	0.82	0.73	61.7	64.4	0.54	0.50	67.62
fixed production assets	1.2	0.99	0.74	1.7	1.8	0.50	0.48	1.8
durable consumer goods	23.0	0.41	0.23	10.2	7.2	0.98	0.32	4.92
other assets	4.5	0.82	0.40	3.5	1.3	0.91	0.38	1.08
non-housing liabilities	-0.4	0.98	-0.12	0.1	-0.7	0.98	-0.26	0.36
China as a whole								
Total wealth (net value) of which:	100.0	0.40	0.40	100.00	100.0	0.55	0.55	100.00
land value	31.6	0.55	0.29	22.92	9.4	0.67	-0.05	-0.77
financial assets	15.8	0.67	0.43	17.08	21.8	0.74	0.63	24.92
net value of housing	35.4	0.64	0.54	48.15	57.9	0.67	0.63	66.32
fixed production assets	4.3	0.75	0.36	3.97	4.0	0.84	0.30	2.16
durable consumer goods	11.9	0.54	0.21	6.41	6.9	0.64	0.48	6.01
other assets	1.4	0.95	0.40	1.46	0.9	0.97	0.69	1.16
non-housing liabilities	-0.5	0.96	0.01	-0.02	-0.8	0.97	-0.17	0.27

Note: The observations with negative value of wealth are not included in computation of Gini coefficients. Observations are for individuals rather than households.
Sources: Household income survey, 1995 and 2002.

Table 5.4 presents the results from our decomposition analysis. It is apparent that the contribution of land value to the inequality of net wealth in rural areas decreases from 40 per cent in 1995 to 20 per cent in 2002. This dramatic drop resulted mainly from a significant fall in the share of land value in net wealth. The concentration ratio of land value decreases slightly, but remains at a relatively lower level compared to the Gini of the net wealth even in 2002. The land value, therefore, had an obvious equalizing effect, which became weaker as its share decreased over time. On the contrary, the housing assets have the biggest increase in their contribution to the inequality of net wealth in rural China, and became the largest contributor in 2002. It is worth noting that the housing value shows not only a rise in its share but also a remarkable increase in its concentration ratio, implying more unequal distribution of housing assets among rural households. As shown in Table 5.4, the third largest contributor to the inequality of net wealth is financial assets. Moreover, the contribution of financial assets increases from 13 per cent in 1995 to 15 per cent in 2002.

5 The Wealth Distribution in Urban China

As shown in Table 5.2, the net wealth of urban households consists of six items: housing assets, financial assets, fixed production assets, durable consumption goods, other assets, and non-housing debt. As above, the housing assets are expressed as the net value of housing, being equal to the total value of housing minus housing debts. Net wealth is then the sum of all assets minus non-housing liabilities.

Unlike rural households, urban households had substantial growth in their wealth from 1995 to 2002. Household wealth per capita increased from 13,700 yuan to 46,000 yuan in constant prices, with an annual growth rate of 19 per cent. Among the six wealth components, housing assets played the most important role in the rise in net wealth of urban households. The market value of housing assets increased by 396 per cent during the seven years and its share in net wealth on average augments from 44 per cent in 1995 to 64 per cent in 2002. Meanwhile, production assets grew at the same speed as housing assets, but their share remained at quite a low level, no higher than 2 per cent. Largely because of the faster growth in housing assets, the share of financial assets dropped by two percentage points, even though the amount of financial assets increased by 211 per cent.

We also examine the distribution of wealth in urban China by looking at the shares of decile groups (see Table 5.3 and Figure 5.2). Since for some urban residents their debts exceeded their assets, the lowest decile group owned less than 1 per cent of total urban wealth in both years. The wealth share of the highest decile group was 39 per cent in 1995 and then decreased to 34 per cent

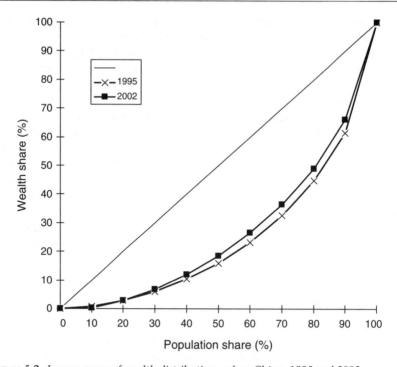

Figure 5.2. Lorenz curve of wealth distribution, urban China, 1995 and 2002

Note: Observations are for individuals rather than households. Those with a negative value of wealth are not included.

in 2002. At the same time, the Gini coefficient of wealth distribution in urban China decreased from 0.52 to 0.48.

When net wealth is broken down into its six components, we find that housing assets are the most unequally distributed in both years (see Table 5.4). The concentration ratio of housing assets was 0.73 in 1995, which was 21 percentage points higher than the Gini of net wealth. Although this ratio became smaller in 2002, it remained at the highest level for any of the six wealth components. It is apparent that housing assets are the greatest contributor to the inequality of wealth distribution in urban China. They explain 62 per cent and 68 per cent of the total inequality in 1995 and 2002 respectively.

Why is housing the most unequally distributed asset in urban areas, and much more unequally distributed than in rural areas? The underlying causes can be traced back to the housing system under the traditionally planned economy. As is well known, prior to the reforms basic necessities such as food, cotton, edible oil, and so on were rationed on a per head basis. Housing was distributed according to one's official rank or political power. As a result, housing was unequally distributed based on political considerations.

During the mid-1990s, the market-oriented housing reform not only inherited the pre-existing inequality of housing distribution, but further increased that inequality (Zhao and Li 1997). When public housing was sold to urban households, the price was set with a consideration only of housing space. The other factors, such as locations and housing quality, were not reflected in the selling prices. Consequently, those living in apartments with high quality and in good locations obtained much higher capital gains after purchasing public housing. In addition, some cities and work units linked the housing distribution with official positions, which created opportunities for some officials to obtain housing with higher potential market values. The selling prices were set artificially, much lower than the market prices. According to a study of cities in eleven provinces by Wang and Wei (1999) in 1995, this price differential was 8:1 (see Table 5.5). Because of such institutional arrangements, housing is much more unequally distributed than the other assets (the ratio between the top two deciles and the bottom two deciles was 19:1 for net wealth and 35:1 for housing assets in 2002). Moreover, the inequality in housing assets was larger in urban areas than in rural areas. The ratio of housing assets between the top two deciles and the bottom two deciles in rural areas was only 11:1 (Zhao and Ding 2006). However, the distribution of housing assets was more equal in 2002 than in 1995, because more households had purchased the public apartments that they lived in. As our data show, 57 per cent of urban households were in public housing in 1995, but the percentage had fallen to 16 per cent in 2002. Table 5.4 also indicates a rapid growth of housing assets of urban households because of a larger scale of housing privatization.

It should be noted that the value of usage rights of the households living in public housing is not taken into account as part of their housing assets. As shown in Gustafsson et al. (2003), including the value of usage rights of public housing would significantly reduce inequality of wealth distribution in urban China in 1995, its Gini coefficient decreasing by nearly 10 percentage points.[8] Therefore, inclusion of the value of the usage rights of public housing would lead to a reversed change in wealth inequality in urban China. The distribution of wealth would be more unequal in urban China in 2002 than in 1995. Compared to housing assets, the distribution of financial assets was quite equal among urban households in both years. They had a concentration ratio of 0.42 in 1995 and 0.44 in 2002. As mentioned earlier, financial assets were more evenly distributed in urban areas than in rural areas. More equal distribution of financial assets implies that less wealthy households have a fairly high saving rate compared to their net wealth or income. This can be explained by many uncertainties arising during the period of economic transition. Ongoing

---

[8] One of our exercises indicates that, if the percentage of urban households living in public housing in 1995 were the same as in 2002, the inequality of wealth distribution in 1995 would go down by 7 percentage points.

Table 5.5. Market and subsidized housing prices, urban China, 1995

Province	Market housing price (yuan/m²)	Public housing sales price (yuan/m²)	The ratio between market price and public housing sale price
Beijing	3,226.52	403.68	7.99:1
Shanxi	919.06	238.56	3.85:1
Liaoning	1,491.45	272.85	5.47:1
Jiangsu	1,247.26	191.28	6.52:1
Anhui	897.80	105.83	8.48:1
Henan	780.02	166.80	4.68:1
Hubei	2,187.50	98.53	22.20:1
Sichuan	1,050.20	87.04	12.50:1
Guangdong	3,100.00	247.59	12.07:1
Yunnan	1,276.34	201.01	6.35:1
Gansu	1,169.87	241.53	4.84:1
Mean price	1,576.91	204.97	7.69:1

Source: Wang and Wei (1999).

reforms of social security related to pension, healthcare, and education cause urban people to save more for precautionary reasons. In addition, traditional Chinese culture places a high value on saving.

6 The Distribution of Wealth in China as a Whole

We now turn to the distribution of wealth in China as a whole. Table 5.2 also contains the basic results for household net wealth per capita and its various components nationwide. The net wealth per capita is 12,102 yuan and then increases to 25,897 yuan in 2002, with a growth rate of 114 per cent. The fast growth of net wealth was mainly driven by a rapid growth of housing assets, which rose by 249 per cent during the period of 1995–2002. At the same time, housing assets increased their share of net wealth from 34 per cent to 58 per cent, becoming the largest component in 2002. Financial assets also had very fast growth, becoming the second largest component in 2002; their share in net wealth went up from 16 per cent to 22 per cent. Therefore, housing and financial assets together account for 89 per cent of the net wealth in 2002, compared with only 51 per cent in 1995. Since urban households have no land, average land value was only 2,421 yuan in 2002, declining by more than one third; its share in net wealth decreased from 32 per cent to 9 per cent.

As for the distribution of net wealth, Table 5.3 also presents the estimated wealth share and cumulative share for each decile group and the national Gini coefficients as well. It is clear that the inequality of wealth distribution in China as a whole rose fairly substantially between 1995 and 2002. The top decile possessed 31 per cent of all the net wealth in 1995 and then 41 per cent in 2002, increasing by 10 percentage points in just these seven years. Meanwhile,

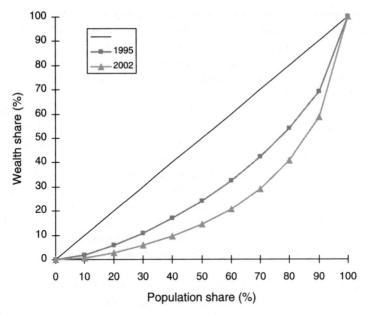

Figure 5.3. Lorenz curve of wealth distribution, all China, 1995 and 2002

Note: Observations are for individuals rather than households. Those with a negative value of wealth are not included.

the share of the two bottom deciles decreased from 5.8 per cent to 2.8 per cent. Moreover, the ratio of the share of the top decile to the bottom decile went up from 15:1 in 1995 to 59:1 in 2002, and the ratio of the top two deciles to the bottom two deciles from 8:1 to 21:1. The Gini coefficients of net wealth in the two years provide further evidence for widening inequality of wealth distribution in China as a whole. As shown in Table 5.3, the Gini coefficient mounts from 0.40 to 0.55, a substantial rise indeed. The Lorenz curves of the national wealth distribution also indicate a significantly wider inequality in 2002 than in 1995, as illustrated in Figure 5.3.

The decomposition analysis for the Gini coefficient can be also applied to the national distribution of household wealth. The results from our decomposition analysis are presented in Table 5.4. Clearly, there are three wealth components—housing asset, financial assets, and other assets—which have concentration ratios higher than the Gini coefficient of net wealth, so they have disequalizing effects. Among the three components, housing assets play the most important role in widening inequality of the wealth distribution. They had a share of 35 per cent in net wealth and a concentration ratio of 0.54 in 1995. The corresponding numbers went to 58 per cent and 0.66 in 2002. Thus, the contribution of housing assets to the inequality of net wealth increased from 48 per cent to 66 per cent. It seems that the housing privatization had little impact on the share of financial assets of households. Conversion of financial assets by some urban households to housing assets by purchasing public apartments might seem to account for financial assets declining as a percentage of net wealth. Actually, it is not the case. As shown in Table 5.4, the share of financial assets increased from 16 per cent in 1995 to 22 per cent in 2002. Meanwhile, the distribution of financial assets became more unequal in 2002 than it was in 1995, because both the Gini coefficient and concentration ratio of financial assets rose considerably. As a result, the contribution of financial assets to total inequality of net wealth in China as a whole went up from 17 per cent to 25 per cent. Nevertheless, there was a remarkable change in the role of land value in the wealth distribution. It accounted for 32 per cent of the net wealth in 1995, and the percentage fell to 9 per cent in 2002. The concentration ratio of land value was 0.29 and then fell to −0.045. Moreover, it explains −0.8 per cent of the total inequality of net wealth in 2002. That implies that land is more important for the less wealthy households whereas housing and financial assets are relatively more important for wealthy households.

The national Gini coefficient of wealth was considerably higher than that in either urban or rural China in 2002, which implies there is a big gap of wealth between urban and rural households. As our results in the previous tables have shown, the wealth gap between urban and rural areas was almost absent (1.20:1) in 1995, but it went up to a high level (3.57:1) in 2002. The widening urban–rural gap of wealth was the result of two factors. The first was housing privatization in urban areas, which started in the early 1990s and spread out in the late 1990s. There is no doubt that the housing reform enabled urban households to gain substantially in measured wealth. As a result, the housing reform widened the estimated urban–rural wealth gap. The second factor was the declining value of rural land, which was a large part of the net wealth of rural households in 1995 but no longer played such an important role in 2002.

To investigate how large the impact of the urban–rural gap in household wealth is on the inequality of wealth in China as a whole, we conducted decomposition using the following formula for the popular Mean Logarithmic Deviation (MLD) measure:[9]

$$I(y) = \sum_{g}^{k} \frac{n_g}{n} I_g + I(u_1, u_2, \ldots, u_k) \tag{5.2}$$

Using (5.2), total inequality, as measured by the MLD, can be decomposed into between-group and within-group inequality. The results from our decomposition analysis are presented in Table 5.6. It is apparent that between-group urban–rural inequality was very small in 1995, accounting for only 1 per cent

[9] For an analysis of the decomposition properties of the MLD index, see Shorrocks (1984).

Table 5.6. Decomposition of national wealth inequality into urban and rural components, China, 1995 and 2002

Date	National inequality	Between urban and rural areas	Within urban and rural areas	Within urban areas	Within rural areas
1995					
MLD	0.276	0.003	0.273	0.141	0.132
Contribution (%)	100	1.1	98.9	51.1	47.8
2002					
MLD	0.538	0.200	0.338	0.172	0.166
Contribution (%)	100	37.2	62.8	32.0	30.8

Note: The observations with negative value of wealth are not included. Observations are for individuals rather than for households.

Sources: Household income survey, 1995 and 2002.

of the national inequality of wealth distribution. However, the between-group inequality as a percentage of the national inequality increased significantly to 37 per cent in 2002. These results indicate that, when China entered into the new millennium, her wealth distribution became increasingly unequal and the wealth gap between urban and rural households displayed a comparable pattern to the urban–rural income gap (Li and Yue 2004).

How should China's distribution of wealth be assessed in the context of international comparison? By international standards (Davies and Shorrocks 2000; Schneider 2004; Davies et al. 2007), the Gini coefficient of wealth distribution in China is not very high.[10] However, the speed at which inequality is rising is very fast, although it is not comparable to Russia. Household wealth in developed countries has been accumulated over several hundred years, while wealth accumulation in China has taken place only in around twenty years. This suggests that wealth accumulation and the increase in wealth inequality in China are unusually speedy. Moreover, since 2002, the increase in wealth inequality has accelerated as suggested by the latest *Forbes* lists. The number of billionaires from China grew from 1 on the 2002 list to 8 on the 2006 list, and again to 20 on the 2007 list.

7 Conclusion

Since the economic reform, both rural and urban households have been transformed from a proletariat to property owners. Especially since 1990, the Chinese people have experienced rapid accumulation of wealth. Housing and

---

[10] Davies et al. (2007; see also Chapter 19, this volume) reports the Gini of wealth distribution for twenty-six countries, among which the lowest are 0.547 for Japan, 0.570 for Spain, and 0.579 for South Korea apart from China. Among developing countries the lowest are 0.660 for Bangladesh and 0.669 for India.

financial assets have become the largest components of net wealth for both urban and rural households. At the same time, the distribution of wealth became more unequal in China as a whole during the period under study. The rising inequality is largely due to the widening household wealth gap between urban and rural areas. From the mid-1990s, the housing reform in urban areas has speeded up, through which most public apartments have been privatized. In this process urban households have purchased their apartments at extremely low prices, so the majority of urban households have gained from the reform and have their housing assets increased substantially. As a result, the gap of household wealth between urban and rural areas was significantly wider in 2002 than in 1995.

The housing reform does narrow the inequality of housing wealth within urban areas as more and more households purchase their apartments, but housing assets increase their share in household net wealth and become the largest contributor to the inequality of household wealth in urban China. Even in 2002, housing assets had substantial disequalizing effects on the distribution of wealth in urban areas and in China as a whole. It should be pointed out that, if the value of the usage rights of public housing was imputed, then the inequality of wealth distribution would be wider in 2002 than in 1995.

Another major contributor to the widening wealth gap between urban and rural households is declining land value for rural households. Land value was the largest part of net wealth of rural households in 1995, but it became the second largest part in 2002. Although land value still plays a significant role in narrowing the wealth inequality within rural areas, the importance of this role is decreasing considerably over time.

The inequality of wealth distribution in China is larger than that of income distribution. Twenty years ago, Chinese residents had little property income except interest (World Bank 1981). The present and future situations, however, are completely different. Because of the differences in the methods of calculating land values in 1995 and 2002, the inequality of wealth distribution was more or less underestimated in rural areas in 2002 and in China as a whole as well. In the long run, wealth will serve as an important determinant of individual income. For instance, in cities more and more households will have property income such as housing rent. As a result, the inequality of wealth will exacerbate income inequality. If China wishes to prevent this from happening, redistributive measures may be required.

Taxation and transfers may play a direct role in reducing inequality of wealth, but the fundamental measures are those enabling the less wealthy people to accumulate their wealth more speedily. One of these measures is improvement of education in quantity and quality for the less wealthy people. To a large extent, improving the ability of the labour force depends on education. Improving the education status of less wealthy groups is an important way to reduce the inequality of wealth. In other words, improving education so as to reduce the inequality of human capital can create equal opportunities for people to gain income and wealth.

A second relevant measure is to have a more flexible policy for rural–urban migration, which will greatly help to narrow the wealth gap between urban and rural households. Reduction in the barriers to labour migration allows people more equal opportunity to take part in the process of income and wealth generation. It has been demonstrated that labour migration, especially between rural and urban areas, can play an important role in reducing the inequality of income and wealth. Although some of the systemic barriers to migration such as the *hukou* system, welfare system, housing system, and employment system have been reduced, China is still far away from a competitive labour market. To make the labour market more competitive, especially in labour mobility between rural and urban areas, is thus an important and relevant policy thrust to be considered in the future.

6

The Distribution of Household Wealth in India

S. Subramanian and D. Jayaraj

1 Introduction

This chapter presents some major findings from an analysis of the five decennial Reserve Bank of India–National Sample Survey Organization's *Surveys on Debt and Investment* (NSSO 1961–2, 1971–2, 1981–2, 1991–2, and 2002–3) in respect of magnitudes and trends for indebtedness, the composition of wealth, and inequalities in the distribution of wealth at the level of the household. A more detailed treatment of the subject is available in Subramanian and Jayaraj (2006), while issues relating to the nature and quality of the data in the surveys have been discussed in an appendix to that paper.

2 Some Findings from the Survey Data

2.1 *Debt*

Indebtedness can be captured in two indicators, the *incidence* measure (or proportion of households reporting indebtedness) and the *debt–asset ratio*. At the all-India rural level, the data (see Table 6.1) suggest that in respect of both indicators there has been a decline over time in indebtedness (though the

This chapter owes much to the detailed and constructive suggestions, with respect to both form and content, made by Jim Davies. The authors also acknowledge the helpful suggestions made by an anonymous referee. The chapter could not have been written without the help of R. Dharumaperumal, who provided superb computational assistance under tremendous pressure of time. This work has also benefited from very helpful discussions with A. Vaidyanathan, and from the cues suggested by his own earlier work on the subject. A. Arivazhagan, Lorraine Telfer-Taivainen, and R. Senthil helped with the word-processing and formatting, for which our thanks are expressed.

Table 6.1. Indebtedness over time, all India, 1961/1962–2002/2003

Year	Rural		Urban	
	Proportion of indebted households	Debt–asset ratio	Proportion of indebted households	Debt–asset ratio
1961–2	62.80	n.a.	n.a.	n.a.
1971–2	42.87	4.43	n.a.	n.a.
1981–2	19.97	1.83	17.36	2.54
1991–2	23.40	1.78	19.30	2.51
2002–3	26.50	2.84	17.80	2.82

Sources: Reserve Bank of India (1965); NSSO (1985; 37th Round, Report No.318); NSSO (1998; 48th Round); and NSSO (2005; 59th Round, Report No.500).

Table 6.2. The inverse monotonicity between indebtedness and asset holdings, India, 2002–2003

Size-class of household asset holdings (rupees)	Average value of cash loans (rupees)	Average value of asset holdings (rupees)	Debt–asset ratio (%)
0–15,000	1,443	6,317	22.84
15,000–30,000	2,510	22,353	11.23
30,000–60,000	3,251	44,595	7.29
60,000–100,000	4,323	78,359	5.52
100,000–150,000	5,279	123,453	4.28
150,000–200,000	5,729	173,397	3.30
200,000–300,000	7,458	244,483	3.05
300,000–450,000	10,201	367,066	2.78
450,000–800,000	16,772	592,415	2.83
>800,000	36,712	1,752,321	2.10
Aggregate	8,694	306,967	2.83

Source: Computations based on data in NSSO (2005; 59th Round, Report No.500).

1981–2 survey report itself acknowledges that the incidence figure for this year is suspiciously low). While the incidence of indebtedness appears to be lower, the debt–asset ratio is generally higher for the urban areas than for the rural, as revealed by the data for 1981–2 and 1991–2. The burden of debt is typically higher for the asset-poor households than for the asset-rich ones, as reflected in a monotonically declining debt–asset ratio with the size-class of asset ownership (see Table 6.2, which presents data for India, rural and urban combined, in 2002–3).

There is reason to believe that the extent of indebtedness is understated in the surveys. This issue is explored by Rao and Tripathi (2001) and Satyasai (2002), with particular reference to the 1981–2 and 1991–2 surveys. Among other things, Rao and Tripathi point out that the extent of institutional credit, as available from figures provided by the lending agencies, is considerably higher than debt owed to these sources as reported in the 1991–2 survey. Based on their work, Subramanian and Jayaraj (2006) calculate that the extent of indebtedness in 1991–2 was perhaps around 3.15 times larger than the estimate yielded by the survey. A similar qualification seems to be indicated for the 2002–3 survey as well: in particular, rural indebtedness and debt-induced farmer suicides, which have been widely reported in the media in the time after the year 2000, are not commensurately reflected in the 2002–3 data.

2.2 Assets: Average Holdings across Space and over Time

Table 6.3 presents information, at the all-India level, on the nominal and real values of asset holdings per household, and inequality in their distribution, over the period of the five surveys. On the assumption that the wholesale price index (see Vaidyanathan 1993) or the consumer price index can serve as at least rough surrogates for an asset price indicator, Table 6.3 suggests that there has been a clear survey-to-survey increase in the real value of asset holdings per household.

There is a fair degree of stability over time in the rankings of states according to average asset holdings per household (for details, see Subramanian and Jayaraj 2006). Data for the years 1971–2, 1981–2, 1991–2, and 2002–3 suggest that, in rural India, the five worst-performing states have been Orissa, Tamil Nadu, West Bengal, Assam, and Andhra Pradesh, while the top five states have been Punjab, Haryana, Kerala, Uttar Pradesh, and Rajasthan. In the urban areas, the five worst-performing states have been Orissa, Andhra Pradesh, Bihar, Assam, and West Bengal, while the front-rankers have been Kerala, Haryana, Punjab, and Maharashtra. Taking both urban and rural areas into account, the polarities are described by Punjab, Haryana, and Kerala, at the top and, systematically, Orissa at the bottom. The gap between the best and the worst performer has been large, and it has grown larger with time. Briefly, all the states of the Indian union have registered improvements in their mean asset-holding position, but in the rural areas the initially better-off states have outpaced the worse-off ones over time.

2.3 Asset Composition

It should be noted straightaway that there is one feature of asset composition that sharply differentiates a developing country from an industrialized one: a predominantly rural and agrarian economy like India displays an asset portfolio that is significantly more strongly weighted in favour of physical assets than one would expect from the experience of industrialized economies in which financial assets play a relatively vastly more important role. A comparative picture of the division between tangible and financial assets as it obtains for India and for selected industrialized countries reveals the following: the

Table 6.3. Nominal and real values of asset holdings per household, and inequality in the inter-household distribution of assets, India, 1961/1962–2002/2003

| | Asset holdings per household (rupees) | | | | | | | | | Gini coefficient of inequality | | Theil index of inequality | |
| | Nominal | | | Real (deflated by WPI) | | | Real (deflated by CPI) | | | | | | |
	R	U	C	R	U	C	R	U	C	R	U	R	U
1961–2	5,267	n.a.	n.a.	27,290	n.a.	n.a.	22,900	n.a.	n.a.	0.6440	n.a.	0.8031	n.a.
1971–2	11,343	n.a.	n.a.	30,740	n.a.	n.a.	25,780	n.a.	n.a.	0.6564	n.a.	0.8471	n.a.
1981–2	36,089	40,566	37,157	36,089	40,566	37,157	36,089	40,556	37,157	0.6354	0.7037	0.8013	1.0224
1991–2	107,007	144,330	116,873	51,570	69,557	56,324	49,540	65,904	53,865	0.6207	0.6805	0.7123	0.881
2002–3	265,606	417,158	306,967	66,640	104,664	77,017	66,568	90,099	72,990	0.6289	0.6643	0.7501	0.8241

Note: WPI = Wholesale Price Index; CPI = Consumer Price Index; R = Rural; U = Urban; C = Combined. Data on WPI and CPI, for the years before 2002–3, are from Centre for Monitoring Indian Economy: *Basic Statistics for the Indian Economy (August 1993)*; and for the year 2002–3 are from *Annual Statistical Abstract 2002–2003*. Time-series data on the official exchange rate are available on the statistical website Indiastat.com. The data indicate that the annual average exchange rates, as expressed in Indian rupees per US dollar in 1961–2, 1971–2, 1981–2, 1991–2 and 2002–3 were, respectively, 4.76, 7.43, 8.97, 24.47, and 48.40. The all-India combined mean asset-holding per household, in US dollars at current domestic prices and exchange rates, were then of the order of: US$4,142 in 1981–2, US$4,776 in 1991–2, and US$6,342 in 2002–3.

Sources: Computations based on data in Reserve Bank of India (1965), Reserve Bank of India (1975), NSSO (1985; 37th Round, Report No.318), NSSO (1998; 48th Round), and NSSO (2005; 59th Round, Report No.500).

share of financial assets in all assets was 5.01 per cent for India in 2002–3, 18.2 per cent for Italy in 1991 (Brandolini et al. 2004: table 7), 21.2 per cent for Canada in 1984 (Morisette et al. 2003: table 1), 24 per cent for Sweden in 1975 (Spånt 1981: table 2), and 22.1 per cent for Germany in 1983 (Hauser and Stein 2003). Thus, while financial assets in the industrialized countries could easily account for a fifth of the value of all assets, the corresponding share in India is less than a twentieth. We shall return to this theme a little later.

Table 6.4 presents a comprehensive picture of the composition of household assets (rural and urban combined) at the all-India level, for 1981–2, 1991–2, and 2002–3, disaggregated by the size-class intervals of household asset holdings relevant for the respective surveys. The table also affords a consolidated profile of asset composition, separately for rural and urban India. The data for India in 2002–3 are typical of a pattern in which asset diversification is a declining function of aggregate wealth, with specialization in land rising with wealth. This pattern of asset diversification contrasts with that in the developed countries, where there is some suggestion—see, for instance, King and Leape (1984), who employ survey data for the late 1970s in the USA—that diversification tends to increase with wealth. Land continues to remain the symbol and substance of both wealth and power in rural India.

The numbers in Table 6.4 confirm that wealth in rural India is heavily land-dominated. There is a fair measure of inter-temporal stability in the asset composition, with land accounting for about two-thirds of the value of all assets, followed by buildings that account for about a fifth, and durable household assets edging out the share of livestock and poultry over time. Among themselves, these four asset components account for about 95 per cent of all wealth. In the urban areas, land and buildings together claim between two-thirds and three-quarters of the total value of assets, with buildings being somewhat weightier than land. The third most important asset component in the urban areas is durable household assets, followed by financial assets, though the latter overtook the former in 2002–3: these two components, along with land and buildings, claim about 94 per cent of the value of all assets. Financial assets are significantly more important in the urban areas than in the rural. Between 1991–2 and 2002–3, at the combined all-India level, the share of financial assets rose from 3.6 per cent to 5 per cent, but, given the large weight of rural population in total population, the overall picture was still very heavily biased in favour of physical assets, in particular, land. Even in 2002–3, financial assets were overwhelmingly constituted by bank deposits (92.3 per cent of the total), with shares accounting for only 4.5 per cent.

It is worth remarking that the picture presented above is seldom reflected in the pink press or the visual media: entire television channels are devoted to a continuous monitoring of the stock market, and to the consumer-durables-oriented lifestyle of the urban elite. The dominant reality on the ground

Table 6.4. Size-class-wise (rural and urban combined), and consolidated (rural/urban), composition of assets, India, 1981–1982, 1991–1992, and 2002–2003

Year	Size-class	Land	Building	Livestock and poultry	Agricultural machinery	Non-farm business equipment	All transport equipment	Durable household assets	Financial assets	All assets
1981–2	1	10.65	23.85	3.44	1.12	2.61	2.94	52.50	2.89	100.00
	2	25.00	33.56	7.52	0.74	1.41	1.63	24.88	5.29	100.00
	3	35.09	30.44	7.66	0.69	0.99	1.16	17.83	6.14	100.00
	4	42.91	27.07	7.34	0.89	0.65	1.21	14.38	5.55	100.00
	5	50.25	25.76	5.76	1.27	0.59	1.13	11.26	3.99	100.00
	6	54.16	25.46	4.10	1.59	0.49	1.16	9.47	3.57	100.00
	7	59.19	23.30	2.39	2.46	0.71	1.48	6.98	3.48	100.00
	8	62.42	20.68	1.59	3.23	1.83	1.96	4.25	4.04	100.00
	1–8: Rural	62.12	20.71	4.98	2.47	0.30	0.96	7.10	1.37	100.00
	1–8: Urban	32.36	35.65	0.83	0.41	2.05	2.51	15.14	11.05	100.00
1991–2	1	11.96	24.94	3.72	0.77	1.93	3.89	47.38	5.40	100.00
	2	24.20	34.31	5.52	0.59	1.48	2.33	27.84	3.73	100.00
	3	31.05	35.72	6.17	0.57	0.95	1.70	19.94	3.90	100.00
	4	37.95	33.74	5.54	0.62	0.82	1.41	15.92	4.01	100.00
	5	43.17	32.57	5.40	0.74	0.70	1.48	12.56	3.38	100.00
	6	45.81	30.95	4.48	0.82	0.58	1.41	10.79	5.16	100.00
	7	49.40	30.00	4.15	1.07	0.56	1.42	9.78	3.62	100.00
	8	52.06	29.11	3.33	1.09	0.52	1.30	8.84	3.74	100.00
	9	54.48	27.75	2.68	1.17	0.50	1.55	8.03	3.83	100.00
	10	59.61	25.15	1.27	2.07	0.79	2.08	5.62	3.40	100.00
	1–10: Rural	64.25	21.40	3.38	2.23	0.32	1.21	5.88	1.33	100.00
	1–10: Urban	35.80	39.46	0.42	0.26	1.48	3.03	11.29	8.26	100.00
2002–3	1	14.80	21.86	2.19	0.67	1.87	2.97	48.43	7.22	100.00
	2	25.84	36.96	3.14	0.54	1.06	1.77	26.40	4.30	100.00
	3	31.86	41.09	3.40	0.48	0.71	1.55	17.13	3.79	100.00
	4	39.55	38.77	3.34	0.53	0.68	1.50	12.06	3.73	100.00
	5	44.35	35.87	3.06	0.56	0.64	1.35	9.82	4.35	100.00
	6	47.75	34.45	2.90	0.68	0.62	1.14	8.30	4.19	100.00
	7	51.14	32.02	2.37	0.74	0.51	1.43	7.47	4.33	100.00
	8	51.66	31.59	1.85	0.99	0.58	1.47	6.92	4.95	100.00
	9	53.35	29.81	1.29	1.44	0.56	1.86	6.27	5.44	100.00
	10	59.11	25.03	0.67	1.69	0.88	3.05	4.29	5.26	100.00
	1–10: Rural	63.22	23.53	2.10	1.98	0.35	1.39	5.11	2.32	100.00
	1–10: Urban	38.54	37.84	0.21	0.22	1.38	3.85	8.37	9.58	100.00

Source: Calculations based on data in NSSO (1985; 37th Round), NSSO (1998; 48th Round), and NSSO (2005; 59th Round).

presents a stark contrast to this construction. From a major country-wide household survey conducted in 2000 by the National Council of Applied Economic Research (NCAER) for the Securities and Exchange Board of India (SEBI), it emerges that only an estimated 8 per cent of all Indian households had invested in either or both of equity shares and debentures at the end of the financial year

1998–9. Comparison with a 1986 *Survey of Financial Assets* conducted by the NCAER suggests that investor households have grown at a compound rate of 22 per cent per year between 1985–6 and 1998–9; further comparison with the results of a SEBI survey conducted in 1991–2 reveals that this growth has been much sharper in the post-1991–2 period (the watershed year for economic liberalization in the country). Despite these developments, by the turn of the millennium, 92 per cent of all Indian households had no direct investment in equity shares (see the *Rediff Money Special*, August 2000).

The situation is not very different in the matter of durable household assets. Despite their relatively large presence in the wealth portfolio of the poor, there is reason to believe that the nature and quality of durables owned by the poor is of doubtful value. Data on the ownership of assets and amenities provided by Census of India 2001 (tables on houses, amenities, and assets are available on compact disk) confirm this proposition. For a class of consumer durables constituted by radios/transistors, television sets, telephones, bicycles, scooters, motorcycles and mopeds, and cars, vans and jeeps, it turns out that the headcount ratio of households that do not own *any* of these durables—not even a transistor—is as high as 34.5 per cent. These deprivation statistics are compatible with the positive relationship between consumer expenditure and wealth: as the 1991–2 survey unsurprisingly reveals, for both rural and urban India, average household asset holdings systematically rise with the per capita expenditure class in which the households fall.

Briefly, and in the light of the statistics reviewed above, it would appear to be premature, unrealistic, and essentially diversionary to construct India's wealth status in the image of a small, enclave, urban elite's aspirations. In the larger scheme of things, financial assets and durables in India are still nowhere near imitating their relative significance in the industrialized West. It is worth underlining the issue: misplaced priorities can not only cost a government its seat (as happened in India's general elections of 2004), but derail important programmes and policy orientations. The proposition is nowhere more evident than in the sadly discredited and all-but-forgotten role of land reform as an egalitarian and anti-poverty instrument in India's economic development. This brings us directly to a consideration of distributional questions.

2.4 Vertical Inequality in the Distribution of Household Assets

THE POLARITIES: ASSETLESSNESS AND THE TOP 1 PER CENT

Sample data at either end of a distribution are in general not very reliable. Further, 'assetlessness' is a necessarily somewhat vague notion: it is unlikely to describe exactly the state of being literally in possession of *no assets of any kind whatever*, and what constitutes 'assetlessness' could also well be temporally, spatially, and culturally variable. Subject to these qualifications, and confining ourselves to 1991–2 and 2002–3, we find that the proportion of assetless households in the country as a whole has declined from 0.41 per cent to 0.12 per cent. The immensity of India's population allows very large numbers to be absorbed in very small proportions. Thus, the number of households without any asset base to fall back upon in the event of an adverse state of nature is distressingly huge: this figure, in 2002–3, was 0.26 million—a little more than one-twelfth of Portugal's total number of households of 3.15 million, and 1.7 times Luxembourg's 0.15 million households. The issue is one not just of relative deprivation, but of stark and absolute destitution.

The microdata for 1991–2 permit us to explore the upper end of the asset spectrum. The wealthiest household in urban India is reported to have had assets of the value of Rs14.30 million, with a corresponding figure of Rs12.70 million in rural India. The data suggest that, at the all-India level, the wealthiest 1 per cent of households—call these the 'rich' households—accounted for 16.67 per cent of the value of all assets. The caste-related distribution of the burdens and benefits of society are revealed starkly in the following summary statistics. The ratio of the incidence of scheduled caste and scheduled tribe (SCST) assetlessness to that of non-SCST assetlessness is in excess of 3, while the ratio of the incidence of non-SCST 'richness' to that of SCST 'richness' is 15. It is doubtful that, in the absence of deliberate over-sampling of the very rich, the true wealth status of this category of households will have been captured in the sample surveys. We shall return to this issue at a later stage.

INTER-HOUSEHOLD INEQUALITY IN THE DISTRIBUTION OF ASSETS: THE PICTURE AT THE ALL-INDIA LEVEL

Table 6.3 presents information for India on the Gini coefficient (calculated from the various surveys' grouped distributional data by the usual 'geometric' method) and the Theil index of inequality. The overall picture yielded by the relevant numbers is one of greater inequality in the urban than in the rural areas, with, by and large, an indication of over-time decline in both areas.

As has been discussed in Subramanian and Jayaraj (2006), there is a case for interpreting these figures, especially the temporal pattern, with a good deal of caution. Apart from the possibility of increasing under-reporting and under-valuation of assets (especially land and buildings) over time, there are also problems of comparability of grouped data occasioned by variable numbers of size-classes over time and unverifiable impacts of inflation, *via* the particular size-classification that has been resorted to from survey to survey, on the estimate of inequality. Thus, the all-India (combined rural and urban) estimate of the Gini coefficient obtained from the published grouped data of the 1991–2 survey, at 0.6434, is lower than the estimate, at 0.6683, obtained by employing the individual household observations available in the microdata set.

Table 6.5. Decile shares in total value of assets, India (rural and urban combined), 1991–1992 and 2002–2003

Decile	1991–2		2002–3	
	Asset share	Average asset holding per household (Rs)	Asset share	Average asset holding per household (Rs)
1st	0.00133	1,558	0.00246	7,539
2nd	0.00726	8,487	0.00786	24,118
3rd	0.01441	16,836	0.01447	44,418
4th	0.02323	27,144	0.02277	69,890
5th	0.03447	40,279	0.03352	102,895
6th	0.04943	57,769	0.04808	147,596
7th	0.07069	82,607	0.06913	212,197
8th	0.10423	121,810	0.10294	315,989
9th	0.16956	198,154	0.16997	521,752
10th	0.52540	614,005	0.52881	1,623,273
Share of top 5%	0.38225		0.38319	
Share of top 1%	0.16222		0.15717	
Gini coefficient	0.66820		0.66875	

Source: Computations based on NSSO (1998; 48th Round) and NSSO (2005; 59th Round), after estimating the equation of the Lorenz curve by the GQ method using POVCAL.

It would be distinctly helpful to be able to present distributional information in the form of fractile shares. This is aided, when we are working with grouped data, by the ability to estimate the equation of the Lorenz curve. Two methods of estimation based on parametrized Lorenz curves are the so-called Beta method of Kakwani (1980) and the General Quadratic (GQ) method of Villasenor and Arnold (1989). By employing the algorithmized computational procedure for the GQ method available in the 'POVCAL' package created by Chen et al. (1991), it proved possible to obtain fitted Lorenz curves for the distribution of household asset holdings at the all-India (combined rural and urban) level for 1991–2 and 2002–3.

Table 6.5 presents a picture of considerable inequality. The asset share of the poorest 50 per cent of the population was just 8.07 per cent in 1991–2 and 8.11 per cent in 2002–3. The average asset holding of the richest decile exceeded that of the poorest decile by a factor of around 39,400 per cent in each of the years 1991–2 and 2002–3. The asset share of the very rich (top 1 per cent) was a little higher, at 16.22 per cent, in 1991–2 than it was, at 15.72 per cent, in 2002–3. The median asset value, at Rs48,123 (respectively, Rs122,809) was just 41.2 per cent (respectively, 40.01 per cent) of the mean value, at Rs116,873 (respectively, Rs306,967) in 1991–2 (respectively, 2002–3). The cumulative density functions are plotted in Figure 6.1, and the Lorenz curves of the distributions in Figure 6.2. Each of the cumulative density functions in Figure 6.1 is typical of a concentrated distribution, as reflected in the small clearance between the curve and its western and northern boundaries. Each of the Lorenz curves likewise displays a

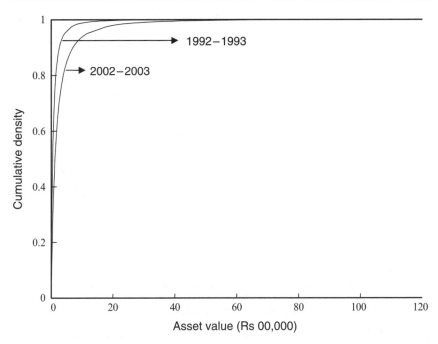

Figure 6.1. Cumulative density functions for asset distribution, India (rural and urban combined), 1991–1992 and 2002–2003

substantial deviation from the diagonal of the unit square, and it is virtually impossible to distinguish the two curves. The Gini coefficients calculated from the fitted Lorenz curves are larger than those obtained through the usual 'geometric' method from the grouped survey data: 0.6682 for 1991–2 and 0.6688 for 2002–3. It may be added that the distribution of household assets is pronouncedly more unequal than the distribution of household consumption expenditure: the microdata for 1991–2 suggest that the asset Gini is 0.6683, while the consumption expenditure Gini is 0.3505. Also, the asset share of the top 1 per cent, in 1991–2, at 16.2 per cent, is much higher than the income share of the top 1 per cent, which is estimated at 7 per cent, on the basis of income-tax returns, by Banerjee and Piketty (2003: fig. 3).

As was noted earlier, the true wealth status of the very rich is unlikely to be accurately reflected without resort to deliberate over-sampling of this category of households. Comparison with alternative sources of information for the 1991–2 and earlier surveys has proved to be difficult. For more recent years, data from journalistic sources on the very rich are available. For instance, *Forbes* magazine mentions nine Indians among the world's wealthiest persons in 2004. *Business Standard* magazine (2005) provides a list of the 178 wealthiest individuals/families in India, and the list is available for 2003 and 2004 (as on

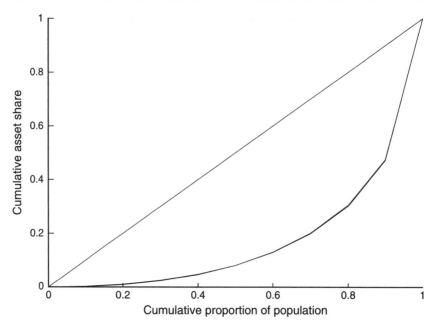

Figure 6.2. Lorenz curves for asset distribution, India (rural and urban combined), 1991–1992 and 2002–2003

31 August of the respective years). Sinha (2006) has analysed these data, and he shows that the distribution of wealth of these ultra-rich households is well approximated by the Pareto distribution. The richest entity, according to the *Business Standard* list, increased its wealth from Rs189,636 million in 2003 to Rs311,984 million in 2004—this sort of quantum leap is very much a feature of the burgeoning information and technology sector of corporate industry. The wealth of the least wealthy on the 2003 list is Rs192.4 million (around $US3.98 million at the 2002–3 exchange rate); the lower bound on the highest (open ended) size-class interval for asset ownership, as reported in the 2002–3 survey, is, by comparison, a paltry Rs0.8 millions (or $US16,529).

The purist may frown upon an attempt at directly incorporating these rough-and-ready orders of magnitude based on journalistic sources in any calculation of inequality that requires 'adjusting' the survey data. There is, nevertheless, strong reason to believe—see Davies (1993) and Davies and Shorrocks (2000)—that such an exercise could be suggestive of a more realistic picture of wealth concentration than is afforded by the 'uncontaminated' survey data. With this in mind, we have added the *Business Standard* 2003 wealth data on the richest 178 households to the open-ended class interval of the grouped 2002–3 survey data on asset distribution, and re-estimated the general quadratic equation of the Lorenz curve: the asset share of the richest 1 per cent is now found to rise from 15.72 per cent to 17.77 per cent. Combining the *Business Standard* data with the survey data suggests that the wealthiest 178 households account for 0.00009 per cent of all households, and for 2.045 per cent of the country's estimated wealth: the ratio of asset share to population share of the *Business Standard*'s ultra-wealthy is a small matter of 23,239. We do not have to accept these numbers at face value, but it would seem to be hard to deny that the surveys underestimate the wealth of the very rich by a significant margin.

INTER-HOUSEHOLD INEQUALITY IN THE DISTRIBUTION OF ASSETS: THE PICTURE AT THE LEVEL OF THE STATES

At the level of individual states, we find (see Subramanian and Jayaraj 2006 for details) that inter-state disparity in inequality levels is quite muted when compared to inter-state disparity in average asset holdings. The wealth status of a state can be described in terms of its average level of asset holding and how unequally it is distributed. Letting μ stand for mean asset holdings per household and G for the Gini coefficient of inequality in the distribution of assets, $W \equiv \mu(1 - G)$ is Sen's (1976) measure of the 'distributionally adjusted mean', and can be employed, in the present context, as an *ad hoc* way of combining information on the level (interpreted as a 'good') and inequality (interpreted as a 'bad') of wealth. In rural India, the best-performing state, Punjab, has a W-value of Rs394,111 and the worst performer, Orissa, has a W-value of Rs41,055, the proportionate difference between the two being of the order of 0.8958. In urban India, the best performing state is Kerala, with a W-value of Rs351,374, and the worst-performing state is Orissa, with a W-value of Rs85,475; the proportionate difference between the two is a high 0.7567. The data suggest that vertical inequality in the distribution of wealth is generally high for India and its states, and higher for some states than for others; and identifiable states like Orissa, Andhra Pradesh, and Tamil Nadu labour under the twin burdens of high inequality and low average wealth.

INTER-HOUSEHOLD INEQUALITY IN THE DISTRIBUTION OF NET WORTH

Net worth, defined as assets *less* liabilities, is obviously a more accurate indicator of wealth than asset holding. Unfortunately, distributional analysis of net worth based on the published data provided by the surveys is not possible because the households are ranked by asset holding rather than by net worth. The availability of unit level data for 1991–2, however, enables us to examine the distribution of net worth. Using the 1991–2 microdata, we have ranked households according to net worth, and then classified them into the same size-classes as are to be found in the published 1991–2 survey, with one further size-class added. The additional size-class relates to households for which debt is in excess of asset holding. At the combined (rural and urban) all-India level,

Table 6.6. Coordinates of the Lorenz curve for the distribution of net worth, India (rural and urban combined), 1991–1992

Size-class	Without correcting the debt figure		After correcting the debt figure	
	Cumulative population share	Cumulative share in net worth	Cumulative population share	Cumulative share in net worth
<0	0.00907	−0.00086	0.03481	−0.01041
0–5,000	0.11429	0.00108	0.13912	−0.00839
5,000–10,000	0.18481	0.00568	0.20825	−0.00369
10,000–20,000	0.29735	0.02005	0.32070	0.01135
20,000–30,000	0.38581	0.03917	0.40646	0.03078
30,000–50,000	0.51733	0.08432	0.53248	0.07590
50,000–70,000	0.61239	0.13372	0.62633	0.12693
70,000–100,000	0.71035	0.20562	0.72098	0.19958
100,000–150,000	0.80408	0.30601	0.81159	0.30114
150,000–250,000	0.89459	0.45818	0.89874	0.45419
>250,000	1.00000	1.00000	1.00000	1.00000
Gini coefficient	0.6588		0.6820	

Note: The debt figure is corrected by blowing up each household's reported debt by the factor by which the aggregate debt figure is blown up when corrected for the possible under-estimation of institutional debt, as detailed in the section on 'debt' in the text.

Source: Computations based on unit-level data made available by NSSO on CD ROM (marked as 48th Round, Schedule 18.2, Debt and Investment).

an estimated 1.43 million households are reported to have negative net worth. Grouped data on cumulative population and net worth shares, derived from the microdata, are presented in Table 6.6. When a variable (like net worth) assumes negative values, the Gini coefficient can be computed along the lines suggested by Chen et al. (1987).

As we have seen earlier, the debt–asset ratio declines monotonically with the size-class of asset holdings. Debt, like taxation, is a drain. Therefore, the distribution of net worth when the debt–asset ratio is a declining function of asset size can be expected to be like a post-tax income distribution under a regressive tax scheme. It is not surprising, then, that the Gini coefficient for net worth, at 0.6692, is higher than the Gini coefficient for assets, at 0.6436. The actual difference is perhaps larger, because the extent of total indebtedness reported by the survey is very small, the aggregate debt–asset ratio being just 2.01 per cent. If each household's debt figure is blown up by the factor (3.15) obtained after correction for the under-reported extent of institutional debt (see the earlier section on debt), and if households are reclassified by net worth corresponding to these revised debt estimates, then we obtain an 'adjusted' net worth distribution (see Table 6.6 again). The Gini coefficient for this 'adjusted' distribution is, as might be expected, higher, at 0.6820, than the coefficient for the unadjusted distribution. Our general sense is that the underestimation of both asset holdings and debt in the survey has worked in such a way as to understate the true extent of inequality in the distribution of net worth.

2.5 Inequality Decomposition by Asset Components

Table 6.7, based on the 1991–2 microdata, provides information on the Gini coefficient of inequality in the inter-household distribution of each asset component, separately for the rural and the urban areas. As can be seen from the table, financial assets display an extraordinarily high order of concentration, as do agricultural machinery and non-farm business equipment, but these assets together account for less than 6 per cent of the value of all assets at the combined (rural and urban) all-India level. The Gini coefficients for land and buildings are also particularly high in the urban areas, and these categories of assets together constitute a weighty part of the asset portfolio, accounting, between them, for 82 per cent of the value of all assets. It is these asset components that might be expected to drive aggregate inequality, to the decomposition of which we now turn.

A *decomposition rule R* is a procedure by which the proportionate contribution of each asset component to aggregate inequality can be reckoned, with the proportionate contributions adding up to unity. The *'Variance Rule' R_V* of decomposition advanced in Shorrocks (1982, 1983) is given by R_V: $s_k =$ $cov(A_k,A)/Var(A)$, where s_k is the proportionate contribution to aggregate inequality of the kth asset component, A is the distribution for total assets, A_k is the distribution for the kth asset component, cov stands for co-variance, and Var stands for variance. Shorrocks observes that, as it happens, R_V is the 'natural' decomposition rule for the variance and the squared coefficient of variation: hence the label 'Variance Rule' for R_V.

Table 6.8 presents information, for all the survey years under review, on each of the various asset components' proportionate contribution to aggregate inequality in the distribution of assets (*s*) under the decomposition rule R_V;

Table 6.7. Inequality in the distribution of asset components, India (rural and urban), 1991–1992

Asset component	Gini coefficient of inequality	
	Rural	Urban
Land	0.7280	0.8265
Building	0.6094	0.7997
Livestock and poultry	0.6883	0.9557
Agricultural machinery	0.9147	0.9885
Non-farm business equipment	0.9786	0.9677
All transport equipment	0.8978	0.9209
Durable household assets	0.6566	0.6523
Financial assets		
Shares	0.9858	0.9919
Deposits	0.9629	0.8730
Loan receivable in cash	0.9955	0.9960
Loan receivable in kind	0.9995	0.9995

Source: See Table 6.6.

Table 6.8. Per cent contribution of asset components to total value of assets (*c*) and to aggregate inequality (*s*) under the 'variance rule', India, 1971/1972–2002/2003

Year	Land	Building	Livestock and poultry	Agricultural machinery, etc.	Non-farm business	All transport equipment	Durable household assets	Financial assets	All
Rural									
1971									
c	66.22	18.42	6.46	2.73	n.a.	n.a.	4.61	1.55	100
s	74.78	13.4	3.36	3.64	n.a.	n.a.	2.80	2.02	100
s/c	1.13	0.73	0.52	1.33	n.a.	n.a.	0.61	1.30	
1981									
c	62.12	20.71	4.98	2.47	0.30	0.96	7.10	1.37	100
s	71.84	14.71	2.66	4.03	0.32	1.16	4.12	1.16	100
s/c	1.16	0.71	0.53	1.63	1.07	1.21	0.58	0.85	
1991									
c	64.25	21.4	3.38	2.23	0.32	1.21	5.88	1.33	100
s	74.09	14.29	1.81	3.23	0.25	1.37	3.98	0.98	100
s/c	1.15	0.67	0.54	1.45	0.78	1.13	0.68	0.74	
2002									
c	63.22	23.53	2.10	1.98	0.35	1.39	5.11	2.32	100
s	73.98	14.83	1.11	2.92	0.30	1.80	2.97	2.10	100
s/c	1.17	0.63	0.53	1.48	0.85	1.30	0.58	0.91	
Urban									
1981									
c	32.36	35.65	0.83	0.41	2.05	2.51	15.14	11.05	100
s	40.87	35.67	0.57	0.60	3.16	2.79	7.76	8.59	100
s/c	1.26	1.00	0.69	1.46	1.54	1.11	0.51	0.78	
1991									
c	35.8	39.46	0.42	0.26	1.48	3.03	11.29	8.26	100
s	38.99	41.55	0.24	0.32	1.58	3.16	7.20	6.96	100
s/c	1.09	1.05	0.57	1.23	1.07	1.04	0.64	0.84	
2002									
c	38.54	37.84	0.21	0.22	1.38	3.85	8.37	9.58	100
s	42.85	36.71	0.10	0.30	1.53	4.47	5.13	8.91	100
s/c	1.11	0.97	0.48	1.36	1.10	1.16	0.61	0.93	

Source: See Table 6.6.

and also on each component's contribution to the total value of assets (*c*). Table 6.8 reveals considerable stability in the decomposition pattern over time. Component contributions to inequality are generally consistent with component shares in the total value of assets, with land and buildings between them accounting for between three-quarters and four-fifths of all inequality in both the rural and the urban areas: the division is heavily weighted in favour of land in rural India and more balanced between the two in urban India. The ratio s_k/c_k is of significance: when it is in excess of unity for any asset component k, the suggestion is that asset k has a disequalizing impact on the aggregate distribution, which is disproportionately greater than its share in the aggregate value of assets. Table 6.8 reveals that the s/c ratio is *consistently* at least equal to one for three categories of assets in the rural areas—land, agricultural machinery, and all transport equipment—and for four categories of assets in the urban areas—

land, agricultural machinery, transport equipment, and non-farm business equipment (for buildings, s/c is in excess of unity in 1981–2 and 1991–2, and falls just short of unity in 2002–3). The component-wise decomposition invites attention to those components for which both s and s/c are high. By this reckoning, Table 6.8 signals a simple message: land and buildings between them in the urban areas, and land by itself in the rural areas, must be seen to be the major driving force behind aggregate inequality in the distribution of assets. This is of a piece with what we have seen earlier: the centrality of land in India's wealth picture is re-emphasized.

2.6 India and China: A Very Quick Comparison

While it would be interesting to undertake a comparative time-series analysis of the evolution of wealth distribution across the developing nations of the world, such an exercise is rendered very difficult by the severe paucity of data that obtains. However, some information is available that permits a comparison between India and China at a proximate point in time. Around about 2000, the net worth per capita, on a purchasing power parity (PPP) basis, was nearly twice as high for China (at $US11,267) as for India (at $US6,513); see Davies et al. (Chapter 19, this volume). Li and Zhao (Chapter 5, this volume) estimate that the Gini coefficient of inequality in the household distribution of net worth in 2002 was of the order of 0.55 in China; in India, in 2002–3, the corresponding figure was substantially higher, at 0.68. The relatively low level of inequality in China probably has much to do with its history of land reform and an equitable distribution of land, particularly in the rural areas. However, the dynamics of inequality have also been markedly different in the two countries: while the Gini coefficient in India has displayed a rough stationarity over four decades from 1961–2 to 2002–3, the Gini coefficient in China has shot up from 0.45 to 0.55 in just the period from 1995 to 2002 (again, see Li and Zhao, Chapter 5, this volume). The market reform process in China, accompanied by a widening inequality between the rural and the urban areas, would appear to have contributed to this overall spurt in inequality. Among some developing countries for which estimates are available (see Davies et al., Chapter 19, this volume), it appears that, apart from China, only South Korea (a successful history of land reform again?), Bangladesh, and Vietnam have levels of wealth inequality not higher than for India, with Gini coefficients of 0.58, 0.66, and 0.68 respectively. Pakistan, Thailand, Nigeria, Argentina, Mexico, Indonesia, and Brazil all have higher levels of wealth inequality, with the Gini coefficient ranging from 0.70 for Pakistan to 0.78 for Brazil. In so far as the composition of wealth is concerned, a marked difference between China and India is that the share of financial assets in China (which is in excess of 20 per cent) is more than five times that in India (see Li and Zhao, Chapter 5, this volume). The salience of financial assets in China's portfolio probably has something to do with the fact that the share of private housing in the asset structure has been historically low, with much of housing being state owned—consumer durables and financial assets have therefore accounted for a larger share of all assets in China than in India.

2.7 Horizontal Inequality in the Distribution of Assets

Table 6.9 provides information, for 1991–2, on average asset holdings per household, the Gini coefficient of inequality, and the Theil index of inequality, for each of the all-India rural and urban populations, partitioned by caste and by occupational category. The caste categories employed are the SCST and the rest, labelled 'others'; the occupational categories employed are cultivators and non-cultivators in the rural areas, and the self-employed and the non-self-employed in the urban areas. Among other things, Table 6.9 indicates that (particularly) in the rural areas, both caste and occupational divisions are very pronounced. When the population is partitioned into the SCST and others caste categories, the 'between-group' contribution to the aggregate Theil measure of inequality (which is a decomposable index) is quite substantial, at nearly 11 per cent. When the population is partitioned

Table 6.9. Mean asset holdings, inequality, and inequality decomposition by caste and occupational categories, India (rural and urban), 1991–1992

| | Data relating to caste | | | | Data relating to occupational categories | | | |
	Rural India		Urban India		Rural India		Urban India	
Assets per household (rupees)	All	107007	All	144330	All	107007	All	144330
	Others	134501	Others	159746	Cultivator	142308	SE	189710
	SCST	50363	SCST	58873	Non-cultivator	38180	NSE	120928
Gini coefficient of inequality	All	0.6207	All	0.6805	All	0.6207	All	0.6805
	Others	0.5954	Others	0.6695	Cultivator	0.5545	SE	0.6410
	SCST	0.5707	SCST	0.6466	Non-cultivator	0.6463	NSE	0.6962
Theil index of inequality	All	0.7123	All	0.8810	All	0.7123	All	08810
	Others	0.6410	Others	0.8480	Cultivator	0.5521	SE	0.7713
	SCST	0.6079	SCST	0.7898	Non-cultivator	0.8382	NSE	0.9296
% contribution to Aggregate Theil index of inequality	Among others	76.12	Among others	89.96	Among cultivators	68.13	Among SE	39.13
	Among SCST	13.10	Among SCST	5.58	Among non-cultivators	14.23	Among NSE	58.20
	Between groups	10.78	Between groups	4.56	Between groups	17.63	Between groups	2.67

Note: SCST = scheduled castes and tribes, SE = self-employed, NSE = non-self-employed.
Source: Calculations based on data in NSSO (1998; 48th Round).

Table 6.10. Differences in 'distributionally adjusted' levels of wealth between best and worst performing groups, India, 1991–1992

Item	State and group	μ (rupees)	G	$W \equiv \mu(1-G)$ (Rs)	(MaxW–MinW)/ MaxW
Rural polarization	AP, SCST	27,931	0.5956	11,295	0.9582
by caste	Punjab, others	474,913	0.4317	269,893	
Urban polarization	Orissa, SCST	23,291	0.5811	9,757	0.9242
by caste	Punjab, others	292,328	0.5594	128,800	
Rural polarization	AP, NC	18,109	0.6128	7,012	0.9841
by occupation	Punjab, C	614,888	0.2824	441,244	
Urban polarization	Orissa, NSE	66,521	0.6830	21,087	0.8725
by occupation	Punjab, SE	328,101	0.4961	165,330	

Note: μ = mean asset holdings per household; G = Gini coefficient of inequality; SCST = scheduled castes and tribes; NC = non-cultivators; C = cultivators; SE = self-employed; NSE = non-self-employed.
Source: See Table 6.9.

into the cultivator and non-cultivator occupational categories, the 'between-group' contribution is even higher, at nearly 18 per cent.

As we have noted earlier, the wealth status of a group can be seen as an increasing function of its level and a declining function of the extent of inequality in its distribution. Sen's 'distributionally adjusted mean', $W \equiv \mu(1 - G)$, where μ is mean asset holdings per household and G is the Gini coefficient of inequality, can be employed as a means of combining information on the level and inequality of wealth with a view to conveying a summary picture of how well or badly a group is performing on the wealth front. The gulf in wealth status (in terms of Sen's index) that separates identifiable sub-groups of the population is captured in a stark and summary form in Table 6.10. The table presents the values of μ, G, and W for each pair of polar cases of grouping by caste and by occupational category, in each of the rural and the urban areas, and the last column measures the proportional difference in welfare between the best-off and the worst-off groups. The gulf in each case is enormous, and the gap between rural Punjabi cultivators and rural Andhra Pradesh non-cultivators is as close to the theoretical maximum as makes no difference!

A finer partitioning of the population is rendered possible by employing the 1991–2 microdata, which facilitate a caste-*cum*-occupation categorization. We have three castes (scheduled caste, scheduled tribe, and 'others') and four occupation groups (agricultural labourers, artisans, cultivators, and 'other labourers' in the rural areas, and casual labourers, self-employed, regular/salaried employees, and 'other labourers' in the urban areas). In combination, these castes and occupations yield twelve groups for the rural areas that can be derived from the Cartesian product {scheduled caste, scheduled tribe, 'others'} × {agricultural labourers, artisans, cultivators, 'other labourers'}, and similarly twelve groups for the urban areas derived from the cartesian product {scheduled caste, scheduled tribe, 'others'} × {casual labourers, self-employed, regular/salaried employees, 'other labourers'}. We do not present the detailed calculations here, but simply note that, in any given occupational category, the worst-off caste groups are either the scheduled castes or the scheduled tribes, while, in any given caste category, the worst-off occupational groups are the agricultural labourers in the rural areas and the casual labourers in the urban areas. The proportionate difference between best- and worst-performing caste-*cum*-occupation groups, in terms of Sen's 'distributionally adjusted mean' indicator W, also turns out to be huge (in excess of 90 per cent in both the rural and the urban areas). Group differentiation by wealth in India is clearly massive.

3 Summary and Conclusions

A. K. Sen (1981) emphasizes the view that the level and distribution of assets are an important determinant of the success or failure of entitlements. This is borne out on the ground in an important empirical study, by Jain et al. (1989), on the determinants of poverty in India. In a cross-sectional analysis of fifty-six regions of the country for 1971–2, employing national sample survey data, the authors have attempted to explain the inter-regional variations in levels of living and poverty. Their major finding is that, at the margin, mean asset security has a greater impact on poverty than even agricultural performance.

In developing countries like India, with a preponderantly rural population, land is the single most important component of the asset portfolio. The composition and distribution of assets, with particular emphasis on the land component, and their role in the 'dynamics of rural transformation', have been studied by Kurien (1989) in the context of the state of Tamil Nadu. His analysis of agricultural production, technology, and the household distribution of assets by land ownership suggests that, while agricultural technology is largely scale-neutral, its benefits are unequally distributed in favour of the larger landowners on account of their superior ability to take advantage of the complementarities of modern inputs, implements and machinery, and farm processes. Janakarajan's field-related work (1992) on Tamil Nadu shows that improved irrigation, technology, high-yielding crop varieties, and the availability of credit have all contributed considerably to a dynamic growth of agricultural output in the state, but inequalities in the distribution of both land and access to private (lift) irrigation have played a large part in preserving feudal social relations of dependence and oppression even in an environment of modernizing, 'capitalist' forces of production in agriculture.

Given the centrality of land in the asset structure of rural India and of other developing countries, and its driving force in precipitating inequalities in the distribution of assets, one would imagine that land reform must constitute an important component of anti-poverty policy. Implementation of land reform has often been compromised by both the political power of 'land-lobbies' and that aspect of ideological orientation that insists on seeing equity as endangering efficiency. Increasingly, however, the conservatism underlying such positions has been undermined by a number of careful empirical studies. Bandyopadhyay (2003) provides an instructive account of the role of land reform in explaining agricultural growth and poverty reduction in the state of West Bengal. The Indian experience, employing state-level data, has been analysed by Besley and Burgess (2000), who conclude that, of the four components of land-reform policy in India, two (tenancy reform and abolition of intermediaries) have had a depressing effect on poverty, while the other two (land redistribution and land consolidation) have been very poorly implemented:

Although the effects on poverty are likely to have been greater if large-scale redistribution of land had been achieved, our results are nonetheless interesting as they suggest that partial, second-best reforms which mainly affect production relations in agriculture can play a significant role in reducing rural poverty. (p. 424)

Similarly optimistic appraisals are available for South Africa in the study by Deininger and May (2000), who say: 'The good news is that the data on land reform implementation provide strong support in favour of the hypothesis that land reform was able to target the poor and that there is little difficulty in combining equity and efficiency objectives.' Deininger et al. (2000) present the case of the contribution of land reform to economic growth and poverty reduction in Zimbabwe, a study in which they cite a number of other cases of success, reported by other authors, relating to Japan, Korea, Taiwan, the Philippines, Brazil, and Colombia.

Against this background, one can appreciate the importance of a study of India's wealth statistics for an understanding of the structural features of the country's economy, and for being guided in the formulation and implementation of pro-egalitarian and anti-poverty policy. The principal source of India's wealth distributions statistics is constituted by the five major decennial sample surveys of 1961–2, 1971–2, 1981–2, 1991–2, and 2002–3. A number of difficulties confronting the user of these data have been discussed, in a non-nihilistic spirit, in Subramanian and Jayaraj (2006). One has to allow for the strong possibility that both the level and inequality in the distribution of asset holdings are increasingly understated over time in the surveys. This problem is so much a function of the general environment of untruthful voluntary disclosure that it would amount largely to token exhortation if one were to urge more accurate reporting by the surveys, although there is a case for some internal cross-checking in the matter, for example, of land operations. The construction of wealth statistics must also be accompanied, importantly, by the construction of appropriate asset-specific prices, so that meaningful real comparisons, in both cross-section and time-series exercises, are rendered possible. Third, for a number of reasons, it would greatly enhance both freedom and accuracy of analysis if the survey results were available in the form of unit record data, a situation that presently obtains only for 1991–2 and 2002–3. This would call for discussions between the data-generating agency and data-users on how best the data may be arranged and computerized, with a considerable measure of urgency attached to the process.

Section 2 has presented some salient findings (subject to the data limitations just mentioned) from the five wealth surveys. Levels of debt, levels of asset holdings across space and over time, the composition of wealth, vertical inequalities in its distribution, decomposition of inequality by asset components, and questions of horizontal inequalities, in terms of the highly skewed distribution across caste and occupation groups, have been investigated. The general picture that emerges is one of considerable concentration of wealth both vertically and horizontally, considerable inter-state differentials, and the continuing centrality of land and real estate in the wealth composition of the country. These findings only underscore the importance of land reform, especially its redistributive component, as a policy instrument for the cure of deeply entrenched structural inequality and poverty—an issue of centrality that has got lost in a regrettable policy mix of neglect, political unpreparedness, and denial.

Principal Data Sources Employed

Census of India (2001). Tables H-13, H-13 SC, and H-13 ST (Number of Households Availing Banking Services and Number of Households having each of the Specified Assets) accessed on CD ROM.

Centre for Monitoring Indian Economy (1993). *Basic Statistics Relating to the Indian Economy* (Aug. 1993), vol. 1, Bombay.

Ministry of Agriculture (1998). *All-India Report on Agricultural Census: 1990–91*, Department of Agriculture and Cooperation, Government of India, New Delhi.

NSSO (1968). National Sample Survey Organization, *Tables with Notes on Some Aspects of Land holdings in Rural Areas (State and All-India Estimates)*, 17th Round, September 1961–July 1962, Report No. 144, Department of Statistics, Government of India, New Delhi.

NSSO (1976). National Sample Survey Organization, *Tables on Land Holdings: All-India*, 26th Round, Report No. 215, Department of Statistics, Government of India, New Delhi.

NSSO (1985). National Sample Survey Organization, *Assets and Liabilities of Rural and Urban Households (States and All-India Estimates)*, 37th Round, Jan.–Dec. 1982, Report No. 318, Department of Statistics, Government of India, New Delhi.

NSSO (1986). National Sample Survey Organization, *Report on Land Holdings—1: Some Aspects of Household Ownership Holding*, 37th Round, Jan.–Dec. 1982, Report No. 330, Department of Statistics, Government of India, New Delhi.

NSSO (1986). National Sample Survey Organization, *Report on Land Holdings—2: Some Aspects of Operational Holdings*, 37th Round, Jan.–Dec. 1982, Report No. 331, Department of Statistics, Government of India, New Delhi.

NSSO (1996). *Land Holdings Survey: Some Aspects of Household Ownership Holdings*, 48th Round, Jan.–Dec. 1992, Report No. 399, Department of Statistics, Government of India, New Delhi.

NSSO (1997). *Land and Livestock Holdings Survey: Operational Land Holdings in India: 1991–92—Salient Features (Report 2)*, 48th Round, Jan.–Dec. 1992, Report No. 407, Department of Statistics, Government of India, New Delhi.

NSSO (1998). *Debt and Investment Survey: Household Assets and Liabilities as on 30.6.1991*, 48th Round, Jan.–Dec. 1992, Report No. 419. Department of Statistics, Government of India, New Delhi.

NSSO (1998). *Household Assets and Indebtedness of Social Groups as on 30.6.91, Debt and Investment Survey*, 48th Round, Jan.–Dec. 1992, Report No. 432 (Part I). Department of Statistics, Government of India, New Delhi.

NSSO (2005). *Household Asets and Liabilities in India (as on 30.06.2002)*, Report No.500 (based on data of the 59th Round [Jan.–Dec. 2003] *All-India Debt and Investment Survey*). Ministry of Statistics and Programme Implementation, Government of India, New Delhi.

NCAER (2000). National Council of Applied Economic Research, *Survey of Indian Investors*, New Delhi.

Reserve Bank of India (1965). 'All India Rural Debt and Investment Survey', *Reserve Bank of India Bulletin*, 19/6 (June).

Reserve Bank of India (1975). *All-India Debt and Investment Survey 1971–72: Assets and Liabilities of Rural Households as on 31st June 1971 (Statistical Tables)*, vol. 1, Bombay.

Unit level data made available by NSSO on CD ROM (marked as 48th Round, Schedule 18.2, Debt and Investment).

7

The Evolution of Personal Wealth in the Former Soviet Union and Central and Eastern Europe

Sergei Guriev and Andrei Rachinsky

1 Introduction

Transition from plan to market is a natural experiment of historical significance. It has affected economic relationships, social and political structures, and, what is most important, the lives of 1.5 billion people in almost thirty countries. While the transformational recession, subsequent recovery, and other aggregate processes have been studied extensively, our understanding of the evolution of personal wealth and of the distributional effects of transition is still far from complete. This is not because these issues are unimportant. Transition countries are, on average, rather wealthy. Figure 7.1 and Table 7.1 show the standing of transition countries in terms of wealth with regard to other economies' comparable per capita GDP.[1] Unlike the pre-transition years, much of this wealth is now owned by individuals. Privatization has provided many citizens of transition countries with property rights for assets they were de facto controlling and using during the communist era.

Yet this wealth is not equally distributed among the citizens of post-communist countries, which has significant implications for economic growth and sustainability of reforms. Indeed, inequality, both income and wealth inequality, has an important and lasting effect on the institutional change (Glaeser et al. 2003; Sonin 2003). Moreover, as financial markets are imperfect, wealth inequality is crucial for economic development, as wealth-constrained entrepreneurs cannot implement their business ideas. Banerjee and Newman (1993) show that, in the absence of an effective court system and well-functioning financial markets,

---

[1] Figure 7.1 presents national wealth including natural resources, production capital, infrastructure but excluding human capital. The graph for production capital/GDP looks similar.

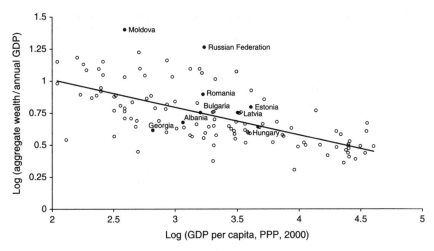

Figure 7.1. Transition countries are on average richer than other countries with comparable per capita income

Note: The graph presents aggregate national wealth around the world and in transition countries in 2000.

Source: World Bank (2006a).

wealth inequality breeds wealth inequality and may lock the economy in an underdevelopment trap.

The research on wealth inequality is plagued by an array of data problems (see Davies et al., Chapter 19, this volume). First, there are no consistent microeconomic data on personal wealth for transition countries. Whatever data are available are not comparable, either cross-country or over time. The wealth data for the pre-transition period are problematic for a number of reasons (see next section). Also, transition has been accompanied by a substantial growth of informal sector (Shleifer and Treisman 2005). What is more important, the growth of informal sector may have been very different in different countries (Alexeyev and Pyle 2003) and cannot be accurately measured (Hanousek and Palda 2005). Even given the imperfect data, there are a few strands of studies that promote our understanding of wealth inequality in transition.

First, as much personal wealth distribution today is driven by the privatization process, the existing research on privatization provides important insights. Although the scholars of privatization also complain about the lack of data, substantial progress has been made (Megginson 2005; Guriev and Megginson 2007). In addition to privatization of industrial assets, the reforms have also transferred real estate to urban citizens and farm land to farmers. Prior to transition, socialist economies provided each citizen with virtually free access to public housing. Transition has transformed these rights-to-use into private property rights essentially creating a market for real estate—consistent with the

Table 7.1. Per capita wealth, transition countries and selected OECD countries ($US)

Country	2000, total wealth	2005, financial wealth	2000, produced capital + urban land only	2000, total wealth excluding human capital
Albania	17,199		1,745	5,637
Armenia	15,294			
Azerbaijan	11,447			
Belarus	25,447			
Bulgaria	22,866	1,381	5,303	8,751
Croatia	29,437	6,198		
Czech Rep.	25,697	7,564		
Estonia	31,180		18,685	24,967
Georgia	21,115		595	2,394
Hungary	38,411	6,222	15,480	20,427
Kazakhstan	23,348			
Kyrgyzstan	9,745			
Latvia	27,468		12,979	18,464
Lithuania	29,091			
Macedonia	24,144			
Moldova	11,577		4,338	7,598
Poland	35,566	4,493		
Romania	22,127	818	8,495	13,003
Russia	25,755	1,136	15,593	32,809
Slovak Rep.	35,786	4,236		
Slovenia	46,461			
Tajikistan	5,443			
Ukraine	15,141			
China	11,965		2,956	5,179
France	83,016		57,814	64,150
Germany	89,871		68,678	73,124
Italy	119,704		51,943	56,621
UK	124,861		55,239	62,406
Eurozone		54,300		
Canada	89,252		54,226	88,997
Japan	115,237		150,258	151,771
USA	147,665		79,851	94,603

Sources: Column 1: Davies et al. (2007) (predicted or actual, PPP adjusted); Column 2: Unicredit (2006); Columns 3 and 4: World Bank (2006a) (PPP adjusted).

logic of de Soto (2000). In addition to registering the private property titles, transition has resulted in a significant increase of supply of housing in real terms. For example, in Russia, a country traditionally plagued by the lack of housing, an average citizen has seen a 20 per cent increase in terms of per capita square metres during 1990–2004. The transfer of housing has contributed to an increase in wealth inequality as the value of housing in different locations varies greatly.[2]

---

[2] This is certainly a measurement issue—except for de Soto's collateral argument, the rental service flow was the same before transition. Yet, as the differences in the value of the rental service flows were not properly measured, transition has resulted in an *observed* increase in inequality. See Yemtsov (Chapter 15, this volume) for a thorough empirical study of the effect of housing privatization on inequality in Poland, Serbia, and Russia. Gustafsson and Li (2001) argue that in China much of the urban–rural inequality is due to the high value of the user rights for urban real estates that urban workers obtain at low rates.

Figure 7.2. Russians in the *Forbes* billionaires list, 2002–2006

Note: Forbes estimates of the billionaires' wealth are shown at the date of the publication of the list. The numbers next to bars indicate the number of Russian individuals in the *Forbes* list.

Source: Forbes (2002–6), Russian Trading System website (www.rts.ru), and authors' calculations.

Second, there is substantial research on one of the most intriguing phenomena in transition: the emergence of a handful of super-rich tycoons in Russia— so called 'oligarchs'. Out of 691 billionaires in the *Forbes* list of 2005, 27 are from Russia, which is substantially more than from the other transition countries combined, including China (see Figure 7.2).[3] It is interesting to compare Russia's standing in the *Forbes* billionaire list and in the World Wealth Report that cover the 'second-tier rich'—individuals with at least $US1 million in financial assets. While Russia has 4 per cent of the world's billionaires in terms of both wealth and number of individuals, there are only 103,000 Russian *millionaires* (only 1.2 per cent of the world's total) who have about $US670 billion wealth (2 per cent of the world's total).[4] The comparison of the *Forbes* list and the World Wealth Report suggests that there is a huge inequality at the very top end of Russia's wealth distribution: 25 Russian

[3] Actually, in the 2005 *Forbes* list, the total wealth of all non-Russian billionaires from transition countries (including China but excluding Hong Kong) was below the wealth of the single richest Russian. In 2004 the wealth of 26 Russian billionaires was about 19% of Russian GDP; the total wealth of all 262 billionaires in the USA was just 7% of US GDP. The role of oligarchs increased even further in 2006, when their wealth doubled to $US174 billion (23% of Russian GDP). Out of 1,062 billionaires in the *Forbes* list of 2008, 87 are from Russia.

[4] The 2005 World Wealth Report does not provide an estimate of the total wealth of Russian billionaires. We use the numbers of 544 billion and 573 billion for 2002 and 2003 mentioned in the presentation of the 2004 World Wealth Report (Vedomosti 2004) and extrapolate them for the next year.

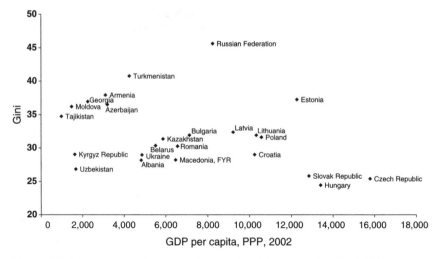

Figure 7.3. Income inequality Gini estimates, transition countries, 1996–2002
Source: World Bank (2006b).

oligarchs have about 12 per cent of the combined wealth of 103,000 Russian millionaires.[5]

How and why did these 'oligarchs' arise? Why did they emerge in Russia but not in other transition countries? What is the impact of their wealth on the economic development of Russia? We address these issues in detail below.

Third, the *income* inequality is studied and understood very well. Milanovic (1998) provides a comprehensive analysis of income inequality in transition based on the comparable data from household surveys in transition. Figure 7.3 illustrates the variety of transition experiences in terms of increases in income inequality.[6]

Given that prior to transition personal wealth inequality as well as personal wealth *per se* were quite low, the current wealth inequality is essentially a function of income inequality during the transition process. As transition countries are essentially middle-income countries, the poor face a subsistence constraint, so that, within each economy, the savings rates increase with income. Foley and Pyle (2005) show that the lower half of Russian income distribution essentially saves nothing or even dissaves; the savings rates are

[5] The World Wealth Report (2005) is based on 2004 data; hence it has to be compared to the *Forbes* list in 2004 when Russia had 25 billionaires jointly owning US$80 billion.

[6] This scatterplot is very intuitively divided into three clusters. Within each cluster there is a positive correlation between levels of income and inequality (interestingly, the relationship between *changes* in Gini and per capita is actually negative; Keane and Prasad 2002). One cluster is the advanced transition countries other than Poland; another is the war-torn countries plus resource-rich Russia and Turkmenistan; other countries are in the third cluster. The fact that Poland is in the intermediate cluster may be explained by the high pre-transition inequality: actually the change in Poland's Gini was very small (Keane and Prasad 2002).

substantial only in the top income quartile. The lower saving rates by the poor imply that the wealth inequality is much higher than income inequality.

This argument is incomplete without taking into account capital gains, in particular those on the public housing and productive assets transferred to private hands in the course of transition. While there are no data for such an adjustment, it would probably further increase the estimated inequality. Indeed, the opportunities to earn higher income would be higher for individuals, regions, and sectors where such assets are more valuable and vice versa.

2 Initial Conditions

Our knowledge of inequality in the socialist economies is highly incomplete. The first problem is the lack of primary data. The official data have not been collected, so the most reliable information on inequality has come from the emigrant surveys. Ofer and Vinokur (1992) have surveyed 1,250 Soviet Jewish emigrants to Israel who provided information on their wealth prior to their decision to emigrate. These surveys suffer from two important methodological problems. The emigrants are certainly not a representative sample. Among other things, their decision to emigrate could be linked to their low wealth (it is therefore not surprising that 58 per cent of emigrants in the survey had no assets at all). Ofer and Vinokur recognize these problems and suggest that one should be very careful interpreting their wealth inequality estimates (indeed, the 0.7–0.8 Gini coefficient for the wealth distribution obtained by Ofer and Vinokur is strongly influenced by the large share of assetless migrants).

The other more important problem is that the pecuniary income/wealth inequality does not measure the true inequality of living standards in a command economy. First, there have been many missing markets (including real estate and financial markets). Second, the real inequality is not in having the wealth but in the ability to use this wealth to buy goods in shortage at state prices. These were driven by connections that in turn were a function of people's standing in the soviet hierarchy.[7] The acuteness of shortage differed geographically. Those residing in larger cities would have access to much better provision of goods in stores. The mobility was constrained through the system of residence permits, so that relocation to a large city was a crucial non-monetary incentive. The factories were also happy to provide the skilled workers with fringe benefits such as good healthcare and housing—this legacy was still important during transition (Commander and Schankerman 1997; Juurikkala and Lazareva 2004; Friebel and Guriev 2005). Moreover, these problems differed across countries. While the share of public-sector employment was very high everywhere, only in

[7] See Shleifer and Vishny (1994) for this theory explaining why centrally planned economies needed shortages to provide incentives.

Yugoslavia and Poland was public employment below 90 per cent (Milanovic 1998), and the share of private income varied from 5 to 25 per cent (Table 7.2).

Table 7.2. The share of private income in socialist economies before transition, 1988–1989

Income source	Czechoslovakia	USSR	Bulgaria	Hungary	Yugoslavia	Poland
Primary income	72.9	78.8	71.2	71.7	83.1	78.2
Labour income	69.5	72.0	56.5	55.0	62.2	53.0
Self-employment income	3.4	6.8	14.7	14.0	20.9	25.2
Property income	n.a.	n.a.	n.a.	2.7	n.a.	n.a.
Social transfers	25.4	13.6	21.2	22.4	13.3	20.7
Pensions	16.5	8.0	16.6	13.4	12.1	14.3
Child benefits	5.6	1.2	2.3	6.0	1.2	5.2
Other cash transfers	3.3	4.4	2.3	3.0	0.0	1.2
Other income	1.7	7.6	7.6	6.0	3.6	1.1
Gross income	100.0	100.0	100.0	100.0	100.0	100.0
Personal taxes	14.2	n.a.	n.a.	16.5	1.2	1.6
Direct taxes	0.0	n.a.	n.a.	10.7	1.2	1.6
Payroll tax (employee)	14.2	0.0	0.0	5.8	0.0	0.0
Private income	5.1	14.4	22.3	22.7	24.5	26.3

Note: Private income is calculated as the self-employment income, property income, and other income.
Source: Milanovic (1998).

3 Reform Strategies and Inequality

One of the most commonly held beliefs about transition is that the rise of inequality is due to the reform and to privatization in particular. This argument is especially popular among the scholars of Russian transition (Stiglitz 2003) and goes as follows: Russian reform has channelled state assets into the hand of a few, and drastically reduced the government funding of public goods, therefore leaving the majority of citizens at or below the subsistence levels. The existing evidence suggests that the situation is more involved. First, the income inequality has risen in all transition countries including China and Vietnam. Second, even in Russia the major increase in inequality occurred prior to privatization. Third, as shown by Milanovic (1999), most of the increase in income inequality in post-communist countries is due to wage decompression (see Figure 7.4).[8]

Yet, all of the above refers to income inequality.[9] The dynamics of wealth inequality was also driven by the privatization process. Transition countries

[8] Milanovic's study ends in the 1990s, but the levels of inequality in transition economies have remained roughly constant since then.

[9] Given the presence of a score of billionaires ('oligarchs') and another 0.2% of households of millionaires in Russia, the effect of high *wealth* inequality on the measurement of *income* inequality may be larger than in other countries (owing to undersampling of the super-rich in household surveys). In section 4.1 of Guriev and Rachinsky (2006), we use the only dataset (the census of Moscow taxpayers) that does include the super-rich and show that the resulting Gini coefficient of income distribution is about 20–30 percentage points higher than the estimate obtained through household surveys.

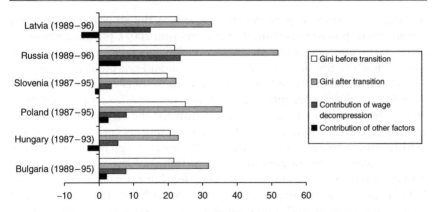

Figure 7.4. Change in Gini coefficient and the contribution of wage decompression, transition countries, 1987–1996

Source: Milanovic (1999).

have chosen very different privatization strategies (Megginson 2005): some (most importantly, Russia and the Czech Republic) opted for voucher-based mass privatization, others sold in open auctions allowing foreigners to bid, some sold to insiders, some did not privatize at all.

The outcomes, however, do not depend very much on the privatization strategies. Rather, there is a clear distinction between Central and Eastern Europe (CEE) and the former Soviet Union (FSU) transition experiences— Berglof and Bolton (2002) refer to this distinction as the Great Divide of transition. For example, despite all the difference between Polish and Czech privatization strategies, the ownership structures in these countries are converging (Grosfeld and Hashi 2003). Even though the Czech Republic has had its share of corporate governance scandals (Johnson et al. 2000), market institutions have emerged since the country joined the EU. Also, Russia has privatized extensively and is now renationalizing important sectors of the economy.

The simplest explanation of the Great Divide is the outside anchor of EU accession available to CEE countries. In these countries, the commitment to reforms was credible, while in the FSU there has always been a fear of reversal and expropriation; the risk actually materialized in Russia, Belarus, and some other countries. This determined the choice of reform strategies. In order to provide demand for market institutions, reformers had to create a critical mass of private owners, and do that quickly. While the voucher privatization is suboptimal in terms of efficiency (Megginson 2005), it had to be implemented to make the reforms irreversible.[10] On the other hand, as reformers already

[10] The risk of policy reversal was the major factor for not adopting China's gradualist approach. The renationalization of a few key enterprises in 2004–5 implies that this risk was and still is very tangible. Unfortunately for the reformers, the rise in inequality owing to hasty privatization has only strengthened public support for policy reversal.

141

realized at the beginning of the reforms and as the empirical research on privatization showed later (Guriev and Megginson 2007), privatization works better in the presence of complementary reforms of market and state institutions. Therefore the reformers faced a chicken-and-egg problem. In Russia, they chose to launch a rapid mass privatization to transfer tens of thousands of industrial enterprises into private hands (usually those of incumbents) within the course of a couple of years.[11] Initially, the assets were owned by tens of millions of Russians, but the ownership quickly consolidated. As the market institutions were underdeveloped, there were huge 'institutional economies of scale'—large owners were able to influence the rules of the game through capturing regulators, courts, and legislatures (Glaeser et al. 2003; Hellman et al. 2003; Sonin 2003; Slinko et al. 2005). Hence the shares changed hands from workers and retired workers to managers or outside majority owners.[12]

The next wave of privatization was the so-called loans-for-shares programme. This programme was designed to overcome the parliament-imposed ban on privatization of mining industries. The government did not sell the assets; rather, the government borrowed cash from private banks, using the assets as collateral; as the government never intended to make repayment, the assets were actually transferred to the bankers. As the auctions were run by the banks themselves, they were rigged, and the assets were privatized at a small fraction of their market value (Freeland 2000).[13] Both loans-for-shares privatization and post-voucher-privatization consolidation of ownership resulted in an emergence of a few large business groups, each owned by a handful of entrepreneurs known as oligarchs.

4 Oligarchs

According to Plato, 'oligarchy' is a form of government by a small group; Plato distinguished oligarchs from nobles, as the latter are few but rightful rulers while oligarchs come to power unlawfully. In its current meaning in Russia, the term 'oligarch' denotes a large businessman who controls sufficient resources to influence rules of the game—politics, regulation, and judiciary—to

---

[11] Beck and Laeven (2006) show that the institutional challenges were especially important in transition countries with natural resources and with many years under communism. Russia has both.

[12] One of the important factors in this process was the spread of wage arrears in Russia in the mid-1990s (Earle and Sabirianova 2002). As workers were not paid wages in time, they were desperate to get cash and sold their shares at very low prices.

[13] The important factor was the 1996 presidential elections; loans-for-shares helped Yeltsin enlist support of the bankers (future oligarchs), as these assets would remain their property only in case of Yeltsin's victory.

further his fortunes. As mentioned above, transition has created oligarchs in Russia but not in other post-communist countries. Russia differs from other transition countries in several important respects. First, it holds vast natural resources, which creates enormous potential for rent-seeking. Second, unlike the CEE countries, it spent more time under communism; it was, therefore, more difficult to rebuild market institutions (no living Russian had memory of life in a capitalist economy). Besides, Russia did not have an outside anchor such as EU accession, which has created commitment to building these institutions in the CEE. Third, Russia has undertaken a democratic and decentralized path of political reform, which allowed for private agents to build their estates independent of the rulers. The latter factor is important for understanding the difference between Russia, on the one hand, and authoritarian post-soviet regimes, on the other. While the latter have successfully eliminated all private oligarchs, it is not clear how much wealth has been amassed by the rulers themselves. Because of the oppression of the free press, such data are not available, but even the sketchy evidence suggests that the post-soviet authoritarian rulers are rich enough to be considered the 'ultimate oligarchs' within their own countries.[14]

These distinguishing features of Russia's economy have predetermined the emergence of Russian oligarchs. While the conventional wisdom is that the Russian oligarchs were created by the loans-for-shares scheme discussed above, this is only a part of the picture. Indeed, among the twenty-two business groups listed in Table 7.3, only three (led by Potanin, Abramovich, and Khodorkovsky) owe their fortunes to this particular event, as they have used the loans-for-shares auctions to acquire the crown jewels of the mining industry. Two more oligarchs—then industry incumbents Bogdanov and Alekperov—have used loans-for-shares to reinforce their control over their own enterprises. Others have risen through voucher privatization or through purchasing privatized firms from incumbents.[15] Moreover, the first list of

---

[14] One of the most liberal of these rulers, Kazakh President Nursultan Nazarbayev, has allegedly tunnelled at least $US1 billion of oil export revenues to one of his private accounts; his family controls many other key enterprises in the country (Hiatt 2005; Kramner and Norris 2005). Another common example is Ukraine, where three groups (those of Taruta, Akhmetov, and Pinchuk) have become the pillars of President Kuchma's regime (not surprisingly, Kuchma is Pinchuk's father-in-law) and did suffer a certain fallout after the Orange Revolution of 2004. Gorodnichenko and Grygorenko (2005) list thirteen Ukrainian oligarchs (including Pinchuk, Ahmetov, and Taruta) who jointly control about 40% of the Ukrainian economy. Yet only three of them—the very same Pinchuk, Ahmetov, and Taruta—showed up in the *Forbes* list.

[15] Guriev et al. (2006) track all the private Russian owners in the World Bank's dataset (2004) and find that 42% of Russian firms were controlled in 2003 by owners who were industry insiders at the beginning of transition; 48% of the firms are controlled by owners who have served in high government positions at some point in 1990s. The preliminary evidence in the paper suggests that, while political connections help to get better assets, the politically connected owners are less efficient owners in terms of productivity *growth*.

143

omnipotent tycoons of Russia—the so-called Berezovsky's Group of Seven—included four businessmen who actually lost all loans-for-shares tenders they took part in.

Table 7.3 is borrowed from Guriev and Rachinsky (2005), who used a unique dataset on ownership of Russian industry in 2003 to classify the largest owners as oligarchs. In their sample covering about 75 per cent of Russian industry, the twenty-two oligarchs control about 40 per cent of sales and employment. It is, therefore, not surprising to see astonishing estimates of their personal wealth in the *Forbes* list. What do we know about Russian oligarchs? First, they do control enterprises in natural-resource industries and in protected industries such as automotive (Guriev and Rachinsky 2005). Their market shares in the industries that they control are very large. Yet, it should not be a concern for the antitrust policy, as almost all these industries produce globally tradable goods. What is more important is the 'political antitrust' (Rajan and Zingales 2003) policies restricting the state capture by the large influential business groups. Even though the oligarchs are small in the global economy, they have a huge weight within Russia.

Most of the oligarchs in Table 7.3 are relatively young. The average/median Russian billionaire is about 45 years old, twenty years younger than an average/median billionaire in the USA. Most of them control majority or supermajority stakes in their companies, which they are still actively managing. The absence of separation of ownership and control and resulting agency problems have provided the oligarchs with strong incentives to restructure their firms. Boone and Rodionov (2002) argue that, since the oligarchs established—often through expropriation and dilution of other shareholders including the state—the control over their assets, they have been running them very well. This claim is consistent with preliminary evidence in Guriev and Rachinsky (2005) and Shleifer and Treisman (2005), who show that oligarchs seem to outperform other Russian owners and almost catch up with foreign owners.

Moreover, consistently with reformer's expectations, oligarchs began to lobby for certain further pro-market reforms (Guriev and Rachinsky 2005). This process, however, took more time than the reformers expected and was also less comprehensive. First (as suggested by Glaeser et al. 2003; Sonin 2003), oligarchs originally benefited from continued rent seeking. Second, unlike robber barons in the USA, Russian oligarchs are a part of a globalized economy (a few oligarchs from Table 7.3 live in London, most prominently Roman Abramovich), and hence their commitment to building long-term security of property rights in Russia is rather limited.

The oligarchs' incentives are also weakened by the insecurity of their property rights. A median Russian voter deems oligarchs' property rights illegitimate and supports their expropriation (see a discussion of poll data in Guriev

Table 7.3. Russian oligarchs, mid-2003

Senior partner(s)	Holding company/firm, major sector(s)	Employment (000) (% of sample)	Sales (R bn) (% of sample)	Wealth ($US bn)
Oleg Deripaska	Base Element/RusAl, aluminum, auto	169 (3.9)	65 (1.3)	4.5
Roman Abramovich	Millhouse/Sibneft, oil	169 (3.9)	203 (3.9)	12.5
Vladimir Kadannikov	AutoVAZ, automotive	167 (3.9)	112 (2.2)	0.8
Sergei Popov, Andrei Melnichenko, and Dmitry Pumpiansky	MDM, coal, pipes, chemical	143 (3.3)	70 (1.4)	2.9
Vagit Alekperov	Lukoil, oil	137 (3.2)	475 (9.2)	5.6
Alexei Mordashov	Severstal, steel, auto	122 (2.8)	78 (1.5)	4.5
Vladimir Potanin, and Mikhail Prokhorov	Interros/Norilsk Nickel, non-ferrous metals	112 (2.6)	137 (2.6)	10.8
Alexandr Abramov	Evrazholding, steel	101 (2.3)	52 (1.0)	2.4
Len Blavatnik, and Victor Vekselberg	Access-Renova/TNK-BP, oil, aluminum	94 (2.2)	121 (2.3)	9.4
Mikhail Khodorkovsky	Menatep/Yukos, oil	93 (2.2)	149 (2.9)	24.4
Iskander Makhmudov	UGMK, non-ferrous metals	75 (1.7)	33 (0.6)	2.1
Vladimir Bogdanov	Surgutneftegaz, oil	65 (1.5)	163 (3.1)	2.2
Victor Rashnikov	Magnitogorsk Steel, steel	57 (1.3)	57 (1.1)	1.3
Igor Zyuzin	Mechel, steel, coal	54 (1.3)	31 (0.6)	1.1
Vladimir Lisin	Novolipetsk Steel, steel	47 (1.1)	39 (0.8)	4.8
Zakhar Smushkin, Boris Zingarevich, and Mikhail Zingarevich	IlimPulpEnterprises, pulp	42 (1.0)	20 (0.4)	1
Shafagat Tahaudinov	Tatneft, oil	41 (1.0)	41 (0.8)	2.9
Mikhail Fridman	Alfa/TNK-BP, oil	38 (0.9)	107 (2.1)	5.2
Boris Ivanishvili	Metalloinvest, ore	36 (0.8)	15 (0.3)	8.8
Kakha Bendukidze	United Machinery, engineering	35 (0.8)	10 (0.2)	0.3
Vladimir Yevtushenkov	Sistema/MTS, telecoms	20 (0.5)	27 (0.5)	2.1
David Yakobashvili, Mikhail Dubinin, and Sergei Plastinin	WimmBillDann, dairy/juice	13 (0.3)	20 (0.4)	0.2
Total		1,831 (42.4)	2,026 (39.1)	

Note: Each entry lists the leading shareholder(s) in a respective business group, the name of the holding company or the flagship asset, and one or two major sectors. We report several individuals per group only when there is equal or near equal partnership. Ranking is based on employment in the sample and may therefore be different from actual, as the sample disproportionally covers assets of different oligarchs. Employment and sales are based on official firm-level data for 2001.

Source: Employment and sales are from World Bank (2004) and Guriev and Rachinsky (2005). The percentages in parentheses are the share of employment/sales of the World Bank's sample, which in turn covers a substantial share of the economy. Wealth is the market value of the oligarchs' stakes in spring 2004 calculated by authors using *Forbes* 2004 and stock market data. Wealth includes stakes of all the partners identified by the survey (in most cases, there is just one major owner, but in some cases there are 2–3 or even 7). The exchange rate was $US1=29 roubles.

and Rachinsky 2005; see also Vedomosti 2003b). This is well understood by all Russian politicians, who use the threat of expropriation to obtain political or pecuniary contributions from the oligarchs. In particular, President Putin used the anti-oligarch sentiment in his campaign in 2000; once he had come to power, he offered the oligarchs the following pact. As long as the oligarchs paid taxes and did not use their political power (at least not against Putin), Putin would respect their property rights and refrain from revisiting privatization. This pact defined the ground rules of the oligarchs' interaction with central and regional government for Putin's first term (2000–4). Although the pact could never have been written down, even the general public was well aware of its existence. A poll by FOM (an independent non-profit Russian polling organization) a week after the meeting of Putin and the oligarchs showed that 57 per cent of Russians knew about it.

Putin proved the credibility of the expropriation threat in 2003, when the prominent oligarch Mikhail Khodorkovsky, the majority owner of the Yukos oil company, deviated from the pact by openly criticizing corruption in Putin's administration[16] and supporting opposition parties and independent media (Vedomosti 2003a). He and his partners were soon arrested or forced into exile, and their stakes in Yukos expropriated. Khodorkovsky was sentenced to eight years in prison, and his personal estate is now estimated to be only $US2 billion (down from $US15 billion).

The Yukos affair clarified the rules of the game between oligarchs and the Kremlin. Oligarchs learned the risks related to violating the pact, and so, in the future, they will be less likely to interfere in national politics. Ironically, by crushing Russia's most transparent company, Putin pursued the 'political antitrust' policy that was crucial in building US democracy and economy at the beginning of twentieth century (Rajan and Zingales 2003). Even though oligarchs remain economically powerful, they no longer have any role in politics. This in turn removed any counterweights to bureaucracy, which then followed a steady course for renationalization. The nationalization occurs through the buy-out of oligarch firms by state-owned companies. In some cases, the oligarchs receive a large share of their assets' market value, in others just a fraction.[17] Therefore any wealth estimate based on the assets' market value (as those provided by *Forbes*) may substantially overestimate the true wealth of the oligarchs; the wealth depends both on the value of the assets and on the relationship with the government.

[16] 'Tycoons Talk Corruption in Kremlin', *Moscow Times*, 20 Feb. 2003, 5.

[17] As the threatpoint is the full expropriation, one should expect that, even if assets are acquired by the state at the market value, the seller is asked to make substantial side payments. A prominent Russian journalist, Yulia Latynina, suggests that this was the case in the purchase of Sibneft from Abramovich (*Echo Moskvy*, 11 Mar, 2006, www.echo.msk.ru/programmes/code/42280).

The nationalization of the key oligarch-controlled assets will continue. At the time of writing the study, 4 out of the 22 groups in Table 7.3 are nationalized (Abramovich's Sibneft, the main division of Khodorkovsky's Yukos, Kadannikov's Avtovaz, Bendukidze's UMZ) and 2–3 more nationalizations are being discussed. Given the notorious inefficiency and corruption of Russian bureaucracy, these companies will eventually have to be reprivatized. If they are privatized in an open and competitive fashion, the public will respect the new owners' property rights which will in turn result in efficient incentives to invest. Yet another option is to reprivatize these companies to dispersed owners. This will provide the Russian middle class with a stake in the financial development and economic growth and even increase their personal wealth. As shown in Megginson (2005), privatization IPOs are usually underpriced by about 30 per cent. Yet, if government fails to enforce post-IPO corporate governance, the dispersed owners may fail to reap the value of their investment.

Whether a direct sale to a strategic investor or share issue privatization (SIP) is selected or the two approaches are combined is yet to be seen. In principle, these companies are sufficiently large so that SIPs may be more efficient (Megginson 2005). The management of state-owned companies is biased towards SIP; indeed, if they have stakes in their companies, they would rather benefit from a liquid market where they can cash in. They will also be better-off under dispersed ownership as there will be less shareholder monitoring so they will preserve the private benefits of control.

However, the most important choice is not the one of the method of privatization but about the government's commitment to transparent rules of reprivatization.[18] If the privatization auctions/IPOs are rigged again, the new buyers will benefit in the short term, but the vicious circle of illegitimate property rights will result in another expropriation. This may create a stable equilibrium like in Acemoglu and Robinson (2001)—high wealth inequality breeds support for expropriation, but as political institutions are underdeveloped, the redistribution benefits the bureaucrats (who become the new rich) rather than the poor; therefore high inequality may persist for quite a while.

5 Policy Issues

Is there a simple solution for the wealth inequality problem? Given high corruption (often driven by the very same inequality), redistribution does

---

[18] A reprivatization of Krivoryzhstal in Ukraine provides an important illustration of the argument (Kramer and Timmons 2005). In 2004 this crown jewel of the Ukrainian steel industry was privatized to two out of the three most influential Ukrainian oligarchs at $US0.85 billion. The public outrage over the rigged auction was one of the important drivers of the Ukrainian Orange Revolution. The new government cancelled the privatization of the plant and resold it in an open tender for $US4.8 billion to a leading global player. The high price and the transparency of the auction secured public support for the property rights.

not necessarily benefit the poor. And, unless the corruption is reined in, the expropriation of oligarchs will create only new oligarchs. It is, therefore, crucial to remove the fundamental cause of growth in wealth inequality, the 'institutional economies of scale'. As the market and government institutions are underdeveloped, the rich have an advantage in furthering their riches while the poor are denied opportunity. The transition countries should therefore focus on providing equal access to education and healthcare,[19] to the judiciary system, and to financial markets.

The institutional reforms of this kind require the government's commitment. Unfortunately, commitment to reform is, in its turn, harder to assure in unequal societies; high wealth inequality reduces stability of economic policy in both democratic and authoritarian regimes (in the latter, the stability of the regime itself is undermined). In the CEE countries, such commitment is provided by the outside anchor of the EU accession, and most of the preconditions for reducing the inequality are already in place.

Commonwealth of Independent States (CIS) countries have mostly lagged behind the accession countries in terms of building market institutions, albeit to a varying extent. The list of institutions to be introduced is long. First, households need to have access to savings, investment, credit, and insurance. For this, the government should support competition in the financial markets, but also introduce prudential regulation, regulation of the stock market, credit history bureaux, deposit insurance system. Second, property rights for real estate should be established, and the real-estate market should be efficient. This is a major innovation for post-communist countries and it requires an overhaul of legislation and the creation of a land registry. Third, the government should protect the property rights of entrepreneurs, both from racketeering and from predation from its own corrupt bureaucrats.

Every CIS country has taken some of the steps above, and none has completed all of them. It is probably going to take more time than the reformers envisioned in the beginning of transition. While these institutions benefit the median voter, the problem is that in some of these countries the democratic transition is stifled or even reversed. Hence the policy choices may be biased in favour of the ruling elite, which is happy to continue redistribution from the middle class. Moreover, reducing the wealth inequality may empower the middle class and therefore endanger the power of the entrenched elites. Thus it remains to be seen whether and how CIS countries manage to break out from the high inequality trap.

---

[19] In this respect, the transition countries, especially the CIS, are yet to make the turnaround (World Bank 2005b). The access to public goods, to quality education, and to healthcare is still not improving after a decline in the beginning of transition, and the situation is especially dire for the poor.

6 Conclusions

Given the lack of reliable data on personal wealth, it is hard to speculate on the evolution of personal wealth and of wealth inequality in transition countries. Yet, the indirect evidence points to a stark increase both in average personal wealth and in wealth inequality, especially in the former Soviet Union. While much of the *income* inequality is explained by the wage decompression, the *wealth* inequality was in many cases driven by privatization and the subsequent consolidation of ownership. In particular, in Russia, the transition resulted in an emergence of a new class of rich individuals. While these oligarchs have restructured their companies and lobbied for further pro-market reforms, the median voter's perception of their illegitimacy has undermined the government's incentive to continue reforms. It is, therefore, not surprising that in Russia, as well as in the other CIS countries, inequality has remained high and reforms that could eventually bring it down have been abandoned or even reversed. On the other hand, in the CEE countries, the outside anchor of EU accession has provided governments with a commitment device to introduce institutions for greater equality of opportunity.

Like many other studies on wealth inequality, ours concludes by restating the obvious need for more data. To illustrate the sheer extent of potential mismeasurement, we have estimated the Gini index for income using the only database that includes Russia's super-rich individuals; we found that the official data may underestimate Gini by about 25 percentage points. The wealth inequality data are probably even more distorted. An informed policy debate can be based only on reliable and comparable data on personal wealth coming from representative household surveys, which would indeed include some very rich individuals. Unfortunately, such data are still non-existent.

8

Household Wealth in Latin America

Florencia Torche and Seymour Spilerman

1 Introduction: The Importance of Household Wealth and Asset Holdings

This chapter reviews the empirical and historical literature on wealth owner-ship and inequality in Latin America. Although much has been written about the distribution of education and income in the region, to date there has been little systematic study of wealth inequality. This study uses various available sources and primary data analysis to draw inferences about the distribution of different types of assets—housing, land, and capital wealth—in Latin America, and highlights the areas in which new information is needed.

With few exceptions—Uruguay, Costa Rica, Venezuela—the countries of Latin America have the highest levels of income inequality in the world. In the late 1990s, for example, the income share received by the highest income decile was 47.2 per cent in Brazil, 47.0 per cent in Chile, and 43.1 per cent in Mexico, in contrast to 30.5 per cent in the United States (de Ferranti et al. 2004: 2). While estimates of household net worth that would permit a calculation of wealth inequality are not available for Latin America, there are reasons to expect more extreme concentration in this continent than in Asia or the industrialized countries. First, in all countries for which wealth data are available, the Gini index for household wealth exceeds the Gini for household income. Second, the initial conditions of European settlement in Latin America involved conquest and the appropriation of much of the arable land and natural resources, followed by the persistent political dominance by European

We thank James Davies, Edward Wolff, John Muellbauer, Carmen Deere, and participants at the UNU-WIDER project meeting 'Personal Assets from a Global Perspective', Helsinki, 4–6 May 2006, for comments. Support from Ford Foundation grant #1040–1239 is gratefully acknowledged. We would like to thank Eva Quintana and Tatiana Alves for excellent research assistance.

150

settlers and economic exploitation of the indigenous population. This sort of historical legacy also argues for a high concentration of wealth. In fact, Davies et al. (Chapter 19, this volume) estimate wealth Ginis of 0.78, 0.75, and 0.74 for Brazil, Mexico, and Argentina, which place these countries among the most unequal of the (mostly industrialized) countries compared.

1.1 Household Wealth in Developed Countries

Historical estimation of wealth distributions based on estate and wealth tax data goes back to the early twentieth century in a few industrialized nations, including the USA, the UK, France, and the Scandinavian nations (Ohlsson et al., Chapter 3, this volume; Atkinson, Chapter 4, this volume). In contrast, survey-based wealth information, which allows analysis of determinants and outcomes of net worth, is a relatively new development (see Jäntti and Sierminska, Chapter 2, this volume). Public-use datasets containing modules on household wealth are now available for some twenty countries. As a result, a literature on household wealth has swiftly developed. This literature includes descriptive studies of wealth holdings and the shape of wealth distributions, investigations into the determinants of household accumulation, studies of parental 'motives' for transfers, and a growing body of work on the *effects* of household wealth on various outcome measures. The last serves as a bridge between studies of household wealth in developed countries and the comparable literature in Latin America.

It is useful to formulate wealth effects in three categories: contributions to living standards and labour-force behaviour; precautionary savings; and effects of parental wealth on the life chances and attainments of offspring. The first topic has not been the focus of sustained research, though there have been studies of wealth effects on entrepreneurship (e.g., Lindh and Ohlsonn 1998) and on entrance into home ownership (e.g., Mulder and Wagner 1998; Chiuri and Jappelli 2003). However, in the measurement of household wealth in these studies, inheritances and parental transfers are often entangled with life-cycle accumulation, so we defer our remarks on this material to the discussion of parental wealth effects.

The second theme, precautionary savings, has received more attention—possibly because the recent contraction in public-support programmes in the USA and Europe has shifted much of the risk of job loss and illness to families, compelling them to rely more on private savings (e.g., Carroll and Samwick 1998; Wolff 2001: table 2.13; Haveman and Wolff 2004). While these studies have focused on the vulnerabilities of families in the developed world, the same concerns are evident in examinations of population welfare in Latin America, especially in light of the weak social safety net in most countries (e.g., Filgueira 1998; Ruggeri Laderchi 2003; Fay and Ruggeri Laderchi 2005).

The third category addresses the impact of parental resources and parental transfers on various outcome measures of offspring. These studies delve into the effects of *initial conditions*: the extent to which the attainments and living standards of children are conditioned by parental wealth and other resources. Parental wealth can affect educational attainment both directly, such as through payments for private school tuition, and indirectly, as in the purchase of a home in a neighbourhood with a quality public school (e.g., Green and White 1997; Boehm and Scholttman 1999). Parental wealth can reduce the waiting time from marriage to home ownership or permit the purchase of a more expensive home (Engelhard and Mayer 1998; Guiso and Jappelli 1999; Spilerman 2004). More generally, parents can allocate their transfers strategically to assist children at critical points along the life course, either to facilitate career development or to assist at times of economic distress.

In the main, the studies noted here have been carried out with data from the USA and Europe, though household wealth should be an even more relevant resource in Latin America, given the limited access to the credit market and the weakness of the social safety net. Furthermore, wealth should be critical to the replication of Latin American inequality, because it is household assets, rather than an income stream, that is transferred across generations. While the issue of wealth transmissions in Latin America is not addressed in the current chapter, the reader is referred to Spilerman and Torche (2004) and Torche and Spilerman (2006) for an analysis of parental wealth effects on various outcome measures. It is important to highlight, however, that the Latin American literature on household wealth approaches the topic in ways that are distinct from the formulations used in industrialized countries, as we highlight in the following section.

1.2 Formulations of Household Wealth in Latin America: The Asset Approach

The literature in the industrialized world underlines four sources of evidence from which to construct proxies for household health: wealth tax data, estate tax data, investment income tax data, and sample surveys (Davies and Shorrocks 2000; Atkinson, Chapter 4, this volume). At the time of writing, there is no survey of household wealth for any Latin American country, and the weakness of taxation systems in many countries of the region makes tax-based information partial and unreliable. An alternative for Latin America, and for the developing world in general, is the use of more widely available survey information on household asset holdings. Indeed, a common situation for researchers is one of having binary data on various household assets (ownership/non-ownership) but no information on the value of the items, or on income received from different types of assets. In part, this state of affairs has motivated an interest in examining *asset holdings* in studies of household wealth in Latin American countries.

A second important difference with the industrialized world is that the notion of assets in the Latin American literature references a broader portfolio of items than in the developed world. While in industrialized countries the term *asset* is restricted to material items that have market value, students of Latin America tend to associate assets with 'productive resources' and count among them educational attainment and social capital (e.g., Moser 1998; Szekely 2001; Fay and Ruggeri Laderchi 2005). This different formulation reflects more than semantics or the lack of data on household net worth. At the theoretical level, it is based on the framework of Sen (1992), who associates productive assets with 'capabilities'; as such, inequality of asset holdings relates to the distribution of opportunity. Furthermore, the focus on assets in Latin America is driven by the sensitivities of researchers for whom the alleviation of poverty, widespread on this continent, is an overriding concern. Influenced by this objective, household assets have come to encompass whatever 'income producing resources' can reduce poverty (Attanasio and Szekely 2001). Thus, a home is important, because it can serve as a storefront or as the locus of household-based production. An automobile can serve as a taxi or be used in a carting business, and tool ownership opens other income-generation possibilities.

Education, then, is viewed as another productive asset, though one of immense consequence (de Ferranti et al. 2004: 151–7). Given high economic fluctuations, lack of universal social protection, and weakness of credit markets, Latin American households are acutely vulnerable to events such as illness or job loss. This vulnerability is blamed for the early school withdrawal by poor children and teenagers (de Ferranti et al. 2004: table A47; see also Moser 1998; Spilerman and Torche 2004). Attempts have been made to redress this problem by means of cash payments to poor households, conditional on the children's school attendance—for example, the *Oportunidades*, formerly *Progresa*, programme in Mexico (Schultz 2004); and *Bolsa Escola*, now subsumed into *Bolsa Familia*, in Brazil (Bourguignon et al. 2003). However, what is deeply implicated is the lack of material assets or savings that could be drawn upon to smooth consumption (Szekely 1998: ch. 8; Fay and Ruggeri Laderchi 2005).

This Latin American focus on income-generating assets has given rise to a literature on the 'asset vulnerability' of poor families. Moser (1998: 3) has examined the sensitivity of families to risks and shocks, and their resilience to stressful events, in terms of asset portfolios, though in conformity with this literature her asset specification includes human and social capital as well as material resources. Similarly, Escobal et al. (2001: 227–9), assessing urban poverty in Peru, found, not surprisingly, that savings, durable goods, and home ownership are buffers against economic crisis. Trejos and Montiel (2001), analysing data from Costa Rica, also conclude that material asset ownership reduces a family's prospects of falling below the poverty line. In sum, a nascent Latin American literature highlights the crucial relevance of asset holdings—broadly defined in the current formulations—for the economic well-being of households.

1.3 The Measurement of Wealth Distribution with Asset Data

An obvious starting point to construct a proxy for household wealth using survey information on asset holdings is by a count of asset items. Filmer and Pritchett (1999, 2001) have suggested a more refined approach based on principal component analysis. Essentially, this involves constructing a sequence of linear combinations of binary terms for the presence of an asset item. The first component is the linear combination with assigned weights so that it accounts for the largest amount of variance in the correlations among the items. Additional components can be extracted, each explaining the maximum amount of remaining variation in the asset items.

Filmer and Pritchett (1999, 2001) constructed an asset index using the first principal component with a set of household items. Their objective was not to estimate wealth inequality, but rather to explore the effects of household wealth on various outcome variables, especially the educational attainments of children. Using this wealth proxy in regressions, they concluded that the asset index is superior to consumption measures of wealth because 'the major problem with current expenditures as a proxy for long-run wealth is the presence of short term fluctuations' (Filmer and Pritchett 2001: 116). While theirs is an attractive approach for utilizing asset information, the formulation is problematic with respect to producing a wealth proxy. In particular, Filmer and Pritchett do not distinguish between living standard measures and wealth indicators in their choice of assets. Living standard indicators are items that reflect a family's well-being but have little resale value, such as a radio or a telephone, and that can be purchased from household income by all but the very poorest households. Filmer and Pritchett also include indicators of residence amenities—presence of electricity, a flush toilet, piped water—though their population samples appear not to be restricted to homeowners. For residents who do not own, however, these amenities are questionable as indicators of wealth.

If many of the Filmer and Pritchett items tap household income as much as wealth, one approach might be to add an instrument for income to the regressions on outcome variables so that the effect of the asset index could be examined net of income. Such partial regression effects could more reasonably be interpreted as wealth effects. Perhaps a better approach would be not to restrict the principal component analysis to a single component. A common strategy in factor analysis is to rotate the several extracted components to approximate some specification of 'simple structure' (Bennett and Bowers 1976). This approach can be informative about the intercorrelations among asset items and might well reveal both an income factor and a household wealth factor; each could then be used in the study of wealth and income effects.

In a variant of this approach, Torche and Spilerman (2006) used confirmatory factor analysis to model separate latent variables for living standard and household wealth in Chile. The living standard construct was measured by four consumption indicators; the household wealth construct by four investment assets—ownership of financial assets, rental property, other real estate, and business property—items that clearly tap wealth and not living standard. This formulation was used to assess the paths by which parental wealth in Chile, net of other parental resources, affects a range of outcomes in the lives of adult children.

The measurement of wealth *inequality* from asset items poses additional challenges. As McKenzie (2005) has noted, the asset items must span a sufficient cost range to allow for differentiation across the wealth distribution. If few items are used, there will be a tendency for households to clump together in small groups. If, for instance, the distribution of assets is skewed towards the low end (by the omission of assets associated with great wealth), then wealthy households will not be differentiated from middle-class ones. The consequence will be a downward bias in the estimate of wealth inequality. A similar problem arose in an attempt by Fay et al. (2002) to calculate inequality in home values from housing quality items. Because the items did not tap the extremes of housing quality, the estimates of home value fell in a more narrow range than the reported values. In sum, given limited availability of wealth data in Latin America, asset-based measures provide a promising approach to estimation of the wealth distribution. However, the value of this method crucially depends on the ability of the asset items to capture the scope of wealth holdings in a particular country.

1.4 *Wealth Distribution in Latin America: Chapter Outline*

This study provides a survey of the wealth distribution in Latin America, using published data and our own analysis of household surveys in fourteen countries in the region. Sections 2, 3, and 4 present estimates of the distribution of home ownership, land holdings, and capital assets, respectively. Land has historically been the main form of wealth in Latin America. Consequently, analysts tend to use land concentration as a proxy for overall asset inequality (Alesina and Rodrik 1994; Birdsall and Londono 1997; Deininger and Squire 1998; Deininger and Olinto 2000). This assumption is questionable today. With three-quarters of Latin Americans living in urban areas, other forms of wealth have become relevant. Paramount is owner-occupied housing. Interestingly, Section 2 shows that home ownership is much more evenly distributed in Latin America than in developed countries such as the USA or the UK, in spite of the deeper poverty in the region. As we will discuss, this pattern is explained by the prevalence of squatting settlements in urban areas, and by governmental housing policies in some countries.

Section 3 shows that land concentration in Latin America is among the highest in the world, although there is some cross-national variation, correlated with the experience of agrarian reform. When we compare two distinct dimensions of land distribution—access to land, and concentration among landowners—we also find substantial variation across Latin American countries. Another component of the household wealth portfolio is capital assets, including rental and commercial real estate, and financial resources. While land and residences have high functional value for owners, capital assets provide liquidity and fungibility, and therefore serve a consumption storage function. Our analysis in Section 4 suggests that the ownership of capital assets is highly concentrated in Latin America, and that the large majority of the population, up to 90 per cent in some countries, does not have access to this type of wealth.

While the legal ownership of assets is taken for granted in the developed world, this is not the case in Latin America. Current estimates indicate that about one-third of owners lack formal title for their home or plot. According to de Soto (2000), untitled property is 'dead capital' that cannot be used as collateral for investment purposes. Section 5 reviews the literature on informal wealth and the relevance of formal title. Finally, Section 6 discusses the historical origins and development of the unequal wealth distribution in Latin America since colonial times, focusing on the institutional mechanisms through which wealth concentration has been maintained over time. Section 7 summarizes and concludes.

2 Home Ownership

Home ownership has not been a major theme in the asset literature of Latin America (though see World Bank 2002a, b; Fay and Wellenstein 2005), despite the inclusion of residences in the category of productive assets. Nonetheless, housing is the most widespread asset in Latin America; indeed, for the vast majority of the population owner-occupied housing is the only asset in their portfolio (de Ferranti et al. 2004: 194). Furthermore, housing is a tractable instrument if the intent is to alter the wealth distribution, because it is not a finite asset and it does not require redistribution, as does land (Fay et al. 2002).

Table 8.1 reports the home tenure status for fourteen Latin American countries, based on household surveys around 2000 (survey descriptions can be found in the Appendix). The last column in the table presents the tenure status in the USA, as a baseline for comparison. As in the USA, a very large proportion of Latin American households own their homes. Home-ownership rates range from 55 per cent in Colombia to more than 75 per cent in Nicaragua, Panama, and Paraguay with a population-unweighted Latin American average of 69 per cent. Only 15 per cent of Latin American households rent against 31 per cent

Table 8.1. Home tenure status, Latin American countries and the USA, c. 2000

Tenure arrangement	Argentina	Bolivia	Brazil	Chile	Colombia	Costa Rica	Ecuador	Guatemala	Mexico	Nicaragua	Panama	Paraguay	Peru	Uruguay	USA
Own	71.6	64.5	71.6	72.0	55.3	74.4	66.7	70.5	72.6	77.6	77.2	76.7	74.3	67.2	66.3
Rent	13.0	15.0	15.3	15.6	35.9	15.3	18.1	9.7	13.7	3.1	11.3	9.9	6.8	17.5	30.7
Provided by employer or family member		15.7	11.6	11.5	8.0		14.2	14.4	13.2	11.9	8.6	12.6	15.0	14.4	
Squatting	1.4			0.3	0.6						2.9		3.9		
Other	14.0	4.8	1.5	0.6	0.2	10.3	1.0	5.4	0.5	7.4		0.7	0.1	0.9	3.0
Total	100	100	100	100	100	100	100	100	100	100	100	100	100	100	100

Note: All samples weighted to represent national populations (urban in the case of Argentina and Uruguay).

Sources: Latin American countries: author's calculations based on household surveys; see Appendix for survey descriptions. USA: Survey of Consumer Finances 1998.

in the USA. This 16 percentage point difference is partly accounted for by two customary tenure arrangements in Latin America: dwellings provided by a family member or friend (most frequently as a 'long term loan'); and dwellings provided by an employer, an arrangement frequent among rural workers and manual employees in remotely located manufacturing or extractive plants.[1] The most striking finding from Table 8.1 is that home-ownership rates are as high as in the USA, in spite of much deeper poverty in the region. In addition to high rates of ownership, Latin America is characterized by remarkably even access to home ownership across socio-economic strata. Table 8.2 reports home-ownership rates by income decile.[2]

Table 8.2 reveals low inequality of home ownership in Latin America, in sharp contrast with the high income concentration in the region. While in the USA (last column) home-ownership rates increase monotonically from 41 per cent in the poorest quintile to 94 per cent in the wealthiest decile, in Latin America home ownership increases only slightly across the income distribution, and even declines in some countries. There is a small positive gradient of the home-ownership rate with income in Argentina, Brazil, Colombia, Costa Rica, Mexico, Panama, and Uruguay. However, the poor are *more likely* to be homeowners than the middle class and the wealthy in Bolivia, Chile, Guatemala, Paraguay, and Peru. We suggest that two factors account for this widespread access to home ownership in Latin America: the prevalence of squatter settlements in the region, and the role of housing policy in some countries.

Latin America experienced a massive migration from the countryside to the cities during the second half of the twentieth century, leading to an increase from 42 per cent in 1950 to 74 per cent in 2000 in the urbanization rate (United Nations 1990; Population Reference Bureau 2000). Governments were not able to meet the housing demands of these rural migrants, and the newcomers opted to seize unoccupied land and build precarious dwellings, creating enormous neighbourhoods that today contain much of the population in some urban areas. These neighbourhoods go by various names: *tugorio* in Colombia, *poblacion callampa* in Chile, *favela* in Brazil. As a consequence, a large proportion of the poor do not hold formal title. Fay and Wellenstein (2005: 92) estimate that one-third of homeowners in Latin America lack legal title and the proportion reaches 40–50 per cent in some of the larger cities (Grimes 1976). Indeed, many self-declared homeowners in household surveys

---

[1] With the exception of Argentina, Guatemala, and Nicaragua, the residual 'other' category is small and captures different, nationally specific arrangements.

[2] Throughout this chapter we produce asset distribution data by decile whenever possible because of evidence that what appears to be unique about inequality in Latin America is the extraordinary concentration of income, and most probably of other resources, in the wealthiest decile, together with relatively less inequality across the bottom nine deciles (IADB 1999; Portes and Hoffman 2003; Torche 2005). Rates by income quintile for a larger number of countries can be found in de Ferranti et al. (2004: table A40).

Table 8.2. Home tenure by income decile, Latin American countries and the USA, c. 2000

Income decile	Argentina			Bolivia			Brazil			Chile			Colombia			Costa Rica			USA*
	Own	Rent	Other	Own	Rent	Other	Own	Rent	Other	Own	Rent	Other	Own	Rent	Other	Own	Rent	Other	Own
D1	69	9	22	92	3	5	60	21	20	71	9	20	59	26	15	75	6	18	41
D2	72	10	18	77	10	13	66	14	20	70	11	19	54	34	12	74	9	17	
D3	70	11	19	61	16	23	65	16	19	69	15	16	53	34	13	66	13	21	57
D4	69	13	18	59	16	25	69	14	17	71	14	15	48	39	13	71	15	14	
D5	66	17	17	50	24	26	69	15	15	72	15	12	49	42	9	71	16	12	66
D6	68	15	17	56	20	24	71	16	13	73	15	12	47	41	12	72	18	10	
D7	72	16	12	60	15	25	74	15	11	70	19	11	51	40	8	74	16	10	82
D8	75	15	10	60	16	24	73	15	12	70	20	10	54	41	6	77	17	7	
D9	76	14	9	62	16	22	75	17	8	69	22	9	55	40	4	80	16	4	91
D10	81	13	7	66	15	19	81	14	5	64	30	6	70	27	3	84	14	2	94
Total	72	13	15	64	15	21	72	15	13	70	17	13	54	37	9	74	14	12	68

Income decile	Guatemala			Mexico			Panama			Paraguay			Peru			Uruguay			USA*
	Own	Rent	Other	Own	Rent	Other	Own	Rent	Other	Own	Rent	Other	Own	Rent	Other	Own	Rent	Other	Own
D1	63	2	35	78	9	14	85	5	11	82	6	12	85	2	13	58	10	32	41
D2	62	2	35	67	13	20	75	9	16	80	7	12	85	2	14	59	15	26	
D3	51	5	44	67	15	18	78	9	13	81	8	11	82	5	14	61	17	22	57
D4	57	5	38	70	16	14	79	10	10	82	6	13	77	5	18	63	20	16	
D5	53	11	36	65	17	18	79	14	7	79	9	12	78	5	17	67	19	14	66
D6	52	9	40	69	14	17	76	12	12	79	8	13	76	8	16	68	22	11	
D7	53	13	33	74	14	12	79	14	7	74	13	13	76	9	15	71	19	9	82
D8	56	15	30	76	14	10	81	14	5	76	12	13	76	10	14	74	19	7	
D9	59	19	22	77	13	10	81	15	4	73	15	13	75	9	16	76	19	5	91
D10	66	17	17	82	12	5	89	10	2	69	16	15	75	13	13	81	15	4	94
Total	57	10	33	73	14	14	80	11	9	77	10	13	78	7	15	67	18	15	68

* US figures are homeownership rates for first four income quintiles, and the two wealthiest deciles.

Sources: Latin American countries: author's calculations based on household surveys; see the Appendix for survey descriptions. USA = Survey of Consumer Finances 2001, reported in Aizcorbe et al. (2003).

might actually be squatters, which is consistent with the low percentage reporting a mortgage.[3]

We speculate that the low reporting of squatting status (see Table 8.1) is due to two factors. First, families have been living in these *de facto* arrangements for a long period, sometimes more than a generation, and consider themselves legitimate owners even in the absence of legal title. Second, respondents are reluctant to acknowledge that they lack legal title. Survey evidence suggests that the former reason has more explanatory power. For instance, in Nicaragua, when the survey response options are formulated as 'dwelling owned, with formal title' and 'owned, no formal title', as many as 30 per cent of home-owners select the latter option. Similarly, in Ecuador, only 67 per cent of respondents who report having paid in full for their dwelling have legal title. In Guatemala, 18.1 per cent of owners indicate that they do not have a legal title to the house, while another 26.8 per cent indicate that they have 'unregistered title'. These responses suggest that legal ownership is severely over-reported in surveys, with clear implications for a household's ability to collateralize its home equity (see Section 5).

Housing policy is the second factor explaining the high overall rate of home ownership in Latin America. In several countries home ownership by the poor has been fostered through generous government subsidies (see Arellano 2000: 161; Fay and Wellenstein 2005: 110, on Costa Rica; Torche and Spilerman 2006, on Chile). Given budget constraints, government-sponsored housing projects tend to be located in the urban periphery, where land is cheap but infrastructure is deficient and employment is distant. As a consequence, housing policy may have exacerbated class segregation in Latin American cities (see Ducci 2000 for the case of Chile).

2.1 Housing Wealth

Given the widespread access to home ownership, and the lack of legal title by many low-income homeowners, the market value of 'owned' housing may be low for a large proportion of the population. Since direct measures of home value are not available in household surveys, we proxy it by rental value, as estimated by the homeowners. This approach is supported by studies that find home value estimates based on rental income to be quite accurate (Kain and Quigley 1972). Admittedly, this approach may suffer from bias if some households systematically over- or underestimate the rental value of their dwellings, and it assumes that the relation between market value and rental income in a country is constant across regions and neighbourhoods.

---

[3] The proportion of homeowners who have an outstanding mortgage ranges from 1–2% in Nicaragua, Paraguay, and Peru, to 28% in Chile.

Table 8.3a. Share of total housing wealth by income decile (non-homeowners coded as having zero housing wealth), selected Latin American countries, c. 2000

Income decile	Bolivia	Brazil*	Chile	Colombia	Guatemala	Mexico	Panama	Paraguay	Peru	Uruguay
D1	1.3	8.0	5.0	6.7	5.2	2.1	2.1	4.0	2.0	4.6
D2	2.1		5.6	5.9	4.0	2.9	2.8	4.7	3.3	5.6
D3	3.2	9.0	6.5	6.1	4.5	3.4	4.1	6.0	3.4	6.1
D4	3.2		6.9	5.4	5.0	4.6	5.2	6.9	6.0	6.4
D5	3.8	13.0	7.9	8.0	5.5	5.2	6.0	7.7	7.8	7.5
D6	5.0		9.1	6.7	7.2	6.9	7.6	8.1	9.3	8.6
D7	7.1	20.0	9.7	8.4	8.9	8.9	8.7	9.0	9.2	9.6
D8	12.6		11.0	10.8	10.1	10.8	11.5	11.5	12.8	11.2
D9	17.3	50.0	14.2	12.4	14.3	15.1	15.9	13.9	15.2	14.1
D10	44.5		24.2	29.7	35.3	40.2	36.1	28.1	31.1	26.2
Total	100	100	100	100	100	100	100	100	100	100

* Brazil figures are housing wealth by income quintile. Obtained from Reis et al. (2001), figures are for 1999.

Note: Estimates of housing wealth obtained from survey question asked of homeowners 'If you were to rent this property, which monthly rent would you be able to charge?'.

Source: Author's calculations based on household surveys (except for Brazil); see the Appendix for survey descriptions.

Table 8.3b. Distribution of housing wealth, selected Latin American countries c. 2000

	Bolivia	Chile	Colombia	Guatemala	Mexico	Panama	Paraguay	Peru	Uruguay
Housing wealth Gini*	0.85	0.60	0.71	0.84	0.70	0.64	0.63	0.74	0.56
Household income Gini[†]	0.58	0.57	0.58	0.58	0.55	0.56	0.57	0.49	0.45
Share of housing value by housing wealth percentile[‡]									
Quintile 1	0.9	6.6	5.3	2.7	3.0	3.6	3.2	1.6	8.5
Quintile 2	2.6	10.3	13.1	6.8	5.6	7.8	8.0	3.0	13.3
Quintile 3	3.9	14.6	11.1	8.5	13.4	15.0	14.0	8.0	14.3
Quintile 4	11.4	20.1	18.7	16.1	15.9	15.4	22.2	17.2	21.1
Quintile 5	81.3	49.5	51.8	65.9	62.1	58.3	52.6	70.1	42.8
Decile 10	65.2	34.3	36.5	51.6	43.0	40.4	37.2	51.9	25.6
Total (across quintiles)	100	100	100	100	100	100	100	100	100

* Housing wealth Gini based on the full sample, non-homeowners coded as having zero housing wealth.
[†] Obtained from de Ferranti et al. (2004 table A3).
[‡] Calculation excludes non-homeowners.

Note: Estimates of housing wealth obtained from survey question asked of homeowners 'If you were to rent this property, which monthly rent would you be able to charge?'. Quintiles are not exact in some countries because of clustering in cutpoints. In all cases clusters in cutpoints were put in the lower category.

Source: Author's calculations based on household surveys; see the Appendix for survey descriptions.

Table 8.3a presents estimates of the share of housing wealth by income decile for homeowners in the ten countries with available survey data. The concentration in the highest decile is evident, ranging from some 25 per cent in Chile and Uruguay to more than 40 per cent in Bolivia and Mexico. In contrast with the previous findings for access to housing, these results show a significant association of housing wealth with income. Table 8.3b examines the distribution of housing wealth using the Gini index (non-homeowners are coded as having zero wealth), and the distribution of home values by housing wealth quintiles (non-owners are excluded). The Gini scores indicate extremely high concentrations of housing wealth, higher than the concentration of income. Chile is an exception, with similar inequality of housing wealth and income— probably a result of its widespread programme of housing assistance. The share of housing wealth held by different percentiles indicates high inequality among homeowners, with the top quintile receiving more than 50 per cent of the total housing wealth in all countries, with the sole exception of Chile and Uruguay.

3 Land Distribution

Land is a prominent resource in contemporary Latin America, even after the large-scale urbanization of the second half of the twentieth century. Although 74 per cent of Latin Americans live in urban areas, there is significant variation across countries. Some (Argentina, Brazil, Chile, Uruguay, Venezuela) feature urbanization rates higher than 80 per cent, while in others, such as Bolivia, Guatemala, and Nicaragua, about half of the population is still rural (UN-Habitat 1999). In the latter countries, land remains a major economic resource and a component of the asset portfolio of many families. The best sources of information on land inequality are the datasets assembled by UNDP (1993), Deininger and Squire (1998), and Deininger and Olinto (2000). These datasets were constructed from the decennial FAO World Censuses of Agriculture, complemented with other sources. The FAO data are based on official national agricultural surveys conducted at the beginning of each decade, and refer to rural areas. The unit of analysis is an operational holding, 'an economic unit of agricultural production under single management, comprising all livestock kept and all land used wholly or partly for agricultural production purposes, without regard to title, legal form, or size' (FAO 2001).

The level of standardization across countries is considerable in the FAO data. However, measures of inequality based on these data have limitations. First, they refer to land operation rather than ownership. According to Deininger and Squire (1998), measures of concentration based on the former are a lower bound for ownership concentration because the rental market seems to contribute to a more equal distribution. Also, the measures of land distribution do not adjust for soil quality or land improvement, and they rarely account for land held under communal tenure arrangements, such as the *ejido* in Mexico.

Table 8.4a displays land inequality measured by the Gini coefficient for world regions from the 1950s to the 1990s (Deininger and Squire 1998). Latin America consistently shows the highest inequality in the world. In the 1990s, the Gini was 0.77 for Latin America, versus 0.42 for East Asia, 0.49 in sub-Saharan Africa, and 0.59 in the OECD countries, and was only surpassed

Table 8.4a. Land concentration (Gini coefficient) across regions of the world, 1950s–1990s

Region	1950s	1960s	1970s	1980s	1990s
Sub-Saharan Africa		48.6	56.9	47.7	49.0
East Asia and Pacific	44.8	47.3	48.9	46.9	42.1
OECD and high income	58.4	59.4	52.3	54.6	59.0
South Asia	67.8	59.6	62.0	61.4	58.4
Middle East and North Africa	78.3	64.6	71.9	67.5	
Latin America	82.0	81.2	81.3	80.5	77.4
Eastern Europe	62.0	52.4	75.1	98.0	92.0

Source: Deininger and Squire (1998: table 2).

Table 8.4b. Land concentration (Gini coefficient), Latin American countries, South Korea, and the USA, 1970s–2000s

Country	1970s	1980s	1990s	2000s	Average 1970–2000
Mexico	0.61*				0.61
Honduras	0.77*		0.66		0.72
Nicaragua				0.72	0.72
Bolivia	0.77*	0.77[†]			0.77
Uruguay	0.81*	0.80[†]		0.80	0.80
Costa Rica	0.81[†]				0.81
Colombia	0.83		0.89	0.80	0.84
Chile				0.84[‡]	0.84
Ecuador	0.84*				0.84
Argentina	0.86*		0.83		0.85
Brazil	0.84	0.85	0.85	0.85	0.85
Panama	0.89		0.82[†]		0.86
Peru	0.91		0.86		0.89
Venezuela	0.92*			0.88	0.90
Paraguay	0.86*	0.93	0.93		0.91
USA	0.72		0.71[‡]		0.72
South Korea	0.37	0.35	0.34		0.35

Note: Average includes all available figures between 1970 and 2000.

Sources: * Deininger and Olinto (2001), based on FAO, *World Censuses of Agriculture*. [†] De Ferranti et al. (2004: table A.39), based on Deininger and Olinto (2001) and UNDP (1993). [‡] Frankema (2005: appendix table 4), based on FAO, *World Censuses of Agriculture*. Otherwise, FAO, *World Censuses of Agriculture* (1970–2000).

by Eastern Europe after the post-socialist transformation. When countries are ranked based on land inequality, the top twenty include sixteen Latin American nations (Frankema 2005: 10).

Table 8.4b presents measures of land inequality for Latin American nations, South Korea, and the USA from the 1970s to 2000s. Among the countries of Latin America, the land Gini ranges from a low of 0.61 in Mexico, to a high of 0.90 in Venezuela and Paraguay. The lowest concentration figures are comparable to the USA, which features a Gini of 0.72, and are much higher than South Korea, with a Gini of 0.35. The discrepancy between income and land inequality is substantial in some countries. Argentina and Uruguay display relatively

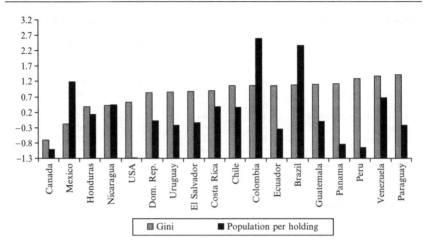

Figure 8.1. Standardized value of agricultural population per holding and land concentration (Gini coefficient), Latin American countries, USA, and Canada, 1960s–2000s

Note: Land concentration Gini and agricultural population per holding reported are the average of available figures from 1960s–2000s. Both values are standardized using the total world sample (54 countries) mean and standard deviation.

Sources: Authors' calculations based on Erickson and Vollrath (2004), FAO *World Censuses of Agriculture* (selected years), and Deininger and Olinto (2001).

high land concentration, in spite of having some of the lowest income inequality scores in the continent, a fact that is driven by the historical patterns of extensive cattle production (de Ferranti et al. 2004: 191).

Land inequality also highlights the relevance of agrarian reform in Latin America. Some of the countries displaying the lowest levels of land concentration, particularly Bolivia, Mexico, and Nicaragua, experienced the most extensive agrarian reform during the twentieth century (Cardoso and Helwege 1992: 261). The first Latin American country to implement agrarian reform was Mexico in the wake of the 1917 revolution. The Mexican experiment was followed by Bolivia and Cuba in the context of socialist revolutions in the mid-twentieth century, each benefiting some 70 per cent of the rural population. In the 1960s agrarian reform was promoted by the Alliance for Progress in an attempt to quell revolutionary fervour following the Cuban revolution; the deepest of these reforms was in Chile. An additional round of land reforms was instituted in Central America in the 1980s (Thiesenhusen 1995). The most extensive was in Nicaragua: land reform after the overthrow of the Somoza dictatorship in 1979 benefited some 30 per cent of rural households. In general, however, the effect of agrarian reform in Latin America has been limited when compared with that in other regions (Deininger 2003: xi).

A weakness of measures of land concentration using FAO data is that they are based on landowners only. A substantial number of rural Latin Americans, however, do not have access to land (Deininger 2003). In order to include the landless population, Erickson and Vollrath (2004) produced the agricultural population per holding (APH), calculated as the ratio of total rural population to number of holdings, based on the FAO Agricultural Censuses. A higher value of the APH indicates more restricted access to land and greater inequality. Figure 8.1 presents the standardized values of two measures of land inequality for Latin American countries: the Gini coefficients of land concentration among land-holders and the APH for the entire rural population. These two dimensions of land inequality are only weakly correlated (correlation coefficient = 0.06).

Two patterns of land inequality emerge in Figure 8.1. The most common one features high concentration among landholders, but relatively widespread access to land. This pattern applies to Chile, Costa Rica, the Dominican Republic, Ecuador, El Salvador, Guatemala, Panama, Paraguay, Peru, Uruguay, and Venezuela, and also to the USA and Canada. The second pattern—characteristic of the largest Latin American countries, Brazil, Mexico, and Colombia—displays a large landless rural population, but relatively low inequality among landholders (for the factors explaining this pattern in Brazil, see Assunção, Chapter 9, this volume). These findings highlight the relevance of distinguishing the two dimensions of land concentration in Latin America to understand different forms of rural inequality.

4 Capital Asset Ownership

In developed countries the value of investment and capital assets is consider-ably more concentrated than that of home equity (e.g., Wolff 2001: table 2.5; Headey et al. 2005) and we have no reason to believe that the story is different in Latin America. One way to estimate the value of capital assets when data are lacking is to extrapolate from investment income, inflating by a multiplier that reflects the rate of return to the asset (Davies and Shorrocks 2000: 642). We use questions about asset income in Latin American surveys to estimate the distribution of asset values. Since our focus is not on total wealth but on the distribution of different asset types across socio-economic strata, we do not adjust investment income by a multiplier, avoiding the serious difficulties of selecting an appropriate rate of return for the different asset categories.

The main problem with this approach is the downward bias in the estima-tion caused by non-reporting and underreporting of income, particularly among wealthy families (Szekely and Hilgert 1999).[4] While this is a problem in all countries, it is especially severe in Latin America because the wealthy

[4] This problem is well acknowledged in the estimation of household income in Latin America and routinely corrected using national account information. Correction is not pos-sible in the case of wealth given that estimation of total wealth holdings is dispersed in a number of sources (tax records, land registries, registrar and recorder offices, etc.), and com-prehensive balance sheets are not available to researchers.

Table 8.5. Households receiving income from selected investments, Latin American countries, c. 2000 (%)

	Share of household income derived from capital and profits	Proportion of households receiving income from selected assets		
		Rental property (includes land)	Stock dividends	Interests from deposits and savings
Argentina	3.0			
Bolivia	2.0	5.1	0.7	2.4*
Brazil	2.8	5.2	0.1	
Chile	11.5	6.1	0.4	1.5
Colombia	5.4	9.8	2.8*	
Dominican Republic	1.8			
Ecuador	3.3			
El Salvador	3.3			
Guatemala	2.7	4.1	0.5	
Mexico	1.6	3.8	0.1[†]	0.4
Nicaragua	2.5			
Panama	1.6			
Paraguay	2.4	3.3		
Peru	2.0			
Uruguay	3.4	4.4	0.4[†]	0.5*
Venezuela	1.8			

* Includes interest from loans.
[†] Includes bonds and mutual funds.

Sources: Column 1: De Ferranti et al. (2004: table A21); survey dates: Argentina (2001), Bolivia (1999), Brazil (2001), Chile (2000), Colombia (1999), Dominican Republic (1997), Ecuador (1998), El Salvador (2000), Guatemala (2000), Mexico (2000), Nicaragua (1998), Panama (2000), Paraguay (1999), Peru (2000), Uruguay (2000), Venezuela (1998). Columns 2–4: author's calculations based on household surveys; see the Appendix for survey descriptions.

tend to live in guarded residences or in gated communities, making access difficult for interviewers. This limited representation of the upper class in surveys is particularly consequential in Latin America, given the extreme concentration of income (IADB 1999; Portes and Hoffman 2003; Torche 2005). Thus, we agree with de Ferranti et al. (2004: 64) that 'capital income, land rents and profits are seriously underestimated in household surveys', and that calculations of asset concentration provide, at best, a lower bound.

With these caveats, we present two measures of investment asset inequality in Table 8.5. The first is the share of total household income that is attributable to capital, profits, and rents, compiled by de Ferranti et al. (2004: table A21) for sixteen Latin American countries. This income stream does not exceed 3 per cent of total income in most countries. The exceptions are Chile and Colombia, with shares of 11.5 per cent and 5.4 per cent, respectively. The second is the proportion of households receiving income from rental property, stocks, and interest from deposits and savings, which we calculated for the eight Latin American countries for which data are available. We restrict our analysis to these three types of asset, because they are the only comparable ones across countries. As can be seen in Table 8.5, a minority of households report income

Table 8.6. Distribution of investment income by household income percentiles, for types of investment income, Latin American countries

Country	Panel 1 Capital, rents, and profits					Panel 2 Rental property						Panel 3 Stock dividends						Panel 4 Interest from savings and deposits					
	Q1	Q2	Q3	Q4	Q5	Q1	Q2	Q3	Q4	Q5	D10	Q1	Q2	Q3	Q4	Q5	D10	Q1	Q2	Q3	Q4	Q5	D10
Argentina	1.5	4.6	7.4	16.3	70.3																		
Bolivia	0.5	2.0	5.9	15.7	75.8	1.6	5.7	6.5	12.5	73.7	57.1	0.0	0.0	0.1	0.9	98.9	97.1	0.5	3.2	6.7	9.4	80.3	67.9
Brazil	3.2	3.4	4.5	10.5	78.4	0.7	1.6	5.3	13.3	79.1	58.8	0.0	0.0	0.8	11.0	88.2	76.8						
Chile	0.0	0.0	1.1	9.7	89.1	1.4	3.8	6.1	15.9	72.7	56.4	1.2	1.3	2.2	4.4	90.8	76.3	3.0	3.7	3.5	7.1	82.7	76.1
Colombia	2.0	3.2	5.5	13.5	75.7	5.7	8.4	13.3	22.7	50.0	35.5	1.8	3.2	2.7	16.2	76.1	63.9						
Dominican Republic	4.4	6.4	8.8	16.4	63.9																		
Ecuador	1.2	3.1	4.5	8.7	82.5																		
El Salvador	2.1	3.2	4.0	9.9	80.8																		
Guatemala	0.1	0.2	1.4	2.3	95.9	0.0	0.1	0.1	0.8	98.9	96.6	0.0	0.0	0.0	0.1	99.9	99.0						
Mexico	1.6	1.8	6.0	7.1	83.4	2.5	1.9	4.5	7.4	83.7	79.9	0.0	0.0	0.2	0.2	99.6	99.1	1.5	1.7	0.2	1.8	94.7	87.2
Nicaragua	0.2	0.8	1.3	4.1	93.6																		
Panama	0.7	2.4	8.4	9.1	79.3																		
Paraguay	1.1	1.8	3.9	11.4	81.7	0.8	2.5	4.9	12.9	79.0	66.0												
Peru	0.8	2.9	5.6	12.3	78.5																		
Uruguay	0.6	2.2	5.2	10.8	81.2	1.3	2.1	3.8	7.0	85.8	79.9	0.0	0.0	0.0	0.1	99.9	99.5	0.2	0.1	0.6	2.5	96.6	94.0
Venezuela	3.6	7.4	8.9	12.1	68.1																		

Note: Sum across income quintiles adds up to 100 per cent for each income type. In Colombia stock dividends (panel 3) includes interests from loans. In Bolivia and Uruguay interest from savings and deposits include interest from loans. In Mexico and Uruguay dividends from stocks include bonds and mutual funds.

Sources: Panel 1: De Ferranti et al. (2004: table A37); survey dates are the following: Argentina (2001), Bolivia (1999), Brazil (2001), Chile (2000), Colombia (1999), Dominican Republic (1997), Ecuador (1998), El Salvador (1998), Guatemala (2000), Mexico (2000), Nicaragua (1998), Panama (2000), Paraguay (1999), Peru (2000), Uruguay (2000), Venezuela (1998). Panels 2–4: authors' calculations based on household surveys; see the Appendix for survey descriptions.

from these assets. This is the case even in countries that have well-developed financial systems such as Uruguay and Chile. The most widespread asset is rental property, and the proportion of households receiving income from this source ranges from 3.3 per cent in Paraguay to 9.8 per cent in Colombia. Asset scarcity is even more pronounced for financial resources such as stocks, with the proportion of households receiving income from this source ranging from 0.1 per cent in Brazil and Mexico to 0.7 per cent in Bolivia (the figure for Colombia includes interest from loans and therefore is not strictly comparable).

Given the high concentration of income in Latin America, it is expected that capital assets will also be clustered in the top percentiles. Table 8.6 presents the distribution of capital income sources by household income percentiles. The table covers 'capital, rents, and profits' for sixteen Latin American countries, produced by de Ferranti et al. (2004: table A37), as well as our estimates of the distribution of the three main sources of investment income (rental property, stocks, and deposits and savings), by quintile and for the top decile, for the eight Latin American countries with comparable survey data.

As expected, income from 'capital, rents, and profits' is concentrated in the top income quintile in all countries (panel 1). This category accounts for more than 80 per cent of asset income in the majority of Latin American countries, ranging from 68 per cent in Venezuela to 96 per cent in Guatemala (the comparable figure for investment asset concentration in the USA is 70.1 per cent).[5]

Concentration varies sharply across asset category. Inequality is particularly high for stocks; with the exception of Colombia the top decile's share exceeds 75 per cent in the seven countries for which information is available (however, as indicated, the figure for Colombia includes income from loans and it is not fully comparable). In Bolivia, Brazil, Mexico, and Uruguay, the four bottom quintiles have virtually no income from stocks. The asset that is most equally distributed is rental property, with the share of the top decile averaging 66 per cent, and ranging from a low of 36 per cent in Colombia to 97 per cent in Guatemala. In the case of Colombia, low inequality in real-estate income is driven by an active residential rental market; in other nations it is driven by widespread land rentals. This is particularly the case in Bolivia and Mexico, two countries that experienced extensive agrarian reform; in each, the share of rental income flowing to the top decile is approximately 40 per cent.

In summary, much more than housing wealth, financial and real-estate assets are highly concentrated in Latin America. As in developed countries, this is particularly the case for financial resources—stock, savings, and deposits—the most liquid form of equity. The counterpart of this high concentration is exclusion: the majority of households in the region appear not to

[5] The US estimate is for 'financial net worth' as defined in Wolff (2001: 36–7). This category is similar to capital or investment assets, as specified in the text, except for the inclusion of individual retirement accounts in the US figure. We thank Ed Wolff for calculating the US value.

have access to these forms of wealth. It is important to emphasize, however, that the survey information on investment income used in this section is limited. A more refined assessment requires adding dichotomous questions on financial, business, and real-estate ownership to the household surveys in the region, if not questions on monetary values.

5 Informal Capital and Property Rights

As indicated, an important characteristic of asset ownership in Latin America is that a large proportion of the population lacks legal title to land and home. In urban areas, 30–35 per cent of the population (up to 40–50 per cent in some of the largest cities) live in squatter settlements (Grimes 1976). The situation is not better in rural areas, where a large proportion of farmers also lack legal title. The proportion of farmers without a secure title is 39 per cent in Chile, 17 per cent in El Salvador, 37 per cent in Colombia, 44 per cent in Honduras, and 50 per cent in Paraguay (Lopez and Valdes 2000: table 1.1).

Prompted by the work of de Soto (1989, 2000) a vibrant debate has emerged about the relevance of formal title for household well-being and economic development. De Soto (2000: 35) argues that in the developing world the poor own significant amounts of property ($US9.3 trillion according to his calculations).[6] The assets are, however, 'dead capital' because the owners lack clear, enforceable property rights. This limits financial transactions and impedes the use of property as a consumption reserve or as collateral, thus hampering development.

Besides de Soto's calculations, there are no reliable estimates of how much wealth has been accumulated in the form of informal property across Latin America. Our discussion, therefore, will focus on the evidence about the relevance of legal title for wealth creation, cast in the larger context of the importance of property rights (North and Thomas 1973; North 1981; Johnson et al. 2002; Acemoglu and Johnson 2005). According to de Soto, widespread access to and enforcement of legal title is critical to reducing poverty in so far as property rights increase security from eviction or boundary disputes; and give new owners legal claims in the property transaction. Partly under the influence of de Soto's claims, land titling programmes have been launched in several Latin American countries. In Peru, property titles were given to 1.2 million urban households during the 1990s (World Bank 1998), and land titling programmes are currently being implemented in Colombia, Mexico, Honduras, Paraguay, and Brazil (Galiani and Schargrodsky 2006).

A recent set of studies in Latin America and other regions of the developing world assesses the effects of property rights on investment, real-estate values, access to credit, household income, and children's education in urban areas.

[6] However, see Woodruff (2001) for a critique.

The impact of land titles in rural areas appears to be mixed. Studies in Brazil (Alston et al. 1996), Ghana (Besley 1995), and Thailand (Feder et al. 1998) found that plot titling raised land values, facilitated investment in the plot, and improved access to credit. Somewhat more equivocal results were reported by Do and Iyer (2002), who concluded that the conferral of land rights in Vietnam led to an investment increase in plots in urban areas, but did not have an impact on agricultural productivity. A study in rural Paraguay (Carter and Olinto 2003) introduces a note of caution, finding that titling increased agricultural investment, but the effect varied across socio-economic groups; benefits accrued mainly to wealthy households.

Other research in rural areas, especially in sub-Saharan Africa, has detected little impact of titling on investment, land productivity, and access to credit (Pinckney and Kimuyu 1994; Brasselle et al. 2002; Place and Otsuka 2002). These authors argue that the weak effects of titling show that informal land-tenure arrangements can provide considerable investment security, especially in stable communities. A study by Lanjouw and Levy (2002) is important because it tests whether efficiency of informal property rights is an African particularity or also applies to Latin America. Based on data from Guayaquil, Ecuador, they found that land titling raised property values by 24 per cent. Nonetheless, informal property rights can effectively substitute for formal tenure. The importance of formal title appears to diminish when communities are more settled and have established informal governance structures. More vulnerable households (those with low education and income, little savings, and few years of residence) tend to benefit more from formal titles, because they appear to command less authority in an informal system.

In part, the mixed results have been attributed to the difficulty of addressing endogeneity of tenure status. Two case studies in Latin America are particularly relevant in so far as they deal with potential endogeneity of property rights by using natural experiments in which titles were allocated randomly. Field (2005) analysed the effect of a nationwide titling programme in Peru in the late 1990s, which provided titles to about 1.2 million urban households. She found that obtaining a title led to an increase in the rate of housing renovation of more than two-thirds. However, the effect of titling on access to credit was small and mostly driven by government credit (Field and Torero 2004). Similar small effects on the formation of a healthy housing market and on access to credit have been reported in Colombia by Gilbert (2002). In the second study, Galiani and Schargrodsky (2006) used a natural experiment to explore the effects of titles given to poor squatters in Buenos Aires. They found that titling resulted in increased housing investment, reduced household size, and improved children's education. The effects on credit access, however, were modest.

In sum, these studies in Latin America and in other developing countries suggest that: (1) land titling has positive effects on investment and access to credit; (2) the impact of land titling on living standards (measured by income or welfare indices) is quite small; and (3) the effect of formal titling depends substantially on the strength of informal arrangements and is more effective for households or in communities unable to enforce their informal rights.

6 Historical Sources of Wealth Inequality in Latin America

To explore the roots of high wealth concentration in Latin America we use a comparative historical perspective based on the work of the economic historians Engerman and Sokoloff (Engerman and Sokoloff 1997, 2002; Engerman et al. 1999; Engerman et al. 2000: 108–34; Sokoloff and Engerman 2000; also see de Ferranti et al. 2004 for a summary). This perspective highlights the influence of initial factor endowments in colonial times on the unequal distribution of assets, especially the control of land and labour. The initial concentration of assets in the hands of a small *criollo* elite gave rise to institutions through which the elite maintains its privilege. This perspective suggests the continuous influence of colonial conditions via two avenues. First, elite ownership of land and natural resources was successfully 'converted' into urban-based assets in the nineteenth and twentieth centuries. Second, institutions supported by the initial concentration of wealth have persisted over time, preventing access to capital, non-land property, education, and political power by the majority of the population.

The basic tenet in this approach is that variation in factor endowments— broadly defined to include size and quality of land, climate, and available native population—gave rise to sharply different productive and social regimes, characterized by varying levels of inequality. To this, the features of the colonizing powers should be added: Mercantilist Spain focused on resource extraction in areas where large native populations could provide free labour, while liberal Britain promoted profit making through market exchange (Lange et al. 2006). Three productive regimes can be distinguished in the Americas on the basis of factor endowments and characteristics of the colonizing powers. The first, prevalent in the Caribbean and parts of South America (especially Brazil), had climate and soil well suited to the production of staple crops and was characterized by large economies of scale, as in sugar, tobacco, and coffee production. These conditions encouraged the use of African slaves. The established social structure thus consisted of a small elite and a large number of slaves with minimal human capital; this resulted in a massive concentration of resources. When slavery was abolished in the mid-nineteenth century, the concentration of land, education, and other assets in the white elite remained pervasive (Skidmore 1999: 70).

The second regime can be associated with Spanish colonies such as Mexico and Peru. In these areas, a large native population survived contact with the Europeans, and the Spanish Crown allocated to European settlers large plots of lands, mineral resources, and the rights to enslaved native labour and tribute (institutionalized as the *encomienda* or *mita* systems). As in the first regime, this type of productive organization gave rise to the concentration of resources, and a sharp dichotomy along racial (European/indigenous) lines. In contrast, a very different productive regime developed in northern USA and Canada. There, the geographic and soil characteristics and the scarcity of native populations did not provide comparative advantages for large-scale crops, but was conducive to small-scale grain production. Given the abundant land and low capital requirements, most households were able to operate as independent producers. Additionally, the population was mostly of European descent and had roughly similar human capital, in comparison with sharp disparities among peoples in the other two regimes. This agrarian system provided the basis for a social structure of small, relatively equal landholders (Engerman and Sokoloff 2002: 60).[7]

In the two Latin American regimes, high asset concentration allowed elites to establish an institutional framework that favoured the maintenance of privilege. In the northern USA and Canada, in contrast, the relative equality of resources generated a dispersal of power and promoted the formation of equalitarian institutions. Two early institutional arrangements were particularly relevant for solidifying inequality in Latin America: land policy and immigration policy. Governments in the Spanish and Portuguese colonies distributed land through grants of large plots, fostering concentration, whereas, in the northern USA and Canada, sales of small plots were prevalent. Subsequent land policies continued these initial paths. In the USA the Homestead Act of 1862 made household farm-sized plots free to all who settled and worked the land; in Canada, the Dominion Lands Act of 1872 did the same. Nothing like these policies was implemented in Latin America, with the partial exception of Argentina.

Immigration policy was also critical. The British, responding to labour scarcity in the colonies, actively encouraged immigration from England and other European countries to their colonies, generating a diversified white population. In contrast, the Spanish Crown tightly controlled immigration, under the influence of the local *criollo* elites who resisted competition. This restrictive stance was possible because there was a substantial supply of native labour. Only in the nineteenth century did the Hispanic colonies promote immigration, but at that point most migrants chose to go to North America, lured by greater opportunity.

---

[7] Conditions were different in the American south (see Engerman and Sokoloff 2002: 60–1).

In terms of political institutions, the Latin American elites successfully blocked the expansion of voting rights. As late as the early twentieth century none of the Latin American countries had a secret ballot and only a minuscule proportion of the population voted, ranging from 4 per cent in Bolivia to 18 per cent in Costa Rica (Engerman and Sokoloff 2002: 74). In contrast, in the USA and Canada, initial equality among settlers provided the basis for the early expansion of democracy. The USA and Canada were pioneers in eliminating property and literacy restrictions to voting, and in implementing secret ballots. By the early twentieth century about 40 per cent of the Canadian and US populations typically voted in national elections.

Canada and the USA also became pioneers in the expansion of primary education. By the mid-nineteenth century, every locality in the northern USA had free schools, open to all white children and supported by general taxes. By 1900 the literacy rate was 90 per cent in the USA for whites. In contrast, the Latin American elites fiercely resisted taxation for educational purposes and opposed educational expansion. As a result, even in the most highly educated Latin American countries the literacy rate reached only some 50 per cent in 1900 (for example, 52 per cent in Argentina, 43 per cent in Chile, 54 per cent in Uruguay). And in the Latin American countries with the lowest educational attainment, only a small minority was literate in that year: 17 per cent in Bolivia, and 15 per cent Guatemala (Engerman et al. 2000).

In terms of capital formation, financial institutions developed very early in North America, facilitating the ability of the population to use land as collateral. The government prevented monopoly concentration, leading to competition among numerous small banks. In contrast, in Latin America, where the elite retained vast political power, the chartering of banks was tightly controlled by the central government, leading to monopolistic financial systems. This institutional set-up greatly reduced access to credit, savings, and investment capital.

In summary, we suggest that the initial conditions of colonization led to the formation of institutions that served to maintain high levels of wealth concentration in Latin America. However, during the nineteenth century, at the time of achieving independence from Spain, liberal elites rose to power and tried to implement progressive policies across the region, giving rise to a 'liberal reform' period (Mahoney 2001). Concerned about the high level of land concentration, and inspired by the examples of North America and Europe, these liberal elites sought to reduce inequality, but their attempts failed dramatically. Examples of the failure can be found in Mexico, Brazil, and Bolivia. In Mexico the so-called Lerdo Law (1856) prohibited ecclesiastical and civil institutions from owning property not used in day-to-day operations (Meyer and Sherman 1987). As a consequence, a vast amount of land controlled by the Catholic Church was put up for auction. Intended by liberals to weaken the Church and by conservatives to increase government revenue, the law produced neither. The land was not purchased by peasants, but by large proprietors and foreign investors, resulting in increased inequality. A similar failed reform took place in Brazil, where a law intended to reduce inequality instead favoured land concentration (Dean 1971). In Bolivia, an 1874 law turned all communal Indian land into individual holdings; the land was then largely appropriated by the elite (Klein 1993; Thiesenhusen 1995). By the early twentieth century, the institutionally ingrained patterns of social exclusion in Latin America prevented the region from joining the trend towards greater equality experienced in Europe and the USA (Morrison 2000; Piketty and Saez 2003) and led to the persistence of high asset concentration in this region.

7 Summary and Conclusions

While inequalities in education, earnings, and income have been extensively studied in Latin America, relatively little is known about the distribution of wealth in this region. This chapter provides an introductory survey. Given the lack of data on household net worth, we use published data and our own analysis of household surveys in fourteen Latin American countries to produce estimates of the distribution of land, housing wealth, and financial assets. We also discuss the prevalence and consequences of lacking legal title for owned property and the historical roots of wealth concentration in the region. We find that access to home ownership is widespread, with very little variation across income levels. This sharply contrasts with patterns in developed countries such as the USA and the UK, where home ownership is highly stratified by income. The explanation of the Latin American pattern is to be found in the prevalence of squatting settlements and untitled tenure, and in effective public housing programmes in some countries such as Costa Rica and Chile. However, when the value of the dwellings is analysed, we find high concentration and a significant correlation with household income. Still, concentration of housing wealth among the top income percentiles is less than that of income itself.

Examination of land ownership in Latin America indicates the importance of distinguishing two dimensions of the distribution of land: access to land and concentration among landowners. These two dimensions correlate weakly, suggesting that country-specific historical and institutional factors determine the type of inequality in different nations. The largest countries—Brazil, Mexico, Colombia—feature very restricted access to land and therefore a large landless population, but relatively less inequality among landowners. When concentration among landowners is analysed in an international comparative perspective, Latin American countries consistently rank among the most unequal in the world.

Financial assets are the most unequally distributed type of wealth in Latin America. Indeed, we find a pattern of sharp concentration in the top percentiles and exclusion of the vast majority of the population—up to 90 per cent concentration at the top in some countries.

The historical section claims that the substantial concentration of wealth in Latin America has roots in the colonial structure of natural resource accumulation by a small European elite. This distributional pattern was sustained over time through exclusionary economic, political, and educational institutions that guaranteed the maintenance of privilege.

Our empirical analyses rely on survey information, and use actual or estimated income from different asset types to estimate their value. This is undoubtedly an imperfect approach, subject to random and, probably, systematic error. More precise analyses would require specialized surveys, such as those conducted in India or China, and other sources of data, such as balance sheets and tax returns (for a review, see Davies and Shorrocks 2000, 2005).

Important advances can be attained, however, with minor modifications of survey data routinely collected in Latin America. For instance, asking homeowners the follow-up question 'do you have a legal title for this property?' would permit ascertaining the extent of formal property ownership. Also, adding questions for homeowners about estimated rent and estimated market value of dwelling to all national surveys would permit international comparisons, and it would provide the basis to conduct sensitivity analysis of proxies of monetary value of properties. Finally, a simple set of dichotomous questions about ownership/non-ownership of different types of assets, such as land, commercial real estate, holiday homes, bank deposits, stocks, bonds, etc. could be added to standard household surveys. These questions are less affected by problems of recall, refusal, reliability, and stability endemic in enquiries about value of household assets.

In addition to better data, the application of innovative methods can yield important progress in the study of the wealth distribution in Latin America. Strategies such as the estate multiplier approach (see, e.g., Pinto 2006 for the Brazilian city of Campinas), and principal component, factor, or multiple correspondence analysis of a set of assets (such as those used by Spilerman and Torche (2004), Torche and Spilerman (2006), and Burger et al., Chapter 12, this volume), can provide useful estimates of household wealth when direct measures of net worth are unavailable. Naturally, no data source or method is perfect, and all have important limitations. However, their combination will certainly help refine wealth estimates in Latin America and will produce increasingly accurate bounds on the quantities of interest. We hope that this introductory survey will motivate research on the thus far largely neglected topic of wealth distributions in Latin America, and on its effects on the living standards and opportunities of people in the region.

Appendix

Table 8.A1. Household surveys, coverage and characteristics, Latin America

Country	Year	Name	Coverage	Sample size (households)
Argentina	2003	Permanent Household Survey	Urban	16,924
Bolivia	2002	Living Standards Survey	National	5,746
Brazil	2002–3	Survey of Family Budgets	National	48,470
Chile	2003	National Socioeconomic Characterization Survey	National	68,153
Colombia	1997	Survey of Quality of Life	National*	9,121
Costa Rica	2004	Household Survey of Multiple Purposes	National	43,779
Ecuador	1998	Living Standards Measurement Survey	National	5,760
Guatemala	2000	Living Standards Measurement Survey	National	8,046
Mexico	2004	National Survey of Household Income and Expenditure	National	22,595
Nicaragua	2001	Living Standards Measurement Survey	National	4,191
Panama	2003	Living Standards Measurement Survey	National	8,000
Paraguay	2004	Integrated Household Survey	National	7,823
Peru	2004	National Household Survey	National	5,093
Uruguay	2004	Continuous Household Survey	Urban	6,363

* Except for the housing module, which includes only 'cabeceras municipales'.

Source: See text.

9

Land Reform and Land Holdings in Brazil

Juliano Assunção

1 Introduction

The distribution of wealth is extremely unequal in Brazil—the Gini coefficient is the highest (0.784) among the countries reported in Davies et al. (Chapter 19, this volume). Throughout Brazilian history, wealth has been largely associated with land. At the very beginning of colonization, only thirty years after the discovery, the Portuguese Crown divided the huge territory into large tracts of land that were donated to grantees with hereditary succession. This pattern is persistent and today Brazil has one of the most skewed land distributions in the world. Facing the challenge of reducing inequality of land ownership and intensifying land use, the Brazilian government began a land-reform programme in 1964, with the enactment of the Land Act. There have been important differences in the implementation of that programme through time and space.

This chapter studies the structure of land ownership and land distribution in Brazil, investigating the consequences of the land-reform programme as it was implemented in the 1990s. The empirical strategy is based on the use of time and space variation of the land-reform programme as a means of identifying a causal impact of land reform on land ownership and inequality. This strategy is implemented with household-level data from the National Household Survey (PNAD), covering the period 1992–2002 (except 1994 and 2000), and land disappropriations reported by the National Institute for Rural Settlement and Agrarian Reform (Brazil) (INCRA).

I gratefully acknowledge the comments from James Davies, Carmen Deere, Patrick Honohan, Branko Milanovic, John Muellbauer, Daniel Waldenström, and other contributors to the UNU-WIDER project meeting 'Personal Assets from a Global Perspective', Helsinki, 4–6 May 2006. Also, I would like to thank Michel Azulai and Flavia Feres for providing excellent research assistance. All errors are my own.

The main findings of the study are the following. The investigation of the effect of the land reform on landownership suggests that (1) there has been no increase in the access to land of the typical Brazilian rural household; and (2) the effect is differentiated with respect to household income and the educational level of the household head—there has been an increase in land ownership of the poorest households and those with the least educated heads, and a decrease for the other classes of rural households. Concentrating on the families with land holdings, the analysis of the land-reform effect provides evidence of an increase of land inequality. This result is obtained both with the decomposition of the effect of land reform by household income group and using quantile regression analysis. Land reform seems to reduce the size of holdings for small landowners (poor households) and to increase the size of holdings for those above the median (richer households).

These results should contribute to a better understanding of the impact of redistributive land reform in Latin America. Although there is a vast literature addressing land reform and agrarian organization, there is relatively little evidence about the Latin American experience (Binswanger and Deininger 1997; Carter and Zegarra 2000; Deininger and Feder 2001; and Torche and Spilerman, Chapter 8, this volume). Although some authors—such as Conning (2001) and Conning and Robinson (2001)—have constructed models that exhibit features often observed in Latin America to analyse agrarian organization and land reform, most of the literature considers general aspects or case studies from Asia (Horowitz 1993; Grossman 1994; Besley and Burgess 2000; Banerjee et al. 2002).

The study is presented in six sections. Section 1 presents the historical determinants of land concentration in Brazil. Section 2 describes the institutional background regarding the Brazilian land-reform programme. Data are depicted in Section 3. Section 4 investigates the correlation between land and wealth indicators. Sections 5 and 6 evaluate the impact of the reform on land ownership and land inequality, respectively. A summary of the results and final remarks are presented in the conclusion section.

2 Historical Determinants of the Land Distribution and Land Access in Brazil

The highly concentrated Brazilian land distribution is deeply rooted in the colonization process. In the 1530s, inspired by the success of land settlements in the Madeira Islands, Portugal's King João III divided Brazil into fifteen territories called *capitanias hereditárias* (hereditary captaincies)—areas donated to Portuguese grantees (captains) with hereditary succession. Each captain had complete authority over his land. However, owing to a series of obstacles, only a few *capitanias* remained intact through the generations, and six of the captains never took possession of their claims (Bueno 1999).

Another wave of settlements occurred in the seventeenth century, with the increase in the global demand for sugar. In another land-concentrating initiative, the Crown offered large tracts of land (*sesmarias*) freely to Portuguese grantees in order to encourage settlement and production. The holders of *sesmarias* experienced complete property rights over their holdings whenever land was kept under cultivation. It is worth noting that such a condition regarding land use remained throughout Brazil's history and was reasserted in the constitution of 1988. The *sesmaria* system ended in 1822 with Brazilian independence (Alston and Mueller 2003).

From 1822 to 1850 no land policy changes took place and settlers obtained land by squatting, enforcing their claims by social norms. In 1850 the landowners of the coffee plantations passed the Land Act, which set the pattern for modern land holding. The Land Act of 1850 forbade the colonial practice of obtaining land through squatting, limiting the acquisition to purchase. All existing squatters were legalized and, surprisingly, all *sesmarias* were revalidated (Alston and Mueller 2003). Concentration of land was the rule, and the great majority of the people (especially after the 1888 abolition of slavery) were forced to work on large plantations and farms without any hope of acquiring a small farm of their own.

In addition to the heritage from the colonial period, the macroeconomic environment since the 1970s the last forty years has played a key role as a determinant of land distribution in Brazil. The following analysis considers land holdings as a hedge against inflation and macroeconomic instabilities, both of which tend to set a wedge between the price of land and the capitalized value of the income stream generated from agriculture. Especially in periods of high macroeconomic instability, people demand land as a mechanism of protection against aggregate uncertainty. Assunção (2008) argues that this feature, coupled with imperfections in the land rental market, leads to inefficiently high concentration of land holdings. The existence of a non-agricultural component in the demand for land is identified through the comparison between land prices and rental rates of croplands and pastures—while an increase in macroeconomic instability raises the land prices, the same is less likely to occur with the rental rates. The study shows that the heterodox economic plans launched in the 1980s and 1990s to contain inflation[1] promoted significant increases in land prices for sales of both meadows and

---

[1] The implementation of economic plans aimed specifically at containing inflationary inertia through a set of measures including the de-indexation of the economy, temporary price freezes, and a freeze on financial assets to reduce the economy's liquidity and generate resources for the budget. The uncertainty introduced into the economy by those drastic measures generated a large shift in the demand for safe assets, including land.

cropland in the current and next semester, accounting for more than 15 per cent of the total variability of these prices from 1966 to 2000. The effects upon rental rates are much smaller and even statistically insignificant for cropland.

This suggests that the response of land sale prices to an exogenous increase in macroeconomic instability is larger than the response to rental rates, which is consistent with the existence of a non-agricultural purpose of land holding. For pastures, the economic plans have caused an increase of almost 40 per cent in land prices of sales in the current semester and up to 50 per cent in the next one. The rental rates have experienced a much lower increase, around 20 per cent. For cropland, there were significant increments only for land prices, both in the current and in subsequent semesters.

The pattern of land concentration and its roots in colonial history are also observed in many other Latin American countries. Torche and Spilerman (Chapter 8, this volume) discuss the salient features of the land distribution in Latin America in comparison to other parts of the world.

3 Brazilian Land Reform

3.1 *A Brief History*

Recent land-reform history in Brazil begins with the Land Act of 1964, brought about by the military regime. The long and comprehensive text embodied a detailed plan for agrarian reform. The law created the Brazilian Institute for Agrarian Reform (IBRA) and the National Institute for Agricultural Development (INDA) in order to carry out the Act. In 1971 IBRA and INDA were merged into the National Institute for Rural Settlement and Agrarian Reform (INCRA). The Act was a means of defusing the pressure for land redistribution created by social movements, especially the 'peasant leagues', and the emerging activism of Catholic priests. The political context in Latin America in the early 1960s was characterized by peasant militancy and threats of agrarian rebellion. However, instead of redistributing property, the economic strategy of the military regime aimed at the modernization of large land holdings with the help of subsidized rural credit. Soybean cultivation—the main target of the rural policies—generated large surpluses for export and, simultaneously, resulted in the absorption of small farmers by medium- and large-sized properties, concentrating the land distribution.

With the return of democracy in 1985, the first National Agrarian Reform Plan (1985–9) was prepared and launched, establishing the unrealistic target of settling 1.4 million families in five years. But, as shown in Table 9.1, the Sarney government disappropriated less than 5 million hectares, only a little more than 10 per cent of the initial proposal. On the other hand, Sarney's

Table 9.1. Land-reform expropriation processes, Brazil, 1979–2003

Brazilian presidents	Brazil		North region		North-east region		Central-west region		South-east region		South region	
	No. of events	Total area	No. of events	Total area	No. of events	Total area	No. of events	Total area	No. of events	Total area	No. of events	Total area
J. Figueiredo (Mar. 1979–Mar. 1985)	131	2,845,029	21	1,503,700	34	488,966	26	532,296	11	47,557	39	272,510
J. Sarney (Mar. 1985–Mar. 1990)	701	4,811,507	128	1,789,716	258	1,276,426	89	1,290,367	85	281,368	141	173,630
F. Collor de Mello (Mar. 1990–Oct. 1992)	7	15,065	2	5,550	0	0	3	3,041	1	3,584	1	2,890
I. Franco (Oct. 1992–Jan. 1995)	245	1,365,263	36	402,473	113	476,309	48	419,772	15	30,746	33	35,962
F. H. Cardoso I (Jan. 1995–Jan. 1999)	2,323	7,561,048	358	2,181,950	999	2,260,640	431	2,414,377	253	442,025	282	262,056
F. H. Cardoso II (Jan. 1999–Jan. 2003)	1,265	2,785,296	186	511,376	633	1,175,412	189	775,182	156	249,238	101	74,089

Note: Total area in hectares.

Source: INCRA (1999).

government determined the first of two significant waves of disappropriations in recent Brazilian history.

In the following Collor government the programme came to a halt—only 15,065 hectares were disappropriated. With the impeachment of Collor and the substitution of a new president in 1995, the land reform process was resumed and more than 20,000 families were settled on almost 1.5 million hectares. During his first term of office (1995–8), President Fernando Henrique Cardoso accelerated the rhythm of the settlements. As shown in Table 9.1, more than 7.5 million hectares were disappropriated in the period.[2] Table 9.1 shows that the disappropriation wave undertaken in Cardoso's administration is substantially different from the disappropriations under the Sarney government. While the disappropriated areas in each year of the two governments are comparable, the number of processes established under Cardoso is much higher, suggesting that the settlements were more decentralized across the Brazilian territories. The period was also characterized by conflicts and land invasions, mostly associated with the Landless Workers' Movement, which is the largest social movement in Latin America with more than 1.5 million members. In the second term of Cardoso's administration the focus of land reform changed from the disappropriation model to a new form of 'negotiated land reform' (Deininger 1998).

Figure 9.1 shows the spatial distribution of the disappropriations during the Cardoso period. The process is clearly heterogeneous, restricted to subregions of the country. In order to focus our analysis on the areas where the process was more concentrated, a sub-sample of selected Brazilian states is built. This study evaluates the consequences of this modern wave of land redistribution based on disappropriations, covering the period 1992–2002 and corresponding to the governments of Itamar Franco and Fernando Henrique Cardoso.

3.2 Land Disappropriation: Procedures and Costs

Introduced by the Land Act, the land disappropriation legislation was significantly changed by Brazil's 1988 Constitution. Since then, only unproductive land is under the risk of disappropriation, for which the state needs to pay a 'fair price'. After the 1993 amendment, the 'fair price' became the 'market price'. Therefore, at the same time that there is a permit of confiscation, the government needs to pay the market price, which, in principle, is determined by buyers and sellers rather than anything else.

---

[2] The official report indicates that the first Cardoso government settled landless households on 12 million hectares. On the other hand, the data on disappropriation process from INCRA indicate 7.5 million hectares. The difference of 4.5 million hectares (37%) may be due to settlements on public lands or even to errors in the computation of the 12 million hectares.

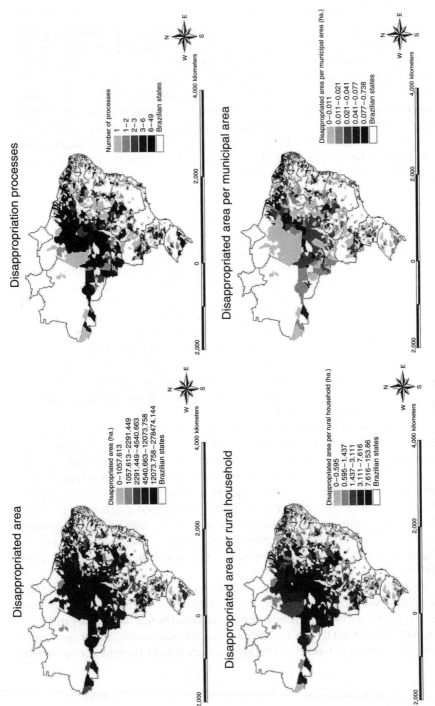

Figure 9.1. Land disappropriation in Cardoso's government, Brazil

This conceptual confusion in the legislation of disappropriation along with other institutional failures imposed high costs on the land reform. According to INCRA (1999), the final cost stipulated by the judicial system in the end of a disappropriation process is, on average, five times the initial evaluation. In the south-eastern part of the country the average multiplier was 14. Reydon (2000) describes eight necessary steps of the disappropriation process. The process begins with an act signed by the Brazilian president and finishes, usually, with a judicial decision. There are three issues addressed in the judicial demands: the items to be compensated, the amount of the indemnity, and the form of payment (public bonds versus cash).

4 Data

The following analysis is based on combined data from two sources. The first is the database on the disappropriation processes publicly available on the INCRA's website.[3] The data comprise the date, farm's name, area, and municipality of each approved process of land disappropriation since 1979. The second source of information is the National Household Survey (PNAD), collected annually[4] since 1981 by the Brazilian Census Bureau (IBGE). Since 1992 the PNAD survey has provided information on land holdings and, therefore, the period considered in the analysis is 1992–2002. The sample consists of all rural households available in the PNAD survey, from 1992 to 2002. The information across years refers to repeated cross-sections. It is not possible to form a panel with PNAD data.

For each household, there is information on land holdings, household-head characteristics, spouse characteristics, and household characteristics. Since the PNAD survey is representative at the state level, the information of each household is combined with information on land disappropriation in the corresponding state in the previous year. It is assumed, implicitly, that settlements take about one year after the disappropriation to be established. The results are robust to the use of different lags of the information about land reform. Actually, the disappropriation in the current year is highly correlated with disappropriation in the previous year or two years before.

Table 9.2 reports the variables considered in the analysis and gives their summary statistics. We consider two main dependent variables: a binary variable indicating whether the household owns land or not, and the logarithm of land-holding area. Of the 131,775 households in the sample, 39 per cent held a positive amount of land. The average farm size was 41 hectares for those with

---

[3] www.incra.gov.br. [4] Except for the years of 1991, 1994, and 2000.

Table 9.2. Description of the variables

Variables	Obs	Mean	Std Dev.	Min	Max
Dummy (household with land holdings=1)	131775	0.3948473	0.48882	0	1
Total area of the land holdings	131775	16.56629	149.48	0	10000
Log (total area of the land holdings)	52031	11.25869	1.72691	0	18
Dummy (positive disappropriation until the previous year=1)	131775	0.7775223	0.41591	0	1
Disappropriated area per rural household in the state until the previous year	102458	0.0001445	0.00034	0	2.56E-03
Log (disappropriated area per rural household until the previous year)	102458	−9.85296	1.27841	−13.554	−5.967
Household head characteristics					
Gender	131775	0.8706887	0.33555	0	1
Age	131757	46.59258	16.0858	10	106
Years of schooling	131589	3.44639	2.95841	1	16
Dummy (employer=1)	115555	0.0461598	0.20983	0	1
Dummy (employee=1)	115555	0.4219116	0.49387	0	1
Dummy (self-employed=1)	115555	0.4730648	0.49928	0	1
Income	128465	417.0069	833.528	0.000	43032.780
Spouse characteristics					
Dummy (spouse is present=1)	131775	0.7849972	0.41083	0	1
Gender	103443	0.013727	0.16513	0	1
Age	103429	39.84355	14.4284	11	98
Years of schooling	103179	4.053121	3.06749	1	16
Income	103111	83.39452	277.456	0	22258
Number of household members	131775	4.140178	2.1597	1	24
Number of members above 60 years old	131775	0.3645987	0.65412	0	6
Number of members under 10 years old	131775	1.073899	1.29223	0	10
Household characteristics					
Per capita income	127691	174.228	348.246	0	16749
Dummy (lives on own land=1)	92928	0.8836949	0.32059	0	1
Dummy (access to piped water=1)	131274	0.472226	0.49923	0	1
Dummy (house with bathroom=1)	131271	0.6342223	0.48165	0	1
Dummy (access to electricity=1)	131267	0.6907905	0.46217	0	1
Dummy (has water filter=1)	131265	0.4307774	0.49519	0	1
Dummy (has colour TV=1)	131271	0.3636523	0.48105	0	1
Dummy (has refrigerator=1)	131255	0.4637538	0.49869	0	1

Source: IBGE, National Household Surveys (PNAD) (various).

land holdings.[5] The main independent variables in this study are those with information on land reform. There are two variables measuring land disappropriation in the state in the previous year. The first one is a dummy variable indicating whether or not there was any disappropriation in the state, until the previous year. More than three-quarters of the sample had at least one disappropriation process in their state. The second variable aims at capturing the intensity of the disappropriation, and it is defined as the ratio between the disappropriated area (measured in hectares) and the number of rural households of each state until the previous period. There are also three sets

---

[5] If we include the households with no land, the average becomes 16.6 hectares, as shown in Table 9.2.

of control variables regarding characteristics of the household, household head, and spouse.

5 Wealth and Land

This section assesses the relationship between land and wealth indicators in Brazil. Since there is no information on personal assets, the focus is restricted to an approximation of household wealth. This approximation is comprised by three components. The first component is the per capita household income. Under imperfect credit markets, expected household income is an increasing function of wealth (Banerjee and Newman 1993; Galor and Zeira 1993). Thus, information on the total household income reflects, to some extent, information on family wealth. The first column of Table 9.3 presents a regression of the logarithm of household land holdings on the logarithm of per capita income. The estimated coefficient suggests a very tight relationship between income and land, statistically significant at 1 per cent. In the next two columns, Table 9.3 shows the relationship between land and other components of household wealth. The second wealth component consists of

Table 9.3. The relationship between wealth indicators and land holding

Dependent variable: log (area of the household land holdings)				
	(1)	(2)	(3)	(4)
Log (per capita income)	0.569***	0.460***	0.400***	0.317***
	(0.007)	(0.008)	(0.008)	(0.012)
Dummy (has water filter=1)		0.293***	0.270***	0.165***
		(0.015)	(0.015)	(0.015)
Dummy (has colour TV=1)		0.067***	0.095***	−0.021
		(0.020)	(0.019)	(0.020)
Dummy (has refrigerator=1)		0.462***	0.422***	0.244***
		(0.018)	(0.022)	(0.023)
Dummy (access to piped water=1)			0.508***	0.402***
			(0.021)	(0.022)
Dummy (house with bathroom=1)			0.299***	0.212***
			(0.019)	(0.020)
Dummy (access to electricity=1)			−0.620***	−0.570***
			(0.020)	(0.021)
Household head characteristics	No	No	No	Yes
Spouse characteristics	No	No	No	Yes
Household characteristics	No	No	No	Yes
Constant	8.879***	9.070***	9.319***	7.409***
	(0.037)	(0.038)	(0.038)	(0.217)
Year dummies	Yes	Yes	Yes	Yes
Observations	48957	48860	48859	40860
R-squared	0.13	0.16	0.19	0.26

* significant at 10%; ** significant at 5%; *** significant at 1%.

Note: Robust standard errors in parentheses.

Source: IBGE, National Household Surveys (PNAD) (various).

durable goods: water filter, colour TV, and refrigerator. And the third wealth component on which there is information in the PNAD survey is related to the value of houses and, in particular, to the housing infrastructure. The underlying assumption of this exercise is that wealthier families live in better equipped houses, both in terms of durable goods and in terms of infrastructure.

Column (2) of Table 9.3 shows that the presence of all durable goods is highly correlated with land. Moreover, when information on durable goods is incorporated in the regression, the coefficient of income is reduced from 0.569 to 0.460. This is evidence that income in column (1) reflects part of the household wealth that is incorporated in column (2). The same seems to occur with the introduction of information about infrastructure in column (3). The only exception is access to electricity, which has a statistically significant and negative coefficient. The results might reflect the fact that households with larger tracts of land are located in more isolated areas. In this case, access to electricity is more related more to urbanization than to wealth. Finally, in column (4), all available information about the characteristics of the household head and spouse is introduced in the regression to control for observed heterogeneity. Even after controlling for all these characteristics, land remains highly correlated with the three wealth components: per capita income, durable goods, and infrastructure. Thus, the following analysis of land distribution can, roughly speaking, also be interpreted as a study of the wealth distribution in Brazil.

6 Land Reform and Land Ownership

This section estimates the impact of land reform on the fraction of rural households with land holdings, through household-level data. The sample comprises all surveyed rural households, whether they held a positive amount of land or not, for the period from 1992 to 2002. Households are pooled across years—that is, households of different periods are considered distinct. The results are estimated considering the following linear probability model:[6]

$$\Pr\{L_i > 0 | D_i, X_i\} = \alpha \cdot I\{D_i > 0\} + \gamma \cdot \log(D_i) \cdot I\{D_i > 0\} + \beta' X_i \qquad (9.1)$$

where L_i stands for the total area owned by household i, $I\{D_i > 0\}$ is a binary variable indicating whether or not there is disappropriation until the previous year in the state where household i lives, $\log(D_i) I\{D_i > 0\}$ is the logarithm of the disappropriated area per rural household in the state with positive disappropriation until the previous year, and X_i is a vector of control variables

---

[6] For ease of notation, it is considered $\log(0) \cdot 0 = 0$ in the interpretation of (9.1).

including household-head characteristics, spouse characteristics, household characteristics, and year dummies.

Under the assumption that, given the observed characteristics, the disappropriation until the previous year is not correlated with the unobserved determinants of land holding, parameters α and γ measure the effect of land reform on the fraction of rural households with land holdings. Manipulating (9.1) it is possible to show that:

$$\alpha = \Pr\{L_i > 0 \mid D_i > 0, X_i\} - \Pr\{L_i > 0 \mid D_i = 0, X_i\} \tag{9.2}$$

and

$$\gamma = \frac{d\Pr\{L_i > 0 \mid D_i > 0, X_i\}}{d\log(D_i)} = \frac{d\Pr\{L_i > 0 \mid D_i > 0, X_i\}}{\frac{dD_i}{D_i}}. \tag{9.3}$$

Thus, the parameter α measures the effect of the first disappropriated hectare per rural household on the fraction of rural families with land holding, and the parameter α represents the effect of a 1 per cent change in the disappropriated area per rural household on land ownership. Results from the estimation of (9.1) are presented in Table 9.4, considering nested specifications for the vector of control variables. In column (1), which controls only for the year dummies, the existence of land disappropriation in the previous year has an effect of 31.7 percentage points on the fraction of households with land. The effect of 1 per cent of variation in the disappropriated area per rural household is to increase land holding by 3.1 percentage points. However, when the full set of control variables is introduced, column (2) shows that the effect vanishes. Thus, on average, results from columns (1) and (2) of Table 9.4 suggest that land reform does not increase the proportion of rural families with land holdings. On the one hand, these results might be true in the sense that Brazilian experience with land reform does not increase the access to land. On the other hand, the estimated zero effect might be the result of countervailing effects. As shown in Section 2, the Brazilian land-reform programme consists of redistributive transfers from large landowners to small farmers and landless peasants. Unimproved and large tracts of land are under risk of expropriation, while small and productive farms cannot be taken. Consequently, the process by itself has differentiated effects on the rural households.

In order to investigate possible differentiated effects, Table 9.4 presents estimates of (9.1) in which the parameters α and γ are decomposed according to the household per capita income, age, and years of schooling of the household head. For the cases of income and age, the sample was divided into quintiles, and, for the case of schooling, terciles were used because of the large number of heads with one year of schooling or less. The results reported in columns (3) to (5) suggest that the absence of effect shown in column (2) is the result of heterogeneity, related to income and education. Columns (3) to

Table 9.4. Effect of land reform on the fraction of the rural population with land holdings, Brazil

Dependent variable: Dummy variable indicating whether the household owns land

	Without controls (1)	With controls (2)	Decomposition of the effect with respect to		
			income (3)	age (4)	schooling (5)
Dummy (positive disappropriation until the previous year=1)	0.317*** (0.013)	0.01 (0.014)	0.135*** (0.024)	0.089*** (0.030)	0.077*** (0.020)
Dummy (positive disappropriation) × dummy (2nd quintile)			-0.104*** (0.034)	-0.076* (0.040)	-0.043 (0.030)
Dummy (positive disappropriation) × dummy (3rd quintile)			-0.135*** (0.037)	-0.057 (0.040)	-0.141*** (0.029)
Dummy (positive disappropriation) × dummy (4th quintile)			-0.243*** (0.039)	-0.117*** (0.039)	
Dummy (positive disappropriation) × dummy (5th quintile)			-0.173*** (0.038)	-0.178*** (0.041)	
Log (disappropriated area per rural household)	0.031*** (0.001)	0.002 (0.001)	0.013*** (0.002)	0.011*** (0.003)	0.007*** (0.002)
Log (disappropriated area per rural household) × dummy (2nd quintile)			-0.010*** (0.003)	-0.009** (0.004)	-0.002 (0.003)
Log (disappropriated area per rural household) × dummy (3rd quintile)			-0.011*** (0.004)	-0.007* (0.004)	-0.012*** (0.003)
Log (disappropriated area per rural household) × dummy (4th quintile)			-0.022*** (0.004)	-0.013*** (0.004)	
Log (disappropriated area per rural household) × dummy (5th quintile)			-0.014*** (0.004)	-0.020*** (0.004)	
Household head, spouse, and household characteristics	No	Yes	Yes	Yes	Yes
Constant	0.407*** (0.003)	-0.063*** (0.011)	-0.055*** (0.012)	-0.041*** (0.015)	-0.083*** (0.012)
Year dummies	Yes	Yes	Yes	Yes	Yes
Observations	131775	63562	63562	63562	63562
R-squared	0.00	0.59	0.60	0.59	0.59

* significant at 10%; ** significant at 5%; *** significant at 1%.
Notes: Terciles rather than quintiles were considered for the case of years of schooling owing to the large proportion of heads with 1 year of schooling or less. Robust standard errors in parentheses.

Source: IBGE, National Household Surveys (PNAD) (various).

(5) indicate that land reform increases the access to land of low-income households and those with a less educated head, considering both the occurrence of land reform (α) and its intensity (γ).

Land disappropriation increases by 13.5 percentage points the fraction of the rural families with land holding, in the first quintile of the per capita income distribution, as shown in column (3) of Table 9.4. For all other income groups, the effect is substantially lower or even negative. The effect of the intensity of the land reform, which is measured by the disappropriated area per rural household, is also positive and statistically significant for low-income households. A similar pattern is shown for the educational level of the household head in column (5). Only the lowest tercile, which corresponds to the household head with one year of schooling or less, is affected positively by the land reform.

7 Land Reform and Land Distribution

The previous section investigated the effect of land reform on land ownership. Here, the analysis is restricted to landowner households, aiming at estimating the effect of the reform on the land distribution. It is not possible to assert, a priori, whether a redistributive land reform as implemented in Brazil increases or reduces the average land-holding size. It depends on the relationship between the holdings affected and not affected by the reform. If the farm size of the beneficiaries is smaller than the average non-affected farm, land reform tends to reduce the typical farm size. On the other hand, if the confiscated farms are not the largest, it is possible to have an increase in the average post-reform land holdings.

The empirical analysis that follows is presented in two steps. First, the effect on the average farm size is considered. Then, quantile regressions are used to investigate the effect of the land reform on each decile of the land distribution. The first set of results uses the following linear specification[7] focusing on the average land holding size:

$$E(\log{(L_i)}\,|\,D_i,\,X_i) = \phi \cdot I\{D_i > 0\} + \lambda \cdot \log{(D_i)} \cdot I\{D_i > 0\} + \delta' X_i. \qquad (9.4)$$

Again, if the disappropriation until the previous year is not correlated with the unobserved determinants of land-holding size, conditional on the observed variables X_i, the parameters ϕ and λ measure the effect of land reform on the fraction of rural households with land holdings. Simple computations with (9.1) show that:

---

[7] As in the previous section, it is assumed that $\log(0)\cdot 0 = 0$ in the interpretation of (9.4) for the sake of simplification.

$$\phi = E\left(\log(L_i^{D=1}) - \log\left(L_i^{D_i=0}\right) \mid X_i\right) \approx E\left(\frac{L_i^{D=1} - L_i^{D_i=0}}{L_i^{D_i=0}} \mid X_i\right) \tag{9.5}$$

And

$$\lambda = \frac{dE(\log(L_i) \mid D_i > 0, X_i)}{d\log(D_i)} = E\left(\frac{\frac{dL_i}{L_i}}{\frac{dD_i}{D_i}} \mid D_i > 0, X_i\right). \tag{9.6}$$

Thus, the parameter ϕ represents the percent change of the first disappropriated hectare per rural household on the size of the land holdings. The parameter λ is the elasticity of the size of the land holdings with respect to the disappropriated area per rural household, for those states with positive disappropriation.

Panel (i) of Table 9.5 shows the estimates of (9.4), using different sets of control variables and decompositions. Column (1) suggests that land reform reduces the average farm size. However, controlling for all observed characteristics, the effect becomes positive. The first disappropriated hectare per household increases the average farm size by 57.3 per cent. It is important to keep in mind that the average of this variable in the sample, according to Table 9.2, is substantially smaller than 1. Similarly to the analysis of land ownership, column (3) shows that land reform has differentiated effects with respect to the household per capita income. There is a reduction in the average farm size of the 20 per cent poorest households and an increase in land holdings of the others. The decomposition in terms of age does not present a clear pattern, while there is also some heterogeneity with respect to the head's schooling.

Thus, this first set of results suggest that land reform has increased the average size of the land holdings, but this effect is not homogeneous with respect to household per capita income—poorer households experienced a reduction while richer households experienced an increase in the average farm size. Comparing these results with those of Section 4, in which land is highly correlated with income, Table 9.5 indicates that land reform increases the inequality in the distribution of land. In order to address this question in a more systematic way, quantile regressions are estimated. The specification presented in (9.4) is estimated for each decile of the land distribution. Results for 10, 30, 50, 70, and 90 percentiles are depicted in panel (ii) of Table 9.5, and the coefficients ϕ and λ are plotted in Figures 9.2 and 9.3, respectively.

The results suggest that Brazilian land reform has, surprisingly, increased the inequality of land distribution. Land reform has negative effects on holdings with size below the median and positive effects on holdings above the median of the distribution.

Table 9.5. Effect of land reform on the size of land holdings, Brazil

Dependent variable: Log (area of the household landholdings)
Panel (i): OLS estimates

	Without controls (1)	With controls (2)	Decomposition of the effect with respect to		
			income (3)	age (4)	schooling (5)
Dummy (positive disappropriation until the previous year=1)	−0.300*** (0.077)	0.573*** (0.082)	−0.458*** (0.143)	0.192 (0.198)	0.071 (0.125)
Dummy (positive disappropriation) × dummy (2nd quintile)			0.876*** (0.207)	0.314 (0.252)	0.482*** (0.186)
Dummy (positive disappropriation) × dummy (3rd quintile)			1.171*** (0.226)	0.397 (0.243)	1.175*** (0.174)
Dummy (positive disappropriation) × dummy (4th quintile)			1.464*** (0.233)	0.597** (0.245)	
Dummy (positive disappropriation) × dummy (5th quintile)			2.118*** (0.221)	0.452 (0.285)	
Log (disappropriated area per rural household)	−0.002 (0.007)	0.075*** (0.008)	−0.029** (0.014)	0.033* (0.019)	0.028** (0.012)
Log (disappropriated area per rural household) × dummy (2nd quintile)			0.099*** (0.020)	0.031 (0.025)	0.047** (0.018)
Log (disappropriated area per rural household) × dummy (3rd quintile)			0.123*** (0.022)	0.049** (0.024)	0.113*** (0.017)
Log (disappropriated area per rural household) × dummy (4th quintile)			0.147*** (0.023)	0.068*** (0.024)	
Log (disappropriated area per rural household) × dummy (5th quintile)			0.201*** (0.021)	0.044 (0.028)	
Household head, spouse, and household characteristics	No	Yes	Yes	Yes	Yes
Constant	11.389*** (0.016)	8.424*** (0.197)	8.286*** (0.200)	8.484*** (0.209)	8.466*** (0.200)

Year dummies	Yes	Yes	Yes	Yes	Yes
Observations	52031	35652	35652	35652	35652
R-squared	0.00	0.27	0.29	0.27	0.28

Panel (ii): Quantile regressions

	10%	30%	50%	70%	90%
Dummy (positive disappropriation until the previous year=1)	−0.585***	−0.649***	0.071	1.132***	1.663***
	(0.099)	(0.088)	(0.085)	(0.106)	(0.120)
Log (disappropriated area per rural household)	−0.034***	−0.041***	0.028***	0.126***	0.174***
	(0.009)	(0.008)	(0.008)	(0.010)	(0.011)
Household head, spouse, and household characteristics	Yes	Yes	Yes	Yes	Yes
Year dummies	Yes	Yes	Yes	Yes	Yes
Observations	35652	35652	35652	35652	35652

* significant at 10%; ** significant at 5%; *** significant at 1%.

Notes: Terciles rather than quintiles were considered for the case of years of schooling owing to the large proportion of heads with 1 year of schooling or less. Robust standard errors in parentheses.

Source: IBGE, National Household Surveys (PNAD) (various).

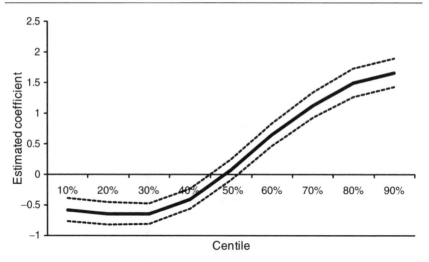

Figure 9.2. Quantile estimates of the effect of land reform on the size of land holdings, Brazil

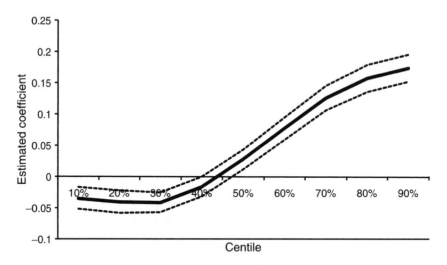

Figure 9.3. Quantile estimates of the effect of the disappropriated area on the size of land holdings, Brazil

8 Conclusion

Throughout Brazil's history, wealth has been highly associated with land ownership. In this sense, this study looks at the recent Brazilian experience with redistributive land reform in order to shed light on its effect on the distribution of wealth in rural areas. After presenting the historical determinants of land concentration and the institutional background for land reform in Brazil, the study evaluates the impact of land disappropriation on land ownership and land distribution.

Two main conclusions arise from the investigation of the impact of land disappropriations on the fraction of the rural families with land holdings. First, land reform does not increase the percentage of households with land in rural areas, at least from an aggregate perspective. Second, the decomposition of this impact according to household income and education of the head reveals important differences. There is an increase in landownership among the poorest households and those for which the head has no more than one year of schooling. For all other household classes there is a reduction in the percentage of landowners. Thus, considering the whole rural population, land reform points towards a less unequal distribution of assets, since it increases land ownership among poor households and reduces land ownership among rich households.

Interestingly, the analysis of the effect of land reform on the distribution of land *among landowner households* seems to suggest the opposite. Both the quantile regressions and the decomposition of the impact according to income indicate an increase in the inequality of holdings. Land reform increases the number of poor landholders with very small holdings, which tends to increase measures of land inequality among landholders. Concomitantly, it increases the relative holdings of rich families with large holdings, which again raises measures of inequality in land holding. Whether land reforms are equalizing or disequalizing thus depends on whether one regards the full population, or simply the population of landholders, as the appropriate frame of reference.

10

Estimating the Balance Sheet of the Personal Sector in an Emerging Market Country: South Africa, 1975–2005

Janine Aron, John Muellbauer, and Johan Prinsloo

1 Introduction

Substantial changes in equity values and the value of residential real estate over the past decade have generated new interest internationally in the potential influence of household-sector wealth on the final consumption expenditure of private households (Boone et al. 2001; Aoki et al. 2002; Catte et al. 2004; Muellbauer 2008). This is equally true in South Africa. Final consumption expenditure by households relative to gross domestic product rose from an average of 56 per cent in the 1980s to an average of 62 per cent between 1990 and 2005. By contrast, gross saving as a percentage of gross domestic product declined from an average of 24.5 per cent during the 1980s to only 16 per cent on average between 1990 and 2005. Likewise, gross saving by the household sector relative to gross domestic product declined from 6.5 per cent to 3.5 per cent for the corresponding period. Household balance sheet evidence is likely to help explain these phenomena.

Official balance sheet estimates for the household sector are not available in South Africa at the time of writing, similar to many emerging market economies. Yet with South Africa's well-developed financial sector and deep capital

The authors are grateful to H. Wagner, M. Kock, and D. Meyer of the South African Reserve Bank for data discussions, and to J. Van den Heever for comments. We are grateful to R. Ward, R. Dagnall, and N. Griffin of the UK Office of National Statistics for advice. This collaborative research was funded by the Department for International Development (UK), grant number R8311, and the South African Reserve Bank.

markets, asset market channels are likely to be important in the determination of aggregate consumer spending and saving, consumers' demand for credit, and their broad money holdings. As other emerging market countries develop their credit markets, stock markets, and other financial institutions, the monetary transmission mechanism will alter and asset price fluctuations will become more relevant; see Coricelli et al. (2005). The macroeconometric models that inform policy for these economies will need to take these behavioural shifts into account. But, in the absence of liquid and illiquid household-sector wealth measures, the important domestic asset and credit channels of the monetary policy transmission mechanism will be poorly estimated. Household balance sheets are also required for an assessment of the distribution of wealth and liquidity. This is a first step towards the analysis of wealth inequality within a country. Further, while there are good wealth data at the level of the Organization for Economic Cooperation and Development (OECD), there is a dearth of such data for intermediate income countries, like South Africa, to facilitate international comparisons of household wealth (Davies et al., Chapter 19, this volume). These considerations motivate the effort to construct time series of market value data for the main components of household-sector wealth in South Africa.

This chapter produces comprehensive quarterly estimates of household balance sheets for South Africa to 2005.[1] The main balance sheet categories are liquid assets, household debt, and various categories of illiquid financial and tangible assets, including private pension wealth, directly held shares and bonds, and housing. Another aim is to draw lessons from South Africa for emerging market countries, not only in terms of how to create balance sheets, but also of how the liquid and illiquid asset composition can alter over time as markets deepen.

The national income and expenditure accounts of South Africa are long established. Estimates of final consumption expenditure by households[2] and net savings have been available annually since 1946 and quarterly since 1960. The South African Reserve Bank (SARB) has published flow-of-funds data back to 1970. Information on household holdings of government and public-enterprise debt securities, their interest in unit trusts (mutual funds), and pension and long-term insurance funds (using a mix of book values and market values) and household debt data also date back to the 1970s. From

---

[1] The South African Reserve Bank (SARB) will shortly publish selected items of the quarterly household balance sheets in the *Quarterly Bulletin* of the SARB on an ongoing basis.

[2] In the 1993 System of National Accounts, households as final consumers consist predominantly of individuals and families, but currently household sector data in South Africa, as in many countries, also include non-profit institutions that serve households. Unincorporated business enterprises, such as sole proprietorships, farmers, unincorporated professional firms, and the informal sector, are also included in the household sector, despite the fact that they are production units rather than or as well as final consumers.

these data and other sources, it is possible to construct a profile of the main components of household-sector wealth stretching back to the 1970s.

The chapter extends the earlier work of Aron and Muellbauer (2006a), particularly in a broader treatment of tangible assets and foreign assets (though still incomplete), and some refinements in the measurement of housing wealth and liquid wealth. The historical data for liquid assets and the pension liabilities of long-term insurers from 1970 to the early 1990s were constructed using the methodology in Aron and Muellbauer (2006a), as were private pensions up to 1998. The methods rely, where relevant, on accumulating flow of funds data using appropriate benchmarks, and, where necessary, converting book to market values using appropriate asset price indices. Thereafter these estimates are linked to data published in the *Quarterly Bulletin* of SARB. For ordinary shares, government and corporate stocks and official pension funds, these methods provide data up to 2005. Debt estimates and comprehensive estimates of tangible assets for households and unincorporated businesses were mainly compiled from money and banking and national accounts statistics obtained from SARB.

This study draws, where feasible, on best practice from the Office of National Statistics (ONS) of the United Kingdom. Section 2 describes, in the absence of fully integrated balance sheets for the institutional sectors, elements of balance sheet estimates for the household sector in South Africa. Cross-references are made to the methodology used in the UK for estimating the various asset and liability categories. Section 3 discusses the trends in the components of household wealth. Section 4 explores the paucity of such data in developing and emerging market countries, and draws lessons from the South African research for the compilation of household balance sheets. Section 5 concludes.

2 Household Balance Sheet Estimates for South Africa

This section explains the methodology for estimating fixed assets and financial assets available for the household sector in South Africa. The methodology for the liabilities of the household sector is presented in the second part of the section. Household balance sheets are currently compiled in the UK by the ONS as an integral part of the Integrated Economic Accounts of the National Accounts. A summary of the UK methodology is given in Aron et al. (2006), and provides a useful platform to evaluate the appropriateness of balance sheet estimation methods and the ultimate calculation of net wealth for households in South Africa. The sources for the data used in constructing South African estimates of fixed and financial assets, and liabilities, are summarized in Aron et al. (2006: table 1).

2.1 Tangible Assets

The fixed or tangible assets[3] of households in the compilation of aggregate wealth numbers for the household sector in South Africa comprise the market value of residential buildings and the capital stock (derived from fixed capital formation, and the book value of inventories) of unincorporated business enterprises.

RESIDENTIAL BUILDINGS

The asset value of residential buildings owned by households, including unincorporated business enterprises in the agricultural sector, is derived from the existing capital stock at constant values using the Perpetual Inventory Method (PIM). The capital stock at constant prices for private dwellings[4] is inflated by an average house price index[5] obtained from one of the larger commercial banks, Absa. These calculations provide a fairly reliable proxy of the market value of residential buildings owned by households. The land value of residential property is calculated, using an average ratio of the land value for existing and new houses relative to the purchase prices of the buildings excluding the value of the land. An average ratio of 32.7 per cent was obtained from unpublished surveys conducted by Absa between 1966 and 2004. By comparison with the UK, the valuation of property for assessment rate purposes is not conducted on a uniform basis by local government throughout all the provinces in South Africa. Consequently, employing the tax records of the local authorities to estimate the market value of housing stock, as in the UK, is not currently a viable option.

NON-RESIDENTIAL BUILDINGS AND NON-RESIDENTIAL LAND

Unfortunately, the asset value of fixed investment of non-residential buildings and other fixed assets by unincorporated business enterprises can be estimated only indirectly. By using information obtained from the Economic Activity Surveys (EAS) per industry, conducted annually by Statistics South Africa since 1998, it is possible to make a distinction between incorporated and unincorporated business enterprises. Fixed ratios (per industry) as calculated by the National Accounts Division of SARB from the most recent EAS are applied to capital stock data[6] obtained from the National Accounts Division,

---

[3] Although calculations of the stock of durable consumer goods are available, in keeping with international practice they do not form part of the institutional sector balance sheets and are therefore not included in the wealth estimates.

[4] Note that, since private dwelling includes some residential rented property owned by corporations and pension funds, this will overstate the ownership by the household sector.

[5] The average house price index is based on the total purchase price of houses, comprising of small, medium, and large houses within a range of 80–400 m². In addition, the index covers the nine provinces and twelve regions within the provinces.

[6] The capital stock data are based on the PIM of non-residential buildings and other fixed assets in the private sector.

199

to allocate a certain portion of fixed assets (per industry) to the household sector.

There are no appropriate official price indices to define market values, so the stock of non-residential buildings at constant values is inflated by a derived price index of the market value of non-residential buildings. This annual index back to 1974 is calculated from rental values and capitalization rates of industrial buildings, offices, and shopping centres in the larger metropolitan areas. The value of the land for non-residential property is estimated from unpublished balance-sheet ratios calculated from the 2002 EAS. The ratio of the book value of land relative to non-residential buildings for the various industries excluding agriculture—estimated at an arithmetic average of about 14 per cent—is applied to the derived market value of non-residential buildings of unincorporated business enterprises. This ratio was used to obtain approximate values of land for 1975–2005. For agricultural land, annual estimates at market value were obtained from the National Department of Agriculture. The allocation of land value to the household sector is based on an annual average ratio of the operating surpluses of incorporated and unincorporated enterprises in the agricultural sector, obtained from the National Accounts Division.

The difference between the UK's and South Africa's methodologies for fixed asset values of unincorporated enterprises is that the UK surveys capture fixed assets at market values, while in South Africa the surveys on these balance sheet items reflect only book values. Balance sheet items are included in the questionnaires of Statistics South Africa only since 1998.

OTHER FIXED ASSETS

Estimates of the replacement value (a proxy for market value) for vehicles, plant and machinery, construction works (structures), and cultivated assets recorded in the balance sheet of the household sector were derived from net capital stock measures (calculated using the perpetual inventory method (PIM) per industry, as compiled by the National Accounts). The allocation of the asset values of these types of assets was derived using the ratios between incorporated and unincorporated enterprises by industry, as discussed above, from the EAS. These ratios were also used to obtain a split of the market value of inventories between incorporated and unincorporated enterprises. The market value of inventories is available from quarterly surveys conducted by Statistics South Africa, which is similar to the UK case, where information is obtained from direct returns.

2.2 Financial Assets

The financial assets incorporated in the calculation of wealth estimates for households in South Africa are deposits with banks and mutual banks, interest in pension funds and the pension business of the long-term insurers, participation mortgage bond schemes, unit trusts, equities, issues of bonds by government and by publicly owned enterprises, and corporate bonds. In addition, an assumption of the average value of coin and bank notes in possession of the household sector (that is, in circulation outside the monetary sector) is also included. Unfortunately, only limited information exists on individual ownership of foreign assets and liabilities (see below).

LIQUID ASSET STOCKS

Household liquid asset data include deposits of individuals, unincorporated enterprises, and non-profit organizations with banks and mutual banks, the Postbank, and the Land and Agricultural Bank. It also includes deposits with non-monetary financial institutions. These deposits cover the entire maturity spectrum from cheque and transmission accounts to long-term fixed and notice deposits. SARB publishes a quarterly analysis of bank deposits by type of depositor, but only from the third quarter of 1991. The quality of these data sources[7] is sound and in keeping with the methodology used in the UK. Prior to the third quarter of 1991, in the absence of other data, the methodology in Aron and Muellbauer (2006a) was employed to cumulate the relevant flow of funds categories[8] using a second benchmark for 1969Q4 and matching the 1991Q3 benchmark. The benchmark calculation draws on US and UK experience (ibid. for details).

From the third quarter of 1991, summing the components for the personal sector provides a series for personal broad money holdings and a benchmark for the third quarter of 1991. Unpublished counterpart data obtained since 1995 from the Land and Agricultural Bank comprise the deposits of forced stock sales by the unincorporated business enterprises in the agricultural sector. Before 1995 an average of 35 per cent of call money deposits with the Land and Agricultural Bank was used as a proxy of forced stock sales. The 35 per cent assumption was based on the average ratio of forced stock sales relative to call money deposits between 1995 and 2003. The cumulated stock of deposits with 'other financial institutions' (item 13), obtainable from the flow of funds, was added to this total (see details in Aron and Muellbauer 2006a).

Finally, notes and coin held by the household sector outside the banking sector was added. Notes and coin held by institutions outside the banking sector are derived from the total issued by SARB, less the total notes and coin

---

[7] Deposits by households at banks, the Postbank and Land and Agricultural Bank are counterpart data obtained from direct returns to SARB. These aggregates are included in the balance sheet of the institutions as total liabilities of the banks to the household sector.

[8] 'Liquid assets' comprise the following flow-of-funds categories: (10) cash and demand monetary deposits; (11) short/medium-term monetary deposits; (12) long-term monetary deposits; (13) deposits with other financial institutions. An adjustment was made for missing data on unincorporated businesses (see Aron and Muellbauer 2006a).

Table 10.1. Household balance sheet of assets and liabilities relative to personal disposable income, South Africa, selected years

	1975	1980	1985	1990	1995	2000	2005
Liquid assets[1]							
Liquid assets total	0.900	0.829	0.771	0.514	0.435	0.502	0.544
Other deposits[2]	0.004	0.004	0.004	0.003	0.002	0.003	0.007
Participation bonds	0.055	0.028	0.030	0.018	0.012	0.006	0.003
Government and public enterprise assets[3]							
(19) Short-term government stock	0.003	0.006	0.002	0.002	0.002	0.002	0.000
(20) Long-term government stock	0.009	0.004	0.007	0.006	0.005	0.002	0.001
(22) Securities of local authorities	0.003	0.002	0.000	0.000	0.000	0.000	0.000
(23) Securities of public enterprises	0.003	0.004	0.017	0.014	0.008	0.005	0.004
Corporate bonds and equities							
(24) Other loan stock and preference shares	0.038	0.024	0.012	0.011	0.008	0.008	0.006
(25) Ordinary shares	0.722	1.087	0.886	0.754	0.928	0.782	1.028
Equity in unincorporated businesses	—	—	—	—	—	—	—
Equity in other unlisted securities	—	—	—	—	—	—	—
Pension funds[4]							
Private self-administered pension funds	0.216	0.311	0.381	0.406	0.595	0.440	0.391
Pensions with long-term insurers	0.156	0.268	0.370	0.469	0.536	0.499	0.444
Official pension funds	0.146	0.140	0.176	0.229	0.405	0.525	0.789
Foreign assets[5]	—	—	—	—	—	0.030	0.037
TOTAL financial assets	2.254	2.708	2.658	2.427	2.935	2.805	3.255
Liabilities							
Total household debt	0.482	0.466	0.574	0.595	0.624	0.553	0.693
Mortgage debt	0.269	0.249	0.250	0.279	0.342	0.301	0.408
Consumer credit	0.176	0.183	0.263	0.270	0.248	0.212	0.254
TOTAL liabilities	0.482	0.466	0.574	0.595	0.624	0.553	0.693
Tangible assets							
Residential buildings (incl. land)	1.100	0.970	0.959	0.753	0.605	0.618	1.056
Other tangible assets	1.028	0.851	0.664	0.455	0.298	0.240	0.226
TOTAL non-financial assets	2.128	1.822	1.624	1.208	0.903	0.858	1.282
Consumer durables (total)[6]	0.590	0.494	0.603	0.526	0.433	0.448	0.412

TOTAL net wealth (incl. consumer durables, using shares benchmark of 25:1 for 1969) [7,8]	4.490	4.558	4.310	3.566	3.646	3.558	4.257
TOTAL net wealth (excl. consumer durables, using shares benchmark of 25:1 for 1969) [7,8]	3.901	4.064	3.708	3.040	3.213	3.109	3.844
TOTAL net wealth (excl. consumer durables, using shares benchmark of 15:1 for 1969) [7,8]	3.609	3.632	3.359	2.747	2.875	2.823	3.470
Total personal disposable income (R millions)	16857	35860	76213	181531	349183	587724	969402

Notes and sources: Household debt data (published from 1991) and income data from the *Quarterly Bulletin*, South African Reserve Bank. Pensions with long-term insurers from Capital Market Statistics, South African Reserve Bank (market value data reported from 1991). Unit trusts data from Capital Market Statistics, South African Reserve Bank. Unpublished data on total household debt (pre-1991), household mortgage debt, consumer credit (after 1992); see also Prinsloo (2002), and constant price housing stock, were kindly provided by the South African Reserve Bank. All other data: authors' calculations, as explained in the text. Note that for liquid assets and long-term insurers, the first set of assumptions apply as regards the sensitivity analysis in Aron and Muellbauer (2006a: table 1); but for ordinary shares, the second assumption is also shown, of a 15:1 benchmark for 1969, for directly-held equity relative to unit trusts held.

1. Liquid assets up to 1991 comprise categories: (10) cash and demand monetary deposits; (11) short/medium-term monetary deposits; (12) long-term monetary deposits; and (13) deposits with other financial institutions, where numbers in parentheses refer to flow of funds categories from the National Financial Account, South African Reserve Bank. A correction was made for missing data on unincorporated businesses (see Aron and Muellbauer 2006a). After 1991, stock data on bank deposits are used directly to construct liquid assets.

2. Other deposits comprise the category: (14) deposits with other institutions.

3. Government and public enterprise assets also include categories: (15) treasury bills; (16) other bills; and (21) non-marketable government bonds. Category (21) became negative and the series was omitted. Categories (15) and (16) are omitted because the flow of funds record zero transactions for the household sector.

4. Pension funds comprises category: (29) interest in retirement and life funds, from Capital Market Statistics, South African Reserve Bank, which combines private self-administered pension funds (reported at book values until 1998Q4), pensions with long-term insurers (reported at book values before 1985, at a mix of book values and market values between 1985 and 1991, and at market values from the end of 1991), and official pension funds (note: as of March, 2007, these have been reported at market value, back to 2002). The assumptions refer to the proportions of funds (prop) reporting at market value in the following periods: (i) 1961:4 1985:2: prop=0; (ii) 1985:3 1986:4: prop=0.15; (iii) 1987:1 1987:3: prop=0.3; and (iv) 1987:4 1991:3: prop=0.15.

5. The following data were unavailable: equity in unincorporated businesses and in other unlisted securities. Data on foreign assets are incomplete, but for 1998–2003, annual Coordinated Portfolio Investment Survey data on foreign equity and debt are available (see section 2.2, unit trusts). We have included these in total net wealth. However, we have not included data on foreign assets derived from the Amnesty Unit, National Treasury (see section 2.2, foreign deposits).

6. Consumer durables comprise categories: (A) furniture, household appliances, etc.; (B) personal transport equipment; (C) recreational and entertainment goods; (D) other durable goods (jewellery etc.). There are published figures for consumer semi-durable goods.

7. Total net wealth sums the above categories.

8. For ordinary shares, finding the appropriate benchmark for 1969 is controversial. The proportion of equities held directly by the household sector could be expected to be at least as large as in the UK and the USA, given a similar culture of share ownership but greater inequality in share ownership in South Africa. We compare two alternative benchmarks for South Africa in 1969, of 15:1 and 25:1 to unit trusts (details on benchmark construction in Aron and Muellbauer 2006a).

held by banks. This approach is similar to that of the UK and seems to be the best available option. To allocate an asset value of this balance to households, the operating surpluses between 1975 and 2005 of the household sector and the corporate sector were used to obtain a proxy for such a division.[9] Over the long run, 1975 to 2005, an average of about 70 per cent of notes and coin held outside the banking sector can be allocated to the household sector.

OTHER DEPOSITS

In the flow of funds, a further type of deposit is listed 'deposits with other institutions', such as households' deposits with municipalities. This is a very small category throughout the period. It was decided to group this category with directly held illiquid financial assets. The series is derived by cumulating the relevant flow of funds category (item 14) with respect to a benchmark for 1969, as in Aron and Muellbauer (2006a).

FOREIGN DEPOSITS

Households' foreign-exchange denominated deposits, made in terms of the relaxation of exchange control since 1997, should be included in the liquid asset data. Previously, individual residents could not acquire any foreign assets, while all residents had to obtain permission to borrow funds abroad. Historically, however, many South Africans took funds offshore illegally, commencing well before the 1980s, but probably increasing substantially between 1985 and 1994—a time of international sanctions against South Africa and the eventual change over to a new political dispensation. There are no data on the build-up of these assets over the past twenty-five years—it would be difficult to provide realistic estimates for balance sheet purposes—and we exclude it from the total wealth measure given in Table 10.1.

INTEREST IN PENSION FUNDS

Households' vested interest in pension funds comprises the accumulated funds of official pension and provident funds (providing pensions for public-sector employees) as well as private funds. The official pension funds are those funds administered by the Department of Finance, Transnet, Telkom, and the Post Office. The privately administered funds consist of funds registered in terms of the Pension Funds Act of 1993, foreign funds registered in South Africa, funds established in terms of individual agreements, and state-controlled funds exempted from the requirements of the Act. To avoid double counting, underwritten funds covered by insurance policies or group

[9] The gross operating surpluses of the corporate sector and the household sector were published in a supplement to the June 2005 *Quarterly Bulletin* of SARB, and became part of official estimates published annually in the *Quarterly Bulletin* of SARB during the course of 2006.

insurance schemes and included with long-term insurers, discussed below, are excluded.

Data for both private and official pension funds are obtained from returns submitted by these institutions to SARB, and are published in the *Quarterly Bulletin* of SARB. The interest of households in pension funds and long-term insurers, below, are well captured. However, in the case of private funds, data at market value became available only as from March 1999; and for official pension funds, only from March 2007, backdated to 2002. Book value data for both categories of pension fund were accordingly adjusted to market values employing the methodology in Aron and Muellbauer (2006a). To derive the corresponding market values, the net holding gains by the end of the period on the market value of the stock at the beginning of the period have to be added, as well as any holding gains on net purchases made during the period. The revaluation adjustment can be explained as follows. Let A_{t-1} be the market value of an asset at the end of the period, $t-1$. Let π_{t-1} be the corresponding price index. Let NPA_t be net purchases of the asset in the period. Then

$$A_t = A_{t-1}(\pi_t/\pi_{t-1}) + (NPA_t)(\pi_t/\tilde{\pi}_t) \tag{10.1}$$

where $(\pi_t/\tilde{\pi}_t)$ is the revaluation adjustment of net purchases made in period t, and $\tilde{\pi}_t$ is the average price level recorded during the period of purchases, since purchases are assumed to be spread over the period. Given an asset benchmark at an initial date, data on the net purchases in the period and the corresponding price indices, the revaluation adjustment in (10.1) can be used to derive market-value data.

For private self-administered pension and provident funds, there are quarterly data on the portfolio composition of assets from 1963, and annual data from 1958, both on a book value basis. There are seven groups of assets subject to revaluation. The adjustment of the book values of the assets to market value was made by applying (10.1), and using end-1961 benchmarks and constructed price indices for each of the seven groups. Details on price index construction are provided in Aron and Muellbauer (2004: app. 2). For official pension funds, there are annual book value portfolio composition data from 1974. Prior to 1974, there are annual data for total assets at book value, from 1948. These funds started investing in ordinary shares, other company securities, and fixed property only in 1990, when quarterly data begin. Prior to 1990, government, local authority, and public enterprise bonds accounted for more than 85 per cent of total assets purchased. To convert book to market values throughout the period, end-1961 benchmarks were employed with (10.1) on quarterly, interpolated data.

INTEREST IN LONG-TERM INSURERS

Household interest in long-term insurers is derived from the pension activities of long-term insurers. Around half the liabilities of long-term insurers represent personal-sector pension assets.[10] The pension business represents those activities of the long-term insurers conducted on behalf of the pension funds and the underwriting of annuities. The data for unmatured policies of pension business are directly surveyed from the relevant institutions by the Research Department of SARB and published in the *Quarterly Bulletin*. However, as with the pension funds, the earlier data are reported at book rather than market value. The first reliable market value data are reported from the fourth quarter of 1991. Consequently, data prior to this were adjusted to reflect market values using the methodology in Aron and Muellbauer (2006a). For long-term insurers, quarterly data on the portfolio composition began in 1963, and annual data in 1946. The procedure outlined above for pension funds can be followed using end-1961 benchmarks. However, there is one quite serious difficulty. Between the third quarter of 1985 and the third quarter of 1991, some insurers reported at market values and others at book values, while from the fourth quarter of 1991, all insurers were required to switch to the market-value basis. Unfortunately, the proportions that reported on either basis are not known, and the proportions appeared to alter after the stock market crash in October 1987. Details of the assumptions made that give the most plausible outcome are found in Aron and Muellbauer (2004: app. 2).

UNITS IN DOMESTIC AND FOREIGN UNIT TRUSTS

The unit trust data are *not* included separately; they are subsumed into other categories, which are summed to achieve the total wealth aggregates (namely, liquid assets, directly held illiquid assets, and pension funds and insurance companies). The market values of unit trust security holdings, including cash, deposits, and accrued income, are published in the *Quarterly Bulletin* of SARB. For further discussion on definitions and the avoidance of double counting, see Aron et al. (2006).

Exchange control relaxation in 1998 allowed resident households to make investments directly into foreign portfolio assets. Unpublished estimates of resident households' portfolio investment in foreign assets (excluding cash deposits) for the period 2001–3 have been extrapolated back to 1998, and they are incorporated as part of the foreign asset component part of total net wealth in the balance-sheet estimates for the household sector (see Aron et al. 2006 for details).

---

[10] In this study it is assumed that the non-pension business of long-term insurers does not contribute to personal sector assets.

PARTICIPATION MORTGAGE BOND SCHEMES

Participation mortgage bond schemes are in some respects similar to unit trusts. A pool of funds of a large number of smaller lenders is constructed in order to finance large mortgage loans. The participation is similar to long-term deposits of five years or longer. Investors are largely households seeking high, yet secure, returns on their capital. Deposits received from participants (individuals) are directly reported in the *Quarterly Bulletin* of SARB. Funds are also loaned to individuals, and these funds are treated as liabilities on the households' balance sheet. Similar deposit and loan instruments are not available in the UK.

GOVERNMENT AND PUBLIC ENTERPRISE ASSETS

In the absence of other data, the flow of funds data were used to construct measures of household holdings of the bonds issued by government and by publicly owned enterprises, using the methodology in Aron and Muellbauer (2006a). The government and public-enterprise components of the flow of funds comprise short-term and long-term government stock, and the securities of local authorities and public enterprises.[11] The benchmarks for short-term and long-term government stocks come from data on the ownership of end-1969 stocks in *Public Finance Statistics* of SARB, while quarterly figures on the personal-sector ownership of the securities of local authorities and public enterprises are available from 1970 in *Capital Market Statistics* of SARB. All these figures are on a book value rather than on a current market value basis, and require the revaluation adjustment using (10.1). The methodology for estimating price indices for fixed interest securities is given in Aron and Muellbauer (2004: app. 1).[12] However, short-term yields are roughly constant during 1965–9, suggesting the 1969 book values are reasonable approximations to the market values.

CORPORATE BONDS AND EQUITY

An accurate assessment of the direct investment in shares by households is one of the most difficult calculations to make, owing to the lack of reliable information in South Africa. The available data ownership by the personal sector is unsatisfactory, since surveys of share registers and of household finances are

---

[11] Non-marketable government debt was omitted owing to data inconsistencies; but the holdings fortunately are small (for instance, relative to liquid assets).

[12] Historical data on government bond price indices from JSE Ltd begin in 1980, while the Reserve Bank has published a bond price index only from 1999. Aron and Muellbauer (2004, 2006a) therefore use standard price–yield relationships to derive price indices for short- and long-duration government bonds before 1980. Coupons and maturities are held fixed for quarter to quarter comparisons, and these indices are chained.

not carried out in South Africa (as they are in the USA and the UK). The stock of shares directly held by households was estimated using the flow of funds data of ordinary shares held by households, from the methodology in Aron and Muellbauer (2006a). The flow of funds categories were cumulated using a benchmark of the value of ordinary shares held by households in 1969, calculated from relevant ratios in the UK and USA.[13] Conversion from book to market value of stocks was carried out using the JSE Ltd all-share index, adjusted for assumed trading or management costs (see Aron and Muellbauer 2006a).

2.3 Liabilities

On the liability side of the household-sector balance sheet, the two main components of debt are mortgage advances and other credit extended to households. The latter, sometimes referred to as 'consumer credit', is, in turn, subdivided into open account credit, personal loans extended by banks, credit card facilities, instalment sale transactions and lease agreements, other personal loans and non-bank loans. The bulk of household debt is borrowings from the banking sector. However, a comprehensive analysis of household debt should also take into account of the securitization of leasing and mortgage transactions, a relatively new development in South Africa, which accounted for approximately 4 per cent of total household debt by 2005 (see Aron et al. 2006 for discussion).

MORTGAGE ADVANCES

Mortgage advances are extended to households using residential property and other fixed property as security for the loan. South African credit markets developed markedly during the 1980s and 1990s. From 1995 special mortgage accounts ('access bond accounts') allowed households to borrow and pay back flexibly from these accounts up to an agreed limit set by the value of their housing collateral. Strong competition among the various financial institutions has caused mortgage advances to be used extensively for purposes other than the financing of transactions for fixed property. Greater transparency on these forms of credit and improved data will obviously be helpful in monetary policy making.

---

[13] For ordinary shares, estimates are sensitive to the chosen benchmark for 1969. The assumptions made in this chapter imply that households owned 41% of market capitalization of the JSE Ltd at the end of 1969 and 18% at the end of 1997 (see details in Aron and Muellbauer 2006a).

OPEN ACCOUNTS

Open accounts of households include all outstanding debits to retailers,[14] and also those amounts payable to buy-aid associations[15] for the purchase of goods and services from retailers. Estimates for outstanding debt on open accounts are indirectly derived from information on retail sales using credit financed by the retailers themselves (as opposed to banks), which is reported monthly by Statistics South Africa in its news release on retail sales. In the UK, the outstanding debt to trade creditors is derived as a residual of unpaid bills of accounts of individuals with companies.

PERSONAL LOANS AT BANKS

Personal loans granted by banks consist of overdraft facilities made available by banks to their clients and other advances granted to individuals. Only that part of the overdraft facility that is actually drawn by the consumer is included in household debt.

CREDIT CARDS

Banks make credit card facilities available to consumers, offering a convenient method of making purchases and deferring the payment of the purchase price. Debit balances on credit card accounts are usually payable within one calendar month after the cardholders receive their accounts, but budget facilities are also provided to postpone the payment over longer periods. The outstanding debit balances at the end of each calendar month, and not the total credit available, are taken into account in calculating total consumer credit.

INSTALMENT SALE AND LEASE AGREEMENTS

An instalment sale agreement (hire-purchase agreement) is a transaction in terms of which goods or services (typically durable consumer goods) are provided to the buyer, but where the purchase price is paid in instalments over a period in the future. Lease agreements are transactions in terms of which goods are leased with or without an arrangement that the debtor will become the owner of the goods at any time during or after the expiry of the lease period. If the lessee does not acquire ownership in terms of the agreement, the outstanding commitments can be regarded as rent and the leased

---

[14] Balances of trade creditors and debtors on households' balance sheets are difficult to estimate. The numbers are not fully incorporated into the current analysis. However, changes in these aggregates are not volatile and this omission should not have a meaningful impact on trends in the overall net worth position.

[15] Buy-aid Associations are clubs that negotiate benefits such as trade credits and trade discounts for consumer members at various suppliers. The traders are paid by the associations after three months, while the members pay the buying associations one or two months after purchase of the goods. At year-end, members are rewarded with a bonus (from net profit) in accordance with their purchases during the year.

goods remain an asset on the balance sheet of the lessor. In the case of a financial lease agreement, the transaction can either be a conditional sale or a hire purchase, and all the risks and economic value related to the right of ownership of the asset concerned are transferred from the lessor to the lessee. Consequently, the commitments in terms of a financial lease are included in household debt.

OTHER PERSONAL LOANS

Other personal loans consist of loans granted to individuals by long-term insurers and through participation mortgage bond schemes where the surrender value of a policy serves as security for the loan (so-called loans against policies). This information is directly obtained from quarterly surveys from all long-term insurers. These data are published with a lag of two quarters in the *Quarterly Bulletin* of SARB. Similar estimates in the UK are obtained from surveys of the annual accounts of long-term insurers.

OTHER NON-BANK LOANS

The exponential growth of the micro-lending industry, especially during the 1990s, firmly established the role that micro-lenders have played in increasing access, particularly by low-income households, to credit extension. However, relative to total household debt outstanding, estimated at a level of about R672 billion at the end of 2005, the debt extended by micro-lenders amounted to less than 5 per cent. About 52 per cent of the debt granted by micro-lenders comes from banks and is consequently already measured as part of household debt (data from the Micro-Finance Regulatory Council (MFRC)). The bulk of the remaining micro-debt granted to individuals arises from close corporations (for example, small retailers)[16] and public and private companies, and about half of this debt is already captured in the total debt figures (the debts households owe to retailers). The balance is included in total household debt under the category 'other non-bank loans'. This was interpolated backwards and forwards and incorporated in the total debt from 1969 to 2005.

3 Trends in Assets, Liabilities, and Net Wealth

Real household spending has increased in recent years, and is partly explained by trends in the net wealth of the household sector. The considerable fluctuations

---

[16] A close corporation may be formed by between one and ten persons who are referred to as members. The Close Corporations Act 69 of 1984 governs this form of ownership. It requires compliance with some formalities and registration of a founding statement with the Registrar of Companies.

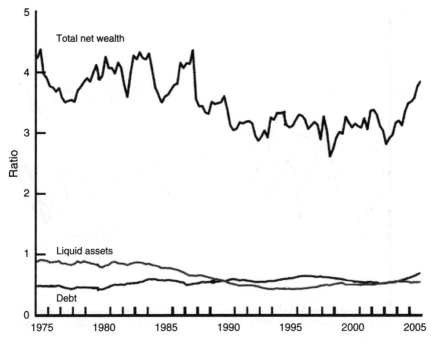

Figure 10.1. Ratios of household net wealth, debt, and liquid assets to personal disposable income, South Africa, 1975–2005

Note: Net wealth excludes consumer durables.

in total net personal wealth (excluding consumer durables) are shown in Figure 10.1, relative to a four-quarter moving average of personal disposable income.[17] The relatively high wealth to income ratio in the early 1970s, associated with strong economic growth and high gold prices, declined in the mid-to-late 1970s as the world economy faltered and as domestic political difficulties increased (for example, the schools boycott in 1976). The ratio rose following a gold price boom around 1980, when buoyant share prices were followed by house price and investment booms. Economic and political difficulties increased in the 1980s, and the debt crisis of 1985 and international trade and financial sanctions severely constrained access to capital and trade. Growth weakened and real

---

[17] In modelling household expenditure or portfolio decisions in the current quarter, one would normally use asset data at the end of the previous quarter, and current quarter personal disposable *non-property* income rather than the moving average of personal disposable income (PDI), see Aron and Muellbauer (2000a, b). However, PDI is more comparable internationally, while its non-property variant is subject to approximations of varying complexity (see Blinder and Deaton 1985).

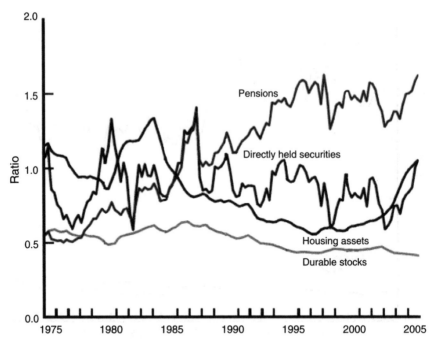

Figure 10.2. Ratios of pension assets, housing assets, directly held illiquid financial assets, and stocks of consumer durables to personal disposable income, South Africa, 1975–2005

house prices began a long-term decline. Recovery in the gold price in the late 1980s temporarily raised the wealth to income ratio; but, since 1988, it has fluctuated in a relatively narrow range, despite the positive political changes in South Africa.

Net wealth as a percentage of personal disposable income of households fell from 406 per cent in 1980 to a recent low of 273 per cent in 1998. Current estimates indicate that this ratio increased again to more than 380 per cent in 2005, exceeding earlier average levels. This can mainly be attributed to substantial increases in asset values, particularly in the private property market and equity prices.

However, there are considerable compositional changes in the components of net wealth underlying this trend. Most striking are the rise in the value of pension wealth and the trend decline of directly held securities, the decline and recent recovery of housing wealth, and the rise in household debt and concomitant decline of liquid assets from the early 1980s to the late 1990s. Figure 10.1 also shows debt and liquid asset to income ratios, while Figure 10.2

shows pension assets, gross housing assets, directly held financial assets and consumer durables, relative to income.

3.1 Household Debt

Van der Walt and Prinsloo (1995) and Prinsloo (2002) publish detailed charts of total household debt and its main components, and information on the institutional framework, data sources, and determination of household debt. Table 10.1 includes entries on consumer credit and mortgage debt. The growth of consumer credit and mortgage debt can be examined from several points of view: as a fraction of total debt extended to the private sector, as a proportion to income, as a proportion of wealth, and in terms of debt service ratios.

The rising household debt to income ratio over the past two decades can be attributed to the financial deregulation from the beginning of the 1980s; and, more recently, the reduction in interest rates, in both nominal and real terms. Both have contributed to a significant easing of liquidity constraints on households. There are important macroeconomic implications arising from the larger stock of household debt. Lower inflation has two effects on the debt to income ratio: it boosts the numerator of the ratio as a result of increased borrowing by households at lower nominal interest rates; and it lowers the growth of nominal household income. Consequently, households may be surprised in future years by the proportion of income still required to service debt, and hence have to lower their desired consumption. The higher aggregate debt to income ratio implies that households will be more exposed to interest-rate shocks.

Figure 10.3 displays the real prime interest rate, followed closely by mortgage rates.[18] The *positive* correlation between the real interest rate on borrowing and the debt to income ratio (Figure 10.1), particularly since 1980, with a correlation coefficient of 0.7 for 1980–2005, contradicts conventional expectations. This is likely to be the result of two factors. Inflation has tended to be correlated with negative real returns until monetary policy shifted, and correlated also with a fall in the value of nominal debt outstanding relative to nominal income. The correlation coefficient between annual inflation and the debt to income ratio for 1980–97 is -0.52. A second factor is financial liberalization. The removal of quantitative controls over credit in the early 1980s, associated with a move to controlling credit expansion via higher interest rates, induces a positive correlation between a

---

[18] The ex-post real interest rate is measured by $r - \Delta_4 \ln pc$ where r is the four quarter moving average of the nominal prime interest rate and pc is the consumer expenditure deflator.

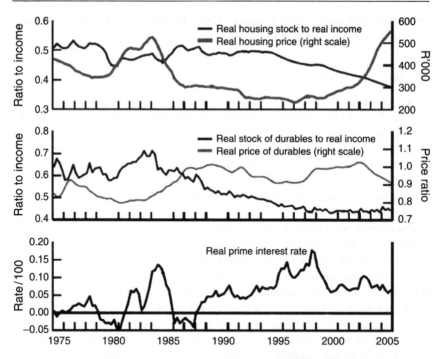

Figure 10.3. Ratios of stocks of housing and consumer durables to personal disposable income versus relative prices and real interest rates, South Africa, 1975–2005

supply-driven credit expansion and higher interest rates. This phenomenon has been observed in other countries that underwent financial liberalization in the 1980s, such as the UK and Scandinavia (see Lehmusaari 1990; Berg 1994).

The determination of the debt to income ratio in South Africa was the subject of an econometric investigation by Aron and Muellbauer (2000a, b, 2006b). Interest rates, financial liberalization, income and population growth, and housing, pension, directly held illiquid and liquid assets components of wealth were the key determinants, and the role of gross housing assets apparently increased with financial liberalization. The rise in the debt to income ratio occurred despite the decline after 1983 in the ratio of housing assets to income, and high real interest rates in the mid-1980s and the 1990s. However, although South Africa's ratio of household debt to disposable income increased strongly in the 1980s and again in the first half of the 1990s, it was lower than most of the OECD countries, and significantly lower than in the USA, Japan, Canada, and the UK.

Household debt relative to *tangible* assets (largely residential housing, Table 10.1) for 1980, 1990, 2000, and 2005 was, respectively, 25, 49, 64, and 54 per cent. Household debt relative to total financial assets in these same years was 17, 24, 20, and 21 per cent, respectively. Household debt relative to total net wealth in these years was 12, 20, 18, and 18 per cent, respectively. All three indicators suggest that, in recent years, capital gearing (debt ratios to various measures of total assets) has been at moderate levels. The debt service ratio of households (measured using the prime rate of interest) rose from an average of 5 per cent in the 1970s to a high of 13 per cent at the end of 1998. The reduction in interest rates from the high levels of 1998 contributed to its subsequent decline.

For a detailed discussion of the changing composition of household liabilities, see Aron et al. (2006). Buoyant demand since 1991 saw mortgage advances as a percentage of total household debt rise to 61.5 per cent by the end of 2005. The other category, consumer credit, has seen personal loans (including overdraft and credit card facilities), instalment sale credit, and leasing rise in importance relative to open accounts. This may have raised the interest-rate sensitivity of aggregate demand—the impact of interest rates changes is likely to fall more heavily on personal loans, instalment sale, and lease agreements than on open accounts.

3.2 The Liquid Asset to Income Ratio

The ratio of liquid assets to income underwent a long-term decline to the mid-1990s, after which there was a slow recovery. Some of the decline is accounted for by financial liberalization from 1981 and extending into the 1990s—with improved access to credit, the precautionary, buffer-stock, and consumption smoothing motives for holding liquid assets (see Deaton 1992) declined. There may have been an overall wealth effect, with the net wealth to income ratio influencing the liquid asset ratio; see Thomas (1997) for such an effect in the UK. Political credibility effects, inducing currency substitution away from domestic assets and towards illegal foreign assets, may have been a factor in the declining liquid asset to income ratio from 1976 and after the debt crisis of September 1985, reversing with the democratic elections of 1994. However, the main factor is likely to have been that, for an average taxpayer, the real after-tax return on liquid assets has been negative from the early 1970s to the early 1990s, apart from a brief spell in 1984–5 (see Prinsloo 2000: 17). The weighted average of marginal tax rates rose from around 10 per cent to over 30 per cent from 1970 to the 1990s, before declining again in recent years. Higher returns help explain the renewed rise in the liquid asset to income ratio from the late 1990s. On balance, it seems that household saving in the form of deposit-type investments was adversely affected by negative or low after-tax real interest rates.

3.3 *The Gross Housing Assets to Income Ratio*

The ratio of housing wealth to income can be decomposed into the ratio of the constant price housing stock to real income and the ratio of house prices to the consumer price deflator. These ratios are shown in Figure 10.3. Since the housing stock evolves only very slowly, poor income growth between the early 1980s and 1990s is reflected in a rise in the real stock to real income ratio, while stronger growth since 1994 has seen a fall in the ratio. However, most of the rise in the early 1980s and subsequent decline in the value of housing assets relative to income is due to the rise and then decline in the real house price index (see Figure 10.3). Despite an increase at an average annual rate of 8 per cent between 1999 and 2003, the real value of houses at the end of 2003 still remained about 28 per cent below the peak in 1984. The subdued real rate of return, over a long period, on investment in fixed property seemed to have encouraged households to concentrate their saving in risk-averting institutions and financial assets rather than in riskier undertakings and fixed assets. However, from 2003 to the end of 2005, South Africa saw exceptionally strong house price rises (which amounted to a real average annual rate of almost 20 per cent) alongside rising income, reductions in nominal interest rates, and buoyant business and consumer confidence.

Several factors can explain the changes in real house prices. Econometric work on house prices in South Africa (see Aron et al. 2003) suggests plausible long-run income effects on house prices in line with international evidence, with the income elasticity in the range 1.5 to 2. Interest rates, credit growth, and inflation volatility (linked to interest rate uncertainty) are important in explaining house prices. Borrowing costs are ingredients in the user cost of housing. The latter depends on the interest rate minus the expected rate of house price appreciation. Figure 10.3 shows the prime rate of interest to which mortgage and other borrowing rates are closely linked. The relatively high level of mortgage interest rates, on average about 18 per cent during 1984–98, made it difficult for individuals, especially first-time buyers, to enter the property market. Further discussion can be found in Aron et al. (2006).

3.4 *The Durables to Income Ratio*

Figure 10.3 shows the real stock of consumer durables relative to real income and the relative price of durables.[19] The stock obviously lags behind purchases. It seems likely that income growth, a declining relative price, net wealth, and relatively low real interest rates help to explain the relatively strong accumulation of durable stocks between the mid-1970s and early 1980s. The temporary

---

[19] This is measured as the durables deflator relative to the deflator for total consumer expenditure.

decline in 1980 is largely explained by the surge in disposable income given the gold price boom, and the lagged response of stocks to durable purchases. Stocks rose strongly subsequently relative to income, with low real interest rates in 1981–2 a contributing factor. From the early 1980s, real stocks of durables declined relative to real income until the late 1990s. Trade sanctions between 1985 and 1990 help to account for the rise in the relative price of durables, raising the valuation of the existing stock seen in Figure 10.2, but also contributing to the rapid fall in the real stock to real income ratio. This began to be reversed from 1990, when the economy was opened to international competition. Real per capita household income in the 1990s and net wealth to income ratios show no sustained increases, while real interest rates rose, peaking in 1997–8, so providing little stimulus for rises in real purchases. Since 2000, stronger income growth and lower interest rates have contributed to stabilizing the real stock to real income ratio, though the relative prices of durables remain at high levels.

3.5 The Ratio to Income of Pension Assets and Directly Held Securities

Households' interest in financial assets is mostly concentrated in pension funds and at long-term insurers. Over the long run, these assets constitute on average 52.5 per cent of total household financial assets. During the 1990s this ratio rose to more than 60 per cent compared with an average of about 40 per cent during the 1970s. The relatively high level of investment by households in pension funds and long-term insurance is not surprising given the fact that South Africa has a well-developed contractual saving and investment industry. The assets of insurance companies alone amounted to an average of about 73 per cent of the annual gross domestic product between 1995 and 2005. If pension funds are included, the ratio will be even higher.

The rise in the pension assets to income ratio relative to that of directly held securities to income was illustrated in Figure 10.2. In Figure 10.4, the log pension ratio is plotted against the log total return indices in equities and long bonds.[20] It also shows the rising proportion of pension assets invested in equities, from 20 per cent in the early 1970s to over 50 per cent by the 1990s. The correlation between the pension to income ratio and the total returns index for equities is high throughout (the decade by decade correlation coefficient exceeds 0.87 for all three decades from 1970). A substantial part of the rise in the log ratio of pension assets to income can be explained by a weighted average of the total returns indices for equities and bonds. This correlation is

---

[20] See the note for Figure 10.4.

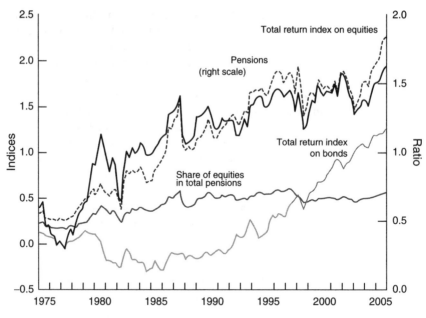

Figure 10.4. Ratio of pension assets to personal disposable income versus total return indices for equities and bonds, and the share of equities in pension assets, South Africa, 1975–2005

Note: The share of equities is a proportion between 0 and 1. The quarterly total return index is defined as: $(P_i/P_{i-1}) \times (1 + QY_i)$, where P_i is the price index of an asset, i, and the per-quarter yield is QY_i. Cumulating quarterly log return indices gives cumulative log total return indices. While the equity and bond yields are assumed free of tax in the case of pensions, this would not be the case for private households holding these assets directly. For equities, a 0.4% per quarter management charge is subtracted from the quarterly return. Both cumulative return indices are deflated by the consumer expenditure deflator to convert to real terms.

likely to be even greater for a more sophisticated weighted total returns measure, giving cash, short-term bonds, real estate, and other asset classes their due. Thus, a fairly passive investment strategy of holding securities and reinvesting the income in the same securities could account for a considerable part of trends in the pension ratio, and its short-term fluctuations.

Regulatory changes have also played an important role, however. The early 1980s saw a relaxation of government-prescribed asset ratios applying to private pension funds and pensions invested with insurance companies, making it possible to expand the proportion invested in equities, on which rates of return were higher. From 1990 official pension funds were no longer restricted to invest only in public fixed-interest securities. And the concern to move official pension funds to an approximately fully funded basis raised contribution rates into these funds.

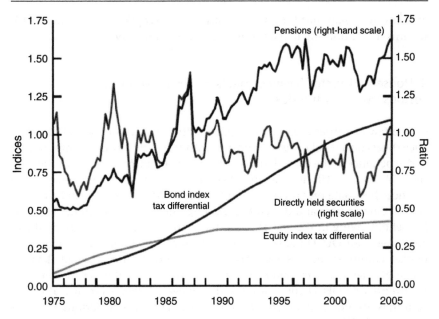

Figure 10.5. Ratios of pension assets and directly held illiquid financial assets to personal disposable income versus the difference between taxed and untaxed total return indices in bonds and equities, South Africa, 1975–2005

Note: The bond (or equity) tax differential is defined as the log (cumulative real return index with dividends untaxed) minus the log (cumulative real return index with dividends taxed). For equities, we apply the tax factor $(1 - mtd)$, where mtd is the tax rate on dividends, 12.5% in recent years; and for bonds, the factor $(1 - mt)$, where mt is the average of marginal income tax rates.

Relative, after-tax returns in alternative assets—directly held financial securities, liquid assets, and housing—are probably also part of the explanation for the rise in pension wealth relative to income. Tax incentives favoured investment in pensions over directly held financial securities. The tax disadvantage of directly held securities is shown in Figure 10.5, where the pensions and the directly held securities ratios are plotted against the differentials between taxed and untaxed total return indices for bonds and for equities. For pensions there were no taxes on dividends or interest,[21] while, for directly held securities, dividend income was taxed.[22] Real returns on liquid assets, particularly

---

[21] Following the Katz Commission (1996), pension fund income began to be taxed. Pension payments are taxed at the respective tax rates of the individuals in receipt of pensions. These tend to be low, since other income is usually low during retirement. Also, a substantial part of the pension is paid out as a tax-free lump sum at retirement.

[22] See the note for Figure 10.5. South Africa had no capital gains tax until after the budget of 2000.

after tax, were poor until the 1990s (with a brief exception in the mid-1980s). Returns in the housing market were weak during 1983–99.

4 Household Sector Balance Sheets in Developing Countries: Lessons from South Africa

Only a few countries currently compile institutional sector and national balance sheets on a regular basis. Countries with relatively advanced information and experience in the compilation of balance sheets include Australia, Canada, the USA, and the UK. Babeau and Sbano (2003) contains useful comparative balance-sheet data on European countries, the USA, and Japan, and a discussion of data sources and difficulties. An ongoing study by Lequiller et al. on household saving in the OECD has entailed the collection of household balance sheets for OECD (2004) countries, now also including a few emerging market countries such as Hungary, Mexico, and Poland. Though data on financial balance sheets comprising financial assets and liabilities are compiled for twenty-one OECD countries, the disaggregated details for several OECD countries are not available or remain partial. The United Nations Statistics Division (UNSD) collects detailed national accounts data on an annual basis from all its member countries, published in 'National Accounts: Main Aggregates and Detailed Tables' (UN, New York). However, there are no balance-sheet data for any country published by the UN in its annual statistical publications, nor are these available from the UN database for member countries.[23]

We carried out an informal survey regarding the status of balance sheet developments for the household sector on a small number of developing countries (comprising those attending Advisory Expert Group meetings on the update of the 1993 System of National Accounts for UNSD).[24] Eight countries responded—namely, Brazil, Costa Rica, Czech Republic, Ethiopia, Jordan, Lithuania, Malaysia, and Trinidad and Tobago. Of this sample, the Czech Republic is the only country that compiles institutional-sector balance sheets (annually) and could provide detailed information.

Many developing countries do not regard the compilation of balance sheets as a priority in the national accounts. In addition to resource constraints, the resource requirements to generate balance sheet data compared with the potential use of the accounts, and the lack of effective users, has hampered the expansion of the national accounts to include balance sheets. Obtaining reliable and timely stock data beyond the traditional requirements to compile the flow data for a set of current accounts within the framework of the national

[23] Personal communication.

[24] An invited group of country experts advises the Inter-Secretariat Working Group on National Accounts (ISWGNA) on updating the 1993 System of National Accounts (SNA).

accounts presents a serious challenge to many developing countries. Preparing balance sheets for any sector requires the availability of detailed data on the stocks, or indicators of the stocks of assets, or at least data on all relevant assets for a relatively long period. Such information is typically not available because economic surveys covering all economic activities are often only introduced and collected for the most recent past. In general, the focus is on the data needed to compile the current accounts, rather than for the accumulation accounts. Further, there is often no information to distinguish the establishments operating under the household sector from other sectors, making institutional sector classifications almost impossible. Data on the assets held by the households collected through general household surveys are often of poor quality because most households tend not to report accurately what they possess. The collection of balance-sheet data is subject to greater problems in valuation than transaction data. Often stock data in business accounts are valued at book value instead of at market value, which implies that adjustments are required. Even in the Czech Republic many problems remain. The basic data source for the assets and liabilities of unincorporated enterprises is usually statistical sample surveys for subsets of selected production industries. More often than not, such a primary data source for the household sector as consumers is not readily available. Consequently, secondary or indirect information from different institutions and other sectors has to be used to get a comprehensive picture of the household sector.

In countries with developed banking systems, the banking regulator, often the central bank, collects and collates basic data on deposits and loans of various types. This is the standard source for data on liquid assets and debt. Insurance companies and pensions funds are typically regulated also, so that the regulator should be regularly monitoring market values of assets and liabilities. In countries with developed equity and bond markets, share registers, in principle, are the data source, though these registers need to be surveyed. However, as we saw from South Africa, this can be problematic, and dividend payments and tax records can offer corroborating information on the fraction of market capitalization held by the domestic household sector. Business surveys can be used as a guide to the capital held in unincorporated enterprises and corporate enterprises whose securities are not publicly traded.

In many poor countries, tangible assets in agriculture measured from household surveys and censuses will be an important component of household wealth, though more relevant for the study of inequality, poverty, welfare, and agricultural supply than for macroeconomic management. Residential housing wealth is typically the most important tangible asset held by households outside agriculture. Most countries have property taxes, often to raise local revenue. If local government tax records can be coordinated, they are a useful source for numbers, types, and values of housing, at least for some base year. Censuses are an alternative source, refreshed from annual data on new construction based on building permits, and estimates of demolition. However, a critical set of data to arrive at market valuations are transactions data on houses traded by type and location. Often, where credit markets are well developed, a large mortgage lender, or an association of mortgage lenders, or an association of real-estate agents can collect data in a systematic form. If mortgage markets are not well developed, it is probable that housing wealth has little macroeconomic significance, as noted above. But transition economies would be well advised to start monitoring the housing price and wealth data, as these markets develop.

For distributional studies as well as for helping to construct national balance sheets, when there are gaps in national sources, there is no substitute for household surveys such as the US Survey of Consumer Finances or Spain's new Survey of Household Finances.[25] Indeed, South Africa itself could benefit from instituting a specialist survey of this kind. Such benefits include improvements in macroeconomic management and in the understanding of the macroeconomic to poverty linkages.

5 Conclusion

There is no doubt about the strategic importance of the household sector and the influence it has on consumption and saving in any economy, but the lack of balance sheet data for the household sector in many countries is a serious shortcoming that hampers the effective assessment of households' consumption behaviour and how a country's national wealth is managed. The South African research provides an example to data-poor countries suggesting it is unnecessary to compile the full sequence of the national accounts, including the financial accounts and balance sheets, before obtaining usable wealth estimates for the household sector. The judicious use of other data sources, the indirect calculation of assets and liabilities, the use of counterpart data, and the exploitation of all relevant data sources and administrative records can go a fair way in the compilation of wealth estimates. An alternative approach would compile the financial account and balance sheet for a single institutional sector, like the household sector, rather than for the full sequence of institutional sector accounts. This could be an opportunity to use the framework of the national accounts to get a proxy of wealth estimates for the household sector, avoiding the constraint of reconciling the integrated economic accounts across all sectors when adequate data sources are not yet available.

Moreover, the trends found in South Africa, of the falling importance of liquid assets and the rise of share holding, pension assets and debt, with deepening financial markets, would be expected to occur more generally as

---

[25] www.bde.es/estadis/eff/effe.htm.

countries liberalize markets and develop more fully. Yet while saving and borrowing flows provide a window on how the household sector is adjusting its balance sheet, it is the balance sheet itself—the stock position—that matters for the assessment of the economic outlook. In practice, changes in the household sectors' net financial wealth are dominated by valuation changes, in particular changes in share prices. In South Africa, notwithstanding the fact that net saving flows have declined over the past decade, the net worth to income ratio rose during the 1990s and beyond as a result of the buoyancy of asset markets. The effect of any wealth revaluation remains difficult to quantify and can vary between countries and evolve within a country as financial development takes place.

Muellbauer (2008; see also Aron and Muellbauer 2006b) distinguishes three facets of financial liberalization, which the previous literature does not bring out clearly. The three facets imply both a shift in the average propensity to consume and important interaction effects—for example, with housing wealth, income growth expectations, interest rates, and indicators of uncertainty. First, financial liberalization reduces credit constraints on households engaging in smoothing consumption when they expect significant income growth. Second, it reduces deposits required of first-time buyers of housing. And, third, it increases the availability of collateral-backed loans for households already possessing collateral. The pure 'housing wealth effect' could be quite small and is uncertain. Individuals planning to purchase their own houses may reduce their consumption because of higher house prices, as they will have to save more in order to meet higher deposits and repayment requirements, offsetting the wealth effect from owners.

For these reasons, the aggregate housing 'wealth effect' can even be negative if access to credit is very restricted. Changes in house values may influence household consumption, even if pure wealth effects are absent, to the extent that they influence the borrowing capacity of households. Households' ability to borrow will in practice depend strongly on their capacity to provide collateral as security for repayments, and real estate is the most widely used collateral asset. Consumers can withdraw part of the increase in housing equity by increasing their borrowing secured on rising property values, and use part of the proceeds to finance additional consumption. Aron and Muellbauer (2006b) provide evidence that the collateral effect in South Africa is strong. Between 2003 and 2005, strong house-price and share-price growth have plausibly made important contributions to strong consumption growth and a lower household saving rate. It is likely that similar developments will occur or are already under way in other emerging market economies as their financial and legal systems develop.

11

Asset Portfolios in Africa: Evidence from Rural Ethiopia

Christian Rogg

1 Introduction: Asset Holdings in Rural Africa

This chapter is concerned with the left-hand tail of the global asset distribution. In other words, it considers some of the poorest people in the world: agricultural households in Ethiopia. The objectives of this chapter are to present a detailed picture of household-level asset portfolios in rural Ethiopia, to discuss some of the factors that shape the composition and size of asset holdings, and to shed light on the roles that assets play in the lives of these households. The study stands alongside the investigation by Burger et al. (Chapter 12, this volume) for Ghana. Relatively little work has been done on asset holdings in Africa. This is true for both rural and urban households. A number of studies have looked at specific assets in isolation, particularly land, but very few have considered the full gamut of assets. Even fewer studies have quantified the various assets and estimated total wealth. Hence, it is difficult to gain a clear picture of who owns what in Africa. This chapter aims to give an overview of what we have learned to date and, more specifically, to provide detailed information on one particular country: Ethiopia. It focuses on rural areas, as this is where 63 per cent of African households are located (World Bank 2006b).

There are several reasons why asset information has not been compiled in a systematic way. First, household data are notoriously poor in Africa, and not many surveys have collected information on assets. Second, the existing asset data are often not easily comparable. For example, some surveys include cash holdings while others report only physical assets; some quantify the value of land

Much of the evidence presented here is drawn from my doctoral thesis at the University of Oxford. The views in this chapter are my own and should not be attributed to the institutions that I am affiliated with. I am grateful for comments received from Jim Davies and other contributors to this project at, and after, the UNU-WIDER project meeting 'Personal Assets from a Global Perspective', Helsinki, 4–6 May 2006.

holdings while others provide only the size of plots. Third, the existing asset data were often collected as a by-product—for example, to control for wealth in regression analyses—and are therefore reported only in passing in many studies.

I begin by discussing the motivations for asset accumulation before considering the types of assets that households in rural Africa own. The reasons why households save have been categorized in several different ways. Keynes (1936) considered 'eight main motives...which lead individuals to refrain from spending out of their incomes'. Gersovitz (1988: 382–424) distinguishes between four such considerations—the life cycle, precaution, investment, and bequests. For each of these motivations, clear differences can be drawn between developing and developed countries. Concepts such as saving for retirement or bequests are sometimes of limited relevance in the context of rural Africa, where formal employment is rarely available and several generations of the same family often cohabitate. The presence of borrowing constraints (and high interest rates) means that saving for self-financed investment is crucial. The high level of exposure to risk—for example, droughts and illnesses, combined with an absence of formal insurance services—means that the precautionary saving motive is of particular importance.

Households in rural Africa, as elsewhere in the world, own a variety of assets. But their choice of assets differs from that in more developed regions. The most important factor in explaining asset holdings in rural Africa is that households tend to derive the majority of their income from agricultural activities, either directly (through farming or rearing of livestock) or indirectly (through processing and selling agricultural produce). Sinha and Lipton (1999) cite evidence that farm income accounts for 55–71 per cent of total income in developing regions around the world. The lowest share (55 per cent) is found in east and southern Africa, while it is significantly higher in western Africa at 64 per cent. Reardon et al. (1988) show that agricultural and livestock income accounted for 44–61 per cent of household income in rural Burkina Faso in the mid-1980s. In western Tanzania, farm income accounts for 79 per cent of total household income (Dercon and Krishnan 1996; Dercon 1998). In rural Ethiopia, the sum of net crop income and livestock income accounted for 83 per cent of total income in 1994, and 94 per cent in 1997 (Rogg 2005). Earlier research by Dercon and Krishnan (1996) showed that farm and livestock income accounted for 61–85 per cent of total income in 1989 for a smaller subset of Ethiopian villages.

As a result of the predominance of agricultural activities, land holdings tend to account for a significant share of household wealth. Burger et al. (Chapter 12, this volume) report that land and housing account for 79 per cent of household wealth in Ghana (when one excludes livestock).[1] Livestock

---

[1] Note that Li and Zhao (Chapter 5, this volume) and Subramanian and Jayaraj (Chapter 6, this volume) find very similar shares for aggregate land and housing wealth in rural China and India (74% and 87%, respectively).

holdings also play an important role and are usually the largest non-land asset in the portfolio. For example, Fafchamps et al. (1998) cite evidence that livestock accounts for 54 per cent of household wealth in Burkina Faso. Given the prominence of livestock in asset portfolios, it is important to disaggregate these holdings. Cattle usually make up a significant share, if not the majority, of livestock wealth. For example, of the two-thirds of households in western Tanzania that owned livestock in 1989–90, 75 per cent owned cattle (Dercon and Krishan 1996). Depending on the season, households may also hold large stocks of harvested produce. Farm tools and other durable assets used in agriculture account for much of the remaining wealth. On the other hand, cash and financial assets play a limited role. The same is true for consumer durables and other luxury goods. While there are good reasons for why we observe limited cash holdings—namely, the fact that most households engage in subsistence farming and carry out only a limited amount of market transactions—it is also likely that financial assets are under-reported and therefore subject to measurement error. In fact, the notorious unreliability of cash data has led numerous researchers to exclude financial assets.

Finally, let me highlight one other important characteristic of portfolios in rural areas of developing countries: they are strongly influenced by seasonal variations. In particular, crop and food stocks make up a much larger share of the portfolio after the harvest than before. Udry (1995) provides an indication of the magnitude of this effect for households in northern Nigeria. He shows that livestock accounts for 68 per cent of asset portfolios early in the harvest season, but falls to around 30 per cent after the harvest has been completed. This points to the importance of ensuring that panel data on assets are collected at approximately the same time each year.

2 Asset Holdings in Rural Ethiopia

The previous section discussed asset portfolios in rural Africa. I now turn to a more in-depth analysis of one particular country—namely, Ethiopia. The reason for focusing on Ethiopia is a pragmatic one: the data collected as part of the Ethiopia Rural Household Survey (ERHS) probably includes the most detailed and reliable asset information of all large panel datasets on African households.

2.1 *Data and Overview of Key Characteristics of Sample Households*

The focus here is on household-level asset holdings in rural Ethiopia in the mid-1990s; more specifically, the period 1994–7. These were eventful, but comparatively stable, years for Ethiopia. In the words of Bigsten et al. (2003), it was 'a period of economic recovery driven by peace, good weather, and much improved macroeconomic management'. Civil war had come to an end in 1991, a structural adjustment programme was agreed in 1994, and parliamentary elections were held in 1995. This period of peace and progress lasted until war broke out with Eritrea in May 1998—see Marcus (2002) for a more detailed discussion of these events. As a result of the peace and stability in the mid-1990s, the economic conditions for most households improved significantly. Dercon (2004) finds that consumption in a subset of the fifteen ERHS villages grew on average by 12 per cent per annum during 1989–97. Bigsten et al. (2003) and Bigsten and Shimeles (2004) study the period 1994–7 and show that poverty in rural areas fell from 42 per cent to 36 per cent. Bigsten and Shimeles (2004) find that poverty fell in eleven of the fifteen ERHS villages. For the following analysis, I employ rounds 1–4 of the ERHS.[2] The ERHS is a panel dataset with approximately 1,450 households in fifteen villages. Dercon (2001) and Rogg (2005) provide further information on the data and the key descriptive statistics. Dercon and Krishnan (1998) discuss the sampling methodology. Bevan and Pankhurst (1996) review the key socioeconomic aspects of the fifteen village communities.

The ERHS sample is broadly representative of households in rural Ethiopia. Dercon (2001) compares it to the much larger Welfare Monitoring Survey and shows that the ERHS is reasonably representative in terms of key demographic variables—for example, household size, percentage of female-headed households, and levels of education. Another notable feature of the ERHS is its low attrition rate (7 per cent between 1989 and 1994, and only 2 per cent between 1994 and 1995 according to Dercon and Krishnan 1998). In part, this may be due to mobility constraints resulting from households' inability to buy or sell land. Finally, the data quality of the ERHS is generally considered to be high in comparison to other household surveys in Africa. Dercon (2001) states that 'the panel provides highly comparable data on [food] consumption, assets, infrastructure, activity choice, household composition, etc.'.

The vast majority of the sample households are landholders and depend on rain-fed crop agriculture for a large share of their income. The remaining income is earned through the trading of livestock, the sale of livestock products, engagement in off-farm activities (such as crafts, petty trading, casual labour, food processing, or the sale of collected firewood) and, to a very small degree, transfers (such as food aid and income from food-for-work programmes). Agricultural production consists of cereals, pulses, and tubers, which are either consumed or traded in local markets. Surprisingly, most ERHS households are net buyers of food (Dercon 2001). Export crops, such as

[2] Other data used in this chapter include rainfall information, village-specific price data to obtain money-metric values for livestock, grain, and other assets (see Dercon and Krishnan 2000 for further details), consumption data, and income data. I am grateful to the Meteorological Institute of Ethiopia, Stefan Dercon, Bereket Kebede, and Agnes Quisumbing for providing me with this data.

coffee and chat, are important in some villages, but only a minority of farmers in the sample grow such crops. Ploughing is usually done by oxen or by hand.

Given that savings are measured at the household level, and that demographic variables play an important role in determining saving (see Section 7), it is worthwhile elaborating on what is of interest in the typical household structure. In rural Ethiopia, most households are nuclear, with five to six people, and monogamic (Dercon and Krishnan 2000). Bevan and Pankhurst (1996) provide more details on the regional variation of household structures among the survey villages. For example, kinship seems to play a more prominent role in determining household membership in the south than it does in the northern and central regions. There are also differences with respect to transgenerational continuity. While there is little evidence of this in central and northern regions, households in the south tend to be more extended and often include three generations as well as the spouses of children and their offspring.

2.2 Average Asset Portfolios in Rural Ethiopia

In line with the earlier discussion, the fact that most households in rural Ethiopia are farmers has a significant impact on portfolio composition. Agricultural assets—land, livestock, farming tools, and stored produce—account for the bulk of household wealth. The ERHS collected information on all these non-financial assets. It paid less attention to financial assets. While lending and borrowing transactions were captured, cash holdings were not recorded. The available evidence indicates that financial assets and even cash play only a very limited role in these village economies. This is to be expected for subsistence farmers. For example, very few households had access to formal financial services: only 1 per cent of households had bank accounts in 1994. However, approximately 19 per cent were members of rotating savings and credit associations (*equbs*) over the survey period; see Ayalew (2003) for more detail.

For these reasons, the emphasis here is on non-financial assets, which account for nearly all household wealth. The discussion includes land holdings. But an important caveat is that there is no real market for land in Ethiopia, as land sales are illegal. The Ethiopian constitution states that 'ownership of rural and urban land is vested "in the state and in the peoples of Ethiopia . . . and [is] not subject to sale or to other means of transfer"' (Marcus 2002: 243). It is, therefore, difficult to quantify the monetary value of land as can be done for all other assets.[3] Kebede (2006) provides a more detailed account of land holdings among the ERHS households and shows that the

---

[3] Note that one approach would be to impute a value for land holdings based on plot size and derived agricultural income. For an example, see Li and Zhao (Chapter 5, this volume). While this approach would make it possible to obtain a monetary value for land holdings, it also introduces potential problems. For example, the value of land holdings would automatically fall if agricultural earnings were to fall, even if the underlying quality of land and its

current distribution of land is as much the result of the socialist redistribution in the 1970s as of feudal structures that existed before.

Tables 11.1 and 11.2 provide information on the prevalence and value of key assets: land, livestock, durables, and crop/food stocks. They show that very few households own no assets (less than 2 per cent), while nearly all households own land (95 per cent), which is either self-cultivated or rented out. The average land holding is 1.51 hectares. Nearly all households also own durable assets. It is important to distinguish between two types of durables. The first group (termed 'productive assets') is used in the production process and includes tools and equipment, such as ploughs and spinning wheels. The second group (referred to as 'unproductive assets') are consumer or luxury goods, such as furniture, electronic appliances, and jewellery. In terms of value, durables account for approximately one quarter of total assets (see Table 11.2). As mentioned earlier, livestock plays an important role in asset portfolios in rural Ethiopia. Livestock is owned by approximately 80 per cent of sample households and accounts for more than half of the portfolio value (see Tables 11.1 and 11.2).[4] The ERHS collected information on twenty-two types of animals. Again, I will consider two different groups. The first is small livestock, which includes goats, sheep, and chicken. The second is large livestock, which can be further subdivided into pack animals (horses, donkeys, mules, and camels), traction animals (oxen), and cattle (bulls, cows, heifers, and calves). Very few households own all types of livestock (only 12 per cent in 1994, rising to 24 per cent by 1997). In particular, around a quarter of sample households do not own large livestock, the purchase of which is beyond their means.

Two further features of livestock portfolios are worth noting. First, the percentage of households that own livestock rises during the survey period. This increase is particularly significant for pack and traction animals. Second, the value of livestock holdings also rises significantly over the survey period. Dercon (2004) documents a similar increase in the volume of livestock holdings. He shows that the number of livestock units held by a sub-sample of the ERHS households rose by 16 per cent per annum between 1989 and 1997.

Food/crop stocks are the last asset category considered here. The most frequently kept stocks are teff, barley, wheat, maize, sorghum/millet, and horse beans. They are held by 61–82 per cent of sample households, depending on the survey year. The value of such assets is difficult to compute, as they are dependent on the season in which the data are collected. As mentioned above, they account for a higher share of the total asset portfolio after the harvest.

---

income-generating capacity were unchanged (e.g., because the household merely decided to dedicate more time to off-farm work).

[4] Dercon (2004) indicates that 75% of households owned livestock before the great famine in the mid-1980s, but lost or sold many animals during the crisis. As a result, only 50% had livestock in 1989.

Table 11.1. Asset ownership, Ethiopia, 1994–1997

	Households owning the respective asset (%)		
	1994	1995	1997
Land*	95	n.a.	n.a.
Durable assets	97	97	98
Productive	89	91	96
Unproductive	86	89	86
Livestock	78	82	85
Small stock	50	53	60
Large stock	72	75	77
Pack	29	31	38
Oxen	40	41	52
Cattle	62	64	67
Crop/food stocks	61	82	76
No assets	2	1	0
Observations	1,463	1,460	1,401

* Given that there is no market for land and that land transactions are illegal, this figure is provided only for the first survey year.

Source: Author's calculations based on the Ethiopia Rural Household Survey.

Table 11.2. Value of asset holdings, Ethiopia, 1994–1997

	1994			1995			1997		
	Mean	Std Dev.	Median	Mean	Std Dev.	Median	Mean	Std Dev.	Median
Land (hectares)*	1.51	1.61	1.00	n.a.	n.a.	n.a.	n.a.	n.a.	n.a.
Durable assets	350.2	1702.3	81.0	399.9	1722.5	110.5	400.7	1158.3	175.0
Productive	62.1	166.6	28.0	82.9	235.7	43.0	101.0	210.9	58.0
Unproductive	288.1	1666.1	40.5	317.0	1675.8	55.0	299.7	1109.7	101.0
Livestock	1721.8	2398.5	891.3	1704.3	2338.8	850.0	2050.3	2941.1	1127.5
Small stock	180.7	451.2	0.0	168.8	428.9	13.8	287.3	907.6	20.0
Large stock	1541.1	2159.6	800.0	1535.5	2117.7	785.0	1763.0	2448.8	1000.0
Pack	154.9	570.1	0.0	158.4	552.7	0.0	213.9	760.6	0.0
Oxen	471.2	853.2	0.0	476.5	883.6	0.0	672.7	1013.2	0.0
Cattle	914.9	1510.3	400.0	900.5	1487.2	400.0	876.4	1270.9	500.0
Crop/food stocks	735.9	1756.2	138.5	1192.7	2098.8	402.0	859.1	2361.8	120.0
TOTAL	2807.9	4103.1	1331.2	3330.1	4383.9	1726.0	3493.8	4690.1	1932.0

* Given that there is no market for land and that land transactions are illegal, this figure is provided only for the first survey year.

Note: Values in birr, except land, which is measured in hectares. Figures are calculated only for those households holding the respective assets; i.e. not for all households. For comparison, the average income per adult was 447 birr in 1994 (Dercon 2001). This figure is for six villages only. The exchange rate at the time was approximately 5 birr = $US1, i.e. the income per adult was around $US90 per year.

Source: Author's calculations based on the Ethiopia Rural Household Survey.

This difference might well be large.[5] For the ERHS households, crop/food stocks account for 25–35 per cent of the portfolio. In summary, nearly all households own durables, around 80 per cent own livestock, and three-quarters hold

[5] It is difficult to tease these differences out of the ERHS data because information on crop/food stocks is available at only one point in time for two of the three survey years. A simple correction is carried out: I assume a linear decrease in crop/food stocks over the period after

crop/food stocks. In terms of value, livestock accounts for more than half, while crop/food stocks and durables account for much smaller shares.

Tables 11.1 and 11.2 show that the value of individual asset holdings, and consequently the composition of asset portfolios, varies over time. Rogg (2005) analyses asset transactions during the survey period and shows that nearly all households were net purchasers of durables (96 per cent), while only a small minority were net sellers (4 per cent). The picture is very different for livestock: 59 per cent of households were net sellers, while only 40 per cent were net purchasers (for 1 per cent of households, the value of their livestock holdings remained constant). This is true for all types of livestock: the number of net sellers is larger than the number of net purchasers. This is to be expected if rearing and trading of livestock are an income-earning activity.[6]

3 How Do Asset Portfolios Vary with Wealth?

So far, I have explored only average asset portfolios. The next step is to consider the distribution of assets across the sample households. I will do so by disaggregating the sample into quartiles for each of the two key asset categories (land and non-land wealth). Table 11.3 presents the results. While 86–100 per cent of households in the wealthiest quartile own the various assets considered here, the figures are much lower for households in the poorest quartile. The differences between the top and bottom quartiles are particularly striking for livestock and crop/food stocks. For livestock, the results are driven by substantial inequality in the holdings of large animals. Taking 1997 as an example, Table 11.3 indicates that 43 per cent of households in the lowest quartile and 100 per cent of households in top quartile owned livestock (using the non-land wealth classification). For cattle, which account for around half the value of the average livestock portfolio, the respective figures are 18 per cent and 93 per cent; for oxen, they are 3 per cent and 91 per cent (results not reported here; see Rogg 2005 for details).

In addition to considering the prevalence of asset holdings, it is also interesting to explore portfolio composition. This is done in Table 11.4. As before, I disaggregate the sample into wealth quartiles (using both land and non-land assets as proxies). Table 11.4 shows that the portfolio share of individual assets varies greatly across wealth quartiles. In general, the portfolio shares of livestock and food/crop stocks increase with wealth, while the share of durable assets decreases. The differences are most striking for durables and livestock. Durable assets account for 25–68 per cent of portfolios in the poorest quartile,

the harvest and adjust the value of such stocks depending on how much time has lapsed between the harvest and the interview date. More complicated consumption rules were experimented with, but yielded similar results.

[6] Information on sales of crop/food stocks is not provided here, as it is difficult to account for the trading of such stocks. Such an assessment would require detailed information on harvests, own consumption, trading, wastage, and storage for all crop/food subcategories.

Table 11.3. Asset ownership, comparison of wealth quartiles, Ethiopia, 1994–1997

Proxy for wealth	Households owning the respective asset (%)								
	1994			1995			1997		
	Durables	Crop/food stocks	Livestock	Durables	Crop/food stocks	Livestock	Durables	Crop/food stocks	Livestock
1. Land									
Lowest quartile	93	33	61	94	74	69	99	67	69
Second quartile	95	46	71	96	74	77	98	64	75
Third quartile	100	82	88	100	87	89	98	74	84
Top quartile	99	86	94	100	90	96	99	86	94
2. Non-land assets									
Lowest quartile	88	18	26	92	52	44	95	55	43
Second quartile	99	49	88	98	80	87	99	74	95
Third quartile	100	82	99	100	94	98	100	80	99
Top quartile	100	96	99	100	98	99	99	96	100
AVERAGE	97	61	78	97	81	81	98	71	79

Source: Author's calculations based on the Ethiopia Rural Household Survey.

Table 11.4. Composition of asset portfolios, comparison of wealth quartiles, Ethiopia, 1994–1997

Proxy for wealth	Share of the portfolio that is held in the respective asset								
	1994			1995			1997		
	Durables	Crop/food stocks	Livestock	Durables	Crop/food stocks	Livestock	Durables	Crop/food stocks	Livestock
1. Land									
Lowest quartile	0.40	0.12	0.48	0.25	0.34	0.41	0.36	0.18	0.46
Second quartile	0.31	0.16	0.53	0.23	0.33	0.44	0.28	0.17	0.55
Third quartile	0.19	0.27	0.54	0.16	0.36	0.48	0.23	0.21	0.56
Top quartile	0.12	0.22	0.66	0.11	0.29	0.60	0.12	0.20	0.68
2. Non-land assets									
Lowest quartile	0.68	0.11	0.21	0.42	0.29	0.29	0.58	0.20	0.22
Second quartile	0.17	0.15	0.68	0.13	0.32	0.55	0.20	0.13	0.67
Third quartile	0.12	0.22	0.66	0.12	0.33	0.55	0.12	0.16	0.72
Top quartile	0.10	0.27	0.63	0.10	0.38	0.52	0.10	0.27	0.63
AVERAGE	0.26	0.19	0.55	0.19	0.33	0.48	0.25	0.19	0.56

Source: Author's calculations based on the Ethiopia Rural Household Survey.

depending on the year and proxy that are used. But they account for only about 10 per cent in the wealthiest quartile. Conversely, the share of livestock is much greater for the wealthiest households (52–68 per cent) than for the poorest (21–48 per cent).

4 Asset Inequality

I now turn to a more formal exploration of asset dispersion in rural Ethiopia by employing two standard inequality measures: the coefficient of variation and the Gini coefficient (see Cowell 1995 for a comprehensive overview of approaches to measuring inequality; Litchfield 1999 and McKay 2002 for shorter introductions). As before, I will consider both the total portfolio and disaggregated asset categories.[7] To ensure robustness of the results, I treat the three survey years as repeated cross-sections. As before, the assessment of inequality in land holdings is limited to the first survey year.

The coefficient of variation (CV) is the standard deviation divided by the mean. The CVs for the full sample are presented in Table 11.5a. Given that the sample consists of fifteen villages, it may be more appropriate to calculate the average of the fifteen village-level CVs (denoted CV')—i.e. $CV'_j = \frac{1}{V} \sum_{v=1}^{V} CV_{jv}$, where $V=15$ is the number of villages and subscript j denotes the asset under consideration. The resulting CVs are shown in Table 11.5b.[8] Note that CV_j captures both variations within and between villages, while CV'_j calculates the average of within-village variations. As a result, the values in Table 11.5a (CV_j) are generally larger than those in Table 11.5b (CV'_j).

The second inequality measure used is the Gini coefficient—calculated as per Deaton (1997: 139). As for CVs, Gini coefficients are calculated for both total wealth and individual asset subcategories. The three years are treated as repeated cross-sections. Table 11.6a provides Gini coefficients for the full sample (γ). Table 11.6b presents averages of the fifteen village-level Gini coefficients (γ'), where $\gamma'_j = \frac{1}{V} \sum_{v=1}^{V} \gamma_{jv}$.[9] As expected, the latter are larger than the former ($\gamma_j > \gamma'_j$ for all assets and years).[10]

---

[7] The discussion here concentrates on wealth inequality. See Fafchamps (2003) for a discussion of how different types of inequality are related.

[8] Note that the CVs in Table 11.5b are weighted by the number of households in each village. This is done to ensure that each household carries equal weight (a standard value judgement) independent of which village it is located in. In most cases, the weighted averages are very similar to the simple averages.

[9] As the CVs before, the Gini coefficients presented in Table 11.6b are not simple averages of the village-level Gini coefficients, but are weighted by the number of households in each village.

[10] Note that these results are somewhat at odds with those presented in Bigsten et al. (2003). They find a very similar expenditure-based Gini coefficient for 1994 (0.39), but identify a significant increase in inequality by 1997 (Gini of 0.43). This increase in expenditure inequality is somewhat puzzling, given that none of the other inequality measures presented above shows a similar trend.

Table 11.5a. Coefficients of variation for consumption, income, and assets, Ethiopia, full sample, 1994–1997

Year	Consumption			Income	Assets							
	Total	Food	Non-food	Harvest	Total	Durables	Livestock total	Livestock large	Livestock small	Food stocks	Land
1994	0.90	0.93	1.30	2.23	1.37	4.86	1.39	1.40	2.50	2.39	1.07
1995	0.93	0.95	1.95	1.84	1.25	4.31	1.37	1.40	2.54	1.76	—
1997	0.87	0.91	1.39	1.92	1.34	1.99	1.43	1.39	3.16	2.75	—

Sources: Author's calculations based on the Ethiopia Rural Household Survey; consumption and income data compiled by Stefan Dercon.

Table 11.5b. Coefficients of variation for consumption, income, and assets, Ethiopia, weighted average of village CVs, 1994–1997

Year	Consumption			Income	Assets							
	Total	Food	Non-food	Harvest	Total	Durables	Livestock total	Livestock large	Livestock small	Food stocks	Land
1994	0.75	0.80	1.05	1.55	1.23	2.44	1.19	1.25	1.99	2.52	0.77
1995	0.78	0.83	1.13	1.43	1.10	2.24	1.17	1.24	1.96	1.74	—
1997	0.79	0.84	1.28	1.37	1.05	1.44	1.17	1.20	2.34	2.25	—

Sources: Author's calculations based on the Ethiopia Rural Household Survey; consumption and income data compiled by Stefan Dercon.

Table 11.6a. Gini coefficients for consumption, income, and assets, Ethiopia, full sample, 1994–1997

Year	Consumption			Income	Assets						
	Total	Food	Non-food	Harvest	Total	Durables	Livestock total	Livestock large	Livestock small	Food stocks	Land
1994	0.43	0.44	0.58	0.69	0.63	0.78	0.63	0.64	0.79	0.77	0.53
1995	0.43	0.43	0.62	0.65	0.59	0.75	0.63	0.64	0.79	0.70	—
1997	0.42	0.43	0.58	0.72	0.59	0.65	0.62	0.62	0.80	0.82	—

Sources: Author's calculations based on the Ethiopia Rural Household Survey; consumption and income data compiled by Stefan Dercon.

Table 11.6b. Gini coefficients for consumption, income, and assets, Ethiopia, weighted average of village Gini coefficients, 1994–1997

Year	Consumption			Income	Assets						
	Total	Food	Non-food	Harvest	Total	Durables	Livestock total	Livestock large	Livestock small	Food stocks	Land
1994	0.38	0.40	0.50	0.56	0.55	0.68	0.56	0.58	0.77	0.72	0.38
1995	0.37	0.38	0.50	0.56	0.52	0.65	0.56	0.58	0.77	0.61	—
1997	0.37	0.38	0.52	0.55	0.49	0.54	0.55	0.57	0.77	0.71	—

Sources: Author's calculations based on the Ethiopia Rural Household Survey; consumption and income data compiled by Stefan Dercon.

The coefficients of variation (Tables 11.5a and 11.5b) and the Gini coefficients (Tables 11.6a and 11.6b) tell a similar story. All inequality measures are comparatively stable over time, with some evidence of decreasing asset inequality over the survey period. The overall Gini coefficient for asset holdings in rural Ethiopia in 1997 is estimated at 0.59, which is comparable to the value of 0.652 imputed by Davies et al. (Chapter 19, this volume) for Ethiopia as a whole (given higher incomes in urban areas, it is expected that the national Gini coefficient is higher than the one for rural areas alone). Land is by far the most equally distributed asset. Both the coefficients of variation and the Gini coefficients for land are much lower than those for total wealth and all other asset subcategories.[11] This could be attributed to the aforementioned prohibition of land sales, which is a heritage of Ethiopia's socialist past. However, Kebede (2006) shows that land inequality among ERHS households is at least as high as in other African countries, if not higher. By international comparison, the Gini coefficient for land of 0.53 in 1994 is indeed above the sub-Saharan African average of 0.49 during the 1990s, but it is relatively low compared to countries in other regions, particularly Latin America (see Torche and Spilerman, Chapter 8, this volume). Note also that our discussion here focuses on the size of land holdings and therefore ignores the quality of the land. In hilly countries like Ethiopia, for example, households in low-lying villages may have larger plots of lower quality, while households higher up may have smaller plots of better quality. However, Kebede (2006) finds that there is no statistically significant correlation between the size and quality of land holdings for ERHS households.

Inequality is surprisingly high for all other assets, with Gini coefficients well over 0.5 in most cases. Small livestock, crop/food stocks, and durables tend to be most unequally distributed, while large livestock have the most equal distribution. This picture is confirmed by the standard deviations presented in Table 11.2. In general, inequality appears to increase with asset liquidity: more liquid assets, like crop/food stocks and small livestock, are more unequally distributed than less liquid assets, such as land and large livestock (but note that the 1994 and 1995 figures for durables do not fit this pattern).

Tables 11.5a and 11.5b provide information not only on asset inequality but also on consumption and income inequality. The picture that emerges is consistent across survey years and across the two measures of inequality. Not surprisingly, consumption inequality is much lower than the other two types of inequality. The Gini coefficient is around 0.4, with inequality in food consumption much lower than inequality in non-food. Surprisingly, income

---

[11] Li and Zhao (Chapter 5, this volume) find that land is also the most equally distributed asset in rural China. But Subramanian and Jayaraj (Chapter 6, this volume) conclude that some other assets, such as buildings, durables, and livestock, are more equally distributed than land in rural India. In fact, land is found to be the major driving force behind inequality in rural India.

inequality is higher than both consumption and asset inequality. The income data presented here are limited to harvest income. To check the robustness of this result, I also computed the Gini coefficients for another income data series, which includes a broader set of income sources.[12] The respective Gini coefficients for 1994, 1995, and 1997 are 0.67, 0.64, and 0.69—that is, slightly lower than those presented in Table 11.6a. However, the overall picture is unchanged: income inequality is higher than asset inequality.

This finding is in contrast to the general belief that asset inequality is higher than both consumption and income inequality. Davies et al. (Chapter 19, this volume) estimate that the global Gini coefficient for *wealth* was 0.893 in 2000 (or 0.804 if measured in purchasing-power-parity terms) and cite other analyses, which estimate that the global Gini coefficient for *income* was 0.795 in 1998.[13] However, when considering the various asset subcategories included in this study, it becomes obvious that the usual pattern also holds for most assets in rural Ethiopia. If we leave aside land because of the aforementioned measurement issues, then we see that three of the four monetized assets (small livestock, food/crop stocks, and durables) are more unequally distributed than income. It is the comparatively low inequality in large livestock, which accounts for the majority of the portfolio, that lowers overall asset inequality significantly. In general, asset inequality in rural Ethiopia appears to be relatively low in comparison to other countries around the world (Davies et al., Chapter 19, this volume).

5 Asset Holdings, Income, and Consumption

It was stated above that most of the assets held by sample households are involved in production. As a result, we would expect that households with more assets generate more income and enjoy higher levels of consumption.[14] However, one could also argue that causality runs the other way—that is, that households with more income are able to invest more and acquire more assets. A detailed analysis of this two-way causality is beyond the scope of this study. Here, I will limit myself to a discussion of correlation coefficients. We would

[12] The data on harvest income was provided by Stefan Dercon (University of Oxford). The more comprehensive income dataset was provided by Agnes Quisumbing (International Food Policy Research Institute). Given that I am using consumption figures that were computed by Stefan Dercon, I am using the corresponding income data, albeit limited to harvest income, to ensure consistency.

[13] Torche and Spilerman (2006) indicate that the Gini index for household wealth exceeds the Gini index for household income in all Latin American countries for which wealth data are available.

[14] I use households as the unit of analysis. A correction for adult-equivalent units in all key variables (i.e. assets, income, and consumption) changes only the magnitude of the values but not the overall conclusions (see Rogg 2005 for more details).

expect that there is a clear positive correlation between assets, on the one hand, and income or consumption, on the other. This hypothesis is confirmed by the data. Table 9 in Rogg (2006) provides the correlations between the value of asset holdings and income and consumption. Land and non-land assets are treated separately in light of the different measurement units (as mentioned above, land is measured in terms of the size of land holdings while non-land assets are measured in terms of their monetary value).

The correlations indicate that the two main asset categories—land and non-land wealth—have a significant positive correlation (between 0.41 and 0.44 for the three survey years). Also, both have a strong positive correlation with household income. This is particularly true for harvest income. Wage income and aid (which tends to take the form of food aid or income from public works projects)—two relatively unimportant sources of income—show a small negative correlation with both asset categories. This is not surprising: households with large land holdings are less likely to dedicate labour to non-farm employment, and aid is usually received by poorer households. There is also clear evidence that households with greater land holdings and non-land assets enjoy higher consumption levels. Finally, the correlation coefficients for land are consistently lower than for non-land assets. This is not surprising given that there is much less variation in land than in non-land holdings (see standard deviations in Table 11.2).

This evidence points not only to a clear link between asset wealth and higher income/consumption, but also to the strong correlation between low asset holdings and consumption/income poverty. Indeed, numerous empirical studies have shown that the value of a household's assets is an important determinant of its probability of being poor. McKay and Lawson (2003) survey the literature and conclude that the characteristics most commonly associated with chronic and transient poverty include limited physical assets and human capital (alongside demographic composition, location, and occupation).

Evidence for rural Ethiopia confirms this link between asset holdings and income or consumption poverty. It also shows that asset ownership seems to place households in a better position to reap the benefits from economic reforms. Dercon (2001) and Dercon and Krishnan (1998) assess the impact of reforms introduced in Ethiopia in the early 1990s. They find that the reforms led to significant welfare gains in rural areas, but that these gains were very unevenly distributed. Households with more physical assets (particularly better land) and more human capital were the main beneficiaries, alongside households with better market connections.

Finally, threshold effects are important in this context. The acquisition of many assets is very 'lumpy'—that is, the indivisibility of key assets means that households need to have either sufficiently high incomes or access to a safe facility for storing savings in order to be able to purchase such assets. Neither may be the case. Let me provide an example. The acquisition of cattle is a 'lumpy' investment that is beyond the means of many rural households. Dercon (1996, 1998) and Dercon and Krishnan (1996) find that the 'lumpiness constraint' prevents rural households in Ethiopia and Tanzania from adopting cattle-rearing as a livelihood strategy and forces them to resort to other, usually less profitable, income-earning activities. This constraint is most binding for the poorest households. Table 11.4 indeed indicates that the asset portfolios of the poorest households differ significantly from those of richer ones.

6 The Impact of Uncertainty on Asset Holdings

Uncertainty is a key aspect of life in rural areas of developing countries. Households are exposed to many risks, ranging from illnesses and theft to flooding and price changes. While all households around the world are subject to risks, poor rural households in low-income countries are particularly affected—see Fafchamps (1999), Sinha and Lipton (1999), and World Bank (2000). For example, they are more exposed to diseases, while often having only very limited access to medical facilities. And their incomes tend to be highly dependent on favourable weather, while having no recourse to hedging such risks on insurance markets.

Economic theory tells us that exposure to risk will affect the choice of asset holdings. More specifically, it predicts that households in riskier environments will hold a lower share of their portfolio in assets with risky returns (e.g. Pratt and Zeckhauser 1987; Kimball 1991, 1993). While the theoretical underpinnings are well developed, little empirical work has been carried out to explore whether this prediction holds for poor rural households in developing countries.[15]

Rogg (2005) tests this hypothesis for the ERHS households, exploring whether residing in a village with more uncertainty provides a disincentive to holding assets with riskier returns. The analysis employs a standard (two-asset) portfolio model with a 'safe' asset (that has certain returns) and a 'risky' asset (that has uncertain returns). The analysis focuses on crop/food stocks and livestock, the two most important liquid assets for households in rural Ethiopia. Following Fafchamps et al. (1998), the returns to crop/food stocks are treated as constant and the returns to livestock as (relatively) uncertain. The hypothesis is that households exposed to more background risk will hold a smaller share of their portfolio in the riskier asset—that is, the portfolio share of livestock holdings decreases as uncertainty increases. Table 10 in Rogg

[15] This is primarily due to limited data availability. Some researchers who have endeavoured this type of analysis are Rosenzweig and Binswanger (1993) for India, Jalan and Ravallion (2001) for China, and Fafchamps et al. (1998) for Burkina Faso.

(2006) shows that, on average, livestock accounts for 56 per cent of the asset portfolio. This share is significantly lower for households that are most exposed to uncertainty (measured by rainfall variability) than for those least exposed.

The figures in Rogg (2006: table 10) provide strong support for the hypothesis, which is confirmed by regression analysis on portfolio composition measures. Following the approach of Jalan and Ravallion (2001), Rogg (2005) also shows that there are important differences across wealth quintiles. In particular, the impact of uncertainty is greatest for the poorest households. These results, which are robust across different years and different proxies for uncertainty and wealth, confirm that households exposed to more uncertainty hold a smaller share of their portfolio in risky assets.

7 How Do Asset Portfolios Vary with Demographic Variables?

The empirical literature consistently finds that demographic variables play an important role in shaping portfolios. This is in line with the predictions of the theoretical literature on saving and asset holdings. Here, I will concentrate on four demographic variables: (1) age of the household head, (2) education of the head, (3) household size, and (4) household illnesses.

A person's *age* plays a central role in the savings literature. The life-cycle/permanent-income hypothesis stipulates that people aim to smooth consumption over their lifetime. They will do so by saving during their adult (or working) years, borrowing when they are young and in education, and running down their savings in retirement; see Attanasio and Banks (2001) for a fuller discussion. There is clear empirical support for the assumption that age has a significant impact on saving patterns in developing countries (see, e.g., Deaton 1990: 61–96). However, while there is clearly a link between the age of the household head and the value and pattern of asset holdings, this link does not tend to follow the predictions of the life-cycle/permanent-income hypothesis. As discussed above, many households in developing countries, particularly in rural areas, are unable to borrow, have difficulties finding safe stores of value for their savings, and cohabit (and pool their income and assets) with several other generations. For example, Burger et al. (Chapter 12, this volume) find no dissaving among families with older household heads in Ghana; instead, the wealth-over-age curves either remain flat or increase with the age of the head.

The link between *education* of the head and the shape and size of the household's asset portfolio is less intuitive. One possible channel is via the income variable. More educated household heads are likely to earn higher incomes and become wealthier. Burger et al. (Chapter 12, this volume) show that more educated household heads in Ghana have higher asset holdings and that a higher level of education is also associated with increasing asset holdings over the lifespan of the household head (while households with low education do not tend to accumulate additional assets as the head ages). A second channel is through investment decisions. There is some evidence that more educated people invest in different assets (see, e.g., Browning and Lusardi 1996). The evidence presented above indicates that the portfolios of wealthier households indeed differ systematically from those of their poorer neighbours. Hence, even if education did not lead to income differentials, it would lead to different portfolio allocations. A third channel, which is likely to be important in agricultural settings, is the choice of income-generating activity. More educated households are likely to be better placed to find off-farm employment. As a result, they may own less land and livestock.

Household size and composition are also likely to be important in explaining saving. It is more difficult to save out of a given income draw if more mouths need to be fed. The link between household size and wealth is likely to be particularly evident in developing countries owing to high uncertainty and the resulting strength of the precautionary saving motive. It has long been argued that larger households can internalize more risk (Kotlikoff and Spivak 1981). For example, falling ill is less likely to be a problem for someone who is part of a large household than for the sole income-earner in a family. Similarly, it is easier to diversify the household's income sources if there is more than one working-age adult. In extreme, households can be considered infinitely lived units ('dynastic households').

The final demographic variable considered here is household proneness to *illness*. Again, there are several channels through which this variable may affect the size and composition of portfolios. Let us start again with the income channel. Ill health is likely to have a negative impact on income. Not only does it result in foregone income, particularly if the illness strikes a working-age adult, but it also necessitates some financial outlay to cover medical costs. Another channel is through risk aversion. There are several theoretical motivations for why greater exposure to uninsurable background risk, such as prevalence of diseases, should orient allocations away from assets whose uncertain returns introduce additional risks—see Pratt and Zeckhauser (1987), Kimball (1991, 1993), Gollier and Pratt (1996).

Table 11.7 overviews the key demographic variables for the sample households. It shows that, on average, household heads are around 47 years old and have less than two years of formal education. The average size of households is around six. Households affected by illness lose between 13 per cent and 23 per cent of their working days. The figures also indicate that the average age of heads increased over the survey period, while average household size fell. These trends are to be expected in mostly poor rural areas where at least some of the younger generations are attracted to migrate to urban areas.

Table 11.7. Demographic characteristics, Ethiopia, 1994–1997

Year	Age of household head			Education of head (yrs)		
	Mean	Std dev.	Median	Mean	Std dev.	Median
1994	46.5	16.3	45	1.79	3.11	0
1995	47.4	16.1	46	1.78	3.11	0
1997	48.4	15.7	48	1.75	3.09	0
	Household size			Share of working days lost to illness*		
1994	6.1	3.0	6	23.1%	n.a.	0
1995	6.0	3.0	6	13.9%	n.a.	0
1997	5.8	2.7	5	15.8%	n.a.	0

* The survey asked interviewees to indicate how many days they had been off owing to illness over the preceding four weeks. The percentages presented are derived by dividing the answer by 28. This is clearly not a comprehensive measure of the household's proneness to illness, but a good proxy nonetheless. Given the derived nature of the percentages, standard deviations are not presented.
Source: Author's calculations based on the Ethiopia Rural Household Survey.

How do the size and composition of asset portfolios vary with these demographic variables? This question is answered in Table 11.8, which provides correlations between the four demographic variables and the various asset holdings. I also carried out regression analysis to ascertain that the story told by the individual correlation coefficients still stood after controlling for non-linearities and the simultaneous effect of the other demographic variables. More specifically, I regressed the various types of assets on the group of four demographic variables, included squared terms, and controlled for heteroscedasticity. The results (not shown here) give a similar picture.

Table 11.8 shows that the only correlations that are consistently negative are those for the number of working days lost to illness. This is not surprising. As mentioned, households that are more prone to illnesses are likely to earn lower incomes. In turn, households with lower incomes tend to own fewer assets than households with higher incomes. The remaining three sets of correlations tend to be positive across the board (the few exceptions with negative correlations are insignificantly low). By far the strongest positive correlations are found for household size. Larger households tend to own more land and more of any of the other assets. In fact, regressing land or non-land assets on household size, while controlling for non-linearities and the impact of the other demographic variables, yields significance at the 1 per cent level across all three years, with the largest coefficients being recorded for livestock. The high positive association for livestock holdings points to the importance of household labour in looking after the animals.

The correlations for characteristics of the household head (age and education) also tend to be positive, but of a smaller magnitude. More educated heads of household tend to be wealthier. This effect has high statistical significance in the regression analysis. Durables and crop/food stocks are the main causes

Table 11.8. Correlations between asset holdings and demographic variables, Ethiopia, 1994–1997

Type of asset	1994		1995		1997	
	Age of head	Education of head	Age of head	Education of head	Age of head	Education of head
Land (plot size)	0.08	0.01	n.a.	n.a.	n.a.	n.a.
Durables	− 0.02	0.09	− 0.02	0.10	− 0.03	0.14
Livestock	0.11	0.04	0.12	0.04	0.07	0.08
Crop/food stocks	0.01	0.08	0.00	0.11	0.01	0.07
Total portfolio	0.06	0.10	0.06	0.11	0.04	0.12

Type of asset	1994		1995		1997	
	Size	Days lost to illness	Size	Days lost to illness	Size	Days lost to illness
Land (plot size)	0.13	0.02	n.a.	n.a.	n.a.	n.a.
Durables	0.06	− 0.03	0.07	− 0.02	0.12	− 0.01
Livestock	0.24	− 0.02	0.22	− 0.02	0.27	− 0.07
Crop/food stocks	0.12	− 0.07	0.15	− 0.03	0.15	− 0.02
Total portfolio	0.21	− 0.05	0.22	− 0.03	0.28	− 0.06

Source: Author's calculations based on the Ethiopia Rural Household Survey.

for this positive association. The near-zero correlation between education and land holdings, and the (unreported) insignificant regression coefficients, are in line with the aforementioned possibility that more educated household heads derive a greater share of their income from off-farm activities. While older heads of household tend to be wealthier, this effect was often not statistically significant in the regression analysis. In fact, much of this positive association is driven by an increase in livestock holdings as the head of household gets older.

8 The Role of Assets in Marriage Decisions

A person's wealth, or lack thereof, has a fundamental impact on most aspects of life. While this chapter has focused mostly on economic aspects relating to asset holdings, the sociological literature provides rich insights into other functions of assets—for example, in determining a person's status in society; see Bevan and Pankhurst (1996) for a sociological survey of the ERHS villages. Here, I will concentrate on one such function, which is often overlooked— namely, the role that assets play in marriage markets. The discussion draws on three recent studies by Fafchamps and Quisumbing (2002, 2005a, b), who investigate this issue for the ERHS households. A more comprehensive overview of the issues is provided by Deere and Doss (Chapter 17, this volume).

Marriages in rural Ethiopia tend to be arranged by the couple's parents, often without consulting their children. Two-thirds of the survey respondents indicated that they had never spoken to their future spouse before the marriage (Fafchamps and Quisumbing 2002). Furthermore, remarrying is comparatively frequent, with 43 per cent of husbands and 32 per cent of wives having been married more than once (Fafchamps and Quisumbing 2005b).

In rural areas of developing countries, a marriage is not only the union of two people and the formation of a family. As most households are engaged in farming, a marriage also constitutes the formation of a new 'production unit'. The assets that a couple is endowed with at the time of marriage can thus be considered as the 'start-up capital' with which this new enterprise gets established. Such assets, therefore, have an effect not only on a household's immediate income, but also on its long-term prosperity (Fafchamps and Quisumbing 2002, 2005a). The extent to which spouses receive assets at the time of marriage, and the type of assets they receive, vary across cultures. Deere and Doss (Chapter 17, this volume) analyse land ownership by women in Africa and conclude that marriage is the most common way for women to gain access to land. Rather than receiving land from their parents at the time of marriage, women are allocated land by their husbands through either use rights or permanent rights. Given that most marital regimes in Africa maintain the separation of spouses' property, women's claims to land do not extend beyond the marriage (for example, women lose their rights if there is a divorce).

In rural Ethiopia, marriage is an occasion for substantial asset transfers—in fact, intergenerational asset transfers take place primarily at the time of marriage (Fafchamps and Quisumbing 2005b). These transfers do not usually take the form of ritual gifts, such as dowries or bride prices. Instead, the wealth transferred takes the form of assets that will enable the new household to earn an independent income. The most important asset that the new couple inherits is land, which is usually brought to the marriage by the groom. Indeed, grooms may have to wait until they are allocated land before they are able to marry. As a result, the value of assets that the groom brings to the marriage is ten times greater than what the bride contributes: 4,270 birr versus 430 birr (Fafchamps and Quisumbing 2002, 2005a). Numerous studies have shown that this pattern holds true for other countries as well (see Deere and Doss, Chapter 17, this volume, for a summary). In fact, two-thirds of brides in rural Ethiopia bring no assets to the marriage. If they do contribute assets, these usually take the form of livestock rather than land. The value of assets brought into the marriage is shown to have a significant effect on the control over assets during the marriage and the distribution of assets upon divorce.

Family wealth also plays an important role in the selection of marriage partners (Fafchamps and Quisumbing 2005b). In particular, it can be shown that households in rural Ethiopia engage in 'assortative matching'. In other words, the rich marry the rich while the poor marry the poor. In line with such behaviour is the finding that the value of assets brought to the marriage is positively correlated with parents' wealth.[16] Finally, there is also evidence that the parents of brides act strategically in endowing their daughters with assets. For example, they tend to give more to daughters if that will raise their chances of marrying a wealthy groom. Parents do not, however, compensate for outcomes in the marriage market—that is, they do not allocate more assets to those siblings who were less successful in finding wealthy spouses (Fafchamps and Quisumbing 2005a).

In summary, the distribution of assets at the time of marriage plays an important role in the matching of spouses and is likely to have a significant impact on the household's future prosperity. The positive correlation between parental wealth and transfers to spouses as well as the positive correlation between the wealth of the groom's family and of the bride's family imply a perpetuation of wealth inequality and constitute a limitation on intergenerational mobility. However, Fafchamps and Quisumbing (2005b) show that the Gini coefficient for current asset holdings is significantly lower than for asset holdings at the time of marriage. This could be the result of continuing asset accumulation by less wealthy households, parental bequests after marriage, or public redistribution policies. Furthermore, it is worth pointing out that schooling and other measures of human capital are likely to become more important than physical asset holdings as a country becomes more developed.

9 Conclusions

Evidence on household-level asset holdings in Africa is scarce. We know much more about consumption and income patterns of African households than we know about their wealth. This chapter contributes to filling this gap by investigating the distribution of asset holdings in rural Ethiopia. It is one of only a few efforts to provide a detailed and disaggregated analysis of household-level asset portfolios in Africa. I show that non-financial assets make up the majority of household wealth. Furthermore, the composition of asset portfolios varies significantly across sample households. For example, it depends on the size of the portfolio and the household's exposure to uncertainty. Finally, asset holdings are positively correlated with income and consumption.

I show that asset inequality is lowest for land and much higher for all other assets. Asset inequality is found to be higher than consumption inequality but, somewhat surprisingly, lower than income inequality. The chapter also explores the importance of demographic variables in shaping asset portfolios

---

[16] This finding is in line with evidence presented by Torche and Spilerman (Chapter 8, this volume) for Chile, where children's wealth is almost entirely determined by parental wealth.

and demonstrates that asset holdings increase with household size and with the education of the household head. Finally, it is shown that assets play a critical role in marriage markets in rural Ethiopia.

The chapter also points to some gaps in our knowledge and identifies methodological challenges when compiling and analysing household-level asset data in very poor rural environments. As regards gaps in our knowledge, the chapter does not claim to present a full account of asset holdings in Ethiopia. For example, it covers only rural areas and does not include financial assets. It also focuses only on positive asset balances. The absence of information on indebtedness means that it is not possible to assess the net wealth of households—that is, assets minus liabilities.[17]

As regards methodological challenges, the chapter identifies several issues that are particular to the context of poor rural households in sub-Saharan Africa and other developing countries. Comprehensive panel datasets on assets do not yet exist in Africa. Data on assets are patchy, as household surveys are generally more concerned with the collection of accurate consumption data than wealth data. Furthermore, the quantification of asset holdings—and their monetization in the case of non-financial assets—is often tricky. One approach is to ask survey participants about the value of the respective asset, but this may lead to measurement error if households do not have accurate information (for example, because an asset is not readily traded) or if they have an incentive to under- or over-report the value of their assets. An alternative is to use location-specific price data gathered at the closest market, but this approach requires significant additional effort (and the data may not be accurate because many assets are difficult to standardize: the price of an ox varies significantly depending on the health and age of the animal).[18] Another challenge that is peculiar to gathering asset data for rural households in developing countries is the important role played by seasonal variations. Given the predominance of agricultural activities, asset portfolios vary significantly between the pre-harvest and post-harvest seasons. Hence, it is critical to measure household wealth at the same point of time for all households in the sample and to ensure that future survey rounds are conducted again at the same point in the agricultural season.

As noted above, there are still big gaps in our knowledge of asset holdings in Africa, and the methodological challenges are formidable. But the research presented in this volume, and the multitude of approaches applied to a broad range of countries and datasets, shows that it can be done. This gives hope that soon we will have a clearer picture of who owns what in Africa.

---

[17] Burger et al. (Chapter 12, this volume) find that wealthy households are more likely than poor households to incur debt in Ghana. They find that the proportion of households that incur debt is 49% among the richest wealth quintile and only 33% among the poorest wealth quintile.

[18] A combination of these two approaches is used for the present study.

12

Marketable Wealth in a Poor African Country: Wealth Accumulation by Households in Ghana

Ronelle Burger, Frikkie Booysen, Servaas van der Berg, and Michael von Maltitz

1 Introduction

Accumulated wealth is clearly important for the survival and advancement of poor households. Although wealth is traditionally associated with the upper end of the income distribution, it may play a more pivotal role in the lives of the poor. Recent empirical and theoretical analysis has shown that drawing on wealth can help keep poor households afloat after an income or expenditure shock. Udry (1995), for instance, demonstrated that farmers in northern Nigeria appear to smooth consumption through dissaving after negative income shocks.[1] Accumulated wealth can create a buffer for the most vulnerable.

Empirical and theoretical evidence also suggests that assets may be pivotal to help the poor get ahead.[2] For instance, the theoretical work of Aghion and Bolton (1997) proposes that households with little accumulated wealth may find it difficult to acquire capital to fund an income-generating venture. Owing to their lack of wealth, they are not able to have a large financial stake in the proposed income-generating venture. This can cause incentive

This study builds on previous research by the authors investigating poverty and inequality trends in seven African countries (Booysen et al. 2008), which was funded by the Poverty and Economic Policy (PEP) research network of the International Development Research Centre (IDRC). More information on the research network's activities is available from: www.pep-net.org. The authors are grateful to Jim Davies, Cheryl Doss, Seymour Spilerman, and Florencia Torche for helpful comments on an earlier draft of the study. All errors and omissions remain the responsibility of the authors.

[1] Although there is controversy regarding the extent of the smoothing, it is a well-established finding in the literature that there is a substantial amount of smoothing that occurs and that smoothing is often achieved via the sale of assets. See Rosenzweig and Wolpin (1993) and Fafchamps et al. (1998) on the sale of livestock following an income shock.

[2] See, e.g., Bhide and Mehta (2006) and Aghion and Bolton (1997).

problems, making the project more risky and hence also more expensive to fund. In some cases these incentive problems may make projects prohibitively expensive, thus shutting off a possible escape out of poverty.

For the reasons cited above, wealth may significantly enhance a household's prospects of exiting poverty. However, a high proportion of the poor in Africa has no or extremely low levels of marketable wealth (Rogg, Chapter 11, this volume). For many African households it is difficult to save. Low and variable income makes it hard to save in at least two ways. First, in African countries where many households struggle to survive, there is often little opportunity to build up a buffer. Most households also face a further obstacle: finding a liquid and safe store of value. Owing to the high overheads and institutional ineffi-ciencies associated with banking in these countries, few African households have access to financial products and banking services. Informal community savings schemes are suboptimal because they do not provide a safe value store for households, as households in the same community are often exposed to similar (covariate) risks. Non-financial assets may present an alternative saving form, but it comes with its own risks. These assets can easily be expropriated through theft and, in the case of livestock, also drought and are hence not secure stores of value (Collier and Gunning 1999a). In addition, assets often require investments that are large relative to the household's income, which makes it more difficult to use assets to 'smooth' income.

In an attempt to learn more about these processes, this study examines the accumulation of marketable wealth in an African country. The focus is on marketable wealth because the welfare-improving mechanisms of wealth for poor and vulnerable families described in the paragraphs above are reliant on liquid stores of value.

Constructing estimates of the marketable wealth of households in develop-ing countries is far from straightforward. As far as the authors know, there are no wealth surveys for developing countries, and regular household surveys do not traditionally gather sufficient information to track the wide variety of savings forms found in developing countries, including financial assets such as pension funds, bonds, and shares as well as non-financial assets such as land, livestock, and housing. There are also problems with the reliability of data on financial assets reported in surveys. It is difficult to obtain reliable financial information from poor households because of the long recall periods and often also the inadequate levels of numeracy and literacy. Because of these deficiencies in existing data sources and approaches, this study investigates the merits of an alternative approach that can be applied to any representative household survey containing information on consumer durables. The ap-proach uses data on the ownership of a number of non-financial assets to construct an index to approximate accumulated wealth holdings. It has been established that questions regarding the ownership of non-financial assets are more reliable than self-reported valuations of the respondent's financial assets.

Although admittedly less than ideal in many respects,[3] this method may provide a way to study wealth in developing countries where there are no wealth surveys available.

The proposed index of consumer durables appears to be an appropriate approach here given the study's focus on marketable wealth. Wolff (2001) defined marketable wealth as a store of value that can be readily converted to cash. Because of the peculiarities and complexities of savings behaviour in African countries, consumer durables have been shown to be widely held and are expected to have a strong correlation to marketable wealth for the 'representative' individual, despite it comprising a relatively small share of wealth.[4] Wolff's definition (2001) of marketable wealth excludes consumer durables, but the inclusion of consumer durables under this umbrella term can be justified in this context. As discussed earlier, for many households in African countries it is difficult to find investments that are liquid and safe stores of value. While consumer durables are admittedly not as liquid as savings or stocks, they may as a rule be 'more readily converted to cash' than assets such as land and houses. For instance, Collier and Gunning (1999b: 7) claim that 'most land in Africa is still not readily marketable'. They argue that land titling schemes have not improved marketability of land as much as hoped. Aryeetey (2004) reports that in the rural areas of Ghana 53 per cent of households did not own their farmland and 40 per cent of those households who did did not have title deeds for the land.[5] Evidence presented by Torche and Spilerman (Chapter 8, this volume) regarding the misreporting and misinterpretation of questions about house ownership in Latin American countries may make it reasonable to assume that a large proportion of house ownership captured in surveys should not be regarded as marketable wealth.[6] Additionally, there is little indication that conventional stores of marketable wealth such as houses and land are necessarily better stores of value than durable assets in Ghana.[7]

---

[3] The shortcomings of the approach are investigated in Sections 3 and 5 of this chapter.

[4] Rogg (Chapter 11, this volume) reports that, while nearly all households own durable assets, this accounts for only roughly one-quarter of total assets.

[5] The low incidence of use of land as a guarantee for loans and houses can be interpreted as providing further support for this view. Udry (1995) finds that in Nigeria land was used as a guarantee for loans in only 3% of cases. According to the GLSS 1998, only 1.4% of the 2,662 loans tracked in the survey used land as collateral. Housing was used as a guarantee for only 0.2% of these loans. Most of the loans had no guarantee, but 4.4% of these loans were backed by 'other' unspecified assets. This may suggest that the limited use of housing and land as collateral is due not merely to the informal nature of the market for loans, but also possibly to the fact that these assets are not considered to be marketable forms of wealth.

[6] There is also some evidence of this in the GLSS 1998. Almost 20% of those who report owning a house in the module on household assets claim not to own a house elsewhere in the survey. The survey asked no more detailed questions regarding house ownership.

[7] According to the GLSS 1998, the median depreciation rate for land is positive (indicating appreciation in terms of the median) and ranks top of a list of twenty-four household assets, but land has the second highest variation in the depreciation rate. Housing ranks seventh highest in terms of median depreciation (performing worse than cameras, cars, motorcycles,

When using a household survey to study wealth, it is important to bear in mind that household survey samples are designed to give an adequate representation of the country's population, not the country's wealth. Because of the high concentration of wealth at the upper end of the distribution, it has been shown that household surveys are likely to under-represent total wealth and the extent of inequality in its distribution (Davies and Shorrocks 2005). This is less of a concern for this study, as the emphasis here falls not on assessing total wealth or investigating the inequality of wealth or changes in wealth levels, but rather on identifying patterns in wealth accumulation and drivers of wealth accumulation.

The authors choose to apply this method to Ghana because it is viewed as an interesting case for examining wealth accumulation in the light of the stable growth and the increase in the general levels of education experienced in recent years. Since 1990 per capita growth rates have been consistently positive and since the mid-1990s these have been reasonably stable around 2–3 per cent (ISSER 2005). The average number of years of education had increased by 27 per cent between 1991 and 1998, rising from 4.5 to 5.7 years (Teal 2001). According to Teal (2001) this period was also marked by an improvement in the incidence of poverty.

Ghana is also an appropriate choice because it appears to typify the problems associated with household wealth accumulation in African countries in many ways. Owing to the dominant role of agriculture in the economy,[8] most households are exposed (either directly or indirectly) to the high levels of uncertainty associated with agricultural production. There are few safe and liquid stores of value available to the largely rural population.[9] Access to formal sector financial services is remarkably low in Ghana.[10] Combined housing and land account for more than 65 per cent of total wealth,[11] but, owing to complex ownership arrangements and claims, thin markets and the 'lumpiness' of these assets, housing and land can often not be used to smooth consumption and are

---

air conditioners, shares, and also, land) and has the fourth highest variation in rate of depreciation. Shares and motorcycles both have reasonably high variation in depreciation rates, but air conditioners, cars, and cameras have considerably lower variation in depreciation rates. The calculated depreciation is based on the self-reported (recalled actual) purchase prices and the self-assessed current market worth of assets. Adjustments were made for inflation.

[8] It is an economy dominated by agriculture, even more so than the average African country. In 2005 agriculture was responsible for 60% of employment and represented 37% of GDP (World Bank 2006b).

[9] In 2003, 54.6% of the population resided in rural areas (World Bank 2006b).

[10] The market penetration of banks in this country is extremely low, even by African standards. On average, claims on the private sector by deposit money banks and other financial institutions constituted barely more than 3% of GDP between 1980 and 1995, according to Demirgüç-Kunt and Levine (2001). This is much lower than the African median of 15% and considerably lower than the OECD average of 78%.

[11] These estimates are from the GLSS 1998. The share of average wealth is, however, much lower at 14% and 18% for housing and land respectively.

frequently not accepted as collateral (Collier and Gunning 1999b). For instance, Aryeetey (2004) reports that in 1993 only 21.2 per cent of farm-owning households held the right to sell their farms. The country is in many ways a typical African country. According to 1999 estimates the poverty head count ratio in Ghana was 44.8 per cent, just slightly lower than the 45.7 per cent ratio for sub-Saharan Africa (World Bank 2006b). According to the Penn World Tables, Ghana's GDP per capita was $US1,349 in 2000, higher than the population weighted average GDP per capita for the continent of $US1,006 (Heston et al. 2002).

2 Data

There are four main data sources available for Ghana that could be used for this analysis: the Population Censuses, the Core Welfare Indicators Surveys, the Ghana Living Standards Surveys (GLSS), and the Demographic and Health Surveys (DHS). The first two data sources have obvious deficiencies. There are no recent population censuses and the Core Welfare Indicators Survey is not detailed enough. This leaves the GLSS and DHS. The GLSS tracks a long list of assets, but its surveys are more dated than the DHS series and do not allow us to observe the full impact of the high growth and the recent increase in educational levels on wealth accumulation. The last GLSS was conducted in 1998 and the three preceding surveys were in 1991, 1987, and 1988. The last DHS was in 2003 and there are also DHS available for 2002, 1998, 1993, and 1988.

As the name suggests, the DHS are focused on issues affecting health and demography, including data on marriage, fertility, family planning, reproductive health, child health, and HIV/AIDS (Rutstein and Rojas 2003). These surveys are available for seventy-five developing countries, and in most of these countries there have been more than one survey. The surveys were initiated by the United States Agency for International Development (USAID), and, although they have little information of a financial or economic nature, they contain questions on ownership of a range of durable household assets that can be used to construct an indicator of wealth.

The DHS series may appear to be an unorthodox choice of data source for the questions we intend to examine, but the surveys have a number of strengths that make them particularly attractive for a comparison of asset indices over time. The standardization of a number of sections of the survey enhances the comparability across time for variables in sections. Because of the continuity associated with a large, centrally coordinated programme of surveys, one would also expect the survey samples of the DHS series to be more comparable across years than the samples of household survey samples designed by national statistical offices. Three nationally representative DHS were selected for this analysis: 1993, 1998, and 2003. There are ten private assets that are tracked in each of these surveys.

3 Constructing an Asset Index

Asset indices are widely used to construct welfare measures for poverty analysis. The World Bank (2003) reports that there is generally a significant, but modest correspondence between these indices and monetary measures of welfare, ranging between 0.20 and 0.40. Asset indices often include a wider range of indicators than what may be suggested by the name, including ownership of assets, quality of housing, and access to public services. In the development literature there are two competing motivations for using this approach. According to the first approach it is assumed that the correspondence between the index and the welfare measures is strong enough that asset indices can mimic the more traditional monetary measures of welfare in cases where a survey contains no income or expenditure data. The work of Sahn and Stifel (2000) provides an example of this approach. Conversely, others advocate the use of the asset index approach, not because of the correspondence between the asset index and monetary measures of welfare, but because of discrepancies (e.g., Asselin 2002). According to this view, asset indices are used to construct a broader measure of welfare, incorporating more dimensions of deprivation and well-being than are included in conventional monetary measures.

This study examines whether this approach can also be used to compile an index to approximate wealth. For this purpose we deliberately select a set of indicators that are likely to be correlated with personal wealth. Section 5 investigates how closely the constructed index resembles wealth.

There is a wide array of techniques available to calculate the weights for the assets in the index. Although the principal component approach (PCA) is widely used for the construction of indices in development economics literature, most of these analyses are reliant on discrete and categorical variables, and multiple correspondence analysis (MCA) is a more appropriate technique for these types of variables. PCA was essentially designed for continuous variables, as it assumes a normal distribution of indicator variables. In contrast, MCA makes fewer assumptions about the underlying distributions of indicator variables and is more suited to discrete or categorical variables. Hence, the authors opt for MCA rather than PCA.

Asselin (2002: 14) describes the calculation of a composite poverty indicator using MCA as a four-stage process. First, one constructs an indicator matrix (of ones and zeros) that shows the asset ownership of each household. The households, for example, are displayed as rows, and each asset is represented by the inclusion of a column for each of the set of mutually exclusive and collectively exhaustive ownership categories for that asset. In other words, each categorical asset ownership variable is reduced to a set of binary indicators. In this way, every household will indicate a '1' in exactly one of each asset's set of columns or categories, and a '0' in every other column. Second, the profiles of the households relative to the categories of asset ownership are calculated. The row profiles of a matrix are the rows of that matrix, each divided by its row sum. Third, MCA is applied to the original indicator matrix, and provides a set of category weights from the first dimension or factorial axis of the analysis results. Fourth, these MCA category weights are applied to the profile matrix. A household's MCA composite indicator score is calculated by adding up all of that unit's weighted responses. The calculation of the household's asset index score can be represented as follows:

$$MCAi = Ri_1W_1 + Ri_2W_2 + \ldots + RijWj + \ldots + Ri_jW_J \tag{12.1}$$

where $MCAi$ is the ith household's composite wealth indicator score, Rij is the response of household i to category j, and Wj is the MCA weight for dimension one applied to category j.

In using the asset indices to consider the evolution of marketable wealth over time, it is also necessary to construct asset indices that are comparable over time. There are two possibilities that would enable comparison over time. On the one hand, the asset index can be constructed using pooled weights obtained from the application of MCA to all three surveys or the index can be based on baseline weights obtained from an analysis of the first period survey. We opted for the latter. To ensure comparability across time, only variables that appear in all three surveys and were coded from similarly phrased questions were included in the analysis.

4 Estimating Wealth Using an Asset Index

Table 12.1 lists the weights assigned to each of the assets using the MCA approach. There are nine binary household-level consumer durables: radio, television, refrigerator, bicycle, motorcycle, car, horse and cart, video recorder, and tractor. In addition, there is also a categorical indicator on the type of flooring with four options (smart floor,[12] cement floor, earth floor, and other). While it is unlikely that any of these items would be purchased primarily as investments, Aryeetey (2004) argues it makes sense for less affluent households to invest in productive assets that may have a dual role for the household. On average consumer durables represent 74 per cent of marketable wealth in Ghana.[13] Also, consumer durables are expected to have a positive and significant relationship with other forms of marketable wealth because households may reveal information regarding their risk profile, demand for savings, and wealth holdings in their acquisition of specific consumer durables.[14]

---

[12] 'Smart' floors are generally carpeted, wooden, or tiled floors.

[13] Based on our own calculations from GLSS 1998.

[14] According to the GLSS, the correlation coefficient between consumer durables and non-consumer durable forms of wealth is highly significant and positive (0.22).

Table 12.1. Weights assigned to assets by multiple correspondence analysis, Ghana

Asset	Loss in asset index score associated with not owning this asset	Gain in asset index score associated with owning this asset	Increase in score associated with ownership
Bicycle	− 0.009	0.045	0.054
Horse and cart	− 0.001	0.300	0.301
Radio	− 0.171	0.247	0.418
Tractor	− 0.001	0.670	0.671
Motorcycle	− 0.009	0.757	0.766
Television	− 0.115	0.764	0.879
Refrigerator	− 0.095	0.949	1.044
Car	− 0.034	1.252	1.286
Video recorder	− 0.035	1.518	1.553
Mutually exclusive flooring options			Increase in score for each floor option relative to earth floor
Earth floor		− 0.188	
Cement floor		− 0.095	0.093
Other floor		0.114	0.302
Smart floor		0.545	0.733

Source: Authors' calculations using Ghana DHS (1993).

The first dimension of the index accounts for 0.969 of the total inertia in the data. In other words, almost all the variation in household asset ownership can be summarized by the first dimension of the MCA. This provides adequate justification for use of only the first dimension from the MCA in the weighting of the survey responses when calculating the asset index scores.

In line with intuition, Table 12.1 shows that possession of any of the nine binary assets would increase a household's asset index score (although in the case of bicycle ownership, only barely). In most cases there is an asymmetry between the gain associated with ownership and the loss associated with not owning the asset. For instance, owning a horse and cart will increase the index score of a household by 0.3, but there is little cost to not owning a horse and cart. While ownership of this asset may be associated with a higher value of this latent variable, the lack of ownership is not necessarily associated with a lower value of this latent variable. There are only two assets—namely, radio and television—where the loss in the index score associated with non-ownership exceeds 0.1. If the latent variable that this asset index is approximating is assumed to be wealth, this would mean that, for the remainder of the consumer durables,[15] not owning a particular asset does not appear to be a good predictor of wealth deprivation.

[15] The term 'consumer durables' is not traditionally applied to the flooring categories listed here. Although mud or cement floors may have a relatively long life, they can hardly be regarded as manufactured goods. However, these two categories can be interpreted as representing the decision not to purchase other categories of flooring that could be classified as manufactured goods (e.g., tiles).

Generally there also seems to be some correlation between the weight assigned to the ownership of the asset and the cost of acquiring the asset. The pattern is, however, not consistent. The weight associated with ownership of a video recorder is more than double that of the weight of tractor ownership. This may be because in such an index this variable may represent far more than merely ownership of a video recorder. A video recorder is strongly associated with a high position on the scale of this latent variable. If the latent variable is presumed to be wealth (as intended), then it may for instance be that ownership of video recorders is highly correlated with large wealth holdings and ownership of other, more expensive assets so that this variable can effectively be used to identify the most affluent households among our sample. An increase in the index score is usually associated with a rise in the number of assets, but this does not hold true in all cases. Also, for most assets the likelihood of ownership generally increases monotonically as one progresses from the bottom towards the top of the asset index distribution. Bicycles and horse carts are exceptions and appear to be inferior goods that are traded in when households become sufficiently wealthy.

There is also evidence of a hierarchy or ladder of assets: the households in the bottom asset quintile tend to own very few assets: they have a cement or earth floor and a small proportion also own a bicycle. None of the households in the bottom quintile possesses any of the other eight assets in the index. All households in the quintile second from the bottom have bicycles and cement floors. Households in the third quintile are the first to report ownership of other floors, horse and carts, and radios. Ownership of smart floors, televisions, motorcycles, refrigerators, tractors, and cars start appearing in the second quintile from the top. Ownership of video recorders is restricted to the top quintile of households only.

It appears that the index has difficulty distinguishing the relative wealth of observations at the bottom end of the distribution. Figure 12.1 depicts the cumulative density function for the asset index pooled across the three surveys, showing much crowding in the left-hand side of the curve, with more than 70 per cent of observations crammed in between -0.7 and 0, a space that represents less than one-tenth of the full range of the index. This crowding at the bottom end of the distribution could merely reflect how difficult it is for some households to acquire assets. Alternatively, it could be a symptom of censoring due to shortcomings in the set of assets available (for example, that the list does not include enough of the assets in which the very poor invest).

The index has 215 unique values, but the bottom 44 per cent of the households in this pooled sample attained 10 different index values only. This is in contrast with the top 10 values that account for only 0.14 per cent of the sample. There are 47 unique values for the asset index that occur in the top 5 per cent of the distribution, ranging from 3.33 to 7.05. In principle censoring

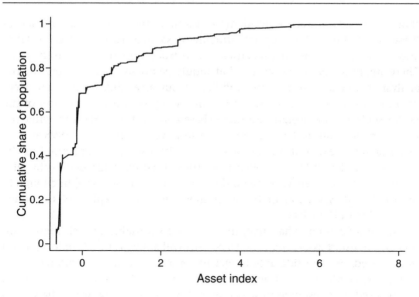

Figure 12.1. Cumulative density curve for asset index, Ghana

may occur on both ends of the asset index, but in this case it appears to be a much larger concern at the bottom end of the distribution.

5 Assessing the Accuracy of the Asset Index as an Approximation of Wealth

To measure how well the constructed asset index approximates wealth, an asset index similar to the one compiled with the DHS data is estimated using the GLSS of 1998 and then compared to various monetary estimates of wealth from the same survey. According to the GLSS 1998 user guide, the main objective of this survey was to gather information on individual wages, household income, and household expenditure (Ghana Statistical Service, n.d.). The survey sample is stratified according to ecological zones and rural and urban location. The survey covers 5,998 households. The definition of households is similar to that employed in the DHS: all individuals who slept in the same house and ate their meals together for nine of the previous twelve months were regarded as members of the same household.

The GLSS dataset is well suited to testing the adequacy of the asset index constructed in the DHS. The survey tracks ownership for an expanded list of household assets including land and houses and also financial assets such as shares. The survey asks respondents to estimate the resale value of each of these assets. It includes a separate module on savings. Furthermore, the GLSS also contains all of the 10 assets used to construct the asset index in the DHS. There are, however, some caveats that should be noted when interpreting the analysis below as a test of the validity of our asset index approach. First, because of the implementation of baseline weights, the 1998 version of the DHS asset index uses weights estimated based on the 1993 DHS data, while the GLSS survey's asset index is computed using weights from the 1998 survey. Additionally, the definitions and coverage of the assets used for compiling the GLSS asset index differ somewhat from those used for constructing the DHS index.[16] These differences between the indices are considered slight enough to regard the GLSS version of the asset index as a near replica of the index compiled with DHS data.

Although far from exhaustive, the 1998 GLSS contains a much more comprehensive list of assets than the DHS. This will allow us to estimate a second index based on a considerably longer list of assets, including amongst other things ownership of land, housing, and also shares. This expanded asset index can be used to investigate to which extent discrepancies between the wealth variable and the parsimonious asset index (akin to the index estimated with the DHS data) is attributable to shortcomings of the asset index approach or to problems relating to a small number of assets.

The 1998 GLSS contains ample information on wealth, which enables the calculation of a reasonable proxy for household wealth. An estimate of total household wealth is derived by adding the respondent's savings and the sum of the estimated resale values of assets owned (including consumer durables, farming equipment, land, houses, and shares).[17] A measure for marketable wealth is calculated by excluding land and houses, assets that are often inherited or passed down rather than bought and that the owner may frequently not have the right to sell. The most notable omission in these estimates of wealth is debt. The survey contains information on whether or not any household member had debt and the amount of the initial debt, but no information that would allow the calculation of the outstanding amount of debt. Survey

---

[16] The GLSS asks only agricultural households about the ownership of tractors. The question regarding the ownership of a cart or trailer is asked of agricultural households and business owners. Some of the asset classifications deviate from those employed in the DHS. In the GLSS, horse and cart is not listed as a separate category. The only available comparable category is cart and trailer. Refrigerator is also not specified separately as a category, but occurs only in a pairing with freezer. The video category is broadened to video equipment in the GLSS. Also, the earth-floor category is coupled with mud floors, and the concrete or cement floors are paired together. Lastly, the categories provided to describe the type of floor of the dwelling in the GLSS do not include smart floors.

[17] The appendix of the UNU-WIDER Research Paper (2006/138) version of this chapter provides more detail on the construction of the wealth variable (Burger et al. 2006).

information regarding the distribution and prevalence of household debt indicates that wealthy households are more likely to have debt.

To simplify the evaluation of the tests performed here, the wealth variables are assumed to provide a more accurate representation of household wealth than the asset index, and a closer correspondence to these wealth variables is interpreted as evidence that the asset index is approximating wealth better. However, because of reliability concerns regarding responses to questions about savings and the resale estimates and the omission of debt,[18] it would be naive to assume that wealth estimates based on these numbers will provide a perfectly accurate representation of the wealth of households in the survey sample. There is ample reason to suspect that the measurement error of the wealth and also the marketable wealth variable may be high. If it is assumed that the measurement error of the wealth variables is 'noise' and independent of the measurement error of the asset indices, then the correlation coefficients reported here may underestimate the actual correlations.

The parsimonious asset index and the measures of marketable wealth have highly significant and positive correlation coefficients, ranging between 0.12 and 0.28 depending on what is included in the measure. To investigate whether the correlation may be improved by increasing the number of assets, an expanded asset index is estimated including fifteen additional assets listed in the household assets and durable goods module of the 1998 GLSS.[19] However, the correlation coefficients with wealth were not higher for the expanded asset index.

The positive and highly significant correlation coefficient between the basic index and marketable wealth variable supports the interpretation of this index as a measure of marketable wealth. The basic index's correlation with marketable wealth is virtually identical to the correlation with total wealth, but alternative measures of fit suggest that a narrower interpretation of the index as representing marketable wealth rather than total wealth may be more appropriate. There is, for instance, a higher degree of overlap in terms of the allocation of households to quintiles (based on their rank) between the basic asset index and marketable wealth than between the basic index and the total wealth variable. Also, the wealth by age curves for the basic index have a closer resemblance to the curves for the marketable wealth variable than to those for total wealth. According to the asset index variable, the wealth age curve is flat for households with heads without any secondary education. This is in contrast

---

[18] There are small discrepancies between the correlation coefficients reported here and those shown in Burger et al. (2006), because the wealth estimates reported in this chapter include livestock values. Because of the ambiguity of the phrasing of the question with regards to the stock of livestock held, the livestock estimates were omitted in the original calculations of total wealth.

[19] See the appendix of Burger et al. (2006) for more details on what assets the module listed.

to the low, but steady gradient of wealth increase over age that the total wealth variable shows for this group. If land and homes are excluded from the wealth variable, the slope of the wealth asset curve for the households with less-educated household heads disappears. The possibility of interpreting the index more generally as an approximation of welfare was also investigated, but there is little support for such an argument. The correspondence with per capita household income is considerably lower than that reported for wealth. Much of the observed correlation between income and the asset index may be mediated via the strong relationship between income and wealth.

The next two sections use the basic asset index constructed with the DHS data to investigate patterns and determinants of wealth accumulation. As argued in the previous section, we opt to use the DHS rather than the GLSS, because the last GLSS survey available is from 1998—versus 2003 for DHS—and does not allow us to study the full effect of the recent growth and increase in education. Also, the DHS series has a reputation for cross-survey comparability.

The next section examines the accumulation of marketable wealth using the basic asset index constructed with the DHS data. The analysis is rooted in the literature on savings behaviour. The accumulation of marketable wealth as defined here is expected to be well approximated by models of savings behaviour, because the list of durable assets is comprised mainly of assets that are normally acquired via market transactions and seldom obtained by claim or received via inheritance or as a gift. To avoid unnecessary verbosity, 'wealth' is often substituted for 'marketable wealth' from this point forward.

6 The Accumulation of Wealth over the Life Cycle

There is disagreement regarding the extent to which developed country savings models are relevant to developing country settings. Deaton (1990: 61–96) argues that the popular life-cycle model pioneered by Modigliani and Brumberg (1954: 388–436) may not be suitable to describe wealth accumulation over the life cycle of households in developing countries. According to the life-cycle model, an individual's or household's patterns of saving and dissaving will be determined by their life stage. Households accumulate savings during the productive part of their lives to ensure that they have sufficient resources to consume in the unproductive phase of their lives. Age is consequently viewed as a key determinant of savings behaviour. Deaton (1990) claims that savings behaviour in developing countries cannot be modelled accurately using this traditional theory. According to him the assumptions of the model are unrealistic in the context of developing countries.

In developing countries there are more multi-generational extended family networks, and members of these networks may not need to save for retirement. The extended family structure can provide benefits resembling an old age pension: providing for unproductive individuals (some of these presumably the individual's children) during the productive life stage can be seen as buying provision for the less productive life stage that will follow (assuming that children and other relatives reciprocate).

The high levels of uncertainty that poor individuals face (owing amongst other things to the unpredictable character of agricultural income) and the presence of borrowing constraints further reduce the usefulness of this model in poorer countries. The life-cycle model assumes that savings behaviour is to a large extent driven by the independence motive, an aim that may be less significant in poor, large, multi-generational households. Deaton (1990) suggests that, owing to a borrowing constraint and the high levels of uncertainty that households in developing countries often face, the precautionary motive may be the most important reason for saving. In many cases poor households save to build up a 'buffer' to shield them against unforeseen or unavoidable income shocks.

Is the life-cycle model expected to hold in Ghana's case? There is ample evidence of uncertainties plaguing agricultural households in rural Ghana (Doss 2001) and there is tentative support for claims that many households may be credit constrained (Aryeetey 2004). Additionally, many authors have highlighted the importance of extended family ties and kinship networks in Ghana (La Ferrara 2003; Aryeetey 2004).[20] Deaton's criticism against the life-cycle model is thus expected to be applicable in Ghana's case. If Deaton's criticism is valid, the wealth-over-age curve will exhibit no hump. However, even if this were the case, one would still expect some correlation between age and wealth because an older household head has had a longer period over which to accumulate funds. These predictions are explored by graphing the relationship between wealth and the age of the household head using Lowess smoothing graphs. Lowess smoothing graphs are drawn using locally weighted regressions of the asset index score on the age of the household head for the pooled sample of survey observations. The smoothing occurs because the aggregate asset index score is derived by using all households within a specified span, not just those at the specific point (household head age).[21]

[20] It was also possible to detect multi-generational families based on the information given about each respondent's relationship to the household head. According to these rather crude estimates, roughly 18% of the households in the sample contain more than one generation of adults. Given the geographical basis of the definition of the household in this survey (people who eat and live together), these numbers tell us little about the extent and reach of the individual's obligations towards his or her relatives. According to the pooled version of the three DHS samples, the average household size is 3.9 and the average number of adults is 1.9—both much lower than the sub-Saharan African averages of 5.3 and 2.5 respectively estimated by Bongaarts (2001).

[21] According to the Stata manual, the central point within the span receives the highest weight and points further away receive lower weight, with weight depending on the distance from the central point. The process is repeated for every span/set of data points in data.

Separate curves are mapped based on the highest level of education achieved by household heads.[22] This is partly an attempt to control for the variation in the level of permanent income. King and Dicks-Mireaux (1982) claim that failure to control for permanent income may be a reason why many studies examining the wealth–age relationship do not detect a hump-shaped curve. The mapping of separate curves for different educational levels of household heads may also help to address one of Shorrocks's criticisms (1975) of the use of cross-sectional data for life-cycle analysis—namely, that it does not take into account that survival is not a random selection mechanism. According to Shorrocks, the wealthy may be expected to live longer and thus it is expected that they will be over-represented in older cohorts of cross-sectional data. By analysing the relationship between wealth and age by educational group we may moderate this selection bias to some extent. It will help control for some of the changes in the 'representative individual' that occur over generations (Shorrocks 1975: 160).

Figure 12.2 depicts the age-over-wealth curves for four different household head educational levels (using averages across the three surveys). There are no signs of a hump in any of the curves. The wealth-over-age curves are flat for all households with household heads without completed secondary education. The curves of households with households heads with completed secondary education increase with the household heads' age, but there is no evidence of dissaving among the oldest cohorts. There are at least three possible explanations for the lack of a hump. It may indicate that it is frequently not necessary for Ghanaian families to dissave as the household head advances in age, because there is an extended family structure to look after the older members. Alternatively, the household may not be able to dissave because of the unpredictability of the future and its inability to borrow. A third option may be that Ghanaians continue to work for much longer than individuals in developed countries. The GLSS 1998 suggests that a substantial portion of Ghanaians older than 60 may continue to work. Only 31 per cent of the survey's sample of 1,556 individuals older than 60 years were not working or receiving income. Twenty per cent of those older than 60 reported that they continued to earn an income.

The graph also shows that there are large differences in both the level and the slope of the curves for the four household head educational levels. The flat curves for household heads without completed secondary education provide evidence that little wealth accumulation occurs over time in such households. The upwards slope of the curves for household heads with completed secondary school education signify that wealth accumulation does take place in these households.

---

[22] The educational level variables are here interpreted as representing permanent income. According to Friedman's permanent income hypothesis (1957), individuals' savings decisions are mainly driven by their perceived long-term income. Individuals distinguish between permanent (long-term) and transitory (short-term) changes in their income level and alter their consumption habits only when they believe that their permanent income has changed.

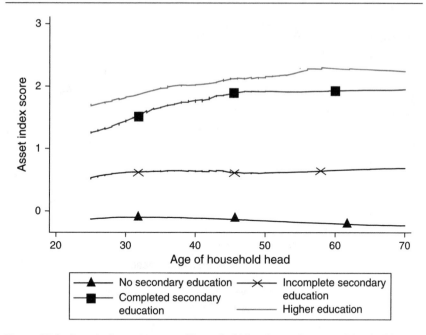

Figure 12.2. Asset index versus age of household head per educational level of household head, Ghana

The literature would suggest that there would be a strong relationship between education and wealth, mediated mainly through earnings. It is hence not surprising that the wealth-over-age curve for higher education lies above that for completed secondary school. The flat wealth-over-age curves for households with heads who had either incomplete or no secondary schooling may suggest that a certain level of education is required to enable an individual to earn sufficient income to facilitate saving. Encouragingly, the analysis shows that in rural areas there is also strong growth in asset holdings with age for households with heads who have completed secondary education (not shown here).

Figure 12.3 plots separate curves for the three survey years. Although we cannot, of course, deduce causality, what is observed here is consistent with the expected impact of the reduction in poverty and increases in educational attainment at the end of the 1990s. As mentioned in the introduction, Teal (2001) estimates that the average Ghanaian level of education rose by 27 per cent during the 1990s while poverty fell from 53 per cent in 1988 to 45 per cent in 1998.[23]

Table 12.2 provides average asset index scores per birth cohort for each survey period. It is clear that there is an improvement over time in the index

[23] For this calculation Teal uses the GLSS, applying the Ghana Statistical Service's 2000 estimate of the poverty line. The appendix of Burger et al. (2006) shows the increase in educational levels over the survey years for the DHS.

263

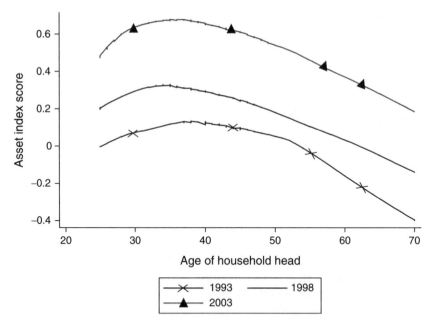

Figure 12.3. Asset index for household head per survey, Ghana

scores of each of these household head cohorts. For the last two survey periods, asset scores are noticeably higher for the younger cohorts, but in the first survey period, the pattern is more ambiguous. The negative relationship between the asset index and the age of the household head in the last two surveys may be due to missing control variables. For instance, the DHS data show that younger cohorts tend to be more educated. When the same table is compiled for each educational level, this trend disappears.

The observed rise in asset scores per cohort over survey periods could be due either to higher savings (as ratio of income) or to improved economic conditions. Given the substantial size of these jumps (compared to other variation patterns in the index), it is unlikely that the higher asset scores can be attributed solely to the former. The rise in average asset scores for cohorts across survey periods is detected for all education groups.[24]

The preceding non-parametric analysis showed that age appears to be an important determinant of wealth, but it also revealed the complexity of distinguishing differences in taste or other generational variations from accumulation over the life cycle. The next section turns to regression analysis in an

---

[24] The general trend appears to be robust for all educational groups, although there are exceptions. In many cases the deviations from the trend may be due to small cell sizes.

Table 12.2. Average asset index per household head cohort, Ghana, 1993–2003

Age in 1993	1993	1998	2003
26–30	0.31	0.37	0.70
31–35	0.17	0.43	0.71
36–40	0.09	0.34	0.63
41–45	0.26	0.22	0.51
46–50	0.19	0.20	0.51
51–55	− 0.02	0.17	0.31
56–60	− 0.13	− 0.03	0.41

Source: Authors' calculations using Ghana DHS (1993, 1998, 2003).

attempt to control for more of the influences on households' pattern of wealth accumulation.

7 Explaining Differences in Households' Levels of Wealth

In constructing an empirical model, the authors take the traditional life-cycle model as a starting point and incorporate modifications proposed by the empirical literature on wealth. Several authors, including Wolff (1981), White (1978), and Steckel (1990), have proposed that life-cycle variables should be supplemented with earnings proxies from a Mincerian human capital model.[25] Indicator variables on educational level (primary, secondary, completed secondary, higher) are used to represent the influence of education. This will allow for non-linearities, which may be useful for capturing threshold effects (for example, having the level of education required to allow the household to earn a living that facilitates saving). Household size, an urban–rural indicator, and the gender of the household head are added to the model as additional controls. The following model is thus estimated:

$$w = \beta_0 + \beta_1 a + \beta_2 a^2 + \beta_3 e + \beta_4 u + \beta_5 n + \beta_6 g \qquad (12.2)$$

where w is the household's accumulated wealth, a is the head of the household's age, e is the education of the household head, u is the urban–rural indicator, n is the household size, g is the gender of the household head, and

---

[25] Information on occupation is excluded, so that the education coefficient will capture the full effect of any changes in the returns to education. The exclusion of variables on occupation could introduce omitted variable bias, but tests with the GLSS 1998 dataset indicate that the impact may not be vast. The omission of occupation variable causes a slight upward bias in the coefficients of the educational variables. If the size of the bias suggested by the test with GLSS 1998 is presumed to be accurate, then any possible omitted variable bias will be of a considerably smaller magnitude than the trend in coefficients between years. Additionally, there is little reason to suspect that the omitted variable bias would fluctuate wildly between years.

Table 12.3. Regressions comparing determinants of asset holdings across surveys, Ghana, 1993–2003

	1993	1998	2003
Some primary education	0.061**	0.099**	0.109**
Completed primary education	0.342***	0.439***	0.580***
Completed secondary education	1.149***	1.463***	1.470***
Higher education	1.733***	1.587***	1.965***
Household size	0.030***	0.044***	0.045***
Urban	0.756***	0.852***	1.039***
Age of household head	0.020***	0.004	0.020***
Squared age of household head	0.0002***	0.00003	0.0002***
Male household head	0.178***	0.202***	0.216***
Constant	− 1.190***	− 0.842***	− 1.147***
R-squared	0.352	0.331	0.323
Overall significance (Prob>F)	0.000	0.000	0.000
Observations	5,779	5,878	6,160

* Significance at 10% level.
** Significance at 5% level.
*** Significance at 1% level.
Source: Authors' calculations using Ghana DHS (1993, 1998, 2003).

the β-terms are the coefficients. If this model is viewed as the sum of a series of fixed-period savings models, then it becomes evident that in the above specification age has a dual role: it may determine how much is saved (or dissaved) in each period and over how many periods these savings are accumulated.

Table 12.3 shows the coefficient estimates for separate regressions for each of the three surveys. The regressions were estimated with provision for the effects of the sampling structure (strata, clusters). There is a considerable amount of stability in coefficients across the survey periods. The main exception is the age variable and its squared value, which are insignificant in the regression for the 1998 survey. The two age variables are also not jointly significant. Apart from this result, there are not many surprises: both of the age variables are significant in both other surveys, with the coefficient on the linear term having a positive sign and the quadratic term's coefficient carrying a negative sign. However, the net effect of age is minor, which is surprising given the various reasons to expect a substantial positive impact. This may be because of the overwhelming influence of education, which has a large, significant, positive impact.[26] It is predicted that in 1998 an individual with higher education will score 1.593 points more on the asset index than someone with no education, a gap that on the asset index scale is equivalent to the

---

[26] Similarly, Rogg (Chapter 11, this volume) finds that the years of education of the household head have a positive correlation with various assets across three survey years in rural Ethiopia.

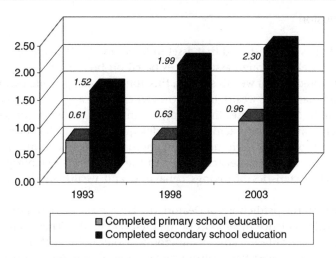

Figure 12.4. Secondary schooling's influence, Ghana, 1993–2003

gain realized by owning a video recorder or, alternatively, a motorcycle and a television.

The coefficient on household size is significant and positive, but small. Urban residency has a positive impact that is large, except for 2003. Having a male household head also appears to provide a significant benefit for asset accumulation, although its impact is not substantial.

The results from the pooled regression[27] (with dummies and interaction effects for 1998 and 2003, with 1993 as the reference or base period) allow the detection of shifts over time in the structural relationships (not shown here). The effect of higher education and male household heads has remained remarkably stable across the three periods. To guard against the influence of data imperfections, we identify changes in coefficients as trends only when they are observed for both periods. There is evidence of a growing premium on completed secondary education and increase in the urban advantage. Figure 12.4 illustrates this effect by comparing predicted index scores for household heads with completed primary schooling with those for heads with completed secondary schooling over the three survey periods. In all cases the household is presumed to be a five-person urban household with a 50-year-old male household head. There is a general upward trend in asset ownership between 1993 and 2003, accompanied by a widening asset score gap between household heads with secondary schooling and those without, especially between 1993 and 1998.

---

[27] Note that the pooled regression did not constrain the residual variances to be equal.

7 Conclusion

This study has demonstrated that asset indices can mimic marketable wealth reasonably well. Although asset indices based on household surveys cannot match the precision of wealth surveys, this approach can provide useful information on marketable wealth in countries where more appropriate sources are not available. Such an asset index may, for instance, be useful for detecting broad trends and patterns across asset index quintiles and education categories. Needless to say, the usefulness of this approach remains conditional on the number and variety of assets contained in the survey, the reliability of data, and the characteristics of savings behaviour and wealth in the applicable country.

In line with the predictions of Deaton, the Lowess curves of wealth over age provide little evidence in support of the life-cycle model. There is no sign of dissaving in later life for any of the groups. Households with less-educated household heads have a flat wealth-over-age curve. Given the interpretation of education as a proxy for permanent income, these flat curves may suggest that there is a threshold level of income required for wealth accumulation. Households with household heads with secondary education have wealth curves that rise with age.

Education level has a considerable impact on wealth accumulation, presumably working via income. The exploratory analysis with the Lowess curves of wealth over age indicates a clear separation in the level of the asset index based on the household head's educational level. The educational level variables have large and highly significant coefficients in the regression results. The regressions also show that education's influence on wealth appears to have increased over time. It is encouraging to find such large positive benefits to investment in education in a country where a considerable share of work occurs outside the formal sector.

There has been a strong increase in the average asset index scores over this period. Although the analysis here is not rigorous enough to be conclusive, there is evidence that this increase could be associated with improved economic conditions and the higher levels of education.

Part III

The Role of Personal Assets in Economic Development and Performance

13

Household Financial Assets in the Process of Development

Patrick Honohan

Introduction

The financial sector plays a multidimensional role in the process of development. It mobilizes and concentrates resources for investment and allocates them based on an assessment of risk and return, judging creditworthiness and monitoring performance. It offers risk-reduction and risk-pooling services that have both direct effects on welfare (by providing insulation from shocks) and indirect effects on growth, by making riskier—but potentially high-yield—investments in human and physical capital accessible. While much of the recent literature focuses on the interaction of enterprises, large and small, with financial markets and financial intermediaries, households are important consumers of financial products, and household behaviour influences the scale and asset mix of finance. Furthermore, poverty and welfare can be strongly influenced by the degree to which households have *access* to the formal financial sector.

This chapter reviews these three dimensions (mobilization, access, and risk reduction) in a quantitative context, concentrating on illustrating some of the very limited data that are available for developing countries. Because the discussion combines data with econometric and conceptual issues, we begin with an extended introduction and summary allowing the main threads of the story to be presented without technical digression.

I am grateful to the project director Jim Davies and to participants at the UNU-WIDER project meeting 'Personal Assets from a Global Perspective', Helsinki, 4–6 May 2006, as well as to Priya Basu, Francesco Gaetano, Tae Soo Kang, Jaechil Kim, Li Shi, Steve Peachey, Ding Sai, Daniel Waldenström, and Jae Hoon Yoo for suggestions and advice on data sources, and to Ying Lin for excellent research assistance.

Mobilization and concentration

The first dimension relates to the role of household financial asset accumulation in helping mobilize resources that can be effectively deployed for productive investment, thereby accelerating growth. There is clearly something to this mechanism, inasmuch as the well-documented link between banking depth and subsequent economic growth almost necessarily entails household accumulation of bank deposits to back the intermediation that is involved here. However, it needs to be recognized that financial asset holdings are highly concentrated, even more so than non-financial assets, to the extent that the financial assets of the lower quartiles can be largely ignored in any discussion of national resource mobilization. This is true for the USA and other advanced economies, and probably holds with even more force for developing countries.

Wealthy households in many developing countries prefer to hold a relatively large fraction of their assets in safer, more transparent, more diversified, and more efficient financial markets offshore.[1] Since such holdings may be illegal because of remaining exchange controls, or because taxes were not paid, offshore holdings would not show up in survey data, and this is probably one of the reasons why most developing countries have not conducted comprehensive surveys of financial asset holdings of households. The share of financial assets in the average household's domestic portfolio increases with the national level of development (and in advanced economies it increases also with the wealth of the household). Within financial assets, holdings of risky assets are even more concentrated: for these, holdings below the top 5 per cent of wealth holders are nationally negligible. Curiously, even though the financial assets of the poor are in aggregate negligible, it appears that countries with deeper financial systems have less absolute poverty, even after taking account of mean national income. This suggests that a deep financial system also affects the structure of the economy in subtle ways that are relevant for the inclusiveness of economic development.

Access

The main focus of current policy concern with regard to household finance in developing countries is the perceived need to increase the access of poor households to basic financial services: deposits, payments, insurance, and credit. In other words, policy-driven research for such countries has focused not on allocation decisions between different assets, or on total amounts held, but simply on whether a participation threshold has been reached.

---

[1] Identified offshore banking deposits as a share of GDP are statistically uncorrelated across countries with per capita GDP (Hanson 2003). Hence, since the elasticity of total bank deposits with respect to income is well over one, we may conclude that poorer countries tend to hold a higher share of their financial assets offshore.

Whether examined from household survey data, or from inference based on numbers of bank and other financial intermediary accounts, it is clear that the fraction of households using[2] the services of formal[3] financial intermediaries is small in most developing countries. In contrast, access figures above 80 per cent and up to 100 per cent are recorded for households in advanced economies (where the relevant policy issues are best discussed in the language of exclusion rather than of access). Despite the lack of concrete evidence, it is also generally believed that there is also a *direct* role for the financial system in reducing poverty by reaching more households with microfinance services. But the scale of this impact remains unclear. Access percentages are correlated with poverty rates and national per capita income, but not very closely. However, conditional on mean national income, attempts (including in this chapter) to detect a relationship in cross-country data between financial *access* and poverty have found no statistically robust causal relationship to date. Intriguingly, then, the strongest cross-country econometric evidence for a financial sector impact on poverty relates to financial depth (total value of private credit in relation to GDP) and not to financial access (percentage of households with an account). Whether this is a causal effect is unclear.

Microeconomic studies on the impact of microfinance on poverty are also surprisingly inconclusive. Although beneficiaries of microfinance schemes are vocal in their praise and gratitude, a comprehensive assessment needs to consider displacement effects and endogeneity of financial access. Only in a few cases so far has it been possible to devise convincing ways of adjusting for, or excluding, these complicating factors. On balance, most observers regard microfinance interventions as poverty reducing, while continuing to call for further analysis of methodologies for increasing cost-effectiveness and sustainability of these initiatives, most of which continue to benefit from external subsidies.

Risk reduction and the asset mix

Turning to the allocation of household assets among financial assets with different risk profiles, the focus shifts to risk reduction for these households. After all, given the ability of intermediaries to pool risk, household behaviour is of only limited importance in influencing the national supply of risk finance. Much of the recent literature on household financial asset allocation has been driven by a concern that households are not allocating their savings in an optimal manner.

---

[2] There is an obvious and important conceptual distinction between access and usage, and surveys often explore this (for further discussion, see Honohan 2004b). In the present chapter we treat the terms synonymously, which may not be too bad an approximation when equating access to the use of *any* financial product.

[3] The discussion is generally confined to the formal financial system and as such excludes borrowing from informal lenders and participation in, for example, informal rotating savings and credit schemes.

The suggestion is often made that, whether because of erroneous risk calculations, or simply out of ignorance, households fail to adopt strategies and products that would give them a dominant risk–return mix. To the extent that household investment allocation errors are confined to lower-wealth households, they are unlikely to significantly affect macroeconomic aggregates.

For developing countries, the bulk of the population has no practical access to sophisticated financial instruments (or even to such products as medium-term residential mortgages). As economies become more prosperous, increasing proportions of the population begin to move beyond deposit products into life insurance, loans, and other more sophisticated products. To that extent, despite considerable interest in the topic, the relevance of such concerns for poverty reduction and growth remain for the present limited.

Implications

In considering policy with respect to household finance in developing countries, it is not unreasonable to distinguish rather sharply between the objectives of 'finance for growth' and 'finance for all'. Sustained national economic growth calls for the intermediation of sizeable resources through an efficient financial system. To the extent that these resources come from the savings of households, it refers to relatively prosperous households—in this context only the top few deciles need to be considered. The more developed the economy, the more deciles become relevant. Policy designed to mobilize a larger volume of funds for intermediation should therefore be directed to matters that affect behaviour of the upper deciles. Such policies would include those affecting political confidence, macroeconomic stability, and expected after-tax returns on financial savings.

A rather different set of policies comes to the fore in seeking to expand the number of households with access. These include regulatory design for micro-finance institutions, ensuring that measures designed to protect consumers against loss do not impose costs so heavy as to deter entry into this low end of the market, characterized by low margins but potentially high volume. Current policy concerns in advanced economies on suboptimal allocation of the household portfolio remain of secondary importance in most developing countries. Instead, legal, regulatory, and tax policies affecting the cost and availability to lower-income households of such products as insurance and home-construction lending, loom large on the policy agenda.

The remainder of the chapter is divided into five sections. The first presents some known statistical regularities about the variation across income groups and countries of household financial asset holdings. Section 2 discusses the channels through which household financial asset holdings affect national growth and poverty. Section 3 turns to the question of how widespread is access by households to financial assets, presenting new data for over 150 countries, and using these data to assess whether such access *per se* helps to reduce aggregate poverty. Section 4 briefly discusses household choice among different financial assets. Concluding remarks are in Section 5.

1 Household Financial Assets: How Holdings Vary across Income Groups and Countries

Our knowledge of the pattern of household financial asset holdings varies greatly by country. The USA has the most comprehensive and apparently reliable data in the form of the triennial Survey of Consumer Finances; preliminary results of the wave from 2004 were recently published by the Federal Reserve Board (Bucks et al. 2006, updating Aizcorbe et al. 2003). Earlier waves of the US survey are thoroughly compared with data for four other advanced economies, Germany, Italy, Netherlands, and the UK, in Guiso et al. (2002). Other advanced countries for which data are available include Korea and Japan. Data for developing countries are, however, very sketchy, and current data-collection exercises in this area are focused more on measuring access or participation than on quantifying asset magnitudes. In this review we draw on much more limited data mainly on savings balances collected in general household surveys for Ghana, Jamaica, and Vietnam, on a 2003 module on household assets and liabilities in India collected as part of the 59th National Sample Survey (NSSO 2005), on a survey of investment in stock-market assets in India (Kar et al. 2003), and on a household survey carried out in 2002 in rural and urban areas in China by CASS (Li and Zhao, Chapter 5, this volume). They show some commonalities with other advanced economies, but also some differences possibly due to survey limitations.

Despite the sketchiness of data sources, some stylized facts can be adduced by reasonable extrapolation and interpolation from what we do have. One cannot, of course, rely wholly on the assumption that cross-sectional patterns within economies—variations in the pattern of asset allocation by such characteristics as age, education, and wealth—can be extrapolated from the rich countries for which we do have cross-sectional data to the poor. Nevertheless, some of those patterns probably do hold up qualitatively (and we will show the extent to which some of them are confirmed in our handful of developing countries for which some data are available) and the patterns can be scaled to the aggregate magnitudes for which data are available in the poor countries.

Financial assets represent a sizeable proportion of the aggregate wealth[4] of households—over 50 per cent in Norway (Jäntti and Sierminska, Chapter 2, this volume) and over 40 per cent in the USA, even if we take the results of household surveys, which may disproportionately understate financial assets if compared

---

[4] Excluding human capital, as is customary.

to data from national balance sheets computed from national accounts sources (Davies et al., Chapter 19, this volume). The share of financial assets in total wealth tends to increase with mean income. For Australia, Canada, Germany, Italy, the Netherlands, and Sweden, the figure obtained from household surveys is about 30 per cent (Guiso et al. 2003; Jäntti and Sierminska, Chapter 2, this volume); in China it is 22 per cent (Li and Zhao, Chapter 5, this volume), in Korea only 17 per cent (Yoo 2005) and in India about 4 per cent (NSSO 2005; Subramanian and Jayaraj, Chapter 6, this volume).[5]

Household financial liabilities also need to be considered for a rounded view; indeed, it would be very artificial to look only at the asset side when it comes to financial assets and liabilities, since both are endogenous and thought to be determined in large part by the same explanatory variables. In aggregate, household financial liabilities amount to as much as 30 per cent of gross household financial assets in the USA, where consumer and household finance is very well developed. Indeed, for all but about the top decile of the *income* distribution in that country, borrowing exceeds gross financial asset holdings. In other words, *net* financial assets for the lower 90 per cent are negative. The largest category of debt is mortgage and home equity debt, reflecting the fact that a homeowner's residence can represent valuable collateral. Instalment credit (mainly related to the purchase of automobiles and other household durables) and credit-card debt are also used in rich countries, but amount to smaller sums.

Borrowing possibilities for low-income households from formal intermediaries are more limited in less-advanced economies. In these countries, middle-class employee households may borrow unsecured, but often under arrangements whereby servicing charges are deducted from wage payments by the employer and remitted to the financial intermediary.

1.1 *Concentration of Financial Asset Holdings*

Just as the share of financial assets in the total increases with mean income across countries, the distribution of financial wealth within advanced economies appears to be more concentrated than non-financial wealth (and than human capital or income). This may be less true in developing countries. For example, Indian survey data suggest that the share of financial assets in wealth is not monotonically increasing in wealth (Subramanian and Jayaraj, Chapter 6, this volume). The relatively undeveloped equity markets—limiting the availability of sophisticated financial claims on the local capital stock—the importance of land holding, and the fact that most businesses are closely held would be contributing factors to this difference.

In China, too, financial wealth as surveyed is *not* more concentrated than other wealth (Li and Zhao, Chapter 5, this volume). However, China's status as

[5] The figure for Japan has been highly volatile in view of the housing boom and bust of the 1980s and 1990s (Iwaisako 2003).

a transition economy must be taken into account in considering the relevance of this observation for other countries. Nevertheless, it is true for all countries that the bulk of financial assets is held by relatively wealthy households. Indeed, the bottom half of the wealth distribution in the USA holds no more than 3 per cent of the system's financial assets. The same group holds about 4 per cent of the risk-free assets and 2 per cent of the risky assets (see Figure 13.1).

Given the fact that a much larger fraction of the population in poor countries holds no financial assets at all, and given that income is in most cases more unequally distributed in developing countries, it would seem likely that the share of financial assets held by the lower deciles would be even lower in the typical low- or middle-income country. In other words, concentration of financial-asset ownership is surely even higher in poor countries. This conjecture is not, however, strongly confirmed by the available survey data. In India—where the data on risk-free financial assets includes cash holdings—the bottom half of the wealth distribution hold about 6 per cent of risk-free assets, and less than 3 per cent of risky assets (shares). Surveys for three other countries, Ghana, Jamaica, and Vietnam, also show surprisingly high percentages of financial assets being held by lower-income groups (details in the working paper version). But these surveys do not capture the top end of the distribution as well as the specialized financial-asset surveys for advanced economies, given that their purpose is not mainly to cover wealth issues. We prefer to discount these particular findings, and rely on the patterns observed more reliably in advanced economies to conclude that policy directed at mobilizing investable funds through the issue of financial assets can safely ignore the lower quartiles of the wealth distribution at least as far as the aggregate sums mobilized are concerned.[6]

Taking account also of the net financial indebtedness of all but the highest income groups, it seems that the net provision of investable funds from the household to the business and government sectors depends essentially on the top decile of the wealth distribution—for the USA, this group contributes 91 per cent of net household financial assets (as compared with 72 per cent of *gross* household financial assets).

For advanced economies, the increased share of financial assets in total wealth is more a function of increased participation[7] as we go up the income scale, more than an increase in the value of holdings conditional on participation.

---

[6] That is not to say that banks will necessarily ignore the smaller depositor. Handling small deposits is costly, but potentially more profitable per dollar transacted. There is value at the 'bottom of the pyramid' for intermediaries who can master the necessary cost efficiencies. But the volume of resources mobilized is negligible in terms of aggregate national intermediation.

[7] By participation is meant whether or not holdings are non-zero. Fixed costs, including those of acquiring information, help explain why households hold only a subset of available assets. King and Leape (1998) estimate a decision model incorporating such costs as well as non-negativity constraints on the US SCF data.

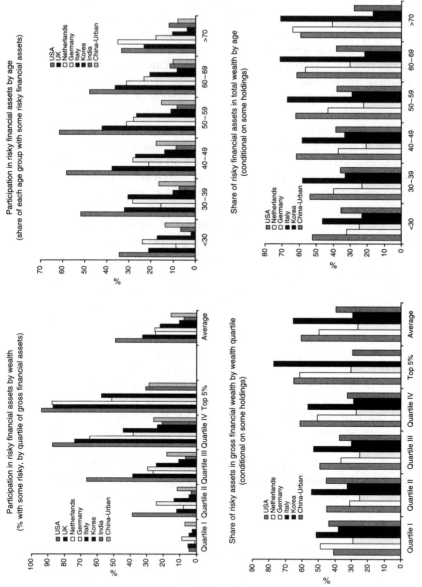

Figure 13.1. Use and portfolio share of risky assets in total financial assets by financial wealth and age, selected economies, 1990s

Note: For India and South Korea the quartiles are income, not wealth.

Sources: Based on data in Guiso et al. (2002); for China, special tabulations by Ding Sai based on CASS 2002 survey (Li and Zhao 2007); for South Korea special tabulations by JaeChil Kim of KSRI based on the Korea Household Income and Expenditure Survey of the National Statistics Bureau.

1.2 *Households' Share of Aggregate Bank Deposits*

Wealthy households hold a sizeable fraction of aggregate bank deposits. The household sector in aggregate holds more than 63 per cent of total deposits at financial intermediaries in the USA, and 80 per cent of deposits from non-financial non-government domestic sectors.[8] For the eurozone, comparable percentages are reported: 60 per cent and 78 per cent respectively. Individuals hold 43 per cent of all resident deposits in the UK, a figure that rises to over two-thirds if deposits of financial institutions and public administration are excluded. Just over a half of the large deposit base of Chinese financial institutions is in the form of household savings deposits. In Egypt, households account for 78 per cent of total deposits. In the Eastern Caribbean Currency Union, household deposits are 60 per cent of the total, or 68 per cent if financial and government deposits are excluded.

1.3 *Offshore Assets and Liabilities*

Although households, like other investors, still tend to display a degree of home preference that discourages cross-border holdings of financial assets (Huizinga and Jonung 2005), nevertheless, reasons of political risk and tax avoidance can provide an important push in the opposite direction, resulting in capital flight and the holding of sizeable and often covert offshore assets. It is difficult to measure the scale and pattern of this flight capital, but it is undoubtedly large (Hanson 2003 and references therein). Omission of offshore holdings will inevitably tarnish any analysis of household financial assets in developing countries.

2 Household Financial Assets and Growth

Numerous econometric studies have established a causal link between financial depth and GDP growth.[9] The indications are that it is through its influence on the productivity of investment, rather than on its magnitude, that bank intermediation exerts its pro-growth effect, at least in higher-income economies. It is the aggregate stock of bank credit to private-sector borrowers, rather than the aggregate stock of money, that has been found to be the most robust explanatory variable in these regression analyses. But, without mobilized funds for onlending, the banks would not be able to increase the volume of credit. Given the importance of household asset accumulation in easing the challenge for

---

[8] Sources for the figures in this paragraph are given in the working paper version.

[9] The finance and growth literature is surveyed in detail by Levine (2005), and summarized more briefly by Honohan (2004a). There remains some doubt as to whether this effect is more important at low or intermediate levels of income, or of financial development (Rioja and Valev 2004; Aghion et al. 2005).

local banks to mobilize funds for onlending, household financial asset holdings do make a potentially significant indirect contribution to growth.[10] It needs to be underlined that this extra link in the chain (from money to credit) is not a very tight one. For example, banks in much of sub-Saharan Africa hold sizeable excess reserves, either finding insufficient bankable lending opportunities to deploy the deposits that they have mobilized, or preferring to invest in high-yielding government securities in cases where domestic financing of government deficits in effect crowds out private lending; in this case, additional household deposits are unlikely to be lent on. Furthermore, other countries have experienced the opposite phenomenon, where banks draw on external credit lines to finance more private lending than could be funded out of domestic resources—direct offshore borrowing by larger enterprises has also been observed in those cases. Nevertheless in broad terms (and in an echo of the Horioka–Feldstein savings-investment correlation across countries), banking depth on the deposit and private credit side remain strongly correlated across countries, suggesting that there is a link, even if it is not a rigid one.

If the poor have limited access to credit, might this imply that financial development is pro-rich, disproportionately benefiting the wealthy? Or is it for outsiders and newcomers that a well-developed financial system most provides opportunities in terms of smoothing consumption, diversifying risk, and overcoming indivisibilities in investment? An interesting but rather rarified theoretical literature has explored a variety of channels through which financial development could affect the evolution of income distribution. Generally speaking, these models pivot on credit constraints and on such aspects as collateral as a prerequisite for credit, and are driven by such considerations as the possibility that improvements in financial intermediation will be seized first by the already wealthy. There has been no professional consensus on which of the various models, with their mutually contradictory conclusions, is most likely to fit reality. Empirical evidence is accumulating, though, that financial development appears to be correlated not only with aggregate income growth, but also with lower poverty, even conditional on average income levels. Somewhat ironically, this seems to be the case more for financial depth indicators than for financial access indicators (see below).

Li et al. (1998) were the first to look at this kind of issue in a cross-country econometric framework. They found that income inequality (Gini coefficient) was lower in cross-sectional regressions with deeper financial systems. Honohan (2004a: 1–37) showed that absolute poverty (proportion of the population below the $US1-a-day or $US2-a-day poverty line) was lower in deeper financial systems, even conditional on the mean income level achieved by the non-rich, and these findings are confirmed on an updated and expanded data set in Table

[10] The household dimension is often not taken into account, so it is overall financial depth and not the household's share that is considered in the literature on finance and growth.

13.2. Beck et al. (2004) looked at income growth rates of the poor and found that they were disproportionately high where financial intermediary development was deep. So there is a double effect on poverty—finance boosts mean income growth and it also promotes a more equal income distribution.[11]

So far, this apparent pro-poor twist to financial depth remains something of a black box. It could reflect the mechanism proposed by Rajan and Zingales (2003), whereby a developed financial system is one where availability of credit undermines the economic power of incumbent elites, thereby generally diffusing development more widely and opening more opportunities. More household saving in financial assets fuels this credit availability and represents an important anti-poverty force.

3 Does Access to a Bank Account Help Reduce Poverty?

Casting our eyes to the bottom of the pyramid, we need to remind ourselves that, for lower-income groups, it is not a question of how much financial assets they choose to hold, and even less a question of how much they choose to borrow from the financial system. These households encounter barriers to accessing financial services.[12] In the advanced economies, this has led to a growing debate around the issue of financial exclusion. It is noted that a small but multiply deprived group—perhaps 10 per cent of the adult population—do not have access to financial services such as a transactions account, or even a savings account, much less a loan from a formal intermediary or an insurance policy. In some cases, product features, such as a high minimum cover for an insurance product, or heavy penalties for unauthorized overdrafts (hard for poor people to avoid if they are using checking/cheque accounts), or having a fixed address as a prerequisite to open an account represent material obstacles to use of such products. In other cases, customers may be screened out because of risk characteristics. Or rationalization of branches and service points may result in many poor customers having too far to travel to a branch to make an account worthwhile. Given the increasing extent to which full participation in economic life in the advanced economies depends on having an account at a financial intermediary, and given the material extra costs often imposed on non-account holders, several countries have adopted policies in recent years to reduce financial exclusion (Porteous 2004; Carbo et al. 2005).

In low- and middle-income countries, however, exclusion is normal for the bulk of the population; hence it becomes more natural to speak of broadening

[11] These findings receive a nice confirmation from the results of Dehejia and Gatti (2005), who found a favourable cross-country effect of financial development on child labour.

[12] Including transactions services—an important dimension for such households, which can be associated with the holding of balances in transactions accounts, but which will not be discussed further in this chapter.

Table 13.1. Composite measure of access to financial services

Country		Code	Value	Code		Country	Value	Country		Code	Value
Albania	b	ALB	34	DEU	s	Germany	97	Panama	s	PAN	46
Algeria		DZA	31	GHA		Ghana	16	Papua New Guinea	b	PNG	8
Angola		AGO	35	GRC	s	Greece	83	Paraguay	s	PRY	30
Antigua & Barbuda		ATG	48	GRD		Grenada	37	Peru		PER	26
Argentina	b	ARG	28	GTM	s	Guatemala	32	Philippines	s	PHL	66
Armenia	s	ARM	9	GIN		Guinea	20	Poland	s	POL	66
Austria	s	AUT	96	GUY	s	Guyana	14	Portugal	s	PRT	84
Azerbaijan		AZE	17	HTI		Haiti	15	Romania		ROM	23
Bahamas, The		BHS	53	HND	B	Honduras	25	Russian Federation		RUS	69
Bangladesh		BGD	32	HKG		Hong Kong, China	[38]	Rwanda		RWA	23
Barbados		BRB	56	HUN	S	Hungary	66	Samoa		WSM	19
Belarus		BLR	16	IND		India	48	Saudi Arabia		SAU	62
Belgium	s	BEL	97	IDN		Indonesia	40	Sao Tome & Principe		STP	15
Belize		BLZ	46	IRN		Iran, Isl. Rep.	31	Senegal		SEN	27
Benin		BEN	32	IRQ		Iraq	17	Seychelles		SYC	41
Bermuda		BMU	48	IRL	s	Ireland	88	Sierra Leone		SLE	13
Bhutan		BTN	16	ITA	s	Italy	75	Singapore	b	SGP	98
Bolivia		BOL	44	JAM		Jamaica	59	Slovak Republic		SVK	83
Bosnia & Herzegovinia		BIH	17	JOR	b	Jordan	37	Slovenia		SVN	97
Botswana		BWA	47	KAZ		Kazakhstan	48	Solomon Islands		SLB	15
Brazil	s	BRA	43	KEN	s	Kenya	10	South Africa		ZAF	46
Bulgaria	s	BGR	56	KOR		Korea, Rep.	63	Spain	s	ESP	95
Burkina Faso		BFA	26	KGZ		Kyrgyz Republic	1	Sri Lanka		LKA	66
Burundi		BDI	17	LVA		Latvia	64	St Kitts and Nevis		KNA	49
Cambodia		KHM	20	LBN	b	Lebanon	[79]	St Lucia		LCA	40
Cameroon		CMR	24	LSO		Lesotho	17	St Vincent & Gren.		VCT	45
Cape Verde		CPV	52	LBR		Liberia	11	Sudan		SDN	15
Central African Rep.		CAF	19	LBY		Libya	27	Suriname		SUR	32
Chile		CHL	60	LTU	s	Lithuania	70	Swaziland		SWZ	35
China		CHN	42	LUX	s	Luxembourg	99	Sweden	s	SWE	99
Colombia	s	COL	41	MAC		Macao, China	[14]	Switzerland	b	CHE	88
Comoros		COM	20	MKD		Macedonia, FYR	20	Syrian A.R.		SYR	17

Country		Code	No.	Country		Code	No.	Country		Code	No.
Congo, Rep.		COG	27	Madagascar		MDG	21	Tajikistan		TJK	16
Costa Rica		CRI	29	Malawi		MWI	21	Tanzania		TZA	5
Côte d'Ivoire		CIV	25	Malaysia	b	MYS	57	Thailand		THA	59
Croatia		HRV	42	Mali		MLI	21	Timor-Leste		TMP	13
Cuba		CUB	45	Malta	s	MLT	90	Togo		TGO	28
Cyprus	s	CYP	85	Mauritania		MRT	16	Trinidad & Tobago		TTO	53
Czech Republic	s	CZE	85	Mauritius	b	MUS	60	Tunisia		TUN	42
Denmark	s	DNK	99	Mexico	s	MEX	25	Turkey	b	TUR	49
Dominica		DMA	66	Moldova		MDA	13	Uganda		UGA	20
Dominican Rep.		DOM	29	Mongolia		MNG	30	Ukraine		UKR	24
Ecuador	s	ECU	35	Morocco	s	MAR	39	United Arab Emirates	b	ARE	[33]
Egypt		EGY	41	Mozambique		MOZ	12	United Kingdom	s	GBR	91
El Salvador		SLV	26	Myanmar		MMR	19	United States	s	USA	91
Eritrea		ERI	12	Namibia	s	NAM	28	Uruguay		URY	42
Estonia	s	EST	86	Nepal		NPL	20	Uzbekistan		UZB	16
Ethiopia		ETH	14	Netherlands		NLD	100	Venezuela	b	VEN	28
Fiji	b	FJI	39	Nicaragua	s	NIC	5	Vietnam		VNM	29
Finland	s	FIN	99	Niger		NER	31	West Bank & Gaza		WBG	14
France	s	FRA	96	Nigeria		NGA	15	Yemen, Rep.		YEM	14
Gabon		GAB	39	Norway	b	NOR	84	Yugoslavia, FR		YUG	21
Gambia		GMB	21	Oman		OMN	33	Zambia		ZMB	15
Georgia	b	GEO	15	Pakistan	b	PAK	12	Zimbabwe	b	ZWE	34

Note: 's' means household survey data used; 'b' means fitted data using bank deposit numbers and not WSBI numbers. [Square bracketed data are considered less reliable.] This is Mark IIc version of the data series. As more refined information on specific countries is obtained, it is envisaged that this series will be updated.

Source: Author's calculations based on Beck et al. (2007), Christen et al. (2004), Claessens (2006), European Commission (2005), Peachey and Roe (2006). For definitions and method see the UNU-WIDER Research Paper (2006/91) version of this chapter (Honohan 2006: app 2).

access to financial services rather than elimination of exclusion as the immediate goal. The exploding microfinance movement is driven by this motivation (Robinson 2001; Honohan 2004b; Armendáriz de Aghion and Morduch 2005). Microfinance pioneers have emphasized the very high rates of return that can be earned by the poor and the near-poor, especially in urban and peri-urban settings, resulting in a high demand for borrowings even at high interest rates. Some microfinance institutions work on a credit-only basis, funding themselves from charitable donors and other sources; some employ forced savings elements to the loan scheme. The modern trend is to emphasize deposits as well as loans as the key tool for efficient financial management, whether they represent precautionary savings, or a means of accumulating capital. Transactions accounts are also important for receiving and making internal and international remittances between family members. And micro-insurance is beginning to be a significant element in the microfinance movement.

Does access to financial services through deposit or loan accounts reduce poverty? Numerous anecdotes illustrate paths to relative prosperity being paved by such financial services. However, there is typically a large element of selection bias, both at the level of the individual client (with the more energetic likely to experience growing loan and deposit balances) and at the level of the village selected for establishment of a microfinance institution (sometimes this is a negative bias, as charitable sponsors seek out the more deprived villages). Furthermore, there can be displacement effects, with non-beneficiaries of microfinance suffering in local markets from the beneficiaries. Despite an extensive quasipromotional literature, detailed microeconometric analyses are, for these technical reasons, surprisingly non-committal about whether direct financial access has a major effect in reducing poverty (Honohan 2004b). Recent controlled experiments have begun to expand the reliable evidence in this area (for a review, see Demirgüç-Kunt et al. 2007).

What can be said at the macro-level? Addressing this question evidently requires a cross-country data series on access. There are many dimensions to financial access, but, to simplify matters, given the shortage of data, it is preferable to concentrate on one summary indicator. The most widely accepted indicator is the percentage of adults who have any type of account (including all types of transactions, savings or loan accounts) at a bank or other formal financial intermediary (World Bank 2005a). How many people in developing countries have access to a bank or other formal financial intermediary account? This empirical question is the subject of vigorous current investigation. Piecing together elements from several other studies (revised for this purpose), the working paper version of this chapter details the methodology of a new composite indicator available for over 150 countries (see Table 13.1 and Figure 13.2). It is based on an estimated non-linear relation between survey data on household access (cf. Claessens 2006), the number of accounts in commercial banks (Beck et al. 2007), savings banks (Peachey and Roe 2006),

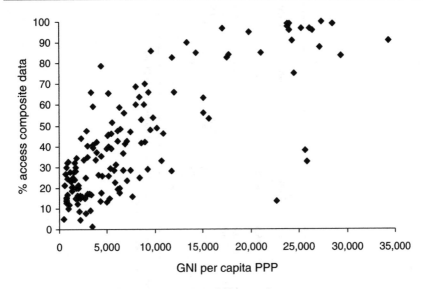

Figure 13.2. Access and per capita income, 160 countries

Note: This uses the composite access indicator—for definition see Table 13.1. GNI per capita data from WDI. The three outliers on the lower right-hand side are Hong Kong, China; Macao, China; and United Arab Emirates.

and various forms of microfinance institutions (Christen et al. 2004), and the average size of these accounts. This relationship is extrapolated to more than one hundred countries for which household survey data are not available.

While the shortcomings of the imputation procedures used to construct the composite indicator, as well as the limitations of the underlying data sources, are recognized, the resulting dataset is nevertheless interesting. Appropriate econometric techniques can limit the consequences of random error.

Returning then to the question of whether financial access reduces poverty, we may use the new access data to obtain a macro cross-country perspective on this issue. Earlier work failed to find any significant cross-country correlation between the density of microfinance accounts and poverty rates (Honohan 2004b). But, given the extensive differences between the old data and the new composite series, it is worth repeating the experiment. In fact (see Table 13.2) we do find that access is correlated with poverty rates (2.D). But access percentages are, of course, strongly correlated with per capita income (see Figure 13.2),[13] and, since the latter is highly correlated with poverty rates, the more

[13] In a regression of data on the summary access indicator for 147 countries, per capita income explains 60% of cross-country variation. After exclusion of five outliers, Hong Kong, Lebanon, Luxembourg, Macao, and United Arab Emirates, this jumps to 73%. It is likely that these five outliers should be omitted from most analyses with these data.

Table 13.2. Poverty and financial access

Equation:	2.A Coeff.	t-Stat	2.B Coeff.	t-Stat	2.C Coeff.	t-Stat	2.D Coeff.	t-Stat	2.E Coeff.	t-Stat
Constant	173.6	**11.6	170.6	**12.8	137.8	**8.5	61.1	**5.7	140.0	**8.5
GNI per cap (log)	−18.8	**10.4								
GNI per cap lower 90% (log)			−19.2	**11.4	−17.5	**10.4			23.4	**8.8
Share of top 10%					0.574	**3.3			0.948	**3.1
Access (log)							−12.4	**3.9	−2.0	0.8
R-squared/NOBS	0.546	91	0.598	89	0.643	89	0.151	89	0.645	87
Adjusted R-squared	0.541		0.593		0.634		0.141		0.632	
S.E. of regression	15.2		14.2		13.5		21.0		13.7	
Log likelihood	−375.7		−361.5		−356.2		−396.2		−348.8	

Note: This table shows regressions relating the $1 per day poverty percentage to financial access percentages across countries. ** and * indicate significance at the 1% and 5% levels, respectively. Cross-section: all available countries. Note GNI per cap is measured at PPP. (Mark IIa of the composite series was used here.)

Sources: For poverty and inequality measures: GPID; for GNI: World Bank (2006c).

interesting question is whether access remains significant in a regression that also includes per capita income. In fact, when per capita income and other controls found to be significant in earlier work (see 2.A–C) are added to the specification, access is no longer significant (2.E).

Given the numerous deficiencies of the aggregate access data series, these negative macro cross-country results should not be taken as proving that access has little effect, but neither do they provide any strong evidence in favour of that hypothesis. Besides, the equation is clearly under-specified; the omission of relevant variables could mask or bias the estimated role of access. For instance, access might be more effective in the presence of other elements of the financial infrastructure such as credit registries or effective protection of property rights (Johnson et al. 2002; Djankov et al. 2007), or if financial liberalization were more advanced (Waldenström and Vlachos 2005). The strength and presence of informal credit channels could also be a factor. Several other control variables reflecting, for example, education and labour-market conditions deserve to be included also. Future work will report the results of further analysis along these lines.

4 Allocation between Different Assets

Turning to the composition of the household financial portfolio, one distinctive stylized fact is that the rich hold a much riskier financial asset portfolio.[14] In making this judgement, we rely on the conventional classification that treats bank deposits (and other liquid assets largely free of default risk such as mutual funds solely invested in short-term money market assets and certain government-sponsored savings schemes) as largely risk free.[15] US data suggest that these display a wealth elasticity of close to unity.[16] Though subject to market risk, government bonds are also often classified with the risk free; lower wealth deciles do not hold much of these, but, even when they are included with the other risk-free assets, this broader category still displays a wealth elasticity little more than unity (constant share of wealth held in this form). Up to a certain level,[17] other risky financial assets have a wealth elasticity

---

[14] Carroll (2002) has shown that a strong bequest motive could explain not only higher savings rates for high-income households but also a higher risk tolerance. Carroll also notes that rich households hold a relatively high share of non-financial business equity. He suggests that this is due to capital market imperfections inducing owners of technology or other productive assets to invest in their own enterprises. An alternative explanation is that true total Haig–Simon income from non-financial wealth is higher than measured. After all, what is wealth but capitalized Haig–Simon income?

[15] Even though subject to inflation risk as well as (in less-advanced economies) a small but sometimes not insignificant default risk.

[16] Inferred from data on asset multiples of income for deciles of *wealth* in Kennickell (2003).

[17] To about the 90th decile of wealth in the US data: non-financial business equity assets represent an increasing share of the portfolios of the very rich.

much higher than unity—this reflects the declining share of total wealth held in non-financial form as wealth increases. If these observations are extrapolated to conditions in low-income countries, the share of risky financial assets in the national totals is likely to be smaller in poor countries. This, indeed, is confirmed by the observation that the ratio of aggregate national bank deposits to market capitalization is negatively correlated with per capita income—though the correlation is rather weak when attention is restricted to data from developing countries, because of outliers such as Israel, Jamaica, and Slovenia.

The pattern of increasing risk as wealth increases appears to be driven mainly by higher participation by rich households in the riskier assets. In other words, a higher proportion of wealthy households hold risky financial assets, but among households with financial assets there is relatively little systematic variation in the ratio of risky financial assets to other assets as wealth increases. This can be seen in Figure 13.1 for six advanced economies (based on Guiso et al. 2002; cf. their tables 1.5 and 1.7), and for Korea. If this can be extrapolated to low-income countries, then it implies that patterns of ownership can be inferred from *participation* rates for different assets and products. Participation data for risky financial assets are available for India (Kar et al. 2003), and these also show a strong upward trend with income (see Figure 13.1). Conditional on some holdings of risky assets, the share of risk in total financial assets rises slightly with income in China. It seems safe to assume that the unconditional share of risky assets increases with wealth in both China and India. Note that participation rates are much lower for all quintiles in India than for the advanced economies shown—as is surely the case in all developing countries. But is household portfolio allocation efficient? There are various reasons to suppose that it is not. For instance, it is hard to rationalize the lack of diversification in most household portfolios.[18] The existence of an equity premium has contributed to a perception that risky assets form too low a share in household portfolios. Other kinds of portfolio allocation error are also conjectured, such as reliance on fixed-interest mortgages, when choice of floating might place the household on a higher indifference curve. Reviewing this literature for the USA, Campbell (2006) concludes that 'many households are reasonably effective investors, but a minority make significant mistakes', and that there may be a persistent cross-subsidy from naive to sophisticated households.

---

[18] For example, M. Kelly (1995) showed that the median US investor held just one equity stock. More recently, Goetzmann and Kumar (2005) showed that, while diversification is increasing among the clients of a large US brokerage, many are still demonstrably insufficiently diversified and forgo substantial returns on a risk-adjusted basis, even after allowing for transactions costs. Bergstresser and Poterba (2004) discuss tax inefficient portfolio allocation by US households.

Various explanations have been advanced for deviations from household portfolio efficiency, including inadequate financial education,[19] weak investor protection,[20] and lack of trust (Guiso et al. 2005).[21] These issues have been little considered in the developing country context, and the limited data on age and education patterns are only moderately informative here. In practice, the use of non-cash financial assets is highly correlated with educational levels in China, Ghana, and Vietnam (but education in turn is correlated with income).[22] In addition to advocating a more adventurous portfolio, financial planners often recommend that the riskiness of the household portfolio should decline as households near retirement—a form of turnpike theorem for investment planning. Looking, therefore, at variations in the share of risky assets with age, no strong pattern emerges consistently across countries for which data are available. There is a hump-shaped pattern—as would be recommended by financial planners—for the USA, the UK, and Germany (see Figure 13.1), but a trend increase for the Netherlands and (at least as far as participation is concerned) for India. The reduced share of risky assets held by older people in the USA is less than would be recommended by financial planners (Ameriks and Zeldes 2004).[23] There is no pronounced age–risk correlation for any of the developing countries for which we have data. Given that different age groups also represent different cohorts in these data, however, there is an identification problem in separating the effects of calendar time and age.

Supply conditions can also strongly affect household portfolio composition in developing countries, including the choice between risky and safe assets, especially, but not only, when exchange controls limit international diversification. Legal, regulatory, and tax policies can strongly affect the cost and availability to lower-income households of such products as insurance and mortgage finance. Equity is the prime risk product, and availability of traded equity has been greatly increased in many developing countries through privatization. This process has been enormously influential in increasing participation in equity markets (Boutchkova and Megginson 2000), even though the voucher-based experiments towards popular capitalism in Eastern Europe were quite problematical (Ellerman 2001). In turn, the political commitment,

---

[19] Lusardi and Mitchell (2006) found astonishing levels of financial ignorance when they added a module on financial education to a 2004 US survey on health and retirement issues.

[20] Giannetti and Koskinen (2004) present data for twenty-six, mostly advanced, economies on the percentage of households holding equities; they find a positive correlation between these percentages and measures of investor protection.

[21] Rosen and Wu (2004) show that households with poor health status hold less risky assets.

[22] For urban households in China, the share holding risky assets increases monotonically with educational categories from 0.1% of those with below primary level education to over 10% for those with post-graduate qualifications (CASS survey special tabulations).

[23] However, as Ameriks and Zeldes (2004) show, the apparent downward trend with old age is not confirmed by a more thorough multivariate microeconometric analysis of the US data—an observation that should act as a caveat for conclusions based on the simpler univariate approach adopted here.

Table 13.3. Use of different financial products, EU countries, 2005 (%)

		Access a/c	Checking a/c	Credit card	Deposit a/c	Debit card	Life assurance	Cheque book	Over-draft	Occupa-tional pension	Mort-gage	Shares	Collective investment	Car loan >1 year	Other loan >1 year	Bonds	None	Don't know	Checking or deposit account
EU25 median		90	73	30	29	35	30	7	12	18	9	8	6	6	8	2	9	1	78
EU25 mean		89	71	34	30	30	28	25	19	17	16	10	10	7	7	5	10	1	80
Belgium	BE	97	93	43	68	38	64	6	27	27	25	17	14	9	4	7	1	2	95
Denmark	DK	99	47	48	26	39	59	20	43	44	40	29	8	16	17	19	1	0	62
Germany	DE	97	92	23	41	40	28	6	24	19	9	11	16	7	8	5	1	1	94
Greece	EL	83	10	26	59	15	28	2	2	5	8	4	2	5	5	1	17	0	65
Spain	ES	95	50	36	54	18	30	3	3	11	19	6	5	7	3	1	4	1	89
France	FR	96	87	62	21	35	10	75	38	11	23	8	10	10	8	2	2	1	89
Ireland	IE	88	57	40	36	36	42	29	16	19	22	10	4	23	12	5	11	1	72
Italy	IT	75	62	20	9	10	6	24	4	4	6	6	6	3	3	4	24	1	70
Luxembourg	LU	99	74	65	29	38	59	9	39	18	25	18	16	17	11	6	1	0	85
Netherlands	NL	100	95	43	30	45	65	7	4	26	49	21	23	3	3	7	0	0	96
Austria	AT	96	73	28	56	39	61	5	31	25	5	7	6	9	11	4	2	2	84
Portugal	PT	84	74	20	12	21	43	35	4	6	10	4	1	4	3	2	14	2	77
Finland	FI	99	82	42	31	22	39	1	8	11	23	17	14	13	11	2	1	0	87
Sweden	SE	99	75	64	50	54	51	9	18	49	49	39	57	16	12	14	7	0	85
UK		91	76	51	37	40	50	64	38	31	30	19	9	10	14	10	7	2	83
Cyprus	CY	85	46	34	40	33	8	28	12	2	13	19	0	17	18	10	14	1	71
Czech Rep.	CZ	85	73	14	14	36	16	0	20	30	5	3	3	6	9	1	14	1	79
Estonia	EE	86	74	20	15	16	25	1	4	31	4	4	1	3	8	0	11	3	78
Hungary	HU	66	49	10	9	24	12	1	12	20	3	1	1	6	3	1	33	1	54
Latvia	LV	64	29	29	7	10	26	2	10	11	5	2	0	3	9	1	35	1	32
Lithuania	LT	70	42	14	9	9	30	1	1	15	0	2	1	1	5	0	25	5	47
Malta	MT	90	53	30	46	26	69	32	6	7	9	13	6	5	3	9	9	1	75
Poland	PL	66	46	14	8	26	5	3	12	9	2	2	2	3	6	2	32	2	49
Slovakia	SK	83	62	13	20	37	7	2	8	18	4	3	3	5	7	2	17	0	74
Slovenia	SI	97	87	35	8	37	56	9	40	8	1	24	8	6	10	2	3	0	90
Predicted @ 50% access		50	50	21	18	22	22	10	11	14	6	5	2	5	7	2			
Predicted @ 100% access		78	78	44	40	49	38	24	20	23	25	18	15	11	10	7			

Note: 'Access' means reporting at least one product.

Source: European Commission (2005) and author's calculations.

which privatization to domestic households can represent, lowers political risk and increases stock-market valuations, which in turn can favourably affect growth (Oijen and Perotti 2001). Beyond the risky/safe dichotomy, available data are not only limited but hard to bring to a common base, given the different types of financial asset and financial product and the different ways in which information about holdings have been measured in different countries. One large cross-country database that avoids these difficulties is that assembled in recent years for the twenty-five member states of the EU, which now includes some middle-income countries.[24]

The pattern of usage of different financial products found in the EU data (see Table 13.3) suggests a fairly clear pecking order for some products, in that there is a fairly regular progression in the use of these products as overall financial access increases. (Here overall financial access is measured by the percentage of respondents who report use any of the products.)

5 Concluding Remarks

Financial asset holdings by households are highly concentrated; in the USA one-half of households own about 97 per cent of financial assets. The savings they represent are pooled and transformed by financial intermediaries and markets, enhancing their risk and return. Although firms are also providers of funds to intermediaries and markets, the savings of prosperous households ultimately represent a large fraction of the resources employed by the financial sector in its provision of risk-reduction services and investable funds. As such, they are a key ingredient in the growth-promoting process of financial intermediation.

Data on the financial asset holdings of households in developing countries are very sparse indeed. The quality of data for the handful of countries for which systematic surveys have been conducted is suspect, with indications that asset holdings of the highest income groups are systematically understated. For low-income countries, the relevant question for poor households is not how much financial assets they have, but whether they have access to

---

[24] The European Commission has conducted financial surveys in member states almost every year since the late 1990s. The objective of the survey includes analysis of satisfaction with products, confidence in intermediaries, and the effectiveness of cross-border competition. The data discussed here were collected in 2005 and reported in European Commission (2005). Thanks to Francesco Gaetano for the special tabulation in the final column of Table 13.3 showing usage of *either* checking *or* deposit account. The European Commission stresses, however, that the Eurobarometer survey was designed to elicit attitudes about the importance of various financial issues rather than measuring usage; therefore the statistics on usage should be treated with caution. In particular, it warns that 'the given response rate should not be misinterpreted as implying that the remaining proportion of respondents do not have the corresponding item'.

financial intermediaries at all. We have drawn on and synthesized recent work by several authors using information provided by banks and microfinance institutions in combination with household survey data to produce estimates of access percentages for some 150 countries. These estimates can be progressively refined as the results of a new wave of access surveys currently under way or planned become available.

The new access percentages are negatively correlated across countries with poverty rates, but the correlation is not a robust one and loses significance in multiple regressions that include mean per capita income. Thus the supposed anti-poverty potential of financial access remains econometrically elusive. Data for developing countries is insufficiently rich to assess whether asset choice by households is consistent with rational choice, a question on which there has been much discussion for advanced economies. Once again, it is more a question of whether households actually use any of a range of different types of financial instruments than of whether they have chosen the optimal quantities of each in their portfolio. Analysis of data from the European Union suggests a ranking of different financial instruments and products in terms of the level of income at which each will be widely used—checking and deposit accounts and their associated cards come first, followed by life assurance and then loans.

14

Housing and Personal Wealth in a Global Context

John Muellbauer

1 Introduction

Housing markets are now internationally recognized as rivalling financial markets for understanding economic fluctuations in economies with developed financial systems. Real estate has emerged as an asset class central to both household and business portfolio decisions. Housing wealth accounted for 41 per cent of net wealth of UK households at the end of 2004, almost twice the percentage represented by pension wealth. The comparable figure for the USA at the end of 2004 was 39 per cent. In recent years, international institutions such as the Organization for Economic Cooperation and Development (OECD), the International Monetary Fund (IMF), and the Bank for International Settlements (BIS) have raised concerns over the potential overvaluation of residential housing markets—by as much as 30 per cent—and the potential implications for an increased risk of a serious downturn in the world economy. The European Central Bank (ECB) has also taken a great interest in the issues posed for monetary policy in the eurozone. In commercial property, the deepening of cross-border markets and the search for investment opportunities by pension funds and other large investors is leading to increased professionalization of commercial property portfolio management, not just in Europe but in the major economies of Asia. Households, via owner-occupied

This study was prepared for the UNU-WIDER project meeting 'Personal Assets from a Global Perspective', Helsinki, 4–6 May 2006. This chapter draws on underlying research for which support is acknowledged from the ESRC under grant RES-000-23-0244: Improving Methods for Macroeconometric Modelling, and from the Department for International Development (UK), under grant number R8311: Monetary Policy, Growth and Stability in SSA. Comments from Janine Aron, Jim Davies, Jim MacGee, Ed Wolff, and a referee are gratefully acknowledged.

293

housing and their pension assets, are exposed to fluctuations in real-estate markets as well as in equity and bond markets.

The first reason why housing and personal wealth matter is thus their importance for understanding macroeconomic fluctuations and debates about longer-run national saving and pensions policies. The global credit crisis that erupted in 2007 has increased the intensity of debates about the role of housing for monetary transmission and financial stability, a major theme of the Federal Reserve's 2007 Jackson Hole Symposium. A critical question about which there is much controversy is how consumer spending is affected by a rise in housing wealth, particularly via its role as collateral for borrowing. In these controversies, the role played by institutional differences in housing and credit markets through time and across countries is often neglected. Section 2 of this chapter addresses the question of monetary transmission to household spending and of the link between housing wealth and consumption. Section 3 briefly reviews international empirical evidence on the housing-to-consumption link. It argues that most studies are flawed by the failure to include relevant 'controls'.

The second reason why housing and personal wealth matter is concern over inequality. Thus recent debates about housing supply policies—for example, land-use planning, construction of social housing, and policies on rent controls—reflects concerns about housing affordability behind which lie serious distributional worries. In a number of countries, the real house price appreciation of the last decade marks one of the largest wealth redistributions from young to old in recorded history. Governments are subject to pressure both from the young who would like housing to be more affordable and the middle-aged and old who are concerned with preserving the value of their wealth. The 'social exclusion' of the young without wealth-owning relatives to transfer a housing deposit or guarantee a mortgage is likely to have widened long-term economic inequality, despite efforts by governments to use social benefits to help the poor. The spatial variation in house prices within a country, reflecting varying land prices, is another important aspect of inequality—between households at different locations.

In most poor countries and transition economies, housing finance systems are still developing, so that housing wealth plays a different, but evolving, distributional as well as macroeconomic role, as the collateral function of housing wealth develops. In many poor countries, formal property titles are missing, particularly for urban squatters and many of the rural poor. Lack of access to shelter is often a major characteristic of poverty. Policies on land use, title registration, and the legal framework, and on how limited resources should be spent on providing housing outside the market system, will then have important repercussions on inequality and the generational transmission of inequality. Section 4 discusses these distributional issues. To illustrate the practical relevance of both macro and distributional concerns, Section 5 reviews some recent policy debates. Section 6 concludes.

2 Consumer Expenditure, Housing Wealth, and Institutions

Consumer expenditure accounts for the greater part of GDP and is central to monetary transmission—that is, the mechanism whereby short-term interest rates affect GDP. Interest rates have both direct and indirect effects on consumer spending.[1] There are three indirect effects: via expected income growth; via income uncertainty or volatility; and through asset prices. Together, these appear to be quantitatively more important than the direct effects, which tend to be of ambiguous sign both in theory and in empirical work.[2]

The indirect effects of an increase in interest rates tend to lead to a decline in consumer spending. However, the size of these effects depends on institutional features that differ across countries and on the definition of consumer spending. The standard definition of aggregate consumption in the national accounts includes an imputation for housing consumption. With this definition, Muellbauer (2008) shows that, in a simple life-cycle model of consumption and housing with infinitely lived households and no credit constraints, the 'housing-wealth' effect is likely to be small and probably even negative. Once credit constraints are taken into account, a liberal credit market tends to result in a positive effect from house prices on consumption as collateral constraints on owners are relaxed and because the need to save for a housing deposit by the young is limited even at higher prices. With an illiberal credit market, the collateral effect is weak, while the need of the young to save for a housing deposit is greater with higher house prices; see Engelhardt (1996) for micro-evidence. In the latter case, higher house prices reduce consumer spending, as seems to have been the case in Italy and Japan. Then higher interest rates via this indirect channel may actually lead to higher spending, tending to offset any negative effects via other channels.

While a decrease in interest rates will generally increase the market value of housing, it has sometimes been argued that the rise in personal wealth that results is illusory. In a closed economy with a fixed population, if households in general tried to make use of their capital gains on housing by selling their property, they would force down house prices. While, at the individual level, housing wealth appears spendable, for the economy as a whole it is not. A super-rational representative household would take this into account. However, one should not exaggerate the degree to which economies are 'closed' with respect to housing. International migration is another reason why the closed economy view is out of place. For example, in the cases of Ireland, Spain, and the UK, immigration has been an important contributor to the rise

---

[1] For a more detailed discussion see MacLennan et al. (2000).

[2] However, the evidence is clearer that expenditure on durable goods is interest sensitive and also that, in countries where floating rate debt is important, rises in rates affect cash flows of borrowers and hence their spending.

in house prices of the last decade, while significant numbers of UK retirees have capitalized on their housing wealth in choosing to live abroad. The upper end of the housing market in London and the south-east of the UK now also has a considerable element of foreign ownership. Even more important, the internationalization of credit markets implies that, as long as foreign lenders are willing to advance credit to households on the basis of domestic collateral values, these values will be far less constrained by domestic income and domestic saving than was once the case.

The size of the housing wealth or collateral effect depends on a number of factors. As noted above, liberal credit markets increase the collateral role of housing wealth, so that higher house prices release constraints on household borrowing and spending. In countries such as Italy, where the legal system impedes the functioning of this collateral mechanism, this credit channel will be weaker than elsewhere. Another institutional feature affecting the efficiency of credit markets concerns the sharing of information on individuals' credit histories by financial institutions, thus reducing the problem of asymmetric information that impedes lending. The USA, for example, is highly developed here, and moreover has national institutions, such as Fannie Mae, Freddie Mac, and the Federal Home Loan Banks, which reduce loan risk for individual lenders.[3] Another factor is the size of transactions costs for housing: the lower these costs, which include taxes, and the charges of real-estate agents and lawyers, the more liquid and so potentially spendable is housing wealth. The tax system can have other effects: for example, if housing is tax advantaged for inheritance tax, as is the case in Japan, older people will be less inclined to reduce their housing equity to maintain spending. This reduces the housing-wealth effect.

A high rate of owner-occupation can be another factor increasing the housing wealth or collateral effect. Over half of German households are renters, for example. While the household sector directly or indirectly owns much of the rental stock, for example, via pension funds, a rise in the value of the rental stock has a smaller wealth or collateral effect than a similar rise in value of the owner-occupied stock. This is partly because the collateral mechanism is missing—pensions cannot usually be used for collateral. Moreover, pensions are far less liquid than other assets.

Offsetting the wealth and collateral effects of house price rises are income and substitution effects. If housing is relatively expensive, consumers have less to spend on other goods. A rise in house prices should cause renters to save more: not only will future rents tend to follow house prices, but those with

---

[3] The securitization of loans and hedging through the derivatives markets, spreading the incidence of risk into the financial system, is another factor easing credit availability. In view of the burgeoning incidence of bad loans in the US sub-prime market in 2007, this was clearly taken too far in recent years; see Rajan (2005) and DiMartino and Duca (2007).

hopes of becoming owners one day need to save more for the initial deposit, unless they give up altogether on owner-occupation. The credit system is again important here. As noted above, in countries like Italy, where large deposits are required of first-time buyers, the young need to save a lot harder in response to house price rises than in the UK or the Netherlands, where loan-to-value ratios can be as high as 100 per cent. This could imply a negative impact of house prices on consumer spending in countries with illiberal credit systems.

So far, we have discussed only the house-price-to-consumer spending linkage. But institutional and historical differences can also impact profoundly on the link between short-term interest rates and house prices themselves. Most obviously, for a given response of consumption to house prices, countries with high ratios of housing wealth to income, such as the UK, will experience greater interest-rate sensitivity than countries with lower ratios. Second, the degree to which mortgage interest rates are sensitive to variations in short-term market rates will be important. Countries where most of the mortgage stock is in the form of fixed-rate loans will have far less sensitivity to short-term interest rates.

Cameron et al. (2006) have studied UK house price determination with regional panel data for 1972–2003. In the UK, one can distinguish several components in the interest-rate-to-house-price transmission channel. The first is a negative real interest rate effect, strengthened by the financial deregulation of the 1980s. The second is a negative nominal interest rate effect, which has become somewhat weaker with the easing of credit conditions.[4] The third effect is non-linear, and operates through a downside risk measure that is zero if the rate of return in recent years was positive, but equals the average lagged return if this return is negative. There are also various indirect effects via income, uncertainty proxies, and other asset prices. MacLennan et al. (2000: 80) investigate the theory of house price volatility and explain that

price volatility increases with more volatile demand and supply, and lower elasticities. Characteristics favouring high demand volatility are low transactions costs, easy credit availability as reflected in high loan-to-value ratios, thus permitting high levels of gearing, and a high proportion of floating rate mortgages. The market rented sector offers a potential safetyvalve which can divert demand from the owner-occupied market when prices are very high. This suggests that countries with small market rented sectors are more likely to have volatile house prices, *ceteris paribus*.

Countries with bigger feedbacks from house price shocks are likely to experience greater house price volatility: a house price shock, which raises expenditure and therefore income, feeds back on itself, thus amplifying the

---

[4] Controlling for the easing of credit conditions greatly improves the significance and robustness of these estimates, particularly of the real rate of interest.

initial shock. One might expect that countries with a less elastic supply of housing should also experience greater house price volatility; see Malpezzi and Maclennan (2001) for a comparison of the USA and the UK, and Glaeser et al. (2006) for the impact of variations in this elasticity over US locations and over time. However, there is an important proviso. In countries with a more elastic response of residential construction to house prices, volatile cyclical fluctuations in construction can contribute to the volatility of national output and employment. The downturns in the sizeable construction sectors in the USA, Spain, and Ireland in 2007–8 are playing an important role in their economic slow-downs.[5] Finally, *ceteris paribus*, one expects an economy with greater income and inflation volatility also to have more volatile house prices. MacLennan et al. (2000) argue that, in countries with pay-as-you-go social-security and pension systems, large market rented sectors, high transactions costs for housing, restricted consumer credit availability, or fixed-rate mortgage markets, consumer expenditure is likely to be driven mainly by income and income uncertainty, with relatively weak or even perverse house price and interest rate effects. The opposite will tend to be true in countries such as the UK, where institutional features lie at the other end of the spectrum, and where liberal credit markets increase asset price volatility.

3 A Brief Survey of the Evidence on the Effects of Housing Assets on Consumption

Recent empirical studies of the housing–consumption link on macro-data include Boone et al. (2001), Ludwig and Sloek (2002), Byrne and Davis (2003), Dvornak and Kohler (2003), Barrell and Davis (2004), Catte et al. (2004), Iacoviello (2004), Case et al. (2005), Caroll et al. (2006), and Slacalek (2006). Earlier studies include Hendry et al. (1990), Kennedy and Andersen (1994), and Muellbauer and Murphy (1995).

Case et al. (2005) claim that, for a panel of US states and a panel of fourteen countries, the housing wealth effect is larger than the stock-market wealth effect. However, as argued by Muellbauer (2008), though the results, at least for the USA, may be broadly correct and consistent with Carroll et al. (2006), their robustness is questionable. The quality of the data for US states leaves much to be desired. For the OECD part of their study, pooling fourteen countries denies heterogeneity between countries implied by institutional differences, as discussed above. Shifts in credit conditions are also omitted, though, for example, Finland, Norway, Sweden, the UK, and the Netherlands all went through revolutions in credit availability. The rise in house prices is highly

---

[5] This will come as no surprise to those who have studied the historical record; see Abramovitz (1964) or Leamer (2007) for a more recent account.

correlated with the shift in credit conditions, so the study is likely to exaggerate the causal role of house prices. Slacalek (2006) studies an international panel of countries allowing for heterogeneity and using a technique that reduces sensitivity to long-term shifts in credit conditions. He finds considerable evidence for heterogeneity, with larger effects in the Anglo-Saxon economies than in core Europe, and has evidence for a negative effect for Italy.

Barrell and Davis (2004) estimate equations for the G5 countries with an equilibrium correction allowing a constant elasticity long-run net wealth effect and real interest rate effects, but no controls for shifts in credit conditions, unemployment rates, or expected income growth. They estimate both single-country equations and pooled equations imposing common long-run coefficients. Byrne and Davis (2003) estimate equations for G7 countries with no controls for shifts in credit conditions, interest rates, unemployment rates, or expected income growth. They do not distinguish housing wealth but test for differences between liquid and illiquid assets effects. For most countries they find net liquid asset effects smaller than those from illiquid assets, and typically negative for the USA and especially for the UK. Since they define liquid assets as gross liquid assets minus debt, this is a classic symptom of omitted variable bias: credit market liberalization is associated with rises in debt relative to income and relative to gross liquid assets. The omitted variable has a positive effect on consumption but is negatively correlated with net liquid assets, and so biases the latter's effect in a negative direction.

In contrast to Case et al., Catte et al. (2004) note institutional differences and, like Slacalek (2006), find major heterogeneity for the parameters in different OECD economies. They estimate ECM models that do have long-run wealth effects, as well as interest rate and unemployment effects. However, they do not control for income expectations explicitly or for the effects of financial liberalization, and this is liable to bias up the estimated housing wealth or collateral effects on consumption. This is also true of Kennedy and Andersen (1994), who study consumption in the form of saving ratios. Nevertheless, this study confirms the heterogeneity of wealth effects across countries, including an apparently negative housing wealth effect for Italy, which could be the result of an ill-functioning mortgage market there.[6]

Boone et al. (2001) are sensitive to the potential importance of credit market liberalization and find some evidence for shifts in long-run relationships, particularly for the UK, USA, and Canada, using dummies for credit market liberalization. They control for interest rate and unemployment dynamics. They also find a negative housing wealth coefficient for Italy. However, they do not attempt to control for income growth expectations or the effect of credit market liberalization on the long-term consumption/income ratio.

---

[6] It may be that the modest liberalization of credit that has occurred in Italy in recent years could attenuate such findings on the latest data.

Muellbauer and Murphy (1995) study UK regional panel data for eleven regions and include a more complete set of controls than earlier studies. They handle income growth expectations through the fitted values from parsimonious income forecasting equations, and check for interaction effects of these with uncertainty indicators. The shifts in credit conditions are proxied using an indicator derived from data on loan-to-value ratios for mortgages to first-time buyers, a forerunner of the one discussed below. They include interest rate and unemployment effects. Assets are aggregated into net liquid and illiquid categories (measured at the end of the previous year), where the latter includes housing wealth, and shifts in wealth effects with credit conditions are checked. As a check on the aggregation of physical and financial illiquid wealth, a separate allowance is made for a real house price effect, but this always proves insignificant. One problem with the study is the omission of the direct effect on consumption of credit conditions discussed below. The other was the authors' scepticism over the accuracy of the regional accounts income data. Subsequently, Cameron and Muellbauer (2000) established that these data seriously understated the rise in relative incomes in the south-east in the 1980s, probably resulting in an upward bias in the housing wealth effects being estimated.

Regarding micro-data evidence, Muellbauer (2008) reviews some of the recent literature, including the finding that, on UK micro-data, Campbell and Cocco (2005) and Attanasio et al. (2005) reach diametrically opposite conclusions. The latter argue that housing wealth or collateral effects are merely proxies for omitted income expectations, while the former find large, sometimes implausibly large, effects. These contradictions have not yet been reconciled but are likely to be due to differences in methodology and in controls for income, credit conditions, unemployment, and other variates.

For aggregate time series data, the failure to control for shifts in credit conditions is often likely to be critical. Although the implications of financial liberalization have aroused interest, controversy, and a growing literature (such as Bayoumi 1993a, b; Schmidt-Hebbel and Serven 1997; Honohan 1999; Bandiera et al. 2000), there has not been an entirely satisfactory applied analysis of these implications in the consumption literature. One major difficulty has been to find an indicator of credit market deregulation with which to model the direct and interaction effects of financial liberalization. Another has been to find a model encompassing the insights from life-cycle theory with a role for the credit channel and shifts in credit supply conditions. As Aron and Muellbauer (2000a) observe, financial liberalization reduces credit constraints on households engaging in smoothing consumption when they expect significant income growth. This is the standard mechanism addressed in the literature on credit constraints. Second, credit liberalization reduces deposits required of first-time buyers of housing. This involves a rise in the long-term consumption/income ratio, particularly for younger households. Third, it increases the availability of collateral-backed loans for households that already possess collateral. This should make housing assets effectively more spendable. The three facets thus imply both a shift in the average propensity to consume and important interaction effects—for example, with housing wealth, income growth expectations, interest rates, and perhaps indicators of uncertainty.

In the absence of shifts in credit conditions, a sensible time series specification for a consumption function comes from generalizing the log approximation of a consumption function where consumption depends on human capital, other wealth, and permanent income. Following Muellbauer and Lattimore (1995), this has a long-run solution as follows:

$$\log c_t \approx [\alpha_0 - \alpha_1 r_{1t} - \alpha_2 \theta_t + \alpha_3 E_t \Delta \log ym_{t+k} + \gamma_1 LA_{t-1}/y_t + \gamma_2 IFA_{t-1}/y_t + \gamma_3 HA_{t-1}/y_t + \log y_t]$$

(14.1)

Here c is consumption, r is the real interest rate, θ is an indicator of income uncertainty, $E_t \Delta \log ym_{t+k}$ is a forecast of the growth rate of non-property income,[7] LA/y is the ratio of liquid assets minus debt to non-property income, IFA/y is the ratio of illiquid financial assets to non-property income, and HA/y is the ratio of housing wealth to non-property income. Asset to income ratios give a better approximation to the underlying linear additive structure of human and non-human capital than does the more conventional log-assets formulation. The γs are marginal propensities for the different assets, which are allowed to differ. If they are equal, assets can be combined into net worth, here an easily testable hypothesis. The specification enforces long-run homogeneity, in that doubling real income and real assets doubles consumption. A higher propensity to spend for liquid assets is consistent with a formal model by Otsuka (2006) which builds on Carroll's buffer stock theory of saving (1997, 2001) and Zeldes (1989).

Habits or adjustment costs (see Muellbauer 1988), result in partial adjustment to the consumption target defined by (14.1). Another component of short-term adjustment of consumption is the change of the nominal rate of interest on debt, nr, weighted by the debt to income ratio, DB/y, to measure the short-term impact of higher debt service costs on cashflow constrained consumers with debt.

If credit conditions ease, one can expect shifts in a number of these parameters. The following should increase: α_0, α_1, α_3, γ_3;[8] while the short-run impact of debt service costs should ease when refinancing is easier. The effect on α_2, which measures the impact of income uncertainty, is ambiguous: better credit access should allow households to borrow if income turns down, but greater debt also makes them more vulnerable.

This model is used by Aron et al. (2008) for consumption in the UK and Aron and Muellbauer (2008) for South Africa. The contrast is interesting, since

---

[7] With horizon k and near future growth rates more heavily weighted than more distant growth rates.

[8] For an example, see Poterba and Manchester (1989).

South Africa is unusual in experiencing an easing of credit conditions without the usual house price boom. For the UK, we use the consumer credit conditions index (CCI), derived by Fernandez-Corugedo and Muellbauer (2006). This comes from modelling data on ten credit indicators, from which a common credit indicator and a risk indicator are extracted, after controlling for standard economic and demographic variables.

We allow the relevant parameters to shift for the UK with the CCI. The expected shifts in parameters all occur, though a few are not very significant. The marginal propensity to spend out of housing assets at the maximum value of CCI is estimated to be a little larger (0.032) than that for illiquid financial assets (0.02), which, in turn, is below that of net liquid assets, at around 0.11. These are lower values of the housing assets effect than commonly found in the literature. We find that a 4-quarter moving average of observations on illiquid financial assets fits far better than the end of previous quarter value, consistent with findings by Lettau and Ludvigson (2004).[9] Since much of illiquid financial assets is in pension funds, this plausibly reflects the slow adaptation of contribution and pay-out rates to changes in asset values. The real interest rate effect is negative and significant, and there is mild evidence that it strengthens as CCI rises, while the debt-weighted nominal interest rate change, also negative, weakens significantly as CCI rises. This is exactly what one should expect: easier access to credit weakens the spending restrictions on indebted consumers when interest rates rise. With easier access to credit, intertemporal substitution should play a bigger role: hence the enhanced real interest rate effect, and indeed the enhanced role for income growth expectations, for which there is also strong empirical evidence.

For the USA, a similar model has been estimated in Muellbauer (2008). The results support the hypothesis that the housing collateral effect has increased with credit market liberalization, and this effect on consumption is now substantially larger than the effect of stock-market wealth on consumption.

The data for South Africa support most of the shifts in the parameters of (14.1) outlined above. An important difference from the UK study is that, without a separately estimated CCI, we estimate a CCI for South Africa using information from jointly estimated debt and consumption equations with common dummies linked to known episodes of credit market liberalization. As noted above, credit market liberalization in South Africa, beginning around 1981, coincided with a long down-trend in real house prices after the gold boom of the late 1970s and early 1980s had driven the market to a peak. The 1980s continuing into the 1990s were marked by high and volatile real interest rates, poor income growth, and political uncertainty, in which the housing market suffered. Yet the debt-to-income ratio trended up, as a consequence of

---

[9] However, Lettau and Ludvigson (2004) understate the empirical significance of the stock-market effect over one- or two-year horizons.

domestic liberalization of credit. This helps distinguish direct from indirect effects of credit liberalization. Our model implies a highly significant housing asset effect on consumption in South Africa. Indeed, all three marginal propensities to consume out of assets are estimated to be higher in South Africa than in the UK. In part, this could be due to underestimation of some assets. But it could also reflect the correlation of asset prices with South Africa's economic and political turmoil, which, despite our efforts, the income growth expectations and uncertainty proxies included in our model may not fully measure.

Interestingly enough, in research on Japanese consumption (Muellbauer and Muarata 2008), we find no evidence of significant credit market liberalization in the 1980s or 1990s in Japan. Furthermore, we find a negative land price effect on consumption. As noted above, this is also likely to be partly a consequence of the structure of inheritance tax in Japan, which advantages inheritance of land or housing and so causes most households to refrain from home equity loans. Financial wealth effects are significant, however.

4 The Inequality of Wealth and of Housing Wealth

One of the key findings of the research on consumer spending discussed in this chapter has been that different propensities to spend are associated with different types of wealth and that these propensities depend on property rights, the credit market, and other institutions. This will also be true for welfare analysis. For example, households having the benefit of the use of publicly owned housing with long-term security of tenure effectively 'own' an asset, even though they cannot trade these rights or use them as collateral. As Yemtsov (Chapter 15, this volume) notes and the discussion by Jim Davies highlighted (Chapter 1, this volume), in the analysis of the privatization of housing in transition economies, some value needs to be associated with these use rights, making the gain in wealth when privatization occurs less pronounced than if they are ignored. There could be a number of obstacles towards the achievement of full property rights even after privatization—for example, ill-defined obligations in apartment blocks for collective maintenance, heating, etc., the lack of a developed property market and/or high transactions costs, and, of course, an undeveloped use of housing collateral in the banking system. This introduces problems of valuation.

Problems of valuation are nothing new, of course. They are also rife in the context of pensions. For example, how is one to value state pensions due to be paid out in twenty years, when governments may devalue these rights in the context of rising but uncertain ratios of retired to working age populations? Occupational pensions, whether linked to final salary or to funds invested, are subject to obvious risks to salaries and to asset returns, and may even be at risk when companies fail. Transfer values can often lie below the value of historical contributions cumulated at some market return. In divorce cases where the spouses' pension rights are part of the overall asset 'pot', it is usual to apply substantial discounts to these rights.

Credit constraints and transactions costs typically imply that values are context-dependent and can differ from individual to individual without the market being able to correct for these differences. The liquidity advantages of cash are obvious and compensate for lower returns. When economists discuss 'the distribution of wealth', they typically add cash and other assets together using market values or approximations to these values. Sometimes valuation problems are acknowledged by examining the robustness of inequality measures to alternative valuation assumptions. The point being made here is that these problems are more pervasive than generally acknowledged. For example, from the point of view of financing consumption in a short-run perspective, the findings reviewed in this chapter suggest applying substantial discounts to illiquid assets of various kinds, and that these discounts will vary with each economy's institutional environment. From a longer-term welfare perspective and from the point of view of intergenerational transmission of inequality, one might well wish to value illiquid assets closer to cash. This is analogous to the point that the inequality of short-term consumption and the inequality of discounted utility over a longer horizon could differ considerably.

Closely related issues arise in the discussion of gender and the distribution of wealth in developing countries by Deere and Doss (Chapter 17, this volume). They argue that assets have functions of well-being and empowerment and that ownership can have complex dimensions, such as the ability to farm, the right to bequeath, and security of tenure, in the context of land. Assets can be more or less community owned and less or more individually owned, and divorce or separation can have very different implications for different types of assets and ownership. Differences in the inheritance regime could have a significant impact on the value an individual places on assets of different types and, of course, on the transmission of inequality. Both for macroeconomics and for welfare analysis, therefore, this more nuanced view of wealth is needed.

Housing wealth inequality matters in its own right, and because differential access to goods funded by government, such as good education, good transport, clean air, and low crime, tends to be capitalized in differential land and house prices (see Gibbons and Machin 2008). Since differences in income, financial wealth, and access to credit influence access to housing in expensive locations, this is an important channel by which such differences affect inequality of life chances more generally.

5 Some Policy Debates

Some issues for macro-policy and inequality will be illustrated with examples from South Africa, the UK, and the eurozone. These have resonance elsewhere, particularly in emerging-market and transition countries with rapidly developing credit markets.

5.1 South Africa

South Africa's credit regime is globally one of the most innovative and liberal, and the easy acquisition of debt has fuelled consumption. Falling nominal interest rates from 2003 to 2006, more affordable mortgages, and ease of remortgaging have generated large rises in mortgage debt, house prices, and consumer spending. The inflationary consequences via the output gap, the trade balance, and hence the exchange rate—unless there are other factors keeping the exchange rate high—are well understood. The potential trade-off for interest rate policy has posed serious dilemmas for the monetary policy committee (MPC). Higher consumption occurs at the expense of personal saving, constraining the domestic funds potentially available for corporate investment and implying an increased reliance on foreign saving, exacerbating the economic vulnerability to reversible capital inflows.

The MPC's interest-rate policy should not have to take sole responsibility for these issues, given the policy trade-offs. Among the available complementary policies, one is to tighten capital adequacy rules on banks. A somewhat less liberal credit market, achievable through increased capital requirements for risky mortgage lending, would enhance saving.

The second lies in complementary fiscal measures on households to help stabilize the property market and the macro-economy—namely, well-designed property and land taxes. Denmark, which has a very liberal and efficient mortgage market and the highest mortgage stock relative to GDP in the world, has had a record of remarkable macroeconomic stability (see Muellbauer 2005). The reasons for this are threefold. First, fixed-rate mortgages are the dominant form of borrowing. This means mortgage costs respond only slowly to short-term interest rates. Second, in the Danish system of property taxes, there is a national, progressive tax with annual revaluations of property.[10] In economic upswings when house price rises outpace incomes, tax revenue rises faster than income, so stabilizing spending. Also, knowing that tax liabilities will increase as values rise discourages the portfolio demand for property. Furthermore, local land taxes tend to encourage the supply of land. Finally, by law, a maximum of 90 per cent of the value of a home can be used as collateral. Borrowing above this limit is unsecured and so more expensive and influenced by credit-rating criteria.[11]

---

[10] To protect those with low incomes relative to their housing wealth, pensioners have the option to defer payment until the property is sold. However, from 2001 the automatic link between the tax and current housing wealth was abandoned, losing an important ingredient in Denmark's automatic stabilizers.

[11] In South Africa in 1998, capital requirements on banks were raised for lending at mortgage loan-to-value ratios in excess of 85%. Legal limits would clearly be a stronger response.

With all three measures in place, the automatic stabilizers function powerfully, greatly reducing the risks of overshooting, permitting lower interest rates and encouraging saving. Not surprisingly, no European country had more powerful automatic stabilizers according to the UK Treasury's fiscal report for the Five Economic Tests for euro entry (HM Treasury 2003).

Large real house price rises also have disturbing implications for the distribution of resources between the young and older households already owning homes, and between poorer and more affluent households. In the context of South Africa's extremes of wealth inequality, a progressive and transparent property tax would keep housing more affordable for the young and the poor, and tap the wealth of the most affluent, without much effect on their incentives to engage in economic activity. Such a tax is therefore ideally placed to meet growth, distribution, and stability objectives.

Housing supply policy could also be regarded as a fiscal measure. South Africa is a deeply unequal society and has one of the highest unemployment rates in the world. According to the 1995 and 2000 household surveys, Statistics South Africa (2002), the percentages of total household spending accounted for by the top quintile in 2000 and 1995 (in parentheses) were 64 per cent (63 per cent), the top two quintiles 82 per cent (82 per cent), and the top three quintiles 92 per cent (93 per cent). If anything, such surveys are likely to understate the spending of the most affluent. As Turner (1976), Mayo et al. (1986), and many others have argued, providing subsidized housing in the form of 'site and basic service'[12] allows poor families to expand their housing shelter over time, as savings and resources permit. Using their own labour develops skills, so contributing to human as well as physical capital accumulation, and helps develop the habit of saving and a stake in the community. In the South African context, using tax revenue to subsidize site and service for many poor households should be preferable to providing higher quality and costly subsidized housing for the few or inducing lower-income households to take on risky levels of debt. Since 1994, housing policy in South Africa has vacillated between the two, as some housing ministers felt site and service were 'too demeaning'. However, recently, policy has again been more progressive.

5.2 The UK

In the UK, housing market developments continue to be a major issue for the Bank of England, HM Treasury (HMT), and the Department for Communities and Local Government (DCLG). The question of whether the UK's different housing and credit market institutions posed too high a risk for the UK to adopt the euro currency emerged as the single most important factor in the negative outcome of the Five Economic Tests (report published by HMT in

---

[12] For example, concrete foundations, sewage, and access to water and electricity.

June 2003). As a consequence, HMT commissioned the Miles Review of the Mortgage Market, which reported in March 2004. Also reflecting concerns over housing affordability and the UK's unusually weak new building response to high house prices, HMT commissioned a series of reviews from Kate Barker on housing supply and the planning system (see below). However, the balance between private renting and owner-occupation, which could have implications for flexible labour markets and the exposure of households to risk, has received little explicit public analysis in the UK. The same is true of the scope for property taxes in addressing stability, affordability, distributional, and efficiency issues.

The Bank of England follows housing and mortgage markets very closely but seems puzzled by the shifts in the correlation of real house price growth and consumption in recent years.[13] Bivariate relationships are never stable for long when the true relationships are multivariate. Aron et al.'s results (2008) explain substantial shifts in the bivariate relationship, given the major downturn in illiquid financial asset values in the early years of the millennium, and from other changes, including the decline in net liquid assets relative to income.

The Bank has also had to concern itself with potential risks to financial stability. There have been debates about whether there is a 'bubble' in the housing market—with more than 30 per cent overvaluation estimated by the OECD—and whether therefore heavily indebted UK households, and UK domestic demand more generally, face a bleak future. The econometric evidence in Cameron et al. (2006) is that, in 2003–5, values were close to fundamentals, given incomes, interest rates, and the tax and land planning regimes. By mid-2007, prices looked a little overvalued on then prevailing economic conditions. The upward trend in world interest rates to mid-2007, the sub-prime crisis, and the more general credit contraction that followed, uncertainties about the degree and timing of the unwinding of global macroeconomic imbalances, and the global oil and food price shocks, imply a sharp deterioration in the fundamentals and suggest extended falls in prices are likely.

In principle, fiscal policy, land-use planning policy and other interventions, such as building subsidized social housing, also have an influence on the level of house prices, and so on the macro-economy as well as on housing affordability and the intergenerational distribution of wealth. The UK government has clearly found this a difficult area for decision making. On the fiscal side, the phasing-out of mortgage interest tax relief was completed in 2000. Stamp duty rates on transactions have been raised several times. The 50 per cent discount on property tax (council tax) on second and further homes has

---

[13] See, for example, minutes of the Monetary Policy Committee meeting held on 8–9 Feb. 2006, para. 9, and Minutes of Evidence by Mervyn King to the Treasury Select Committee, 30 Nov. 2004. See also Aoki et al. (2002) and Benito et al. (2006), who document the breakdown in the new Bank of England model on this point.

been made optional for local authorities. But the zero marginal tax rate for more expensive homes[14] and the additionally regressive tax structure below that threshold, have been retained, while the scheduled revaluation of properties in 2007 after sixteen years has been postponed again. It is clear that property taxes without regular revaluations or indexation to prices are far less useful for macro-stabilization.

The UK, along with many other countries, is perceived to be facing a pensions crisis. One fiscal policy contribution has been to extend tax advantages for Real Estate Investment Trusts and for self-invested pension funds investing, for example, in collective schemes owning rental properties. That such tax breaks for relatively wealthy investors may make housing affordability more problematic for lower-income younger households seems not to have been a major consideration.[15] The government has instead focused on the weak supply response of the UK house-building industry, behind which lies a sluggish planning system, last revised in 1991 in the direction of greater restrictiveness. Since 1997 planning controls have effectively been tightened further, both by forcing more building onto 'brownfield' sites and away from 'greenfield' sites, and by increased use of 'Section 106' agreements, by which land for social housing and other side payments are negotiated, often with long delays, from developers in return for planning permission. The Barker Review (2003, 2004) of new housing and the Barker Review (2006) of land-use planning have been developing policy alternatives.

5.3 *The Eurozone*

The UK is far from alone in facing such policy dilemmas. The Dutch government, also faced with a great house price boom, has struggled with fiscal issues, finding it politically difficult to reduce tax relief on mortgage interest, or to raise property taxes. The Dutch planning system, once well known for its relative efficiency, is perceived to have been overwhelmed by demand. The Dutch boom, together with higher domestic inflation and so a loss of competitiveness, has been an important factor in the economic difficulties faced by the country in recent years. It illustrates well the dilemmas for monetary policy in the eurozone stemming from the institutional differences discussed earlier.

While the Netherlands experienced a major credit market liberalization in the 1990s, Italy remains one of the least developed mortgage markets in core Europe. As noted above, this has much to do with the legal system, which

---

[14] To put it simply, the tax bill on a £GB20m home is the same as on a £GB1m home.

[15] Though it probably was a factor in the late exclusion of individual property investments from self-invested pensions in December 2005, when the Treasury had earlier signalled their inclusion and the financial services industry was geared up in readiness.

makes mortgage repossession very difficult, so undermining the housing collateral function. While low interest rates and increased banking competition have led to rising debt levels in recent years, Italian household debt remains far below the levels in the European countries with more liberal credit regimes. Two of the studies of G7 consumption functions with fairly comprehensive controls found negative housing wealth effects for Italy. The interpretation is that, with high deposit requirements, potential first-time buyers need to save more when house prices rise, while tenants may take higher house prices as an indicator of future rent rises. It is likely that the rises in Italian house prices in recent years are due to low interest rates and foreign demand, fuelled by easy credit and earlier capital gains in northern Europe. This part of the monetary transmission mechanism appears to run in reverse for Italy, contributing to weak domestic demand conditions in recent years. While it is possible that some improvement has taken place in credit availability in Italy, so that the negative housing wealth effect is weaker or may even have been neutralized by now, it is clear that these asymmetries in monetary transmission are holding back growth in the eurozone. For Italian society, with the oldest first-time buyers in Europe, the ill-performing credit market contributes to low rates of household formation and birth rates, and so indirectly to Italy's demographic and pensions problems. Unfortunately, the level of economic literacy on these complex issues by the general public everywhere and by most politicians is such that reasoned debate is difficult. As we have seen, even among professional economists there is widespread confusion about the macroeconomic role of housing and the empirical magnitudes involved.

Related issues arise in the context of policies for economic development. De Soto (2000) argues that, in the context of developing countries, the access to credit that well-developed property rights for land provide has profound implications for entrepreneurship, investment, and growth. He goes so far as to argue that the development of such rights in the West explains why capitalism has been so productive there, while the absence of proper land titles in many developing countries explains the failure of capitalism there. However, this is overstating the case, since other factors are also involved in generating a deep institutional structure of financial intermediation.[16]

6 Conclusions

This chapter has argued that housing wealth plays a potentially very important role for macroeconomic fluctuations and for the distribution of welfare. However, this role is dependent on the institutional framework governing property rights, access to credit, financial architecture and regulation, and trading costs.

[16] See Buckley and Kalarickal (2006: 28–38) for a more detailed discussion of the issues and policy lessons for titling and land-use regulation.

The simplistic view, that for spending power and macroeconomic consequences housing wealth is just like financial wealth, has also been disputed here. Logic and evidence suggest that net worth does not capture fully the relevant information in wealth portfolios to explain consumption. Liquid assets tend to be more spendable that illiquid assets, and the liquidity of housing is quite context dependent. Housing is both an asset and a good providing important services, and this implies that changes in its price have different implications from changes in other asset prices. Moreover, the collateral role of housing varies greatly with the structure of institutions. This implies that important differences exist between countries and over time, as increased access to credit increases the impact of house prices on consumption.

An important reason why this matters for macroeconomic stability and the stability of the financial system is that house prices can overshoot their fundamentals. The empirical evidence is that housing markets are not 'efficient'; see Stein (1995) for reasons to do with credit constraints and lack of 'deep pockets' by traders. There is evidence that in many countries house price expectations contain an element based on the extrapolation of recent gains. Then a sequence of positive shocks can cause further appreciation beyond the fundamentals. The second chief reason why house prices can overshoot is because credit markets tend to do so, as so clearly illustrated by the US sub-prime explosion of lending and its subsequent collapse (see DiMartino and Duca 2007). The reasons have been much debated in recent years and include the skewed incentives for bankers selling products from which they personally make short-term gains, even though the bank as a whole may lose in the long run. Since banks collectively are essential to the functioning of the global economy, they know that public agencies will save them from the worst consequences of their risk-taking excesses.

Increases in the average real price of housing change the distribution of welfare in favour of older households, who tend to be owners, and away from the young, who tend not to be owners and may not even be old enough to vote. The effects on the intergenerational distribution of welfare are similar to those of higher government budget deficits (see Weale 2007). An important difference, however, is that, while deficits may be used to fund generally available goods such as health and education, the redistribution from an increase in average house prices is towards the haves from the have-nots. Because access to a clean environment and publicly funded goods such as transport and education is reflected in land or house prices, inequality of income and wealth is transmitted into differential access to such goods. Thus, higher average prices amplify market inequality and social exclusion. The lack of voting power of the young and the disproportionate influence of wealth via the media and the funding of political parties tend to make governments complicit in policies resulting in higher house prices. This includes planning or zoning policies favouring incumbents as well as tax policies.

The failure of governments generally to grasp the nettle of reforms that would help both stabilize their economies and financial systems and reduce inequality and social exclusion thus has deep roots in political economy. The widespread misunderstandings in the economics profession about the causes and consequences of the operation of housing and credit markets have contributed to this failure.

15

Housing Privatization and Household Wealth in Transition

Ruslan Yemtsov

1 Introduction

There is a growing recognition of the importance of studying wealth distribution globally, as well as in developing and transition economies (Davies et al., Chapter 19, this volume). Understanding the distribution of wealth is important in its own right as an indicator of social cohesion. The stock of available assets also determines the ability of households to withstand shocks, and inequality in its distribution is linked to intergenerational transmission of poverty. Even in rich countries with diversified portfolios, housing represents the largest part of household wealth. From an analysis of the balance sheets of a number of rich countries one can infer that housing accounts for an average of 35–45 per cent of total household wealth. In developing countries housing accounts for a similarly large share (see Davies et al., Chapter 19, this volume, for a review).

Distribution of housing is typically determined by institutional factors and changes relatively slowly (see Muellbauer, Chapter 14, this volume, for a review). Rapid shifts in the distribution of property titles are therefore of particular interest to researchers. Land reforms represent one type for such a change. Massive privatization programmes form another type. Studying their outcomes may help to gain insights about how redistribution policies affect inequality. During 1991–9 as much as 28 per cent of housing stock in transition countries of Eastern Europe and the former Soviet Union (FSU) was

This study has been revised following presentation at the UNU-WIDER project meeting 'Personal Assets from a Global Perspective', Helsinki, 4–6 May 2006. The author is grateful to the meeting participants and Tony Shorrocks for useful comments. Special thanks to the project director, Jim Davies, for his review of the first draft, encouragement, and suggestions. Views expressed are the author's and do not necessarily represent those of the World Bank.

privatized (World Bank 2001b). This figure ranged from 7 per cent in Georgia, to over 60 per cent in Estonia and Kazakhstan. Privatization of housing was part of a much broader programme that affected the distribution of productive assets and the functioning of the economy as a whole, again with important cross-country differences.

The sheer size of asset value affected by housing privatization in transition countries appears to be extremely large. An influential report of the World Bank (2001b) estimated a total wealth transfer due to housing privatization across all European and Central Asian (ECA) countries to equal as much as $US1.1 trillion, which is equivalent to roughly $US3,300 per capita transfer of wealth.[1]

These are large values, but little is known about the effects of this process on inequality in housing wealth distribution. To illustrate this, it is sufficient to mention that, to the best of the author's knowledge, not a single transition economy is included in the Luxembourg Wealth Study and no data on a Gini index for housing values are available for ECA countries.

Based on the survey data from three transition countries—Poland, Russia, and Serbia—this chapter attempts to provide empirical evidence about the distribution of housing stock, its relative role compared to other forms of wealth holding, and its effects on the distribution of current consumption.[2] The three countries selected for this study pursued different types of privatization programmes and were characterized by different initial conditions, thus offering an interesting field for comparisons.

2 Housing Ownership in Transition Economies

Transition countries in ECA began housing reform by simple give-away schemes (most frequently by selling housing units to tenants at prices well below market valuations), accompanied by a series of reforms aimed at creating institutions for housing markets. The housing sectors as a whole moved closer to a market system with dominating private ownership of housing assets, elimination of subsidies for utilities, emergence of private finance,

---

[1] The estimate derived in World Bank (2001b) is based on opportunity cost approach.

[2] The chapter does not discuss land reforms. Land privatization was an important reform in many transition economies redistributing vital assets in the low-income CIS countries, with significant variation across countries. As much as 90% of arable land was transferred to households on highly beneficial terms in Albania and Armenia, between one-half and three-quarters in Romania, Estonia, Latvia, and Moldova, one-third in Kyrgyzstan and Georgia, but only 10–20% in Russia, Kazakhstan, Ukraine, and Uzbekistan (Rozelle and Swinnen 2004). Despite initial fears of potential regressive effects (Flemming and Mickewright 1999), restitution of land to former owners was not shown empirically to have a sizeable effect on inequality (Macours and Swinnen 2005).

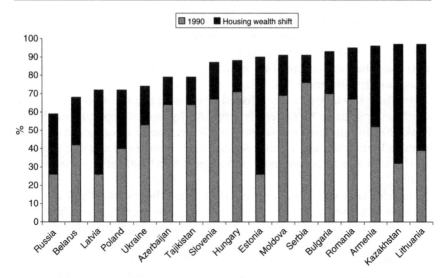

Figure 15.1. Privatization outcomes, share of housing in private hands, transition countries, 1990–1999

Source: World Bank (2001b).

and land markets. The result of these combined trends is presented in Figure 15.1.

Figure 15.1 shows the share of housing in private hands (measured by square metres of living space) at the start of transition and by 1999 in seventeen countries of the region. The scale of ownership transfer is massive in some countries (Estonia, Latvia, Kazakhstan), and is quite impressive everywhere, with a median value of one-third of housing stock moving from public to private home ownership. In many countries, however, a substantial portion of the stock continues to remain in public hands.

Figure 15.1 suggests that by early 2000 most transition countries had converted to rather high ownership rates (above 80 per cent) when compared to 50–60 per cent as typically observed in developed market economies. Moreover, as shown in Yemtsov (2007)[3] the housing ownership rates differed little across deciles of current consumption, with poor and rich having similar share of house-owners.

High ownership rates in transition economies is a puzzling outcome; as discussed in Dübel et al. (2005), multi-family (MF) structures, which dominate the housing stock, are more efficiently managed by large private companies renting out individual units to tenants. Overly developed private ownership therefore suggests that privatization of housing in transition has not yet produced an efficient market. Scholars studying housing markets point out

---

[3] An extended version of this chapter.

that often changes in supporting legislation (governing land markets and financial sector) lagged behind ownership reforms, and there were various policy biases against rental market participants (Dübel et al. 2005). The in-depth review of legislation (the United Nations Economic Commission for Europe (UNECE)) shows that privatization and housing market reforms were not conducted seamlessly anywhere. Such distortions are likely to result in inequitable welfare outcomes, despite seemingly homogenous ownership rates.

3 Effects of Housing Privatization in Transition on Inequality

Liberalization of markets led to rapid increases in inequality during the early years of transition, and, despite an apparently common legacy and common circumstances of transition, the outcomes appear to show great variations across countries.[4] Housing privatization was part of transition and deeply affected distributional outcomes, with some common features of housing reform (Flemming and Micklewright 1999). But how this affected inequality is much less clear—according to one view (Alexeev 1998) privatization of housing was an equalizing factor; according to others it might have led to real or spurious increases in inequality.

3.1 Stylized Facts on Housing Ownership under Socialism: Implication for Inequality in Transition

Countries in transition have a common legacy of suppressed inequality; this was also true for the housing conditions. Typically a household in a planned economy would reside in a small publicly owned unit (by state or enterprise), pay (subsidized) rent, and enjoy protection and security of tenure that would make it similar to extended user rights (Alexeev and Gaddy 1993). Universal privatization by transferring the ownership titles to *all* tenants would have had little effect on the distribution of economic wealth as an outcome, but in the process it might have created a spurious hike in inequality.[5]

   To illustrate this point, it is useful to imagine a simplistic model assuming that there are only four households in an economy. They occupy identical public housing units each worth $US10,000. Since they are not part of private assets holdings, initially inequality in housing wealth is zero (Gini = 0). Let us assume that the housing privatization in this economy gradually (over four

---

[4] Commander et al. (1999). For the most recent review of empirical evidence on inequality in all transition economies of Eastern Europe and FSU, see Mitra and Yemtsov (2007) and Guriev and Rachinsky (Chapter 7, this volume).

[5] This is, of course, an oversimplification, given deviations from the 'standard' in all countries discussed above.

years) gives property rights to the occupants at a constant rate of one household per year. At the end of the exercise all housing is in private hands, and, since it is all identical, inequality will be zero again, but in the process spurious wealth inequality between 'owners' (each possessing $US10,000) and 'tenants' (with zero ownership) will be generated reaching a maximum in the second year of the programme (Gini of 0.167).

Similar dynamics can be inferred for housing as a component of current consumption (and income). Originally, all households have to pay an equal amount as rent to the state, and, if we look at their expenditures, the inequality is zero. As tenants who decide to privatize no longer have to pay the rent to the state, spurious inequality emerges if the owner-occupied rent is ignored. This bias may be blurred by the fact that the state may wish to decide to charge owners higher utility payments compared to those who remain in public housing (then privatization serves as a screening device to identify those who are able to afford utility payments reflecting full cost recovery). How exactly these two factors will affect measured inequality will depend on the definition of household welfare aggregate. If imputed rents for the privatized housing are included in the measure of welfare, but only actual rents are used for public housing (typical statistical practice), inequality measures will be upward biased (because they will include a spurious difference in housing costs and will ignore rent subsidies). There are two approaches that avoid this bias: either the simple exclusion of all rents and utilities from the measured consumption data, or the comprehensive imputation of all rents and real economic cost of utility services (based on market valuation).

The existing empirical literature on inequality and housing distribution in transition relies on both approaches. As a rule, the most accurate imputations reveal that proper accounting for housing cost and value of owner-occupied housing has an equalizing effect on measured household welfare. An example of such careful analysis by Milanovic (1990) of the pre-transition situation in a number of economies in East Europe shows an overall egalitarian pattern of distribution for housing wealth, leading to a small reduction in the measured inequality levels.[6] Only a handful of studies directly address the distributional effects of housing-sector reform for the Commonwealth of Independent States (CIS). Perhaps the most well-known example is a study by Buckley and Gurenko (1997). Using Russia Longitudinal Monitoring Survey (RLMS) data and estimating imputed rent, they report that the inequality in the total consumption was significantly lower in Russia in 1993 than measured by reported expenditures alone: the Gini index falls from an apparent 0.417 (with no housing imputations) to an actual 0.354 when proper accounting is made for imputed rents. In a more recent and comprehensive attempt by

[6] This needs to be qualified as very approximate, given underdeveloped housing markets in these countries and very arbitrary valuations of wealth.

Tesliuc and Ovcharova (2007), using data for 2003, accounting for imputed rents (and utility subsidies) reduces the Gini index for per capita consumption from 0.29 to 0.26.

Studies so far have not linked the inequality in current consumption with the privatization of housing assets. Contrary to the equalizing effects of housing ownership and use, the effects of housing privatization may be disequalizing for a number of reasons. First, those who benefited from housing privatization also had higher chances to gain from other aspects of reform. For example, rural residents and dwellers in small cities typically owned their own home before the transition; these groups have not participated in housing privatization, but they were the ones who lost out as a result of economic restructuring in transition (World Bank 2005b).

Second, there was a significant stratification of housing quality under socialism, which became evident in different market valuations for different properties. It is well documented that the socialist system favoured elites in providing significantly better housing, free of charge (in that respect the experience of ECA countries was not different from China; see Li and Zhao, Chapter 5, this volume). They typically benefited from transition using their social capital, and the housing transfer provided to them dwarfs what the poor received as a result of marketization of their poorly constructed buildings on city outskirts (see Bertaud and Renaud 1997). Additionally, housing quality varied significantly by age of construction.

Third, the housing stock transferred through privatization may not be as marketable, and the process itself if badly managed could be value subtracting. Years of central planning resulted in construction without reference to land values, producing spatial patterns of housing stock at odds with those that would have been produced in response to market forces. Bertaud and Renaud (1997) made evident the stark contrast between residential density by distance from the city centre in a market-based economy and distorted allocation inherited from the command system. The resulting spatial misallocation of housing creates costs for residents (who need to commute longer distances) and the city (which has to provide city services to remote locations).

Fourth, the housing privatization was also often partial, increasing the hidden disparities of socialist housing legacy. The apartment units were privatized; but not the land under the buildings, nor the common areas and structures. Local governments were much more concerned with the ability of households to absorb additional current utilities costs than with maintaining the value of housing stock. As a result, multi-story apartment buildings have on the whole not been maintained (see Struyk 1996). Leaking roofs and internal piping and energy losses from poorly insulated buildings are the most prevalent problems, and buildings are estimated to use two to three times as much heating as buildings in comparable climates in Western Europe (World Bank 2003). This suggests that a considerable part of the housing stock in transition countries functions inefficiently in meeting the population's housing needs, and its market value is significantly below a common standard.

Early empirical evidence pointed to rather unequal outcomes of housing privatization, which were disequalizing (see Guzanova 1998; and most recently Zavisca 2005). Whether this result is consistent with the overall equalizing effects of housing distribution will be analysed in this chapter using the most recent available data. But, before turning to micro-level sources, it is useful to confront aggregate outcomes in terms of inequality with the scale of housing privatization.

3.2 Outcomes of Housing Privatization and Inequality at the Aggregate Level

Figure 15.2 puts side by side the size of ownership transfer between 1990 and 1999 and the change in inequality measured with official data. It shows no apparent relationship between the size of the housing privatization programme and changes in inequality. Clearly, a larger transfer of housing to tenants does not imply less increase of inequality. If anything, there are some signs of positive association (especially if the clear outliers of Turkmenistan and Georgia are removed). Every country with a shift in housing ownership of more than 30 per cent has an increase of over 6 percentage points in the

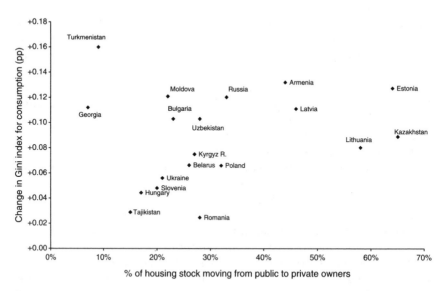

Figure 15.2. Housing wealth shift and change in inequality, transition countries, 1990–1999

Source: Author's estimates based on World Bank (2001b) and from Mitra and Yemstov (2007).

Gini index. That positive link is contrary to a belief according to which housing privatization counteracts inequality increases induced by other aspects of reform (Alexeev 1998). Two reasons can explain this gap between the expectations and the outcome. First, contrary to earlier beliefs, housing privatization was not universal, but affected a selected group of households. Second, because of biases in the existing readily available welfare measures, readily available inequality may reflect a spurious correlation between (incorrectly) measured inequality and privatization of housing stock.

It is obvious that housing privatization programmes created winners and losers depending on where people happened to be living at the beginning of transition. To see how this affected overall inequality, to correct possible biases in measuring inequality it is necessary to turn to survey data.

4 Data and Features of Housing Privatization for Poland, Russia, and Serbia

Given significant variations of housing privatization programmes across countries, it will be particularly interesting to study its effects in a comparative perspective. Recent advances in data availability in transition economies[7] have led to a proliferation of studies on household welfare. However, so far none of the countries in the region has had special surveys of household assets or debts, which have been carried out for many OECD countries.[8] The choice of countries for the analysis was, therefore, not very wide. Within a subset of countries with suitable surveys, three were selected based on the quality and comprehensiveness of collected data: Poland, Russia, and Serbia. They also displayed a very different approach to housing privatization.

4.1 Housing Privatization in Poland, Russia, and Serbia

In each of these three countries the privatization programme included giveaway schemes for tenants of public housing. The terms of such transfers differed, and, even more so, the supporting changes in housing policy and legal framework.

Poland started the transition with a significant share of housing stock already in private hands, mostly as housing cooperatives (Markham 2003). One of the first acts of the new government in 1990 was to devolve ownership of public housing to the newly established local governments, transferring the reponsibility for housing maintenance. In addition, state-owned land was

---

[7] Discussed in World Bank (2005b), and in Mitra and Yemtsov (2007).

[8] See Jäntti and Sierminska (Chapter 2, this volume) on the Luxembourg Wealth Survey, or even in developing countries—see, e.g., Subramanian and Jayaraj on India (Chapter 6, this volume).

made available for private development. There was a one-time title transfer at below market price and a package of reforms that created a proper framework for the housing sector, including rapid reform of utilities to achieve cost recovery, proper titling of cooperative stock, enabling legislation for private investors, land reform, clear delineation of property rights, and restitution to former owners. Social policy and affordability concerns played a significant role in retaining municipal ownership as a sizeable fraction of the housing (Dübel et al. 2005).

Russia pursued a policy of effectively giving away public- and enterprise-owned housing, while continuing large public housing construction. House-holds were given an option to privatize at a symbolic (book value) price, and that option remained open till the adoption of the New Housing Code in 2006. In parallel, housing stock owned by enterprises has been divested to the municipalities. The rental controls and utilities price policy were providing significant subsidies to households opting not to privatize; owners were also expected to pay property taxes not paid by renters. Tenancy rights remained strong (eviction is still nearly impossible). At the same time, the country was developing a legal framework to ensure housing market operations. The main impediment was controversy over the public ownership on land and struc-tures/common areas in multi-family buildings (Struyk 1996).

Serbia, while historically possessing the largest private housing stock, under-took privatization as a one-time give-away scheme, transferring publicly owned units to their tenants for a symbolic price. But there was a missing legal frame-work, contradictions between different laws governing housing market, and unclear delineation of ownership and user rights for housing and maintenance obligations. Vast parts of the country (rural areas) were practically excluded from any housing reform (UNECE 'Serbia and Montenegro').

4.2 Surveys

This chapter relies on income and expenditure surveys with sufficient housing data for each country, and with the information on whether the dwelling occupied by a participating household was privatized, privately owned, or remained in public ownership. Details of surveys used are reported in Yemtsov (2007). Here only basic information is presented.

For Poland the study is based on a household budget survey (HBS) con-ducted by the Central Statistical Office (CSO) with a sample of about 30,000 households. For Russia the analysis is based on the official statistical agency of Russia multi-topic survey, or NOBUS,[9] conducted in 2003 on a sample of

---

[9] Data, documentation, and a selection of papers based on the NOBUS data are available online at http://nobus.worldbank.org.ru.

about 45,000 households. In Serbia the data used come from the Living Standards Measurement Survey (LSMS) conducted in 2002 and 2003 on a panel sample of 2,500 households. The survey was accompanied by a unique (in the region) real-estate survey to measure housing values for participating households.

4.3 Valuing Housing as an Asset and as an Element of Current Consumption

In the absence of direct observations on the value of housing assets, the *opportunity cost* approach is used to assess the value of household housing. It relies on the observation that housing value and the flow of services from housing are two sides of the same coin. If we have one of them, we can estimate the other. Purchase of a housing unit under common financial terms of housing finance (down payment, real interest rate, years of mortgage repayment, closure cost) has an annual cost that is equivalent to an estimated cost of homeownership. That cost (plus maintenance) is an indication of the rent that should be charged by the owner of the unit to a renter to recover the investment. It has to be equal to the flow of services from housing enjoyed by a dweller.

Technically, for estimating the flow of services from housing three methods are used: market costs, self-assessment, and extrapolation through hedonic regressions or stratification (Eurostat 2005). Among those, the market cost method can be applied only to households that pay rent or repay mortgages and can assess the annual financial cost of their home ownership. To impute the flow of services from own housing to their owners, a stratification method is most frequently used in conjunction with surveys of expenditures and incomes. It consists of dividing the housing stock into strata (by location, quality, size, etc.) and in using actual average market values paid by renters to impute values to all units in a stratum, regardless on their ownership. Hedonic regressions are often combined with self-assessment by survey respondents of how much they would have to pay on the market for the housing unit with the same characteristics as they own. Following Rosen (1974), it consists of regressing a set of characteristics of housing quality on the observed market or self-assessed rents (with subsequent extrapolation to non-renters or non-evaluated units). Predicted values by the regression are often used to remove the outliers that are frequent in self-assessed variables.

The same approach can be used to construct housing wealth estimates when no data are available. Imputing back from the flow of imputed rents to the values of housing stock is a defendable way to assess unobserved housing wealth: empirical studies of the housing markets consistently find a tight and linear relationship between the rent and the market price for the housing unit (for an example of tight links between average rent and house prices in Germany's *Länder*, see Palacin and Shelburne 2005). Such a relationship depends on the prevailing interest rate (and mortgage finance terms), and expected changes in housing prices.

Using this approach in Poland, the household housing value was imputed through a two-stage procedure. At the first stage, (log) current market rental charge (for about one-third of all households that were market renters—that is, excluding those in social publicly owned units, and owners) was regressed on housing quality measured with its amenities and access to various facilities, its space, type of building, location, and so on. Location was measured with the following variables: region (voivodship), place of residence (rural or urban, plus the size of the city), and rate of unemployment in the region (as a proxy of the general quality of the neighbourhood). All coefficients had correct signs and were significant, but the fit (R^2 of only 0.08) was low (see Topińska and Kuhl 2003). At the second step, owners' imputed rent was recalculated into the housing price for each household using the mortgage calculator (parameters of the typical mortgage reported in UNECE were summarized as Housing Asset Value = Monthly Rent * 750 − 166.67).

In Russia, imputing housing values had to use a different information base given a much smaller market rental segment—less than 5 per cent of the tenants rented their dwellings from other private agents (households or companies). Of these, only half have reported the monthly rent they pay; a third of households nationwide rented their dwellings from government or municipal authorities paying 'social rent'. The procedure to estimate housing values had to rely on reported subjective (implicit) rent by owners. In the NOBUS survey, the households that own their dwellings were asked to estimate the rental value of their dwelling—the amount of money they would have to pay if they would have to rent such a dwelling from a third party. These implicit rents were consistent with the private market range (see Tesliuc and Ovcharova 2007 for details), and substantially above the 'social rents'. Tesliuc and Ovcharova used a hedonic rent regression in which all rents (market based or implicit rents) were regressed on a set of housing characteristics (number of rooms and measures of dwelling quality such as type of roof, floors, construction material of walls, type of sanitation, etc.), as well as regional and area dummies. The model had a reasonable fit, explaining 66 per cent of the variation in rents. Moreover, the coefficients of the model had the expected signs. Next, the parameters obtained from this model were used to predict rental values for all households. The final step was identical to that used for Poland and consisted of converting the flow of rents into an estimation of housing asset value using typical terms of financing a house purchase.

Serbia is the only country where the housing wealth calculation is direct. Assessment of home prices was conducted as part of the household survey based on the data that were provided by the local real-estate agencies in areas where the survey has been conducted. Housing assets values were used to derive imputed rents based on the assumed depreciation rates and cost of capital, thus reversing the logic applied in Poland and Russia. Interestingly enough, the rent imputed this way has turned out to be similar in both its median and the shape of the distribution to actual rents paid by those renting their dwellings (see Bjeloglav et al. 2007).

There are a number of issues related to these procedures. Households may not be aware of the actual housing values of their dwellings. However, when comparisons between self-assessed and actual market values are made, self-reported data are found to be accurate (Bucks and Pence 2005). There are also issues of self-selection when estimates from renters are used to impute values for owners. Finally, the questionnaires help to identify (with more or less precision) whether the respondent resides in a housing unit that was privatized, but it does not capture movers who purchased their current properties by selling a privatized unit, excluding a fraction of privatized stock from the analysis. Given very low residential mobility rates—for example, less than 2 per cent in Russia (World Bank 2005b, 2005c)—this omission introduces only a minimal bias.

5 Outcomes of Housing Privatization in Three Countries: Results for Poland, Russia, and Serbia

The first check on the survey data is to ascertain that statistics on housing stock are consistent with macro-level estimates. In three countries, housing ownership rates (measured as the percentage of the population residing in housing units that belong to them) in surveys is in line with official data (and close to the rates depicted in Figure 15.1). Rates of privatization also are in line with the aggregate statistics. Russia, among the three countries, has the highest incidence of privatized housing: almost a third of the population directly benefited from housing privatization. Simple physical characteristics of housing stock reveal little inequality in the distribution of living space. The Gini index for square metres per capita varied between 0.22 in Russia and 0.26 in Serbia, and the average space per capita varies between 37 square metres in Russia and 73 square metres in Serbia. Interestingly, these statistics show little change in the distribution of physical space compared to pre-transition period: the Gini index for per capita living space in Russia and Ukraine was around 0.25 in 1985 (Alexeev 1998).

Ownership conditions reported by the respondents are also quite informative. Only in Poland are mortgages reported by a sizeable fraction of households (4 per cent), and mortgage-use rates are not statistically different from zero in Russia and Serbia. This is confirmed by the banking statistics on outstanding mortgages to households reported by Palacin and Shelburne—in Poland at the end of 2001 they amounted to only 1.8 per cent of GDP; in Russia the earliest data for 2004 show only 0.4 per cent of GDP. Serbia by

2003 had no sizeable lending to households for housing finance. This information allows one to focus directly on housing value without worrying too much about liabilities while estimating household wealth in transition economies.

5.1 Parameters of Housing Wealth Distribution

Table 15.1 uses results of housing assets valuation described in the previous section. All local currencies are converted into euros using market exchange rates. Households are grouped in quintiles according to the estimated value of their own housing unit. Focusing first on basic descriptive statistics, we see that the average price of a housing unit was similar in Serbia and Poland (around €25,000) and was much less in Russia (around €9,000) in 2003. These values are estimates (except for Serbia, where they come directly from real-estate valuations) but seem to be in line with what is reported by real-estate agents in Poland and Russia. Palacin and Shelburne report average prices of around $370/m^2 in Poland (2001), and $455/m^2 in Russia (2003). Multiplying by the average size of the unit and exchange rate gives values that are similar to the estimates reported in Table 15.1 (for Russia 2003: $455*35 m^2/1.15$/€ ~ €13,000); Poland 2001: $370*60 m^2/0.9$/€ ~ €24,000).

There is a sizeable inequality in housing values between the top (households holding the most valuable 20 per cent of housing stock) and bottom quintiles: 10 times difference in Russia, 12 times in Serbia, and 3.5 times in Poland. Inequality in housing values for Russia and Serbia (Gini ~0.4) is similar to what is measured in the OECD (for the USA, UK, and Israel, as reported by Sierminska and Garner 2002). When zero values are used for non-owners to get overall measure of inequality of housing wealth, Russia and Serbia are in line with Latin American countries (0.60 for Chile, 0.56 for Uruguay, but 0.70 for Mexico and 0.85 for Bolivia; see Torche and Spilerman, Chapter 8, this volume). Poland stands out as having lowest inequality in housing wealth overall and between homeowners. This again does not contradict indirect evidence from real-estate agencies. As reported by Palacin and Shelburne (2005) in Russia, prices per square metre ranged from $US2,000 for Moscow city centre versus $US160 for Magadan. In Poland the variation was €1,600/m^2 for Warsaw city centre versus €260/m^2 in a secondary city, suggesting a much smaller spread.

Turning to the incidence of privatization across housing wealth quintiles, one finds striking differences across countries. In Poland, privatized stock is more or less evenly spread across the distribution. In Russia and Serbia, low-value properties are virtually absent from the privatization (or, more correctly put, prices of housing unit that fell into private hands outside privatization are

Table 15.1. Housing wealth for homeowners and percentage privatized, by quintiles of housing wealth, Poland, Russia, and Serbia, 2001 and 2003

Housing wealth quintile	Poland, 2001			Russia, 2003			Serbia, 2003		
	Housing value, average €	% privatized	HV for privatized €	Housing value, average €	% privatized	HV for privatized €	Housing value, average €	% privatized	HV for privatized €
1st (lowest)	13,394	29.6	13,989	1,884	1.0	2,082	5,305	0.0	0
2nd	18,920	38.7	18,989	3,696	5.1	4,244	9,936	2.9	12,604
3rd	23,106	36.3	23,045	7,171	65.2	7,446	18,477	14.9	19,676
4th	28,405	26.2	28,120	12,379	86.9	12,467	31,165	30.3	32,517
5th (highest)	44,397	8.0	37,890	19,484	92.5	19,378	62,770	54.3	59,557
Average €	25,644	27.8	21,800	8,921	50.1	13,503	25,507	20.5	44,423
Gini, HV	0.239		0.162	0.410		0.227	0.454		0.265
Gini, HW*	0.402		0.162	0.631		0.227	0.504		0.265

* Calculation includes zero value for non-homeowners.

Notes: Weighted by households, non-owners excluded from calculations, average exchange rate for the surveys period used; in all countries except Serbia housing wealth is estimated based on imputed rent, procedure is described in Section 5. HV = housing values for owner-occupied units. HW is housing wealth for all households, including zero for all non-owners.

Sources: Serbia: author's estimates based on LSMS 2003. Russia: author's estimates using NOBUS 2003 based on imputed rent data by Tesliuc and Ovcharova (2007). Poland: author's estimates based on HBS 2001 data with rents imputed by Topińska and Kuhl (2003).

below those of privatized units), and instead middle and especially top-value properties are over-represented.

5.2 Privatization and Inequality in Housing Wealth

To see how privatization affected the level of inequality in housing wealth, one can decompose the final observed inequality into the inequality 'between' privatizers and other owners and inequality 'within' each of these groups. Since the Gini index is not additively decomposable, Theil entropy measure of inequality should be used (Shorrocks 1980). Let the population share of the jth group in the population be given by w_j, and the housing wealth share by v_j. For the *Theil entropy measure $E(1)$ the decomposition is:*

$$E(1) = \sum_{j=1}^{2} v_j E(1)_j + \sum_{j=1}^{2} w_j \left[\frac{v_j}{w_j} \ln \left(\frac{v_j}{w_j} \right) \right]$$

where $E(1)_j$ is the Theil entropy measure calculated for all individuals in subgroup j. The first term gives the component of overall inequality that is due to inequality *within* sub-groups. The second summation term gives the component of inequality that is due to differences *between* groups. Table 15.2 reports results. The effect of privatization on housing wealth inequality can be assessed as a sum of the between component and the inequality within a group of privatizers.

The significance of data presented in Table 15.2 is that each country selected for this study has its unique configuration of inequality decomposition. In Serbia, the country with highest inequality in housing wealth, privatization added about one-quarter to (already high) inequality. In Russia, differences in values between privatized units and other properties combined with the

Table 15.2. Inequality in housing wealth and decomposition: non-privatized versus dwellers residing in privatized units, Poland, Russia, and Serbia, 2001 and 2003

	Poland, 2001		Russia, 2003		Serbia, 2003	
	Theil index of inequality	Contribution to inequality (%)	Theil index of inequality	Contribution to inequality (%)	Theil index of inequality	Contribution to inequality (%)
All homeowners	0.099	100.0	0.277	100.0	0.344	100.0
Homeowners, non-privatized	0.109	85.7	0.289	26.6	0.373	71.1
Homeowners, privatized	0.043	9.9	0.081	21.8	0.114	11.4
Between groups		4.4		51.6		17.5

Notes: Weighted by households; non-owners excluded from calculations.
Sources: See Table 15.1.

significant scale of privatization made it the largest contributing factor of housing wealth inequality: 70 per cent of all inequality in housing wealth observed in 2003 could be attributed to the effect of privatization. In Poland, the limited scope of privatization, its pro-middle class and pro-poor distributional pattern, and the relatively small size of privatization, resulted in minimum impact (less than 15 per cent).

5.3 Consumption Inequality and Distribution of Housing Wealth

This section attempts to link inequality in housing asset with the inequality in current consumption using a simple statistical decomposition. Table 15.3 moves to the question of where the privatizers came from: the poor, middle, or rich classes. Linking housing wealth to the distribution of consumption (gleaned from rental costs and purchases of durables), Table 15.3 puts data on homeownership in the spectrum of living standards distribution. All figures in Table 15.3 are population weighted and thus may differ from averages in Table 15.1.

Ranking of households relies on consumption as a most accurate measure of well-being[10] and excludes all rental costs from consumption aggregates. This helps to avoid biases that are due to housing ownership in measuring inequality. This approach is similar to the 'before housing cost' measurement of expenditures and incomes taken as a benchmark in inequality comparisons across countries (Sierminska and Garner 2002), and assumes no systematic difference in other housing cost (utilities) between owners and tenants. This assumption was probably not accurate in early transition, but had little effect on measured inequality; over time there was a clear equalization of utility payments across types of housing ownership (Dübel et al. 2005).

Share of homeowners varies by quintiles, with expected correlations between homeownership and level of well-being (with a notable exception of Serbia, where it is homogeneous across all quintiles). But even the poorest have homeownership rates that are not dramatically different from the averages—a situation in deep contrast to OECD countries but similar to the one reported in Latin America (Torche and Spilerman, Chapter 8, this volume).

Privatization in all three countries favoured the rich. Particularly in Poland, despite its overall equitable pattern of distribution, only 8 per cent among the poorest quintile benefited from privatization as opposed to 32 per cent at the top.

The three countries studied here exhibit large variations of housing stock values across deciles, even with homogeneous ownership rates. However, there is less inequality in housing wealth among beneficiaries of privatization

---

[10] The choice of consumption rather than income was dictated by practical considerations described in Yemtsov (2007).

Table 15.3. Consumption per capita, housing assets, share of homeowners and 'privatizers' by quintiles of consumption, Poland, Russia, and Serbia

Consumption quintiles	CPC, monthly €*	Housing wealth**, €	% homeowners***	House value for owners, €	% privatizers***	House value for privatizers, €
Poland						
1st (poorest)	60	18,339	72.4	25,320	8.2	21,296
2nd	91	20,766	77.6	26,757	12.5	21,807
3rd	120	22,117	79.9	27,666	17.8	22,544
4th	157	21,981	80.1	27,456	23.3	22,460
5th (richest)	258	23,373	81.8	28,565	32.0	23,458
Average €	137	21,315	78.4	27,197	18.8	22,627
Gini, CPC	0.307					
Russia						
1st (poorest)	25	3,882	55.7	6,973	18.6	13,916
2nd	43	4,874	61.2	7,970	25.9	13,240
3rd	58	5,500	62.3	8,829	30.4	13,332
4th	76	6,310	63.1	10,001	33.3	14,205
5th (richest)	125	7,281	65.2	11,158	40.5	14,275
Average €	65	5,569	61.5	9,057	29.7	13,841
Gini, CPC	0.304					
Serbia						
1st (poorest)	55	16,307	91.0	17,918	9.7	43,198
2nd	85	21,872	90.6	24,139	14.3	45,523
3rd	112	23,946	91.2	26,247	17.8	49,077
4th	146	27,582	91.5	30,134	23.0	46,218
5th (richest)	241	30,516	89.7	34,039	24.5	46,557
Average €	128	24,042	90.8	26,476	17.8	46,440
Gini, CPC	0.290					

* Excluding rental costs for renters and imputed rent for owners.
** Zeros for renters, population weighted.
*** Population weighted.

Note: CPC = consumption per capita.

Sources: See Table 15.1.

than among all homeowners. Privatization transferred a relatively homogeneous stock to a sizeable fraction of households, most of which turned out to be on top of the distribution. It therefore contributed to the *increase* of inequality. To see exactly how, the next section turns to the decomposition of inequality by components.

5.4 Inequality, Housing Wealth, and Asset Ownership

Instead of treating housing assets and current consumption separately, it is now possible to combine them into one comprehensive measure of welfare. Indeed, ownership of housing generates service flows that form a part of current consumption levels. It also affects consumption and saving decisions of different households in a different way and hence the distribution, but studying this channel goes beyond the modest decomposition analysis imposed by the available data from transition economies.

Imputing rents also helps to put privatization into a broader context of housing ownership forms. As mentioned before, households residing in 'socially provided' housing continue to enjoy significant security of tenure and have in fact user rights that should be properly accounted for. So far in the analysis they have been treated as non-owners, with zero housing wealth. If their imputed rent is taken into consideration, it is possible to see whether (more unequal) housing ownership affected the inequality in living standards. To assess the effect of housing ownership on the overall levels of inequality, it is important to integrate other durable assets into the analysis. All expenditures on purchasing durable items are excluded from the consumption aggregate. Instead, rental value of consumer durables is used (see Yemtsov 2007 for details of estimation).

Bringing together imputed and actual rents, flow of services from durables, and consumption, it is possible to examine the joint distribution of wealth and current consumption. Following Shorrocks (1982), the contribution of each component k is presented as the product of its concentration coefficient and share in total consumption; G_k^*, the concentration coefficient for component k is:

$$G_k^* = \frac{2}{\mu n^2} \sum_{i=1}^{n} \left(r_i - \frac{n+1}{2} \right) y_{k,i}$$

where $y_{k,i}$ is component k of the consumption of household i, mean *total* consumption is denoted by μ and r_i is household's i rank in the ranking of *total consumption*. It is different then from component 'own Gini', which shows the inequality in its own distribution (using its ranking). The overall Gini index is a weighted sum of the concentration coefficients:

Table 15.4. Decomposition results for inequality in consumption, Poland, Russia, and Serbia

Components of consumption	Average monthly value, €	Structure (%)	Own inequality, Gini	Concentration coefficient	Contribution to inequality
Poland					
All consumption per capita	151.91	100	0.291	1.000	100
Of which					
Imputed and act rents per capita	10.49	7	0.317	0.204	5
Imputed flow from durables per capita	9.00	6	0.422	0.312	6
All other components of consumption	132.42	87	0.297	0.296	89
Russia					
All consumption per capita	83.52	100	0.282	1.000	100
Of which					
Imputed and act rents per capita	16.21	19	0.449	0.264	18
Imputed flow from durables per capita	1.96	2	0.526	0.288	2
All other components of consumption	65.36	78	0.304	0.286	79
Serbia					
All consumption per capita	165.43	100	0.292	1.000	100
Of which					
Imputed and act rents per capita	34.56	21	0.498	0.359	26
Imputed flow from durables per capita	3.23	2	0.635	0.396	3
All other components of consumption	127.64	77	0.290	0.271	72

Source: See Table 15.1.

$$G = \sum_{k=1}^{K} \frac{\mu_k}{\mu} G_k^* = \sum_{k=1}^{k} S_k G_k^*$$

where S_k is a share of component k in total consumption.

Table 15.4 presents results for three countries and for three components of consumption: housing, flow of services from durables, and the rest of consumption. Data show clearly that the distribution of housing assets has a significant impact on consumption levels and on inequality. In Serbia and Russia the flow of services from housing accounts for 20 per cent of total consumption, with 7 per cent in Poland. Household ownership of durables plays a less significant role as a factor of current consumption levels and hence represents a weaker driver of inequality.

High 'own' Gini for the housing component shows that the underlying distribution of ownership and user rights for housing is more *unequal* than the distribution of consumption. This is particularly the case for Serbia (Gini for rent 0.498) and for Russia (Gini of 0.449). Despite high own inequality, concentration coefficients for imputed rents in Poland and Russia fall well below the overall Gini; only in Serbia is it noticeably above (0.359 versus 0.292). As a result, housing still produces an equalizing effect on the distribution, but the size of this effect is small. In Poland, the Gini moves, from before housing to after housing, from 0.297 to 0.291; in Russia, from 0.304 to 0.282. In Serbia the effect is slightly disequalizing, the Gini moves, with inclusion of rents, from 0.290 to 0.292.

Why is the contribution of housing to inequality not more than 1–2 percentage points of Gini, even though housing itself is not equally distributed? This is due primarily to the closer relationship between the welfare of households, their current consumption, and the quality and quantity of their housing. Such closer correlation represents a change compared to the situation observed in early transition, when connection between household wealth and current consumption was weaker. This change in the distribution of housing is in large part the disequalizing outcome of housing privatization. Thus, it is not surprising that the scale of housing impact on inequality is so much lower in the 2000s than it was when measured by Buckley and Gurenko (1997) for 1993.

6 Discussion and Implications

The results obtained through the analysis of housing values in micro-datasets can help to gauge the parameters of the overall distribution of wealth in transition economies. The scale of housing privatization can be more accurately measured based on estimates in this chapter. Among the three countries studied, Poland transferred the least housing assets through privatization:

only 16 per cent of total national housing stock value. But it represents as much as €53 billion in 2001 prices. Using information from the World Bank (2006b), *World Development Indicators*, analysed in Davies et al. (Chapter 19, this volume), one can estimate overall wealth holdings in the following simple way (statistics that are estimated in this study are marked by an asterisk (*)):

- financial assets   = €77.8 billion
- liabilities   = €18.1 billion
- housing assets*   = €335.9 billion
- durables*   = €11.2 billion

Russia privatized 44 per cent of its housing stock by value. Tenants who privatized their dwellings now constitute about half of all homeowners. Housing privatization had a large effect on national wealth holding. Estimates of housing wealth presented in this chapter can be combined with other data on household balance sheets using data from Rosstat (2003):

housing, all stock	€574.36 billion*
housing, in private hands	€315.64 billion*
of which privatized	€234.84 billion*
durables	€107.82 billion
financial assets	
HH term deposits	€29.90 billion
saving deposits	€52.39 billion
cash holdings (inc. hard currency)	€12.14 billion
actual final consumption of HH	€220.79 billion
GDP	€379.58 billion
Memo:	
housing stock (official balance value)	€199.59 billion
all productive assets (official balance value)	€539.12 billion
incomes from property (SNA)	€19.84 billion

Serbia has the least developed data on wealth among the three countries studied, but, using unusually detailed LSMS data, one can compensate for the shortcomings of official statistics and get some idea of their relative importance in the household balance sheet for 2003:

housing	€65.775 billion*
of which privatized	€20.216 billion*
all agric. HH assets (including land)	€9.691 billion*
durables	€4.427 billion*
financial assets	
banking deposits	€1.768 billion
liabilities	€0.564 billion

These simple estimates show that in the countries studied housing is the main form of household assets.

This chapter has looked at the distribution of housing, and at its effects on the distribution of current consumption. In all three countries we find that inequality in the value of housing was much lower among those who privatized their dwellings than among all homeowners. Those who have privatized their homes seem to enjoy higher levels of current consumption. They also have housing of significantly higher value than the rest of the population. There is a closer correlation between the value of housing and current consumption. Overall, as expected, distribution of housing moved closer to a market system. But housing markets remain highly distorted, especially in Russia and Serbia, and these distortions are generating inequalities that are comparable to those observed in highly unequal societies, such as Latin American countries.

Only Poland seems to be managing housing inequality, even though its privatization programme is much smaller than that of Russia. This shows the importance of broad housing market reforms, which Poland undertook early in transition, to achieve more equitable access to housing. Russia in particular seems to need to implement such a comprehensive housing reform. Despite its seemingly egalitarian housing legacy and apparently generous housing privatization programme, the country appears to have one of the most unequally distributed housing assets. In Serbia, with its deeply unequal distribution of housing, the problem seems to be elsewhere—an insufficient supply of housing owing to a poor financial framework and legal problems in setting up an efficient housing market. A practically missing rental market is a sign of these problems. The result is that a majority of the housing stock in Serbia is not managed and maintained as though it were privately owned.

The spectacular development of housing and rental markets in transition economies makes measurement of housing values possible and allows empirical investigation of changes in the distribution of housing assets—something that was totally out of the question in early transition. The analysis presented in this chapter identifies a number of gaps in the data. In particular, survey data from only three countries among more than twenty transition economies could be used to study the distribution of housing values. Other countries need to invest in better survey data to monitor changes in household wealth. Moreover, an estimate of the housing net worth requires the collection of data on mortgages and housing debts. Overall the information collected through existing household surveys seems to provide enough data to make a first rough measurement of housing wealth distribution, presented in this chapter, but further progress depends on addressing the gaps. This will help to provide more accurate estimates of the increasingly important factor of well-being in transition countries.

16

Land Titles, Credit Markets, and Wealth Distributions

James C. MacGee

1 Introduction

There are substantial cross-country differences in the clarity and security of private titles to land and real estate. In addition, substantial cross-country variations in credit markets cause large differences in the extent to which real estate can be used as collateral for borrowing. While these differences have motivated a substantial literature exploring their role in accounting for cross-country differences in aggregate economic outcomes, relatively little attention has been paid to their potential implications for the distribution of wealth within countries. This chapter addresses this void, and asks whether and how the land administration system and credit market regulations for land and real estate matter for wealth distribution.

This is an interesting question for several reasons. First, land and real estate possess several characteristics that distinguish them from other goods. In particular, land and real estate are fixed in location and often consumed (or used in production) in bulky bundles (Galal and Razzaz 2001). In practice, real estate is often purchased using collateralized financing, or used to secure lending for other purposes. This, combined with the fact that land and real estate comprise a significant share of a typical household's portfolio, suggests that changes in ownership rights and/or the ability to use real estate as collateral could have a large impact upon a household's access to credit and the distribution of wealth.

This question is also of interest since there are large differences across countries in land administration policy. For example, there are large cross-country

This is an updated version of a study presented at the UNU-WIDER project meeting 'Personal Assets from a Global Perspective', Helsinki, 4–6 May 2006. Helpful comments from Jim Davies, Sergei Guriev, and project participants are greatly appreciated.

differences in the fraction of the housing stock lacking formal title, ranging from virtually zero in developed countries to over 50 per cent in sub-Saharan Africa, over 40 per cent in East Asia, and roughly 25 per cent in Latin America and the Middle East (Deininger 2003). Not surprisingly, this variation has motivated substantial work on the economic implications of land title systems. As we discuss in Section 4, this literature suggests that, for most developing countries, improved land registration systems combined with credit markets reforms would probably increase the level of productivity and GDP. Partly as a result of this work, there has been renewed interest by policy-makers in efforts to reform land administration policy in developing countries.

Economic theory suggests several mechanisms via which the land title system and associated credit market regulations could influence wealth distribution. One such mechanism is shifts in the portfolio of assets held by households in response to variations in the extent to which real estate can be used as collateral for personal loans. If legally recognized titles to land are non-existent, or there is no legal mechanism for enforcing mortgage contracts, then real estate will have little value as collateral. This both increases the down payment required to purchase real estate, and makes it difficult for households to access equity in their home should the need arise. Given that personal real estate (mainly residential structures) comprises over one-third of the assets of the median household in developed countries, changes in the value of real estate as collateral could lead to large shifts in household portfolios and thus influence the measured wealth distribution.

Another important channel via which land policy could influence wealth distribution is by changing the borrowing constraints of actual and potential entrepreneurs. Given that real estate often serves as collateral for loans, limits on real-estate titles or restrictions on repossessions of real estate by lenders may make it more difficult for entrepreneurs to borrow to finance their business.[1] This could have an especially large impact on the extreme tail of the wealth distribution, as entrepreneurs comprise a significant proportion of the wealthiest 1 per cent of households in developed countries (Davies and Shorrocks 2000; Cagetti and De Nardi 2005).

The mechanisms sketched above highlight that the effectiveness of land administration policy depends upon the extent to which real-estate assets can be pledged as collateral. Hence, this chapter adopts a broad definition of land titles that includes both formal ownership rights to land as well as credit markets rules that facilitate the usage of real estate as collateral for borrowing.

---

[1] This channel figures prominently in the de Soto (2000) argument that land title systems have a large impact on GDP per capita. In an insightful review of this book, Woodruff (2001) points out some missing links in his arguments, and challenges some of de Soto's estimates.

As we discuss in Section 2, land title systems in most developed countries include both these elements.

Evaluating the relationship between land administration systems and wealth distribution is complicated by a paucity of data on wealth distributions.[2] As a result, there is little comparable cross-country data on the distribution of household wealth that could be used to help identify the effect of different land administration systems. Given the data limitations, this chapter uses current economic theory to obtain a preliminary and rough overview of the qualitative and quantitative effect of land administration systems on wealth distribution. In particular, we draw upon recent work on the relationship between durable goods and wealth distribution, as well as that between entrepreneurship and wealth distribution, using dynamic, incomplete market heterogeneous agent models.

In many ways, the implications of existing theory are surprising. One might expect that limited titles to land and real estate would accentuate wealth inequalities. However, standard existing theory of dynamic general equilibrium models where households face uninsurable income shocks feature several forces which act in the opposite direction. Indeed, recent work suggests that improved land title systems could increase wealth inequality by reducing the need for lower wealth households to accumulate financial assets to use as down payments or as precautionary savings. While the implications of current theory on entrepreneurship and wealth distribution are more ambiguous, improved land title systems may also generate increased wealth inequality by providing high ability entrepreneurs with increased access to credit. Note, however, that this increase in wealth inequality is not 'bad' here, as households always prefer better defined land titles in these models.

Several caveats about the scope of this study are in order. First, this chapter leaves open the question of why countries chose different land administration systems. Instead, we ask what effect varying the land title system would have on the wealth distribution. Second, this chapter abstracts from the possible effect land titles might have on government policy by shifting the distribution of wealth (especially land), and from differential access to formal land titles and credit markets. Finally, this chapter abstracts from possible relationships between improved land titling and economic growth.[3]

This chapter is organized as follows. Section 2 outlines what a land title system involves and discusses the evolution of land and real-estate rights and

---

[2] Davies and Shorrocks (2000) note that obtaining accurate measures of wealth distribution is difficult even for developed countries.

[3] Tressel (2003) argues that the development of modern financial intermediaries is closely associated with the use of collateralized debt by entrepreneurs, and that this financial development is critical for the rise of long-run growth. Aghion et al. (2005) argue that there exists a critical level of financial development below which countries will have a long-run growth rate below that of the world leaders. This suggests land titling systems could influence growth rates via the level of financial development.

credit markets in Western countries. Section 3 reviews some key facts on the role of real estate in the wealth distribution. The literature on the impact land administration has on the level of GDP and productivity is reviewed in Section 4. Section 5 explores the relationship between household real-estate holdings and titles and wealth distribution, focusing on household savings and portfolio decisions. Possible interactions between titles to durable goods, entrepreneurship, and wealth distribution are discussed in Section 6. The final section concludes.

2 Land Title Systems

This section addresses two issues. First, what is a land title system? Second, we provide some evidence that there are large differences across countries in land title systems. In addition, we discuss the development of these rights in developed (particularly North American) countries.

2.1 What is a Land Title System?

Before discussing the implications of different land title systems for wealth distribution, we need to define 'land title system'. Since this chapter adopts a broad view, a land title system encompasses all the processes required legally to recognize, protect, and record trades of real estate by private parties, as well as the legal and administrative processes required to support the efficient operation of the mortgage market.[4] The motivation for this broad definition is to capture the various ways land rights can impact on wealth distribution.

Clearly, a necessary aspect of any land title system is some formal system of granting and recording ownership rights to specific parcels of land and real estate to different parties. In addition, there should be a well-specified mechanism for resolving any disputes over the boundaries or ownership of different properties.[5] These activities are typically referred to as land administration (Deininger 2003). Moreover, these ownership rights should be freely tradeable between consenting parties. To support these trades, the title system thus needs to be able to record the sale or transfer of property between different parties efficiently as well as to provide prospective buyers with accurate information on the current ownership of land.

---

[4] We restrict attention to *private* land titles, and abstract from the question of how to assign wealth shares of public or communal rights to land and real estate to individual households.

[5] This condition is not always satisfied, even in developed countries. For example, in Canada there are a number of ongoing disputes over the ownership of some parcels of lands claimed by aboriginal groups as well as private or public parties.

The process of recording ownership and sales of land is termed a land administration system. Land administration systems have two components. The first is a registry that tracks land ownership and transactions. The second is a database, termed a *cadastre*, which is a public record of interests in land (Deininger 2003). This generally includes maps and other descriptions of land parcels and the identity of the owner of various legal rights to the land. In addition, most cadastres contain information on the valuation of the land, and on land use as well as any buildings or structures present (Williamson 1985).

Many land title programmes have focused on the creation of a cadastre and resolution of outstanding disputes over ownership. However, the successful working of land and real-estate markets requires more than secure and well-defined titles to land. Since property is typically fixed in location and purchased in 'large' bundles, it serves as collateral for a substantial fraction of lending in developed countries.[6] The usage of land and real estate as collateral for borrowing, however, requires a set of (enforced) rules that allow potential lenders to determine not only who has existing title to a property, but also the value of any outstanding liens or other claims. Additionally, lenders must have the legal right to seize these assets in the event of default. The effectiveness of these foreclosure rights (in the event of default) depends upon how expensive they are to use and how quickly they are enforced.[7]

Land title systems in developed countries have land administrative systems and credit market institutions that accomplish these objectives. Generally, a cadastre-type system provides accurate information on property ownership. As well, there exists a well-specified procedure for recording the transfer of property and a well-defined body of law for settling ownership dispute. The legal institutions required to support the credit market for real estate are also well developed. In Canada, for example, the need for accurate and accessible information on outstanding loans is handled through the Personal Property Security Act (PPSA). This act specifies where and what type of information about mortgages (and other secured loans) must be recorded, and how this information can be accessed. In particular, the PPSA requires the names and addresses of the parties, a description of the collateral, and the length of the registration (Cuming et al. 2005). These records are maintained in a single, centralized computer database at the provincial level, which provides a low-cost way of checking for existing liens on real estate. In addition, there is a

---

[6] In Canada and the USA mortgages account for roughly 70% of consumer borrowing.

[7] Several papers have found that variations in foreclosure rules across states within a country matter. Pence (2003) finds that US states with laws that increase the cost and time involved in foreclosures have mortgages 4–6% smaller than states with more lender-friendly rules. Jappelli et al. (2005) look at data on court enforcement of financial contracts and lending across Italian regions, and find that these differences in court enforcement significantly affect households' ability to borrow.

well-defined set of (enforced) procedures for the seizure of real estate in the event of default.

While many developed countries have implemented (broadly) similar rules, in many developing countries substantial fractions of the land and real estate lack full legal title that can be sold (Deininger 2003). In addition, many countries lack public credit registries, or have limited or unenforceable fore-closure proceedings. One potential explanation for these differences is that the benefits of public credit registries and property rights are greater in more developed economies. If so, these differences in land and real-estate markets may simply reflect the lower level of real GDP per capita in developing coun-tries compared to developed countries. To explore this, we briefly document the development of land titling systems in developed countries. Combining this with historical data on real GDP per capita provides a quick check of whether developing country land markets differ from developed countries such as Canada at a comparable stage in their economic development. Par-ticular attention is paid to the Canadian experience, since it is reasonably representative of developed countries.

2.2 Historical Development of Real-Estate Markets

Property rights to land can take various forms. Historically, many property rights were of a communal or group nature, whereby a group of households had joint claims over the usage of certain parcels of land. Standard economic theory suggests that the emergence and development of property rights should be driven by changes in the benefits and the costs of creating and enforcing them (Demsetz 1967). As Deininger and Feder (2001: 288–31) note, establishing and enforcing property rights to land and real estate is costly, as plots of land must be measured, accurate records of land titles maintained, and disputes over land ownership settled. Deininger (2003) ar-gues that the emergence of individual property rights in land can be viewed as an institutional response to higher land values. The general idea is that an increase in the relative scarcity of land creates an incentive for the creation of rental markets for land so as to allocate scarce productive resources to their most productive usages. This requires the recognition of individual rights to specific sections of land.

The evolution of these legal rights in developed nations is roughly in ac-cordance with theory. While there are records of land ownership since at least ancient Egypt, the movement towards systematic cadastre-based land registra-tion systems took place in continental Europe in the early 1800s (Williamson 1985). Many of these systems evolved from land tax systems into one focused on recording who possessed title to different parcels of land. The common-law countries (Australia, Canada, New Zealand, the UK, and the USA) operate variations on the continental system. Unlike many continental countries, the actual administration and recording of titles is much more decentralized to provincial and municipal authorities in common-law countries. However, the basic requirements of having agreed procedures to identify and transfer title to well-defined properties are common to all these countries.

A key element of the legal system in developed countries is the rules on the usage of personal property assets as collateral for lending. The legal and administrative procedures required for lending collateralized by land and real estate is considerable. For example, in Canada and the USA, a closely regulated process requires some form of *public* registration of non-possessory security interests.[8] These public registries have a long history. In Canada, the first public registry predates confederation, dating from the 1849 Bills of Sale Act of the Province of Canada, which required that lending secured by collateral be registered. If a mortgage was not properly registered, priority was granted to any subsequent claims of purchasers or lenders. This requirement continues to exist under current law (the PPSA), which has streamlined the registration process and led to the centralization of records in a single, province-wide computer database, so as to reduce the costs of checking for existing liens.

The Canadian experience is by no means exceptional. As Ziegal (1974) points out, many of the innovations in Canadian law followed changes introduced in the USA. Moreover, the timing in many West European countries is similar. For example, in 1844 a cadastre register and map were established in Denmark, followed a year later by a land registry system established at local courts that could record and secure legal rights of property of ownership and mortgages (Ting et al. 1999).

The dramatically different situation present in many developing countries today can be seen by comparing GDP per capita to that of Canada historically. For example, GDP per capita in Canada in 1913 was similar to that of Ecuador and Peru in 2001, and below that of Argentina. These countries are frequently cited as examples of nations with poor land administration systems and credit market imperfections. This suggests that the lack of these rights in these countries is not due simply to a lower level of GDP per capita than developed nations, but rather reflects other factors.

3 Wealth Inequality and Real Estate

This section sets out some facts on the empirical linkages between land and real estate and wealth distribution. Unfortunately, there is a paucity of data on wealth distribution and real estate in many countries, especially in the developing

---

[8] An ongoing process of legal reform attempts to improve the working of these credit markets (see Cuming et al. 2005).

world. As a result, we devote more attention to reviewing what is known about the distribution of the components of wealth in developed countries such as the USA. There are two stylized facts that we wish to highlight. First, real estate and land account for a significant share of household portfolios. Second, the distribution of residential equity is more equal (at least in some developed countries) than total wealth.

Land and real estate comprise a significant share of household wealth. Bertaut and Starr-McCluer (2002: 181–217) report that equity in the primary residence accounted for roughly 20 per cent of household net worth in the USA in 1998. For the median, home equity was more than twice as important, and accounted for roughly 43 per cent. Moreover, while roughly two-thirds of households owned a home, less than half reported owning equity. The available data suggest that the USA is not atypical. For example, Guiso and Jappelli (2002: 181–217) report that the primary residence accounts for nearly half of the value of total assets held by Italian households. The available data also indicate that real estate comprises a significant share of household portfolios in developing countries. For the three largest (by population) developing countries—China, India, and Indonesia—household survey data indicate that housing and land account for roughly 70 per cent of household wealth (Davies and Shorrocks 2005).

It is well known that the wealth distribution is highly concentrated and unequally distributed, even in countries with well-developed land and real-estate markets (Davies and Shorrocks 2000). For example, in the USA, the top 1 per cent hold roughly one-third of total wealth, while the wealthiest 5 per cent hold more than half (Cagetti and De Nardi 2005).[9] Housing equity, however, is less unequally distributed than total wealth. Diaz and Luengo-Prado (2003) use the 1998 Survey of Consumer Finance and find that the distribution of wealth (net worth) is more concentrated than earnings, with Ginis of 0.796 and 0.611, respectively. The distribution of consumer durables (residential housing and automobiles) is similar to that of earnings, with a Gini of 0.626, and a mean-to-median ratio of 1.52 versus 1.57 for earnings. Financial assets are much more concentrated, with a Gini of 0.953. They also find that the value of durables as a fraction of total wealth is decreasing in household wealth. For the bottom 40 per cent of households, durables account for 317 per cent of their total wealth while the top 20 per cent hold 29 per cent of their wealth in durables.

While the US data suggest that housing wealth is less unequally distributed than total wealth, some countries exhibit a different pattern. Bauer and Mason (1992) review several estimates of wealth inequality in Japan, and find that housing and land are the principal sources of inequality in wealth. Davies and

[9] While Wolff (1996) and others find that wealth inequality is slightly higher in the USA than other OECD countries, the qualitative patterns appear to be similar across countries.

Shorrocks (2000) report that in South Korea land holdings are the single most important determinant of the concentration of wealth. A possible explanation of this difference is that financial assets are a much smaller share of reported household wealth in these countries.[10] As a result, land and housing are much more important as an apparent source of wealth inequality than in the USA.

4 Real Estate Titling and Economic Outcomes

There are several reasons why well-defined and enforced rights to trade land and real estate should be good for economic outcomes. First, well-defined and publicly enforced tradable property rights provide better incentives for investment and labour supply. Second, freely tradable property rights lead to the allocation of resources to their most productive uses (Deininger and Feder 2001). Additionally, if agents face binding borrowing constraints for unsecured credit, the ability to use land assets as collateral for borrowing may significantly relax borrowing constraints and facilitate both investment and intertemporal smoothing.

There is a large and growing literature investigating the potential impact of the system of titles to land on economic performance. Deininger and Feder (2001) argue that this literature suggests that all these forces are at work. In this section, we review some direct evidence of the effects of improving titles on output. This provides us with some initial insights into the potential effects of land titling systems on the wealth distribution. In later sections, we ask what economic theory can tell us about the likely effects of the borrowing constraints on wealth distribution.

4.1 Direct Economic Effect of Land Titling

There are several important effects of differences in the title status of land. First, within a country, there is a significant premium for land with clearly defined title relative to land without title (Deininger 2003). Deininger reports that studies in several countries have found that the premium for titled land ranges from 15 to 81 per cent. Increased security of land titling as well as transferability of land is associated with increased productivity and investment (Feder and Nishio 1999).[11] Several papers have found that increases in

---

[10] The data used for these studies have been criticized for poorly measuring financial assets.

[11] While the existing empirical work focuses on positive level effects, land tenure systems could also impact growth rates. While several studies have argued that higher levels of inequality of ownership of agricultural land is associated with lower growth rates (e.g., Deininger and Olinto 2000), less attention has been paid to the impact of improved land tenure systems on growth rates. However, Keefer and Knack (2002) find that less secure property rights reduce economic growth, which suggests that less secure property rights in land may also have a negative growth effect.

tenure security—the likelihood that the current owner of land will retain possession in the future—lead to increased investment (see Besley 1995; Li et al. 1998). Deininger (2003) also notes that the transition from collective to private farming in China was associated with large increases in productivity. Other studies have found that yields on titled land exceed those on untitled, as do inputs of land and fertilizer. However, in some cases 'traditional' systems of land ownership with limited private ownership also offer sufficient tenure security to generate levels of investment comparable to those on privately owned plots.

Another potential benefit of secure, transferable land titles is better access to credit. The ability to use real estate as collateral gives households access to larger loans and more favourable terms. Deininger (2003) reviews a number of chapters which conclude that land titles lead to increased borrowing by farmers. However, increased access to credit also depends upon the existence of credit markets institutions which facilitate access to information about outstanding liens and allow for easy foreclosure in the event of default. Additionally, there is also some evidence that land titling may not improve credit market access for low-wealth households who own very small plots of land (Deininger and Feder 2001; Carter and Olinto 2003).

An additional benefit of improved access to credit markets may be increased smoothing of income fluctuations. Kilenthong (2005) shows theoretically that an increase in the quantity of assets with clear title can improve intertemporal smoothing of income fluctuations when households face borrowing constraints. However, as Deininger (2003) points out, borrowing to smooth income fluctuation may lead to 'distress sales' in response to adverse income shocks. This may lead to a concentration of wealth distribution over time if the price of land during periods of low income tends to be much lower then during normal times. There is some evidence of this in areas of Bangladesh, where land sales are frequently motivated by a need to purchase necessities, and the Gini of land ownership has increased since 1960.

While there is considerable support for the view that a well-functioning land title system leads to higher levels of GDP, the impact on the wealth distribution is unclear. Given the substantial difference in the relative price of titled and untitled land, measured wealth inequality may be less in countries where all real estate has clear title. Another potentially equalizing force is that better land rights may have the largest impact upon the poorest parts of the income and wealth distribution. In this case, increased inequality between these households may be less of a factor than the increase in their average wealth.

There are several channels, however, via which better land titling might increase wealth inequality. First, when households differ in their ability to take advantage of the increased scope for more efficient production associated with better property rights, better land title systems could make the income and wealth distribution more unequal. For example, if the poorest households remain unable to access credit markets, clear land titles may accentuate wealth inequality as middle- and upper-income households use better credit access to increase their income and wealth. In addition, increased risk sharing may lead to a less equal wealth distribution, as households with risky income reduce their precautionary savings.

These various forces suggest that the overall impact of land title systems on wealth distributions is probably ambiguous. To better understand the probable magnitudes and directions of these forces we turn to recent work on understanding the wealth distribution.

5 Theory: Wealth Distribution and Real Estate

What does current economic theory imply are the probable effects of poorly functioning land title systems on household portfolio choice and the distribution of wealth? The main channel we focus on is variations in the extent to which real estate can be used as collateral to secure borrowing. This is a natural channel to focus on, as imperfect land titles reduce the willingness of lenders to accept personal real estate as collateral. This reduces the fraction of the value of real estate that can be collateralized.[12]

Diaz and Luengo-Predo (2003) and Gruber and Martin (2003) explore the implication of restrictions on the fraction of a durable good (housing) that can be used as collateral for borrowing for wealth distribution. Both papers incorporate a durable good into an incomplete market economy populated by infinitely lived agents similar to that of Aiyagari (1994).[13] These papers assume that adjusting the stock of durables is costly, and that households can only borrow via credit secured by their holdings of the durable good. Diaz and Luengo-Predo (2003) find that their benchmark parameterization generates a distribution of durables wealth similar to the earnings distribution, and a distribution of financial assets that also closely resembles the US data. While Gruber and Martin (2003) also closely match the durable distribution, the distribution of assets is significantly less unequal than the data.[14]

---

[12] The evidence on mortgage lending across countries appears to be consistent with this interpretation. Buckley (1994) reports that a smaller share of investment in housing in developing economics is financed via borrowing (mortgages) than in developed countries.

[13] These papers build upon a recent literature that uses dynamic general equilibrium models with heterogeneous agents *quantitatively* to account for the wealth distribution. Cagetti and De Nardi (2005) provide a useful summary of recent work on the wealth distribution.

[14] This reflects a difference in the calibration of the idiosyncratic shocks to household earnings. Diaz and Luengo-Predo (2003) use an earnings process similar to that of Castaneda et al. (2003), which was chosen to generate a wealth distribution similar to that observed in the USA in a single asset economy. In contrast, Gruber and Martin (2003) use household earnings from the Panel Study of Income Dynamics (PSID), which imply a much more compressed support and persistence of the earnings process than in Diaz and Luengo-Predo.

Diaz and Luengo-Predo (2003) and Gruber and Martin (2003) use their calibrated model to undertake several counterfactual experiments on the effect of restricting the fraction of the durable that can be used as collateral. Both papers find that reducing the down-payment constraint (increasing the fraction of the durable good that can be collateralized) lowers wealth inequality. This is due to two forces. First, because households wish to consume durables, restricting borrowing increases the incentive for low-income low-wealth households to save to purchase durables in the future. When collateralized borrowing is permitted, households can finance durables purchases by holding negative financial assets. This leads to a lower capital stock and higher interest rate, which generates increased wealth inequality by making wealthier households richer and poor households poorer. Second, an increased ability to borrow against the value of durable holdings reduces the precautionary savings of low net worth households, which thus increases wealth inequality.

The credit market channel explored by these papers suggests that imperfectly defined land titles may tend to reduce wealth inequality. This implies that policy reforms which improve the functioning of land and credit markets are likely to increase wealth inequality. However, existing economic theory suggests that this increase in wealth inequality is not bad *per se*, as it is associated with choices made by households that make them better off.

6 Entrepreneurship and Wealth Distribution

The large fortunes accumulated by entrepreneurs (households with a considerable ownership and active management interest in a business) accounts for a significant share both of total wealth and of the wealthiest 1 per cent. Cagetti and De Nardi (2005) report that, in 1989, more than 60 per cent of the richest 1 per cent of American households were entrepreneurs. Hence, if the land title system influences household decisions to become an entrepreneur or the accumulation of entrepreneurial wealth, it could significantly impact the wealth distribution.

One mechanism through which land titles could influence entrepreneurial decisions is via household borrowing constraints. Borrowing constraints matter, since households often borrow to (partially) finance new businesses. In practice, a substantial fraction of borrowing by self-employed business owners is collateralized by personal assets. Using data from the USA Survey of Consumer Finance, Cagetti and De Nardi (2006) find that 29 per cent of self-employed business owners were using personal assets as collateral for business loans. The median ratio of the value of these loans to total business loans was 21 per cent, while for the top 10 per cent the ratio was 77 per cent. This is not just a US phenomenon. Black et al. (1996) report that a significant component of small business lending in the UK is collateralized loans backed by personal assets. Hence, if poor land titles (or poor enforcement of mortgage contracts) make it difficult for (potential) entrepreneurs to use their real-estate holdings as collateral for loans to finance a business, some households may be unable to raise sufficient funds to open a business, or be forced to operate a smaller business than desired. This may be especially important for lower- and middle-class households, who tend to hold a larger fraction of their wealth in real estate than richer households.[15]

Is it likely that land title and credit market regulations *significantly* impact wealth distribution through entrepreneurship? There are two issues that need to be addressed to answer this question. First, do liquidity constraints matter for entrepreneurship? Second, do credit market distortions due to limited rights to utilize real-estate assets as collateral significantly impact on the entrepreneur? Given the paucity of data, we attempt to get some preliminary insights by reviewing existing theory on occupational choice and wealth.

6.1 *Entrepreneurship and Liquidity Constraints*

While the importance of liquidity constraints for entrepreneurship is the subject of current debate, there is some (mainly US) evidence that they influence households' decisions to start a business even in developed countries that have well-developed financial and land registration systems. The limited evidence for developing countries appears to suggest an even larger effect, and also provides some direct support for the relationship between land titles and entrepreneurship.

A number of studies have concluded that borrowing constraints significantly influence a household's decision to pursue entrepreneurial opportunities in developed countries. In a heavily cited paper, Evans and Jovanovic (1989) examined data from the National Longitudinal Survey of Young Men, and found that wealthier men were more likely to start a business. They conclude that liquidity constraints prevent some households from starting a business and lead to the operation of some businesses at lower levels of capital than is economically efficient. Holtz-Eakin et al. (1994) also conclude that liquidity constraints matter for entrepreneurship. They found that receiving an inheritance increases the probability of a household continuing to operate its business and increases the value of sales. Black et al. (1996) used UK data, and found that increases in the value of net housing equity led to a significant increase in the rate of small business formation. They interpret this as supporting the importance of liquidity constraints.

---

[15] De Soto (2000) argues that the lack of effective land titles in developing countries means that the durable assets of poor and middle-class households are 'dead' capital that cannot be used as collateral for loans by small business owners. He argues that this helps to explain the large income differences between developed (Western) countries and developing nations.

Recent work by Hurst and Lusardi (2004) has challenged this view. They argue that the relationship between the probability of starting a business in the USA and household wealth is non-linear. Using PSID data, they find a positive relationship between household wealth and the probability of starting a business for only the top 5 per cent of the wealth distribution. They conclude that borrowing constraints do not appear to be empirically important for most small business formation in the USA. However, their interpretation of the data has been challenged by Cagetti and De Nardi (2005), who claim that models where (potential) entrepreneurs face binding liquidity constraints generate artificial data similar to that reported by Hurst and Lusardi (2004).

Given that the USA and other developed countries have relatively well-functioning land registration and credit markets, one might think that households in countries with limited land titles or credit market distortions would face tighter borrowing constraints. The limited evidence for developing countries suggests that this is the case. Paulson and Townsend (2004) provide one of the few studies of the impact of financial constraints on entrepreneurship in a developing country. They use a survey of households and village financial to determine whether financial constraints play an important role in determining entrepreneurship in Thailand. Their data suggest that financial constraints matter, as wealthier households are significantly more likely to start a business than poorer households. Paulson and Townsend find a large difference between business and non-business households in the percentage of households owning titled land. Roughly 50 per cent of the privately owned land in Thailand has full legal title (and hence can be used as collateral), while the remaining privately owned land cannot be sold or used as collateral. Since the vast majority of formal sector loans in Thailand are collateralized using land, households that own non-titled land face tighter borrowing constraints than similar households holding titled land. Their results suggest that this matters, as the median business operator in their sample had 10 times more land that could be used as collateral than did non-business households. Moreover, this difference was much larger than the difference in total assets or the total value of land holdings.[16]

6.2 Theory: Borrowing Constraints, Entrepreneurship, and Wealth Distribution

The remaining question is what does current theory tell us about the probable qualitative and quantitative effect of land registration systems on entrepreneurship and wealth distribution? Since little work has been done to address

---

[16] In related work, Mesnard and Ravallion (2003) look at data on return migrants to Tunisia to see what factors influence self-employment decisions. Their empirical findings imply that, the higher the initial level of wealth inequality, the lower the rate of business start-ups. This provides further support for the existence of liquidity constraints in developing economies.

this question explicitly, we review related work on the relationship between wealth distribution, entrepreneurship, and borrowing constraints. To adapt these frameworks to our question, we (once again) make the assumption that, the 'worse' the land registration system, the smaller the fraction of real-estate wealth that can be used as collateral for a business loan.[17] Thus, to use existing theory to answer our question, we ask what happens as borrowing constraints are tightened.

Papers examining occupational choice and wealth constraints can be grouped into two categories, both of which assume that households face borrowing constraints because of imperfect financial markets.[18] The first category assumes that households are identical except for their initial wealth holdings. These papers highlight how wealth inequality matters for economic performance and the evolution of wealth distribution over time. The second group of papers assumes that households differ, not only in their initial wealth holdings, but also in other dimensions such as their productivity in different occupations.

We begin by asking what we can learn about the likely effects of land registration systems on entrepreneurship from models where households differ only in their initial wealth holdings. For brevity, we focus on a frequently cited paper by Aghion and Bolton (1997).[19] They examine a model where households choose between being workers or becoming entrepreneurs and operating a more productive 'capital-intensive' technology. This technology requires a fixed amount of capital to operate, and its output is uncertain. However, the probability of success depends upon the (unobservable) effort of the household operating the project. Since effort is costly, there is a moral hazard problem that causes household effort to be decreasing in the amount borrowed. As a result, low-wealth households are unable to borrow enough to operate the capital-intensive project. Instead, they are 'stuck' in the low return sector until they are able to accumulate enough savings to enter the capital-intensive sector.

The comparative statics of reducing the fraction of household wealth that can be invested in the capital-intensive technology is surprisingly complicated, and depends upon the general equilibrium structure one assumes. Given any distribution of wealth, the direct effect of reducing the fraction of wealth that can be directly invested is to increase the number of credit-constrained households that are forced to operate in the less-productive sector.

---

[17] This story also presumes that it is costly to sell/buy real estate, so that households prefer to use their home as collateral instead of selling and investing the proceeds. This seems reasonable, especially since imperfect land title makes it difficult to sell real-estate assets.

[18] Some common reasons for imperfect financial markets include informational asymmetries and moral hazard as well as limited enforcement of debt contracts.

[19] Another frequently cited paper is Banerjee and Newman (1993). Bardhan et al. (2000: 541–603) review the literature on wealth inequality and economic outcomes.

This reduces the income and savings of the newly credit-constrained households relative to what they would have been if the household were able to enter the entrepreneurial sector. This should lead to increased inequality of wealth inequality over time. Thus, one would expect that worse land registration systems should have higher levels of wealth inequality.

This conclusion depends, however, on whether capital is internationally mobile. If capital is mobile, then the domestic return on savings is unaffected by the land registration system, and there are no general equilibrium forces to offset the mechanism discussed above. However, if capital is immobile, then the domestic interest rate may differ along with variations in the land registration system. The reason is that the increased number of credit-constrained households in the poor land registration economy lowers the demand for borrowing, and increases the supply of lendable funds (since credit-constrained households would want to save to be able to start a business in the future). This pushes down the equilibrium interest rate, which reduces the return on asset holdings of the wealthiest households and thus reduces wealth inequality. However, this also means that it takes longer for poor households to accumulate sufficient savings to start a business. As a result, the net effect on wealth inequality is unclear when capital is not mobile.

More recent work on entrepreneurship has relaxed the assumption that households differ only in their initial wealth holdings. The motivation is that there is substantial evidence that households differ along other dimensions that influence both their earnings ability as workers and their ability to run projects. This extra heterogeneity turns out to affect the ability of these models to match the wealth distribution in the data.

We again focus our attention on a representative paper, Cagetti and De Nardi (2006). They examine a quantitative dynamic general equilibrium model where households can choose to become entrepreneurs or work for firms. Households differ in their ability both as workers and as managers. Cagetti and De Nardi examine a life-cycle model in the sense of Blanchard (1985) with two stages of life: youth and old age. Young households face a constant probability each period of becoming an old agent, while old agents have a constant probability of dying each period. New households receive an initial draw from the ability distribution of workers and entrepreneurial ability, both of which evolve stochastically over their life, and inherit the wealth holdings of the old household they replace.

The key elements of Cagetti and De Nardi (2006) are the production structure and borrowing constraints. They assume two sectors: a standard perfectly competitive sector that produces output using capital and labour and an entrepreneurial sector. In the entrepreneurial sector, entrepreneur i produces output y using entrepreneurial ability θ^i and capital according to $y = \theta^i k^v$. This production structure implies that entrepreneurs face decreasing returns from investment and an optimal firm size that is increasing in the ability of the entrepreneur (θ).[20] The borrowing constraint takes a relatively simple form. The only punishment for an entrepreneur absconding with borrowed funds is the loss of fraction f of their total investment. As a result, wealthier households can borrow more to finance their projects, since their cost of defaulting is larger.

Cagetti and De Nardi (2006) calibrate and simulate their model. For reasonable parameter values, their model does a good job of accounting for both the US wealth distribution and the distribution of entrepreneurial wealth. Their ability to match the wealth distribution depends partially on the assumption that some households are very productive entrepreneurs who earn large returns from their managerial abilities and have a significant savings motive because of being borrowing constrained. This saving incentive is amplified by the risk that their entrepreneurial ability may decrease. As a result, the highest earners in the model have high saving rates, which help generate a skewed wealth distribution.

Cagetti and De Nardi (2006) report the results of several experiments with different borrowing constraints. Their results suggest (somewhat surprisingly) that wealth inequality decreases as borrowing constraints become tighter.[21] This is driven by several forces. First, there is a decline in the fraction of the population that become entrepreneurs, because of the increased savings required to become an entrepreneur. This happens despite the fact that the tighter borrowing constraint leads to an increase in equilibrium interest rates, which makes accumulating savings more attractive. The tighter borrowing restriction also means that households that do initiate small businesses find it more difficult to borrow, and hence run smaller, less profitable firms. This leads to less wealth in the upper 1 per cent of the population, as the most productive entrepreneurs accumulate wealth at a slower rate. However, this decrease in wealth inequality is associated with lower aggregate output.

6.3 Summary: Entrepreneurship and Land Titles

There is empirical and theoretical evidence that poor land title systems adversely affect entrepreneurship. As emphasized by de Soto (2000), this lowers output and productivity. However, current economic theory suggests that the

---

[20] In this environment, increased entry of entrepreneurs indirectly impacts on existing entrepreneurs via the rental rate of capital and wage rate. This abstracts from potential effects because of 'crowding' associated with increased number of entrepreneurs attempting to utilize a fixed factor such as a natural resource. As Shorrocks (1988: 241–8) points out, this effect also matters for entrepreneurship and the wealth distribution.

[21] These experiments also provide some support for de Soto (2000), as GDP decreases as the borrowing constraint is tightened. In related work, Antunes and Cavalcanti (2007) examine a model of occupational choice with limited enforcement of debt contracts calibrated to the Peruvian economy. They find that borrowing constraints can account for roughly a quarter of the difference in per capita GDP between Peru and the USA in 1999.

relationship between land titles and the wealth distribution is ambiguous. On the one hand, tighter borrowing constraints associated with the inability to use real estate as collateral for lending make it harder for low-wealth households to become entrepreneurs. This increases wealth inequality, by reducing the earnings and total savings of households that are pushed out of entrepreneurship. If households differ in ability, this also reduces the size of businesses run by high-ability but low-wealth entrepreneurs while having little impact on the size of firms run by high-ability high-wealth households, which also increases wealth inequality. These effects are offset by the fact that tighter borrowing constraints make it harder for high-ability entrepreneurs to accumulate very large fortunes by reducing the size of firms they operate.

This ambiguity suggests that further quantitative work is required to better identify the relationship between entrepreneurs, the wealth distribution, and land titling systems. Such work should also address several shortcomings of existing theory. First, existing models are single-asset frameworks, which focus on the distribution of net worth. Given that land and real estate account for a larger fraction of wealth for middle-income than high-income households, this may be an important abstraction. As a result, a poor land registration system is likely to have the biggest effect on middle-wealth households' borrowing abilities, and a much smaller impact on the borrowing constraints of the very rich and the very poor. This introduces a force towards increased wealth inequality, as middle-wealth households that have significant entrepreneurial ability face tight borrowing constraints, which forces them to operate smaller firms and thus accumulate wealth more slowly than wealthy households of comparable ability.

7 Conclusion

There is growing evidence that well-functioning land and real-estate markets play an important role in economic outcomes. This has led to increased efforts by governments and international institutions to support reforms to land administration systems and credit markets in developing countries (Deininger 2003). The hope is that these reforms will increase output in developing countries, and help reduce the large differences in income across countries.

The potential impact of these reforms to land administration systems and credit markets on within-country wealth inequality is unclear. The theory reviewed in this study suggests, somewhat surprisingly, that these reforms may lead to increased wealth inequality. These reforms should make it easier for households to use real estate as collateral for loans, thus allowing them to borrow more and on better terms. Standard theory suggests that this relaxation in borrowing constraints is likely to generate changes in household portfolio and entrepreneurship decisions that could increase wealth inequality.

However, current theory also implies that the increased access to entrepreneurial opportunities of households currently excluded from borrowing should act to reduce wealth inequality.

This ambiguity suggests further research is needed to better understand the relationship between land administration systems, credit markets, and the wealth distribution. Ideally, this work will also deal with several issues that this chapter and current theory abstract from. First, the discussion abstracted from the possibility of 'dual' systems of land rights. If certain groups in a country had access to land with well-defined titles while others did not, then the implications for wealth inequality could be very different from the predictions of current theory. Another issue is the relationship between the price of land and the type of land title. Land with poorly defined title sells at a discount relative to land with clear title, so, if households can choose freely between the two, poor land title systems may have little effect on the wealth distribution. Finally, we abstracted from political-economy-based arguments that land titling restricts the ability of 'elites' to lobby government agents for preferential access to real estate when land titles are not formally defined (Deininger and Feder 2001). To the extent that this behaviour makes the wealth distribution more unequal, land titles may reduce wealth inequality. Research that can quantify the importance of these questions is likely to offer further insights into the relationship between land titles and the wealth distribution.

17

Gender and the Distribution of Wealth in Developing Countries

Carmen Diana Deere and Cheryl R. Doss

1 Introduction: Why the Distribution of Wealth by Gender Matters

It is well recognized that the ownership of assets improves the lives of the women and men who own and control them. The relationships between asset ownership and reduced poverty and enhanced security have been extensively researched, as has the relationship between asset accumulation and economic and political power. What has only recently garnered attention is that women may not share in the wealth of men, even within the same household or family. Women and men not only have significantly different access to wealth but also may use their assets and asset income differently, which may have consequences for household well-being as well as for the larger society. While the relationships are nuanced and complex, women's asset ownership is associated with their increased empowerment and individual well-being. To the extent that owning assets improves women's productivity and ability to earn a living, women's ownership of assets will contribute to economic growth and development. The evidence strongly supports the claim that the gender distribution of wealth is important.[1]

The first reason why the gender distribution of wealth matters is related to equity. If women systematically have less access to wealth, then the equity issues are similar for the distribution of wealth by gender as by race and ethnicity. The patterns of wealth ownership by gender worldwide suggest

The authors are grateful to *Feminist Economics*, and the journal's editor, Diana Strassman, for the opportunity that led to our collaboration. This paper is a further elaboration of Deere and Doss (2006) and the ideas in the special issue on Women and the Distribution of Wealth, which we co-guest edited. The special issue was funded by a generous grant from The Ford Foundation. Catherine Vaughan provided research assistance on the section on land in Africa.

[1] This section is drawn from Deere and Doss (2006).

that women face greater constraints than men in accumulating and keeping assets.

Second, men and women may use wealth in different ways. This discrepancy can have effects that originate in the household but permeate the larger society. A large body of evidence suggests that the outcomes of household decisions depend on who has more bargaining power within the household. Since bargaining power is usually associated with individual access to income or ownership of wealth, this suggests that the gender patterns of wealth ownership are important, even within households.[2] Studies have shown that household expenditures differ depending on the assets brought to marriage by each spouse (Quisumbing and Maluccio 2003) and that the current asset distribution by gender affects household expenditure patterns on food, health, education, and household services (Thomas 1999; Katz and Chamorro 2003; Doss 2006a). Women's asset ownership may increase the anthropometric status of children (Duflo 2000) and the incidence of prenatal care (Beegle et al. 2001) and reduce domestic violence (Panda and Agarwal 2005; Friedemann-Sánchez 2006).

A third reason the gender distribution of wealth is important is the relationship between assets and poverty. Among the poor, wealth may be very limited, but the assets they own, such as land, housing, small businesses, and even consumer durables, may have an important impact on their well-being. Incorporating gender into studies of wealth and poverty could also illuminate the ways gender intensifies or mitigates financial vulnerability during times of economic stress, when assets can provide a degree of security.[3]

Lastly, asset ownership is related not only to well-being but also to women's empowerment. Agarwal (1994, 1997) has argued forcefully that women's ownership of land leads to improvements in women's welfare, productivity, equality, and empowerment, a proposition that is gaining resonance among the international development community (World Bank 2001a). Owning assets may give women additional bargaining power not just in the household, but also in their communities and other public arenas.

Additional empirical research is needed to demonstrate that women's ownership of assets is likely to keep them out of poverty or safe from destitution; lead to better outcomes for children, such as increased school retention or higher expenditures on education and health; or result in better outcomes for women in case of separation, divorce, or widowhood. Since the same factors

---

[2] This literature on bargaining power and wealth and assets is clearly related to the more extensive literature on women's bargaining power and income.

[3] Unfortunately, since the literature on gender and wealth is so limited, even for advanced countries, there has been little investigation into the relationship between gender earnings and income gaps and the gender asset gap. For the USA, various studies of the baby boomer generation (born between 1957 and 1964) suggest that the gender wealth gap has been reduced in concert with a reduction in the gender earnings gap, and that this has contributed to reducing the risks of women falling into poverty (Yamokoski and Keister 2006).

that influence women's ability to obtain and keep assets also influence their ability to negotiate other outcomes within the household, it is difficult econometrically to determine the causal relationships. But growing evidence, both econometric and qualitative, suggests that these relationships are present and that women's asset ownership is crucial for women's well-being.

2 The Gender Asset Gap: Evidence from Developing Countries

Not much is known about the distribution of wealth by gender in developing countries, particularly at the national level. In many countries, land is still the most important component of wealth, particularly in rural areas. The data on the gender asset gap in land for Latin America and Africa will be reviewed in Sections 4 and 5. Here we summarize the few studies that shed light on the distribution of assets more broadly, highlighting gender differences in assets brought to marriage and in the composition of assets.

The extent to which women are able to accumulate assets prior to marriage varies enormously cross-culturally, depending on such practices as dowry, inheritance patterns, and women's labour-force participation. Quisumbing and Maluccio (2003: table 1) analysed recall data on assets brought to marriage in Bangladesh, Indonesia, Ethiopia, and South Africa. In all these cases, husbands brought greater wealth to marriage than did wives. These differences were substantial, and the gender inequalities tended to persist over the life cycle. Breza (2005) examined data on assets brought to marriage by Hausa households in northern Nigeria. Not only did men bring more assets to the marriage, but also during the marriage they continued to accumulate wealth while women reduced their assets.

Analysing survey data for six developing countries, Quisumbing and Hallman (2003) found that while husband–wife gaps in age and education are closing, the distribution of assets at the time of marriage continues to favour husbands. The authors suggested that, while the reduction of husband–wife gaps in schooling and age may improve the balance of power within the family, the persistent gender asset gap in favour of husbands may impact on family well-being.

Antonopoulos and Floro's study (2005) of low-income urban households in Bangkok, Thailand, demonstrates the importance of asset ownership among the poor and the variations in the composition of assets according to gender. Their 2002 survey of married couples showed that the mean value of men's real assets only slightly exceeded that of women. Whereas women were more likely to own jewellery (an important and relatively liquid means of wealth accumulation in Asia), men were more likely to own transport vehicles. A higher proportion of women than men owned individual financial assets, but the mean value reported was similar.

These micro-level studies provide some information about the distribution of particular assets in a given location, but there are scant data on the gender distribution of wealth at the national level (Deere and Doss 2006). There are a number of reasons for this. First, there is considerably less information on wealth than on income. Second, researchers collect most of the data on wealth at the household rather than the individual level. Most analyses focus on variations in wealth by comparing characteristics of the household head: age, education, occupation, and sometimes gender. But analyses based on the gender of the household head do not tell us much about the distribution of wealth by gender overall. For example, Doss (2006b) demonstrates that, in Ghana, using female-headed households underestimates the gender–land gap, compared with using individual land holdings.

Third, there are conceptual issues in sorting out who owns property within married couples. Marital property regimes define the legal ownership of assets brought to and acquired during the marriage, and these regimes differ radically, both across countries and within countries. Furthermore, an individual's perceptions of ownership within marriage and social norms may not conform to legal norms. Rather than disentangling complex legal issues to determine who owns different assets within the household, economists tend to make the simplifying assumption that all assets are jointly owned.

A fourth issue is that the timing and composition of wealth transfers may differ cross-culturally. In some places the majority of transfers take place at the time of marriage or as *inter vivos* transfers during the marriage, while in other places bequests are more important.[4] Many studies focus on only one component of wealth, but sources of wealth may be gender differentiated.

Fifth, the concept of ownership is itself complex, especially in developing countries. Different individuals may have rights over the same animal or piece of land. For example, in some countries women own the crops but not the land on which they are grown (Gray and Kevane 1999). Ownership and control of an asset may also differ (Agarwal 1994; Deere and León 2001a; Fafchamps and Quisumbing 2002). Researchers often define the owner as the person who can sell the asset, but this may not be the only or even the most important dimension of ownership (Meinzen-Dick et al. 1997; Rocheleau and Edmunds 1997).

3 Constraints on Women's Ownership of Assets

Women's ability to accumulate wealth is conditioned by the state, the family, the community, and the market. Through civil codes and property and family law, the state structures the accumulation, control, and transmission

---

[4] See Quisumbing et al. (2001) for an excellent discussion of how households allocate land and schooling to their children.

of property. Legislation that defines and limits married women's property rights has historically excluded women from owning and controlling assets. Reforms of such legislation as well as those affecting inheritance regimes have facilitated women's accumulation of wealth. Beginning in the late nineteenth century, legislation establishing state pension or social-security systems and reforming agrarian laws have also impacted on women's ability to accumulate and control assets.

Family and community norms regarding the accumulation and transmission of wealth are as important as the state in setting the contours for women's relationship to assets. These norms are particularly important in areas of the world where customary marital and inheritance systems still prevail and carry legal recognition. In addition, often a large gap exists between formal, legal norms, and actual practice. Much more work is needed to understand how social norms interact with legal frameworks to affect women's accumulation of wealth.

Markets, particularly the labour market, also affect women's ability to accumulate assets, since saving out of current income is a primary means of accumulating wealth. Women's lower wages and the gender division of labour within the labour market and between productive and reproductive labour affect women's ability to accumulate wealth. In addition, the historical development of particular markets, such as the financial market, have had important implications for the composition of savings and wealth and the ability of women to accumulate assets. In this section we privilege legal frameworks, given their importance to comparative analyses, and emphasize the importance of these institutions to understanding gendered patterns of asset accumulation.

3.1 *Legal Marital Regimes*

In broad strokes, marital regimes follow three general models: full community property, partial community property, and separation of property. In many countries, couples may accept the legal default regime or opt for a different one. Community property regimes have historically been associated with countries whose legal tradition derives from Roman law, such as southern Europe and Latin America. The distinguishing factor between full and partial community property is what happens to property acquired prior to the marriage as well as to inheritances received during the marriage. While in full community property regimes all assets are pooled, partial community property recognizes as individual property the assets acquired prior to marriage or received as inheritances after marriage. In most partial community property regimes, the income generated by individual property, such as rents and interest, is also pooled. In addition, in full or partial community property regimes, upon dissolution of the marriage the community property is divided equally between the two spouses (or their estates).

The separation of property regime was initially associated with Islamic law, as it evolved in the Ottoman Empire in the fifteenth to nineteenth centuries. After the Married Women's Property Acts were passed in the USA and England in the nineteenth century, the separation of property regime came to prevail throughout the British Empire. In this marital regime the assets acquired by each spouse prior to or during the marriage remain their individual property. If the union is dissolved, there is no community property to divide. Whether a surviving spouse has a claim on the assets of the deceased depends on the inheritance regime; similarly, in the case of divorce, any claim on assets acquired during the marriage depends on divorce legislation. The marital regime itself does not confer property rights.

In both traditional Islamic and Roman law, married women had a legal personality and could own, inherit, and bequeath property. In contrast, under British common law prior to the Married Women's Property Acts, married women did not have their own legal personality. Hence, the importance of these nineteenth-century reforms in the USA, the UK, and throughout the British Empire (Deere and Doss 2006).[5]

Married women under Islamic law had even greater legal control over their property than did women under Roman law, because they retained possession and management of whatever property they brought to or acquired during the marriage (Fay 1998; Esposito 2001). Under the default marital regime of partial community property in Spain and Hispanic America, married women lost the right to manage their individual and community assets during their marriage. Nonetheless, this marital regime was particularly favourable to married women, for it implicitly recognized women's contribution to the formation of community property through domestic labour. Women had a much stronger fall-back position than they did in countries of the common-law or Islamic traditions. If the marriage ended, women retained their own individual property as well as half the community property (Deere and León 2001a, 2005).

The 1981 UN Convention on the Elimination of All Forms of Discrimination against Women (CEDAW) was an important watershed in the consolidation of married women's property rights. To end discrimination against women, CEDAW stipulates that women's rights to own, inherit, and administer property in their own names must be recognized (United Nations 1980). As of 2005, the CEDAW had been ratified by 179 of the 185 UN member countries. Its implementation, nonetheless, has been uneven.

In Latin America, the signing of CEDAW had profound effects. Most countries have reformed or adopted new national constitutions that explicitly

---

[5] In a few countries, such as Lesotho and Swaziland, married women are still considered minors and cannot be allocated or bequeathed land or make decisions about its use (Walker 2002).

guarantee equal rights to men and women. Most that had not already done so reformed their civil and family codes to end statutory discrimination against women in family matters. All but three Latin American countries now legally recognize the dual-headed household, where husbands and wives have equal responsibility for household representation and the management of community property (Deere and León 2001a). Nonetheless, everywhere in the region there is a disjuncture between women's formal equality and real equality in the accumulation and management of assets.

In India, in contrast, the signing of CEDAW has not led to significant changes in married women's property rights. The Hindu Marriage Act of 1955 recognized the property each spouse brought to marriage as their own separate property, individually to manage and to use.[6] This act was silent, however, about the property acquired during marriage. As Datta (2006) argues, this approach disadvantages wives, who upon divorce have no legal right to a share of the property acquired by their husbands during marriage, even though they may have contributed to these assets either monetarily or through their domestic labour. During divorce proceedings, women are entitled only to maintenance and potentially to alimony, but this is at the discretion of a judge. In this context, state policies requiring joint titling of assets is a revolutionary change in married women's property rights, entitling widowed or divorced women to half of this jointly titled property.

Many African countries have passed legislation protecting women's property rights, but the property rights regimes for women in Africa are a combination of customary and legal systems, including remnants of colonial, modern constitutional, traditional, and, in some cases, religious law. These systems entail overlapping and sometimes conflicting rules. For example, in Kenya there are five separate legal systems for marriage: civil, Christian, Islamic, Hindu, and customary. Each system has its own rules (Human Rights Watch 2003). Thus, the rules for women's property ownership are fluid and, depending on the judge, could be used in combination either to advantage or to disadvantage women.

In the contemporary literature on wealth accumulation, little attention has been given to differing marital regimes and their impact on women's accumulation of property. Holding all else constant, given women's disadvantage in the labour market, one would expect women to fare better in countries where the default marital regime was total or partial community of property than in those where separation of property prevails (Deere and León 2001a).[7]

---

[6] The Hindu Marriage Act of 1955 is thus similar to the 1882 Married Women's Property Act in England.

[7] For example, in the USA (where the default marital regime varies by state), in the late nineteenth century it was recognized that widows fared much better in community property states than in common-law states, where separation of property prevailed (Shammas et al. 1987).

3.2 *Inheritance Regimes*

The state plays a major role in the transmission of assets through its potential to limit testamentary freedom, govern intestate succession, and tax estates. The tremendous variation in legal inheritance regimes internationally is reflected, in broad strokes, in the differences among regimes derived from Roman, Islamic, and common law. This picture is further complicated because in many regions the state is not the only source of succession law. Customary law may overlap with civil law, and inheritance systems may differ across religious and ethnic groups. Even in countries with one dominant legal tradition under a federal system of government, such as the USA or Mexico, succession law varies at the state level. And inheritance may differ substantially in practice from the formal legal regime. Here we focus on formal, legal inheritance regimes and highlight five major differentiating factors: the difference between partible versus impartible inheritance; the degree of testamentary freedom; whether male and female children are treated equally; the inheritance rights of spouses; and the role of dowry and dower.

Impartible inheritance is usually associated with primogeniture, whereby the eldest son inherits all or most of his parent's assets. Daughters obviously fare better under partible inheritance regimes, where the parent's wealth may be divided. The best example of an impartible inheritance regime is the tradition of primogeniture and entailed estates in nineteenth-century England, whereby the eldest son inherited the entire estate.[8] Another difference in legal inheritance regimes emerged with the rise of liberalism in the eighteenth and nineteenth centuries; some countries adopted full testamentary freedom and others retained the privileged role of necessary (or forced) heirs—as derived from Roman law. By the eighteenth century in England, men and single women had the right to freely will their property, with the one requirement being that widows retained the use or income rights over one-third of their husband's real property (the dower). With independence, most former British colonies adopted testamentary freedom. In India, the Hindu Succession Act of 1956 established unrestricted testamentary freedom (Agarwal 1994). In Latin America, the countries most influenced by nineteenth-century British and North American liberalism—Mexico and several in Central America—adopted testamentary freedom in the late nineteenth and early twentieth centuries (Deere and León 2005).

The system of necessary heirs derived from Roman law reigned in much of Europe and throughout Latin America until the late nineteenth century and still prevails in southern Europe and South America. In colonial Hispanic America, as in Spain, individuals were free to will only one-fifth of their estate; the remaining four-fifths were reserved for the children or descendants of the

---

[8] See the detailed comparison of the partible and impartible inheritance regimes in Europe and Africa by Platteau and Baland (2001).

deceased, or, in their absence, the deceased's parents or ascendants. After independence, in a nod to testamentary freedom, in most of these countries these shares increased from one-fifth to one-fourth (Deere and León 2001a, 2005). Inheritance regimes based on restricted testamentary freedom and necessary heirs provide the potential for sons and daughters to receive equal treatment. If a parent wills the unrestricted portion to only one child, gender inequality may result; however, the degree of gender inequality that could be introduced because of parental preference is small compared to that possible in a regime of full testamentary freedom. In addition, in countries of the Roman law tradition, if the deceased did not leave a will, sons and daughters are treated equally (Deere and León 2001a).

Islamic law is the primary exception to this pattern of gender equality in legal systems based on partible inheritance and necessary heirs. Under Islamic law generally only one-third of an estate can be willed freely. The remainder is destined for the deceased's children and other necessary heirs. Of this restricted portion, daughters are entitled only to one-half the share of sons. This same discrimination against daughters holds if the deceased died intestate (Fay 1998; Esposito 2001).[9]

There is great variation cross-culturally in the treatment of a widow or widower whose spouse has died intestate, although they are often in the first order of inheritance in countries with separation of property. Under traditional Islamic law, husbands and wives were always in the first order of inheritance, but widows were in a less favourable position than widowers. While husbands were entitled to one-quarter of their deceased wives' estate, widows were entitled to only one-eighth, and, in polygamous marriages, this small share was divided among all the wives (Esposito 2001). In India, under the Hindu Succession Act of 1956, the first order of inheritance includes sons, daughters, the widow or widower, and the parents of the deceased; however, there are a number of variations at the state level, particularly with respect to inheritance of land (Agarwal 1994).

The overall trend internationally has been towards reforms that favour spouses in inheritance, as well as equal treatment of widows and widowers. In the civil codes adopted after independence, Latin American countries began to include spouses among those who would inherit under intestacy in the absence of children or parents, preferring widows and widowers over siblings.[10] In the late nineteenth century, a few countries began to include

[9] See Agarwal (1994) on the differences between Sunni and Shia law with respect to inheritance by daughters.

[10] In Roman law, the ordering of legitimate heirs under intestacy included children (or descendants), parents (or ascendants), siblings, and collateral kin up to the twelfth degree. In most countries where inheritance laws were derived from Roman law, spouses inherited under intestacy only when there were no living blood kin, presumably because they had property rights to half of the community property.

spouses, even in cases with surviving children or parents, in the first order of inheritance under intestacy, dictating that spouses would inherit an equal share. A few countries—including Venezuela, Bolivia, and Argentina—went even further and included spouses as necessary heirs (Deere and León 2005). This change has placed spouses in a privileged position compared to children, since they are also automatically entitled to half of the community property when widowed.

In recent decades, there also have been attempts in Africa to improve the inheritance rights of widows. In Ghana, under customary law, there was separation of property, but wives did not inherit from their husbands. The Intestate Succession Law of 1985 provided that, in the subdivision of farms under intestacy, wives receive a three-sixteenth share, reserving nine-sixteenths for the children, one-eighth for the surviving parent(s), and only one-eighth to be distributed according to customary inheritance law (Fenrich and Higgins 2002).

Overlapping with marital and inheritance regimes is the incidence of dowry and dower, which also vary in content cross-culturally. The most common pattern is for dowry to be given by a girl's parents at the time of her marriage either to her directly or to her husband and/or his family. Dower, in contrast, is usually given by the groom (and/or his family) to the bride either at the time of marriage or to be provided to the wife in case of dissolution of the union, for whatever reason. Where dower differs from bride wealth (or bride price) is that the latter is usually paid to the bride's family by that of the groom, and is more a form of compensation for losing a daughter's labour than a form of protection for the bride.

In India, the dowry goes to the groom's parents. The practice of dowry has been illegal since 1961; however, it continues and is becoming increasingly common in areas where bride wealth had previously prevailed. According to Rao (2005), the introduction of dowry in one such area in southern India has led to enhanced son preference among parents, a reduction in the level of support that married daughters can claim from their natal kin, and a shift away from relatively egalitarian marriages. On the other hand, she notes that a woman married with a dowry—even if she does not control it—tends to have stronger bargaining power vis-à-vis her mother-in-law.

In sum, the study of marital regimes and inheritance norms and practices is crucially important to understanding the constraints and possibilities for women's accumulation of wealth. The fact that individual inheritances by men and women who constitute a couple are rarely taken into account in current survey research is a problem, and such research leads at best to only partial analyses of the underlying dynamics of household wealth accumulation. To illustrate these propositions, we now analyse women's land ownership in Latin America and Africa.

4 Women's Land Ownership in Latin America

The gender asset gap in land in Latin America is substantial. As Table 17.1 shows, in the various national rural household surveys undertaken in the early 2000s, the share of landowners who are female ranged from only 11 per cent (Brazil) to 27 per cent (Paraguay). Not only are women less likely to own land, but female landowners tend to own less land than men. Household surveys for eight Latin American countries revealed that the mean amount of land owned by women was always less than that of men, although only in Chile and Paraguay is the difference statistically significant (Deere and León 2003: table 5). Throughout Latin America, inheritance is much more import-ant for women than for men as a means of land acquisition. As Table 17.2 shows, for the six countries for which data are available, although sons are the preferred heirs, a larger share of women acquired their land through inherit-ance than men. This implies that other forms of land acquisition—market purchases,[11] allocations through land reform, or redistribution by peasant or indigenous communities—are even more biased against women.

Deere et al. (2005) hypothesize that female land ownership is positively associated with whether a woman's parents were landowners; the amount of land they owned; the gender composition of a woman's siblings (those with-out brothers being more likely to inherit land); age; widowhood; household headship; and education. Women with more education should be better able to defend their potential land rights; in addition, education serves as a proxy for labour-market opportunities and hence the possibility of purchasing land independently. In countries with full or partial community property, marriage should also increase the likelihood of women acquiring land through the market, for, if the couple buys land, it legally pertains to both of them. Although they lacked data on a number of crucial variables, such as the land holdings of a woman's parents, Deere et al. (2005: table 4) estimated a Logit

Table 17.1. Distribution of landowners by gender, Latin America, various years (%)

Country/year	Women	Men	Couple	Total
Brazil (2000)	11	89	n.a.	100 (n=39,904)
Honduras (2001)	26	74	n.a.	100 (n=808)
Mexico (2002)	22.4	77.6	n.a.	100 (n=2.9m)
Nicaragua (2000)	22	78	n.a.	100 (n=2,474)
Paraguay (2001)	27	69.6	3.2	100 (n=1,694)
Peru (2000)	12.7	74.4	12.8	100 (n=1,923)

Sources: Brazil, Mexico, Paraguay, and Peru: Deere and León (2003: table 1); Honduras and Nicaragua: Katz and Chamorro (2003).

[11] This may be due to biases within the land markets themselves or due to the fact that women earn lower incomes than men and thus have less access to the funds to purchase land.

Table 17.2. Form of acquisition of land by gender, Latin America (%)

Country	Inheritance	Community	State	Market	Other	Total
Brazil						
Women	54.2	—	0.6	37.4	7.8	100 (n=4,345)
Men	22.0	—	1.0	73.1	3.9	100 (n=34,593)
Chile						
Women	84.1	—	1.9	8.1	5.9	100 (n=271)
Men	65.4	—	2.7	25.1	6.8	100 (n=411)
Honduras						
Women	39.7	—	0.7	57.4	2.2	100 (n=210)
Men	19.1	—	0.7	77.9	1.4	100 (n=598)
Mexico						
Women	81.1	1.8	5.3	8.1	3.7	100 (n=497)
Men	44.7	14.8	19.6	12.0	8.9	100 (n=2,547)
Nicaragua						
Women	37.2	—	15.2	46.9	0.4	100 (n=544)
Men	21.6	—	16.8	61.0	0.4	100 (n=1,931)
Peru						
Women	75.2	1.9	5.2	16.4	1.3	100 (n=310)
Men	48.7	6.3	12.4	26.6	6.0	100 (n=1,512)
Couple	37.3	1.6	7.7	52.6	0.8	100 (n=247)

Sources: Brazil, Chile, Mexico, and Peru: Deere and León (2003: table 1); Honduras and Nicaragua: Katz and Chamorro (2003).

model of the determinants of female land rights. They found that, for both Paraguay and Peru, whether the adult woman in the household has land rights was positively and significantly associated with female headship and a woman's age.

Katz and Chamorro (2003) explored the determinants of the total amount of land owned by women in Honduras and Nicaragua. They found that a woman's age, education, and headship were all positively and significantly related to the amount of land she owned. The land area owned by the parents of the woman or her husband were not significant in explaining women's land ownership. Further work on the determinants of women's land rights will have to await more appropriate data.

Two recent trends in Latin America may mitigate the gender asset gap in land: a growing trend towards gender equality in inheritance of land in certain countries and increasing state attention to gender concerns in land redistribution and titling programmes. Deere and León (2003: 933), in their review of the literature for twelve countries, found the following factors causally associated with a trend towards gender equality in land inheritance: (1) rising literacy, including legal literacy (associated with a greater knowledge of national laws favouring equality of inheritance shares among children and/or the property rights of widows); (2) a move towards partible inheritance practices (associated with smaller family size in rural areas); (3) greater emigration from rural areas by children of both sexes (associated with fewer potential heirs interested in farming activities); and (4) growing land scarcity and/or a decline in peasant agriculture (associated with a decreasing reliance by households on farming as their primary income-generating activity). Quantitative studies are nonetheless needed to confirm the relative importance of these trends.

The other major development of the last several decades has been the growing commitment by Latin American states to gender equity, reflected in the new land laws of the 1990s. In many countries the legal figure of the male head of household as the beneficiary of state land redistribution efforts was replaced either by more gender neutral language, or, in the more progressive cases, by a focus on the dual-headed household (where both adults are present) as the beneficiary of state efforts in land titling programmes. As a result, the share of women beneficiaries, both individually and as a result of the joint titling of land to couples, has risen considerably (Deere and León 2001b). While there are indications that the distribution of land by gender is gradually becoming more equitable, the gender asset gap in land nonetheless remains large.

5 Women's Land Ownership in Africa

Data on land rights in Africa are less available than for other regions and data on women's land rights are even scarcer. In part, this lack of data on land rights is due to the fact that much land in Africa is untitled and held collectively. In southern and eastern Africa, for example, the amount of rural land that is privately owned ranges from 5 per cent in Lesotho to 67.5 per cent in South Africa (Walker 2002). Within the categories of private, communal, and state-owned land are a range of overlapping rights that add layers of complexity to any analysis of land 'ownership' in Africa. For example, the Botswana Tribal Land Act includes and distinguishes between the rights of avail and of way, and the rights to occupy, use, have access to, transact, and exclude (Adams 2003). For Ghana, Goldstein and Udry (2005: 5) note:

Individual claims over land overlap. Who ends up farming a specific plot is the outcome of a complex, sometimes contentious, process of negotiation . . . The act of cultivating a given plot may, or may not, be associated as well with the right to the produce of trees on the land, the right to lend the plot to a family member, the right to rent out the land, the right to make improvements, or the right to pass cultivation rights to one's heirs.

Thus, the ability to farm the land, security of tenure, and the right to bequeath it do not necessarily depend on formal ownership, in the sense of the land being individually titled. But it becomes much more difficult to sort out the meaning of land ownership in these contexts.

The limited data do suggest that the gender gap in land ownership in Africa is substantial. In Cameroon, less than 10 per cent of the land certificates are held by women (ICRW 2005), and in Kenya only 5 per cent of women own

Table 17.3. Women's share of land holdings, selected African countries

Country	Women's land as % of total agricultural holdings	Average size women's holdings (ha)	Average size men's holdings (ha)
Benin	11	0.98	1.76
Congo	25		
Morocco	14	0.50	1.00
Tanzania	25	0.53	0.73
Zimbabwe small-scale commercial	3	1.86	2.73
Zimbabwe large-scale commercial	10		

Source: FAO (1997).

land in their own names. In Uganda only 7 per cent of women own land themselves (Rugadya et al. 2005). An FAO study (1997) finds that, for a number of countries, women have smaller land holdings than men and are less likely to have any land holdings (see Table 17.3). Doss (2006a) found that women held land in only 10 per cent of Ghanaian households, while men held land in 16–23 per cent. The mean value of men's land holdings was almost three times the mean value of women's land holdings. Although women were more likely than men to own business assets, the mean value of business assets owned by men was much higher than that owned by women. Thus, ownership of businesses does not compensate for the lack of land.

Land is acquired through marriage, inheritance, the market, the state, and local community leaders. In Africa, local leaders often control the final allocations and can reallocate land as they deem necessary. Little land is purchased in the market, although this is changing. The challenge in understanding these patterns is that most legal systems in Africa combine several legal systems, including civil and customary law. Customary law varies within individual countries in ways that may or may not coincide with state or regional boundaries. In general, however, the most common way that a woman gains access to land is through marriage. These rights may be either use rights or permanent rights. In effect, most marital regimes are separation of property regimes, where men and women hold their property separately, and women have little or no permanent claim on the property owned by their husbands. Thus, although women gain access to land through their husbands, they do not gain ownership of it. The distinction is important. Their claims to this land usually do not extend beyond the marriage, so that they lose it in cases of death or divorce. In a survey in Nigeria, women distinguished between land that they owned themselves and land that was given to them by their husbands, with the former being the most secure form of access. Fifty-three per cent of the land they held was obtained through their husbands, while they themselves owned only 4 per cent of the total farmland (FAO 1997).

Inheritance patterns in Africa are complex, again with overlapping customary and legal regimes. Given that few countries have community property regimes and husbands and wives do not jointly own land, inheritance practices are particularly important for women. Yet widows do not necessarily inherit anything. This may result in a widow being evicted from the house that she shared with her husband and losing access to the land that she farmed.

There is no clear relationship between the lineage system—whether it is matrilineal or patrilineal—and women's access to land. In patrilineal areas of Malawi, land inheritance is through male lineage; women can access land only through their husbands and sons. Even if the marriage is matrilineal, in situations where women move to their husband's village, widows are likely to experience land insecurity. Where it is common for a man to move to his wife's village, women fare better, although the land is often really under the control of the wife's brothers or uncles (Shawa 2002). Yet, in some areas in Malawi, Zambia, and Mozambique, matrilineal and matrilocal systems result in land being passed both through the female blood lines and directly to women (Roth 2002).

The Akan in Ghana practise uterine matrilineal inheritance, where land is transferred from the deceased man to his brother or nephew. Under customary law, women do not inherit from their husbands. The 1985 Intestate Succession Law does provide for wives to inherit, but it has had limited impact in practice (Fenrich and Higgins 2002). Women in Ghana may fare better under the patrilineal systems, where a man's children inherit his land. They are more likely to support their mother, the widow, than is the deceased husband's brother or nephew. The changes in the laws in Ghana have had limited impact on actual inheritance practices. In Zambia, Munalula and Mwenda (1995: 93–100) report that recent statutory laws provide legal protection to widows, either by allowing a husband to make a will declaring the nature of his wife's or wives' inheritance, or through the Intestate Succession Act of 1989 that permits a widow a 20 per cent share of her husband's property.

Women's inheritance rights do not eliminate the gender gap. For example, in Ethiopia, one study found that the mean value of land inherited by husbands was 10 times greater than that inherited by wives. Wives generally inherited land from either a previous husband or his family, rather than from their own parents (Fafchamps and Quisumbing 2002: 58–9). In Ghana, daughters frequently inherit less than their brothers, especially where land is scarce.

The marriage and inheritance systems interact in complex ways. In some areas, it is common for a widow to herself be inherited by her deceased husband's brother (Human Rights Watch 2003). This practice suggests that widows may have some, even if tenuous, claim to land when their husband dies, because men use this practice to claim their deceased brother's land. In some instances, the state owns and allocates the land. State land redistribution offers an opportunity for women to gain access to land, but their ability to take advantage of this opportunity varies. A survey of couples in Zimbabwe found that 98 per cent of resettlement area permits given for farming and grazing land were held by husbands (Ikdahl et al. 2005). Women lost their rights to stay on the settlement scheme once they were divorced, but there is some suggestion that they were allowed to remain if they were widowed. In Ethiopia's recent land titling process, women have been given access to formal land titles. As of October 2004, there were 721,978 land holdings registered. Of these, 28.9 per cent were registered to women, 32.5 per cent were registered to men, and 38.6 per cent were jointly registered to a couple. The remaining land was registered as communal, or belonging to an NGO or governmental organization (Teklu 2005).

Many states in Africa have recently passed family and land bills that strengthen women's land rights. These are part of a wider effort to redistribute land and increase the security of tenure. Yet numerous researchers have documented situations in which women are unable to take advantage of this legal access to land. For example, Tekle (2001) documents that, in Eritrea, although women have legal access to land, laws conflict with customary practices, and many people are ignorant of the laws. In South Africa, the court ruled in 2004 that primogeniture was unconstitutional, but this information has not yet had an effect on customary land transfer (Ikdahl et al. 2005). In other cases, although gender-equity laws are on the books, there is no pretence that they will be enforced. In Uganda, the State Minister for Lands, Baguma Isoke, described the Land Act as a literature document of no legal consequence (Okore 2006).

Women's rights also depend on land availability. In Sudano-Sahelian West Africa, where women usually have limited rights to cultivate on their own account, growing land scarcity and concentration are shrinking their allotments (Gray and Kevane 1999). In Tanzania, in colonial times, land, unlike livestock, could pass from parents to daughters or sons; as populations increased, there was less land available, and women could inherit land from their parents only when their brothers 'had enough'. In some cases female-owned land was taken back by their male relatives (Yngstrom 2002).

6 The Impact of Women's Land Ownership on Household Income and Welfare

Access to land is important for both men and women. The lack of secure tenure, whether with legal titles or customary rules, limits land-use options. In particular, it encourages farmers to plant annual crops rather than tree crops and to make limited investments in the land itself.[12] These factors are gendered to the extent that women's tenure is less secure than men's. In addition, lack of access to land is correlated with poverty. The lack of women's land ownership feeds the view that women are not real farmers. This, in turn, limits their access to credit, extension services, and access to other inputs. This can be an endless cycle whereby women are not given land because they are seen as less productive, and they are less productive because they have less access to land and other inputs.

Deere et al. (2005) explore whether female land rights lead to higher rural household incomes in landowning households in Paraguay and Peru. Controlling for household and farm characteristics and regional factors, they show that female land rights have different effects in the two countries. In Paraguay, they are negatively related to total household income. In Peru, female land rights are positively and significantly associated with higher total household income. In both countries, while female land rights are negatively associated with farm income levels, they are positively associated with off-farm income. In Peru, where the agrarian structure is relatively egalitarian, with most farms being small, female land rights (in dual-headed households, where both adults are present), evaluated at the mean, increase off-farm income by 400 per cent and net total household income by 47 per cent.

Mardon (2005) analyses the impact of female land rights and collective action on intra-household bargaining power in the Brazilian agrarian reform. Focusing on dual-headed households on agrarian reform settlements in six states, she finds that, holding individual and household characteristics constant, women's land rights are associated with higher rates of autonomous decision-making. She also finds that women's participation in the social movements that coordinate economic and political collective action contribute to women's voices being heard. Women's membership in the Landless Rural Worker's Movement (MST) is associated with higher rates in joint household decision-making.

Katz and Chamorro (2003) suggest that in Honduras and Nicaragua there is a positive correlation between women's property rights and their overall role in the household economy. In Nicaragua, women with land rights in male-headed households tend to administer a greater share of crop and livestock income compared to those with no land rights. In Honduras, women with land rights in male-headed households generate a larger share of household income via their own 'microenterprises' than do other women. In both countries, women with land rights contribute relatively more to the household through their own wage and salary income and are more likely to have received credit.

---

[12] Although in some places, such as Ghana, planting tree crops increases one's security of tenure.

Katz and Chamorro also explore the impact of female land rights on the share of household expenditure on foodstuffs and the schooling attainment of children. Controlling for the level of corn production, household character-istics, household income, and women's income as well as regional effects, they found that the amount of land owned by women and female household headship were positively and significantly related to the share of household expenditures on foodstuffs. Evaluated at the mean, households with female land rights in Nicaragua spend 5.5 per cent more on foodstuffs than house-holds without female land rights. In Honduras, 2.5 per cent more is spent on food. Female land rights had a small positive impact on children's schooling. Controlling for the gender of the child, average age, assets, headship, parents' education, share of farm income, and distance to a primary school, and evaluated at the mean, children in households with female land rights com-plete 0.10 years of school more than in households without them. In both countries, children in female-headed households finish one year less of school.

Mardon (2005) also investigates children's school enrolment and attain-ment rates on Brazilian agrarian reform land settlements. Children progress more rapidly through school in lone-mother beneficiary households, com-pared with those in dual-headed households. This suggests that, given equal access to community resources, lone mothers invest more in their children's human capital. She concludes that the explicit bias in the agrarian reform policy towards dual-headed households may limit the potential social bene-fits. This analysis highlights the importance of considering the combined impact of female land rights and household composition and headship.

Using nationally representative data from Ghana, Doss (2006a) finds that the share of farmland held by rural women impacts on household expend-itures patterns. In 1991–2, women's share of farmland significantly increased budget shares on food and education and decreased budget shares on alcohol and tobacco, household durables, and household non-durables. In 1998–9, women's share of farmland significantly increased budget shares on food and decreased budget shares on household durables, household non-durables, clothing, and the miscellaneous category. Using econometric analyses to examine the issues of the impact of land ownership on women's well-being is fraught with endogeneity issues. The same factors may allow women access to land and improve their well-being; thus, it is difficult to demonstrate that it is necessarily the impact of land ownership that affects women's well-being. Women throughout rural areas frequently claim that their lack of access to land hinders their ability to support themselves and their children, suggesting that land is important to women's welfare.

Owning assets may even be a matter of life and death. Research is beginning to highlight the relationship between asset ownership and HIV/AIDS. Scholars suggest that this relationship may work in either direction. A lack of assets may make women more vulnerable to AIDS, and contracting HIV/AIDS frequently means that women lose access to any property that they had (Strickland 2004). In addition, women's insecure property rights mean that they lose control of their property—and thus their sources of livelihood and security—once their husband dies of AIDS.

7 Conclusion

Considerable progress has been made in measuring the distribution of wealth by gender and in understanding the factors that account for the gender wealth gap and why it matters. Although formidable methodological and data gaps make comparative work challenging, the evidence strongly suggests that it is critical to understand the gender patterns of wealth distribution. Excluding gender from the analysis may lead to only partial understandings of the full distribution of wealth. Since household wealth may not belong jointly to the husband and wife, gender inequality within households biases estimates of the degree of wealth inequality in a given country. At the very least, and only as a first approximation of the gender asset gap, it is important to consider the gender of the household head in analyses of wealth inequality. More precise estimates, however, of the distribution of wealth will require measures of asset inequality at the individual as well as the household level.

Comparative work has been stymied until recently, not only by the lack of comparable data but also by the lack of sufficient understanding of marital and inheritance regimes. That which is available suggests that, given women's disadvantage in the labour force, women fare better under community property than under separation of property regimes. However, a view of the complete picture requires a combined analysis of marital and inheritance regimes. It will be up to future empirical work to demonstrate how particular combinations of marital and inheritance regimes and social norms play out to favour or discourage the attainment of gender equality in wealth. In addition, to understand the patterns of wealth transmission across generations, it is important to consider both *inter vivos* transfers and bequests. Finally, household structure, especially marital status and parenthood, are important determinants of wealth.

While some limited research has focused on differences in attitudes and preferences for risk among men and women in developed countries,[13] we are not aware of any that has looked at the gender differences in risk preferences within developing countries and the possible impact on wealth accumulation. This is an area that needs further research.

Methodological issues will continue to be a challenge. The best estimates of the division of wealth by gender come from probate records, but, when

---

[13] This literature is discussed briefly in Deere and Doss (2006).

available, they are biased towards the wealthy. Large-scale datasets ignore the individual wealth of spouses and the property rights governing the marriage. In addition, studies frequently do not consider all the components of wealth; such studies look at pensions, land, or financial assets, but not all of them together. Given the fragmentary and incomplete nature of the data, it is premature to draw conclusions regarding general trends in the gender patterns of asset ownership. The available evidence nonetheless suggests that in developed countries nineteenth-century policy reforms contributed substantially to reducing the gender asset gap, and that in countries such as the USA and the UK the gender gap is largest among the super-rich (Deere and Doss 2006). For less-developed countries, it appears that the gender asset gap will not decrease without strong, effective policy interventions.

As detailed analysis of Latin America and Africa shows, there are formidable constraints to increasing women's access to assets, particularly land. While the legal systems are changing to improve women's legal access to land, the interaction of legal rights and social norms still limits women's access to land. Not only is it important to study the actual patterns of land ownership by gender; it will also be critical to understand how women's access to land increases or decreases because of broader societal and policy factors, including land titling programmes, changes in the legal system, increased value of land and agricultural products, and non-agricultural opportunities. Women's ability to organize around land issues in various settings will affect the gender land gap as well.

There are a number of directions for future research on women and wealth. Better data collection would allow us better to answer the question of what wealth women already own. It would also allow us to understand the various gendered patterns of asset ownership, including what types of assets are commonly accumulated by men and women. Additional work is needed to conceptualize wealth within households, and detailed ethnographic studies from a variety of contexts would help in this respect. Incorporation of gender into a broader range of studies of the distribution of wealth will be an important first step.

18

The Informal Sector in Developing Countries: Output, Assets, and Employment

Sangeeta Pratap and Erwan Quintin

1 Introduction

According to existing estimates, it is not unusual for the informal sector to account for over half of employment in low-income nations. The prevalence of untaxed, unregulated activities in these nations may well be a natural response to burdensome environments. However, it comes at a cost. Small tax bases constrain fiscal authorities to raise revenues through inefficient means and to delay necessary investments in infrastructure and education. Furthermore, resources are not likely to be directed to their most efficient uses if production is carried out in an environment where formal mechanisms of contract enforcement and dispute resolution are not available.

Governments in developing nations resort to a variety of policies to try and bring more economic units into the tax-paying fold. These range from sporadic crackdowns on undeclared economic activities, to subsidies and tax breaks for firms that agree to register legally and maintain legitimate tax-accounting practices. Understanding the intended and unintended effects of these policies is an important area of research. This requires models that are consistent with the existing evidence on the nature and determinants of informal economic activities.

Our first objective in this study is to document a set of robust empirical regularities with which a satisfactory model of the informal sector should be consistent. These regularities include a strong correlation between institutional

The views expressed in this study are those of the authors and do not necessarily reflect the position of the Federal Reserve Bank of Dallas or the Federal Reserve System. We would like to thank Jim Davies and Basudeb Guha-Khasnobis for many helpful comments and suggestions.

quality, the tax burden, and the size of the informal sector, even among nations at similar stages of economic development. They also include marked differences in the distribution of employee and employer characteristics across sectors. Specifically, the informal sector emphasizes self-financed, under-capitalized, small-scale, unskilled-labour-intensive production.

Our second objective is to evaluate the extent to which current models of the informal sector are consistent with the existing empirical evidence. Early work on the informal sector emphasized barriers to entry into the formal sector for workers as the explanation for the existence of large informal sectors in many low-income countries. In contrast, in the recent literature, large informal sectors arise as the optimal response to burdensome institutional environments. In those models, direct subsidies to formal employment are poor substitutes for improvements in institutional quality. We describe a static model that contains the key ingredients of most modern models of the informal sector and show that it provides potential explanations for much of what we know about the informal sector. Furthermore, because recent work adopts a general equilibrium approach, it is possible to analyse the effects of various public policies on welfare, output, and productivity.

Our final objective is to discuss the difficulties associated with measuring informal sector wealth. The empirical evidence suggests that a large fraction of capital formation takes place in the informal sector. By their very nature, informal assets are difficult to inventory. Given the difficulties inherent in recording hidden economic activities, the large size of informal sectors in many nations makes measures of wealth inequality across households and across countries unreliable. The only solution lies in the continued improvement of national accounting practices worldwide. These measurement issues have important consequences for policy. As de Soto (2000) explains, formal and informal assets are not comparable. Because informal assets seldom carry proper titles, they cannot be used as collateral for formal loans, which implies that many profitable investment opportunities, and hence opportunities to build wealth, are left untapped in the informal sector. These observations lead de Soto to conclude that formalizing property rights is the key to giving the poor better access to credit. This view is controversial,[1] but it is clear that properly accounting for informal wealth will help improve the design of development policies.

2 The Facts

This section provides a survey of the existing evidence on the importance, the characteristics, and the determinants of informal economic activities. As we

---

[1] See Woodruff (2001) for a discussion.

shall see, empirical studies in this area tend to employ very different method-ologies, in part because they rely on different practical definitions of informal activities.[2] Despite these methodological differences, the empirical litera-ture has unearthed a number of robust characteristics of informal sector production.

2.1 Measurement Issues

Given the nature of informal activities, measuring the size of the informal sector is a difficult task. A variety of methods have been used to construct estimates. This section reviews some of the commonly used methods. It draws heavily on Schneider and Enste (2000) and the references contained therein.

Direct approaches to measuring the size of the informal sector rely on survey data. For instance, standard household surveys provide a good estimate of the fraction of workers who fail to receive the benefits that labour law mandates in a given nation (see, e.g., Pratap and Quintin 2006a). Some surveys directly question households about their activities, both declared and undeclared. Clearly, the quality of the resulting estimates depends crucially on the reliabil-ity of responses. Data from fiscal audits can also provide estimates of the magnitude of undeclared income in a given nation, after correcting for the fact that taxpayers selected for audit are a biased sample.

An alternative approach is to estimate the size of the informal sector indir-ectly using macroeconomic variables. One estimate of the importance of undeclared activities is the gap between GDP measured according to the income approach and GDP measured according to the expenditure approach. A second approach (known as the currency-demand method) attributes the fraction of currency demand that is not explained by a standard money demand equation to the informal sector.[3] A third indirect approach uses electricity consumption data to obtain an estimate of total economic activity, from which one can subtract official measures of economic activity to produce an estimate of unofficial activity. This method is often referred to as the physical input method. In addition to assuming that the ratio of electricity use to economic activity is relatively stable, this approach requires reliable electricity consumption data. Finally, the model approach tries to estimate the size of the informal sector in the context of a flexible statistical model. Typic-ally these models have two components: an equation that specifies the infor-mal sector as a latent endogenous variable that is causally related to several

---

[2] See Pratap and Quintin (2006b) for a discussion.

[3] The premise here is that cash is the principal medium of exchange and plays an important role as store of value in the informal sector. Arguments to support this premise include the fact that a share of informal activities is illegal, and the fact that households who operate in the informal sector have limited access to banking services. See Thomas (1992: ch. 7) for a discussion.

factors (such as tax burdens, labour-market restrictions, efficiency of government institutions), and a second equation where the informal sector determines a set of endogenous indicators (such as tax evasion, monetized transactions, official labour market participation rates, and so on). Identification in these models comes from restrictions on structural parameter values and the variance covariance matrix of the error terms.

As we discuss in Section 5, in order to produce all-inclusive measures of economic activities, national accountants worldwide supplement these standard measurement methods with other available data on 'hidden' economic activity in various industries, most notably data on material use. However, for the purpose of studying the determinants of informal activity, macroeconomic models have the advantage of applying uniform procedures to all countries making cross-country comparisons possible.

While estimates of the output and employment size of the informal sector are now available for a large cross-section of nations, estimates of the asset size of the informal sector (of the fraction of physical capital that is employed in the informal sector, for instance) are almost non-existent. One exception is de Soto (2000), who provides rough estimates of informal wealth for a few nations. The lack of informal wealth estimates is not surprising, given the obvious difficulties associated with tracking informal investment. Section 5 discusses some of the issues associated with measuring assets in the informal sector.

2.2 Size of the Informal Sector

All the measurement approaches we have described are based on strong, often unverifiable assumptions, and one should therefore focus on results that are not sensitive to particular methodological choices. In their survey article, Schneider and Enste (2000) list a range of existing estimates of the size of the informal sector for a large cross-section of countries. The range of estimates available for each country is wide in some cases, but the correlation across estimates obtained from different methods is, with a few exceptions, reasonably strong.

Figure 18.1 plots the output size of the informal sector (measured using the physical input method) in 1989–90 against real GDP per worker for all countries for which Schneider and Enste (2000) provide data. The figure illustrates several well-established facts. Most notably, the importance of informal economic activities varies greatly across countries, and it is highly correlated with the level of economic development. The figure also shows that the size of the informal sector varies greatly even among nations at similar stages of economic development. This begs a natural question: do nations with large informal sectors share distinguishing features other than a typically low level of income per capita? In principle, the variance in the importance of informal

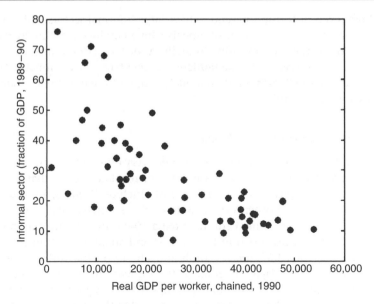

Figure 18.1. Economic development and informality, developing countries

Note: Real GDP per worker is in $US chained around 1990. The size of the informal sector is measured using the physical input method for most countries, and the currency demand approach for a few countries.

Sources: Penn World Tables (mark 6.1) and Schneider and Enste (2000).

activities among nations at a similar income level could simply be the result of the noise inherent in the methods employed to produce those estimates. It turns out, however, that the size of the informal sector is strongly correlated with several country-specific features.

Using a cross-section of Latin American countries in the early 1990s, Loayza (1996) finds that the size of the informal sector depends positively on proxies for the tax burden and labour-market restrictions. The size of the informal sector is also negatively related to a proxy for the quality of government institutions, which reflects the quality of bureaucracy, corruption in government, and the rule of law. Johnson et al. (1998) obtain similar results with a sample of forty-nine countries that include Latin America, the OECD, and the former Soviet Union in the 1990s. They find that the unofficial economy tends to be small in countries with a business-friendly regulatory regime and a comparatively light tax burden. They also find that indices that proxy for the security of property rights and the quality of the legal system account for a significant fraction of the cross-country variance in the size of the informal sector, and that corruption indices are negatively related to the size of the informal sector. Botero et al. (2003) find that heavier regulation of labour is associated with a larger unofficial economy in a cross sample of eighty-five countries.

These and other studies have uncovered a clear pattern in the cross-country evidence. Nations with poorly functioning institutions, a heavy tax burden, and high levels of corruption tend to have large informal sectors. This constitutes strong evidence in favour of models where employers optimally weigh the costs and benefits of operating formally. As de Soto (1989) suggests, informality is a natural response to a burdensome regulatory environment. As we shall see in Section 3, most modern models of the informal sector are founded on this appealing intuition.

2.3 Formal and Informal Employers

Formal and informal producers operate under very different constraints. Most obviously, formal employers bear a number of regulatory costs that unregistered firms can typically avoid. These costs include licences, bureaucratic approvals, bribes, and other fees. De Soto (1989) estimated that setting up a legitimate business in Lima, Peru, required a 10-month waiting period (estimated to cost over $US1,000 in lost profits) and about $US200 in fees. The same operation took 3.5 hours in Florida and 4 hours in New York (Chickering and Salahdine 1991). Djankov et al. (2002) estimate these costs of entry in eighty-five countries and find that they range from 2.63 per cent of per capita GDP in Canada to 463 per cent of per capita GDP in the Dominican Republic.

Perhaps the most important cost borne by producers who choose to enter the formal sector is that they become subject to profit and payroll taxes. Tax rates are often set high in developing nations, since governments are constrained to rely on a very small tax base. Other regulations such as environmental and zoning rules and restrictions in the use of imported inputs are also important in some countries. Finally, formal producers must typically comply with the stipulations of the labour code, including minimum wage restrictions, severance payments, and social-security requirements.

On the other hand, operating legally gives employers better access to public goods such as formal contract enforcement mechanisms. It is difficult to enter into enforceable, verifiable business arrangements with an economic unit that does not exist legally, does not maintain credible accounting practices, and often lacks a clear title to the assets it owns. As a result, informal producers must operate with little or no outside finance. Using survey data from Lima, Peru, Wendorff (1985) calculates that almost 80 per cent of the funds used by informal producers are self-financed and that informal (non-bank) sources of finance account for most of the remaining capital. According to his calculations, bank loans play a negligible role in informal sector production. Furthermore, the loans that informal producers obtain from informal sources are small, often granted on a very short-term basis, and carry exorbitant interest rates.[4]

---

[4] See Mansell-Carstens (1995) for a comprehensive review of the evidence and literature on informal finance, and Straub (2005) for a discussion of the role of informal finance in economies with bad institutions.

Not surprisingly then, informal production tends to be much more labour-intensive than formal production. Paredes Cruzatt (1987) calculates that half of informally employed workers in Lima, Peru, in 1983 operated with less than $US500 worth of capital, while over 90 per cent of formally employed workers operated with over $US6,000 worth of capital. Soderbom and Teal (2000) discuss data from four sub-Saharan African nations[5] that illustrate the heterogeneity in capital intensity across firms in developing countries. Their numbers suggest that manufacturing firms with more than 100 employees operate on average with three to four times more physical capital per employee than firms with fewer than six employees in Cameroon, Ghana, Kenya, and Zimbabwe.

Informal employers also tend to operate on a much smaller scale than formal producers. Fortin et al. (1997) report that 90 per cent of all informal jobs (defined as jobs in establishments that are not legally registered) come from units of production with fewer than six employees in Cameroon. In the private formal sector, that fraction is only 31 per cent. Table 18.1 illustrates the marked scale difference between formal and informal production, with data for Buenos Aires and its suburbs drawn from Argentina's permanent household survey between 1993 and 1995. In these calculations, we restrict our attention to employees between the ages of 16 and 65 who have exactly one occupation. We classify workers as informally employed if they fail to receive social-security coverage in the form of pension contributions and unemployment insurance, two benefits mandated by Argentina's labour laws.[6] As in most developing economies, small establishments account for a significantly higher fraction of employment in the informal sector than in the formal sector in Argentina.

The correlation between scale and formality is so strong that many studies simply equate informality with small-scale production, a definition that has the virtue of being easy to implement, overly simplistic as it may be. This correlation also makes the importance of informal activities a natural explanation for the fact that small firms account for a much higher fraction of employment in developing nations than they do in industrialized nations—see Tybout (2000) for a discussion. Many authors (see, e.g., de Soto 1989; Rauch 1991; Gauthier and Gersovitz 1997) argue that the prevalence of small firms in developing nations is a response to the excessive regulations and taxes that large firms must bear.

---

[5] These data were collected by the Centre for the Study of African Economies via surveys between 1992 and 1998. In these data, the capital stock is the resale value of all structures, equipment and other fixed assets as estimated by the respondent in each firm.

[6] Pratap and Quintin (2006b) discuss these data in detail.

Table 18.1. Individual and job characteristics of formal and informal sector employees, Buenos Aires and its suburbs, 1993–1995

	1993		1994		1995	
	Formal	Informal	Formal	Informal	Formal	Informal
Establishment size (employees)						
5 or fewer	0.129	0.598	0.153	0.590	0.145	0.638
6–25	0.278	0.242	0.273	0.265	0.279	0.242
26–50	0.161	0.054	0.148	0.055	0.138	0.030
51–100	0.122	0.043	0.128	0.040	0.133	0.026
101–500	0.175	0.040	0.167	0.030	0.188	0.043
More than 501	0.136	0.022	0.131	0.021	0.117	0.020
Average age	37.22	33.42	37.00	33.01	37.30	33.22
Education						
None	0.004	0.006	0.003	0.010	0.003	0.009
Primary	0.337	0.491	0.324	0.488	0.351	0.485
High-school	0.429	0.378	0.431	0.389	0.386	0.367
Superior	0.058	0.033	0.074	0.024	0.077	0.027
University	0.171	0.093	0.168	0.089	0.183	0.113
Hourly wages	4.514	3.487	4.750	3.710	4.591	3.360
Observations	2,806	1,780	3,032	1,668	2,965	1,634

Notes: Entries give the fraction of employees in each category. Age is measured in years. Hourly wages are in 1993 pesos and corrected for Christmas bonuses.

Sources: Argentina's Permanent Household Survey and Pratap and Quintin (2006a).

2.4 Formal and Informal Workers

The distribution of employee characteristics also differs greatly across sectors. Among other differences, formal workers tend to be more educated, older, and earn more than their informally employed counterparts, as illustrated in Table 18.1 with data from Argentina's permanent household survey. Given that formal workers tend to have more experience and education than other workers, it is not surprising that hourly wages are higher in the formal sector than in the informal sector. A question that generates much debate is whether observable differences in worker characteristics can account for differences in earnings across sectors. The conventional view is that they cannot; formal workers, it is often suggested, earn more than observably similar informal sector workers. This view is supported by a number of empirical studies that find that some earnings-relevant characteristics of workers are better rewarded in the formal sector.[7]

However, as pointed out by Heckman and Hotz (1986), the fact that parametric estimates of earnings functions differ across sectors does not constitute compelling evidence that labour markets are segmented along formal/informal lines in developing nations. Earnings functions can differ in equilibrium if labour markets are *weakly* competitive, with heterogenous workers choosing

---

[7] See, e.g., Mazumdar (1981) for Malaysia, Heckman and Hotz (1986) for Panama, Roberts (1989) for Guadalajara, Mexico, Pradhan and van Soest (1995) for Bolivia, Tansel (1999) for Turkey, and Gong and van Soest (2001) for Mexico.

the sector where their productivity is higher (Rosen 1978).[8] Earnings functions may also differ if individual skills are bundled (Heckman and Scheinkman 1987). Furthermore, much of the empirical work uses OLS techniques, which may be biased by the endogeneity of sector choice. Pratap and Quintin (2006a) show that, in addition to constituting a weak test of segmentation, parametric evidence that a significant formal sector premium exists may be fragile. Standard tests applied to the data summarized in Table 18.1 suggest that a significant formal premium exists in Buenos Aires. But flexible semi-parametric estimation techniques applied to the same data yield no evidence that formal workers earn more than their observably similar informal counterparts.

In summary, the existing evidence on whether labour markets are segmented along formal/informal lines in developing nations is mixed, at best. Not coincidentally, many recent models of the informal sector do not appeal to any segmentation arguments.

3 Theories

This section describes how models of informal economic activities have evolved over the years and evaluates the consistency of existing models with the facts we documented in Section 2. While we endeavour to mention as many of the many important contributions made in this area in the past half-century as possible, our main goal is for our literature review to be representative. Thomas (1992) provides a more comprehensive review of early work.

The notion that labour markets may be dualistic in developing nations dates back at least to the work of Lewis (1954), who expresses the view that the rural sector constitutes a stock of potential workers for the urban, formal sector, where jobs pay higher wages. This view is formalized by Harris and Todaro (1970). Fields (1975) expands on the Harris–Todaro model by assuming that urban workers can choose to become informally employed rather than search for higher paying formal jobs.

The seminal paper of Rauch (1991) marks the next major break in the modelling of informal economic activities. In the model, agents who choose to operate informally can choose to pay workers below the minimum wage, but they are constrained to operate below a certain detection threshold. This formalizes the view articulated by de Soto (1989) that producers in developing nations weigh the regulatory costs of operating formally against the benefits, in this case the ability to operate on a more efficient scale. This yields a model that is conceptually consistent with the correlation between the regulatory burden and the importance of informal activities and can replicate many

---

[8] This is illustrated by Magnac (1991), who estimates a structural model of earnings and sector choices with Columbian data. He finds that earnings functions differ across sectors, but finds no evidence that moving across sectors is costly.

salient aspects of the organization of production in developing nations. For instance, it provides an explanation for the fact that firms tend to be either very small or very large in those nations (a phenomenon known as the 'missing middle' in the economic development literature).

In addition, Rauch's competitive equilibrium approach is a framework within which one can analyse the effects of various public policies on welfare, the tax base, and the size of the informal sector, taking into account general equilibrium effects (see, e.g., Rauch 1991 for a discussion of the general equilibrium effects of changes in the minimum wage on the size of the informal sector). The computable general equilibrium exercise of Fortin et al. (1997) constitutes perhaps the best illustration of the value of Rauch's framework for thinking about the effects of public policy choices.

Rauch (1991) emphasizes the fact that, like traditional dualistic models, his model predicts that labour markets are segmented along formal/informal lines. Formally employed workers earn more than similar workers who are unable to find formal jobs. But his framework (together with de Soto's thought-provoking 1989 monograph) also paves the way for a drastic change in the perception of informal activities. In recent papers, the informal sector is most often modelled as the optimal, rational response of economic units (producers) to government-induced distortions rather than the disadvantaged end of dualistic labour markets.

Loayza (1996) illustrates this view by describing a model where labour-market segmentation plays no role. Producers can choose to avoid taxation but must then bear an exogenous cost of informality. Similarly, Sarte (2000) and Choi and Thum (2005) describe environments where the option to operate informally mitigates the distortions introduced by a rent-seeking bureaucracy.[9] In Dessy and Pallage (2003), the productivity differential between the formal and the informal sector depends on the amount of taxes levied, which makes the emergence of economies with high tax rates and large informal sectors endogenous.

Quintin (2000) and Antunes and Cavalcanti (2007) explicitly model the cost of informality as the lack of access to contract enforcement and quantify the effects of the tax burden and limited enforcement on the size of the informal sector via calibrated numerical simulations.[10] Straub (2005) studies the impact of limited enforcement on informal activities in a model that explicitly considers the role and quality of informal credit mechanisms. Ihrig and Moe (2004) quantify the importance of various aspects of tax policy on the size of the informal sector.

---

[9] Marcouiller and Young (1995) model the informal sector as a way to avoid 'exploitation' by the state.

[10] Antunes and Cavalcanti (2007) also quantify the importance of regulation costs for the size of the informal sector.

Given the lack of compelling evidence that labour markets are segmented along formal/informal lines in developing nations, the fact that many recent models of the informal sector require no explicit barriers to labour mobility may be welcome progress.[11] However, an important question to ask is whether those models can replicate key features of labour markets in those countries. As documented in the previous section, workers employed in the formal sector tend to be more educated, more experienced, and earn more than informally employed workers. If labour markets are integrated, why does the distribution of worker characteristics differ systematically across sectors? Amaral and Quintin (2006) propose an answer to this question, which we discuss in greater detail in the next section. Because they have limited access to outside sources of finance, informal producers may be constrained to substitute unskilled labour for physical capital. In other words, segmentation arguments are not necessary to account at least qualitatively for salient features of labour markets in developing nations.

The theoretical debate over whether a satisfactory model of informal activities should assume or imply some wage segmentation has important implications for policy. One natural policy response to wage segmentation is to introduce a formal sector wage subsidy—see Ray (1997: ch. 10) for a discussion. If labour markets are approximately integrated, however, such a subsidy could have adverse effects on welfare and net tax revenues. If wage differentials across sectors reflect primarily productivity differentials, policies that aim solely at reducing the size of the informal sector are likely to be a poor substitute (at best) for direct investments in education or investments in the quality of formal institutions. Regardless of the outcome of the debate over segmentation, modern theories of informal economic activities suggest explanations for many salient features of the organization of production in developing countries. We make this point formally in the next section.

4 A Model

We now outline a simple model that contains many of the ingredients of recent models of the informal sector and provides potential explanations for the facts we documented in Section 2. As in Rauch (1991), the model is a general equilibrium model where producers select a sector in which to operate given the economy's institutional features. As in Loayza (1996), Quintin (2000), Sarte (2000), Straub (2005), and Amaral and Quintin (2006), producers who choose to operate formally benefit from better institutions, but they bear a regulatory cost. Specifically, we assume that contract enforcement is better in

---

[11] Most models continue to assume entry costs into the formal sector for producers to reflect, for instance, the cost of legal registration—see, e.g., Straub (2005).

the formal sector but that formal producers need to pay taxes. This creates a trade-off between access to formal sources of outside financing and the burden of taxation. The model, therefore, is consistent with the empirical link between the tax burden, the quality of formal institutions, and the importance of informal economic activities. Clearly, it is also consistent with the fact that finance is scarce in the informal sector.

A difference between the framework we outline below and many alternative models of the informal sector is the fact that labour markets are integrated. As we mentioned in the previous section, a natural question is whether such a model can account for the fact that formal workers tend to be more educated and earn more than informal workers when labour markets are fully competitive. We will argue that it can under the standard assumption that capital and skill are complementary.

Consider then a static economy where agents are endowed with quantity $a > 0$ of physical capital and a level $z > 0$ of managerial ability. We assume that all agents are born with the same endowment of capital but that managerial talent varies across agents. We also assume that the distribution of managerial ability is continuous. Agents of ability $z > 0$ can choose to become workers, in which case they earn an endogenously determined wage w, or can instead choose to operate a technology that transforms inputs $(k, n) \geq (0, 0)$ of physical capital and labour into quantity $z k^{\alpha_k} n^{\alpha_n}$ of the consumption good, where $\alpha_k, \alpha_n > 0$ and $\alpha_n + \alpha_k < 1$.

Managers can self-finance the capital they use in production, but they can also borrow some capital from an intermediary that can borrow and lend without being bound at exogenous rate $r > 0$. Assuming that r is exogenous simplifies this algebra. One can motivate this assumption by supposing that the economy under study is small and open or, alternatively, that the intermediary has access to a storage technology.

Our key assumption is that the market for loans is imperfect. Specifically, managers who borrow some capital can choose to default on the payment they owe the intermediary. In the formal sector, default carries a cost equal to fraction $\eta > 0$ of the manager's income while, in the informal sector, default carries no cost. This will imply that all production is self-financed in the informal sector. These assumptions formalize the fact that informal employers have limited access to formal means of contract enforcement in a simple fashion.[12] On the other hand, we assume that managers who operate in the formal sector must pay fraction τ of their net income as taxes, while informal managers can avoid taxation at no cost.

---

[12] This contractual framework resembles the one described by Banerjee and Newman (1993). One could also generate endogenous borrowing constraints by assuming that informal assets are 'dead' in the sense of de Soto (2000)—that is, that they cannot be used as collateral. In fact, any friction that limits informal producers' access to finance should yield results similar to ours.

Consider an agent of talent $z > 0$ who chooses to become a manager in the formal sector and let w be the price of labour.[13] Let k be the quantity of capital with which the agent operates and s be the amount she uses as collateral for her loan.[14] Then $d = k - s$ is the net (uncollateralized) capital she borrows from the intermediary. The maximum net income the manager can generate is given by:

$$V(z,\tau,\eta) = (1 - \tau) \max_{n \geq 0, s \leq a, d \geq 0} [z(s + d)^{\alpha_k} n^{\alpha_n} - (s + d)(1 + r) - nw]$$

$$= (1 - \tau) \max_{s \leq a, d \geq 0} [A(w) z^{\frac{1}{1-\alpha_n}} (s + d)^{\theta} - (s + d)(1 + r)]$$

subject to the following no-default constraint:

$$a(1 + r) + (1 - \tau)[A(w) z^{\frac{1}{1-\alpha_n}} (s + d)^{\theta} - (s + d)(1 + r)] \geq (1 - \eta)(1 - \tau) A(w) z^{\frac{1}{1-\alpha_n}}$$
$$(s + d)^{\theta} + (a - s)(1 + r)$$

where $A(w) = \left(\frac{1}{\alpha_n} - 1\right) \alpha_n^{\frac{1}{1-\alpha_n}} w^{\frac{-\alpha_n}{1-\alpha_n}}$ and $\theta = \frac{\alpha_k}{1-\alpha_n} < 1$.

The constraint says that loan contracts must be incentive compatible. The left-hand side of the constraint is the end-of period income the manager receives if she chooses to honour her debt, while the right-hand side is her income if she defaults. When she defaults, she economizes on the gross payment $(s + d)$ $(1 + r)$ she owes the intermediary, but she loses the accrued value $s(1 + r)$ of her collateral, and fraction η of her net income as default cost. This formulation of the incentive compatibility constraint assumes that agents who default in the formal sector must pay taxes. Assuming that agents who default on their loan also manage to default on their taxes would not change any of our qualitative results. Note that this statement of the problem also assumes that the intermediary behaves competitively. Among contracts that are incentive compatible and cover the intermediary's opportunity cost of capital, the contract most favourable to the manager prevails.

Solutions to the constrained contracting problem are easy to characterize. Given $z > 0$, there is a unique scale k^* (z) of operation such that the marginal product of capital is $1 + r$. Absent contractual imperfections (when $\eta = 1$), all formal agents operate at this optimal scale. But when $\eta < 1$, one can show (see Amaral and Quintin 2006) that, given $z > 0$ there exists an asset threshold $a^*(z; \eta, \tau)$ such that agents are constrained if and only if $a < a^*$ $(z; \eta, \tau)$. Furthermore, constrained managers use their entire assets as collateral (they set $s = a$), since the marginal product of capital exceeds $(1 + r)$ in constrained establishments.

[13] Because we assume no barriers to labour mobility, the price of labour must be the same in the two sectors.

[14] Assuming that the intermediary can seize all the manager's assets in the event of default would not alter the analysis in any way, since, as we argue below, it is optimal for all constrained agents to choose $s = a$.

Finally, the loan size rises with managerial talent because raising z weakens the incentive compatibility constraint.

A manager chooses to operate formally when $V(z,\tau,\eta) \geq V(z,0,0)$ and agents become workers when max $\{V(z,\tau,\eta), V(z,0,0)\} < w$. In particular, it is agents of low managerial ability who choose to become workers. The choice of sector is also characterized by a talent threshold. This is because agents of high talent can manage a large quantity of resources more effectively and hence stand to benefit the most from access to outside finance. Formally:[15]

Proposition 1 Given w, there exists $\underline{z}$ and $\bar{z}$ such that agents of ability z become workers if $z < \underline{z}$, informal managers if $z \in (\underline{z}, \bar{z})$, and formal managers if $z \in (\bar{z}, 1)$.
Proof. See Pratap and Quintin (2006b).   □

This result implies that optimal policies are fully described by two ability thresholds and by the maximum incentive compatible loan formal managers can obtain from the intermediary. An equilibrium in this environment is a value for the wage rate such that, given optimal policies, the labour market clears. Standard arguments imply that such an equilibrium exists.

It should also be clear that the equilibrium informal share of employment, capital, and output is increasing in the tax rate and declining in the quality of contract enforcement in the formal sector. When $\eta = 0$, for instance, one easily shows that $d(z) = 0$ for all $z \geq 0$ in equilibrium. Since access to finance is the only potential benefit associated with opting for the formal sector in this model, all agents choose to operate informally when $\eta = 0$. When $\eta = 1$, on the other hand, all formal agents are unconstrained, and the corresponding profit increase can be significant for agents of high managerial ability.

The model is thus consistent with the empirical link between the tax burden, institutional quality, and the size of the informal sector. It also predicts that the organization of production should differ across sectors, as our next result states:

Proposition 2 In equilibrium, formal managers employ more capital and workers and are more productive in total factor terms than informal managers.
Proof. See Pratap and Quintin (2006b).   □

Therefore, the model correctly predicts that the informal sector should emphasize small-scale, self-financed production. One can also show that, as long as the enforcement gap between the two sectors is large enough, formal managers operate at a higher capital-labour ratio than informal managers.

---

[15] The negligible mass of agents whose talent level coincides with one of the thresholds is indifferent between two occupations.

This yields a possible explanation for the fact that the informal sector emphasizes unskilled labour, given the well-documented complementarity between skill and physical capital. Because they tend to be more borrowing-constrained, informal employers choose to substitute unskilled labour for physical capital—see Amaral and Quintin (2006) for a formalization of this idea. In other words, despite the fact that labour markets are assumed to be completely integrated in our model, the distribution of worker characteristics can differ greatly in equilibrium. The model also provides a framework to think about the potential link between wealth inequality, output, and the importance of informal economic activities. A redistribution of wealth towards more talented managers could raise aggregate output and consumption by concentrating resources in the hands of the economy's most productive agents. With some ex-post redistribution of income (a challenging prospect, admittedly, in economies with poor quality institutions), welfare could increase.

Note, however, that this redistribution of wealth would have ambiguous effects on the size of the informal sector and the tax base. On the one hand, wealthier agents can borrow more capital in the formal sector (raising s weakens the incentive-compatibility constraint formal managers face), but they also have less of a need for outside finance, all else being equal. Of course, managerial talent is probably difficult to observe or verify, which makes talent-based redistribution difficult to implement in practice.[16]

However, even a wealth-redistribution scheme that is orthogonal to managerial talent could have positive effects on output. Indeed, in a version of the model we have outlined with exogenous wealth inequality, occupation profiles no longer depend solely on talent; they also potentially depend on wealth. Wealthier agents, all else being equal, are more likely to become managers, while more talented but less wealthy agents are forced to become workers. Making wealth more equal mitigates this source of inefficiency.[17]

While qualitatively promising, however, the quantitative impact of wealth redistribution schemes could be small. For instance, Quintin (2000) finds that, in the context of a dynamic general equilibrium version of the model presented here, even drastic wealth redistribution schemes do little to alleviate the impact of limited enforcement. Even when there is little or no wealth inequality, agents need access to outside sources of finance to operate on an efficient scale. Wealth redistribution schemes, therefore, may be a poor substitute for dealing directly with obstacles to the process of financial intermediation.

---

[16] A practical substitute for talent-based redistribution in this environment is a subsidy to formal managers. Because talented managers self-select into the formal sector, more talented managers are more likely to take advantage of the subsidy. Another benefit associated with this scheme is that it has a positive impact on the tax base.

[17] Naturally and by the same logic, a wealth redistribution scheme that is negatively correlated with talent could have adverse effects on output and productivity.

The environment we described in this section also suggests that growth naturally brings about drastic changes in the organization of production and the importance of informal activities. Assume that the distribution of managerial productivity shifts to the right over time. The equilibrium wage rate (the opportunity cost of self-employment) then rises over time, which, under some assumptions on the shape of technological opportunities, could lead ever more people to choose to work for others rather than become self-employed. Therefore we should expect self-employment to fall as an economy develops, and the average scale of operation to rise, making access to formal sources of finance more valuable. This process is illustrated by Gollin (2000), who also argues that this broad pattern of economic development is borne out by the relevant evidence.[18] Finally, the model's prediction that formal production is more capital-intensive than informal production (a prediction that is borne out by the evidence discussed in Section 2) has important implications for the measurement of informal sector assets, an issue to which we now turn.

5 Measuring Informal Sector Assets

While estimates of the output or employment size of the informal sector exist for a large cross-section of nations, estimates of the size of the assets in the informal sector are much less common. One important exception is de Soto (2000), whose rough estimates of the stock of informal capital confirm the strong belief among development economists that massive amounts of wealth are in the informal sector in developing nations.[19]

De Soto's estimates are staggering. He calculates, for instance, that 'the total value of real estate held but not legally owned by the poor' in developing nations approaches $US10 trillion, which is 'about twice as much as the total circulating US money supply'. According to de Soto, the stock of informal wealth is many times greater than the stock of recorded foreign investment in many nations. De Soto's estimates are rough, but they make it clear that omitting informal assets in wealth measurement exercises could lead to highly biased results—see Davies and Shorrocks (2005) for a discussion.

How should one go about measuring informal wealth? Estimates of the output and employment size of the informal sector can in principle provide an upper bound for the stock of informal capital, since all evidence is that informal production is less capital-intensive than formal production. The resulting upper bound is quite imprecise, however, not only because informal output and employment measures are themselves imprecise, but also because

[18] See also Banerjee and Newman (1993).

[19] Woodruff (2001) discusses and questions the quality of de Soto's estimates. He argues that de Soto vastly exaggerates the magnitude of informal assets but acknowledges that even conservative estimates of the asset size of the informal sector are 'quite large'.

the capital intensity of production differs greatly across sectors. Because they have very limited access to outside finance, informal producers are constrained to substitute labour for capital, a theoretical prediction that is strongly borne out by the available evidence.

To illustrate the potential importance of capital-intensity differences across sectors, consider an economy where the stock of capital in the informal sector is K^I while the formal stock of capital is K^F. Similarly, denote informal employment by E^I and formal employment by E^F. The informal share of physical capital is then given by:

$$\frac{K^I}{K^I + K^F} = \frac{E^I \frac{K^I}{E^I}}{E^I \frac{K^I}{E^I} + E^F \frac{K^F}{E^F}} = \frac{s^I}{s^I + (1 - s^I)\left(\frac{K^F}{E^F} / \frac{K^I}{E^I}\right)}$$

where $s^I = \frac{E^I}{E^I + E^F}$ is the informal share of employment and $\left(\frac{K^F}{E^F} / \frac{K^I}{E^I}\right)$ is the quotient of the capital–employment ratio in the formal sector and the capital–employment ratio in the informal sector. In the case of Cameroon, for instance, ILO (2003: table 7, sect. 2) reports that unincorporated, unregistered enterprises with ten employees or fewer account for roughly 60 per cent of employment. The data presented by Soderbom and Teal (2000) suggest, on the other hand, that large manufacturing firms are roughly three times more capital-intensive than micro-firms in Cameroon. Using these numbers as approximations for s^I and $\left(\frac{K^F}{E^F} / \frac{K^I}{E^I}\right)$ in Cameroon yields an asset share of roughly one-third. Because informal production is more labour intensive than formal production, the informal-sector share of the capital stock is noticeably below the informal share of output and employment. However, even after large capital-intensity corrections, the asset share of the informal sector is likely to remain far from negligible in low-income nations.

While indicative, indirect calculations along these lines can yield only rough estimates of the asset size of the informal sector. Properly accounting for informal wealth requires some direct measurement of informal gross fixed capital formation. Standard measures of the stock of physical capital use the perpetual inventory method applied to investment flows available by broad category in national accounts data. Therefore, estimates of the aggregate stock of physical capital reflect the importance of informal activities only if informal gross fixed capital formation is properly represented in national accounts. To evaluate the extent to which this condition is met, it is important first to recognize that, in theory, informal investment is included in gross fixed capital formation series. In accordance with 1993 systems of national accounts standards, national accountants should include in their calculations activities that are 'underground, illegal, informal or undertaken by households for their own final use'. In particular, informal does not mean unmeasured. However, given their nature, informal activities are measured with significant error and bias.

Macroeconomic models such as those described in Section 2 are one of the primary tools national accountants in developing countries use to gauge the importance of informal activities. In its handbook devoted to the problem of measuring 'non-observed' economic activity, the OECD (2002) sharply criticizes this approach. They express a strong preference for the 'transparent' use of 'all available data' to measure non-observed activities directly and to encourage national accountants to use data from 'a variety of sources' on a 'careful, case-by-case basis... These data are capable of producing much more accurate estimates of GDP and its components than macro-models can ever do.'[20]

In practice, national accountants do supplement macroeconomic estimates of the size of the informal sector with various ad-hoc techniques. In many nations, non-observed gross fixed capital formation is estimated using a commodity flow approach. Independent data on material use (with mark-ups designed to correct approximately for under-recording where appropriate) and input–output assumptions are used to arrive at comprehensive capital formation measures. The goal is to try and correct for the fact that establishment surveys (the source of a big part of investment data in most countries) are subject to much measurement error. While respondents have no obvious incentive to under-report investment, small, young establishments are likely to be under-sampled in those surveys. As is well known, developing nations emphasize small-scale production, which makes the problem of tracking down small, transient establishments particularly acute.

Despite the efforts expended by national accountants, the informal sector clearly adds noise to available measures of physical capital stock. Wealth inequality measures based on standard methods and data could be overstated because of the likely magnitude of error in the measurement of informal production and investment, and because a significant part of these activities are not properly taken into account. The only solution to these measurement issues is to improve the precision of national accounting practices. Much progress has been made in this area over the past decade, which bodes well for our ability eventually to arrive at better measures of aggregate wealth and worldwide wealth inequality. These measurement issues notwithstanding, there is little doubt that a very large fraction of wealth is held informally in most developing nations. This, in turn, has important consequences for the growth prospects of these nations.

Informal assets are much more difficult to leverage into loans than assets that carry proper titles, a fact de Soto (2000) describes as 'the major stumbling block that keeps the rest of the world from benefiting from capitalism'.

[20] The strong preference on the part of economists for macro-models is easy to understand, however. A unified methodology is necessary for cross-country comparisons. The use of macro-estimates does not presuppose the understanding of 'case-by-case' procedure choices made by national accountants at all stages of the data-collection process.

Because it is difficult for banks to enforce the stipulations of loans contracts (which includes the collection of collateral in the event of default), lending cannot be supported in the informal sector. According to de Soto (2000), the reason why informal assets are not treated as proper collateral for loans is that property rights over these assets are not clearly defined and legally recorded. As a result, informal assets are 'dead capital', because 'they cannot be turned into capital, cannot be traded outside of narrow local circles where people know and trust each other, cannot be used as collateral for a loan, and cannot be used as a share against an investment'. The most obvious implication of these observations is that titling programmes have the potential to unleash vast amounts of under-utilized resources in developing nations by allowing households to pursue previously untapped investment opportunities.

Yet, as Woodruff (2001) points out, titling programmes have produced disappointing results in many cases. Woodruff views this as evidence that titling programmes can be successful only as part of a broad set of reforms designed to improve the functioning of institutions. Quite obviously, a better definition of property rights, in and of itself, is not likely to have much impact in nations where formal means of contract enforcement are weak. The broad challenge is to create an institutional environment where informal assets, both physical and human, can be directed to their most productive use.

6 Conclusion

Research on the nature, determinants, and consequences of informal activities in developing nations has yielded a number of important insights. Among other empirical regularities, the importance of informal activities is highly correlated with a nation's level of economic development and the quality of its institutions. Furthermore, the informal sector emphasizes small-scale, unskilled-labour-intensive, self-financed activities. Modern models of the informal sector are consistent with these facts and provide natural frameworks for evaluating the potential consequences of pro-growth policies in nations with large informal sectors.[21]

For instance, competition-enhancing reforms and efforts to reduce the burden of regulation can have a big impact on the size of the formal sector as the economy adjusts to these institutional changes and resources move across sectors. The welfare consequences of these shocks to formal employment depend in part on the degree of integration between the formal and the informal labour market. If the informal sector is best viewed as the disadvantaged

---

[21] The impact of a variety of reforms on the importance of informal activities and on poverty was the object of a 2004 conference organized by UNU-WIDER. See Guha-Khasnobis et al. (2006).

end of dualistic labour markets, transitional or permanent reductions in formal employment could induce large welfare losses. On the other hand, precisely because it absorbs some of the cyclical and transitional variations in formal employment, the informal sector may in fact help mitigate the short-run impact of reforms.[22]

Generally speaking, dualistic models provide a rationale for policies that aim directly at shifting more resources to the formal sector. If marginal products are not equated across sectors, increasing formal employment can reduce poverty and increase welfare. If, on the other hand, income differences across sectors reflect productivity differences and the two labour markets are well integrated, policies whose sole objective is to boost formal employment are unlikely to yield large welfare gains. In those models, reducing poverty requires investments in human capital, and broad pro-growth policies are more likely to benefit all workers. In summary, how best to model informal activities is not merely an academic question. It has important consequences for how best to design efforts to alleviate poverty in developing economies.

One area where much work remains to be done is the measurement of informal wealth. The challenges, to be sure, are enormous. Tracking household assets that lack formal titles and the investment choices of small, unregistered establishments is a daunting task. The cost associated with dealing with these difficulties is clearly prohibitive for nations with scarce public resources. For now, estimates of the asset size of the informal sector remain rare and imprecise when they exist. Progress in this area would greatly enhance our ability to analyse wealth inequality across households and across countries.

---

[22] Similarly, recessions triggered, for instance, by financial crises in emerging nations lead to very large swings in the informal share of employment. This is evidence that workers accept lower-paying jobs during downturns, but this also illustrates the key buffer role informal employment plays in those economies.

Part IV

The Global Picture

19

The World Distribution of Household Wealth

James B. Davies, Susanna Sandström,
Anthony Shorrocks, and Edward N. Wolff

1 Introduction

Research on economic inequality—both within countries and between countries—is usually framed in terms of differences in income or consumption. In recent years a number of studies have extended this line of work to the global stage, by attempting to estimate the world distribution of income: see, for example, Bourguignon and Morrison (2002) and Milanovic (2002, 2005). The findings document the very high disparity of living standards amongst the world's citizens, but indicate that the rising inequality seen within many countries in recent decades has not led to a clear upward trend in global income inequality. The lack of trend is due to the rapid increase of incomes in certain developing countries, of which China is by far the most important.

Alongside this work there has been growing recognition of the importance of other contributions to individual well-being, most especially health status, but also education, environment, personal security, and vulnerability to natural disasters. This chapter focuses on another dimension of human well-being—household wealth—by which we mean net worth or, more precisely, the value of physical and financial assets less liabilities.[1]

Valuable comments and suggestions were received from participants at the WIDER project meeting 'Personal Assets from a Global Perspective', Helsinki, May 2006, and at the International Association for Research in Income and Wealth Conference, Joensuu, Finland, August 2006. Special thanks are due to Tony Atkinson, Brian Bucks, Markus Jäntti, and Branko Milanovic. Responsibility for all errors or omissions is our own.

[1] No attempt is made to include the present value of public pension schemes, because estimates are available for very few countries.

Household wealth is important for a number of reasons. First, it provides a means of raising long-term consumption, either directly by dissaving, or indirectly via the income stream of investment returns to assets. Second, by enabling consumption smoothing, ownership of wealth helps to insulate households against adverse events, especially those that lead to a reduction in income, such as ill health, unemployment, or simply growing old. Third, household wealth provides a source of finance for informal-sector and entrepreneurial activities, either directly or by being used as collateral for business loans. These motives are less compelling in countries that have good state pension arrangements, adequate social safety nets, and well-developed sources of business finance. By the same token, private wealth has more significance in countries that lack these facilities, which is the case in much of the developing world. Thus, as our results will make evident, household wealth tends to be lower in precisely those countries where it is needed most.

Despite these reasons for interest in wealth, and other evidence that asset holdings have a disproportionate impact on household well-being and economic success, and more broadly on economic development and growth, data limitations have handicapped research on the topic. However, the situation has rapidly improved in recent years. Many OECD countries now have wealth data derived from household surveys, tax records, or national balance sheets. Household wealth surveys have also been conducted in the two largest developing countries, China and India, and one survey with wealth results is available for Indonesia. Lists of the holdings of the super-rich are reported at regular intervals by *Forbes* magazine and other media outlets. Other sources add insights into the level and spread of personal wealth. We therefore believe that there are sufficient data to support preliminary estimates of the distribution of household wealth across the world, which we attempt for the year 2000.

The remainder of the chapter is organized as follows. The next section summarizes the sources and methods used in our study (these are described in more detail in Davies et al. 2007). Section 3 discusses results for the estimated world distribution of wealth. Likely future trends in wealth holding and wealth distribution are discussed in Section 4. Conclusions are drawn in Section 5.

2 Sources and Methods

2.1 *Wealth Levels*

The estimation of wealth levels is based on the information that can be assembled from household balance sheets and sample surveys. Household balance sheets are often compiled in conjunction with the national accounts or flow of funds data, while sample surveys derive from household interviews. Available household balance-sheet information enables us to construct 'complete' financial and non-financial data for 19 countries and financial data for 15 countries, where 'complete' is interpreted as full or almost full coverage of financial assets, and inclusion of at least owner-occupied housing on the non-financial side.

The country coverage of household balance sheets is not representative of the world as a whole. While Europe and North America, and the OECD in general, are well covered, low- and middle-income countries are under-represented. In geographic terms this means that coverage is sparse in Africa, Asia, Latin America, and the Caribbean. Fortunately for this study, these gaps were offset to an important extent by the availability of survey evidence for the largest developing countries, China, India, and Indonesia.

Altogether we made use of full or partial data on wealth levels for 39 countries. These countries accounted for 61 per cent of world population in the year 2000 and, we estimate, more than 80 per cent of global household wealth. Regressions run on these 39 countries allowed wealth levels to be estimated for other countries. The best predictions were achieved when separate regressions were run on three subcomponents of wealth: non-financial assets, financial assets, and liabilities. Each of the regressions uses real consumption per capita as one of the explanatory variables.[2] Population density also appears in the regression equation for non-financial assets, market capitalization ratio (a measure of the size of the stock market) in the equation for financial assets, and private-sector domestic credits in the equation for liabilities. To control for the mixture of household budget survey (HBS) and survey data sources, a survey dummy was included, although this was significant only for financial assets, reflecting the well-known fact that financial assets are under-reported in survey data.

In the year 2000, the world comprised 229 countries. The regressions yielded 150 countries with observed or estimated average wealth, covering 95 per cent of world population. The remaining 79 countries are mostly small or insignificant in wealth terms. Omitting these countries implicitly suggests that they are representative of the world as a whole, which is patently untrue. We therefore assigned to each country the average per capita wealth of the corresponding continental region (6 categories) and income class (4 categories), an admittedly crude procedure, but one that is preferable to the alternative default option.

2.2 Shape of Wealth Distributions

A complete picture of wealth holdings within a country requires information on the shape of the distribution as well as the average level. A total of 20

---

[2] The regression results are reported in Davies et al. (2007: table 5). Real consumption per capita was used because consumption figures are available for about twice as many countries as income data, and hence allow imputations to be made for many more countries.

countries have reasonably reliable estimates of wealth distribution at the national level. These are listed in Table 19.1 along with the quantile share data assembled for them.[3] The list includes the largest rich countries and the largest poor countries—the USA, Japan, Germany, UK, France, and Italy, on the one hand, and China, India, and Indonesia, on the other. The Nordic and the smaller English-speaking countries (Australia, Canada, and New Zealand) are also well represented. Inclusion of both the large rich countries of the West, on the one hand, and China and India, on the other, may be quite significant. Milanovic (2005) demonstrates that this relatively small number of countries is responsible for most of the recent changes in world income inequality.[4] It seems likely that these key countries are also crucial for understanding and appreciating the global distribution of wealth.

One set of distributional figures was selected for each country, with a preference for the year 2000, *ceteris paribus*. The data differ in some important respects across countries. For 15 of the 20 countries, the data originate from household surveys, which tend to underestimate the share of the top wealth groups due to lower response rates and under-reporting of asset values, particularly financial assets.[5] Tax records are the source of wealth distribution data for the remaining five countries: estate tax returns in the case of France and the UK; wealth tax records for Denmark, Norway, Switzerland, and Sweden. Although these sources have the advantage that 'response' is involuntary and under-reporting is illegal, under-reporting may still occur, and other valuation problems affect both the accuracy of the figures and the degree of comparability across countries.

Table 19.1 shows that the wealth distribution data most often refer to households or families, but can also refer to individuals or adults. The distributional information usually includes the decile wealth shares, plus the share of the top 5 per cent and the top 1 per cent of wealth holders. But there are many gaps in the coverage. The share of the top 10 per cent is reported for all 20 countries, and ranges from 39.3 per cent in Japan to 71.3 per cent in Switzerland.[6] The very high level of wealth concentration is even more evident in the share of the top 1 per cent. Amongst the 11 countries reporting that statistic (a group that excludes China, Germany, and the Nordic countries

---

[3] Because of rounding errors, the shares do not always sum to 100%. In such cases, the computation procedure we adopted scales the shares appropriately.

[4] See Milanovic (2005: 115).

[5] Over-sampling of high-income/wealth groups, as is done in Canada, Finland, Spain, and the USA, can mitigate the differential response rates. Undervaluation of assets can also be addressed in principle by scaling up the reported figures.

[6] The Danish figure of 76.4% is higher still, but probably unreliable given the large negative asset holdings reported for half the Danish population.

Table 19.1. Wealth shares for countries with wealth distribution data (%)

Country	Year	Unit	Share of lowest (%)											Share of top (%)					
			10	20	25	30	40	50	60	70	75	80	90	10	5	2	1	0.5	0.1
Australia	2002	Household	0.0	0.0		1.0	4.0	9.0	16.0	25.0		38.0	56.0	45.0	32.0				
Canada	1999	Family unit				1.0	3.0	6.0	11.0	19.0		30.0	47.0	53.0					
China	2002	Person	0.7	2.8		5.8	9.6	14.4	20.6	29.0		40.7	58.6	41.4					
Denmark	1996	Family unit	−14.4	−17.3		−18.1	−18.1	−17.6	−15.8	−10.5		1.3	23.6	76.4	56.0		28.8	22.2	11.6
Finland	1998	Household	−0.9	−0.9		−0.3	2.2	7.4	15.0	25.0		38.6	57.7	42.3					
France	1994	Person											39.0	61.0			21.3		6.3
Germany	1998	Household	−0.3	−0.2		0.3	1.5	3.9	9.0	18.9		34.0	55.7	44.4					
India	2002–3	Household	0.2	1.0		2.5	4.8	8.1	12.9	19.8		30.1	47.1	52.9	38.3		15.7		
Indonesia	1997	Household	0.0	0.4		1.3	2.8	5.1	8.5	13.5		21.1	34.6	65.4	56.0		28.7		
Ireland	1987	Household	0.0	0.2		2.5	6.6	12.2	18.9	28.5		40.4	57.7	42.3	28.7		10.4		
Italy	2000	Household					7.0					36.2	51.5	48.5	36.4		17.2		
Japan	1999	Household	0.5	2.1		4.8	8.7	13.9	20.7	29.8		42.3	60.7	39.3					
Korea, South	1988	Household	0.5	1.8		4.0	7.4	12.3	18.9	27.9		39.9	56.9	43.1	31.0		14.0		
New Zealand	2001	Tax unit											48.3	51.7					
Norway	2000	Household	0.1	0.7		2.6	5.8	10.4	16.4	24.2		34.6	49.6	50.5					
Spain	2002	Household			2.1			13.2			34.7		58.1	41.9			18.3	13.1	5.6
Sweden	2002	Household	−5.7	−6.8		−6.9	−6.6	−4.8	−0.6	7.1		19.9	41.4	58.6					
Switzerland	1997	Family									25.0		28.7	71.3	58.0		34.8	27.6	16.0
United Kingdom	2000	Adult						5.0					44.0	56.0	44.0	31.0	23.0		
USA	2001	Family						2.8					30.2	69.8	57.7		32.7		

Source: See Davies et al. (2007: app. IIC).

apart from Denmark), the share of the top 1 per cent ranges from 10.4 per cent in Ireland to 34.8 per cent in Switzerland.[7]

To proceed towards an estimate of the world distribution of wealth, a utility programme developed at UNU-WIDER was used to create a synthetic, equal weighted sample of 1,000 observations corresponding to each of the 20 distributions recorded in Table 19.1. This 'ungrouping' programme can be applied to any set of quantile shares (in the form of Lorenz values) derived from a distribution of positive values (for example, incomes). It begins by generating a sample of 1,000 observations that roughly matches the reported distribution, then adjusts the values until the sample properties exactly match the target characteristics.[8] To apply this programme to the distributions in Table 19.1, the non-positive values were discarded, thus treating these cells as missing observations.

Estimating the shape of the wealth distribution for the countries not listed in Table 19.1 requires more heroic assumptions. We took the view that income inequality is likely to be highly correlated with wealth inequality across countries, and hence drew on income distribution data for 144 countries contained in the World Income Inequality Database (WIID).[9] Comparison of the Lorenz curves for wealth and income distributions for the 20 reference countries in Table 19.1 reveals that the cumulative wealth shares are always lower than the corresponding income shares, and suggests that the ratio of the Lorenz ordinates for wealth and income is reasonably stable across countries. Consequently, the average ratio for the 20 reference countries was applied to the other 124 countries in order to estimate the (unknown) wealth distribution data from the available income distribution information. Wealth distribution figures for the remaining countries (which collectively account for less than 4 per cent of the world population) were again imputed using the average values for the corresponding region and income class.

2.3 Computing the World Distribution

The final step in the construction of the world distribution of wealth combines information on the level and shape of wealth holdings. For each country, the

[7] The sampling frame for the US survey excludes the *Forbes* 400 richest families; adding them would raise the share of the top 1% by about two percentage points (see Kennickell 2003: 3). Other differences in data sources and units of analysis mean that cross-country variations should be interpreted with considerable caution. For example, the relatively low shares of top wealth groups in Australia, Ireland, and Japan are probably due in part to the fact that the surveys in these countries do not compensate for differential response by over-sampling the upper tail, and we believe are consequently likely to underestimate the share of the top 1% by about 5–10 percentage points.

[8] See Shorrocks and Wan (2008) for further details.

[9] The 144 countries covered by WIID are not a subset of the 150 nations for which mean wealth was obtained (from actual data or via the regressions) in Section 2. In particular, populous countries are more likely to report income distribution data, so the list of 144 now includes Cuba, Iraq, Myanmar, Nepal, Serbia, Sudan, and Uzbekistan.

ungrouping utility programme generated a sample of 1,000 observations consistent with the actual, estimated, or imputed wealth distribution. These observations were then scaled to match the mean wealth, and weighted by the population size. Merging the countries into a single dataset produced a weighted sample of more than 200,000 observations[10] from which the minimum wealth and the share of each percentile in the global distribution of wealth were estimated, along with the membership of each wealth percentile by country of residence.

Two additional issues must be confronted before the global wealth distribution figures can be interpreted. First, what is the relevant population to which the figures refer: all households in the world, all individuals, or all adults? Studies of global income inequality typically assume that the benefits of household expenditure are shared equally among household members and that each person counts equally in determining overall inequality. Household assets like housing also provide communal benefits, but ownership and control of household assets do not usually extend to non-adult members, nor are the proceeds shared equally in the event of the assets being sold. We therefore took the view that it is best to disregard ownership of wealth by minors (specifically, those aged below 20 years) and to interpret the wealth distribution figures in terms of the distribution across adults.[11]

The second question concerns the appropriate conversion rate for currencies in different countries. Studies of the global distribution of income or consumption usually use PPP (purchasing power parity) exchange rates to compensate for price variations across countries. Here, we focus on global wealth estimates based on official exchange rates on the grounds that wealth is heavily concentrated in the hands of the rich, whose expenditure for both consumption and investment purposes will often be at world prices rather than at the prices prevailing in their home country.[12]

---

[10] There are 229 countries in all, but some small countries with identical imputed wealth levels and distributions were merged at this stage.

[11] Although the three options considered here—households, individuals, and adults—are all present in the data reported in Table 19.1, most country data refer to households. Our implicit assumption that the distribution of wealth across adults is similar to the pattern across households is admittedly heroic, given that almost nothing is known empirically about the relationship between the two distributions. The two distributions would be identical if all households contained two adults, if children had zero wealth, and if wealth was equally divided between the adult members. Our assumption is also plausible if household wealth was proportional to the number of adult members, *ceteris paribus*. But inaccuracies could arise if, for example, single-person widow and widower households own disproportionate amounts of wealth. This is likely to be the case, although the quantitative impact on our results is unclear.

[12] Some alternative estimates using PPP rates are discussed in Section 3. Further details are reported in Davies et al. (2007).

3 The Global Distribution of Wealth

3.1 *Wealth Inequality*

Table 19.2 summarizes our results on the distribution of household wealth across the world population of 3.7 billion adults, based on official exchange rates and figures for the year 2000. According to our estimates, adults required just $US2,138 in order to be among the wealthiest half of the world. But more than $US61,000 was needed to belong to the top 10 per cent and more than $US510,000 per adult was required for membership of the top 1 per cent. The entrance fee for the top 1 per cent seems surprisingly high, given than the group has 37 million adult members. Furthermore, the figure refers to the year 2000 and is now likely to be considerably higher, especially when measured in US dollars.

The wealth share estimates reveal that the richest 2 per cent of adult individuals own more than half of all global wealth, with the richest 1 per cent alone accounting for 40 per cent of global assets. The corresponding figures for the top 5 per cent and the top 10 per cent are 71 per cent and 85 per cent, respectively. In contrast, the bottom half of wealth holders together hold barely 1 per cent of global wealth. Members of the top decile are almost 400 times richer, on average, than the bottom 50 per cent, and members of the top percentile are almost 2,000 times richer.

Additional information on wealth inequality is provided in Table 19.3, which reports the value of the Gini coefficient for the world as well as the values for individual countries. As mentioned earlier, in all countries that have the requisite data, wealth distribution is more unequal than income. The final column of Table 19.3 records wealth Gini estimates ranging from 0.547 for Japan to 0.801 for the USA and 0.803 for Switzerland. The global wealth Gini is estimated to be even greater at 0.892. This is equivalent to the Gini value that would be registered for a 100-person population in which one person receives $900 and the remaining 99 people each receive $1.

By way of comparison, Milanovic (2005: 108) estimates the Gini for the world distribution of income to be 0.795 in 1998 using official exchange rates. Note that, while wealth inequality exceeds income inequality in global terms, the gap between the Gini coefficients for world wealth and income inequality—about 12 percentage points—is less than the gap at the country level, which averages about 30 percentage points. This is to be expected, given the limited possibilities for higher Gini values arising from an income Gini of 0.795 and a Gini upper bound of 1. It is also worth pointing out that the relative insensitivity of the Gini coefficient to the tails of the distribution implies that our likely slight underestimation of the top wealth shares will have little impact on the estimated Gini. Furthermore, concentration in the upper tail of the income distribution is also probably underestimated

Table 19.2. Global wealth distribution, regional details based on official exchange rates, 2000

	Decile									Top (%)			Adult population (m.)	Population share (%)	Wealth per adult ($US)	Wealth (%)
	1	2	3	4	5	6	7	8	9	10	5	1				
World wealth shares (%)	0	0.1	0.2	0.3	0.5	0.8	1.4	2.7	8.7	85.2	70.7	40.1				
Minimum wealth ($US)	0.1	178	448	874	1,384	2,138	3,467	6,220	13,985	61,536	150,182	512,386				
Percentage of adults by region																
North America	0.2	0.6	1.1	1.4	2.0	2.7	4.6	7.5	13.6	27.3	28.7	38.9	225.7	6.1	190653	34.4
Latin America and Caribbean	5.9	7.1	7.0	5.4	6.3	7.6	9.9	13.1	14.8	4.8	3.0	2.2	302.9	8.2	17892	4.3
Europe	9.4	8.4	9.3	7.8	8.2	9.7	13.0	17.1	29.7	36.2	35.6	25.8	550.6	14.9	67315	29.6
Africa	27.2	17.8	14.4	9.2	7.7	7.3	6.9	6.4	4.3	0.7	0.3	0.2	376.3	10.2	3415	1.0
China	6.4	14.6	15.7	37.1	40.6	39.2	35.1	29.6	9.3	0.2	0.0	0.0	842.1	22.8	3885	2.6
India	26.5	27.2	27.5	19.7	16.8	14.8	11.6	7.4	2.6	0.2	0.0	0.0	570.6	15.4	1989	0.9
Rich Asia-Pacific	0.0	0.1	0.3	0.3	0.6	0.9	1.9	4.1	13.2	28.2	31.2	32.2	183.3	5.0	165008	24.1
Other Asia-Pacific	24.4	24.3	24.7	19.0	17.8	17.7	17.2	14.7	12.5	2.4	1.2	0.6	646.1	17.5	5889	3.0
World	100	100	100	100	100	100	100	100	100	100	100	100	3697.5	100	33875	100

Source: See text.

Table 19.3. Global wealth distribution, country details based on official exchange rates, 2000

Percentage of adults by country	Decile 1	2	3	4	5	6	7	8	9	Top (%) 10	5	1	Adult population (m.)	Population share (%)	Wealth per adult ($US)	Wealth share (%)	Gini
USA	0.2	0.5	0.9	1.2	1.6	2.5	4.2	7.2	11.7	24.8	26.7	37.3	202.9	5.5	201,319	32.6	0.801
Japan						0.1	0.4	1.3	5.0	20.5	25.1	27.0	100.9	2.7	227,600	18.3	0.547
Germany	1.1	0.6	1.0	0.4	0.4	0.2	1.0	1.7	3.6	7.6	9.7	3.5	64.8	1.8	109,735	5.7	0.667
Italy				0.4		0.1	0.3	1.1	4.4	6.6	5.0	4.0	46.4	1.3	122,250	4.5	0.609
UK			0.1	0.1	0.2	0.4	0.8	1.7	2.5	5.9	7.8	6.4	43.9	1.2	169,617	5.9	0.697
France			0.1	0.1	0.2	0.4	0.8	1.8	4.4	4.2	4.1	5.2	44.4	1.2	114,650	4.1	0.730
Spain		0.1	0.2		0.1	0.3	0.5	0.7	3.1	3.9	2.4	1.0	32.2	0.9	86,958	2.2	0.570
Canada		0.1	0.2	0.2	0.4	0.3	0.4	0.3	1.8	2.5	2.0	1.6	22.8	0.6	95,606	1.7	0.688
Taiwan		0.1	0.2			0.1	0.3	0.5	1.4	1.8	1.5	1.2	15.5	0.4	105,613	1.3	0.655
Australia			0.1	0.1	0.2	0.1	0.2	0.2	0.8	1.8	1.3	0.7	13.7	0.4	94,712	1.0	0.622
Netherlands			0.1	0.1		0.1	0.1	0.3	1.0	1.7	1.7	1.4	12.0	0.3	144,406	1.4	0.650
South Korea						0.4	0.7	1.6	4.2	1.6	0.6	0.5	33.2	0.9	41,256	1.1	0.579
Brazil	2.2	2.8	2.5	1.9	2.3	2.8	3.4	4.5	4.4	1.4	0.8	0.6	104.2	2.8	14,887	1.2	0.784
Mexico	0.4	0.8	1.2	0.8	1.0	1.2	1.9	2.7	4.0	1.3	0.9	0.6	56.1	1.5	25,468	1.1	0.749
Argentina	0.1	0.3	0.3	0.4	0.3	0.5	0.6	1.0	1.9	0.9	0.6	0.4	23.3	0.6	38,406	0.7	0.740
Switzerland							0.1	0.3	0.5	0.6	0.7	1.2	5.5	0.1	212,394	0.9	0.803
Turkey	0.3	0.7	1.0	0.7	0.7	1.1	1.4	2.2	2.2	0.5	0.2	0.1	40.4	1.1	15,252	0.5	0.718
China	6.4	14.6	15.7	37.1	40.6	39.2	35.1	29.6	9.3	0.2			842.1	22.8	3,885	2.6	0.550
India	26.5	27.2	27.5	19.7	16.8	14.8	11.6	7.4	2.6	0.2			570.6	15.4	1,989	0.9	0.669
Russia	4.1	3.6	3.5	3.1	3.1	3.7	3.8	2.7	1.3	0.1			107.5	2.9	3,897	0.3	0.699
Indonesia	7.5	6.0	5.5	4.2	3.2	2.7	2.9	0.6	0.9	0.1	0.1		124.4	3.4	2,421	0.2	0.764
Thailand	0.8	1.4	1.2	1.1	1.1	2.2	1.5	1.6	1.0	0.1	0.1		40.2	1.1	6,307	0.2	0.710
Pakistan	2.8	2.8	3.3	2.4	2.5	2.2	1.0	0.9	0.5				68.0	1.8	2,504	0.1	0.698
Vietnam	2.3	2.0	2.0	1.5	1.3	1.2	0.9	0.5	0.2				44.0	1.2	1,982	0.1	0.682
Bangladesh	2.5	2.8	2.9	2.3	2.3	2.2	1.7	1.0	0.3				66.5	1.8	2,392	0.1	0.660
Nigeria	5.9	3.0	2.2	1.1	0.6	0.5	0.3	0.2	0.1				51.4	1.4	813	0.0	0.736
World	100	100	100	100	100	100	100	100	100	100	100	100	3697.5	100	33,875	100	0.892

Source: See text.

(although to a lesser extent than for wealth), so that the estimated *gap* between wealth and income inequality is unlikely to be heavily biased.

3.2 Geographic Distribution of Wealth

The world map in Figure 19.1 shows the per capita wealth of different countries. Western Europe, North America,[13] and rich Asia–Pacific economies (principally Japan, South Korea, Taiwan, Australia, and New Zealand) stand out as the richest areas, with per capita wealth exceeding $US50,000 in the year 2000. Next come some prosperous developing and transition countries—for example, Mexico, Chile, Argentina, Poland, the Czech Republic, and Ukraine—in the $US10,000 to $US50,000 band. The large transition countries, Russia and China, fall in the $US2,000 to $US10,000 range along with Turkey, Brazil, Egypt, Thailand, and South Africa. Finally, in the category below $US2,000 are found India, Pakistan, Indonesia, and most of Central and West Africa.

Regional wealth shares are interesting (see the last column of Table 19.2). North America owns about a third (34 per cent) of the world's wealth. Europe has a fraction less (30 per cent), and rich Asia–Pacific is close behind at

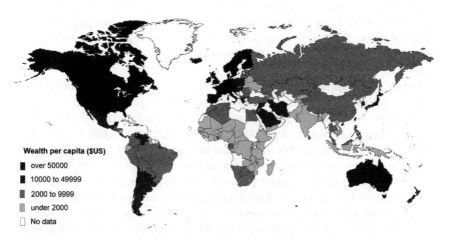

Figure 19.1. World wealth levels, 2000

Wealth per capita ($US)
■ over 50000
■ 10000 to 49999
■ 2000 to 9999
▨ under 2000
□ No data

---

[13] For our purposes, 'North America' includes only Canada and the USA. Mexico and the Central American countries are included in Latin America.

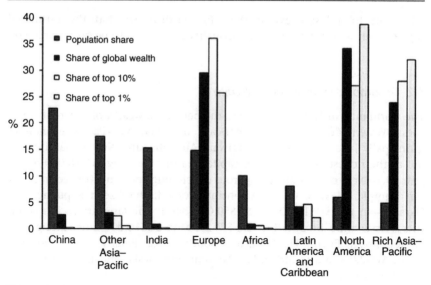

Figure 19.2. Population and wealth shares, by region

24 per cent. The rest of the world shares the remaining 12 per cent. Figure 19.2 shows how these wealth shares compare to population shares. North America has the largest excess of wealth over its 'fair share' according to population, which is a mere 5 per cent. Europe has more than double the population of North America, so that its large wealth share is more aligned with its population. The case of rich Asia–Pacific is intermediate between Europe and North America.

Figure 19.3 compares the asset composition of wealth across a selection of countries. In the USA, according to our estimates, 42 per cent of gross household assets are in financial form. Among the countries for which we have data, this high ratio is approached only by the UK. As illustrated, Japan, Canada, and Germany have a considerably lower share of financial assets—averaging just 28 per cent. Interestingly, estimated financial assets are 22 per cent of the total in China, but just 5 per cent and 3 per cent in India and Indonesia respectively. Like Japan and several other East Asian countries before it, China has been experiencing a period of explosive growth and very high saving rates, which have produced a strikingly different wealth composition than that found in many developing countries. Household assets in the latter are heavily weighted towards land, livestock, and other agricultural assets. Financial development also lags, with the result that non-financial assets dominate the balance sheet.

Figure 19.3 also suggests that debt is higher in the developed world, at least according to official data. However, it is possible that debts are especially

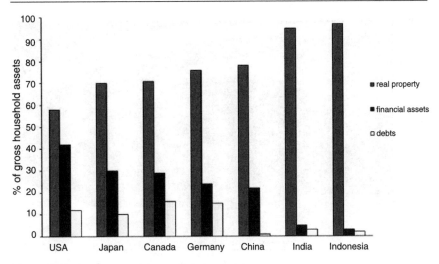

Figure 19.3. Asset composition, selected countries

under-reported in less developed country (LDC) sample surveys. Subramanian and Jayaraj (2006), for example, estimate that the true indebtedness of Indian households is about three times greater than that reported in the survey data. If so, total debt in India would be about 10 per cent of gross assets, similar to the level reported in the USA and Japan.

Turning now to the membership of the wealth quantiles, Figure 19.4 charts the regional composition of the various global deciles. The corresponding numerical data are recorded in Table 19.2. 'Thirds' feature prominently in describing the overall pattern of results. India dominates the bottom third of the global wealth distribution, contributing a little under a third (28 per cent to be precise) of the bottom three deciles. The middle third of the distribution is the domain of China, which supplies more than a third of those in deciles 4–8. North America, Europe, and rich Asia–Pacific monopolize the top decile, each regional group accounting for around one-third of the richest wealth holders, although the composition changes a little in the upper tail, with the North American share rising while European membership declines. Another notable feature is the relatively constant membership share of Asian countries other than China and India. However, as the figures indicate, this group is highly polarized, with the high-income sub-group populating the top end of the global wealth distribution and the lower-income countries (especially Indonesia, Bangladesh, Pakistan, and Vietnam) occupying the lower tail. The population of Latin America is also fairly even spread across the global distribution, but Africa, as expected, is heavily concentrated at the bottom end.

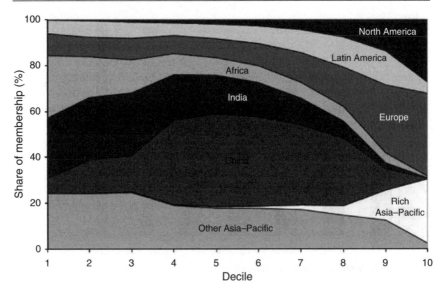

Figure 19.4. Regional composition of global wealth distribution

Table 19.3 provides more details for a selection of countries. The list of countries includes all those that account for more than 1 per cent of global wealth or more than 1 per cent of those in the top decile, plus those additional countries with adult populations exceeding 45 million. They are arranged in order of the number of persons in the top global wealth decile.

The number of members of the top decile depends on three factors: the size of the population, average wealth, and wealth inequality within the country. Unsurprisingly, the USA appears in first position, with 25 per cent of the global top decile (see Figure 19.5) and 37 per cent of the global top percentile. All three factors reinforce each other in this instance: a large population combining with very high wealth per capita and relatively unequal distribution. Japan features strongly in second place—more strongly than anticipated, perhaps—with 21 per cent of the global top decile and 27 per cent of the global top percentile. The high wealth per adult and relatively equal distribution accounts for the fact that the number of Japanese in the bottom half of the global wealth distribution is insignificant according to our figures. Italy, too, has a stronger showing than expected, for much the same reasons as Japan.

Further down the list, China and India both owe their position to the size of their population. Neither country has enough people in the global top 5 per cent in 2000 to be recorded in Table 19.3. While the two countries are expected to be under-represented in the upper tail because of their relatively low mean wealth, their absence here from the top 5 per cent seems anomalous. It may well reflect unreliable wealth data drawn from surveys that do not over-sample

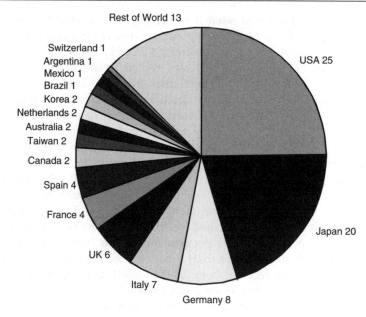

Figure 19.5. Percentage membership of wealthiest 10%

the upper tail, data that could be improved by making corrections for differential response and under-reporting.[14] The representation of both China and India has been rising in the annual *Forbes* list of billionaires, so it is likely that more recent estimates of the membership of the top 5 per cent or top 1 per cent would not only record greater representation from these two countries, but also register an increasing trend over time.[15]

3.3 *Adjusting for Local Prices*

As discussed earlier, it is natural to use official exchange rates to compare the wealth of the world's super-rich in different countries. Lower down the scale, however, the benefits (and valuations) of asset holdings may depend heavily on the local prices of goods and services, so it may be more appropriate to

---

[14] The estimated membership figures for large countries may be especially unreliable, given that our procedures condense the population of each country into a sample of 1,000, so a single sample point for China or India represents more than half a million adults.

[15] Ten years ago the *Forbes* list contained no billionaires from China. In 2007 there were 16. As late as 2004, only 9 billionaires were reported in India. This number had risen to 36 by 2007.

evaluate wealth in terms of what it would buy if liquidated and spent on consumption locally. To address this point, alternative estimates of the world distribution of wealth have been constructed on a PPP basis.[16]

Applying the PPP adjustment increases average wealth in most countries, and hence the global average, which rises from $US33,875 per adult to $US43,494 per adult. The admission fee for membership of the top wealth groups also increases. The price for entry to the top 10 per cent rises from $US61,536 to $US87,876, but entry to the top 1 per cent increases more modestly, from $US512,386 to $US517,601, reflecting the small impact of PPP adjustments within the richest nations. Because the PPP adjustment tends to be greater for poorer countries, switching to PPP valuations compresses the variation in average wealth levels across countries and hence provides a more conservative assessment of the degree of world wealth inequality. For example, the estimated wealth share of the richest individuals falls, from 85.2 per cent to 71.2 per cent for the top 10 per cent of wealth holders, and from 40.1 per cent to 31.9 per cent for the top 1 per cent. The global Gini value also declines, from 0.892 to 0.804 (although the Gini coefficients for individual countries are unaffected).

The overall picture suggested by the PPP results is much the same as the pattern observed earlier with official exchange rates. India moves a little more into the middle deciles of the global wealth distribution, and both India and China are now recorded in the global top 5 per cent, although not in the top 1 per cent. Membership of the top 10 per cent is a little more evenly spread regionally, principally due to a decline in the share of Japan, whose membership of the top 10 per cent falls from 21 per cent to 14 per cent as a result of the decline in Japan's wealth per adult from $US227,600 to $US157,146 when measured in PPP terms.

As regards the rankings of individual countries, Brazil, India, Russia, and Turkey are all promoted to the exclusive group of countries with more than 1 per cent of the members of the global top wealth decile. The most dramatic rise, however, is that of China, which leapfrogs into sixth position with 4.1 per cent of the members. Even without an increase in wealth inequality, a relatively modest rise in average wealth in China in future years will move it up to third position in the global top decile (measured in PPP dollars), and overtaking Japan is not a remote prospect.

In summary, it is clear that household wealth is much more concentrated, both in size distribution and geography, when official exchange rates rather than PPP valuations are employed. Thus a somewhat different perspective emerges depending on whether one is interested in the power that wealth

---

[16] More detailed results are discussed in Davies et al. (2007.) We use the PPP exchange rates from the Penn World Tables.

conveys in terms of local consumption options or the power to act and have influence on the world financial stage.

3.4 *Reliability of Results*

It was noted earlier that the countries for which wealth data are available include those most crucial to the overall world picture—the richest and poorest large nations. Nevertheless, we have had to rely on various estimation and imputation techniques in order to fill the many gaps in data coverage. So it is important to try to assess the robustness of our results to the assumptions and imputations made during the course of the study.

With wealth measured in PPP terms, Davies et al. (2007) show that our main results are very robust to a number of alternative assumptions. The same is true when wealth is valued at official exchange rates. For example, omitting the large number of (mainly small) countries for which the wealth level or distributional shape was imputed using the average value of the corresponding region and income class has little effect on the global figures for wealth levels or inequality. Going further and restricting attention to the 20 countries for which direct data exist on both wealth levels and distributional shape lead to a modest reduction in the Gini coefficient from 0.892 to 0.887, again suggesting that the results are robust. Focusing on the same 20 countries, the use of income inequality as a proxy for wealth inequality was investigated by replacing the 'true' wealth distribution figures with the income distribution derived estimate obtained as for other countries. This reduces the share of the top 1 per cent from 37.6 per cent to 32.9 per cent, and the global Gini value from 0.887 to 0.880, suggesting that the income inequality proxy may lead to an underestimate of global wealth inequality, although the overall impact may be modest, given that the countries involved hold less than 20 per cent of global wealth.

Another way of checking our results is to consider countries that have some information on wealth inequality, although not complete data. Our imputed wealth distributions appear consistent with that partial information, adding to our confidence in the results. For example, Rogg (Chapter 11, this volume) reports a Gini coefficient of 0.59 for rural Ethiopia (which has 84 per cent of the country's population according to the World Development Indicators) in 1997, a moderate figure that does not conflict with our imputed figure of 0.652 for Ethiopia as a whole.[17] Pinto (2006) estimates the distribution of wealth in Campinas, Brazil, a city with a population of about a million people using the estate-multiplier method. He obtains a Gini coefficient of 0.920 for 1996,

---

[17] Per capita wealth is significantly higher in urban than in rural areas in developing countries. Even if inequality in urban areas was no greater than in rural areas, one would therefore expect the national wealth Gini to exceed that for rural areas.

which suggests that our figure of 0.784 for the country as a whole is not extreme.[18] Torche and Spilerman (Chapter 8, this volume: table 8.4b) report a Gini for land holding of 0.85 for Brazil—slightly above the median figure of 0.84 for 15 Latin American countries and well above the US figure of 0.72. Our estimates show above-average wealth inequality for Latin America, consistent with this evidence on land inequality and with data on the distribution of some other important wealth components.[19]

Other considerations also lead us to believe that our estimates of the top wealth shares are conservative. The survey data on which most of our estimates are based under-represent the rich and do not reflect the holdings of the super-rich. Although the Survey of Consumer Finances (SCF) survey in the USA does an excellent job in the upper tail, its sampling frame explicitly omits the 'Forbes 400' families. Surveys in other countries do not formally exclude the very rich, but it is rare for them to be captured. This means that our estimated shares of the top 1 per cent and 10 per cent are likely to err on the low side. A rough idea of the possible size of the error can be gained by noting that the total wealth of the world's billionaires reported by Forbes for the year 2000, $US2.16 trillion, was 1.7 per cent of our estimate of $US125.3 trillion for total world household wealth.

The top tail of wealth distributions is often well approximated by the Pareto distribution, which plots the logarithm of the number of persons above wealth level w against the logarithm of w. The outcome, depicted in Figure 19.6, shows a remarkable correspondence in the range from $US250,000 to $US5 million. Above $US5 million the relationship breaks down, as expected, given the limitations of the data sources and the lumpiness caused by using a single sample observation to represent many tens of thousands of adults. However, it seems reasonable to use a fitted Pareto curve to estimate the number of individuals in the highest echelons of the wealth distribution. This leads us to predict that more than 16,000 adults owned at least $US100 million in the year 2000, and that 553 persons were dollar billionaires (see Table 19.4). The latter figure is very close to the Forbes estimate of 492 billionaires for the year 2000. Furthermore, Forbes magazine classifies 41 per cent of the billionaires as US citizens, a proportion consistent with the figures in Table 19.3, which records a US share of 37 per cent

---

[18] Interestingly, Noyola (2000) obtains a much lower Gini coefficient for wealth in the city of Monterrey, Mexico, in 1998, just 0.54 (this compares to our figure of 0.749 for Mexico as a whole). Noyola's estimate is based, however, on a sample survey of about 1,000 families that did not over-sample the upper tail. The difference between the Pinto and Noyola results illustrates the importance of getting information on the truly rich for obtaining an accurate picture of overall wealth distribution.

[19] Torche and Spilerman (Chapter 8, this volume: Table 8.3b) report the Gini for housing wealth for nine Latin American countries. The range is from 0.56 in Uruguay to 0.85 in Bolivia (in these data non-owners are included in the calculation of the Gini, with zero wealth; in contrast, the Gini for landholding mentioned in our text above is just for landowners). Torche and Spilerman also compare data on the quintile shares for various forms of capital income. For income from capital, rents, and profits in sixteen countries, they indicate a share of the top quintile ranging from 64% in the Dominican Republic to 96% in Guatemala. The median is 80%.

Table 19.4. Estimated global numbers of $US millionaires and billionaires, official exchange rate basis, 2000

Wealth ($US)	Number above
1 million	13,674,966
10 million	469,361
100 million	16,110
1 billion	553

Source: See text.

of the top 1 per cent, and suggests that the share is higher at higher wealth ranges. This degree of similarity may be a little misleading, since the *Forbes* list tends to refer to billionaire *families* rather than *individuals*. Nevertheless, our projections for the number of super-rich adults add to our confidence that our global wealth distribution estimates are plausible.

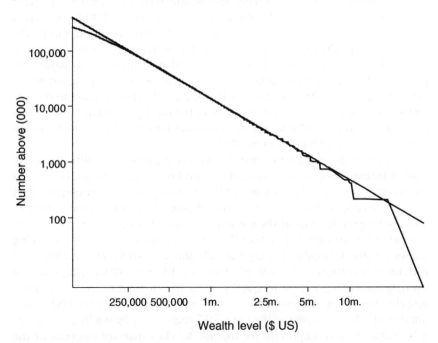

Figure 19.6. Fitted Pareto distribution

4 Trends over Time

This is the first comprehensive study of the world distribution of household wealth ever undertaken. Since our estimates are a snapshot for a single year, no time series exist on global wealth inequality. However, estimates of wealth inequality over time are available for several individual countries, and some comments can be made concerning changes over time in the size of international differences in wealth levels. It is interesting to look at the trends displayed by these pieces of the puzzle, although hazardous to draw conclusions about the trend in global wealth inequality on the basis of the limited evidence.

Long-time series of wealth inequality estimates are available for Denmark, France, Norway, Sweden, Switzerland, the USA, and the UK (see Ohlsson et al., Chapter 3, this volume). From the early years of the twentieth century up to the mid-1970s wealth inequality declined dramatically in all these countries, with the exception of Switzerland. This parallels the decline of income inequality observed over the same period. In contrast, wealth and income inequality have behaved somewhat differently during the last three decades. Increases in income inequality have been strong in the USA and UK, and have been observed in most OECD countries over this period. While the wealth share of the top 1 per cent also increased in most countries during this period (Ohlsson et al., Chapter 3, this volume), the increase in wealth inequality appears to have been generally weaker than that of income inequality. For example, in the USA, while there was a mild increase in wealth concentration between the mid-1970s and the mid-1980s, and a further increase in the late 1990s, inequality then fell, and the share of the top 1 per cent in 2001, at 33.4 per cent according to the Survey of Consumer Finance, did not differ much from the share of 33.8 per cent in 1983.

One part of the explanation for the weaker increase of wealth inequality than of income inequality at the country level is suggested by the findings of Piketty and Saez (2003) who show that the rise in top income shares in the USA in recent decades is due mostly to increased earnings dispersion rather than to increased capital income at the top end. In other words, increased executive compensation and the like, rather than higher returns to rentiers, is driving higher income inequality among the rich and super-rich. This is consistent with the observation of flat or slowly rising wealth inequality during a time of strongly increasing income inequality. A further element in the explanation probably lies in the large increases in house prices in the UK, the USA, and a number of other countries in the last 10–15 years. Housing is a 'popular' asset. It is relatively more important for the middle class than for the poor or the rich. Thus, increases in house prices tend to reduce top wealth shares and other measures of wealth inequality, thus opposing the trend towards higher wealth inequality coming from such sources as higher share prices.

There is also some evidence on between-country trends for the seven major OECD economies: Canada, France, Germany, Italy, Japan, the UK, and the USA. In 1994 the ratio of wealth to disposable income ranged from 4.72 for Canada to 7.47 for Japan. From 1994 to 1997 the unweighted dispersion fell for these countries, as the wealth–income ratio declined somewhat for Japan but rose for the other countries. After 1997 though, dispersion rose because of strong increases in wealth in France, Italy, and the UK, mostly associated with rising real-estate prices. As a result, this group of countries showed about the same dispersion in the wealth–income ratio in 2004 as they did in 1994.[20]

Among developing countries, only China and India offer the prospect of comparisons over time. There is no apparent upward or downward trend in wealth inequality in India, where results from a large asset and debt survey have been available at decennial intervals since 1981–2 (see Subramanian and Jayaraj 2006). On the other hand, wealth inequality has been rising at a strong pace in China, paralleling the rise of income inequality in that country. Between 1995 and 2002 the wealth Gini rose from 0.40 to 0.55 according to survey evidence. As noted earlier, the number of Chinese billionaires on the *Forbes* list has also been rising significantly in the last few years. The disequalizing effect on world wealth distribution is offset, however, by the rise in mean wealth in China, which reduces between-country wealth inequality. Hence the net impact of wealth trends in China on global wealth inequality is unclear.

Russia and the European transition countries also provide evidence of the link between rising wealth inequality and the shift from limited personal property under socialism to a market system (Guriev and Rachinsky, Chapter 7, and Yemtsov, Chapter 15, both this volume). However, the increase in wealth inequality in Central and Eastern Europe has been much less extreme than in Russia. Since the former countries have, on average, been experiencing reasonable economic growth in recent years, their mean wealth, which started from a low level, may have been rising fast enough to offset much of the impact of their higher wealth dispersion on global inequality. This cancellation has almost certainly not taken place for Russia, however, since its increase in wealth inequality has been extreme (see Guriev and Rachinsky, Chapter 7, this volume) and its growth performance has been relatively poor.

While it is difficult to predict future trends in global wealth inequality, a few observations may be offered. First, as in the past, growth in GDP is likely to remain a major determinant of both the overall level of global wealth and the distribution across regions and countries. However, growth in wealth levels may not exactly match income growth rates. Aggregate wealth levels depend heavily on asset prices, especially real-estate and equity values, and are also sensitive to institutional changes affecting property rights, such as moves towards privatization and property registration schemes. On the whole, it seems likely that wealth will grow faster than income in the medium and long run.

---

[20] The unweighted coefficient of variation in 2004 was 0.207, compared with 0.203 in 1994.

A second important factor concerns changes in exchange rates. Exchange-rate movements have little impact on global income inequality measured in PPP dollars, since the PPP currency conversions sterilize most of the change. But, if estimates of global wealth distribution employ official exchange rates, for the reasons discussed earlier, the impact could be significant, especially on the rankings of individual countries. Our estimates for the year 2000 are already likely to be out of date, given the subsequent relative decline in the US dollar. *Ceteris paribus*, figures for more recent years should reduce somewhat the dominance of the USA in the global wealth picture.

Whether wealth inequality will increase or subside in global terms also depends on wealth inequality trends in individual countries, on the level of wealth inequality in the faster growing countries, and on the population weight of the respective countries. Assembling these pieces of the puzzle suggests a crucial role for China during the next twenty years. Strong economic growth coupled with an expansion in private property opportunities provide the foundation for a significant rise in the average level of wealth, which in global terms is reinforced by the population size, but constrained by the managed currency peg to the US dollar. As Figure 19.4 makes clear, China is poised to make big inroads into the echelons of top wealth holders. The relative equality of wealth holdings in China means that even a modest rise in the average level of wealth relative to the rest of the world will promote many into the top global wealth decile, and, given time, into the top global percentile. Indeed, more up-to-date data may reveal that this movement has already begun in earnest.

Although India has a similar-sized population, it is unlikely that Indian nationals will rapidly occupy many of the global top wealth slots for two reasons. First, the recent growth experience has not matched that of China. Second, wealth inequality is much greater, so there are significantly fewer wealth holders who can expect to be promoted into the global top wealth decile. The contrast is captured by the thin right tail of India in Figure 19.4 compared with the fat pattern of China above the global median wealth.

Russia is another country whose super-rich have made headlines in recent years. However, it is unlikely that many Russians will be in evidence among the wealth elite of the world in, say twenty years time, at least compared to Chinese. The much smaller (and shrinking) population and the higher concentration of wealth are the two principal factors limiting the expansion of Russian membership of the global top wealth decile.

5 Conclusions

This chapter has provided a first estimate of the world distribution of household wealth. It is evident that the distribution is highly concentrated—in fact, much more concentrated than the world distribution of income, or the distribution of wealth within all but a few of the world's countries. While the share of the top 10 per cent of wealth holders within a country is typically about 50 per cent, and the median Gini value around 0.7, our figures for the year 2000 using official exchange rates suggest that, for the world as a whole, the share of the top 10 per cent was 85 per cent and the Gini equalled 0.892. By comparison, Milanovic (2005) estimates that the world income Gini was 0.795 in 1998. While wealth (and income) concentration is somewhat less when the estimates are done on a PPP basis, converting at official exchange rates is preferable for many purposes when studying wealth, given the large share of wealth owned by people who can readily travel and invest globally.

Much of the data used in this study derive from household surveys. This is not a big problem for the USA, which supplies 25 per cent of the world's top 10 per cent of wealth holders—sophisticated techniques have been used by the Federal Reserve Board to ensure the reliability of its triennial SCF. Less-striking, but still effective, steps have been adopted in some of the other wealthiest countries. While the super-rich are not represented in these data, this does not significantly compromise measures of the overall degree of inequality. On the other hand, surveys in the major developing countries appear to have difficulties capturing the upper tail. Thus, while we have reasonable confidence in our estimates, a non-negligible error bound is attributable to the limitations of household surveys.

The quality of our results also depends on other sources of data and on the procedures employed to estimate wealth levels and wealth inequality at country level. Full or partial data on household wealth exist for 39 countries, covering 61 per cent of the world's population and all the major OECD economies. The figures are often constructed in conjunction with Flow of Funds data or the National Accounts, suggesting a solid foundation of reliable numbers from financial institutions and government statistical agencies. This generates some confidence in the basic sources.

One of the most fascinating aspects of our results is the light they throw on the geographic distribution of world wealth and of the membership of the top wealth groups. About 34 per cent of the world's wealth was held in the USA and Canada in the year 2000, 30 per cent was held in Europe, and 24 per cent was in the rich Asia–Pacific group of countries. Africa, Central and South America, China, India, and other Asia–Pacific countries shared the remaining 12 per cent. The location of top wealth holders is even more concentrated, with North America hosting 39 per cent of the top global 1 per cent of wealth holders, and Europe and rich Asia–Pacific having 26 per cent and 32 per cent respectively. The high share of top wealth holders in North America is particularly disproportionate, as this region contains just 6 per cent of the world population.

Looking lower down in the global wealth distribution, India supplies about one-third of the bottom three deciles, while China contributes about a third of the people in the fourth to seventh deciles. Latin America is fairly evenly spread across all deciles, reflecting the fact that wealth inequality in the region mimics that in the world as a whole, according to our estimates. Africa and low-income Asia–Pacific are heavily present at the bottom. While North America and rich Asia–Pacific have little representation in the bottom deciles, this is not true for Europe, which comprises about 9 per cent of the world's population in the bottom three deciles.

Information on the geographic distribution of wealth holders produces some straightforward but revealing observations about possible future global trends. For example, if the rapid growth observed in China and India continues, it will probably have different consequences for the two countries' representation in different parts of the global distribution. With its large current representation in the middle wealth deciles, China is poised to contribute a greatly increased number of people to the top deciles, if its mean wealth continues to rise quickly. On the other hand, India has a relatively small number of people in the middle deciles compared with China, so the consequence of continued growth may be that Indians supplant the Chinese as the largest group in the middle-wealth range.

If current trends continue, the bottom deciles in the world wealth distribution may come to be increasingly dominated by Africa, Latin America, and low-income Asia–Pacific countries. While European transition countries are currently found among the bottom deciles, their increasing integration into Europe and fast growth in recent years suggest the likelihood of an upward movement of a large number of people from this region. The success of so many people in rapidly growing Asian countries is very positive in terms of global welfare, but continued low wealth for many in Africa, Latin America, and low-income Asia–Pacific countries is a real concern. From a global perspective, their wealth is relatively lower than income. This points to a serious problem, since these are precisely the countries where having sufficient household wealth is the most crucial, due to the shocks and uncertainty people experience, the lack of social safety nets, and the lack of opportunities to borrow or insure on reasonable terms. Hopefully, one consequence of our study will be to focus attention on developing and improving the institutions and policies needed in these regions to help ordinary people acquire adequate personal assets.

References

Abramovitz, M. (1964). *Evidence of Long Swings in Construction since the Civil War*, New York: National Bureau of Economic Research.

Acemoglu, D., and S. Johnson (2005). 'Unbundling Institutions', *Journal of Political Economy*, 113(5): 949–95.

Acemoglu, D., and J. A. Robinson (2001). 'Inefficient Redistribution', *American Political Science Review*, 95: 649–61.

Adams, M. (2003). 'Land Tenure Policy and Practice in Botswana: Governance Lessons for Southern Africa', *Austrian Journal of Development Studies*, 29(1): 55–74.

Agarwal, B. (1994). *A Field of One's Own*, Cambridge: Cambridge University Press.

Agarwal, B. (1997). 'Bargaining and Gender Relations: Within and Beyond the Household', *Feminist Economics*, 3(1): 1–51.

Agell, J., and M. Persson (1990). 'Tax Arbitrage and the Redistributive Properties of Progressive Income Taxation', *Economics Letters*, 34(4): 357–61.

Aghion, P., and P. Bolton (1997). 'A Theory of Trickle-Down Growth and Development', *Review of Economic Studies*, 64(2): 151–72.

Aghion, P., P. Howitt, and D. Mayer-Foulkes (2005). 'The Effect of Financial Development on Convergence: Theory and Evidence', *Quarterly Journal of Economics*, 120(1): 173–222.

Aiyagari, S. R. (1994). 'Uninsured Idiosyncratic Risk and Aggregate Saving', *Quarterly Journal of Economics*, 109: 659–84.

Aizcorbe, A. M., A. B. Kennickell, and K. B. Moore (2003). 'Recent Changes in US Family Finances: Evidence from the 1998 and 2001 Survey of Consumer Finances', *Federal Reserve Bulletin*, 89 (Jan.), 1–32.

Alesina, A., and D. Rodrik (1994). 'Distributive Politics and Economic Growth', *Quarterly Journal of Economics*, 109(2): 465–90.

Alessie, R., S. Hochguertel, and A. van Soest (2002). 'Household Portfolios in the Netherlands', in L. Guiso, M. Haliassos, and T. Jappelli (eds), *Household Portfolios*, Cambridge MA: MIT Press.

Alexeev, M. (1998). 'The Effect of Privatization on Wealth Distribution in Russia', Working Paper 86, William Davidson Institute, Ann Arbor.

Alexeev, M., and C. Gaddy (1993). 'Income Distribution in the USSR in the 1980s', *Review of Income and Wealth*, 39: 23–36.

Alexeyev, M., and W. Pyle (2003). 'A Note on Measuring the Unofficial Economy in the Former Soviet Republics', *Economics of Transition*, 11(1): 153–75.

Allen, F. (1982). 'On Share Contracts and Screening', *Bell Journal of Economics*, 13: 541–77.

Alston, L., and B. Mueller (2003). 'Property Rights to Land', *Oxford Encyclopedia of Economic History*, Oxford: Oxford University Press.

References

Alston, L., G. Libecap, and R. Schneider (1996). 'The Determinants and Impact of Property Rights: Land Titles on the Brazilian Frontier', *Journal of Law, Economics and Organization*, 12: 25–61.

Alvaredo, F., and E. Saez (2006). 'Income and Wealth Concentration in Spain in a Historical and Fiscal Perspective', CEPR Discussion Paper 5836, Centre for Economic Policy Research, London.

Amaral, P., and E. Quintin (2006). 'A Competitive Model of the Informal Sector', *Journal of Monetary Economics*, 53(7): 1541–53.

Ameriks, J., and S. P. Zeldes (2004). 'How Do Household Portfolio Shares Vary with Age?', available at: http://www.ifk-cfs.de/papers/rtn0505_paper_Ameriks_Zeldes.pdf (accessed 6 Feb. 2008)

Ammermüller, A., A. M. Weber, and P. Westerheide (2005). 'Die Entwicklund und Verteilung des Vermögens privater Haushalte under besonderer Berücksichtigung des Produktivvermögens', mimeo, Mannheim: ZEW.

Andreoni, J., Erard, B., and J. Feinstein (1998). 'Tax Compliance', *Journal of Economic Literature*, 36(2): 818–60.

Antonopoulos, R., and M. S. Floro (2005). 'Asset Ownership along Gender Lines: Evidence from Thailand', Gender, Equality, and the Economy Working Paper 418, Levy Economics Institute, Annandale-on-Hudson NY.

Antunes, A., and T. Cavalcanti (2007). 'Start Up Costs, Limited Enforcement, and the Hidden Economy', *European Economic Review*, 51(1): 203–24.

Aoki, K., J. Proudman, and G. Vlieghe (2002). 'Houses as Collateral: Has the Link between House Prices and Consumption in the UK Changed?', *Economic Policy Review*, 8(1): 163–77.

Arellano, J. (2000). 'Economic Growth, Fiscal Policy, and Social Impact in Chile', in A. Solimano, E. Aninat, and N. Birdsall (eds), *Distributive Justice and Economic Development*, Ann Arbor: University of Michigan Press.

Armendáriz de Aghion, B., and J. Morduch (2005). *The Economics of Microfinance*, Cambridge MA: MIT Press.

Aron, J., and J. Muellbauer (2000a). 'Personal and Corporate Saving in South Africa', *World Bank Economic Review*, 14(3): 509–44.

Aron, J., and J. Muellbauer (2000b). 'Financial Liberalization, Consumption and Debt in South Africa', Centre for the Study of African Economies Working Paper 2000.22, CSAE, Oxford University.

Aron, J., and J. Muellbauer (2004). 'Estimates of Personal Sector Wealth for South Africa', Centre for Economic Policy Research Working Paper 4646, Centre for Economic Policy Research, London.

Aron, J., and J. Muellbauer (2006a). 'Estimates of Household Sector Wealth for South Africa, 1970–2003', *Review of Income and Wealth*, 52(2): 285–308.

Aron, J., and J. Muellbauer (2006b). 'Housing Wealth, Credit Conditions and Consumption', Centre for the Study of African Economies Working Paper 2006.08, CSAE, Oxford University.

Aron, J., and J. Muellbauer (2008). 'Wealth, Credit Conditions and Consumption in South Africa', mimeo, Centre for Economic Policy Research, London (revision of Centre for the Studies of African Economies Working Paper 2006.08).

Aron, J., J. Muellbauer, and A. Murphy (2008). 'Housing Wealth, Credit Conditions and UK Consumption', mimeo, Centre for Economic Policy Research, London.

Aron, J., J. Muellbauer, and J. Prinsloo (2006). 'Estimating the Balance Sheet of the Personal Sector in an Emerging Market Country: South Africa 1975–2005', WIDER Research Paper 2006/99, UNU-WIDER, Helsinki.

Aron, J., J. Muellbauer, and B. Smit (2003). 'Understanding the Inflation Process in South Africa', Keynote Address, 8th Annual Conference on Econometric Modeling for Africa, Stellenbosch University, South Africa, 1–4 July. Available from www.csae.ox.ac.uk.

Aryeetey, E. (2004). 'Household Asset Choice among the Rural Poor in Ghana', paper prepared for the project on Understanding Poverty in Ghana organized by ISSER, University of Ghana and Cornell University, Jan.

Asselin, L. M. (2002). *Multidimensional Poverty: Composite Indicator of Multidimensional Poverty*, Lévis, Quebec: Institut de Mathématique Gauss.

Assunção, J. J. (2008). 'Rural Organization and Land Reform in Brazil: The Role of Nonagricultural Benefits of Landholding', *Economic Development and Cultural Change*, 56: 851–70.

Atkinson, A. B. (2004). 'Top Incomes in the UK over the Twentieth Century', *Journal of the Royal Statistical Society*, 168(2): 325–43.

Atkinson, A. B. (2007). 'Measuring Top Incomes: Methodological Issues', in A. B. Atkinson and T. Piketty (eds), *Top Incomes over the Twentieth Century: A Contrast between European and English-Speaking Countries*, Oxford: Oxford University Press.

Atkinson, A. B., and A. J. Harrison (1975). 'Mortality Multipliers and the Estate Duty Method', *Bulletin of the Oxford Institute of Economics and Statistics*, 37: 13–28.

Atkinson, A. B., and A. J. Harrison (1978). *The Distribution of Personal Wealth in Britain*, Cambridge: Cambridge University Press.

Atkinson, A. B., and A. Leigh (2007). 'The Distribution of Top Incomes in New Zealand', in A. B. Atkinson and T. Piketty (eds), *Top Incomes over the Twentieth Century: A Contrast between European and English-Speaking Countries*, Oxford: Oxford University Press.

Atkinson, A. B., and T. Piketty (2007) (eds). *Top Incomes over the Twentieth Century: A Contrast between European and English-Speaking Countries*, Oxford: Oxford University Press.

Atkinson, A. B., J. P. F. Gordon, and A. Harrison (1989). 'Trends in the Shares of Top Wealth-Holders in Britain: 1923–1989', *Oxford Bulletin of Economics and Statistics*, 51(3): 315–32.

Atkinson, A. B., L. Rainwater, and T. M. Smeeding (1995). 'Income Distribution in OECD Countries: Evidence from the Luxembourg Income Study (LIS)', *Social Policy Studies*, 18, Paris: OECD.

Attanasio, O., and J. Banks (2001). 'The Assessment: Household Savings: Issues in Theory and Policy', *Oxford Review of Economic Policy*, 17(1): 1–19.

Attanasio, O., and M. Szekely (2001) (eds). *Portrait of the Poor: An Asset-Based Approach*, Washington DC: Inter-American Development Bank.

Attanasio, O., L. Blow, R. Hamilton, and A. Leicester (2005). 'Booms and Busts: Consumption, House Prices and Expectations', Institute for Fiscal Studies Working Paper 05/24, Institute for Fiscal Studies, London.

Ayalew, D. (2003). 'Risk-Sharing Networks among Households in Rural Ethiopia', mimeo, Katholieke Universiteit, Leuven.

Babeau, A., and T. Sbano (2003). 'Household Wealth in the National Accounts of Europe, the United States and Japan', OECD Statistics Working Paper 2003/2, OECD, Paris.

Baekgaard, H. (1997). 'The Distribution of Household Wealth in Australia: New Estimates for 1986 and 1993', mimeo, National Centre for Social and Economic Modelling (NATSEM), University of Canberra.

Baekgaard, H., and A. King (1996). 'Modelling the Accumulation and Distribution of Australian Household Assets', paper presented to the 24th General Conference of the International Association for Research in Income and Wealth, Lillehammer.

Bager-Sjögren, L., and A. N. Klevmarken (1998). 'Inequality and Mobility of Wealth in Sweden 1983/84–1992/93', *Review of Income and Wealth*, 44(4): 473–95.

Bandiera, O., G. Caprio, P. Honohan, and F. Schianterelli (2000). 'Does Financial Reform Raise or Reduce Private Savings?', *Review of Economics and Statistics*, 82(2): 239–63.

Bandyopadhyay, D. (2003). 'Land Reforms and Agriculture: The West Bengal Experience', *Economic and Political Weekly*, 1 Mar.: 879–84.

Banerjee, A. V., and A. F. Newman (1993). 'Occupational Choice and the Process of Development', *Journal of Political Economy*, 101(2): 274–98.

Banerjee, A. V., and T. Piketty (2003). 'Top Indian Incomes, 1956–2000', BREAD Working Paper 46, Bureau for Research in Economic Analysis of Development, Harvard University, Cambridge MA.

Banerjee, A. V., P. J. Gertler, and M. Ghatak (2002). 'Empowerment and Efficiency: Tenancy Reform in West Bengal', *Journal of Political Economy*, 110(2): 239–80.

Banks, J., Z. Smith, and M. Wakefield (2002). 'The Distribution of Financial Wealth in The UK: Evidence from 2000 BHPS Data', Institute for Fiscal Studies Working Paper 02–21, University College, London.

Bardhan, P., S. Bowles, and H. Gintis (2000). 'Wealth Inequality, Wealth Constraints and Economic Performance', in A. B. Atkinson and F. Bourguignon (eds), *Handbook of Income Distribution*, vol. 1, Amsterdam: Elsevier.

Barker, K. (2003). *Barker Review of Housing Supply*, London: HM Treasury.

Barker, K. (2004). *Barker Review of Housing Supply*, London: HM Treasury.

Barker, K. (2006). *Barker Review of Land Use Planning*, London: HM Treasury.

Barrell, R., and E. P. Davis (2004). 'Consumption, Financial and Real Wealth in the G5', NIESR Discussion Paper 232, National Institute of Economic and Social Research, London.

Bauer, J., and A. Mason (1992). 'The Distribution of Income and Wealth in Japan', *Review of Income and Wealth*, 38(2): 403–28.

Bayoumi, T. (1993a). 'Financial Deregulation and Consumption in the United Kingdom', *Review of Economics and Statistics*, 75(3): 536–9.

Bayoumi, T. (1993b). 'Financial Deregulation and Household Saving', *Economic Journal*, 103(421): 1432–43.

Beck, T., and L. Laeven (2006). 'Institution Building and Growth in Transition Economies', CEPR Discussion Paper 5718, Centre for Economic Policy Research, London.

Beck, T., A. Demirgüç-Kunt, and R. Levine (2004). 'Finance, Inequality and Poverty: Cross Country Evidence', World Bank Policy Research Working Paper 3338, World Bank, Washington DC.

Beck, T., M. S. Martinez Peria, and A. Demirgüç-Kunt (2007). 'Reaching Out: Access to and Use of Banking Services across Countries', *Journal of Financial Economics*, 85(1): 234–66.

Becker, G. S., and N. Tomes (1979). 'An Equilibrium Theory of the Distribution of Income and Intergenerational Mobility', *Journal of Political Economy*, 87(6): 1153–89.

Beegle, K., E. Frankenberg, and D. Thomas (2001). 'Bargaining Power within Couples and Use of Prenatal and Delivery Care in Indonesia', *Studies in Family Planning*, 32(2): 130–46.

Benito, A., J. Thompson, M. Waldron, and R. Wood (2006). 'House Prices and Consumer Spending', *Bank of England Quarterly Bulletin*, Summer: 142–54.

Bennett, S., and D. Bowers (1976). *An Introduction to Multivariate Techniques for Social and Behavioural Sciences*, New York: Wiley.

Bentzen, J., and J. B. Schmidt-Sørensen (1994). 'Wealth Distribution and Mobility in Denmark: A Longitudinal Study', CLS Working Paper 4, Aarhus School of Business, Aarhus.

Beresford, P. (1990). *The Sunday Times Book of the Rich: Britain's 400 Richest People*, London: Weidenfeld and Nicolson.

Beresford, P. (1991). *The Sunday Times Book of the Rich*, Harmondsworth: Penguin.

Berg, L. (1994). 'Household Savings and Debts: The Experience of the Nordic Countries', *Oxford Review of Economic Policy*, 10(2): 42–53.

Berglof, E., and P. Bolton (2002). 'The Great Divide and Beyond: Financial Architecture in Transition', *Journal of Economic Perspectives*, 16(1): 77–100.

Bergstresser, D., and J. Poterba (2004). 'Asset Allocation and Asset Location: Household Evidence from the Survey of Consumer Finances', *Journal of Public Economics*, 88: 1893–915.

Bernal, P. (2006). Personal correspondence.

Berry, R. A., and W. R. Cline (1979). *Agrarian Structure and Productivity in Developing Countries*, Baltimore: Johns Hopkins University Press.

Bertaud, A., and B. Renaud (1997). 'Socialist Cities without Land Markets', *Journal of Urban Economics*, 41(1): 137–51.

Bertaut, C. C., and M. Starr-McCluer (2002). 'Household Portfolios in the United States', in L. Guiso, M. Haliassos, and T. Jappelli (eds), *Household Portfolios*, Cambridge MA: MIT Press.

Besley, T. (1995). 'Property Rights and Investment Incentives: Theory and Evidence from Ghana', *Journal of Political Economy*, 103(5): 903–37.

Besley, T., and R. Burgess (2000). 'Land Reform, Poverty Reduction, and Growth: Evidence from India', *Quarterly Journal of Economics*, 115(2): 389–430.

Bevan, P., and A. Pankhurst (1996). *Report on the Sociological Dimension of the Ethiopian Rural Economies Project: CSAE and AAU Research Report*, Mar., Oxford: Centre for the Study of African Economies, University of Oxford.

Bhide, S., and A. K. Mehta (2006). 'Correlates of Incidence and Exit from Chronic Poverty in India: Evidence from Panel Data', in A. K. Mehta and A. Sheperd, *Chronic Poverty and Development Policy in India*, London: Sage.

Bigsten, A., and A. Shimeles (2004). 'Dynamics of Poverty in Ethiopia', WIDER Research Paper 2004/39, UNU-WIDER, Helsinki.

Bigsten, A., B. Kebede, A. Shimeles, and M. Taddesse (2003). 'Growth and Poverty Reduction in Ethiopia: Evidence from Household Panel Surveys', *World Development*, 31(1): 87–106.

Binswanger, H. P., and K. Deininger (1997). 'Explaining Agricultural and Agrarian Policies in Developing Countries', *Journal of Economic Literature*, 35(4): 1958–2005.

Birdsall, N., and J. L. Londono (1997). 'Asset Inequality Does Matter: Lessons from Latin America', OCE Working Paper 344, Inter-American Development Bank, Washington DC.

Bjeloglav, D., H. David, G. Krstić, and G. Matković (2007). *LSMS Project 2002–2003: Life in Serbia through Survey Data*, Belgrade: Strategic Marketing.

Bjerke, K. (1956). 'Changes in Danish Income Distribution 1939–52', *Income and Wealth*, 4: 98–154.

Black, J., D. de Meza, and D. Jeffreys (1996). 'House Prices, the Supply of Collateral and the Enterprise Economy', *Economic Journal*, 106(434): 60–75.

Blanchard, O. (1985). 'Debt, Deficits and Finite Horizons', *Journal of Political Economy*, 93(2): 223–47.

Blinder, A. S. (1973). 'A Model of Inherited Wealth', *Quarterly Journal of Economics*, 87: 608–26.

Blinder, A. S., and A. Deaton (1985). 'The Time Series Consumption Function Revisited', *Brookings Papers on Economic Activity*, 2: 465–511.

Boehm, T. P., and A. M. Scholttman (1999). 'Does Home Ownership by Parents have an Economic Impact on their Children?', *Journal of Housing Economics*, 8: 217–32.

Bongaarts, J. (2001). 'Household Size and Composition in the Developing World in the 1990s', *Population Studies*, 55(3): 263–79.

Boone, L., N. Girouard, and I. Wanner (2001). 'Financial Market Liberalization, Wealth and Consumption', OECD Economics Department Working Paper 308, OECD, Paris.

Boone, P., and D. Rodionov (2002). *Rent Seeking in Russia and the CIS*, Brunswick UBS, Moscow: Warburg.

Booysen, F., S. van der Berg, R. Burger, M. von Maltitz, and G. du Rand (2006). 'Trends in Poverty and Inequality in Seven African Countries', paper presented at the Third General Meeting of the Poverty and Economic Policy (PEP) Network, Dakar, 16–20 June.

Booysen, F., S. van der Berg, R. Burger, M. von Maltitz, and G. du Rand (2008). 'Using an Asset Index to Assess Trends in Poverty in Seven Sub-Saharan African Countries', *World Development*, 36(6): 1113–30.

Bostic, R., S. Gabriel, and G. Painter (2005). 'Housing Wealth, Financial Wealth, and Consumption: New Evidence from Micro Data', mimeo, Lusk Center for Real Estate, Singapore.

Botero, J., S. Djankov, R. La Porta, F. Lopez-de-Silanes, and A. Schleifer (2003). 'The Regulation of Labour', NBER Working Paper 9756, National Bureau of Economic Research, Cambridge MA.

Bourguignon, F., and C. Morrison (2002). 'Inequality among World Citizens: 1820–1992', *American Economic Review*, 92(4): 727–44.

Bourguignon, F., F. Ferreira, and P. Leite (2003). 'Conditional Cash Transfers, Schooling, and Child Labor: Micro-Simulating Brazil's Bolsa Escola Program', *World Bank Economic Review*, 17(2): 229–54.

Boutchkova, M. K., and W. L. Megginson (2000). 'Privatization and the Rise of Global Capital Markets', *Financial Management*, 29: 31–76.

Bover, O. (2005). 'Wealth Effects on Consumption: Microeconometric Estimates from the Spanish Survey of Household Finances', Documentos de Trabajo 0522, Bank of Spain, Madrid.

Brandolini, A., L. Cannari, G. D'Alessio, and I. Faiella (2004). 'Household Wealth Distribution in Italy in the 1990s', Temi di discussione, Banca d'Italia, Rome.

Brandolini, A., E. Sierminska, and T. M. Smeeding (2006). 'The Luxembourg Wealth Study: A Cross-Country Comparable Database for Wealth', *Journal of Economic Inequality*, 4(3): 323–32.

Brasselle, A., F. Gaspart, and J. Platteau (2002). 'Land Tenure Security and Investment Incentives: Puzzling Evidence from Burkina Faso', *Journal of Development Economics*, 67 (2): 373–418.

Brenner, M. (2001). 'Re-examining the Distribution of Wealth in Rural China', in C. Riskin, R. Zhao, and S. Li (eds), *China's Retreat from Equality*, New York: M. E. Sharpe.

Breza, E. (2005). 'Intrahousehold Resource Allocation in Hausa-Speaking Nigeria: Uncovering Gender Asymmetries of Wealth and Savings Behavior', mimeo, Yale University Economics Department, New Haven.

Browning, M., and A. Lusardi (1996). 'Household Saving: Micro Theory and Micro Facts', *Journal of Economic Literature*, 34(4): 1797–855.

Buckley, R. M. (1994). 'Housing Finance in Developing Countries: The Role of Credible Contracts', *Economic Development and Cultural Change*, 42(2): 317–32.

Buckley, R. M., and E. Gurenko (1997). 'Housing and Income Distribution in Russia: Zhivago's Legacy', *World Bank Research Observer*, 12(1): 19–32.

Buckley, R. M., and J. Kalarickal (2005). 'Housing Prices in Developing Countries: Conjectures and Refutations', *World Bank Research Observer*, 20(2): 233–57.

Buckley, R. M., and J. Kalarickal (2006). *Thirty Years of World Bank Shelter Lending: What Have We Learned?*, Washington DC: World Bank.

Bucks, B. K., and K. Pence (2005). 'Measuring Housing Wealth', paper prepared for the LWS conference on Construction and Usage of Comparable Microdata on Wealth, Perugia, 27–29 Jan.

Bucks, B. K., A. B. Kennickell, and K. B. Moore (2006). 'Recent Changes in US Family Finances: Evidence from the 2001 and 2004 Survey of Consumer Finances', *Federal Reserve Bulletin*, 92: A1–A38.

Bueno, E. (1999). 'Capitães do Brasil: A saga dos Primeiros Colonizadores', *Coleção Terra Brasilis*, vol. 3, Rio de Janeiro: Objetiva.

Burger, R., F. Booysen, S. van der Berg, and M. von Maltitz (2006). 'Marketable Wealth in a Poor African Country: Using an Index of Consumer Durables to Investigate Wealth Accumulation by Households in Ghana', WIDER Research Paper 2006/138, Helsinki: UNU-WIDER.

Business Standard (2005). 'Ranking'. Available at www.business-standard.com/special/billion/2005/bill05_02.pdf.

Byrne, J. P., and P. E. Davis (2003). 'Disaggregate Wealth and Aggregate Consumption: An Investigation of Empirical Relationships for the G7', *Oxford Bulletin*, 65(2): 197–220.

Cagetti, M., and M. De Nardi (2005). 'Wealth Inequality: Data and Models', Federal Reserve Bank of Chicago Working Paper 2005-10, Federal Reserve Bank of Chicago, Chicago.

Cagetti, M., and M. De Nardi (2006). 'Entrepreneurship, Frictions, and Wealth', *Journal of Political Economy*, 114(5): 835–70.

Cahill, K. (2006). *Who Owns the World? The Hidden Facts behind Landownership*, Edinburgh and London: Mainstream Publishing.

Cameron, G., and J. Muellbauer (2000). 'Earnings Biases in the United Kingdom Regional Accounts: Some Economic Policy and Research Implications', *Economic Journal*, 110: F412–29.

Cameron, G., J. Muellbauer, and A. Murphy (2006). 'Was There a British House Price Bubble? Evidence from a Regional Panel', CEPR Discussion Paper 5619, Centre for Economic Policy Research, London.

Campbell, J. Y. (2006). 'Household Finance', *Journal of Finance*, 61(4): 1553–604.

Campbell, J. Y., and J. F. Cocco (2005). 'How Do House Prices Affect Consumption? Evidence from Micro Data', NBER Working Paper 11534, National Bureau of Economic Research, Cambridge MA.

Carbó, S., E. P. M. Gardener, and P. Molyneux (2005). *Financial Exclusion*, Basingstoke: Palgrave Macmillan.

Cardoso, E., and A. Helwege (1992). *Latin America's Economy: Diversity, Trends, and Conflicts*, Cambridge MA: MIT Press.

Carroll, C. D. (1997). 'Buffer-Stock Saving and the Life Cycle/Permanent Income Hypothesis', *Quarterly Journal of Economics*, 112(1): 1–55.

Carroll, C. D. (2001). 'A Theory of the Consumption Function, with and without Liquidity Constraints', *Journal of Economics Perspectives*, 15(3): 23–45.

Carroll, C. D. (2002). 'Portfolios of the Rich', in L. Guiso, M. Haliassos, and T. Jappelli (eds), *Household Portfolios*, Cambridge MA: MIT Press.

Carroll, C. D., and A. Samwick (1998). 'How Important is Precautionary Saving?', *Review of Economics and Statistics*, 80(3): 410–19.

Carroll, C. D., M. Otsuka, and J. Slacalek (2006). 'How Large Is the Housing Wealth Effect? A New Approach', Economics Working Paper 535, Johns Hopkins University, Baltimore.

Carter, M., and P. Olinto (2003). 'Getting Institutions Right for Whom? Credit Constraints and the Impact of Property Rights on the Quantity and Composition of Investment', *American Journal of Agricultural Economics*, 85(1): 173–86.

Carter, M. R., and E. Zegarra (2000). 'Land Markets and the Persistence of Rural Poverty in Latin America: Post-Liberalization Policy Options', in A. Valdes and R. Lopez (eds), *Rural Poverty in Latin America: Analytics, New Empirical Evidence and Policy*, Basingstoke: Macmillan.

Case, K. E., J. M. Quigley, and R. J. Shiller (2005). 'Comparing Wealth Effects: The Stock Market versus the Housing Market', *Advances in Macroeconomics*, 5(1): 1235–47.

Casteneda, A., J. Diaz-Gimenez, and J.-V. Rios-Rull (2003). 'Accounting for USA Earnings and Wealth Inequality', *Journal of Political Economy*, 111(4): 818–57.

Catte, P., N. Girouard, R. Price, and C. André (2004). 'Housing Markets, Wealth and the Business Cycle', OECD Economics Department Working Paper 394, OECD, Paris.

Chawla, R. (1990). 'The Distribution of Wealth in Canada and the United States', *Perspectives on Labor and Income*, 2(1): 29–41.

Chen, C.-N., T.-W. Tsaur, and T.-S. Rhai (1987). 'The Gini Coefficient and Negative Income', *Oxford Economic Papers*, 34(3): 473–8.

Chen, S., G. Datt, and M. Ravallion (1991). 'POVCAL: A Programme for Calculating Poverty Measures from Grouped Data', DEC-RG, World Bank, Washington DC.

Cheung, S. N. S. (1969). *The Theory of Share Tenancy*, Chicago: University of Chicago Press.

Chickering, L. A., and M. Salahdine (1991) (eds). *The Silent Revolution: The Informal Sector in Five Asian and Near Eastern Countries*, San Francisco: ICS Press.

Chiuri, M. C., and T. Jappelli (2003). 'Financial Market Imperfections and Home Ownership: A Comparative Study', *European Economic Review*, 47(5): 857–75.

Choi, J. P., and M. P. Thum (2005). 'Corruption and the Shadow Economy', *International Economic Review*, 46: 817–36.

Christen, R. P., V. Jayadeva, and R. Rosenberg (2004). 'Financial Institutions with a Double Bottom Line: Implications for the Future of Microfinance', CGAP Occasional Paper 8, CGAP, Washington DC.

Christensen, H. M. (2003). *Skatteberegningsreglerne gennem 100 år*, Copenhagen: Skatteministeriet.

Claessens, S. (2006). 'Access to Financial Services: A Review of the Issues and Public Policy Objectives', *World Bank Policy Research Observer*, 21(2): 207–40.

Coghlan, T. (1906). 'Discussion', *Journal of the Royal Statistical Society*, 69: 735–6.

Coles, S. (2001). *An Introduction to Statistical Modelling of Extreme Values*, London: Springer.

Collier, P., and J. W. Gunning (1999a). 'Explaining African Economic Performance', *Journal of Economic Literature*, 37: 64–111.

Collier, P., and J. W. Gunning (1999b). 'The Microeconomics of African Growth, 1950–2000', thematic paper for the AERC Collaborative Research Project on Explaining African Economic Growth, 1950–2000.

Commander, S., and M. Schankerman (1997). 'Enterprise Restructuring and Social Benefits', *Economics of Transition*, 5(1): 1–24.

Commander, S., A. Tolstopiatenko, and R. Yemtsov (1999). 'Channels of Redistribution: Inequality and Poverty in the Russian Transition', *Economics of Transition*, 7(2): 411–47.

Conning, J. (2001). 'Latifundia Economics', mimeo, Department of Economics, Williams College, Williamstown MA.

Conning, J., and J. A. Robinson (2001). 'Land Reform and the Political Organization of Agriculture', mimeo, Department of Economics, Williams College, Williamstown MA.

Coricelli, F., B. Égert, and R. MacDonald (2005). 'Monetary Transmission Mechanism in Central and Eastern Europe: Surveying the Empirical Evidence', presented at the Finance and Consumption conference on Credit, Consumption and the Macro Economy, 14–15 Oct., European University Institute, Florence.

Cowell, F. A. (1995). *Measuring Inequality*, Hemel Hempstead: Harvester Wheatsheaf.

Croft, T. (n.d.). 'DHS Data Editing and Imputation: Demographic and Health Surveys', available from www.measuredhs.com.

Cuming, R. C., C. Walsh, and R. J. Wood (2005). *Personal Property Security Law: Essentials of Canadian Law*, Toronto: Irwin Law.

Danziger, S., P. Gottschalk, and E. Smolensky (1989). 'How the Rich Have Fared, 1973–87', *American Economic Review, Papers and Proceedings*, 79: 310–14.

Datta, N. (2006). 'Joint Titling: A Win–Win Policy? Gender and Property Rights in Urban Informal Settlements in Chandigarh, India', *Feminist Economics*, 2(1–2): 271–98.

Davies, J. B. (1993). 'The Distribution of Wealth in Canada', in E. Wolff (ed.), *Research in Economic Inequality*, vol. 4, Greenwich CT: JAI Press, 159–80.

Davies, J. B., and A. F. Shorrocks (2000). 'The Distribution of Wealth', in A. B. Atkinson and F. Bourguignon (eds), *Handbook of Income Distribution*, vol. 1, Amsterdam: Elsevier.

Davies, J. B., and A. F. Shorrocks (2005). 'Wealth Holdings in Developing and Transition Countries', paper presented at the Luxembourg Wealth Study conference on Construction and Usage of Comparable Microdata on Wealth, 27–29 Jan., Perugia.

Davies, J. B., S. Sandström, A. F. Shorrocks, and E. N. Wolff (2007). 'Estimating the Level and Distribution of Global Household Wealth', WIDER Research Paper 2007/77, UNU-WIDER, Helsinki.

De Ferranti, D., F. Ferreira, G. Perry, and M. Walton (2004). *Inequality in Latin America and the Caribbean. Breaking with History?*, Washington DC: World Bank.

de Janvry, A., N. Key, and E. Sadoulet (1997). 'Agricultural and Rural Development Policy in Latin America: New Directions and New Challenges', *FAO Agricultural Policy and Economic Development Series* 2, FAO, Rome.

De Long, J. B. (1996). 'Billionaires', www.j-bradford-delong.net/Econ_Articles/billion aires.html (accessed 6 Feb. 2008).

de Soto, H. (1989). *The Other Path: The Economic Answer to Terrorism*, New York: Harper & Row (also published as *The Other Path: The Invisible Revolution in the Third World*).

de Soto, H. (2000). *The Mystery of Capital: Why Capitalism Triumphs in the West and Fails Everywhere Else*, New York: Basic Books.

Dean, W. (1971). 'Latifundia and Land Policy in Nineteenth Century Brazil', *Hispanic-American Historical Review*, 51(4): 606–25.

Deaton, A. (1990). 'Saving in Developing Countries: Theory and Review', *World Bank Economic Review*, Proceedings of the World Bank Annual Conference on Development Economics 1989, Washington DC: World Bank.

Deaton, A. (1992). *Understanding Consumption*, Oxford: Clarendon Press.

Deaton, A. (1997). *The Analysis of Household Surveys: A Microeconometric Approach to Development Policy*, Baltimore: Johns Hopkins University Press.

Deere, C. D., and C. Doss (2006). 'The Gender Asset Gap: What Do We Know and Why Does It Matter?', *Feminist Economics*, 12(1–2): 1–50.

Deere, C. D., and M. León (2001a). *Empowering Women: Land and Property Rights in Latin America*, Pittsburgh: University of Pittsburgh Press.

Deere, C. D., and M. León (2001b). 'Who Owns the Land? Gender and Land-Titling Programmes in Latin America', *Journal of Agrarian Change*, 1(3): 440–67.

Deere, C. D., and M. León (2003). 'The Gender Asset Gap: Land in Latin America', *World Development*, 31(6): 925–47.

Deere, C. D., and M. León (2005). 'The Impact of Liberalism on Married Women's Property Rights in Nineteenth Century Latin America', *Hispanic American Historical Review*, 85(4): 627–78.

Deere, C. D., R. L. Duran, M. Mardon, T. Masterson with M. Correia (2005). 'Women's Land Rights and Rural Household Incomes in Brazil, Paraguay and Peru', *Agriculture and Rural Development Internal Report*, Washington DC: World Bank.

Dehejia, R. H., and R. Gatti (2005). 'Child Labour: The Role of Income Variability and Access to Credit in a Cross Section of Countries', *Economic Development and Cultural Change*, 53(4): 913–32.

Deininger, K. (1998). 'Making Negotiated Land Reform Work: Initial Experience from Colombia', mimeo, World Bank, Washington DC.

Deininger, K. (2003). *Land Policies for Growth and Poverty Reduction*, New York: Oxford University Press for the World Bank.

Deininger, K., and G. Feder (2001). 'Land Institutions and Land Markets', in B. L. Gardner and G. C. Rausser (eds), *Handbook of Agricultural Economics*, Amsterdam: Elsevier.

Deininger, K., and J. May (2000). 'Is there Scope for Growth with Equity?', CSDS Working Paper 29, Centre for Security and Defence Studies, Carleton University.

Deininger, K., and P. Olinto (2000). 'Asset Distribution, Inequality, and Growth', World Bank Policy Research Department Working Paper 2375, World Bank, Washington DC.

Deininger, K., and L. Squire (1998). 'New Ways of Looking at Old Issues: Inequality and Growth', *Journal of Development Economics*, 57: 259–87.

Deininger, K., R. van den Brink, H. Hoogeveen, and S. Moyo (2000). *How Land Reform can Contribute to Economic Growth and Poverty Reduction: Empirical Evidence from International and Zimbabwean Experience*, Washington DC: World Bank.

Dell, F. (2007). 'Top Incomes in Germany throughout the Twentieth Century', in A. B. Atkinson and T. Piketty (eds), *Top Incomes over the Twentieth Century: A Contrast between European and English-Speaking Countries*, Oxford: Oxford University Press.

Dell, F., T. Piketty, and E. Saez (2007). 'Income and Wealth Concentration in Switzerland over the Twentieth Century', in A. B. Atkinson and T. Piketty (eds), *Top Incomes over the Twentieth Century: A Contrast between European and English-Speaking Countries*, Oxford: Oxford University Press.

Demirgüç-Kunt, A., and R. Levine (2001). *Financial Structure and Growth: A Cross-Country Comparison of Banks, Markets and Development*, Cambridge MA: MIT Press.

Demirgüç-Kunt, A., T. Beck, and P. Honohan (2007). *Finance for All? Policies and Pitfalls in Expanding Access*, Washington DC: World Bank.

Demsetz, H. (1967). 'Toward a Theory of Property Rights', *American Economic Review Papers & Proceedings*, 57(2): 347–59.

Dercon, S. (1996). 'Risk, Crop Choice, and Savings: Evidence from Tanzania', *Economic Development and Cultural Change*, 44(3): 485–513.

Dercon, S. (1998). 'Wealth, Risk and Activity Choice: Cattle in Western Tanzania', *Journal of Development Economics*, 55(1): 1–42.

Dercon, S. (2001). 'The Impact of Economic Reforms on Households in Rural Ethiopia 1989–1995', mimeo, University of Oxford, Oxford.

Dercon, S. (2004). 'Growth and Shocks: Evidence from Rural Ethiopia', *Journal of Development Economics*, 74(2): 309–29.

Dercon, S., and P. Krishnan (1996). 'Income Portfolios in Rural Ethiopia and Tanzania: Choices and Constraints', *Journal of Development Studies*, 32(6): 850–75.

Dercon, S., and P. Krishnan (1998). 'Changes in Poverty in Rural Ethiopia 1989–1995: Measurement, Robustness Tests and Decomposition', CSAE Working Paper 98-7, Centre for the Study of African Economies, University of Oxford, Oxford.

Dercon, S., and P. Krishnan (2000). 'Vulnerability, Seasonality and Poverty in Ethiopia', *Journal of Development Studies*, 36(6): 25–53.

Dessy, S., and S. Pallage (2003). 'Taxes, Inequality and the Size of the Informal Sector', *Journal of Development Economics*, 70: 225–33.

Diaz, A., and M. J. Luengo-Prado (2003). 'Durable Goods and the Wealth Distribution', mimeo, Universidad Carlos III and Northeastern University.

Dilnot, A. W. (1990). 'The Distribution and Composition of Personal Sector Wealth in Australia', *Australian Economic Review*, 1: 33–40.

DiMartino, D., and J. V. Duca (2007) 'The Rise and Fall of Subprime Mortgages', *Economic Letter*, 2(11): 1–8.

Djankov, S., R. La Porta, F. Lopez-de-Silanes, and A. Schleifer (2002). 'The Regulation of Entry', *Quarterly Journal of Economics*, 117: 1–37.

Djankov, S., C. McLiesh, and A. Shleifer (2007). 'Private Credit in 129 Countries', *Journal of Financial Economics*, 84(2): 299–329.

Do, Q., and L. Iyer (2002). 'Land Rights and Economic Development: Evidence from Vietnam', mimeo, Massachusetts Institute of Technology, Cambridge MA.

Doss, C. R. (2001). 'Is Risk Fully Pooled within the Household? Evidence from Ghana', *Economic Development and Cultural Change*, 50: 101–30.

Doss, C. R. (2006a). 'The Effects of Intrahousehold Property Ownership on Expenditure Patterns in Ghana', *Journal of African Economies*, 15: 149–80.

Doss, C. R. (2006b). 'Women and Land in Ghana', paper presented at the meeting of the International Association of Feminist Economics, Sydney, July.

Dübel, H.-J., W. J. Brzeski, and E. Hamilton (2005). *Rental Choice and Housing Policy Realignment in Transition: Post-Privatization Challenges in the Europe and Central Asia Region*, Washington DC: World Bank.

Ducci, M. E. (2000). 'Chile: The Dark Side of a Successful Housing Policy', in J. Tulchin and A. Garland (eds), *Social Development in Latin America*, Boulder CO: Lynne Rienner.

Duflo, E. (2000). 'Grandmothers and Granddaughters: Old-Age Pension and Intrahousehold Allocation in South Africa', mimeo, Department of Economics, Massachusetts Institute of Technology, Cambridge MA.

Dvornak, N., and M. Kohler (2003). 'Housing Wealth, Stock Market Wealth and Consumption: A Panel Analysis for Australia', Reserve Bank of Australia Research Discussion Paper 07.

Earle, J., and K. Sabirianova (2002). 'How Late to Pay? Understanding Wage Arrears in Russia', *Journal of Labour Economics*, 20(3): 661–707.

Eichen, M., and M. Zhang (1994). 'The 1988 Household Sample Survey: Data Description and Availability', in E. K. Griffin and R. Zhao (eds), *The Distribution of Income in China*, London: Macmillan Press.

Ellerman, D. (2001). 'Lessons from Eastern Europe's Voucher Privatization', *Challenge*, 44(4): 14–37.

Engelhardt, G., and C. Mayer (1998). 'Intergenerational Transfers, Borrowing Constraints, and Saving Behavior: Evidence from the Housing Market', *Journal of Urban Economics*, 44: 135–57.

Engelhardt, G. V. (1996). 'Consumption, Down Payments and Liquidity Constraints', *Journal of Money Credit and Banking*, 28(2): 255–71.

Engerman, S., and K. Sokoloff (1997). 'Factor Endowments, Institutions, and Differential Paths of Growth among New World Economies', in S. Haber (ed.), *How Latin America Fell Behind: Essays on the Economic Histories of Brazil and Mexico 1800–1914*, Palo Alto CA: Stanford University Press.

Engerman, S., and K. Sokoloff (2002). 'Factor Endowments, Inequality, and Paths of Development among New World Economies', *Economia*, 3(1): 41–109.

Engerman, S., S. Haber, and K. Sokoloff (2000). 'Inequality, Institutions, and Differential Paths of Growth among New World Economies', in C. Menard (ed.), *Institutions, Contracts, and Organizations*, Cheltenham: Edward Elgar.

Engerman, S., E. Mariscal, and K. Sokoloff (1999). 'The Persistence of Inequality in the Americas: Schooling and Suffrage, 1800–1945', mimeo, University of California at Los Angeles.

Erickson, L., and D. Vollrath (2004). 'Dimensions of Land Inequality and Economic Development', *International Monetary Fund Working Paper* 04/158, IMF, Washington DC.

Escobal, J., J. Saavedra, and M. Torero (2001). 'Distribution, Access and Complementarity: Capital of the Poor in Peru', in O. Attanasio and M. Szekely (eds), *Portrait of the Poor: An Assets-Based Approach*, Washington DC: Inter-American Development Bank.

Esping-Andersen, G. (1990). *The Three Worlds of Welfare Capitalism*, Princeton: Princeton University Press.

Esposito, J. L., with N. J. De Long-Bas (2001). *Women in Muslim Family Law*, Syracuse NY: University of Syracuse Press.

Eswaran, M., and A. Kotwal (1985). 'A Theory of Contractual Structure in Agriculture', *American Economic Review*, 75(3): 352–67.

European Commission (2005). 'Public Opinion in Europe on Financial Services', *Special Eurobarometer*, 230, available online via: http://ec.europa.eu/consumers/index_en.htm (accessed 6 Feb. 2008).

Eurostat (2005). 'HBS and EU-SILC Imputed Rent', paper prepared for the First Meeting of the Working Group on Living Conditions, 8–10 June, Luxembourg.

Evans, D. S., and B. Jovanovic (1989). 'An Estimated Model of Entrepreneurial Choice under Liquidity Constraints', *Journal of Political Economy*, 97(4): 808–27.

Eymann, A., and A. Börsch-Supan (2002). 'Household Portfolios in Germany', in L. Guiso, M. Haliassos, and T. Jappelli (eds), *Household Portfolios*, Cambridge MA: MIT Press.

Fafchamps, M. (1999). 'Rural Poverty, Risk and Development', FAO Economic and Social Development Paper 144, Food and Agriculture Organization, Rome.

Fafchamps, M. (2003). 'Inequality and Risk', *Department of Economics Discussion Paper* 144, University of Oxford, Oxford.

Fafchamps, M., and A. R. Quisumbing (2002). 'Control and Ownership of Assets within Rural Ethiopian Households', *Journal of Development Studies*, 38(6): 47–82.

Fafchamps, M., and A. R. Quisumbing (2005a). 'Assets at Marriage in Rural Ethiopia', *Journal of Development Economics*, 77(1): 1–25.

Fafchamps, M., and A. R. Quisumbing (2005b). 'Marriage, Bequest, and Assortative Matching in Rural Ethiopia', *Economic Development and Cultural Change*, 53(2): 347–80.

Fafchamps, M., C. Udry, and K. Czukas (1998). 'Drought and Saving in West Africa: Are Livestock a Buffer Stock?', *Journal of Development Economics*, 55(2): 273–305.

FAO (1990). Food and Agriculture Organization, *World Census of Agriculture*, Rome: FAO.

FAO (1997). *Women: The Key to Food Security*, Rome: FAO, Women and Population Division.

FAO (2000). *World Census of Agriculture*, Rome: FAO.

FAO (2001). 'Supplement to the Report on the 1990 World Census of Agriculture', FAO Statistical Development Series, FAO, Rome.

Fay, M., and A. Wellenstein (2005). 'Keeping a Roof over One's Head: Improving Access to Safe and Decent Shelter', in M. Fay (ed.), *The Urban Poor in Latin America*, Washington DC: World Bank.

Fay, M., and C. Ruggeri Laderchi (2005). 'Relying on Oneself: Assets of the Poor', in M. Fay (ed.), *The Urban Poor in Latin America*, Washington DC: World Bank.

Fay, M., T. Yepes, and V. Foster (2002). 'Asset Inequality in Developing Countries: The Case of Housing', mimeo, World Bank, Washington DC.

Fay, M. A. (1998). 'From Concubines to Capitalists: Women, Property, and Power in Eighteenth Century Cairo', *Journal of Women's History*, 10(3): 118–40.

Feder, G. (1985). 'The Relation between Farm Size and Farm Productivity: The Role of Family Labour, Supervision, and Credit Constraint', *Journal of Development Economics*, 18: 297–313.

Feder, G., and A. Nishio (1999). 'The Benefits of Land Registration and Titling: Economic and Social Perspectives', *Land Use Policy*, 15(4): 25–43.

Feder, G., T. Onchan, Y. Chalamwong, and C. Hongladarom (1998). *Land Policies and Farm Productivity in Thailand*, Baltimore: Johns Hopkins University Press.

Fenrich, J., and T. E. Higgins (2002). 'Promise Unfulfilled: Law, Culture and Women's Inheritance Rights in Ghana', *Fordham International Law Journal*, 25: 259–341.

Fernandez-Corugedo, E., and J. Muellbauer (2006). 'Consumer Credit Conditions in the UK', Bank of England Working Paper 314, Bank of England, London.

Field, E. (2005). 'Property Rights and Investment in Urban Slums', *Journal of the European Economic Association*, 3(2–3): 279–90.

Field, E., and M. Torero (2004). 'Do Property Titles Increase Credit Access among the Urban Poor: Evidence from a Nationwide Titling Program', Harvard Economics Department Working Paper, Harvard University, Cambridge MA.

Fields, G. S. (1975). 'Rural–Urban Migration, Urban Unemployment and Under-Development, and Job-Search Security in LDCs', *Journal of Development Economics*, 2: 165–87.

Filgueira, F. (1998). 'El nuevo modelo de prestaciones sociales en América Latina: Residualismo, efciencia y ciudadanía estratificada' (The New Model of Social Welfare in Latin America: Residualism, Efficiency, and Stratified Citizenship), in B. Roberts (ed.), *Ciudadanía y Política Sociales*, San José de Costa Rica: FLACSO/SSRC.

Filmer, D., and L. Pritchett (1999). 'The Effect of Household Wealth on Educational Attainment: Evidence from 35 Countries', *Population and Development Review*, 25(1): 85–120.

Filmer, D., and L. Pritchett (2001). 'Estimating Wealth Effects without Expenditure Data or Tears: An Application to Educational Enrollments in States of India', *Demography*, 38 (1): 115–32.

Finansdepartementet (1879). *Sammandrag öfver stämpelafgifterna för lagfarter, inteckningar, äktenskapsförord, morgongåfvobref och afhandlingar om lösöresköp under år 1877 samt för bouppteckningar under åren 1873–1877*, Stockholm: Finansdepartementet.

Finansdepartementet (1910). *Bouppteckningar efter aflidna, inregistrerade vid vederbörande domstolar åren 1906–1908*, Stockholm: Finansdepartementet.

Flemming, J., and J. Micklewright (1999). 'Income Distribution, Economic Systems and Transition', in A. B. Atkinson and F. Bourguignon (eds), *Handbook of Income Distribution*, Amsterdam: Elsevier.

Föhl, C. (1964). *Kreislaufanalytische Untersuchung der Vermögensbildung in der Budesrepublik und der Beeinflussbarkeit inhrer Verteilung*, Tübingen: Mohr.

Foley, M., and W. Pyle (2005). 'Household Savings in Russia during the Transition', mimeo, Middlebury College, Middlebury VT.

Fortin, B., N. Marceau, and L. Savard (1997). 'Taxation, Wage Controls and the Informal Sector', *Journal of Public Economics*, 66: 239–312.

Fouquet, A., and D. Strauss-Kahn (1984). 'The Size Distribution of Personal Wealth in France (1977): A First Attempt at the Estate Duty Method', *Review of Income and Wealth*, 30: 403–18.

Frankema, E. (2005). 'The Colonial Origins of Inequality: A Global Investigation of Land Distribution', mimeo, University of Groningen.

Freeland, C. (2000). *Sale of the Century: Russia's Wild Ride from Communism to Capitalism*, New York: Crown Business.

Friebel, G., and S. Guriev (2005). 'Attaching Workers through In-Kind Payments: Theory and Evidence from Russia', *World Bank Economic Review*, Sept.

Friedemann-Sánchez, G. (2006). 'Assets in Intrahousehold Bargaining among Women Workers in Colombia's Cut-Flower Industry', *Feminist Economics*, 12(1–2): 247–69.

Friedman, E., S. Johnson, D. Kaufman, and P. Zoido-Lobaton (2000). 'Dodging the Grabbing Hand: The Determinants of Unofficial Activity in 69 Countries', *Journal of Public Economics*, 76(3): 459–93.

Galal, A., and O. Razzaz (2001). 'Reforming Land and Real Estate Markets', World Bank Policy Research Department Working Paper 2616, World Bank, Washington DC.

Galiani, S., and E. Schargrodsky (2006). 'Property Rights for the Poor: Effects of Land Titling', mimeo, Washington University in St Louis.

Galor, O., and J. Zeira (1993). 'Income Distribution and Macroeconomics', *Review of Economic Studies*, 60(1): 35–52.

Gauthier, B., and M. Gersowitz (1997). 'Revenue Erosion through Tax Exemption and Evasion in Poor Countries', *Journal of Public Economics*, 64: 404–24.

Gersovitz, M. (1988). 'Saving and Development', in H. B. Chenery and T. N. Srinivasan (eds), *Handbook of Development Economics*, vol. 1, Amsterdam: North Holland.

Ghana Statistical Service (n.d.). Ghana Living Standards Survey Round Four (GLSS 4) 1998/9, Data Users' Guide.

Ghatak, M., and N.-H. Jiang (2002). 'A Simple Model of Inequality, Occupational Choice and Development', *Journal of Development Economics*, 69(1): 205–26.

Ghatak, M., and P. Pandey (2000). 'Contract Choice in Agriculture with Joint Moral Hazard in Effort and Risk', *Journal of Development Economics*, 63(2): 303–26.

Giannetti, M., and Y. Koskinen (2004). 'Investor Protection and the Demand for Equity', CEPR Working Paper 4017, Centre for Economic Policy Research, London.

Gibbons, S., and S. Machin (2008). 'Valuing School Quality, Better Transport and Lower Crime: Evidence from House Prices', *Oxford Review of Economic Policy*, 24(1): 99–119.

Gilbert, A. (2002). 'On the Mystery of Capital and the Myths of Hernando de Soto. What Difference does Legal Title Make?', *International Development Planning Review*, 24(1): 1–19.

Glaeser, E. L., J. Gyourko, and R. E. Saks (2006). 'Urban Growth and Housing Supply', *Journal of Economic Geography*, 6(1): 71–89.

Glaeser, E. L., J. Scheinkman, and A. Shleifer (2003). 'The Injustice of Inequality', *Journal of Monetary Economics*, Carnegie-Rochester Series on Public Policy, 50(1): 199–222.

Goetzmann, W. N., and A. Kumar (2005). 'Why Do Individual Investors Hold Under-diversified Portfolios?', Yale School of Management Working Papers YSM454, Yale University and University of Notre Dame.

Goldstein, M., and C. Udry (2005). 'The Profits of Power: Land Rights and Agricultural Investment in Ghana', mimeo, Economic Growth Center, Yale University, New Haven.

Gollier, C., and J. W. Pratt (1996). 'Risk Vulnerability and the Tempering Effect of Background Risk', *Econometrica*, 64(5): 1109–23.

Gollin, D. (2000). 'Nobody's Business but My Own: Self Employment and Small Enterprise in Economic Development', mimeo, Williams College, Williamstown MA.

Gong, X., and A. van Soest (2001). 'Wage Differentials and Mobility in the Urban Labour Market: A Panel Data Analysis for Mexico', IZA Discussion Paper 329, IZA, Bonn.

Gordon, R., and J. Slemrod (1988). 'Do We Collect Any Revenue from Taxing Capital Income?', in L. Summers (ed.), *Tax Policy and the Economy*, Cambridge MA: MIT Press and National Bureau of Economic Research.

Gorodnichenko, Y., and Y. Grygorenko (2005). 'Are Oligarchs Productive? Theory and Evidence', mimeo, University of Michigan.

Gouskova, E., and F. Stafford (2002). 'Trends in Household Wealth Dynamics, 1999–2001', unpublished typescript.

Gray, L., and M. Kevane (1999). 'Diminished Access, Diverted Exclusion: Women and Land Tenure in Sub-Saharan Africa', *African Studies Review*, 42(2): 15–39.

Green, R. K., and M. J. White (1997). 'Measuring the Benefits of Homeowning: Effects on Children', *Journal of Urban Economics*, 41: 441–61.

Grimes, O. (1976). *Housing for Low-Income Urban Families*, Baltimore: Johns Hopkins University Press.

Grosfeld, I., and I. Hashi (2003). 'Mass Privatization, Corporate Governance and Endogenous Ownership Structure', Working Paper 596, William Davidson Institute, Ann Arbor MI.

Grossman, H. (1994). 'Production, Appropriation, and Land Reform', *American Economic Review*, 84(3): 705–12.

Gruber, J., and R. F. Martin (2003). 'Does Housing Wealth Make Us Less Equal?: The Role of Durable Goods in the Distribution of Wealth', mimeo, Econometric Society 2004 North American Summer Meetings.

Guha-Khasnobis, B., R. Kanbur, and E. Ostrom (2006) (eds). *Linking the Formal and Informal Economy: Concepts and Policies*, Oxford: Oxford University Press for UNU-WIDER.

Guiso, L., and T. Jappelli (1999). 'Private Transfers, Borrowing Constraints and the Timing of Homeownership', Centre for Studies in Economics and Finance Working Paper 17, Universita Degli Studi Di Salerno, Fisciano.

Guiso, L., and T. Jappelli (2002). 'Household Portfolios in Italy', in L. Guiso, M. Haliassos, and T. Jappelli (eds), *Household Portfolios*, Cambridge MA: MIT Press.

Guiso, L., M. Haliassos, and T. Jappelli (2002). *Household Portfolios*, Cambridge MA: MIT Press.

Guiso, L., M. Haliassos, and T. Jappelli (2003). 'Household Stock Holding in Europe: Where Do We Stand and Where Do We Go?', *Economic Policy*, 36: 123–70.

Guiso, L., P. Sapienza, and L. Zingales (2005). 'Trusting the Stock Market', CEPR Discussion Paper 5288, Centre for Economic Policy Research, London.

Guriev, S., and W. Megginson (2007). 'Privatization: What Have We Learned?', in F. Bourgoinon and B. Pleskovic (eds), *Beyond Transition: Proceedings of the Annual Bank Conference on Development Economics*, Washington DC: World Bank.

Guriev, S., and A. Rachinsky (2005). 'The Role of Oligarchs in Russian Capitalism', *Journal of Economic Perspectives*, 19(1): 131–50.

Guriev, S., and A. Rachinsky (2006). 'The Evolution of Personal Wealth in the Former Soviet Union and Central and Eastern Europe', WIDER Research Paper 2006/120, UNU-WIDER, Helsinki.

Guriev, S., A. Rachinsky, and E. Zhuravskaya (2006). 'The Genesis of Oligarchs', mimeo, CEFIR, Moscow.

Gustafsson, B., and S. Li (2001). 'Effects of the Transition on the Distribution of Income in China: A Study Decomposing the Gini Coefficient for 1988 and 1995', *Economics of Transition*, 9(3): 593–618.

Gustafsson, B., S. Li, and Z. Wei (2003). 'The Distribution of Wealth in Urban China and in China as a Whole 1995', unpublished typescript.

Gustafsson, B., S. Li, and Z. Wei (2006). 'The Distribution of Wealth in Urban China and in China as a Whole 1995', *Review of Income and Wealth*, 52(2): 173–88.

Guzanova, A. (1998). 'The Housing Market in the Russian Federation: Privatization and its Implications for Market Development', *World Bank Policy Research Working Paper* 1891, World Bank, Washington DC.

Hallagan, W. (1978). 'Self-Selection by Contractual Choice and the Theory of Sharecropping', *Bell Journal of Economics*, 9: 344–54.

Hanousek, J., and F. Palda (2005). 'Mission Implausible III: Measuring the Informal Sector in a Transition Economy using Macro Methods', mimeo, CERGE-EI, Prague.

Hanson, J. A. (2003). 'Are Small Countries Underbanked?', in J. A. Hanson, P. Honohan, and G. Majnoni (eds), *Globalization and National Financial Systems*, New York: Oxford University Press.

Hansson, Å. (2002). 'The Wealth Tax and Economic Growth', mimeo, Department of Economics, Lund University, Lund.

Harbury, C. D., and D. M. W. N. Hitchens (1979). *Inheritance and Wealth Inequality in Britain*, London: Allen & Unwin.

Harris, J. R., and M. P. Todaro (1970). 'Migration, Unemployment and Development: A Two-Sector Analysis', *American Economic Review*, 60: 126–42.

Harrison, A. J. (1979). 'The Distribution of Wealth in Ten Countries', Background Paper 7, Royal Commission on the Distribution of Income and Wealth, London.

Hauser, R., and H. Stein (2003). 'Inequality of the Distribution of Personal Wealth in Germany 1973–1998', paper prepared for the Levy Institute Conference 'International Perspectives on Household Wealth', 17–18 Oct., New York; also Levy Economics Institute Working Paper 398, Levy Institute, Bard College, Annandale-on-Hudson NY.

Haveman, R., and E. N. Wolff (2004). 'The Concept and Measurement of Asset Poverty: Levels, Trends, and Composition for the US, 1983–2001', *Journal of Economic Inequality*, 2: 145–69.

Headey, B., G. Marks and M. Wooden (2005). 'The Structure and Distribution of Household Wealth in Australia', *Australian Economic Review*, 38(2): 159–75.

Heckman, J. J., and V. Hotz (1986). 'An Investigation of Labour Market Earnings of Panamanian Males', *Journal of Human Resources*, 21: 507–42.

Heckman, J. J., and J. Scheinkman (1987). 'The Importance of Bundling in a Gorman-Lancaster Model of Earnings', *Review of Economic Studies*, 54: 243–55.

435

Hellman, J., G. Jones, and D. Kaufman (2003). 'Seize the State, Seize the Day: State Capture, Corruption, and Influence in Transition', *Journal of Comparative Economics*, 31(4): 751–73.

Hendry, D., J. Muellbauer, and A. Murphy (1990). 'The Econometrics of DHSY', in J. Hey and D. Winch (eds), *A Century of Economics: 100 Years of the Royal Econometric Society and the Economic Journal*, Oxford: Blackwell.

Heston, A., R. Summers, and B. Aten (2002). 'Penn World Table Mark 6.1', Center for International Comparisons at the University of Pennsylvania, Oct.

Hiatt, F. (2005). 'Truth-Tellers in a Time of Terror', *Washington Post*, 25 Nov.

HM Treasury (2003). *Fiscal Stabilization and EMU*, London: HM Treasury.

Holtz-Eakin, D., D. Joulfaian, and H. S. Rosen (1994). 'Sticking it Out: Entrepreneurial Survival and Liquidity Constraints', *Journal of Political Economy*, 102(1): 3–75.

Honohan, P. (1999). 'Financial Policies and Saving', in K. Schmidt-Hebbel and L. Serven (eds), *The Economics of Saving and Growth*, Cambridge: Cambridge University Press.

Honohan, P. (2004a). 'Financial Development, Growth and Poverty: How Close Are the Links?', in C. Goodhart (ed.), *Financial Development and Economic Growth: Explaining the Links*, Basingstoke: Palgrave Macmillan.

Honohan, P. (2004b). 'Financial Sector Policy and the Poor: Selected Issues and Evidence', World Bank Working Paper 43, World Bank, Washington DC.

Honohan, P. (2005). 'Measuring Microfinance Access: Building on Existing Cross-Country Data', World Bank Policy Research Working Paper 3606, World Bank: Washington DC.

Honohan, P. (2006). 'Household Financial Assets in the Process of Development', WIDER Research Paper 2006/91, UNU-WIDER, Helsinki.

Horowitz, A. (1993). 'Time Paths for Land Reform: A Theoretical Model of Reform Dynamics', *American Economic Review*, 83(4): 1003–10.

Huizinga, H., and L. Jonung (2005). *The Internalization of Asset Ownership in Europe*, Cambridge: Cambridge University Press.

Human Rights Watch (2003). 'Double Standards: Women's Property Rights Violations in Kenya', *Human Rights Watch*, 15(5A).

Hurst, E., and A. Lusardi (2004). 'Liquidity Constraints, Household Wealth and Entrepreneurship', *Journal of Political Economy* 112(2): 319–47.

Iacoviello, M. (2004). 'Consumption, House Prices and Collateral Constraints: A Structural Econometric Analysis', *Journal of Housing Economics*, 13(4): 305–21.

IADB (1999). Inter-American Development Bank, *Facing Up to Inequality in Latin America: 1998–99 Report*, Baltimore: Johns Hopkins University Press.

ICRW (2005). International Center for Research on Women, 'Property Ownership for Women Enriches Empowers and Protects', *Policy Brief*, Washington DC: International Center for Research on Women.

Ihrig, J., and K. Moe (2004). 'Lurking in the Shadows: The Informal Sector and Government Policy', *Journal of Development Economics*, 73: 541–57.

Ikdahl, I., et al. (2005). 'Human Rights, Formalization, and Women's Land Rights in Southern and Eastern Africa', Studies in Women's Law 57, Institute of Women's Law, University of Oslo.

ILO (2003). International Labour Organization, *Key Indicators of the Labour Market*, New York: Routledge for the ILO.

INCRA (1999). *O Livro Branco das Superindenizações*, Rio de Janeiro: Ministério do Desenvolvimento Agrário.

Inland Revenue Statistics (2006). 'Distribution among the Adult Population of Marketable Wealth', available at: http://www.hmrc.gov.uk/stats/personal_wealth/table13_5.xls (accessed 6 Feb. 2008).

ISSER (2005). Institute of Statistical, Social, and Economic Research, *The State of the Ghanaian Economy in 2004*, Legon: ISSER, University of Ghana.

ISWGNA (1993). Inter-Secretariat Working Group on National Accounts, *System of National Accounts 1993*, Brussels: Eurostat; New York: UN; Paris: OECD; Washington DC: IMF and World Bank.

Iwaisako, T. (2003). 'Household Portfolios in Japan', NBER Working Paper 9647, National Bureau of Economic Research, Cambridge MA.

Jain, L. R., K. Sundaram, and S. Tendulkar (1989). 'Levels of Living and Incidence of Poverty in Rural India: A Cross Section Analysis', *Journal of Quantitative Economics*, 5(1): 187–209.

Jalan, J., and M. Ravallion (2001). 'Behavioral Responses to Risk in Rural China', *Journal of Development Economics*, 66(1): 23–49.

Janakarajan, S. (1992). 'Interlinked Transactions and the Market for Water in the Agrarian Economy of a Tamil Nadu Village', in S. Subramanian (ed.), *Themes in Development Economics: Essays in Honour of Malcolm Adiseshiah*, Delhi: Oxford University Press.

Jäntti, M. (2006). 'Trends in the Distribution of Income and Wealth: Finland 1987–1998', in E. N. Wolff (ed.), *International Perspectives on Household Wealth*, Northampton MA: Edward Elgar.

Jappelli, T., and L. Pistaferri (2000). 'The Dynamics of Household Wealth and Accumulation in Italy', CSEF Working Paper 27, Centre for Studies in Economics and Finance, Salerno, Naples, Milan.

Jappelli, T., M. Pagano, and M. Bianco (2005). 'Courts and Banks: Effects of Judicial Enforcement on Credit Markets', *Journal of Money, Credit and Banking*, 37(2): 223–44.

Jenkins, S. P. (1990). 'The Distribution of Wealth: Measurement and Models', *Journal of Economic Surveys*, 4(4): 329–60.

Johansson, F., and N. A. Klevmarken (2007). 'Comparing Survey and Register Wealth Data', in *Essays on Measurement Error and Nonresponse*, Uppsala: Uppsala University.

Johnson, S., D. Kauffman, and A. Shleifer (1997). 'The Unofficial Economy in Transition', *Brookings Papers on Economic Activity*, 2: 159–239.

Johnson S., D. Kauffman, and P. Zoido-Lobaton (1998). 'Regulatory Discretion and the Unofficial Economy', *American Economic Association Papers and Proceedings*, 88: 387–92.

Johnson, S., J. McMillan, and C. Woodruff (2002). 'Property Rights and Finance', *American Economic Review*, 92(5): 1335–56.

Johnson, S., R. La Porta, F. Lopez-de-Silanes, and A. Shleifer (2000). 'Tunneling', *American Economic Review Papers and Proceedings*, May.

Juster, F. T., J. P. Smith, and F. Stafford (1999). 'The Measurement and Structure of Household Wealth', *Labour Economics*, 6(2): 253–76.

Juurikkala, T., and O. Lazareva (2004). 'The Role of Social Benefits in the Employment Strategies of Russian Firms', mimeo, Helsinki School of Economics, Helsinki.

Kain, J., and J. Quigley (1972). 'Note on Owner's Estimate of Housing Value', *Journal of the American Statistical Association*, 67: 803–6.

Kakwani, N. C. (1980). 'On a Class of Poverty Measures', *Econometrica*, 48(2): 437–46.

Kar, P., M. T. Raju, and S. P. Batra (2003). *Survey of Indian Investors*, Securities and Exchange Board of India, Mumbai.

Katz Commission (1996). *Third Interim Report of the Commission of Inquiry into Certain Aspects of the Tax Structure of South Africa*, Pretoria: Government Printer.

Katz, E., and J. Chamorro (2003). 'Gender, Land Rights, and the Household Economy in Rural Nicaragua and Honduras', paper presented at the annual conference of the Latin American and Caribbean Economics Association, Puebla, Oct.

Keane, M., and E. Prasad (2002). 'Inequality, Transfers and Growth: New Evidence from the Economic Transition in Poland', *Review of Economics and Statistics*, 84(2): 324–41.

Kebede, B. (2006). 'Land Reform, Distribution of Land and Institutions in Rural Ethiopia: Analysis of Inequality with Dirty Data', mimeo, University of East Anglia, Norwich.

Keefer, P., and S. Knack (2002). 'Polarization, Politics and Property Rights: Links between Inequality and Growth', *Public Choice*, 111: 127–54.

Kelly, M. (1995). 'All their Eggs in One Basket: Portfolio Diversification of US Households', *Journal of Economic Behavior and Organization*, 27(1): 87–96.

Kelly, S. (2001). 'Trends in Australian Wealth: New Estimates for the 1990s', paper presented to the 30th Annual Conference of Economists, 23–26 Sept., University of Western Australia, Crawley.

Kennedy, N., and P. Andersen (1994). 'Household Saving and Real House Prices: An International Perspective', Bank for International Settlements Working Paper 21.

Kennickell, A. (2003). 'A Rolling Tide: Changes in the Distribution of Wealth in the United States, 1989–2001', Levy Economics Institute Working Paper 393, Levy Institute, Bard College, Annandale-on-Hudson NY.

Kessler, D., and E. Wolff (1991). 'A Comparative Analysis of Household Wealth Patterns in France and the United States', *Review of Income and Wealth*, 37(1): 249–66.

Keynes, J. M. (1936). *The General Theory of Employment Interest and Money*, London: Macmillan.

Khan, A. R., and C. Riskin (2006). 'Growth and Distribution of Household Income in China between 1995 and 2002', in B. Gustafsson, S. Li and T. Sicular (eds), *Inequality and Public Policy in China*, Cambridge: Cambridge University Press.

Kiær, A. N. (1917). *Indtaegts- og formuesforhold efter skatteligningerne for 1913/14 sammenignet med tidligere og senere aar*, Kristiania: Departementet for Sociale Saker.

Kilenthong, T. W. (2005). 'Collateralized Contracts as a Risk Sharing Mechanism', mimeo, University of Chicago.

Kimball, M. (1991). 'Precautionary Motives for Holding Assets', NBER Working Paper 3586, National Bureau of Economic Research, Cambridge MA.

Kimball, M. (1993). 'Standard Risk Aversion', *Econometrica*, 61(3): 589–611.

King, M. A., and J. I. Leape (1984). 'Asset Accumulation, Information, and the Life-Cycle', NBER Working Paper 2392, National Bureau of Economic Research, Cambridge MA.

King, M. A., and J. I. Leape (1998). 'Wealth and Portfolio Composition: Theory and Evidence', *Journal of Public Economics*, 69: 155–93.

King, M. A., and L. D. Dicks-Mireaux (1982). 'Asset Holdings and the Life Cycle', *Economic Journal*, 92(366): 247–67.

Kitamura, Y., N. Takayama, and F. Arita (2003). 'Household Savings and Wealth Distribution in Japan', in A. Börsch-Supan (ed.), *Life-Cycle Savings and Public Policy: A Cross-National Study of Six Countries*, London: Academic Press.

Klein, H. (1993). *Haciendas and Ayllus*, Palo Alto CA: Stanford University Press.

Klevmarken, N. A. (2004). 'On the Wealth Dynamics of Swedish Families: 1984–98', *Review of Income and Wealth*, 50(4): 469–91.

Klevmarken, N. A. (2006). 'On Household Wealth Trends in Sweden over the 1990s', in E. N. Wolff (ed.), *International Perspectives on Household Wealth*, Northampton MA: Edward Elgar.

Kopczuk, W., and E. Saez (2004a). 'Top Wealth Shares in the United States, 1916–2000: Evidence from Estate Tax Returns', NBER Working Paper 10399, National Bureau of Economic Research, Cambridge MA.

Kopczuk, W., and E. Saez (2004b). 'Top Wealth Shares in the United States, 1916–2000: Evidence from Estate Tax Returns', *National Tax Journal*, 57(2): 445–87.

Kotlikoff, L. J., and A. Spivak (1981). 'The Family as an Incomplete Annuities Market', *Journal of Political Economy*, 89(2): 372–91.

Kramer, A., and F. Norris (2005). 'Amid Growing Wealth, Nepotism and Nationalism in Kazakhstan', *New York Times*, 23 Dec.

Kramer, A., and H. Timmons (2005). 'World's Biggest Steel Maker is Acquiring Ukrainian Mill', *New York Times*, 25 Oct.

Kroll, L., and A. Fass (2006). 'The World's Billionaires', *Forbes*, 9 Mar.

Kurien, C. T. (1989). *Dynamics of Rural Transformation: A Case Study of Tamil Nadu*, Delhi: Orient Longman.

La Ferrara, E. (2003). 'Kin Groups and Reciprocity: A Model of Credit Transactions in Ghana', *American Economic Review*, 93(5): 1730–51.

Laffont, J. J., and M. S. Matoussi (1995). 'Moral Hazard, Financial Constraints and Sharecropping in El Oulja', *Review of Economic Studies*, 62(3): 381–99.

Lampman, R. J. (1962). *The Share of Top Wealth Holders in National Wealth 1922–1956*, Princeton: Princeton University Press.

Lange, M., J. Mahoney, and M. von Hau (2006). 'Colonialism and Development: A Comparative Analysis of Spanish and British Colonies', *American Journal of Sociology*, 111(5): 1412–62.

Lanjouw, J., and P. Levy (2002). 'Untitled: A Study of Formal and Informal Property Rights in Urban Ecuador', *Economic Journal*, 11: 986–1019.

Lavindkomstkommissionen (1979). *Udviklingen i formuefordelingen 1960–1977: Delrapport 2*, Copenhagen: Lavindkomstkommissionen.

Leamer, E. (2007). 'Housing and the Business Cycle', paper presented at Housing, Housing Finance, and Monetary Policy Symposium sponsored by the Federal Reserve Bank of Kansas City, 30 Aug.–1 Sept., Jackson Hole, Wyoming.

Lehmann, F. (1937). 'The Distribution of Wealth', in M. Ascoli and F. Lehmann (eds), *Political and Economic Democracy*, New York: W. W. Norton.

Lehmusaari, O. P. (1990). 'Deregulation and Consumption Saving Dynamics in the Nordic Countries', *IMF Staff Papers*, 37(1): 71–93.

Lettau, M., and S. C. Ludvigson (2004). 'Understanding Trend and Cycle in Asset Values: Reevaluating the Wealth Effect on Consumption', *American Economic Review*, 94(1): 276–99.

Levine, R. E. (2005). 'Finance and Growth: Theory, Mechanisms and Evidence', in P. Aghion and S. N. Durlauf (eds), *Handbook of Economic Growth*, Amsterdam: Elsevier.

Lewis, W. A. (1954). 'Economic Development with Unlimited Supplies of Labour', *Manchester School*, 22: 139–91.

Li, G., S. Rozelle, and L. Brandt (1998). 'Tenure, Land Rights and Farmer Investment Incentives in China', *Agricultural Economics*, 19: 63–71.

Li, H., L. Squire, and H. Zou (1998). 'Explaining International and Intertemporal Variations in Income Inequality', *Economic Journal*, 108(1): 26–43.

Li, S., and X. Yue (2004). 'An Investigation on Income Distribution in China', *Finance and Economics (Cai Jing)*, 3/4: 1–12.

Li, S., and R. Zhao (2007). 'Changes in the Distribution of Wealth in China, 1995–2002', WIDER Research Paper 2007/03, UNU-WIDER, Helsinki.

Lindert, P. H. (1986). 'Unequal English Wealth since 1670', *Journal of Political Economy*, 94(6): 1127–62.

Lindert, P. H. (2000). 'Three Centuries of Inequality in Britain and America', in A. B. Atkinson and F. Bourguignon (eds), *Handbook of Income Distribution*, vol. 1, Amsterdam: Elsevier.

Lindh, T., and H. Ohlsson (1998). 'Self-Employment and Wealth Inequality', *Review of Income and Wealth*, 44: 25–42.

Litchfield, J. A. (1999). 'Inequality: Method and Tools', mimeo, World Bank, Washington DC.

Ljungqvist, L. (1993). 'Economic Underdevelopment: The Case of Missing Market for Human Capital', *Journal of Development Economics*, 40(2): 219–39.

Loayza, N. V. (1996). 'The Economics of the Informal Sector: A Simple Model and Some Empirical Evidence from Latin America', *Carnegie-Rochester Conference Series on Public Policy*, 45: 129–62.

Lopez, R., and A. Valdes (2000). 'Fighting Rural Poverty in Latin America: New Evidence and Policy', in R. Lopez and A. Valdes (eds), *Rural Poverty in Latin America*, New York: St Martin's Press.

Loury, G. (1981). 'Intergenerational Transfers and the Distribution of Earnings', *Econometrica*, 49(4): 843–67.

Lusardi, A., and O. Mitchell (2006). 'Financial Literacy and Planning: Implications for Retirement Wellbeing', presented at American Economic Association, 6–8 Jan., Boston.

Ludwig, A., and T. Sloek (2002). 'The Impact of Changes in the Stock Prices and House Prices on Consumption in OECD Countries', IMF Working Paper 02/1, International Monetary Fund, Washington DC.

Lydall, H. F., and D. G. Tipping (1961). 'The Distribution of Personal Wealth in Britain', *Bulletin of the Oxford Institute of Economics and Statistics*, 23: 83–104.

Macgregor, D. H. (1936). 'Pareto's Law', *Economic Journal*, 46: 80–7.

McKay, A. (2002). 'Defining and Measuring Inequality', *ODI Inequality Briefing Paper* 1/2002, Overseas Development Institute, London.

McKay, A., and D. Lawson (2003). 'Assessing the Extent and Nature of Chronic Poverty in Low Income Countries: Issues and Evidence', *World Development*, 31(3): 425–39.

McKenzie, D. (2005). 'Measuring Inequality with Asset Indicators', *Journal of Population Economics*, 18: 229–60.

McKinley, T. (1993). 'The Distribution of Wealth in Rural China', in K. Griffin and R. Zhao (eds), *The Distribution of Income in China*, London: Macmillan.

Maclennan, D., J. Muellbauer, and M. Stephens (2000). 'Asymmetries in Housing and Financial Market Institutions and EMU', in T. Jenkinson (ed.), *Readings in Macroeconomics*, Oxford: Oxford University Press.

Macours, K., and J. F. M. Swinnen (2005). 'Agricultural Labor Adjustments in Transition Countries: The Role of Migration and Impact on Poverty', *Review of Agricultural Economics*, 27(3): 405–11.

Macours, K., A. de Janvry, and E. Sadoulet (2001). 'Matching in the Tenancy Market and Access to Land', mimeo, University of California at Berkeley, Berkeley CA.

Magnac, T. (1991). 'Segmented or Competitive Labour Markets', *Econometrica*, 59: 165–87.

Mahoney, J. (2001). *The Legacies of Liberalism: Path Dependence and Political Regimes in Central America*, Baltimore: Johns Hopkins University Press.

Mallet, B. (1908). 'A Method of Estimating Capital Wealth from the Estate Duty Statistics', *Journal of the Royal Statistical Society*, 71: 65–84.

Malpezzi, S., and D. Maclennan (2001). 'The Long-Run Price Elasticity of Supply of New Residential Construction in the United States and the United Kingdom', *Journal of Housing Economics*, 10: 278–306.

Mansell-Carstens, C. (1995). *Las Finanzas Populares en México, Centro de Estudios Monetarios Latinoamericanos*, Mexico City: Editorial Milenio.

Marcouiller, D., and L. Young (1995). 'The Black Hole of Graft: The Predatory State and the Informal Economy', *American Economic Review*, 85: 630–46.

Marcus, H. G. (2002). *A History of Ethiopia*, Berkeley and Los Angeles: University of California Press.

Mardon, M. (2005). 'Three Essays on Gender, Land Rights and Collective Action in Brazil's Rural Political Economy', Ph.D. dissertation, Economics Department, University of Massachusetts, Amherst.

Markham, M. (2003). 'Poland: Housing Challenge in a Time of Transition', paper prepared for the project HUT-264 M Housing Policy in the United States: The Intersection of Public and Private Sectors in Housing Finance, Washington DC.

Matsuyama, K. (2000). 'Endogenous Inequality', *Review of Economic Studies*, 67(4): 743–59.

Mayo, S., S. Malpezzi, and D. Gross (1986). 'Shelter Strategies for the Urban Poor in Developing Countries: An Update', *World Bank Research Observer*, 1(2): 183–203.

Mazumdar, D. (1975). 'The Theory of Urban Employment in Less Developed Countries', *World Development*, 4: 655–79.

Mazumdar, D. (1981). *The Urban Labour Market Income Distribution: A Study of Malaysia*, Oxford: Oxford University Press.

Meade, J. E. (1964). *Efficiency, Equality and Ownership of Property*, London: Allen & Unwin.

Meen, G. (2001). *Modelling Spatial Housing Markets*, Boston: Kluwer Academic.

Megginson, W. L. (2005). *The Financial Economics of Privatization*, New York: Oxford University Press.

Meinzen-Dick, R. S., L. R. Brown, H.S. Feldstein, and A. R. Quisumbing (1997). 'Gender, Property Rights, and Natural Resources', *World Development*, 25(8): 1303–15.

Menchik, P. L. (1980). 'Primogeniture, Equal Sharing, and the US Distribution of Wealth', *Quarterly Journal of Economics*, 94: 299–316.

Mesnard, A., and M. Ravallion (2003). 'Wealth Distribution and Self-Employment in a Developing Economy', CEPR Discussion Paper DP3026 and World Bank Paper 2527.

Meyer, M., and W. Sherman (1987). *The Course of Mexican History*, Oxford: Oxford University Press.

Milanovic, B. (1990). 'Poverty in Poland, Hungary and Yugoslavia in the Years of Crisis, 1978–87', World Development Report Working Paper 507, World Bank, Washington DC.

Milanovic, B. (1998). *Inequality and Poverty during the Transition from Market Economy*, Washington DC: World Bank.

Milanovic, B. (1999). 'Explaining the Increase in Inequality during Transition', *Economics of Transition*, 7(2): 299–341.

Milanovic, B. (2002). 'True World Income Distribution, 1988 and 1993: First Calculation Based on Household Surveys Alone', *Economic Journal*, 112: 51–92.

Milanovic, B. (2005). *Worlds Apart: Measuring International and Global Inequality*, Princeton: Princeton University Press.

Miles, D. (2004). *The UK Mortgage Market: Taking a Longer Term View*, London: HM Treasury.

Mitra, P., and R. Yemtsov (2007). 'Increasing Inequality in Transition Economies: Is There More to Come?', in F. Bourgoinon and B. Pleskovic (eds), *Beyond Transition: Proceedings of the Annual Bank Conference on Development Economics*, Washington DC: World Bank.

Modigliani, F., and R. Brumberg (1954). 'Utility Analysis and the Consumption Function: An Interpretation of the Cross-Section Data', in K. Kurihara (ed.), *Post-Keynesian Economics*, New Brunswick NJ: Rutgers University Press.

Moehling, C. M., and R. Steckel (2001). 'Rising Inequality: Trends in the Distribution of Wealth in Industrializing New England', *Journal of Economic History*, 61(1): 160–83.

Mohn, J. R. (1873). 'Statistiske bidrag til belysning af privatformuens fordeling i Norge', *Norsk Retstidende*, 1–2: 1–32.

Mookherjee, D., and D. Ray (2003). 'Persistent Inequality', *Review of Economic Studies* 70 (2): 369–94.

Mookherjee, D., and D. Ray (2006). 'Occupational Diversity and Endogenous Inequality', mimeo, Boston University and New York University, Boston and New York.

Morissette, R., X. Zhang, and M. Drolet (2003). 'The Evolution of Wealth Inequality in Canada: 1984–1999', Levy Economics Institute Working Paper 396, Levy Institute, Bard College, Annandale-on-Hudson NY.

Morrison, C. (2000). 'Inequality in Historical Perspective', in A. B. Atkinson and F. Bourguignon (eds), *Handbook of Income Distribution*, Amsterdam: Elsevier.

Moser, C. (1998). 'The Asset Vulnerability Framework: Reassessing Urban Poverty Reduction Strategies', *World Development*, 26(1): 1–19.

Muellbauer, J. (1988). 'Habits, Rationality and Myopia in the Life-Cycle Consumption Function', *Annales d'économie et de statistique*, 9: 47–70.

Muellbauer, J. (2005). 'Property Taxation and the Economy after the Barker Review', *Economic Journal*, 115: C99–C117.

Muellbauer, J. (2008). 'Housing, Credit and Consumer Expenditure', Symposium on Housing, Housing Finance, and Monetary Policy sponsored by the Federal Reserve Bank of Kansas City, Jackson Hole, Wyoming, 30 Aug.–1 Sept. 2007.

Muellbauer, J., and R. Lattimore (1995). 'The Consumption Function: A Theoretical and Empirical Overview', in H. Pesaran and M. Wickens (eds), *Handbook of Applied Econometrics*, Oxford: Blackwell.

Muellbauer, J., and K. Murata (2008). 'Consumption, Land Prices and the Monetary Transmission in Japan', paper presented at ESRI and the Center on Japanese Economy and Business (CJEB) at Columbia Business School, workshop on Japan's Bubble, Deflation and Long-Term Stagnation, Columbia University, 21 March.

Muellbauer, J., and A. Murphy (1995). 'Explaining Regional Consumption', paper presented at Bank of Portugal Conference on the Microeconomics of Saving, Lisbon, Nov.

Mulder, C. H., and M. Wagner (1998). 'First-Time Home-Ownership in the Family Life Course: A West German–Dutch Comparison', *Urban Studies*, 35(4): 687–713.

Munalula, M., and W. Mwenda (1995). 'Case Study: Women and Inheritance Law in Zambia', in M. Hay and S. Stichter (eds), *African Women: South of the Sahara*, New York: Longman Scientific and Technical.

NBS (1999). National Bureau of Statistics, *Comprehensive Statistical Data and Materials on 50 Years of New China*, Beijing: China Statistical Press.

NBS (2004). *China Statistical Yearbook*, Beijing: China Statistical Press.

North, D. (1981). *Structure and Change in Economic History*, New York: Norton.

North, D., and R. Thomas (1973). *The Rise of the Western World: A New Economic History*, New York: Cambridge University Press.

Noyola, J. (2000). 'The Distribution of Household Wealth in Monterey, Mexico in the 1900s', Ph.D. thesis, University of Notre Dame.

NSSO (2005). National Social Survey Organization, 'Household Assets and Liabilities in India', Department of Statistics, Government of India, New Delhi.

OECD (2000). Organization for Economic Cooperation and Development, 'House Prices and Economic Activity', *OECD Economic Outlook*, 68: 169–84.

OECD (2002). *Measuring the Non-Observed Economy: A Handbook*, Paris: OECD.

OECD (2005a). *National Accounts of OECD Countries*, vol. 1, Paris: OECD.

OECD (2005b). *PPPs and Real Expenditures: Benchmark Year 2002*, Paris: Eurostat-OECD.

OECD Statistics (2004). 'National Accounts of OECD Countries', *Financial Accounts Flows* 111A, and *Financial Balance Sheets* 111B.

Ofer, G., and A. Vinokur (1992). *The Soviet Household under the Old Regime: Economic Conditions and Behavior in the 1970s*, Cambridge: Cambridge University Press.

Ohlsson, H., J. Roine, and D. Waldenström (2006). 'Long-Run Changes in the Concentration of Wealth: An Overview of Recent Findings', WIDER Research Paper 2006/103, UNU-WIDER, Helsinki.

Oijen, P. van, and E. C. Perotti (2001). 'Privatization, Market Development and Political Risk in Emerging Economies', *Journal of International Money and Finance*, 20(1): 43–69.

Okore, M. (2006). 'Land Act Has No Legal Consequence: Baguma', *New Vision* (Kampala), 4 Feb.

Otsuka, M. (2006). 'Essays on Household Portfolio and Current Account Dynamics', ProQuest/UMI.

Palacin, J., and R. Shelburne (2005). 'The Private Housing Markets in Eastern Europe and in the CIS', United Nations Economic Commission for Europe Economic Analysis Division Discussion Paper 6, UNECE, Geneva.

Panda, P., and B. Agarwal (2005). 'Marital Violence, Human Development, and Women's Property Status in India', *World Development*, 33(5): 823–50.

Paredes Cruzatt, P. (1987). 'Segmentacion del Mercado Laboural en Lima Metropolitana', Planificacion del Mercado Laboural, Proyecto Per/85/007, Cuadernos de Informaciones, Lima.

Paulson, A. L., and R. Townsend (2004). 'Entrepreneurship and Financial Constraints in Thailand', *Journal of Corporate Finance*, 10: 229–62.

Peachey, S., and A. Roe (2006). 'Access to Finance, Measuring the Contribution of Savings Banks', World Savings Banks Institute, Brussels.

Pence, K. M. (2003). 'Foreclosing on Opportunity: State Laws and Mortgage Credit', FEDS Working Paper 2003-16, Board of Governors of the Federal Reserve System, Washington DC.

Piketty, T. (1997). 'The Dynamics of the Wealth Distribution and the Interest Rate with Credit Rationing', *Review of Economic Studies*, 64(2): 173–89.

Piketty, T. (2001). *Les Hauts Revenus en France au 20ème siècle*, Paris: Grasset.

Piketty, T. (2003). 'Income Inequality in France, 1901–1998', *Journal of Political Economy*, 111(5): 1004–42.

Piketty, T., and E. Saez (2003). 'Income Inequality in the United States, 1913–1998', *Quarterly Journal of Economics*, 118(1): 1–39.

Piketty, T., and E. Saez (2007). 'Income and Wage Inequality in the US, 1913–2002', in A. B. Atkinson and T. Piketty (eds), *Top Incomes over the Twentieth Century: A Contrast between European and English-Speaking Countries*, Oxford: Oxford University Press.

Piketty, T., G. Postel-Vinay, and J.-L. Rosenthal (2004). 'Wealth Concentration in a Developing Economy: Paris and France, 1807–1994', CEPR Discussion Paper 4631, CEPR, London.

Piketty, T., G. Postel-Vinay, and J.-L. Rosenthal (2006). 'Wealth Concentration in a Developing Economy: Paris and France, 1807–1994', *American Economic Review*, 96 (1): 236–56.

Pinckney, T., and P. Kimuyu (1994). 'Land Tenure Reform in East Africa: Good, Bad or Unimportant?', *Journal of African Economies*, 3(1): 1–28.

Pinto, N. (2006). 'Personal Wealth in Brazil: The Estate-Multiplier Method in a Representative City of the State of São Paulo', Mimeo, Universidade Estadual de Campinas, Brazil.

Place, F., and K. Otsuka (2002). 'Land Tenure Systems and their Impacts on Agricultural Investments and Productivity in Uganda', *Journal of Development Studies*, 38(6): 105–24.

Platteau, J.-P., and J.-M. Baland (2001). 'Impartible Inheritance versus Equal Division: A Comparative Perspective Centered on Europe and Sub-Saharan Africa', in A. de Janvry, G. Gordillo, J.-P. Platteau, and E. Sadoulet (eds), *Access to Land, Rural Poverty, and Public Action*, Oxford: Oxford University Press for UNU-WIDER.

Population Reference Bureau (2000). *World Population Data Sheet*, Washington DC: Population Reference Bureau.

Porteous, D., with E. Hazelhurst (2004). *Banking on Change: Democratizing Finance in South Africa 1994–2004 and Beyond*, Cape Town: Double Storey Books.

Portes, A., and K. Hoffman (2003). 'Latin American Class Structures: Their Composition and Change during the Neoliberal Era', *Latin American Research Review*, 38(1): 41–82.

Portes, A., M. Castells, and L. A. Benton (1989) (eds). *The Informal Economy: Studies in Advanced and Less Developed Countries*, Baltimore: Johns Hopkins University Press.

Poterba, J. M., and J. M. Manchester (1989). 'Second Mortgages and Household Saving', *Regional Science and Urban Economics*, 19(2): 325–46.

Pradhan, M., and A. van Soest (1995). 'Formal and Informal Sector Employment in Urban Areas of Bolivia', *Labour Economics*, 2: 275–97.

Pratap, S., and E. Quintin (2006a). 'Are Labour Markets Segmented in Developing Countries? A Semiparametric Approach', *European Economic Review*, 50(7): 1817–41.

Pratap, S., and E. Quintin (2006b). 'The Informal Sector in Developing Countries: Output, Assets and Employment', WIDER Research Paper 2006/130, UNU-WIDER, Helsinki.

Pratt, J. W., and R. J. Zeckhauser (1987). 'Proper Risk Aversion', *Econometrica*, 55(1): 143–54.

Prinsloo, J. W. (2000). 'The Saving Behaviour of the South African Economy', SARB Occasional Paper 15, South African Reserve Bank, Pretoria.

Prinsloo, J. W. (2002). 'Household Debt, Wealth and Saving', *Quarterly Bulletin*, 63–78, Pretoria: South African Reserve Bank.

Pyatt, G., C. N. Chen, and J. Fei (1980). 'The Distribution of Income by Factor Components', *Quarterly Journal of Economics*, 95: 451–73.

Quintin, E. (2000). 'Limited Enforcement and Economic Development', Ph.D. dissertation, University of Minnesota.

Quisumbing, A. R., K. Otsuka, et al. (2001). 'Land, Trees, and Women: Evolution of Land Tenure Institutions in Western Ghana and Sumatra', Research Report 121, International Food Policy Research Institute, Washington DC.

Quisumbing, A. R., and K. Hallman (2003). 'Marriage in Transition: Evidence on Age, Education, and Assets from Six Developing Countries', Policy Research Division Working Paper 183, Population Council, New York.

Quisumbing, A. R., and J. Maluccio (2003). 'Resources at Marriage and Intrahousehold Allocation: Evidence from Bangladesh, Ethiopia, Indonesia, and South Africa', *Oxford Bulletin of Economics and Statistics*, 65: 283–327.

Rajan, R. G. (2005). 'Has Financial Development Made the World Riskier?', http://www.kc.frb.org/PUBLICAT/SYMPOS/2005/sym05prg.htm.

Rajan, R. G., and L. Zingales (2003). *Saving Capitalism from the Capitalists: Unleashing the Power of Financial Markets to Create Wealth and Spread Opportunity*, New York: Crown Business.

Rao, R., and A. K. Tripathi (2001). 'Indebtedness of Households: Changing Characteristics', *Economic and Political Weekly*, 12 May: 1617–26.

Rao, S. (2005). 'Gender, Liberalization and Agrarian Change in Telangana, India', Ph.D. dissertation, Economics Department, University of Massachusetts, Amherst.

Rauch, J. E. (1991). 'Modeling the Informal Sector Formally', *Journal of Development Economics*, 35: 33–48.

Ray, D. (1997). *Development Economics*, Princeton: Princeton University Press.

Reardon, T., P. Matlon, and C. Delgado (1988). 'Coping with Household-Level Food Insecurity in Draught-Affected Areas of Burkina Faso', *World Development*, 16(9): 1065–74.

Rediff Money Special (2000). 'The SEBI–NCAER Investor Survey', Aug. Available at http://www.rediff.com/money/2000/aug/28spec.htm.

Reis, E., P. Tafner, and L. O. Reiff (2001). 'Distribucao de Riqueza Imobiliaria e de Renda no Brasil: 1992–1999', Seminarios DIMAC N75, IPEA, Rio de Janeiro.

Reydon, B. P. (2000). 'Intervenção estatal no mercado de terras: a experiência recente no Brasil', *Estudos NEAD* 3, Rio de Janeiro: Ministério do Desenvolvimento Agrário.

Ring, A. M. (1998). *Die Verteilung der Vermögen in der Bundesrepublik Deutschland*, Frankfurt am Main: Peter Lang.

Rioja, F., and N. Valev (2004). 'Finance and the Sources of Growth at Various Stages of Economic Development', *Economic Inquiry*, 42(1): 127–40.

Roberts, B. R. (1989). 'Employment Structure, Life Cycle, and Life Chances: Formal and Informal Sectors in Guadalajara', in A. Portes, M. Castells, and L. A. Benton (eds), *The Informal Economy: Studies in Advanced and Less Developed Countries*, Baltimore: Johns Hopkins University Press.

Robinson, M. S. (2001). *The Microfinance Revolution: Sustainable Finance for the Poor*, Washington DC: World Bank.

Rocheleau, D., and D. Edmunds (1997). 'Women, Men, and Trees: Gender, Power, and Property in Forest and Agrarian Landscapes', *World Development*, 25(8): 1351–71.

Rogg, C. (2005). 'Precautionary Saving and Portfolio Management in Uncertain Environments: Evidence from Rural Ethiopia', Ph.D. thesis, University of Oxford, Oxford.

Rogg, C. (2006). 'Asset Portfolios in Africa: Evidence from Ethiopia', WIDER Research Paper 2006/145, UNU-WIDER, Helsinki.

Roine, J., and D. Waldenström (2007). 'Wealth Concentration over the Path of Development: Sweden, 1873–2005', Working Paper 722, Research Institute of Industrial Economics, Stockholm.

Rosen, H. S., and S. Wu (2004). 'Portfolio Choice and Health Status', *Journal of Financial Economics*, 72(3): 457–84.

Rosen, S. (1974). 'Hedonic Prices and Implicit Markets: Product Differentiation in Pure Competition', *Journal of Political Economy*, 82(1): 34–55.

Rosen, S. (1978). 'Substitution and Division of Labour', *Economica*, 45: 235–50.

Rosenbloom, J. L., and G. W. Stutes (2005). 'Re-examining the Distribution of Wealth in 1870', mimeo, University of Kansas.

Rosenzweig, M. R., and H. P. Binswanger (1993). 'Wealth, Weather Risk and the Composition and Profitability of Agricultural Investments', *Economic Journal*, 103: 56–78.

Rosenzweig, M. R., and K. I. Wolpin (1993). 'Credit Market Constraints, Consumption Smoothing and the Accumulation of Durable Production Assets in Low-Income', *Journal of Political Economy*, 101(2): 223–44.

Rosstat (various). *Russian Statistical Yearbook*, Moscow: Rosstat.

Roth, M. (2002). 'Integrating Land Issues and Land Policy with Poverty Reduction and Rural Development in Southern Africa', paper prepared for the World Bank Regional Workshop on Land Issues in Africa and the Middle East, Kampala, Apr.

Rozelle, S., and J. F. M. Swinnen (2004). 'Success and Failure of Reform: Insights from the Transition of Agriculture', *Journal of Economic Literature*, 42: 404–56.

Rubinstein, W. D. (1971). 'Occupations among British Millionaires, 1857–1969', *Review of Income and Wealth*, 17: 375–8.

Rugadya, M., E. Obaikol, and K. Herbert (2005). *Critical Pastoral Issues and Policy Statements for the National Land Policy in Uganda*, Kampala: Associates for Development.

Ruggeri Laderchi, C. (2003). *Drawing on Financial and Physical Assets after a Crisis: The Case of Uruguay*, Washington DC: World Bank.

Rutstein, S. O., and G. Rojas (2003). *Guide to the DHS Statistics*, Calverton, MD: ORC Macro.

Sahn, D. E., and D. C. Stifel (2000). 'Poverty Comparisons over Time and Across Countries in Africa', *World Development*, 28(12): 2123–55.

Sarte, P. G. (2000). 'Informality and Rent-Seeking Bureaucracies in a Model of Long-Run Growth', *Journal of Monetary Economics*, 46: 173–97.

Satyasai, K. J. S. (2002). 'Debt and Investment Survey: An Underutilised Tool', *Economic and Political Weekly*, 2 Mar.: 823–5.

Schmidt-Hebbel, K., and L. Serven (1997). 'Saving Across the World: Puzzles and Policies', World Bank Discussion Paper 354, World Bank, Washington DC.

Schneider, F., and D. H. Enste (2000). 'Shadow Economies: Size, Causes, and Consequences', *Journal of Economic Literature*, 38: 77–114.

Schneider, M. (2004). *The Distribution of Wealth*, Northampton MA: Edward Elgar.

Schöffel, R. (1993). 'Vermögen und seine Besteuerung 1989', *Wirtschaft und Statistik*, 10: 750–8.

Schultz, P. (2004). 'School Subsidies for the Poor: Evaluating the Mexican Progress Poverty Program', *Journal of Development Economics*, 74(1): 199–250.

Sen, A. K. (1976). 'Real National Income', *Review of Economic Studies*, 43: 19–39.

Sen, A. K. (1981). *Poverty and Famines: An Essay on Entitlement and Deprivation*, Oxford: Clarendon Press.

Sen, A. K. (1992). *Inequality Re-examined*, Cambridge MA: Harvard University Press.

Sen, P. K. (1988). 'The Harmonic Gini Coefficient and Affluence Indexes', *Mathematical Social Sciences*, 16: 65–76.

Shammas, C. (1993). 'A New Look at Long-Term Trends in Wealth Inequality in the United States', *American Historical Review*, 98(4): 412–32.

Shammas, C., M. Salmon, and M. Dahlin (1987). *Inheritance in America, from Colonial Times to the Present*, New Brunswick: Rutgers University Press.

Shann, E. (1998). 'Spreading it Around', *Business Review Weekly*, 25 May.

Shawa, M. (2002). 'Gender Implications of the National Land Policy', paper presented at the National Civil Society Meeting on Land Reform Policy, Blanytre, Mar.

Shetty, S. (1988). 'Limited Liability, Wealth Differences and Tenancy Contracts in Agrarian Economies', *Journal of Development Economics*, 24: 1–22.

Shleifer, A., and D. Treisman (2005). 'Normal Country: Russia after Communism', *Journal of Economic Perspectives*, 19(1): 151–74.

Shleifer, A., and R. Vishny (1994). 'The Politics of Market Socialism', *Journal of Economic Perspectives*, 8(2): 165–76.

Shorrocks, A. F. (1975). 'The Age–Wealth Relationship: A Cross-Section and Cohort Analysis', *Review of Economics and Statistics*, 57(2): 155–63.

Shorrocks, A. F. (1980). 'The Class of Additively Decomposable Inequality Measures', *Econometrica*, 48(3): 613–25.

Shorrocks, A. F. (1982). 'Inequality Decomposition by Factor Components', *Econometrica*, 50(1): 193–211.

Shorrocks, A. F. (1983). 'The Impact of Income Components on the Distribution of Family Incomes', *Quarterly Journal of Economics*, 98(2): 311–26.

Shorrocks, A. F. (1984). 'Inequality Decomposition by Population Sub-Groups', *Econometrica*, 52: 1369–85.

Shorrocks, A. F. (1987a). 'Comment', in E. N. Wolff (ed.), *International Comparisons of the Distribution of Household Wealth*, Oxford: Oxford University Press.

Shorrocks, A. F. (1987b). 'UK Wealth Distribution: Current Evidence and Future Prospects' in E. N. Wolff (ed.), *International Comparisons of the Distribution of Household Wealth*, Oxford: Oxford University Press.

Shorrocks, A. F. (1988). 'Wealth Holdings and Entrepreneurial Activity', in D. Kessler and A. Masson (eds), *Modelling the Accumulation and Distribution of Wealth*, Oxford: Oxford University Press.

Shorrocks, A. F., and G. Wan (2008). 'Ungrouping Income Distributions: Synthesising Samples for Inequality and Poverty Analysis', WIDER Research Paper 2008/16, UNU-WIDER, Helsinki.

Sicular, T., X. Yue, B. Gustafsson, and S. Li (2007). 'The Urban–Rural Income Gap and Inequality in China', *Review of Income and Wealth*, 53(1): 93–126.

Sierminska, E. (2005). 'The Luxembourg Wealth Study: A Progress Report', paper prepared for Luxembourg Wealth Study workshop 'Construction and Usage of Comparable Microdata on Wealth', 27–29 Jan., Perugia.

Sierminska, E., and T. Garner (2002). 'A Comparison of Income, Expenditures and Home Market Value Distributions Using Luxembourg Income Study Data from the 1990s', Maxwell School of Citizenship and Public Affairs Working Paper 338, Syracuse University, Syracuse NY.

Sierminska, E., A. Brandolini, and T. Smeeding (2006a). 'Comparing Wealth Distribution across Rich Countries: First Results from the Luxembourg Wealth Study', LWS Working Paper 1, LIS, Luxembourg.

Sierminska, E., A. Brandolini, and T. Smeeding (2006b). 'The Luxembourg Wealth Study: A Cross-Country Comparable Database for Household Wealth Research', *Journal of Economic Inequality*, 4(3): 375–83.

Sinha, S. (2006). 'Evidence for Power-Law Tail of the Wealth Distribution in India', *Physica A*, 359: 555–62.

Sinha, S. H., and M. Lipton (1999). 'Damaging Fluctuations, Risk and Poverty: A Review', background paper for the *World Development Report 2000/2001*, University of Sussex, Brighton.

Skidmore, T. (1999). *Brazil: Five Centuries of Change*, Oxford: Oxford University Press.

Slacalek, J. (2006). 'What Drives Personal Consumption? The Role of Housing and Financial Wealth', mimeo, German Institute for Economic Research, DIW, Berlin.

Slemrod, J., and S. Yitzhaki (2002). 'Tax Avoidance, Evasion, and Administration', in A. J. Auerbach, and M. Feldstein (eds), *Handbook of Public Economics*, vol. 3, Amsterdam: Elsevier, pp. 1423–70.

Slinko, I., E. Yakovlev, and E. Zhuravskaya (2005). 'Laws for Sale: Evidence from Russia', *American Law and Economics Review*, 7(1): 284–318.

Soderbom, M., and F. Teal (2000). 'Skills, Investment and Exports from Manufacturing Firms in Africa', CSAE Working Paper 8, Centre for the Study of African Economies, University of Oxford, Oxford.

Sokoloff, K., and S. Engerman (2000). 'Institutions, Factor Endowments, and Paths of Development in the New World', *Journal of Economic Perspectives*, 14(3): 217–32.

Soltow, L. (1980). 'Wealth Distribution in Norway and Denmark in 1789', *Historisk Tidsskrift*, 59: 221–35.

Soltow, L. (1981). 'Wealth Distribution in Denmark in 1789', *Scandinavian Economic History Review*, 27(2): 121–38.

Soltow, L. (1985). 'The Swedish Census of Wealth at the Beginning of the 19th Century', *Scandinavian Economic History Review*, 33(1): 1–24.

Sonin, K. (2003). 'Why the Rich May Favour Protection of Property Rights', *Journal of Comparative Economics*, 31(4): 715–31.

SOU (1942). Statens Offentliga Utredningar, 'Förutsättningarna för och verkningarna av en engångsskatt å förmögenhet i Sverige', SOU 1942: 52, Stockholm: Finansdepartementet.

SOU (1957). 'Arvsbeskattning, betänkande av Arvsskattesakkunniga', SOU 1957: 48, Stockholm: Finansdepartementet.

SOU (1969). 'Kapitalbeskattningen, betänkande av Kapitalskatteberedningen', SOU 1969: 54, Stockholm: Norstedt.

SOU (2004). 'Egendomsskatter: reform av arvs- och gåvoskatter, slutbetänkande av Egendomsskattekommittén', SOU 2004: 66, Stockholm: Fritzes.

Spånt, R. (1978). 'The Distribution of Household Wealth in Some Developed Countries', CREP-INSEE International Meeting, July, Paris.

Spånt, R. (1979). 'Den svenska förmögenhetsfördelningens utveckling', Statens Offentliga Utredningar 1979: 9, Stockholm.

Spånt, R. (1981). 'The Development of the Distribution of Wealth in Sweden', *Review of Income and Wealth* 27(1): 65–74.

Spånt, R. (1987). 'Wealth Distribution in Sweden: 1920–1983', in E. N. Wolff (ed.), *International Comparisons of the Distribution of Household Wealth*, Oxford: Oxford University Press.

Spilerman, S. (2004). 'The Impact of Parental Wealth on Early Living Standards in Israel', *American Journal of Sociology*, 110(1): 92–122.

Spilerman, S., and F. Torche (2004). 'Living Standard Potential and the Transmission of Advantage in Chile', in E. N. Wolff (ed.), *What has Happened to the Quality of Life in the Advanced Industrialized Nations?*, Northampton MA: Edward Elgar.

Stark, T. (1972). *The Distribution of Personal Income in the United Kingdom, 1949–1963*, Cambridge: Cambridge University Press.

Statistics Canada (2006). 'Table: Household Assets, Debt and Wealth', available at: http://www40.statcan.ca/l01/ind01/l3_3868_1989.htm?hili_famil109 (accessed 8 Feb. 2008).

Statistics Norway (various years). *Statistisk Årbok*, Oslo: Statistics Norway.

Statistics Norway (1915a). *Indtaegs og formuesforhold efter skatteligningen 1911 i forbindelse med Folketællingen 1910*, Kristiania: Statistics Norway.

Statistics Norway (1915b). *Indtaegt, formue og fordelingen av den kommunale skat ifølge skatteligningen for 1913–1914*, Kristiania: Statistics Norway.

Statistics Norway (1934). *Folketellingen i Norge 1 desember 1930. 7 hefte. Inntekt og formue efter skatteligningen 1930–31*, Oslo: Statistics Norway.

Statistics South Africa (2002). *Earning and Spending in South Africa: Selected Findings and Comparisons from the Income and Expenditure Surveys of October 1995 and October 2000*, Pretoria: Statistics South Africa.

Statistics Sweden (2000). 'Förmögenhetsfördelningen i Sverige 1997 med tillbakablick till 1975', SCB Rapport 2000, Stockholm: Statistics Sweden.

Statistics Sweden (2004). *Förmögenhetsstatistik 2002*, Stockholm: Statistiska Centralbyrån.

Steckel, R. (1990). 'Poverty and Prosperity: A Longitudinal Study of Wealth Accumulation, 1850–1860', *Review of Economics and Statistics*, 72(2): 275–85.

Stein, J. C. (1995). 'Prices and Trading Volume in the Housing Market: A Model with Downpayment Effects', *Quarterly Journal of Economics*, 110: 379–406.

Steinmo, S. (1993). *Taxation and Democracy*, New Haven: Yale University Press.

Stewart, C. (1939). 'Income Capitalization as a Method of Estimating the Distribution of Wealth By Size Groups', *Studies in Income Wealth*, vol. 3, Cambridge MA: National Bureau of Economic Research.

Stiglitz, J. E. (1969). 'Distribution of Income and Wealth among Individuals', *Econometrica*, 37(3): 382–97.

Stiglitz, J. E. (1974). 'Incentives and Risk-Sharing in Sharecropping', *Review of Economic Studies*, 41: 219–55.

Stiglitz, J. E. (2003). *Globalization and its Discontents*, New York: W. W. Norton.

Straub, S. (2005). 'Informal Sector: The Credit Market Channel', *Journal of Development Economics*, 78: 299–321.

Straw, K. H. (1956). 'Consumers' Net Worth: The 1953 Savings Survey', *Bulletin of the Oxford University Institute of Statistics*, 18: 1–60.

Strickland, R. S. (2004). *To Have and To Hold: Women's Property and Inheritance Rights in the Context of HIV/AIDS in Sub-Saharan Africa*, Washington DC: International Center for Research on Women.

Struyk, R. J. (1996). *Economic Restructuring of the Former Soviet Bloc: The Case of Housing*, Washington DC: Urban Institute Press.

Subramanian, S., and D. Jayaraj (2006). 'The Distribution of Household Wealth in India, Including an Assessment of the Database', mimeo, Madras Institute of Development Studies: Chennai. See also WIDER Research Paper 2006/116, Helsinki, UNU-WIDER.

Szekely, M. (1998). *The Economics of Poverty, Inequality and Wealth Accumulation in Mexico*, New York: St Martin's Press.

Szekely, M. (2001). 'Where to from Here?: Generating Capabilities and Creating Opportunities for the Poor', in O. Attanasio and M. Szekely (eds), *Portrait of the Poor: An Asset-Based Approach*, Washington DC: Inter-American Development Bank.

Szekely, M., and Hilgert (1999). 'What is Behind the Inequality We Measure? An Investigation Using Latin American Data', IADB Working Paper 409, Inter-American Development Bank, Washington DC.

Tansel, A. (1999). 'Formal versus Informal Sector Choice of Wage Earners and their Wages in Turkey', Working Paper 9927, Economic Research Forum, Cairo.

Teal, F. (2001). 'Education, Incomes, Poverty and Inequality in Ghana in the 1990s', CSAE Working Paper Series 21, Centre for the Study of African Economies, Oxford.

Tekle, T. (2001). 'Women's Access to Land and Property Rights in Eritrea', in *Women's Land and Property Rights in Situations of Conflict and Reconstruction: Towards Good Practice*', New York: United Nations Development Fund for Women (a reader based on the Feb. 1998 Inter-Regional Consultation in Kigali).

Teklu, A. (2005). 'Land Registration and Women's Land Rights in Amhara Region, Ethiopia', Securing Land Rights in Africa Research Report 4, International Institute for Environment and Development, London.

Tesliuc, E., and L. Ovcharova (2007). *Sensitivity of Poverty and Inequality Statistics to Alternative Definitions of Household Welfare Illustration Using the NOBUS Survey*, Washington DC: World Bank.

Thiesenhusen, W. (1995). *Broken Promises, Agrarian Reform and the Latin American Campesino*, Boulder CO: Westview.

Thomas, D. (1999). 'Intrahousehold Resource Allocation: An Inferential Approach', *Journal of Human Resources*, 25(4): 635–64.

Thomas, J. J. (1992). *Informal Economic Activity*, London School of Economics Handbooks in Economics, London School of Economics: London.

Thomas, R. (1997). 'The Demand for M4: A Sectoral Analysis Part 1: The Household Sector', Bank of England Working Papers 61, Bank of England, London.

Ting, L., I. Williamson, D. Grant, and J. Parker (1999). 'Understanding the Evolution of Land Administration Systems in Some Common Law Countries', *Survey Review*, 35: 83–102.

Topińska, I., and K. Kuhl (2003). 'Poverty in Poland: Profile and Changes, 1994–2001', in *Poland: How Far Is Warsaw from Lisbon? Growth, Employment and Living Standards in Pre-Accession Poland*, Washington DC: World Bank.

Torche, F. (2005). 'Unequal but Fluid: Social Mobility in Chile in Comparative Perspective', *American Sociological Review*, 70: 422–50.

Torche, F., and S. Spilerman (2006). 'Wealth, Parental Transfers, and Standard of Living: An Empirical Analysis of Chile', in E. N. Wolff (ed.), *International Perspectives on Household Wealth*, Northampton MA: Edward Elgar.

Trejos, J., and N. Montiel (2001). 'The Capital of the Poor in Costa Rica: Access, Utilization and Return', in O. Attanasio and M. Szekely (eds), *Portrait of the Poor: An Assets-Based Approach*, Washington DC: Inter-American Development Bank.

Tressel, T. (2003). 'Dual Financial Systems and Inequalities in Economic Development', *Journal of Economic Growth*, 8: 223–57.

Tuomala, M., and J. Vilmunen (1988). 'On the Trends over Time in the Degree of Concentration of Wealth in Finland', *Finnish Economic Papers*, 1: 184–90.

Turner, J. F. (1976). 'Housing by People: Towards Autonomy in Building Environments', cited in R. M. Buckley and J. Kalarickal (2005), 'Housing Prices in Developing Countries: Conjectures and Refutations', *World Bank Research Observer*, 20(2): 233–57.

Tybout, J. R. (2000). 'Manufacturing Firms in Developing Countries: How Well Do They Do and Why?', *Journal of Economic Literature*, 38: 11–44.

Udry, C. (1995). 'Risk and Saving in Northern Nigeria', *American Economic Review*, 85(5): 1287–300.

UN-Habitat (1999). *Latin America Country Profiles*, online at http://www.unhabitat.org/categories.asp?catid=2.

UNDP (1993). United Nations Development Programme, *Human Development Report 1993*, New York: UNDP and Oxford University Press.

UNECE (various). United Nations Economic Commission for Europe, *Country Profiles on the Housing Sector*, Geneva: UNECE.

Unicredit (2006). *New Europe Households' Wealth and Debt Monitor*, Prague: Unicredit.

United Nations (1980). *Convention on the Elimination of All Forms of Discrimination against Women*, New York: United Nations.

United Nations (1990). *World Urbanization Prospects*, New York: United Nations.

451

United Nations (2007). *Handbook of the International Comparison Programme, Processing of the Basic Data*, available at: http://unstats.un.org/unsd/methods/icp/ipc5_htm.htm#_0 (accessed 6 Feb. 2008), New York: United Nations Statistics Division.

Vaidyanathan, A. (1993). 'Asset Holdings and Consumption of Rural Households in India: A Study of Spatial and Temporal Variations', in *Agricultural Development Policy: Adjustments and Reorientation*, Indian Society of Agricultural Economics, New Delhi: IBH.

Van der Walt, B. F., and J. W. Prinsloo (1995). 'The Compilation and Importance of Household Debt in South Africa', Occasional Paper 8, South African Reserve Bank, Pretoria.

Vedomosti (2003a). 'Khodorkovsky Confessed: Yukos Shareholders Will Support Union of Right Wing Forces, Yabloko, and the Communist Party', 8 Apr. (in Russian).

Vedomosti (2003b). 'Take Away and Divide: People's Aspirations have not Changed in 86 Years', 18 July (in Russian).

Vedomosti (2004). 'Money Breeds Money', 16 June (in Russian).

Villasenor, J., and B. C. Arnold (1989). 'Elliptical Lorenz Curves', *Journal of Econometrics*, 40(2): 328–38.

Waldenström, D., and J. Vlachos (2005). 'International Financial Liberalization and Industry Growth', *International Journal of Finance & Economics*, 10(3): 263–84.

Walker, C. (2002). *Land Reform in Southern and Eastern Africa: Key Issues for Strengthening Women's Access to and Rights in Land*, Rome: FAO.

Wang, L., and Z. Wei (1999). 'Housing Welfare and Income Distribution in China's Cities', in R. Zhao, S. Li, and C. Riskin (eds), *Re-study on China's Income Distribution*, Beijing: China Finance and Economics Press.

Watkins, G. P. (1907). 'The Growth of Large Fortunes', *Publications of the American Economic Association*, 8: 1–170.

Weale, M. (2007) 'Commentary: House Price Worries', *National Institute Economic Review*, 200: 2–4.

Wedgwood, J. C. (1928). 'The Influence of Inheritance on the Distribution of Wealth', *Economic Journal*, 38: 38–55.

Wedgwood, J. C. (1929). *The Economics of Inheritance*, London: Routledge.

Wendorff., C. (1985). 'Sector Informal Urbano y Crisis Economica: Diagnostico y Alternativa de Politica', in N. Henriques and A. Ponce (eds), *Lima: Poblacion, Trabajo y Politica*, Lima: Pontifica Universidad Catolica del Peru.

White, B. B. (1978). 'Empirical Tests of the Life Cycle Hypothesis', *American Economic Review*, 68: 547–60.

Williamson, I. (1985). 'Cadastres and Land Information Systems in Common Law Jurisdictions', *Survey Review*, 28: 114–29.

Wolff, E. N. (1981). 'The Accumulation of Household Wealth over the Life Cycle: A Micro-Data Analysis', *Review of Income and Wealth*, 27(1): 75–96.

Wolff, E. N. (1987). 'Estimates of Household Wealth Inequality in the US, 1962–1983', *Review of Income and Wealth*, 33(3): 231–56.

Wolff, E. N. (1990a). 'Methodological Issues in the Estimation of the Size Distribution of Household Wealth', *Journal of Econometrics*, 43(1–2): 179–95.

Wolff, E. N. (1990b). 'Wealth Holdings and Poverty Status in the US', *Review of Income and Wealth*, 36: 143–65.

Wolff, E. N. (1996). 'International Comparisons of Wealth Inequality', *Review of Income and Wealth*, 42(4): 433–51.

Wolff, E. N. (1998). 'Recent Trends in the Size Distribution of Household Wealth', *Journal of Economic Perspectives*, 12(3): 131–50.

Wolff, E. N. (2001). 'Recent Trends in Wealth Ownership, from 1983 to 1998', in T. M. Shapiro and E. N. Wolff (eds), *Assets for the Poor*, New York: Russell Sage Foundation.

Wolff, E. N. (2004). 'Changes in Household Wealth in the 1980s and 1990s in the US', Levy Economics Institute Working Paper 407, Levy Institute, Bard College, Annandale-on-Hudson NY.

Wolff, E. N. (2005). 'Is the Equalizing Effect of Retirement Wealth Wearing Off?', Levy Economics Institute Working Paper 420, Levy Institute, Bard College, Annandale-on-Hudson NY.

Wolff, E. N. (2006). 'Changes in Household Wealth in the 1980s and 1990s in the US', in E. N. Wolff (ed.), *International Perspectives on Household Wealth*, Northampton MA: Edward Elgar.

Wolff, E. N., and N. Marley (1989). 'Long-Term Trends in US Wealth Inequality: Methodological Issues and Results', in R. E. Lipsey and H. S. Tice (eds), *The Measurement of Saving, Investment and Wealth*, Chicago: University of Chicago Press.

Woodruff, C. (2001). 'Review of de Soto's "The Mystery of Capital" ', *Journal of Economic Literature*, 39(4): 1215–23.

World Bank (1981). 'China: Socialist Economic Development', World Bank Economic Research Group Report on a Study of China's Economy, China Finance and Economics Press, Beijing.

World Bank (1998). 'Urban Property Rights Project—Peru', World Bank Project Information Document PID6523, World Bank, Washington DC.

World Bank (2000). *World Development Report 2000/2001: Attacking Poverty*, New York: World Bank and Oxford University Press.

World Bank (2001a). *Engendering Development*, Washington DC: World Bank.

World Bank (2001b). *Urban Housing and Land Market Reforms in Transition Countries: Neither Marx nor Market*, Washington DC: World Bank.

World Bank (2002a). 'Brazil: Progressive Low-Income Housing: Alternatives for the Poor', Report 22032-BR, World Bank, Washington DC.

World Bank (2002b). 'Mexico: Low-Income Housing: Issues and Options', Report 22534-ME, World Bank, Washington DC.

World Bank (2003). 'Measuring Living Standards: Household Consumption and Wealth Indices. Quantitative Techniques for Health Equity Analysis', Technical Note 4, World Bank, Washington DC.

World Bank (2004). *From Transition to Development: A Country Economic Memorandum for the Russian Federation*, Moscow: World Bank.

World Bank (2005a). *Measuring Financial Access: Outlining the Scope of Current Data Collection Efforts*, Washington DC: World Bank.

World Bank (2005b). *Growth, Poverty, and Inequality: Eastern Europe and the Former Soviet Union*, Washington DC: World Bank.

World Bank (2005c). *Russian Federation: Reducing Poverty through Growth and Social Policy Reform*, Poverty Reduction and Economic Management Unit, Europe and Central Asia Region, Washington DC: World Bank.

World Bank (2006a). *Where is the Wealth of Nations? Measuring Capital for the 21st Century*, Washington DC: World Bank.

World Bank (2006b). *World Development Indicators* (database), Washington DC: World Bank.

World Wealth Report (various). New York: Capgemini and Merrill Lynch.

Yamokoski, A. and L. A. Keister (2006). 'The Wealth of Single Women: Marital Status and Parenthood in the Asset Accumulation of Young Baby Boomers in the United States', *Feminist Economics*, 12(1–2): 167–94.

Yemtsov, R. (2007). 'Housing Privatization and Household Wealth in Transition', WIDER Research Paper 2007/02, UNU-WIDER, Helsinki.

Yngstrom, I. (2002). 'Women, Wives, and Land Rights in Africa: Situating Gender beyond the Household in the Debate over Land Policy and Changing Tenure Systems', *Oxford Development Studies*, 30: 21–40.

Yoo, K. (2005). 'Empirical Analysis of Portfolio Allocation: The Case of Korea', mimeo, Bank of Korea, Seoul.

Young, A. A. (1917). 'Do the Statistics of the Concentration of Wealth in the United States Mean What They Are Commonly Assumed to Mean?', *Publications of the American Statistical Association*, 15: 471–84.

Zavisca, J. (2005). 'Housing Divides: The Causes and Consequences of Housing Inequality in Russia', mimeo, Center for Russian, East European, and Eurasian Studies, University of Texas at Austin, Austin TX.

Zeldes, S. (1989). 'Optimal Consumption with Stochastic Income: Deviations from Certainty Equivalence', *Quarterly Journal of Economics*, 104(2): 275–98.

Zeuthen, F. (1928). *Den Økonomiske Fordeling*, Copenhagen: Nyt Nordisk Forlag Arnold Busck.

Zhao, R., and S. Ding (2006). 'The Distribution of Wealth in China', in B. Gustafsson, S. Li, and T. Sicular (eds), *Inequality and Public Policy in China*, Cambridge: Cambridge University Press.

Zhao, R., and S. Li (1997). 'Increasing Income Inequality and Its Causes in China', *Journal of Economic Research (Jingji Yanjiu)*, 9: 22–32.

Ziegal, J. S. (1974). 'Canadian Chattel Security Law: Past Experience and Current Developments', in J. Sauveplanne (ed.), *Security over Corporeal Movables*, Leiden: A. W. Sijthoff.

Index

Note: page numbers in *italic* indicate figures and tables.

Index

transition economies (*cont.*)
pre-transition private income *140*
privatization strategies 141
property rights 135–6
wage decompression 140, *140*, 149
wealth inequality 149
wealth of *135*, *136*
see also *individual countries*
Trejos, J. 153
Tressel, T. 336 n. 3
Tripathi, A. K. 113–14
Tuomala, M. 70, 71 n.

Udry, C. 226, 248, 365
Uganda 366, 368
Ukraine 143 n. 14, 147 n., 323
UNECE (United Nations Economic
    Commission for Europe) 315
unit trusts 206
United Kingdom (UK) 3, 279
CCI (consumer credit conditions index) 302
debt 35
entrepreneurship/small business
    lending 345–6
and financial risk 289
home ownership 34, 39
housing market 306–8
housing wealth 293
immigration and house price rises 295–6
income inequality 414
investment income data 83–5
Married Women's Property Acts 358
mean/median wealth 39
SPI (Survey of Personal Incomes) 83
'super-rich' 84–5
top wealth shares 50–1, *50*, *61*
wealth concentration *84*
wealth-income ratio 414–15
wealth inequality 414
women's property rights 358
United Nations (UN): CEDAW 19, 358–9
United Nations Economic Commission for
    Europe (UNECE) 315
United Nations Statistics Division (UNSD) 220
United States Agency for International
    Development (USAID) 252
United States of America (USA) 3, 9, 279
asset income 168
CCI (consumer credit conditions index) 302
debt 34, 35, 38
entrepreneurship 345
estate data 79–81
financial assets, distribution of 277
and financial risk 289
home ownership 34, 38
housing wealth 293
income inequality 21, 414

inheritance regimes 360
land inequality 163, 165
land/real estate and household wealth 341
life insurance 38
literacy 173
loan risk reduction 296
Married Women's Property Acts 358
mortgages 38
mutual funds 38
MWA (mean wealth above) ratio 81, *81*
net worth 30, 31, 41
Panel Survey of Income Dynamics
    (PSID) 30, 31
personal loans 38
primary education 173
retirement accounts 38
stocks 35, 38
'super-rich' 80
Survey of Consumer Finances (SCF) 3, 4, 30,
    31, 412, 417
tax gap 45 n. 10
top wealth shares 51–3, *52*, *61*
voting rights 173
wealth concentration *80*
wealth-income ratio 414–15
wealth inequality 21, 39, 341, 414
women's property rights 358, 359 n. 7
urban poverty 153
Uruguay 412 n. 19
home ownership 158
housing wealth 161, 162
investment income 166–8
land inequality 163–4, 165
literacy 173
stocks 168
urbanization rates 162
USAID (United States Agency for International
    Development) 252

Venezuela 162, 163, 165, 168, 362
Vietnam 12, 127, 170, 277, 289
Villasenor, J. 120
Vilmunen, J. 70, 71 n.
Vinokur, A. 139
Vollrath, D. 165
voting rights 173
voucher privatization 141, 143

Waldenström, D. 45 n. 11
Wang, L. 105, *106*
Watkins, G. P. 66, 86–7
wealth 5, 9, 12, *211*, 412 n. 18
China 10–11
definitions of 2–5, 28–9, 44
education and 262–3, *263*
inherited 88
and living standards 151